From Here to Equality

From Here

to Equality

REPARATIONS FOR BLACK AMERICANS

IN THE TWENTY-FIRST CENTURY

WILLIAM A. DARITY JR. AND

A. KIRSTEN MULLEN

THE UNIVERSITY OF NORTH CAROLINA PRESS Chapel Hill

*This book was published with the assistance
of the William R. Kenan Jr. Fund of the University
of North Carolina Press.*

Manufactured in the United States of America
Designed by Richard Hendel
Set in Utopia and TheSans
by codeMantra, Inc.

The University of North Carolina Press has been
a member of the Green Press Initiative since 2003.

Cover illustration: Memorial Corridor at the National Memorial for Peace
and Justice, Montgomery, Alabama. Photograph by Soniakapadia.

Library of Congress Cataloging-in-Publication Data
Names: Darity, William A., Jr., 1953– author. |
Mullen, A. Kirsten (Andrea Kirsten), author.
Title: From here to equality : reparations for black Americans in the
twenty-first century / William A. Darity Jr. and A. Kirsten Mullen.
Description: Chapel Hill : The University of North Carolina Press,
[2020] | Includes bibliographical references and index.
Identifiers: LCCN 2019046675 |
ISBN 9781469654973 (cloth : alk. paper) | ISBN 9781469654980 (ebook)
Subjects: LCSH: African Americans—Reparations. | African Americans—
Civil rights—History. | Income distribution—United States—History. |
Slavery—United States—History. | Race discrimination—United
States—History. | United States—Race relations—History.
Classification: LCC E185.89.R45 D37 2020 | DDC 323.1196/073—dc23
LC record available at https://lccn.loc.gov/2019046675

*To our sons, Aden and William—members of the fifth
generation born since slavery was outlawed—and to our
ancestors we have identified who were born enslaved
and lived to see emancipation: Rachel King, Jane and
Isaac Mullen, and Sallie Mullen ("wife" of Granville
Spangler); Jennie Davenport; Nelson Strange, Letty
Flippo Hart, Uriah Wise and Hannah Strange Berry
Wise, Walker Taliaferro and Patsy Williams Taliaferro,
and Rev. Walker Taliaferro; Millis Mitchell and Emily
Williams Mitchell; Isham (Isom) Davenport and Annie
Cotton Davenport; Tony Cooper and Bama Cooper and
Jerry Battle and Charlotte Jenkins Battle; Harry Carloss
and Betty Thompson Carloss and Nicholas Leach
and Lucinda Pride Leach; and Nelson and Mahala
Daugherty, Alfred and Phyllis Rhodes, Emanuel Darity
and Caroline Rhodes, Andrew and Lynn Dardie, Logan
Jesse Darity, and Robert Boddie and Lucy Mitchell
Boddie*

Contents

Introduction: Standing at the Crossroads

In order to see where we are going, we not only must see where we have been, but we must also understand where we have been. —Ella Baker, AZ Quotes, 1964

The world has never seen any people turned loose to such destitution as were the four million slaves of the South. . . . They were free without roofs to cover them, or bread to eat, or land to cultivate, and as a consequence died in such numbers as to awaken the hope of their enemies that they would soon disappear. —Frederick Douglass, "Celebrating the Past, Anticipating the Future," 1875

Racism and discrimination have perpetually crippled black economic opportunities. At several historic moments the trajectory of racial inequality could have been altered dramatically, but at each juncture, the road chosen did not lead to a just and fair America.

The formation of the republic provided a critical moment when blacks might have been granted freedom and admitted to full citizenship. The Civil War and the Reconstruction era each offered openings to produce a true democracy thoroughly inclusive of black Americans. Had the New Deal project and the GI Bill fully included blacks, the nation would have widened the window of opportunity to achieve an equitable future. Passage of civil rights legislation in the 1960s might have unlocked the door for America to eradicate racism.

However, at none of these forks was the path to full justice taken.

From Here to Equality is a book primarily about the economic divide between black and white Americans—how it came to be and how it can be eliminated. Specifically, we contend, a suitably designed program of reparations can close the divide. Black reparations can place America squarely on the path to racial equality.

Reparations programs have been used strategically in the United States and throughout the world to provide redress for grievous injustices. These include the U.S. government's provision of reparations for Japanese Americans unjustly incarcerated ("interned") during World War II, the German government's provision of reparations for victims of the Nazi Holocaust, and the Canadian government's provision of compensation to indigenous peoples who were removed forcibly from their families and confined to Christian, church-run, Indian residential schools.[1]

Reversing the effects of slavery for newly emancipated human chattel was the goal of several plans put into action during and immediately following the Civil War. One of the country's earliest efforts to dramatically alter blacks' economic condition was the federal government's post–Civil War plan to give at least forty acres of abandoned and confiscated land as well as a mule to each formerly enslaved family of four (or ten acres per person).

While some maintain that this planned payment of land and a work animal to newly freed men and women in the nineteenth century is a figment of the black imagination, historical records confirm that the promise of reparations was not a myth.[2] It was inscribed in federal legislation. In fact, the allocation, activated in 1865, of forty acres for formerly enslaved Africans was at least the second such measure the federal government had developed to assign land to the former chattel. The idea that reparations could be an effective method of addressing the effects of slavery and white supremacy has a long history, cycling in and out of popular discourse and the national policy arena. Reparations are as timely today as they were in the 1860s.

The ultimate goal of *From Here to Equality* is to help rejuvenate discussions about and to promote reparations for African Americans. As the final chapter of this book will show, there are several mechanisms for reversing gross inequalities between blacks and whites that overcome the frequent reflexive reaction that this is impractical or infeasible. Real equality is a worthy goal, and it can be achieved.

Reparations are a program of acknowledgment, redress, and closure for a grievous injustice. Where African Americans are concerned, the grievous injustices that make the case for reparations include slavery, legal segregation (Jim Crow), and ongoing discrimination and stigmatization.

ARC—the acronym that stands for acknowledgment, redress, and closure—characterizes the three essential elements of the reparations program that we are advocating. Acknowledgment, redress, and closure are components of any effective reparations project. Acknowledgment involves recognition and admission of the wrong by the perpetrators or beneficiaries of the injustice. For African Americans this means the receipt of a formal apology and a commitment for redress on the part of the American people as a whole—a national act of declaration that a great wrong has been committed. But beyond an apology, acknowledgment requires those who benefited from the exercise of the atrocities to recognize the advantages they gained and commit themselves to the cause of redress. Redress potentially can take two forms, not necessarily mutually exclusive: *restitution* or *atonement*. Restitution is the restoration of survivors to their condition before the injustice occurred or to a condition they might have attained had the injustice not taken place. Of course, it is impossible to restore those who were enslaved to a condition preceding their enslavement, not only because those who were enslaved are now deceased but also because many thousands were born into slavery. But it is possible to move their descendants toward a more equitable position commensurate with the status they would have attained in the absence of the injustice(s).

Atonement, as an alternative form of redress, occurs when perpetrators or beneficiaries meet conditions of forgiveness that are acceptable to the victims. Achieving these elements of a reparations program requires good-faith negotiations between those who were wronged and the wrongdoers.[3]

There is no existing mechanism for establishing when African Americans collectively will have reached an agreement that sufficient steps have been taken to justify forgiveness. Consequently, atonement is difficult to accomplish. That is why, in our proposal, we treat restitution as the appropriate form of redress. We have clear metrics for determining when restitution has been achieved that we do not have for establishing the same for atonement.

Specifically, restitution for African Americans would eliminate racial disparities in wealth, income, education, health, sentencing and incarceration, political participation, and subsequent opportunities to engage in American political and social life. It will require not only an endeavor to compensate for past repression and exploitation but also an endeavor to offset stubborn existing obstacles to full black participation in American political and social life.

Reparations demonstrably would be effective if an improved position for blacks is associated with sharp and enduring reductions in racial disparities, particularly economic disparities like racial wealth inequality, and corresponding sharp and enduring improvements in black well-being.

Closure involves mutual conciliation between African Americans and the beneficiaries of slavery, legal segregation, and ongoing discrimination toward blacks. Whites and blacks would come to terms over the past, confront the present, and unite to create a new and transformed United States of America. Once the reparations program is executed and racial inequality eliminated, African Americans would make no further claims for race-specific policies on their behalf from the American government—on the assumption that no new race-specific injustices are inflicted upon them.

A central theme of *From Here to Equality* is the sustained American failure to recognize the pernicious impact of white supremacy and the sustained American failure to adopt national policies that reverse the effects of white supremacy. At each point that the nation stood at a critical crossroads with respect to its racial future, it chose the wrong fork.

The first two chapters comprise part 1 of *From Here to Equality*. In chapter 1, we examine the historical trajectory of the black reparations movement in the United States, demonstrating the consistent denial of efforts to establish a comprehensive program of compensation for black America.

Chapter 2 is devoted to a systematic analysis of the comparative current status of blacks vis-à-vis whites in the United States. We give particular attention to the racial gulf in wealth accumulation, because wealth (or net worth) is the most powerful indicator of the intergenerational effects of white supremacy on black economic well-being. In the same chapter, we also present evidence showing that many Americans are simply wrong about the magnitude and the causes of racial wealth disparities.

Part 2 of the book is devoted to an analysis of the effects of the American system of slavery on the nation's economic and political development. The third chapter identifies the beneficiaries of slavery both in the near and longer terms. We examine the key role that slavery played in American economic development, in both the north and the south. As we stress throughout the volume, the case for justice must include identification of not only the perpetrators of racial harm but also those who gained from the harm—whether or not they inflicted it.

Chapter 4 examines the first major fork in the road for America—the possibility of ending slavery and producing black citizenship at the founding of the new nation. The period of struggle for independence from Britain was rich with possibilities, possibilities that would have been engendered by ending slavery at the origin of the United States but were summarily forsaken.

In part 3 we consider alternative routes not taken during the period of the Civil War. Chapter 5 is an in-depth exploration of the rejected option of *compensated emancipation*, an option that would have prevented or attenuated the war while also ending black enslavement. Chapter 6 details antiblack atrocities that took place during the war. Readers may be surprised to learn the extent to which even the Union army was unwilling to incorporate blacks who had joined their ranks as equals.

Part 4 investigates the lost opportunities for constructing citizenship for the formerly enslaved in the aftermath of the war. Chapter 7 treats a variety of experiments conducted before, during, and after the Civil War to establish communities of freedmen predicated on creating opportunities for full participation in American life. Chapter 8 describes the ferocious postwar conflict over the Radical Republicans' plan for Reconstruction, which included the provision of at least forty acres of land for freedmen and full political participation for black men. The failure to take the Radicals' path set the stage for the subsequent 150 years of black degradation. Chapter 9 records the destruction of the dreams and ambitions embodied in Reconstruction and the restoration of a regime of white rule in the post-Confederate south.

Part 5 of *From Here to Equality* advances a bill of particulars for the outrages and damages wreaked upon black Americans during the century and a half since the Civil War. Chapter 10 focuses on the abuses of the Jim Crow era, the period of legal segregation in America, while chapter 11 is devoted to the insufficiency of the civil rights era to produce racial equality in the United States. Chapter 10 pivots on the sequence of white massacres that resulted in the annihilation of black lives and property. Chapter 11 centers on the prolonged devaluation of black life throughout the post–civil rights era via discrimination and violence.

The final part of the book consists of two chapters and provides a springboard to the design and implementation of a plan for black reparations. Chapter 12 constitutes a systematic response to reparations' critics, while chapter 13 outlines the potential structure of an actual reparations program. These last two chapters, taken together, supply a systematic response to customary logistical concerns raised about black reparations, with the final chapter offering a detailed description of how best to enact them.

From Here to Equality "draws a thick line from the nation's origins to the present."[4] The case we build in this volume is based on all three tiers or phases of injustice: slavery, American apartheid (Jim Crow), and the combined effects of present-day discrimination and the ongoing deprecation of black lives. Most advocates of black reparations have focused exclusively on the injustice of slavery as the basis for redress. Law professor Boris Bittker argued that the case for black reparations should center solely on the harms of legalized segregation, while Roy L. Brooks, also a legal scholar, has argued that the foundation for black reparations is "the legacy of slavery and Jim Crow."[5] We submit that the bill of particulars for black reparations also must include contemporary, ongoing injustices—injustices resulting in barriers and penalties for the black descendants of persons enslaved in the United States.

Sociologist Joe Feagin catalogs the continuing injuries inflicted on black Americans, including wage penalties, physical and psycho-emotional health wounds, and community and institutional damages.[6] Despite the *Brown v. Board of Education* decision in 1954, a wave of federal legislation in the 1960s and 1970s intended to eliminate legal apartheid in the United States, and the enactment of antidiscrimination laws, blacks continue to bear the weight of American racism.

That burden is manifest in labor market discrimination, grossly attenuated wealth, confinement to neighborhoods with lower levels of amenities and safety, disproportionate exposure to inferior schooling, significantly greater danger in encounters with the police and the criminal justice system writ large, and a general social disdain for the value of black people's lives. The legal apparatus created by the civil rights revolution does little to address the complex web of harms imposed upon black Americans today.

Taken individually, any one of these three tiers of injustice—slavery, the regime of legal segregation and subordination, and current discrimination— makes a powerful case for black reparations. Taken collectively, they are impossible to ignore.

Part 1

1

A Political History of America's Black Reparations Movement

The Civil War of 1861–65 ended slavery. It left us free, but it also left us homeless, penniless, ignorant, nameless and friendless. . . . Russia's liberated serf was given three acres of land and agricultural implements with which to begin his career of liberty and independence. But to us no foot of land nor implement was given. We were turned loose to starvation, destitution and death. So desperate was our condition that some of our statesmen declared it useless to try to save us by legislation as we were doomed to extinction. —Ida B. Wells, "Class Legislation," 1893

Black reparations are damages for America's broken contract with black people. —Mehrsa Baradaran, "Black Capitalism Can't Fix the Racial Wealth Gap (Black Agenda Report)," 2018

Just as enslaved Africans were the first abolitionists—liberating themselves and their families whenever possible—so, too, were black Americans the nation's earliest architects of reparations. American reparations advocates were motivated by the federal government's failure to fulfill its promise of an endowment of forty acres and a mule to the formerly enslaved made on multiple occasions toward the end of the Civil War and in the years immediately following 1865.[1]

When Gen. William T. Sherman and Secretary of War Edwin M. Stanton asked Rev. Garrison Frazier, a native of Granville County, North Carolina, what he and other freedmen would need to sustain themselves after the Civil War wound down, Reverend Frazier replied, "Land." Sherman and Stanton had come to Savannah, Georgia, in January 1865 to query black leaders about their vision of the way forward as President Lincoln sought to transform the war-ravaged country. Twenty black leaders, also members of the clergy, had selected the reverend as their spokesman, and he explained, "The way we can best take care of ourselves is to have land and turn and till it by our own labor. . . . We want to be placed on land until we are able to buy it and make it our own."[2]

The Radical wing of the Republican Party, led by Thaddeus Stevens, Charles Sumner, and John C. Frémont, advocated that lands abandoned by and confiscated from the former Confederates be allotted to freedmen. Black abolitionist Frederick Douglass, uncharacteristically, initially was unenthusiastic about the "free land for blacks" strategy. As early as 1853, in a letter to Harriet Beecher Stowe, Douglass complained that once freed, former slaves would not take eagerly to agriculture unless coerced. He also argued that the very nature of slavery robbed freedmen of sufficient self-reliance to be successful as independent farmers.[3]

However, Douglass later came to regret this break with the Radical Republicans. By 1876, before the Republican National Convention, Douglass observed that the ongoing plight of the ex-slaves was due, in large measure, to the failure to grant them land. He favorably invoked the Russian land reform that followed the emancipation of the serfs: "When the Russian serfs had their chains broken and were given their liberty, the government of Russia—aye, the despotic government of Russia—gave to those poor emancipated serfs a few acres of land on which they could live and earn their bread. But when you turned us loose, you gave us no acres: you turned us loose to the sky, to the storm, to the whirlwind, and, worst of all, you turned us loose to the wrath of our infuriated masters."[4]

Subsequently, Douglass repeated, time and again, the phrase "the serfs of Russia . . . were given three acres of land," contrasting this with nothing being given to formerly enslaved blacks in America. On August 1, 1880, in a speech given in Elmira, New York, at a celebration of West Indian slave emancipation, Douglass observed:

He who can say to his fellow-man, "You shall serve me or starve," is a master and his subject is a slave. This was seen and felt by Thaddeus Stevens, Charles Sumner, and leading Republican stalwarts; and had their counsels prevailed the terrible evils from which we now suffer would have been averted. The negro today would not be on his knees, as he is, abjectly supplicating the old master class to give him leave to toil. Nor would he be leaving the South as from a doomed city, and seeking a home in the uncongenial North, but tilling his native soil in comparative independence.[5]

Still later, in a September 24, 1883, speech before the National Convention of Colored Men in Louisville, Kentucky, he repeated the same themes, saying, explicitly, that the ongoing "poverty and wretchedness" of blacks across the south would have been attenuated had the nation heeded the Radical Republicans' call for land distribution to freedmen. The nation's descent into postslavery turpitude was aggravated by going "[a]gainst the voice of Stevens, Sumner, and Wade, and other far-seeing statesmen."[6]

One of the earliest known reparations champions, Callie D. Guy House, born in slavery about 1861 in Rutherford County, Tennessee, was a widow with five children making her living as a self-employed laundry worker and clothes maker.[7] She took up the cause of the ex-slaves after seeing a copy of the pamphlet *Vaughan's Freedmen's Pension Bill: A Plea for American Freedmen*, which began circulating in black communities in central Tennessee around 1890.[8]

Determined to improve the economic independence of the ex-slaves, Callie House initially joined forces with Walter R. Vaughan, the publisher of the pamphlet. Vaughan was a white Nebraska Democrat and a southerner whose own lobbying efforts on behalf of the formerly enslaved dated to 1870. A former mayor of Council Bluffs, Iowa, and the son of a slaveholder, he had proposed an ex-slave pension bill (H.R. 11119) in 1890.[9] Eventually, House broke with Vaughan both on principle and tactics.

Vaughan argued that the measure should be called the "Southern tax relief bill" and promoted it for the benefit of stimulating the southern states' economies. Since whites owned the majority of business enterprises, he reasoned, blacks would have to purchase goods and services from them and would thereby generate economic growth throughout the south. He made a tidy sum from the sale of the brochures, which sold for one dollar. Eventually Vaughan grossed $100,000 against expenses—which included lobbying, printing, and marketing—of about $20,000.[10]

In 1898, House banded with Isaiah Dickerson, a minister and educator, to charter the grassroots National Ex-Slave Mutual Relief, Bounty, and Pension Association (MRBP) in Nashville, Tennessee. Dickerson served as the general manager, and House became the assistant secretary and national promoter of the new organization. Their mission was fourfold: (1) identify ex-slaves and add their names to the petition for a pension; (2) lobby Congress to provide pensions for the nation's estimated 1.9 million ex-slaves—21 percent of all African Americans by 1899; (3) start local chapters and provide members with financial assistance when they became incapacitated by illness; and (4) provide a burial assistance payment when the member died.[11] The MRBP modeled its pension plan for the formerly enslaved on the Civil War program for "disabled veterans and families of deceased veterans" approved by Congress on July 14, 1862.[12]

If the federal government could compensate elderly disabled veterans for their contributions to the war effort, the organizers reasoned, why not also provide support for the aged ex-slaves who had contributed so much to the growth and development of the country over their lifetimes as coerced and unpaid laborers?[13]

One of House's first initiatives was to embark on a two-year lecture circuit to build local chapters and create the infrastructure necessary to connect them to the burgeoning national organization. Her impact was immediate and profound. A phenomenal recruiter, House signed up at least 34,000 members during those two years. By 1916, the MRBP's membership was estimated to be around 300,000.[14] The dues the organization collected from its members made it possible for the staff to pursue its goals. When Reverend Dickerson died in 1909, House assumed the top leadership position.

In 1915, the association went on to challenge the federal government in a lawsuit filed on behalf of ex-slaves. The lawsuit asserted that the U.S. Treasury Department owed the freedmen $68 million—the amount it had collected from the sale of slave-grown and slave-harvested cotton that had been confiscated from Confederates toward the end of and immediately after the Civil War.[15] The claim was denied.

The association's mission and its bulging membership rolls drew the attention of a variety of federal officials and departments. For some in the U.S. government, the association's steadfast belief that involuntary servitude was a human rights violation and that remedies were owed the former slaves was seen as a threat. In 1916, U.S. postmaster general A. S. Burleson sought indictments against leaders of the association, claiming that they had obtained money from the formerly enslaved by fraudulent circulars proclaiming that pensions and reparations were forthcoming. House was convicted and served time in the penitentiary in Jefferson City, Missouri, from November 1917 to August 1918.[16]

While the federal government succeeded in shutting down House's organization, her followers continued to advance the campaign. Many of them joined Marcus Garvey's Universal Negro Improvement Association.[17]

During the twentieth century, there were numerous incidents in which black claims to reparations seemed justified. Chicago was one of twenty-five cities that erupted in racial violence during the summer of 1919, which became known as Red Summer.[18] Black veterans returning from World War I deployments in Europe and across the globe were frustrated to find that discrimination and the routine violent attacks from whites contradicted their status as full citizens in the United States. To compound matters, well-remunerated employment commensurate with the skills the men had honed during their years in the service was in short supply.

On July 27, 1919, a black teenager who was swimming with friends in Lake Michigan drifted across the "color barrier" and was stoned to death by a group of white men. The police officer who arrived on the scene refused to arrest the assailants identified by eyewitnesses. The subsequent uproar led to a week of rioting. Ultimately, twenty-five blacks and thirteen whites were killed, 537 people were injured—some of them severely—and over 1,000 black families lost their homes after they were torched by rioters.

Shaken by the carnage and rancor, Illinois governor Frank Orren Lowden took an unprecedented step and created the Chicago Commission on Race Relations. For the first time since Reconstruction, a governmental agency would investigate white violence against blacks and the social and economic condition of blacks.[19] Detailed accounts of the murders, including the death of Oscar Dozier, a black laborer at Great Western Smelting and Refining Works, are described in the 669-page publication's section titled "Epitome of Facts in Riot Deaths." Dozier, unadvisedly, left work before "adequate protection could be furnished" and was attacked by "a mob of 500 to 1,000 white men at Thirty-ninth Street and Parnell Avenue," who stoned him and cut "a two inch stab wound over his heart." No proposal for compensation for the black victims of the riot was advanced by the commission.[20]

Black nationalist "Queen Mother" Audley Moore, who advocated restitution for African Americans as early as 1950, was a movement pioneer with connections to the Universal Negro Improvement Association. Born in 1898 in New Iberia, Louisiana, at about the same time as the founding of the MRBP, Moore launched the Committee for Reparations for Descendants of U.S. Slaves.[21] One of her grandfathers had been lynched; one of her great-grandfathers, a white slaveholder, had also owned one of her grandmothers.[22] In 1957 and 1959, she formally appealed to the United Nations for reparations for African Americans.[23] Moore's interactions with the UN were forerunners of that global organization's Working Group of Experts on People of African Descent, which was established in 2002 and released its own call for reparations for African Americans in 2016.[24]

Moore also was a key member of the Republic of New Afrika (RNA), an organization formed in 1968 that issued a claim on the territory of the southeastern United States as a location for the formation of a separate majority-black nation. The foundation of the organization's claim was the broken promise of land for ex-slaves embodied in "forty acres and a mule."[25] The RNA sought both land and sovereignty. Moore served as the minister of health and welfare in the RNA's shadow government.

The RNA's first president was Robert Williams, leader of North Carolina's chapter of the National Association for the Advancement of Colored People (NAACP) and a committed advocate of armed black self-defense.[26] Williams's position influenced the Black Panthers' subsequent adoption of a principle of the use of arms for the purpose of group protection from white terror. For Williams and the Panthers, white violence had to be met by black violence.[27]

In 1963, Malcolm X, while still a minister with the Nation of Islam, issued a call for black reparations at Michigan State University. He demanded, foreshadowing the ambitions of the RNA, that the U.S. government grant land and resources that would enable black Americans to establish a separate territory under black control:

> He [Elijah Muhammad, the leader of the Nation of Islam] says that in this section [of the United States] that will be set aside for Black people, that the government should give us everything we need to start our own civilization. They should give us everything we need to exist for the next twenty-five years. And when you stop and consider the—you shouldn't be shocked, you give Latin America $20 billion and they never fought for this country. They never worked for this country. You send billions of dollars to Poland and to Hungary, they're Communist countries, they never contributed anything here.
>
> This is what you should realize. The greatest contribution to this country was that which was contributed by the Black man. If I take the wages, just a moment, if I take the wages of everyone here, individually it means nothing, but collectively all of the earning power or wages that you earned in one week would make me wealthy. And if I could collect it for a year, I'd be rich beyond dreams. Now, when you see this, and then you stop and consider the wages that were kept back from millions of Black people, not for one year but for 310 years, you'll see how this country got so rich so fast. And what made the economy as strong as it is today. And all that, and all of that slave labor that was amassed in unpaid wages, is due someone today.[28]

In May 1969, a decade after "Queen Mother" Audley Moore's historic petitions to the UN, militant activist James Forman interrupted the Sunday services at Riverside Church in New York City to issue the Black Manifesto. The manifesto called for $500 million in reparations from white Americans to be paid by churches and synagogues for the crimes religious institutions had visited upon black Americans in the United States. Forman, in conjunction with the League of Revolutionary Black Workers, had previously presented the manifesto at the National Black Economic Development Conference a month earlier in Detroit.[29]

The Black Manifesto resulted in donations of $500,000 in funds, exactly 0.1 percent of the amount initially demanded. The funds helped establish several organizations intended to support black political and economic advance. These included a black-owned bank, Black Star Publications, four television networks, and the Black Economic Research Center.

The Black Economic Research Center, a nonprofit entity headed by Robert Browne, was a black economic policy think tank.[30] Its mission was to collect data on black economic wealth and income, generate proposals aimed at improving black Americans' economic position, and assist public and private agencies working toward similar goals. The Ford Foundation was a contributor throughout the 1970s, but without further financial support, operations ended in 1980.[31]

Today, there are faith-based organizations that have expressed ongoing commitments to the reparations project in the spirit of their ministry. These include the interfaith Fellowship of Reconciliation based in the suburbs of New York City and the Auburn Seminary located in upstate New York.[32]

There was a surge in the reparations movement in the mid-1980s, and it grew steadily until 2001. Black auteur Spike Lee launched his film production company in Brooklyn, New York, in 1985 and called it 40 Acres and a Mule.[33] In 1987, a new group calling for the repair, healing, and restoration of blacks injured by slavery and American apartheid geared up for a major offensive.

Led by Adjoa Aiyetoro and the late Imari Obadele, the National Coalition of Blacks for Reparations in America (N'COBRA) was founded by the National Conference of Black Lawyers, the New Afrikan People's Organization, and the RNA "for the sole purpose of obtaining reparations for African descendants in the United States." Dorothy Benton Lewis and Irving Davis also were instrumental figures in the development of N'COBRA.

N'COBRA hosted a series of meetings and established chapters across the country as well as in London and Ghana.[34] Then, in 1989, U.S. representative John Conyers (D-Mich.), with assistance from N'COBRA, introduced H.R. 40 in the 112th Congress, a bill to establish the Commission to Study and Develop Reparation Proposals for African Americans. The commission was to be tasked with conducting research and determining "whether . . . any form of compensation to the descendants of African slaves is warranted."[35]

Conyers introduced the bill at the start of every Congress and planned to do so until it was passed into law. As we go to press, with Conyers's exit from Congress in December 2017 amid sexual harassment accusations, Rep. Sheila Jackson Lee (D-Tex.) is now the new sponsor of H.R. 40. Sen. Cory Booker (D-N.J.) is the lead sponsor for the Senate version of the bill, S. 1083.

But H.R.40 never has reached the floor of Congress for a vote. The public visibility of the act has been maintained thanks to Conyers's passion for the cause of reparative justice. "Many people want to leave slavery in the past—they contend that slavery happened so long ago that it is hurtful and divisive to bring it up now," he wrote in 2013. "But the concept of reparations is not a foreign idea to either the U.S. government or governments throughout the world."[36]

Reparations were in the American air. Indeed, between 1993 and 2005, in three separate instances of injustice against blacks, compensation was pursued through different governing bodies to some measure of success. The first instance occurred in 1994, when the Florida legislature decided to investigate atrocities committed against blacks during the 1923 Rosewood white riot, which claimed the lives of an estimated twenty-nine blacks and two whites.[37]

Florida has an abysmal record of mass white terror directed toward blacks, dating at least from 1913. At that time, many white Floridians were incensed by rumors that European women had fraternized with black soldiers during their World War I tours of duty.[38] Between 1913 and 1917, at least twenty-nine lynchings—none of which were prosecuted—were recorded in the state. The greatest number of murders was recorded on Election Day 1920, described by historian Paul Ortiz as "the single bloodiest day in modern American political history." One black town, Ocoee, was burned to the ground after two black men, Mose Norman and Jule Perry, attempted to vote. Walter White, then assistant secretary of the NAACP, estimated that in Ocoee alone, at least fifty blacks were murdered. Thereafter, Ocoee became a whites-only town.[39]

More than seventy years afterward, the Florida legislature commissioned its study to determine the causes of the white massacre in Rosewood.[40] White anger had been ignited when false stories circulated alleging that a white woman had been beaten and raped by a black man. An organized white mob lynched a local black man, Sam Carter, and then proceeded to hunt down other blacks and burn nearly every house in the community. State and local authorities were aware of the carnage but made no arrests.

Many disturbing incidents had occurred in nearby Gainesville immediately before the Rosewood riot. In 1922, the editor of the Gainesville *Daily Sun* had boasted in the pages of his own paper of his membership in the Ku Klux Klan.[41] Furthermore, 100 members of the Klan had marched in Gainesville—fifty miles from Rosewood—the day before the riot.

Local police failed in their duty to protect the Rosewood residents, and they did not investigate the murders. Special Master Richard Hixson, the man who presided over the Florida legislative proceedings, wrote in the culminating report, "It . . . is clear that government officials were responsible for some of the damages sustained by the claimants."[42]

After initially recommending $7 million, the legislative body ultimately approved an award of $2.1 million—$150,000 to each person who could document their residence in the community in 1923—and a separate fund totaling $500,000 for individuals who would receive reparations if they could prove, by application, that they had an ancestor who had lived in Rosewood in 1923.

Nine individuals received payments under the implementation of this law. The claims bill also included a provision for a scholarship fund for the families and direct descendants of Rosewood's residents to attend Florida's public colleges or postsecondary vocational-technical schools.[43] Given the extreme level of terror in Florida early in the twentieth century, it is striking that the Rosewood reparations are *the only instance of compensation provided to victims of white terror by the state.* In chapter 10 we describe numerous mass killings and the barbarity directed against black Americans in the first half of the twentieth century. The evidence notwithstanding, to the best of our knowledge, Florida is the only state to make any compensatory payments to the victims of white riots.

The second instance in which blacks were the recipients of some measure of reparative justice—a class-action lawsuit mounted on behalf of black American farmers against the U.S. Department of Agriculture—was a boost to reparations proponents. The case, *Pigford v. Glickman*—named for Timothy Pigford, a black North Carolina farmer, and Daniel Robert Glickman, then secretary of the Department of Agriculture—was settled in the plaintiff's favor for $1.25 billion in 1999, but ten years later no payouts had been made.

New litigation grew out of *Pigford I*, a class-action lawsuit filed in 1997, in which 400 African American farmers alleged the Department of Agriculture had systematically discriminated against them from 1983 to 1997. The farmers made three charges: the federal agency had procrastinated in processing their loan applications, prevented them from having access to farm loans and benefits programs, and ignored or failed to investigate their claims of discrimination. The result of the second class-action lawsuit, *Pigford II*, was a larger number of eligible claimants. Affected farmers finally began to receive awards in 2013.[44]

Of the 22,505 applicants, 13,348 were approved and received cash or credit up to $50,000. Less than 1 percent pursued larger amounts. The largest award, $13 million, was paid to the now-defunct farm collective New Communities, about a dozen farm families in the southwestern counties of Georgia. Eligible black agricultural producers who joined the *Pigford* lawsuit had been given two options when filing their claims: receive a one-time payment of $50,000 or present extensive documentation to support a larger claim. Missing records, some of which may have been lost or destroyed by the U.S. Department of Agriculture itself, made it impossible for many of the farmers to file for claims larger than the one-time fixed payment.[45]

For adherents tracking these developments, the constellation of advocates uniting around reparations for African Americans in the late 1990s, back-to-back redress successes, and the moral certainty of their cause signified eventual victory. Unlike the apprehension that had stymied the efforts of Callie House and others lobbying on behalf of ex-slaves 100 years earlier, there seemed to be a growing consensus that the timing was right and national sentiments had changed.

In 1997, the Oklahoma legislature authorized funding for the Oklahoma Commission to Study the Tulsa Riot of 1921 to conduct research on the white rebellion and make recommendations.[46] The commission found that the Tulsa riot of 1921 occurred during the epoch of the most deadly wave of white urban antiblack violence in the nation's history. Over a two-day period, a white mob torched more than 1,200 black homes, a hospital, a junior high school, several churches, and 191 businesses in Tulsa's Greenwood community, burning them to the ground. Utilizing six World War I–issue airplanes, whites even pursued blacks from the air with rifles and dropped firebombs on them as they attempted to escape. Estimates indicate that as many as 300 African Americans were murdered.[47]

The late John Hope Franklin, celebrated historian and author, grew up in Oklahoma. His father, Buck "Charles" Colbert Franklin, an attorney, worked in Tulsa's Greenwood business district and was in the city when the massacre occurred. The younger Franklin became a consultant to the commission and eventually a plaintiff in a class-action lawsuit seeking reparations.[48]

In 1997, the same year the Tulsa Riot Commission was formed, President Bill Clinton issued a call for colleges and universities to participate in his National Conversation on Race initiative. John Hope Franklin was appointed to chair the conversation. Bethune-Cookman College participated by recruiting six whites and six blacks from Daytona, Florida, and the surrounding counties to participate in a mock trial and judge the merits of black Americans' reparations claims.[49] The verdict was unanimous in favor of the plaintiffs and included a recommendation that the federal government develop a program to provide restitution to African Americans.

When the Oklahoma Commission to Study the Tulsa Riot of 1921 issued its report three years later, it recommended the 125 survivors be paid reparations. The commission's restorative justice plan also specified solutions such as a scholarship fund for families affected by the riot, an economic development zone in the Greenwood neighborhood where the violence was greatest, and resources for reburial of any human remains that might be found in the unmarked graves of victims.[50] Although the Tulsa riot claimed the lives of ten times more black residents than the Rosewood white riot and destroyed significantly more property, the Oklahoma legislature enacted no mandate and made no payments.

Undeterred, in 2000, a group of accomplished litigators and activist scholars founded the Reparations Coordinating Committee and developed a class-action suit on behalf of the plaintiffs in the 1921 Tulsa massacre. Significantly, their efforts were directed exclusively at the 125 extant survivors still living in 2003, not their descendants. Cochaired by Charles Ogletree (Harvard Law School) and Adjoa Aiyetoro (N'COBRA and the International Association of Black Lawyers), the Reparations Coordinating Committee's legal efforts generated a great deal of attention but, ultimately, were not successful. Later, committee members attempted to develop a general class-action suit for reparations on behalf of all African Americans, but it, too, fell short.[51] It is reasonable to assume that all remaining survivors will die before any compensation ever is delivered.[52]

After the failed attempt to achieve compensation for the survivors of the Tulsa riot, the reparations battleground shifted to Wilmington, North Carolina, and the white insurrection that took place in 1898. The effectiveness of the black male vote in North Carolina, combined with the freedmen's support of the Fusion movement, was an affront to white supremacy. Fusion had brought predominantly white farmers in the Populist movement into a coalition with the Republican Party, increasingly influenced by black voters. Fusion candidates triumphed in the state's 1894 elections, and in 1896 North Carolina elected its first Republican governor since Reconstruction, Daniel L. Russell, breaking the Democratic Party's two-decade hold on the position.[53]

Meticulously planned and systematically encouraged by white supremacist agitation, the goal of the Wilmington massacre was the overthrow of the city's elected Republican municipal administration. More than 2,000 white Democratic Party supporters, determined to reclaim "North Carolina [as] a WHITE MAN'S STATE and WHITE MEN will rule it," forcibly removed lawfully elected black and white officials from government buildings, attacked blacks across the city, and vandalized and burned dozens of black homes and businesses, including the newspaper owned by brothers Alexander and Frank Manly, the *Daily Record*.[54]

Black casualty estimates ranged from 60 to 300. Many blacks left the city permanently. The plotters were drawn from the "best class" of the city's white people, including, most visibly, Alfred M. Waddell, a former Confederate army colonel who installed himself as mayor after the massacre.[55] Waddell, a four-time Democratic incumbent congressman, had lost his seat to Daniel Russell in 1878. Russell, a rare member of the planter class who had been a staunch Unionist, had made the even more uncharacteristic decision to align himself with the Republican Party after the Civil War.

Charles Brantley Aycock became a revered education reformer when he was elected North Carolina's fiftieth governor in 1900, but his white supremacist credentials were unassailable. His inflammatory antiblack rhetoric on the stump in the run-up to the 1898 election played an important role in fomenting the white assault in Wilmington.

After learning that the coup was in motion, Aycock, then living in Goldsboro, made his way to the train station, prepared to fight alongside the white rioters. He canceled his plans and remained in Goldsboro when a telegram reached him and the other 500 armed white men who were ready to board the train to Wilmington informing them that the whites were satisfactorily in control.[56] "Good government in the State and peace anywhere" were within the Democrats' grasp, Aycock said in 1900 when he accepted his party's unanimous nomination for governor, "but [first] we must disenfranchise the Negro."[57]

Julian Carr, an influential tobacco, textile, and banking industrialist born into a slave-owning family, donated sixty-two acres of land that enabled Trinity College to move to Durham, North Carolina, in 1892. Carr's contribution ensured the college's survival and prosperity; it would become Duke University. At the same time, Carr was involved deeply with North Carolina's anti-Fusion Democratic Party. He supported Josephus Daniels in acquiring the Raleigh newspaper, the *News and Observer*, which served as a major organ of the violent white supremacy campaign. In December 1898, a month after the Wilmington massacre, Carr championed the massacre as a "grand and glorious event."[58]

In the aftermath of the butchery in Wilmington, the stage was set for the white supremacists to gain full control of North Carolina's political apparatus. Carr fervently urged white male voters to go to the polls on August 2, 1900, to adopt two amendments, the "grandfather clause" and a poll tax, that effectively would disenfranchise black voters:

It is not my desire to try and stampede your fears by crying "Nigger."
For my part, I would gladly rejoice to strike the word "Nigger" from the

vocabulary of North Carolina politics. But the nigger, in the Providence of God is here, and we believe here to stay. And, I am not ashamed to say in this presence that I have been a friend of the negro, in the negro's place. From my very make-up I am for the "underdog in the fight," so that whenever and wherever the negro has behaved himself, and kept himself in his place, my disposition has been to lend him a helping hand. . . . And yet, after I have said all this; I stand here and declare that as a citizen worthy to enjoy the rights of the franchise the negro is a failure.[59]

Ultimately, the 1898 Wilmington Race Riot Commission recommended, in 2006, that reparations be paid to the descendants of the victims. To this day, the North Carolina legislature has refused to do so.

The third reparations success story—or, at least, partial success story—at the turn of the latest century, involved the 1959 decision of the local school board in Prince Edward County, Virginia, to shut down its school system rather than comply with the *Brown v. Board of Education* desegregation decision. The county's closure of its schools represented one of the most extreme examples of "massive resistance" to the Supreme Court's injunction that the racially dual system of education must come to an end.

While the state of Virginia and Prince Edward County provided vouchers and tax credits to enable white students to attend newly formed all-white academies, no resources were provided for black students to continue their schooling.[60] The school board's refusal to reopen the public schools until 1964 effectively denied many black students the opportunity to further their education. The chains that were placed on the district's school doors to exclude black students from access to education reminded some of the chains that were placed directly on their ancestors during slavery.[61]

Not until 2005—forty-six years after the school closings—did the state of Virginia undertake any effort to atone for the costs of these actions in Prince Edward County. Combining private donations from billionaire John Kluge with state funds, scholarships were offered to the victims of the shuttered school system to enable them to pursue higher education at this much later date. No compensation was offered for past years of lost schooling. Nor was compensation offered to offset the impact of the lost schooling on the affected students' long-term prospects for employment and earnings. Because the victims who still were living were overwhelmingly persons in their fifties and sixties at the time of Virginia's "reparations" plan, only a few were in a position—so deep in adulthood—to take full advantage of a funded opportunity for college and university education.

Despite the widely divergent outcomes of the Rosewood, Pigford, Tulsa, Wilmington, and Prince Edward County claims, excitement surrounded these efforts. They encouraged advocates to speak out about the debt America owed to African Americans. Through diligent research, scholars seeking to broaden the targets of the restitution campaign unearthed and published the names of a dozen present-day corporations that had profited from the Atlantic slave trade in the past. In their view, all slavery-linked profits were unjust enrichment.

The investment bank Lehman Brothers and textile producer WestPoint Stevens, whose fortunes had been built on slave-grown cotton, were called to account, as were the Mobile & Girard Railroad—part of present-day Norfolk Southern Railroad—and the Richmond, Fredericksburg & Potomac Railroad—now CSX—which routinely had rented human chattel by the year to lay rail lines. Dozens of newspaper companies still in circulation founded before and during the antebellum era—Knight Ridder, E. W. Scripps, and Gannett, owner of *USA Today*, among them—had profited from the sale of advertisements promising rewards for the capture and return of runaway slaves, slave auction notices, and recruitment circulars for crews to operate slave ships. Researchers identified dozens of merchants like the Brooks Brothers clothier, which had expanded its operations to capitalize on lucrative southern American and Caribbean plantation markets, the very markets that supplied them with the raw cotton and other slave-made goods the company used to manufacture the clothing it offered to its growing customer base.[62]

Another potential set of targets emerged in 2000: corporations that had "insured slave owners against the loss of their human chattel."[63] Slaves were human property who could be bought, sold, traded, or inherited. The California legislature requested its Department of Insurance make inquiries about "ill-gotten profits from slavery, which profits in part capitalized insurers whose successors remain in existence today."[64] A number of the state's insurance corporations affirmed their "abhor[rence for] the practice of slavery" and expressed "profound . . . regrets that [their] predecessor was associated in any way with that contemptible practice," but none offered to pay reparations.

The American International Group predecessor, United States Life Insurance Company (N.Y.), was founded in 1850. One of the results of its self-study was the discovery of an article published in an unnamed periodical in which a policy, valued at $550, was written on human property listed only as "Charles." Specifically, conditions of death that were excluded from coverage included the following: "Death to said slave by means of any invasion, insurrection, riot, civil commotion, or of any military or usurped power, or in case the slave shall die by his own hand, or in consequence of a duel, or by the hands of justice . . . this Policy shall be void, null, and of no effect."[65]

During the period when reparations advocates were developing restitution strategies based on historical events, few opponents were engaged in the public debate until the emergence, in January 2001, of a singularly energized antireparations pundit. David Horowitz placed an incendiary advertisement in college newspapers across the country, "Ten Reasons Why Reparations for Blacks is a Bad Idea for Blacks—and Racist Too."[66] The ads effectively introduced the subject of reparations to a new generation of Americans and led many to review or acquaint themselves with the country's involvement with the Atlantic slave trade. Horowitz's position held that only those enslaved and their immediate descendants were due recompense. Since all of those individuals were presumed dead, for Horowitz, the matter was closed.

Horowitz's platform possibly had the unintended consequence of setting off a series of heated public and private rebuttals, effectively rekindling the reparations conversation. The United Nations hosted the World Conference Against Racism in Durban, South Africa, from August 31 to September 8, 2001, and declared it would seek compensation for slavery as a goal.

Sensing that the time had come to take a dramatic public stand, Rev. Jesse Jackson insisted it was important for companies that had been founded before or during the antebellum period to reveal the extent of their involvement in the Atlantic slave trade and consider making amends. "All those years of work without wages are the foundation of American wealth," Jackson said. "America must acknowledge its roots in the slavery empire, apologize for it . . . and work on some plan to compensate. An apology is in order. But you must not only apologize with your lips. Repent, repair and remedy go together."[67]

But how would an estimate of those profits be determined? Using arguments based in part on historical documents she received from the defendants, Deadria Farmer-Paellmann began preparation for a lawsuit against FleetBoston Financial (formerly Providence Bank), Aetna, and New York Life Insurance Company. One of the major items Farmer-Paellmann used to document her case was a 1906 history of the New York Life Insurance Company, which indicated that 339 of the first 1,000 policies written by the firm insured slaveholders against losses of their human property.[68] Under the auspices of its subsidiary, Nautilus, New York Life Insurance Company also insured the lives of at least 485 enslaved people for their owners during a two-year period in the 1840s.[69]

Farmer-Paellmann's goal was to force the defendants to provide "an accounting, constructive trust, restitution, disgorgement and compensatory and punitive damages arising out of [their] past and continued wrongful conduct."[70] But momentum, building for the first eight months of 2001, shut down after 9/11, as the nation grieved and attempted to make sense of the events of the day. Farmer-Paellmann's research brought to light a rich potential source for reparations, but the case failed.

Another five years passed before the reparations movement had any prominence again in the news. Between 2007 and 2008, at least six state legislatures issued apologies for slavery or for slavery and Jim Crow, signaling what many believed to be critical encouraging first steps toward reparations. State legislatures in Virginia, Maryland, North Carolina, and Alabama all issued apologies in 2007, while those in New Jersey and Florida made apologies in 2008—and expressed "profound regret" for their state's role in slavery.

When the North Carolina Senate passed its measure denouncing slavery and legal segregation in 2007, state senator Bill Purcell observed that his grandfather was a slave owner, something that had always troubled him.[71] The resolution that Purcell, just two generations removed from slavery times, voted for in North Carolina said, in part, "The General Assembly issues its apology for the practice of slavery in North Carolina and expresses a profound contrition for the official acts that sanctioned and perpetuated the denial of basic human rights and dignity to fellow humans."[72]

Then, in June 2009, the U.S. House of Representatives and the Senate unanimously passed an apology for slavery. Although these formal apologies garnered headlines and brought the country's unequal history to the attention of many Americans, they were frequently—some would say intentionally—worded in such a way as to preempt actual compensation to the descendants of the enslaved.

The reparations conversation vanished from the headlines, not to return visibly to national attention until June 2014, when journalist and public intellectual Ta-Nehisi Coates published a major article in the *Atlantic* titled "The Case for Reparations."[73] The dramatic response to Coates's article reawakened discussion and debate over black reparations in America.

The major compensation strategies pursued over the previous twenty-five years typically have been piecemeal and directed at the courts for remedy. But the courts have not been responsive to class-action suits on behalf of all black Americans for historical injustice, making a large-scale program of reparations via the judicial route unlikely. Not only is there a barrier to suits brought against the government by sovereign immunity, but while private corporations' exploitation of slave labor was immoral, it was also legal under national laws.

An additional disadvantage of approaches like that put forth by Farmer-Paellmann is the absence of a rationale for reparations driven by the unjust practices of the Jim Crow era. No consideration is given to the harms of legal segregation to remaining living victims or younger generations who also bear the cumulative, intergenerational burden of that history.

Claims for the harms of Jim Crow would be more consistent with the enactment of the Civil Liberties Act of 1988, the enabling legislation that mandated reparations for Japanese Americans who had been subjected to incarceration during World War II. This was accomplished by congressional, not judicial, action. We detail a litany of the wrongs committed against African Americans under legal segregation in chapters 10 and 11.

Furthermore, judicial success that is not greeted with broad popular support—*a level of popular support needed to propel Congress to adopt black reparations*—will result in "massive resistance" comparable to the response to the *Brown v. Board* decision in 1954. Therefore, we conclude that a large-scale program of redress will require congressional action to ensure the provision of coverage and amounts of monies that meet the magnitude of the just claim.

While some anticipated that Barack Obama's election might reignite the debate, he short-circuited the conversation before his presidency began. When the NAACP interviewed him in August 2008, Obama said:

> I have a lot of respect for Congressman John Conyers and I'm glad that the NAACP gave him its highest honor this year. While I know where his heart is at, I fear that reparations would be an excuse for some to say "we've paid our debt" and to avoid the much harder work of enforcing our anti-discrimination laws in employment and housing; the much harder work of making sure that our schools are not separate but unequal; the much harder work of lifting thirty-seven million Americans of all races out of poverty.
>
> These challenges will not go away with reparations, so while I applaud and agree with the underlying sentiment of recognizing the continued legacy of slavery, I would prefer to focus on the issues that will directly address these problems and building a consensus to do just that.[74]

As a candidate, not only did Obama have a narrow view of the potential of black reparations; he also assumed that the case for reparations is based exclusively on the grounds of the enslavement of black people in the United States. His comments completely ignored the case in the decades following slavery—nearly 100 years of Jim Crow and ongoing, present-day discrimination.

Of course, neither has his successor, Donald Trump, been an enthusiast for black reparations. That Trump, the most overtly white supremacist president since Woodrow Wilson, does not support a program of compensatory action for the nation's injustices toward black Americans is wholly unsurprising.[75] He made his sentiments quite clear when he reacted to protestors holding "Black Lives Matter" signs at a 2015 press conference in South Carolina, charging that blacks complaining about conditions in the United States should "go back to Africa": "There's no such thing as racism anymore. We've had a black president, so it's not a question anymore. Are they saying black lives should matter more than white lives or Asian lives? If black lives matter, then go back to Africa. We'll see how much they matter there."[76]

Certainly Trump's assertion that "there's no such thing as racism anymore" is discredited by his own presidential campaign and the outlook and actions of his most ardent supporters.[77]

Unexpectedly, the 2018 congressional midterm elections were followed by an even greater surge of interest in black reparations. A movement blossomed in early 2019 on electronic network platforms under the label #ADOS, an acronym for American Descendants of Slavery. This digital campaign asserts that black American descendants of persons enslaved in the United States have a unique and exceptional claim on the nation's government for justice.[78]

Coincident with the emergence of #ADOS, the 2020 major party candidates for the presidency engaged seriously with the reparations project for the first time since the Reconstruction era. Marianne Williamson and Julián Castro were most explicit about their support during the early phase of the primary season. However, only Williamson was bold enough to make an explicit commitment to establishment of a fund and to designate an amount to undertake a black reparations program.[79]

Several Democratic candidates also indicated their support for H.R. 40.[80] As noted above, the bill establishes a congressional commission charged with documenting the long and cumulative trajectory of harms visited upon black Americans and designing remedies for redress that can be translated into enabling legislation for a reparations program. Finally, hearings on H.R. 40 were held before the House Judiciary Committee's Subcommittee on the Constitution, Civil Rights, and Civil Liberties, chaired by Steve Cohen

(D-Tenn.), on June 19, 2019, a signal moment because the bill had never before reached that stage of congressional consideration.[81]

Of course, any sitting president, at his or her own discretion, can appoint a national commission with a similar charge without waiting for congressional approval. The effectiveness of the commission necessarily is contingent on the convictions and expertise of the commissioners and on the designation of an appropriate deadline for completion of their report, preferably no longer than eighteen months.

For black reparations to become a reality, a dramatic change in who serves as the nation's elected officials must take place, both in Congress and in the White House. New national leadership must be committed fully to black reparations. Making this happen requires, in turn, an inspired national movement dedicated to the fulfillment of the goal of racial justice.

2

Myths of Racial Equality

We are basically talking about an economic system that is shot through with discrimination. —Bernard E. Anderson, former assistant secretary of labor, Howard University, 2013

And I want to raise another point about this business about reparations. Palliatives like Affirmative Action will never close the economic gap. This gap is structural. It's not even about salary. Because the black community has been denied so much in wealth-building tools; blacks, even middle-class blacks, have no paper assets to speak of. They may be salaried, but they're only a few months away from poverty if they should lose those jobs, because they have handed—they've had nothing to hand down from generation to generation because of the ravages of discrimination and segregation, which were based in law until recently, and so that the black community economically is very vulnerable, and we have this enormous gap.

Now, this gap was opened, because of the deeds of the United States government, which has a responsibility to make that right. And that has to be a part of our demand. But we have an America that is urging other countries to face up to their past wrongful deeds, while America is unwilling to even acknowledge its past wrongful deed. What crime against humanity could be more horrible than slavery? Or lynching? Or restrictive covenants? Or mortgage discrimination? Or job discrimination? Or housing discrimination? Or all of the varied forms of discrimination that have held people down. —Randall Robinson, interview with Democracy Now, 2000

At the end of the introduction, we identified three tiers of injustice that form the basis for black reparations in the United States: slavery, Jim Crow, and ongoing racial inequality and racism. Most Americans agree that both slavery and legal apartheid were horrific moral outrages, but there are alarmingly large numbers of Americans, both white and black, who do not believe that racial inequality and discrimination continue to exist. For them, blacks are fully engaged in every aspect of American life. For them, the entire third tier of the platform for reparations is a figment of the beholders' imaginations. If blacks are not drowning, they ask, why throw them a special lifeline?

For example, a Pew Research Center survey conducted in 2016 reveals the prevalence of these mistaken beliefs. Researchers found that large proportions of both whites and blacks affirm there is no lingering racial financial disparity. An astonishing 38 percent of blacks contended that blacks are at least as well off or better off financially than whites; among whites, the proportion sharing that opinion was 42 percent.[1]

In addition, 38 percent of white respondents believed the nation has already made all the policy "changes needed to give blacks equal rights with whites." A majority of white respondents thought blacks are treated as fairly as whites in the courts. More than 70 percent of whites thought that blacks are treated similarly to whites when applying for a loan or mortgage, in the workplace, in restaurants, and when voting in elections. Less than 40 percent of blacks shared the same views on their treatment in the courts, in seeking a loan or mortgage, or in the workplace. But a majority of blacks shared the same views as most whites on their treatment in restaurants (51 percent) and in the voting process (57 percent). Half of whites believed blacks are treated as fairly as whites in their encounters with the police, in contrast with a mere 16 percent of blacks.[2]

More than 60 percent of whites did not believe racial discrimination continues to be an important barrier to blacks "getting ahead." Forty-seven percent of whites rejected the notion that lower-quality schools constituted an obstacle for blacks, and 55 percent of whites rejected the idea that a lack of jobs prevents blacks from "getting ahead." In all three of these cases, at least 66 percent of black respondents surveyed thought these factors significantly inhibit black achievement.[3]

However, with respect to factors associated with self-defeating deficiencies in the black community as important reasons for blacks not "getting ahead," white and black respondents held similar views. A striking 43 percent of blacks said a "lack of motivation to work hard" is an important factor producing black-white inequality, in contrast with only 30 percent of whites. Even higher proportions of both groups attributed any ongoing black-white gaps to "family instability" (57 percent of blacks and 55 percent of whites) and to the "lack of good role models" (51 percent of blacks and 52 percent of whites).[4]

So while there were sharp differences in black and white perceptions of the role of societal factors in perpetuating racial economic inequality, there was a sharp convergence on the role of alleged cultural-behavioral factors. A significant proportion of blacks bought the view alleging that black dysfunction helps explain racial inequality in the United States. Moreover, to the extent that the respondents to the Pew survey saw racism as having any ongoing impact, more of them, both white (70 percent) and black (a plurality of 48 percent), emphasized "individual prejudice" as the problem, rather than the system of "laws and institutions."[5]

In *From Here to Equality*, we intend to convince you that America has not transcended racism. Nor has the passage of the Civil Rights Act resulted in economic equality for African Americans. Nor did the election of a black man as president signify the attainment of racial equality. Moreover, the incidence of poverty, unemployment, overincarceration, wealth disparities at all levels of income, and inferior levels of well-being among blacks cannot be explained by defective black behaviors. There is something profoundly wrong with the way we think about how race and racism operate in American society.

In this chapter, we drill down on three key errors that must be corrected. These errors are embodied in the following three erroneous beliefs: (1) Racism and discrimination no longer exist in the United States; (2) there are no significant economic disparities between blacks and whites; and (3) to the extent that there are any residual racial economic disparities they must be due to dysfunctional behavior on the part of blacks.

We rely heavily on statistical findings, rather than anecdotes, to develop a clear portrait of the operation of race and racism in contemporary America. While there always are individuals—some of whom each of us may recognize, at least from afar—who are exceptions to the general pattern, the character of a society is determined most accurately by the typical or average experience of its members.

Economists with a wide range of ideological perspectives also have embraced racial cultural determinism—the idea that race-linked behaviors and attitudes explain racial inequality in the United States.[6] This dangerous line of thinking alleges the black-white economic gap is due not to an acutely unequal playing field but to blacks' deficient skills, training, and motivation. Its defenders allege that group-based inequality ultimately can be eliminated if black Americans exercise enough willpower and do "the right thing."

According to this view, insofar as black Americans possess the capacity to improve their status by altering their own behavior, the nation can be absolved of responsibility. Ostensibly, once blacks as a group take these self-correcting actions, all disparities simply will fall away.

The central problem is, as we demonstrate later in this chapter, positive effort, strong motivation, and high academic achievement never have been sufficient to eliminate disparities in racial economic well-being, security, and opportunity. Moreover, cultural determinism ignores predatory acts on the part of whites, like the seizure of black-owned land and destruction of black-owned property. Indeed, in general, it ignores the history of violent acts against blacks that continue to the present day.

It is important to acknowledge that whites control political and economic power in this country. No shift in the power relationship will be possible unless the society as a whole takes action to transform the structural conditions to make racial equality a real possibility. Given the existing distribution of financial and real resources, *blacks cannot close the racial wealth gap by independent or autonomous action*. One powerful example that challenges the thinking of those who prefer America's feel-good myth of equality is provided by a close analysis of wealth disparity in this country. *Wealth is the best single indicator of the cumulative impact of white racism over time.* Wealth—the difference between what we own and what we owe (or the difference between the value of our assets and our debts, or the net value of our property)—is the economic measure that best captures individual, family, and household well-being:

> Wealth serves as a primary indicator of economic security. Wealthier families are better positioned to finance elite independent school and college education, access capital to start a business, finance expensive medical procedures, reside in higher amenity neighborhoods, exert political influence through campaign financing, purchase better counsel if confronted with an expensive legal system, leave a bequest, and/or withstand financial hardship resulting from any number of emergencies. . . . Wealth provides financial agency over one's life. Simply put, wealth gives individuals and families *choice*; it provides economic security to take risks and shield against financial loss.[7]

Data from the 2016 Survey of Consumer Finances indicates that *median black household net worth ($17,600) is only one-tenth of white net worth ($171,000)*.[8] That means, on average, that for every dollar the middle white household holds in wealth—measured by assets like homes, cash savings, and retirement funds—the middle black household possesses a mere ten cents.[9]

Among black households with positive net worth there is a greater reliance on home ownership as a source of wealth than among white households. Customarily, we have assumed that equity in a home was a secure and stable source of wealth, but recent experience during the Great Recession has torpedoed that belief. The collapse of home ownership and equity value in homes has affected black households adversely and disproportionately.[10]

Moreover, home ownership and total wealth do not track each other as closely as many Americans imagine. For example, a survey conducted in the Los Angeles metropolitan area in 2014–15 demonstrates that the rate of African American home ownership (42 percent) is slightly higher than that of the city's Asian Indians (40 percent), an immigrant community consisting disproportionately of highly educated, affluent professionals. On the basis of home ownership rates, one might expect the two Los Angeles communities to have similar net worth; however, the median Asian Indian household net worth was $460,000, as opposed to only $4,000 for African Americans, less than 1 percent of the former.[11]

The difference appears to be due to far greater rates and levels of ownership of financial assets by Asian Indian households. Fifty-nine percent of Asian Indian households owned stocks, mutual funds, and investment trusts, while only 22 percent of African American households owned the same types of assets.[12] The capacity even to enter markets for remunerative financial assets is contingent on having a significant endowment of wealth in the first place.[13]

From 2005 to 2009, an interval that captures the impact of the Great Recession, median household wealth (all assets minus all debt, the latter including mortgages, credit card balances, and other loans) among blacks actually fell by a whopping 53 percent, compared with a drop of 16 percent among whites.[14] Clearly these vast disparities in black and white wealth are not consistent with claims of any circumstance approximating racial economic equality.

Some have suggested that the racial wealth gap is explained by black profligacy: blacks' unwillingness to commit to a careful plan of saving and blacks' ignorance about proper investment practices. A virtual cottage industry has developed to provide "financial literacy" to black families. But it is striking that there is very little, if any, evidence to support the claim that black saving behavior is the source of the enormous racial wealth gap.[15]

If we consider black and white families with similar income levels, we discover no significant difference in savings rates, nor a difference in rates of return on their personal investments. In fact, in some income categories, blacks display a higher rate of savings. Somehow, blacks manage to have a savings profile comparable to whites with similar income levels, despite the fact that blacks have more kin obligation because their relatives are more likely to be in need than those of comparably situated whites. These family obligations reduce the total income available for saving and wealth building. Nevertheless, the black savings rate is comparable to the white savings rate at each level of household income.[16]

Nor do differences in family structure provide headway in explaining black-white wealth inequality. Single white women with children have as high a median net worth as black women with no children. Single white parents have more than two times the wealth ($35,000), at the median, of married black parents ($16,000). The professed economic benefits associated with having the "ideal" family type do not translate into closure of the racial wealth gap. Being a "stable," married, two-parent black family far from evens black and white wealth levels.[17]

Furthermore, there are vast differences in wealth between black and white women. For example, older (over sixty years of age) single black women with a bachelor's degree have a median net worth of about $11,000, while single white women with a college degree, in the same age range, have $384,000 in median net worth. Single mothers have negligible wealth, but the racial difference still is palpable: white single mothers have a median net worth of $3,000, but black single mothers have a median net worth of *zero*.[18]

While young adult (twenty- to twenty-nine-year-old) single white women who have completed college have a median net worth of $3,400, single black women of a similar age and level of education have a median net worth of *negative* $11,000.[19] A report on the racial wealth gap from Prosperity Now concludes: "The greatest socio-economic disparities for most women of color are rooted in racial inequality, which is then worsened by smaller but significant gendered disparities. It follows that, within the most economically disenfranchised racial and ethnic groups, such as Blacks and Latinos, gendered disparities are usually much smaller than among Whites. African American women and Latinas experience greater gender economic equality within their racial and ethnic groups. However, this parity is more an equality in economic disenfranchisement than an equality in economic wellbeing."[20]

The belief that blacks lack motivation and effort is contradicted by the evidence on racial differences in educational attainment. For comparable levels of family socioeconomic status, black youth obtain more years of schooling and credentials, including college degrees, than white youth.[21] Moreover, unfortunately, motivation and effort are not enough to close the black-white wealth gap. Data from both the Survey of Income and Program Participation and the Survey of Consumer Finances provides the facts.

Black household heads with a college or university degree have about $10,000 less in median net worth than white household heads who never completed high school. Blacks who are working full-time have a lower median net worth than whites who are unemployed. Blacks in the third quintile of the income distribution have similar levels of median wealth as whites in the lowest quintile.[22] That means that, on average, blacks whose incomes were about $60,000 in 2014 had a level of median wealth of about $22,000, while whites whose incomes were less than $26,000 had a median wealth of about $18,000. Blacks in the lowest quintile had a median wealth of a paltry $200.[23]

Furthermore, both black income and wealth levels are much less likely to rise or be maintained across generations than white incomes and wealth. Raj Chetty and his research team found that black Americans display lower rates of upward mobility and higher rates of downward mobility than white Americans across generations.[24] A Vox report on this research summarized the authors' findings on race, ethnicity, and downward and upward mobility as follows:

> White children whose parents are in the top fifth of the income distribution have a 41.1 percent chance of staying there as adults; for Hispanic children, the rate is 30.6 percent, and for Asian-American children, 49.9 percent. But for black children, it's only 18 percent, and for American Indian children only 23 percent.
>
> . . . Conversely, upward mobility for children born into the bottom fifth of the distribution is markedly higher among whites than among black or American Indian children. Among children who grew up in the bottom fifth of the distribution, 10.6 percent of whites make it into the top fifth of household incomes themselves, as do 25.5 percent of Asian-Americans. By contrast, only 7.1 percent of Hispanic children born in the bottom fifth make it to the top fifth, along with 3.3 percent of American Indian children and a tiny 2.5 percent of black children.[25]

Similarly, with respect to wealth, Fabian Pfeffer and Alexandra Killewald have established that intergenerational downward mobility is much greater and upward mobility is much lower for blacks than whites.[26]

Both income and wealth mobility processes contribute directly to the maintenance of high levels of racial economic inequality across generations.

The primary sources of the capacity for sustained wealth building for most people are inheritances, in vivo transfers, and the economic security borne of parental and grandparental wealth. In vivo transfers move resources across generations and are made by donors while they still are living, while inheritances are transfers made upon the death of the donor. Both types of transfers are designed to pass property from one generation to the next, to increase the recipients' economic security, and to maintain and consolidate wealth deep into the future.

In vivo transfers can take a wide variety of forms, some so ordinary that they often are taken for granted as normal or unremarkable. They can include parents paying for a son's or daughter's college education or making the down payment on an automobile or a home; grandparents establishing a trust fund for their newborn grandchild; and an aunt or uncle making a substantial monetary gift to a newly married couple.

At an earlier point in time, gifts from white parents to their children sometimes included a transfer of ownership of both land and enslaved black people. "Slaveholders sometimes set up apprenticeships for their slaves as investments to benefit their heirs," Catherine W. Bishir notes in her copiously researched study of black artisans in New Bern, North Carolina. In 1791, enslaved adolescent Abraham was apprenticed to a local carpenter when William Paxton, his owner, willed him to a nephew. In a separate case, Ann Blackedge, a widow, indicated in her will that a black child she owned named Abram should be trained as a cooper while under the legal guardianship of her son William. When Abram reached the age of maturity, he was to become the property of her granddaughter, Ann B. Hatch, "'or if she be dead to my grandson Richard B. Hatch unless my son William prefers to keep him and pay the said Ann B. or Richard B. Hatch $500,' indicating substantial value anticipated for a skilled slave."[27] In 1839, Theodore Dwight Weld, Angelina Grimké Weld, and Sarah Grimké made the following extended observation about the transfer of enslaved persons as gifts of wealth to the succeeding generation:

> We have said that slaveholders regard their slaves not as human beings, but as mere working animals, or merchandise. The whole vocabulary of slaveholders, their laws, their usages, and their entire treatment of their slaves fully establish this. The same terms are applied to slaves that are given to cattle. They are called "stock." So when the children of slaves are spoken of prospectively, they are called their "increase"; the same term that is applied to flocks and herds. So the female slaves that are mothers, are called "breeders" till past child bearing; and often the same terms are applied to the different sexes that are applied to the males and females among cattle. Those who compel the labor of slaves and cattle have the same appellation, "drivers": the names which they call them are the same and similar to those given to their horses and oxen. *The laws of slave states make them property, equally with goats and swine; they are levied upon for debt in the same way; they are included in the same advertisements of public sales with cattle, swine, and asses; when moved from one part of the country to another, they are herded in droves*

like cattle, and like them urged on by drivers; their labor is compelled
in the same way. They are bought and sold, and separated like cattle:
when exposed for sale, their good qualities are described as jockies show
off the good points of their horses; their strength, activity, skill, power
of endurance, &c. are lauded,—and those who bid upon them examine
their persons, just as purchasers inspect horses and oxen; they open their
mouths to see if their teeth are sound; strip their backs to see if they are
badly scarred, and handle their limbs and muscles to see if they are firmly
knit. Like horses, they are warranted to be "sound," or to be returned to
the owner if "unsound." A father gives his son a horse and a *slave*; by his
will he distributes among them his race-horses, hounds, game-cocks,
and *slaves*.[28]

The most systematic contemporary examination of the relationship between parental and grandparental wealth and the next generation's wealth
has been conducted by Pfeffer and Killewald. Using the longitudinal Panel
Study of Income Dynamics, they demonstrate the close relationship between the older two generations' net worth and the net worth of the third
generation.[29] Given blacks' substantially lower levels of wealth in all past
generations, these intergenerational transmission effects work sharply to
their disadvantage.

Pfeffer and Killewald also show how important family wealth is during a
young person's formative years and that grandparental wealth has a significant independent effect on the wealth outcome for the third generation,
which again operates to the detriment of black wealth accumulation.[30]

Laura Feiveson and John Sabelhaus's study conducted for the Federal Reserve under conservative assumptions demonstrates that *at least* 26 percent
of an adult's wealth position is due directly to transfers of inheritances and
gifts; under less restrictive assumptions, they report that the share could rise
as high as 50 percent. Furthermore, these estimates do not take into account
indirect effects of parental resources on the younger generation's net worth
outcome via greater personal security for risk taking and reduced personal
costs of education.[31] Patently, the fewer resources the older generation has
to transfer to the next, the lower the wealth position attained by the younger
generation.[32]

Correspondingly, in an in-depth study of black and white families in the
southwestern United States, Jennifer Mueller revealed immense differences
in the accumulation and the transfer of wealth over three to four generations. The typical white family in her study reported in excess of six times
as many transfers of monetary assets from older to younger generations as

the typical black family. In addition, transfers of land, residential property, and businesses displayed a similar uneven pattern by race. Mueller provides evidence that the source of these disproportionate transfers to whites is in publicly provided assets, including 246 million acres of land, an area approximating that of Florida, Alabama, Georgia, South Carolina, North Carolina, and Virginia combined. This transfer occurred under the auspices of the Homestead Acts (1860s–1930s).[33]

Blacks largely were excluded from the benefits of Homestead Acts; a mere 4,000 to 5,500 African American claimants ever received federal land patents from the Southern Homestead Act enacted in 1866, according to historian Keri Leigh Merritt; white Southern Homestead Act claimants numbered around 28,000. Gifts of Southern Homestead and Homestead Act land enriched "more than 1.6 million white families—both native-born and immigrant."[34] By the year 2000, the estimate of the number of adult descendants of those original land grant recipients was "46 million people, about a quarter of the U.S. adult population."[35]

The key point is that white parents, on average, can provide their children with wealth-related intergenerational advantages to a far greater degree than black parents. When parents offer gifts to help children buy a home, avoid student debt, or start a business, those children are more able to retain and build on their wealth over their own lifetimes. We examine the historical conditions that led to the initial racial gap in resources in greater detail in subsequent chapters, particularly chapter 10.

Another manifestation of America's huge and growing wealth divide is evident in the scale and type of black corporate ownership. The major black-owned businesses—retailers and service providers primarily—garner less than half of 1 percent of the country's total corporate retail sales. In 2014, the top 100 black-owned firms identified by *Black Enterprise* magazine grossed slightly less than $30 billion—*as a group*.[36]

In comparison, the top-revenue-generating white-owned corporation, Walmart, grossed $482 billion, *sixteen times the combined revenue* of the top 100 black-owned firms. Walmart's gross revenues were more than one-half of the total incomes received by all black Americans during the same year. Furthermore, in 2014, even Nike, which ranked ninety-first on the Fortune 500 list with an estimated revenue of $30.6 billion, grossed more than all of the top 100 black-owned businesses.[37]

Americans widely believe that entrepreneurship is the surest route to wealth accumulation. Those who share this view infer that the lower level of black wealth is due to the lower levels of black self-employment and business ownership. But the reverse is far closer to the truth: lower levels of black wealth drive lower levels of self-employment and business ownership. It takes significant initial wealth to launch and sustain a business, and blacks, generally, have considerably less money to commit to such ventures.[38]

The economists David G. Blanchflower and Andrew Oswald have observed that "people with greater family assets" or who receive an inheritance or gift "are more likely to switch to self-employment from employment."[39] Blacks—whose net family assets typically total less than $10,000—simply do not have access to large amounts of capital to contribute to a new business.[40]

Whether one creates a new business or buys into a franchise, launching a new enterprise requires start-up capital and the capacity to leverage additional credit to maintain the enterprise. Here again, blacks are at a distinct disadvantage. The difficulty in capitalizing a new business is compounded for aspiring black entrepreneurs because of discriminatory practices by lending agencies that frequently outright deny them loans or only offer loans at exorbitant terms.

Blanchflower and his colleagues Phillip B. Levine and David J. Zimmerman have examined these lending practices and found, when you control for creditworthiness, that is, when you take creditworthiness into account, that black-owned firms still are twice as likely to be denied loans as whites with otherwise similar financial backgrounds. When black-owned firms succeed in obtaining loans, they are more likely to pay higher interest rates for approved loans. Discrimination can have an "important impact on the likelihood that the business will succeed."[41]

In 1968, twice as many white households as black households had an income of $100,000 (in 2008 dollars) or more. Fifty years later the relative proportions have not changed; it is still the case that about twice as many white households as black households have an income greater than $100,000.[42] Moreover, black *household incomes* remained mired in the vicinity of 55–60 percent of those of white households between 1967 and 2012, so for at least forty-five years.[43]

Black-white per capita income affords an additional related measure of racial economic disparity. Astoundingly, the ratio of income the average black person receives relative to the average white person *has remained largely unchanged for the past fifty years, at about 60 percent.*[44]

America long has perpetuated the myth that ours is a nation of unbounded opportunity and freedom for all. The belief prevails that ethnic immigrants fortunate enough to reach American shores and enter the country as "tired . . . poor . . . huddled masses" at the feet of the Statue of Liberty will be richly rewarded if they work hard, pledge allegiance to the value of education, adopt delayed gratification as their modus operandi, and harness their energies to American success. Ostensibly, if they follow this prescription aggressively, they will reap the rewards of an uptick in income, membership in the greater social and political arena, and most important, admission to the assimilation club called "American-ness."

We refute this fable of immigrant uplift in America. First, all ethnic immigrant groups that came to the United States at the turn of the twentieth century were not from the same social strata. Nor did they all become members of America's higher social classes. Rather, many of those early immigrants "became white," the ultimate proof of Americanization (or "assimilation").[45] Whiteness itself was a prize, even if those immigrants all did not have the same degree of economic success.

One of the byproducts of the whitening of the immigrants was the blurring of distinctions across each group and the erasure of their particular process of assimilation. Often overlooked is the fact that different groups brought significantly different resources with them, and those differences correspond closely with each group's record of comparative success in the United States. An ethnic immigrant's ability to boost his or her status is based on "the relative social standing of the majority of the members of an ethnic [immigrant] group in their country of origin. . . . The highest social status attained by the adult generation that constitutes the bulk of the migrants will play a critical role in the social status achieved by their children and grandchildren in the receiving country."[46] In fact, what the typical immigrant community achieves is *lateral*, rather than upward, mobility.

Others point to the comparatively high levels of education completed and income earned by descendants of Jewish immigrants to the United States during the late nineteenth and early twentieth centuries as proof that the fable of the American Dream is alive and well. In fact, the relative advantage of Jewish immigrants compared to the descendants of their peers can be best explained by the difference in human capital attributes between them and other groups upon arrival: "Although Eastern European Jewish immigrants entered the United States at the turn of the previous century in comparative poverty, they counted among their numbers a much greater proportion of highly skilled artisans, possessed much higher rates of literacy, and the experience of being part of the urban middle classes than other immigrants at the same time. . . . According to [Nathan] Glazer . . . the Jews had been forced out of their traditional skilled occupations, especially in Russia, by 'governmental anti-Semitism and the industrial revolution.'"[47]

When this wave of Jewish immigrants entered the United States, their appearance gave the mistaken impression that they were drawn from eastern Europe's lower classes. Glazer attributes this disconnect to their history of having been forced out of long-held occupations and deprived of their customary middle-class positions in their countries of origin. Other scholars determined that "[the] proportion of Jews who declared upon entry that they were laborers, farmers or servants averaged less than 25 percent in 1900–1902 compared to 80–90 percent of the other immigrant groups. In addition, [in] 1910 and 1914 . . . about 90 percent of Croatians, Slovenians, Greeks, Hungarians, Poles, [non-Jewish] Russians, and Italians compared to 20 percent of the Jews were laborers, farmers, or servants."[48]

Even the successes of immigrants of color—now frequently labeled with the unfortunate moniker "model minorities"—also can be best explained by *lateral mobility.* When the term "model minority" was first directed at Japanese Americans, by sociologist William Petersen in a 1966 *New York Times Magazine* essay, immigration historian Roger Daniels asserted the term was "as much . . . a way of putting down groups [Petersen] regarded as disruptive as a way of hailing the undoubted achievements of [Japanese Americans] from the disasters of World War II."[49]

Japanese Americans' ability to recover from the depredations of wartime mass incarceration was due to the selectivity of the earlier immigrants to the United States, the Issei generation. In his studies of the Immigration and Naturalization Service, economic historian Masao Suzuki identifies at least three levels of selectivity that explain the Japanese American success story.[50]

The Japanese government conducted the initial screening of immigrants to the contiguous United States to result in optimal success abroad. Consequently, "they tended to come from districts that were less poor and to have higher class status, higher literacy levels, and a smaller likelihood of coming from 'peasant-agriculturalist households' than most Japanese."[51] During that same interval, 80–90 percent of Italian and Polish immigrants who came to start a new life in the United States had been farmhands, laborers, and domestic servants. As other evidence of the Japanese government's selectivity process at work, at the turn of the century, 61 percent of Japanese immigrants to the United States had been farmhands, laborers, and domestic servants; 19 percent had been white-collar professionals, entrepreneurs, and skilled workers; and a remarkable 20 percent had owned and operated their own farms. Japanese immigrants arriving in 1909 not only had considerably higher literacy rates than immigrants from Croatia, Greece, Italy, Montenegro, Poland, Slovakia, and Slovenia, but they also tended to have considerably more formal education than most resident Japanese.[52]

As Japanese immigration continued deep into the first quarter of the twentieth century and self-reports from the most successful of the early immigrants became available, subsequent waves of entrants to the United States tended to have even higher social and economic class backgrounds. During the interval of 1908–24, the proportion of Japanese immigrants who identified as farmhands, laborers, and household servants had been cut in half, to 31 percent; Japanese white-collar workers, entrepreneurs, and skilled workers had more than doubled to 40 percent; and astoundingly, the number of immigrants who *had owned and operated their own farms* rose to over 30 percent.[53] Thus, selectivity progressively targeted more affluent, professional, and literate candidates to the exclusion of all others over time.[54] While the Japanese government's rationale for this decision is an excellent subject for another study, Suzuki makes it clear that the Japanese state played a critical role in regulating the "quality" of immigration to the United States.

Some of the immigrants who were disappointed with their outcomes abandoned the experiment and began a reverse migration back to Japan. As a group, they had been the least successful. Those returning immigrants also were more likely to have been disproportionately drawn from the pool of less literate candidates and those less likely to have owned farms prior to migration to the United States. The absence of these less successful immigrants, in the case of Japanese Americans, created an unusual population remaining in the United States, a population poised for American success.[55]

Suzuki also learned that more economically successful Japanese male immigrants were able to persuade brides from home to come to the United States. Their children, known as Nisei, were born into comparatively well-off Issei households—households designed to provide the children with the best opportunity to do well in their adopted country.[56] Indeed, the visible success of those Japanese immigrants, an affront to white racists, made them targets for mass relocation, incarceration, and seizure of their accumulated property during World War II.[57]

Economists and others seeking to understand the model-minority phenomenon have fixated on the exceptionally high rates of self-employment among Korean Americans.[58] The financial success of Koreans, like that of all other voluntary immigrants, is directly correlated with the attributes they had upon entry to the United States. Economist Timothy Bates's examination of racial and ethnic entrepreneurship reveals that (1) Korean immigrants who are highly educated resort to self-employment because they have been excluded from occupations that are commensurate with their education, and (2) Koreans who immigrate to the United States frequently are in possession of the necessary resources to start up their own businesses.

Bates highlighted a study that revealed the magnitude of those holdings: "[At least as early as] 1979, Korean- and Chinese-immigrant-owned firms began operations with an average initial capitalization of $57,191, nonminority start-ups with $31,939, and firms created by Asian Americans with $43,186."[59] Prospective Korean and Chinese small-business owners arrived with significantly higher levels of investment capital and, importantly, a much smaller share of debt; hence, their "advantage" in the world of enterprise was largely attributable to the resources they had in hand when they arrived in the United States.

Jennifer Lee and Min Zhou define *hyperselectivity* as a condition where the immigrant community to a host country is drawn from the upper strata of the home country's population. In contrast, they define *hyposelectivity* as a condition where the immigrant community is drawn from the lower strata of their country of origin. Educational attainment is the marker these scholars use for gauging immigrant selectivity.[60]

In their analysis, a hyperselected immigrant community, upon entry into the receiving country, has a significantly higher proportion of university degree holders than their conationals who remain in the country of origin; the reverse would be true for a hyposelected immigrant community. Lee and Zhou argue that this type of educational advantage explains the comparative success of post–World War II Chinese immigrants in the United States, and this type of educational disadvantage explains the comparative lack of success of Vietnamese immigrants.[61]

Invariably, the explanation for immigrant participation and success in small business activity is a story of preexisting material assets—tools, machinery, facilities, technological equipment, furniture—that facilitate such engagement. A 2004 newspaper article extolled the business acumen of two Brazilian immigrants, Raquel Siqueira and Rosana Silva, who had established a thriving cheese-flavored-pastry distributorship in Durham, North Carolina. Almost as an afterthought, the reporter revealed that Siqueira and her original partner, Ana Borges, managed to start the enterprise despite having no credit history in the United States by leveraging $300,000 they held in personal savings. To jump-start their production, they used their capital and connections to acquire equipment in Brazil and renovate a portion of a building in their adopted hometown that had been boarded up for twenty years. Moreover, the reporter implies the partners still possessed additional resources—their expenditures had not drained their personal savings in the process.[62]

Land also can be a preexisting material asset that can serve as a springboard to greater comparative prosperity after arrival in the United States.

For example, black West Indian immigrants have come disproportionately from landowning families in their home country. Legal scholar Eleanor Marie Brown's observation that a paradoxical effect of restrictive U.S. immigration policy toward the Caribbean countries "may have [led immigration officials to have] inadvertently selected for propertied 'types,' that is, more elite Blacks" is indicative of the lateral mobility phenomenon.[63]

Their prior position as landowners in their home countries leads Brown to characterize black West Indian immigrants metaphorically as "the blacks who got their forty acres." Access to grants of land dating from slavery times gave them the intergenerational resources necessary for entry into home ownership and entrepreneurship in the United States. She concludes, "Although this group obtained their property *prior* to migrating to the United States, . . . this property provided a base for later business success once this population was in the United States."[64]

Since West Indian immigrants appear to do better economically than black descendants of those enslaved in the United States, and since both groups are phenotypically black, the reasoning runs, oppression and discrimination cannot explain native blacks' failure to advance. In addition to Brown's evidence on their wealth position before entering the United States, sociologist Mosi Ifatunji has shown that although there is some evidence of a West Indian immigrant advantage in outcomes, they, too, lag far behind whites. Moreover, he contends these intrablack differences in outcomes are, again, explained best by the selectivity of immigration and, intriguingly, whites' prejudicial favoritism toward West Indian over native blacks.[65]

While some aspects of the country's voluntary immigrant experience bear a resemblance to "rags to riches" stories, the position of black Americans is completely antithetical to the American Dream myth. Descended largely from enslaved Africans who were *forced* to migrate to the United States and labor as human chattel, this group's history is dissimilar from essentially every other American ethnic group's. Separated from one's family, sold and exported to the Americas, subjected to hard work without pay under the constant threat of violence, enduring Jim Crow laws and white marauders, and experiencing ongoing discrimination in both the public and private sectors—these experiences bear no resemblance to the ideals of the American Dream.

Nevertheless, disciples of the immigrant myth insist the experiences of black Americans also meet this one-size-fits-all-ethnic-groups mold. For example, they frequently assert that black Americans have achieved substantial social progress since the end of legalized segregation in the United States. These disciples contend that any remaining racial inequalities are a consequence of ongoing racial disparities in the quality of schooling. For them, discrimination driven by racism, despite copious evidence to the contrary, is a thing of the past.[66]

Thus, it is misleading to depict as synonymous the experience of ethnic immigrants or immigrants of color and African Americans taken collectively (or Native Americans, for that matter). It would be more apt to compare voluntary immigrants to the United States and African Americans who have chosen to move to other parts of the world, the expatriate black American population. As our research has shown, successful immigrant groups generally have a history of prior success in their countries of origin—whether it be in the form of accumulation of financial wealth, accumulation of educational credentials, or both. These resource advantages are then actualized on the American stage where they often produce even greater financial wealth and a social status niche comparable, in a relative sense, to the one held at some recent stage in the country of origin.

Before the onset of the Great Recession in 2008, the number of Americans living in poverty had fallen for all groups, beginning in the 1960s when the War on Poverty was inaugurated by President Lyndon B. Johnson. But when one considers the *relative* economic position of blacks vis-à-vis whites over the past fifty years, once more, the persistent economic disparities are stark. The proportion of blacks living in poverty from 1959—the first time data was collected—to the present, has stubbornly remained three times that of whites.

The implications for black well-being are critical. In 1959, the poverty rate for white families was 18.1 percent, compared with 56.2 percent for blacks. Expressed in a different way, less than one-fifth of whites lived in poverty in 1959, while over half of blacks were impoverished. Ten years later, the white poverty rate had dropped to 9.5 percent, and the black poverty rate had fallen roughly in lockstep to 31.1 percent. By 2000, the black poverty rate had dropped to 22.1 percent, while the white poverty rate was 7.5 percent, maintaining the gap. This peculiar consistency in the black-white poverty gap was evident even in 2010, when the Great Recession was in full swing; the white poverty rate had risen to 9.9 percent, compared with 27.4 percent for blacks, sustaining an approximate three-to-one black-white poverty rate ratio.[67]

The higher black poverty rate is attributable to two factors: blacks are twice as likely to be unemployed as whites, and blacks with jobs tend to receive lower earnings than whites. Discrimination persists and is a major cause of the gaps in employment and earnings. Sociologist Devah Pager's landmark field experiments in Milwaukee and New York City demonstrate one aspect of the problem. In a disturbing study involving black and white men of similar ages with similar educational attainment, Pager discovered that white male applicants *with felony convictions* were more likely to receive callbacks for job interviews and job offers than black men *without a criminal record*.[68]

In another investigation, economists Marianne Bertrand and Sendhil Mullainathan crafted letters of interest describing the qualifications and employment histories of fictional applicants and submitted them to potential employers who had posted job announcements. Who got called in for interviews? The results of these correspondence tests are also disturbing. Applicants with "black-sounding" names were less likely to be asked to come for job interviews than applicants with "white-sounding" names. And even when Bertrand and Mullainathan enhanced the resumes associated with black-sounding names so that they were stronger than the white resumes, whites still held an advantage in job callbacks.[69]

Another study demonstrated that when blacks' and Asians' resumes are stripped of evidence of their racial or ethnic background, the candidates actually have greater odds of being invited for interviews. This was just as true for applications to firms that advertised their commitment to diversity as for those that did not.[70] Of course, improved odds of reaching the interview stage do not mean that the racial gap in hiring gets closed afterward. A candidate's racial identity typically becomes obvious when they enter the room for the interview.

Furthermore, researchers at the Center for Economic and Policy Research found that there are severe racial employment gaps at the upper end of the educational distribution. In a 2014 study, Janelle Jones and John Schmitt reported that blacks with engineering degrees have much higher unemployment rates than whites with similar degrees.[71]

The import of their finding can be challenged by the possibility that blacks' and whites' engineering degrees may not have been obtained from comparable schools. But a Bloomberg study on MBA recipients provides precisely that kind of evidence. The Bloomberg study reveals that blacks receiving MBAs from Harvard Business School between 2007 and 2009 started their careers earning about $5,000 less than their white peers with degrees from the same program. But by 2015 the racial pay gap for the Harvard MBA recipients had ballooned to a shocking $100,000 annually![72]

S. Michael Gaddis's field experiment is another names study, with false profiles submitted as applications for 1,000 positions advertised by employers. Gaddis paired black-sounding-named applicants whose degrees supposedly were from Harvard, Stanford, and Duke against white-sounding-named applicants whose degrees were from the University of Massachusetts at Amherst, the University of California at Riverside, and the University of North Carolina at Chapel Hill, respectively. *He found that the applicants with black-sounding names with degrees from the higher-cachet institutions were no more likely to receive favorable responses than applicants with the white-sounding names whose degrees were from the less selective institutions.*[73]

Perversely, discrimination in the job market intensifies as blacks become more credentialed. Jones and Schmitt, Gaddis, and reporter Natalie Kitroeff all found that greater educational attainment does not insulate blacks from discrimination—quite the opposite. No matter how much education blacks acquire in quantity or quality, potential employers will not evaluate their credentials and experience on equal footing with those of whites; indeed, the discriminatory differentials rise as blacks attain higher levels of education.[74]

Many employers justify paying lower wages to blacks because they believe blacks are fundamentally different from whites in ways that affect their ability to perform on the job. In 2009, William Julius Wilson, one of the nation's most distinguished sociologists, offered an explanation for the racial gap in male youth unemployment by asserting that young black men, sixteen to twenty-four years of age, lacked the "soft skills" that would enable them to be employed at the same rate as their white peers. Wilson concluded that 52 percent of white males possessed "soft skills," but only 30 percent of black males had attained them, hence their lower representation in service-sector jobs.[75] Soft skills are generally thought to include a range of competencies that typically are not taught formally. They comprise the ability to be punctual, be cordial with clients or customers, and communicate easily with co-workers and supervisors.

Wilson's claim is incorrect on two counts: there is no substantive evidence that, after controlling for their family's socioeconomic status, young black men are more devoid of soft skills than young white men, and furthermore, when they are hired, they do, in fact, land service-industry jobs that frequently require "soft skills." In fact, upon examining the data it is apparent that *the majority of the country's nonprofessional black men between the ages of sixteen and twenty-four holding jobs are crowded into the low-paying service-industry sector.* They typically are excluded from higher-paying employment that does not require "soft skills," such as in the construction sector.[76]

Indeed, young black males are disproportionately confined to low-paying jobs, regardless of whether those jobs require "soft" or "hard" skills. The key divide dictating young black male and young white male employment patterns is not determined by the possession of soft skills versus hard skills; it is determined by differential access to low-paying versus high-paying jobs.[77]

"We're talking about an economic system that is shot through with discrimination against black people that denies them opportunity to participate fully in this economy," Bernard E. Anderson, former assistant secretary of labor, told participants at the Fourth Annual Black Economic Summit. "And until we attack that head on, we are going to continue to have racial inequality."[78]

Today, black-white racial disparities are real, extensive, and quantifiable. They are attributable to the persistence of racism and discrimination in the United States. The current condition of black Americans is a tragic testament to the nation's brutal racial history. The aim of a substantive program of reparations is to produce a *race-fair* America instead of an America that is unable to acknowledge and confront persistent racial inequality.

Part 2

3

Who Reaped the Fruits of Slavery?

Slavery has long been identified in the national consciousness as a
Southern institution. The time to bury that myth is overdue. Slavery is a
story about America, all of America. The nation's wealth, from the very
beginning, depended upon the exploitation of black people on three
continents. —Evelyn Brooks Higginbotham, Foreword to *Complicity*, 2005

As much as it is linked to the barbaric system of slave labor that raised
it, cotton created New York. —Anne Farrow, Joel Lang, and Jenifer Frank,
Complicity, 2005

New England was not a slave society. On the eve of the Revolution, blacks
constituted less than 4 percent of the population in Massachusetts and
Connecticut, and many of them were free. But it was slavery, nevertheless,
that made the commercial economy of eighteenth-century New England
possible and that drove it forward. . . . The dynamic element in the region's
economy was the profits from the Atlantic trade, and they rested almost
entirely, directly or indirectly, on the flow of New England's products to the
slave plantations, and the sugar and tobacco industries that they serviced.
The export of fish, timber, agricultural products, and cattle and horses
on which the New England merchants' profits mainly depended reached
markets primarily in the West Indies and secondarily in the plantation
world of the mainland South. Without the sugar and tobacco industries,
based on slave labor, and without the growth of the slave trade, there
would not have been markets anywhere nearly sufficient to create the
returns that made possible the purchase of European goods, the extended
credit, and the leisured life that New Englanders enjoyed. Slavery was the
ultimate source of the commercial economy of eighteenth-century New
England. Only a few of New England's merchants actually engaged in the
slave trade, but all of them profited by it, lived off it. —Bernard Bailyn,
"Slavery and Population Growth in Colonial New England," 2000

This chapter is devoted to an analysis of how white Americans benefited
from unmerited privileges that flowed from the institution of slavery, particularly the impact on the development of the American economy. The accumulation of wealth among white Americans during this period—elites and

non-elites alike—together with a panoply of entitlements still present today, figures into the reparations calculation.

In their important and accessibly written book, *Complicity: How the North Promoted, Prolonged, and Profited from Slavery*, Anne Farrow, Joel Lang, and Jenifer Frank trace the evolution of the trade in Africans from 1641, when the Massachusetts Bay Colony legally recognized the institution. Though most Americans associate slavery only with the southern states of the United States, or the eventual Confederate States of America, Massachusetts was the first North American colony to give legal sanction to servitude.[1] While there were some who warned against the evils of slavery, the profits the institution promised those who invested in its promulgation, together with the privileges and pampered lives it made possible, were often too alluring to refuse.

From the docks of Providence, Rhode Island, and Boston and Salem, Massachusetts, a round robin of outgoing ships carrying dairy products, fish, and rum followed vessels unloading slaves, sugar, and molasses.[2] Providing provisions for these slaves and for the vast plantations in the U.S. south, the Caribbean, and South America required the efforts of staggering numbers of financiers, merchants, shippers, insurers, real estate brokers, auctioneers, and laborers.

Newspapers like the *Hartford Courant*, which dates from 1764, profited from the sale of advertisements supporting the sale and capture of slaves and notices for slave-ship crews, the provisioning of slave ships and plantations, and the sale of slave-made goods. Railroad companies and sloop, brigantine, schooner, and steamboat owners manufactured specially outfitted vehicles for slave transport.[3] Aetna, the "nation's largest health insurer" as of 2000, and New York Life, the "nation's third oldest insurance company," are just two of a host of insurance firms that provided coverage for slave ships and their cargoes.[4]

At least 5,000 slaves were insured in Connecticut in 1790—when more than half of the state's well-heeled institutions enslaved at least one African. And there were agricultural enterprises throughout Connecticut—generally referred to as "farms"—whose scale and number of unfree personnel would have marked them as "plantations" had they been established in the American south, the Caribbean, or South America.[5]

Slave-grown cotton was the national currency that seeded the growth of several American cities before the Civil War. Between 1821 and 1860, New York City, a major importer of cotton, became the nation's and the world's largest commercial and financial center. In Chester Himes's *Cotton Comes to Harlem*, a satirical novel in his detective ("domestic") series, a bale of cotton in New York City is treated as an anomaly.[6] But there is a very profound sense that the cotton trade made New York City and New York City made the cotton trade.

New York City and southern cotton were a matched pair, sewn together by financial rewards and economic expansion. By the eve of the war, hundreds of businesses in New York, and countless more throughout the north, were connected to, and dependent on, cotton. As New York became the fulcrum of the U.S. cotton trade, merchants, shippers, auctioneers, bankers, brokers, insurers, and thousands of others were drawn to the burgeoning urban center. They packed lower Manhattan, turning it into the nation's emporium, in which products from all over the world were traded. Before the Civil War, the city's fortunes and its economic development were considered by many to be inseparable from those of the cotton-producing states.[7]

In 1861, the city's mayor, Fernando Wood, stunned his constituents when he tapped into the darkling mood and proposed that New York City independently secede from the Union. His speech, given before the New York Common Council, prompted outrage and cries of absurdity. Indeed, Wood's address was precipitated by the long-held close connection the city's tony elite had to the cotton sector. Farrow, Lang, and Frank observe:

> Although many of the city's intelligentsia rolled their eyes, and the mayor was slammed in much of the New York press, Wood's proposal made a certain kind of sense. The mayor was reacting to tensions in Albany, but there was far more behind his secession proposal, particularly if one understood that the lifeblood of New York City's economy was cotton. And cotton was the product most closely identified with the South and its defining system of labor: the slavery of millions of people of African descent.
>
> Slave-grown cotton is, in great measure, the root of New York's wealth. Forty years before Fernando Wood suggested that New York join with the South and exit the Union, cotton had already become the nation's foremost exported product. And in the four intervening decades New York had become a commercial and financial behemoth dwarfing any other U.S. city and most others in the world. Cotton was more than just a profitable crop. It was the national currency, the product most responsible for America's explosive growth in the decades before the Civil War.[8]

Lehman Brothers, widely viewed as one of the nation's most powerful investment banks, filed for bankruptcy in 2008. It collapsed under the stress of the mortgage lending crisis, but Lehman began in 1850 as a cotton brokerage in Montgomery, Alabama. It served as the state of Alabama's fiscal agent at one point and was designated to "service the state's debts, interest payments, and other obligations."[9]

The company's founder, Henry Lehman, immigrated from Rimpar, Bavaria (now Germany), to Montgomery in 1844 and set up a modest shop selling groceries, dry goods, and utensils to area cotton farmers. Buoyed by strong sales, he was joined by his brothers, Emanuel and Mayer, in 1850, and together, they went into the commodities brokerage business, constructed a cotton storage warehouse, and became the area's largest buyers and sellers of cotton. They then phased out their general merchandising enterprises.

Like all southern financial institutions, Lehman Brothers struggled during the Civil War, and as Reconstruction unfolded, family members focused on relocating their operations to New York City. However, cotton continued to trump all domestic trades, and in 1870 the Lehman brothers spearheaded the formation of the New York Cotton Exchange, the first commodities futures trading venture. Mayer Lehman was appointed to its first board of directors.

The extent to which the fortunes of the great New York tycoons of the nineteenth century bore linkages to slavery and the slave trade is impressive. Junius Spencer Morgan, father of J. Pierpont Morgan, had his son study the cotton trade in the south at the start of his business career. "Morgan Sr., a Massachusetts native who became a major banker and cotton broker in London, understood that knowledge of the cotton trade was essential to prospering in the commercial world in the 1850s."[10]

Real estate and shipping magnate John Jacob Astor made his fortune in furs, the Chinese opium trade, and the transportation of cotton to global ports. Jeweler Charles Lewis Tiffany opened the iconic flagship Tiffany's shop on New York City's Broadway Street in 1837 with capital from his father, Comfort Tiffany, whose own fortune had been derived from the operation of a cotton manufacturing company in what would become Danielsonville, Connecticut. Archibald Gracie Jr., the son of the eponymous Scottish international shipper of Gracie Mansion fame, left New York City to become a cotton broker in Mobile, Alabama.[11]

While the campaign to transform the economy of New England and New York using the slave trade and slavery was under way, a similar offensive was taking place across the south. The slave trade and slavery laid the economic foundation for what is now one of the richest countries in the world.

All those who subsequently migrated to the United States have moved to a country whose contemporary promise of opportunity is anchored in its history of exploitation of black lives. The slave trade and slavery extended their tendrils into every fissure of the American economy, producing a hothouse effect that created vast national wealth. America's economic success was built by the unrelenting enslavement of black people. One can hypothesize a counterfactual chain of events where American economic growth took place without slavery, *but this is the actual way in which it all began.*[12]

Throughout New England, shipyards emerged to build the vessels that would become the oceangoing prisons for African slaves, equipped with cannons, muskets, guns, iron chains, shackles, and water tanks. Before the American Revolution, Aaron Lopez, a Portuguese Sephardic Jew living in Newport, Rhode Island, and one of the wealthiest men in British America, earned the sobriquet "merchant of the first eminence" after he built a vertically integrated conglomerate anchored in the trade in enslaved Africans.

Lopez manufactured ships, barrels, bottles, clothing, and textiles, and he owned a rum distillery. He and his father-in-law, the "supremely honorable" businessman Jacob Rodriguez de Rivera, were among the partners in the candle manufacturing concern United Company of Spermaceti Chandlers, one of the country's first cartels. Their donations of lumber and other gifts to the College in the English Colony of Rhode Island and Providence Plantations (present-day Brown University), and those of other members of their religious and business community, led the trustees to open enrollment to Jews.[13]

Capt. James DeWolf and John Brown I, who were from Bristol and Providence, Rhode Island, respectively, were the country's "most audacious" traders who dealt in enslaved black bodies, molasses, and rum and were also the most active and aggressive. The DeWolf family's involvement in the lucrative market in abducted black men, women, and children is documented in two sources produced by DeWolf descendants: the documentary film *Traces of the Trade: A Story from the Deep North*, produced and directed by Katrina Browne, and the book *Inheriting the Trade: A Northern Family Confronts Its Legacy as the Largest Slave Trading Dynasty in U.S. History*, written by Browne's cousin Thomas Norman DeWolf.[14]

Farrow, Lang, and Frank estimate that in the 100 years before the sale of black human beings was banned, Rhode Island's slavers launched at least 934 voyages and captured and transported a minimum of 106,000 Africans to the Americas.[15] Beginning in 1769, with the first of 108 documented expeditions to the continent piloted by captains and crews throughout New England, the DeWolf family alone "transport[ed] more than 12,000 enslaved Africans across the Middle Passage" to plantations and slave markets in the United States and Cuba.[16]

Both enslavers established family dynasties, with John Brown I sharing his enterprise with his three brothers. DeWolf, who helmed a firm that included his seven brothers, had the distinction at one point of being considered the wealthiest person in the American colonies.[17] The first two men alleged to be the richest in the land accumulated their great fortunes from the capture, kidnapping, and compelled labor of black people.

After 1808, when the law abolishing the importation of enslaved people—but not the right to slave owning—was passed, buying and selling black bodies violently imported from abroad simply went underground. By then an elected national official, "U.S. Senator James DeWolf . . . curried favor with President Thomas Jefferson to continue the trade after it was outlawed." The DeWolf family's own research reveals that by 1812 their ancestors owned more ships than the U.S. Navy and conducted their perilous "illegal voyages" to import black bodies from the African continent "most likely until 1820."[18]

Decades before the Civil War, New York City's seaport was the "hub of an enormously lucrative illegal slave trade." Scholars estimate that during the illegal trade's peak years, 1859 and 1860, at least two ships designed to transport enslaved Africans—each built to hold between 600 and 1,000 captives—left lower Manhattan every month.[19]

Historian Bernard Bailyn affirms that feeding and clothing the millions of enslaved blacks working the sugar plantations throughout the Americas was big business, and the income from these enterprises enriched New England and the mid-Atlantic region.[20] Cotton grown by black abductees made the expansion of the area's textile industry possible—some 470 mills were in operation by 1860.[21]

The New York City clothier Brooks Brothers produced "plantation clothing" for slave owners and slave traders preparing the many "head of slaves" in their possession for sale. Brooks Brothers also produced coarse calicos and other rough clothing for the planters' "servants."[22]

From the antebellum period to the start of the twentieth century, two Connecticut towns, Deep River and Essex, became the international epicenter for ivory production, the "plunder for pianos." The towns milled thousands of tons of elephant tusks acquired by the enslavement or death of an estimated 1 million Africans.[23]

During the decades of the 1830s and 1840s, New England mills processed in excess of 100 million pounds of cotton grown in the south. By 1860, ten major cotton-producing states in the south—home to 2.3 million enslaved Africans living on 75,000 cotton plantations—produced "66 percent of the world's cotton, and raw cotton accounted for more than half of all U.S. exports."[24]

Great Britain, France, the Netherlands, Switzerland, Germany, Russia, Italy, Spain, and Belgium were all dependent on U.S. slave–grown cotton by the end of the eighteenth century. The British West Indies trade, driven by sugar grown by enslaved people in the Caribbean, also was a significant spur for New England merchants. By 1776, at the time of the American Revolution, it is estimated that 80 percent of the provisions exported overseas from New England went to the British West Indies.[25]

The reliance of the Caribbean islands on northern products—flour, dried fish, corn, potatoes, onions, apples, cattle, and horses—was so great that when trade was interrupted during the Revolutionary War, famine ensued in the sugar islands. In Jamaica alone, approximately 15,000 enslaved persons died from starvation between 1780 and 1787.[26] Even by 1800, Wethersfield, Connecticut, was exporting most of its 100,000 five-pound ropes of onions to the British West Indies.[27]

Cane sugar was transformed into molasses in the islands and then exported to the north. By 1770, the colonies of Massachusetts and Rhode Island were receiving 3.5 million gallons of molasses. These imports were converted into 2.8 million gallons of rum. While most was consumed by the Yankees themselves, large volumes were exported to other sites in North America and to the African continent to procure more slaves.[28] "When the Newport trade first reached a peak just before the Revolution, its vessels were carrying 200,000 gallons a year to Africa, where ship captains bartered for slaves by the barrel. An African man in his prime could be bought for about 150 gallons."[29]

The reach of slavery was far from contained in the American south, and the economic effects of slavery were far from limited to the south. The destruction of African families and clans was a key element in the wealth equation for America.[30] Black lives were the price paid to lay the foundation upon which this nation was built.[31]

From their very beginnings, America's greatest universities also were connected closely to slavery and the slave trade. Craig Steven Wilder's major study of America's earliest universities and their relationship to slavery, *Ebony and Ivy*, describes "American slavery and the slave trade" as "subsidiz[ing]" both Harvard College and the Massachusetts Bay Colony.[32] The College of William and Mary, receiving its royal charter in the colony of Virginia in 1693, initially was financed by drawing on profits from slave labor deployed in growing tobacco.[33]

The College in the English Colony of Rhode Island and Providence Plantations took its new name, Brown University, after Nicholas Brown made a major gift to the institution in 1804. Collectively, the Brown family already had developed a deep involvement with the university both as donors and as governors of the institution.[34] The Browns were members of the Newport and Providence merchant elite who trafficked heavily in the interlocking trade in slaves, molasses, and rum.[35] As Lorenzo Johnston Greene observed, "The trade was one of the foundations of New England's economic structure; it created a wealthy class of slave-trading merchants, while the profits derived from this commerce stimulated cultural development and philanthropy."[36] One of the key outlets for the merchant class's philanthropic contributions was support for the fledgling American universities.

Seeking students who could meet full expenses of tuition and fees, the early American universities forged relationships with West Indian and southern planters, encouraging them to send their sons to Harvard College, the College of New Jersey (now Princeton University), Dartmouth College, and King's College (now Columbia University), instead of universities in Britain.

The pursuit of wealthy students requiring no financial assistance bears a strong resemblance to contemporary recruitment practices at many colleges and universities. In addition to recruiting students whose parents' fortunes were based on slavery and the slave trade, King's College's leadership committed itself to active fund-raising efforts, making direct solicitations to West Indian planters.[37] Yale's trustees undertook a similar effort.[38]

The College of Philadelphia (now the University of Pennsylvania) made a special attempt to raise funds in South Carolina. Wilder writes, "Struggling to meet their debts, the board of the College of Philadelphia directed Provost William Smith to appeal to the wealthier residents of South Carolina, where the school, particularly through its medical program, had social connections."[39]

Here, again, was a West Indies connection. When Barbados, Great Britain's first successful "experimental tropical agricultural export colony," was settled in 1627, the Anglican Church, the official religion of England, was also established. More than 7,000 Irish indentures were brought in to cultivate sugar initially, working alongside a largely decimated population of enslaved indigenous American Indians, making Barbados the site of the "largest white population of any English colonies in the Americas." The sugar capital became the "springboard for English colonization in the Americas, playing a leading role in the settlement of Jamaica and the Carolinas" through the first quarter of the eighteenth century.[40]

However, by 1684, when the Barbadian population had increased more than thirty-five-fold, unfree Africans comprised more than 60 percent of the inhabitants.[41] Smith, the College of Philadelphia provost, "was an Anglican priest and, because of the Barbados migration, Anglicans had come to power in South Carolina."[42] These efforts appear to have had a significant payoff. Smith came back to Philadelphia in 1772 with £1,000 in commitments, and thereafter, "Professor John Morgan, a member of the first undergraduate class and a founder of the medical school . . . secured £6000 in one trip."[43]

Princeton's linkages to the southern slaveholding class run deep.[44] The College of New Jersey's president in the late eighteenth century, Presbyterian minister John Witherspoon, had influential and affluent relatives in South Carolina:

> The Witherspoons of Society Hill [South Carolina] were part of President John Witherspoon's family web. . . . It was the Witherspoons who helped bring Presbyterianism to Carolina. . . . Gavin Witherspoon's sons became legislators and his grandsons matriculated at South Carolina College (University of South Carolina). There were more than a hundred thousand enslaved people in the Tidewater region. The Witherspoons acquired numerous plantations and significant wealth, and some later fought and died for the Confederacy. Grandson John Dick Witherspoon and his wife, Elizabeth "Betsey" Boykin Witherspoon, had owned as many as five hundred black people.[45]

John Knox Witherspoon, the only college president and clergyman who was a signatory of the Declaration of Independence, was a slave owner himself, as were many of his cosigners on the document. Indeed, the first *eight* presidents of the College of New Jersey were slave owners.[46] Witherspoon's immediate descendants were tightly interlocked with slave ownership, related enterprises, and the further development of America's universities.

When John Knox Witherspoon's son David died, David's human property and land were passed on to his children. In his will, the younger Witherspoon also stipulated that three of the captives be leased out and that the income from their labors be used to pay the tuition and fees for his son John to attend Princeton. In fact, John Witherspoon enrolled at the University of North Carolina and became a physician. He and his wife, Susan Davis Kollock, "a distant cousin," lived in Charleston, South Carolina. Their "daughter Frances married physician, historian, and legislator Dr. David Ramsey (Ramsay)," also of Charleston, a graduate of the College of New Jersey and a delegate from South Carolina to the First Continental Congress.[47]

Ramsay, leader of the Medical Society of South Carolina, was instrumental in reopening the foreign importation of slaves into South Carolina by urging relaxation of yellow fever quarantine laws.[48] South Carolina had closed its ports to the overseas slave trade in 1792 due to fear of slave revolts, disease, and other financial considerations.[49] With Ramsay and the Medical Society of South Carolina arguing that there was insufficient danger from the importation of slaves to generate new epidemics, renewal of the trade became a live option.

During the five-year period that preceded the cessation of the legal overseas slave trade in 1808, at least 40,000 enslaved persons were imported to South Carolina, more than 10 percent of all enslaved persons brought to North America between 1525 and 1866. The United States' acquisition of vast land to the west of the thirteen original colonies, under the terms of the Louisiana Purchase, may have produced the pecuniary incentive for South Carolina to reintroduce the slave trade.[50] Ramsay's enthusiasm about the economic opportunities posed by the new frontier was explicit.[51]

Some universities managed to establish fiscal stability by engaging in the direct buying and selling of enslaved blacks. In 1838, Georgetown University avoided bankruptcy by selling 272 persons owned by the Jesuit priests who were seeking to secure the institution's survival.[52] Ironically, that was the same year in which the abolition movement had attained sufficient gravitas for the radical activist Angelina Grimké to declare, "We Abolition Women are turning the world upside down."[53] Today, Georgetown University's students have voted to add $54.40 to their annual fees to support a fund to assist descendants of enslaved persons.[54]

In addition to slave owning being the norm among early faculty members at Yale, the 1732 gift to the institution from George Berkeley of Whitehall, his Newport, Rhode Island, plantation, enabled the college to inaugurate a fellowship in his name. Among the beneficiaries of Berkeley's largesse were Eleazar Wheelock, founder of Dartmouth College, and several other college presidents.[55]

In the early part of the nineteenth century, Washington College's administrators hired out slaves owned by the institution as a source of revenue.[56] The use of enslaved laborers as "servants" for both faculty and students at Queens College (now Rutgers University) was commonplace across the early American universities.[57]

The University of North Carolina at Chapel Hill, founded in 1789, was the product of efforts of Presbyterian slaveholders and missionaries to build the first public university. The connection to the older northern universities was direct. One of the university's first presidents, Joseph Caldwell, was an alumnus of the College of New Jersey. The first professor at the University of North Carolina, David Ker, stayed only one year in that position before moving to Mississippi to run a cotton plantation.[58]

Major slaveholders in the state were the institution's trustees: "Members of the Board of Trustees were among the largest slave owners in the state. Representative of this group were Benjamin Smith with 221 slaves, Willie Jones with 120, Samuel Johnston with 96, Stephen Cabarrus with 73, and Richard Dobbs Spaight with 71. Of these men, Smith, Johnston, and Spaight served as governors of North Carolina; Cabarrus was Speaker of the General Assembly; and Jones was president of the North Carolina Committee of Safety in 1776 and first Governor ex officio of the new state."[59]

At least thirty of the university's first forty trustees were slave owners.[60] Major slaveholders in the Chapel Hill area donated the land for the college. Among these were John Hogan, who gave 200 acres and received the contract to have his enslaved black workers produce the bricks for the first building, Old East, and Christopher "Old Kit" Barbee, who gave 211 acres in 1792. By 1778, Barbee owned more than 2,000 acres, including 800 acres he had received as the first of three grants from the state.[61] In a sense, his donation merely returned to the state a small share of what he had been given.

Benjamin Smith had been given 20,000 acres of land to the west—acreage that had been appropriated from the Chickasaw Indians—for his service as a colonel during the Revolutionary War. His transfer of ownership to the fledgling university in 1789 constituted a property grant of land that he himself had received without paying a single dollar.[62] A significant portion of the University of North Carolina's pre–Civil War revenue was attributed to sale of the land in Tennessee that Smith had donated to the university.[63]

The late historian John Chapman confirmed that enslaved blacks cleared the land and built the physical structure for the new public institution:

In the summer of 1793, seventeen years after American revolutionaries declared, "all men are created equal," slaves began clearing land to build the first public university in the new nation. Black workers labored through the summer heat to clear a main street for the village of Chapel Hill and to construct the foundations of Old East, the first building at the University of North Carolina. While building contractors during this era were seldom wealthy enough to purchase many slaves, they often rented slaves or found other ways to benefit from slave labor. As architectural historian Catherine W. Bishir noted, "One practice was for a slave owner to furnish laborers to a builder in exchange for a share of the profits. James Patterson, a Chatham County builder, joined with two local slave owners, Patrick St. Lawrence and George Lucas, to erect the first major structure at the new University of North Carolina in 1793."[64]

South Carolina College (now the University of South Carolina) shares a similar history of intense reliance on enslaved laborers at its inception: The campus we experience today would not exist without the labor of slaves, who both built and maintained it. Official records only credit the white builder or contractor in charge of the project, but these men owned and frequently hired slaves with building skills to carry out their projects. These contractors, who were responsible for providing all of their own materials, often purchased bricks from Columbia brick makers. Slaves owned and hired by brickyards performed the work of making bricks by hand, not only to be used at the college, but also for construction of structures all over the relatively young city.[65]

In addition to building the first structures on the campus, enslaved blacks played a critical role in maintaining the college's operations: "[Slaves] also performed daily maintenance work by building fences and making repairs, as well as domestic tasks like cooking and tending gardens. Professors were provided with outbuildings in which to house their personal slaves, and although students were forbidden from bringing slaves to campus, hired-out or college-owned slaves cleaned student living quarters and served their meals. Slaves even played a role in the college's educational mission by cleaning library books and taking care of laboratory equipment."[66]

It is uncanny how closely Chapman's description of the conditions that prevailed at the University of North Carolina mirrored those at South Carolina College:

> In Chapel Hill, large numbers of slaves serviced the needs of the
> young men from wealthy families who attended the university, freeing
> them to pursue their studies or their leisure. Slave laborers liberated
> the professors from mundane chores and enabled them to lead lives
> devoted to intellectual pursuits, participate in town affairs, and spend
> more time with their families and their students. Slave cooks, nurses,
> housekeepers, and washerwomen relieved the normal drudgery of
> women's work for the wives of professors, merchants, and professionals.
> Without the unpaid labor of slaves, such elite lifestyles would have been
> far more costly to maintain. Thus, slave labor provided a direct financial
> subsidy to the university.[67]

The faculty and administrators of South Carolina College also were implicated deeply in the slave system. Francis Lieber, a German-born polymath, legal scholar, and political philosopher, was a professor of history and political economy from 1835 to 1856. Unlike many of his colleagues, Lieber believed that abolition was the moral course, but he tried to hide his beliefs out of fear that he would lose his position or even his life.

During his tenure at South Carolina College, the embattled academic hired an enslaved fourteen-year-old, "Tom, as we call him," into "service" for $4.50 a month, presumably to mask his antislavery sentiments. When other faculty and the trustees learned about Lieber's beliefs, "he was denied the college presidency, [for] which he was the obvious choice, and was forced to resign in 1856."[68]

James Henley Thornwell, a graduate of the college, served both as a professor and as president of the school in the early 1850s. A slave owner, and an ardent advocate of slavery from his pulpit as a Presbyterian minister, Thornwell supported secession and war.[69]

Brothers John and Joseph LeConte were physicians, scientists, *and* slave owners. The elder brother, John, anticipated that a major university would be inaugurated under the Confederacy "where his work would flourish." When the Union army entered Columbia, South Carolina, he and his family left the city with more than twenty slaves. The two brothers landed on their feet after the war. In 1869, both moved to California to join the faculty at the new university in Berkeley.[70]

Thomas Cooper, originally from England, the second president of the college in the interval of 1820–34, was an abolitionist as a youth. Nevertheless, he reversed his position when he moved to South Carolina. The convert became more devout than those raised in the proslavery faith. Not only did he silence all opposition to slavery at South Carolina College, but he also bought slaves and outlined the case in favor of slavery in two 1826 pamphlets, *On the Constitution* and *Lectures*.[71]

Cooper's brief in support of slavery was far from unusual for scholars at both southern and northern universities. Indeed, one of the most potent activities among America's professoriate was crafting the ideological case for slavery as a beneficial system of social stratification. Establishing black inferiority and proclaiming slavery as an appropriate school for civilization or an essential mechanism of behavioral control for alleged black barbarism was a major academic enterprise. For example, the notion that blacks had the smallest cranial capacity of any "racial" group and therefore were cognitively inferior was a product of both northern and southern scholarship.[72]

And, indeed, these were not innocent or idle inquiries. The case for the physical and mental inferiority of blacks made its way directly into several court cases and into the larger arena of national policy making. And there were professional advantages to mounting the case for slavery; for example, a contributing factor to slaveholder Thomas Dew's appointment as president of the College of William and Mary was his strident defense of slavery following the Nat Turner Rebellion in Virginia.[73] Dew had boasted that "Virginia is in fact a *negro* raising state for other states," producing "enough for her own supply and six thousand for sale."[74]

While the toil of enslaved blacks and the profits from their unpaid labor were essential to the development of American universities, those same universities did not admit the sons and daughters of the freedmen through their doors as students after emancipation. An all too brief exception occurred in South Carolina during the Reconstruction era.

South Carolina's Reconstruction legislature moved aggressively to desegregate higher education in the state, and by 1876, the student body at the College of South Carolina was predominantly black. Segregationist faculty members angrily left the college when black students were admitted, making it possible for the Radical Republicans to reconfigure the school's faculty. At one point, Richard Greener, recognized as the first black graduate of Harvard University, was offered chair of Mental and Moral Philosophy, Sacred Literature, and Evidences of Christianity. But in 1877, with the "redemptionists" in control of the state's general assembly, white supremacist governor Wade Hampton closed the university, only to reopen it under its original status as an all-white institution. Thereafter, the University of South Carolina did not, knowingly, admit black students until 1963.[75]

Enslaved blacks played a critical role in building the American railway system, whether they were the direct human property of the railroad companies or "hired" (rented) from their owners. Theodore Kornweibel Jr. reports:

> In 1859, one-third of all southern lines employed 100 or more slaves, ranging from 1,200 at work building the Atlantic & Gulf Railroad in Georgia, to 500 building the Vicksburg, Shreveport & Texas Railroad, to 400 or more toiling on 7 other lines. In contrast, [by 1859] no single plantation was home to as many as 1,200 slaves, and 400 bondsmen were to be found on only a very few large estates. Perhaps the largest single concentration of enslaved railroaders was the 1,493 men and 425 boys at work constructing the North Carolina Railroad in 1852.[76] . . .
>
> Whether for construction and maintenance, or sometimes operations, southern railroads could not do without enslaved black labor.[77]

Sometimes owners actually were reluctant to hire out their enslaved laborers because of the extreme danger associated with rail construction and train operations; if they did so, they often would take out insurance policies on their property, or they would structure contracts that precluded their property from working on the riskiest tasks. Of course, those contractual provisions were not always obeyed, leading contractors and slave owners to the courtroom.[78]

Racial stratification operated in the rail system with enslaved blacks—and subsequently emancipated blacks—assigned the most dangerous work. Prior to the widespread adoption of air brakes and automatic couplers early in the twentieth century, one of the riskiest assignments was the role of brakeman:

> Many railroads used slaves for this [hazardous] position [the lowest ranking on the train]. Their main tasks were helping to stop the train and coupling and uncoupling cars. Brakemen lost their lives by falling off the tops of moving, swaying freight cars, especially at night or in inclement weather, while manually applying brakes on each car. Even on passenger trains, they had to jump back and forth from car to car to apply brakes. Coupling with link and pins required the brakeman to attach an oval iron link with an iron pin in a pocket at one end of one car, stand between it and the other car, and be ready to drop a pin as the new link entered the new car's pocket, and avoid being crushed as the two cars came together.[79]

Under improved safety conditions, brought about by innovations in braking equipment, white laborers seized the brakeman positions, driving black workers out of the jobs.

The history of railroad work is illustrative of a general American tendency to disregard the value of black life. Slaveholders who hesitated to hire out their human chattel to the railroads appear to be an exception, but not because they placed any intrinsic worth on black people; rather it was because they merely were seeking to protect their investment to assure a longer-term return. Whether pay was made to slave owners or directly to black laborers after slavery as wages, the following comment from Kornweibel is apposite: "It is part of the perverse genius of capitalism that a dangerous job does not usually warrant a higher wage. Among the operating crews, brakemen were paid the least."[80]

Slavery and slaveholding were direct and intimate parts of the lives of many white Americans, particularly those in the southern states that would form the Confederacy. Far from slave ownership being the purview of a tiny few, slaveholding families enjoyed a wider presence and prevalence than frequently is acknowledged. Among whites, particularly those in the south, slavery truly was a family affair on the eve of the Civil War.

In 1860, at the national level, approximately 8 percent of all American families owned at least one slave. But this seemingly low aggregate national percentage was influenced heavily by the twenty-one nonsouthern states where *no* families owned slaves during the last days of the antebellum period.[81] By 1860, the southern experience with slaveholding stood in marked contrast with the northern pattern.

Among the eleven states that seceded from the Union in 1861 to establish the Confederacy, Arkansas, Tennessee, Virginia, North Carolina, Texas, and Louisiana registered at the lower end with *at least 20 percent* of white families owning slaves (20, 25, 26, 28, 28, and 29 percent, respectively). The remaining five states all registered proportions of 34 percent or higher, peaking at staggering rates of 46 and 49 percent in South Carolina and Mississippi, respectively.[82]

A still more dramatic indicator of the scope of white engagement with slave ownership is the proportion of white people who were *members of slaveholding families*. While the national figure was 13 percent, in 1860, one-quarter of whites in Arkansas and Tennessee lived in families that owned at least one slave. In Texas, Virginia, and North Carolina, at least one-third of whites lived in slave-owning families. This proportion rose well above 40 percent in Florida, Georgia, Alabama, and Louisiana, cresting at a fantastic *55 and 57 percent in Mississippi and South Carolina*, respectively.[83]

A U.S. Census Bureau report titled "Slave Statistics" provides 1850 data on the distribution of slaveholding families based on the numbers of enslaved persons they owned in North Carolina, South Carolina, and Virginia. More than half of the slaveholding families across the three states owned between two and ten persons, at least 17 percent in each of the three states owned between ten and twenty persons, and more than 10 percent owned between twenty and fifty persons. It is not until we reach the rarified atmosphere of ownership of 200 or more persons in those three states that we locate the 1850 equivalent of the Occupy movement's "1 percent."[84]

In the Army of Northern Virginia, led by Robert E. Lee, soldiers who either owned slaves in their own name or lived in families where slaves were owned constituted almost 40 percent of the enlistees. Because of backward and forward linkages from the slave plantation system, arguably the majority of Confederate soldiers had economic ties to slavery, at least as renters of land from, employees of, or traders with slaveholders.[85] More than half of the officers were slave owners.[86] At the onset of the Civil War, southern whites and slave ownership were intertwined tenaciously.

Black people overwhelmingly were the objects of enslavement.[87] While there was an extended period of white immigrant indentured servitude during the colonial period, their numbers were dwarfed by coerced immigrants from the African continent. Even at the height of importation of white indentures, while 216,000 whites came to British North America as bonded laborers, 300,000 Africans were forcibly imported to the colonies.[88] By the time of the Declaration of Independence in 1776, the practice of white indentureship was in sharp decline.[89] On the other hand, by 1790 there were close to 700,000 enslaved blacks in the United States, a number that grew to 4 million by the start of the Civil War.[90]

Moreover, black enslavement had a unique severity that obviates any equivalence that might be drawn to white indentured servitude.[91] As historian Dominic Sandbrook observes, "It was almost always much better to be a European servant than an African slave. Not only were servants transported in better conditions; they could also hope to be free men, if they survived their term of service. Above all, they were white, which meant that they were automatically different from the West African slaves. As the servants would have pointed out, the racial codes of the American colonies were a lot more than window-dressing. Calling them slaves might be a marketing ploy, but it stretches the meaning of slavery beyond breaking point."[92]

One of the eventual beneficiaries of the relatively advantaged position of white indentures appears to be actor and country music star Reba McEntire. Unlike enslaved blacks who could not obtain property rights in land under any circumstances, after the 1660s in Virginia, indentures were given grants of land or could purchase land on credit. No relatives are known to have accompanied nine-year-old George Brassfield, six generations removed from McEntire, on his passage from England to colonial Virginia. Brassfield was contracted out to work for a tobacco farmer in Essex County, Virginia, and he completed his indenture by 1710. Via the headright system, which we discuss in greater detail in the next chapter, he was able to purchase 300 acres of land with 1,600 pounds of tobacco in 1721.

By 1819, less than a century later, his grandson and namesake, George Brassfield, born in 1765, owned 1,615 acres of land and ten slaves in North Carolina and also was the owner of record of the Brassfield Tavern. The headright system always had been implemented with severe limitations on the participation of enslaved blacks that did not extend to indentured whites, and it laid the foundation for the wealth of George Brassfield and his descendants.[93]

Suffice it to say that in the United States, slave ownership was a white affair and enslavement was a black affair, and the benefits and damages were distributed accordingly. The sale and forced labor of black bodies drove the commerce of the United States from the earliest days of the nation and made possible the world we inhabit today.

4

Roads Not Taken in the Early Years of the Republic

He [the king of Britain] has waged cruel war against human nature itself, violating its most sacred rights of life & liberty in the persons of a distant people who never offended him, captivating & carrying them into slavery in another hemisphere or to incur miserable death in their transportation thither. This piratical warfare, the opprobrium of *infidel* powers, is the warfare of the Christian King of Great Britain. —Thomas Jefferson, draft of the Declaration of Independence

The idea of land and freedom held out a powerful allure for African Americans. As a result, thousands of slaves absconded from their owners and reached the British lines. Still other African Americans escaped to pursue other opportunities for freedom, such as migrating to Florida (a Spanish possession), settling with Native groups, creating their own Maroon communities on the fringes of American society, living as free people in the north, or migrating after the war to other countries. Despite the displacements and confusion caused by the Revolutionary War, the Continental Army eventually prevailed over the British forces, who evacuated the Loyalists, black and white, from Savannah, Boston, Charleston, and New York. As part of this exodus, approximately 3,500 Black Loyalists migrated to Nova Scotia along with hundreds of black slaves owned by Loyalist Americans. —Harvey Armani Whitfield, *Blacks on the Border*, 2006

This chapter begins with an examination of the steps taken by whites to harden the legal definition of "slave" in colonial America, making it a permanent condition. The enslaved were stripped of all rights, isolated, and differentiated from other groups, even as one country after another liberated their bondsmen.

Black enslavement could have ended with the making of the new nation. That was not the path that was taken. In this chapter, we explore the circumstances that resulted in slavery's continuation and growth into the nation-building years of the United States of America.

Slavery and the republic were connected intimately from the outset. In 1776, approximately 25 percent of the 2.5 million inhabitants of the thirteen colonies were black—some 500,000 people. The first post–Revolutionary

War census, conducted in 1790, indicates that over 90 percent of blacks in colonial North America were enslaved and a mere 8 percent were free. There were as many enslaved persons as there were free colonists in Virginia, and there were twice as many enslaved persons as there were free colonists in South Carolina; slavery was practiced in every one of the thirteen colonies.[1]

For a very brief period during the colonial era, black and white laborers were treated equally and their wages and their punishments for comparable offenses were undifferentiated. County court records from the period reveal that some slaves owned personal property and were allowed to contract for their services; others were able to procure freedom for themselves and their families.[2] In England throughout the sixteenth century, the status of "slave" was not a life sentence (conversion to Christianity was a proven route to freedom) nor was it determined by phenotype. But as the demand for manpower grew in the colonies so, too, did the legal strictures on enslaved people, transforming them comprehensively into human chattel devoid of individual rights.

Eager to realize the wealth and expansion opportunities Portugal's and Spain's overseas empires had provided them, mercantile England made repeated attempts to establish its own colonies and monopoly trading partners in the Americas and elsewhere.[3] In 1619, the first enslaved Africans were brought to Jamestown, Virginia for sale, under the auspices of the Virginia Company of London.[4] From then until the 1660s, the majority of blacks in the colonies were contract servants, not persons with the status of slave.[5] According to historian Lerone Bennett Jr., "Before the introduction of slavery, they accumulated land, voted, testified in courts and mingled with the masses of Whites on a basis of relative equality. . . . Freedom preceded slavery, and integration preceded racism."[6]

As tobacco farms were established and began to become profitable, the demand for additional labor intensified. Faced with the escalating cost of hiring white indentures from Europe and replacing those who had cycled through their indenture terms, British investors began to view African slavery as a more viable long-term solution to England's labor shortage problem across the colonies.[7]

This "solution" addressed two problems—one in the colonies and one at home. In addition to solving the colonial labor shortage problem, enslavement of Africans enabled European mercantilist policy makers—and British mercantilists in particular—to maintain a regime of low wages in the home economy. The exportation of too large a fraction of the domestic labor force would put upward pressure on the cost of hiring laborers at home.[8]

An added "bonus": blacks generally possessed a more distinctive phenotype—darker skin shades and other physical markers of being African—that made them easier to both recognize and capture when they sought escape. In contrast, white indentures generally were physically indistinguishable from other white colonists, and at the conclusion of the period of indenture, they frequently were afforded the opportunity to become landed, slave-owning gentry themselves.

One avenue for indentures to obtain land was the headright system. To attract workers to Virginia for tobacco production, the Virginia Company of London, and later the Plymouth Company, gave settlers who made the cross-Atlantic trip at their own expense plots of land anywhere from 1 to 1,000 acres. At no point did there appear to be a plan to include blacks, fully, as candidates for the headright system.

The majority of colonial Virginia's settlers who hailed from the British Isles were indentured servants who worked off the expense of their transport as contract labor for a period of four to seven years. Investors who financed the passage of laborers received headrights, or legal grants of fifty acres of land per person.

Surviving the period of indenture was not assured—in the seventeenth century some estimates indicate that more than half of all indentures died while still in debt bondage.[9] But indentures who completed their terms of service and reimbursed their benefactors for the expenses incurred to transport them to the colony were allowed to purchase land on credit or, occasionally, to receive outright grants of land.[10] Typically required to move to the unimproved territory on the edge of the frontier—further extending the reach of the colony—indentures were thus brought into direct conflict with the native population.

Skirmishes over land encroachment with the native population had long been commonplace. When frustrations with the ineffectiveness of policing the area by the colonial governor William Berkeley boiled over, some 500 mutinous colonists—led by English aristocrat Francis Bacon—took matters into their own hands and attacked several native tribes.

Irritated with what many viewed as the British leadership's ineptitude and tin-eared governance, the latest in a series of tax increases, and an immense property ownership gap that had stifled the aspirations of the colony's large lower class, the rebels demonstrated their discontent by torching the governor's residence in Jamestown, Virginia, in 1676. The uprising became known as Bacon's Rebellion.[11] It took British troops several *years* to bring the Chesapeake under control.[12]

White indentures, yeoman farmers, and blacks joined forces and partici-pated in the revolt, an alliance that greatly disturbed members of the planter elite. Organizing cross-racial coalitions and arming blacks threatened the Tidewater's social order. To "thwart . . . class conflict," white elites wrote laws modeled on and encouraged by "social practices that persuaded" whites "to imagine that tremendous social significance—inherent difference and inferiority—lay beneath black skin."[13]

Some historians have argued that Bacon's Rebellion led Virginia's colo-nial gentry to expand existing laws to create a race-based alliance between wealthy elites and poorer whites. The status of white indentures was ele-vated to encourage them to distance themselves from blacks, while simul-taneously hardening the identification of blackness with slavery.[14] While the headright system predated Bacon's Rebellion, it provided a useful mecha-nism to strengthen the boundary between indenture and slave status.

As early as 1662, the Virginia House of Burgesses—the body of representa-tives North American colonists of English descent established during British rule—eager to find ways to increase its slave population as inexpensively as possible, passed the *partus sequitur ventrem* doctrine, reversing a practice dating back to Roman civil law that conferred the legal status of a child's father to the child.[15]

Historically, fathers were designated as heads of households, and they were legally bound to acknowledge and provide support for their offspring—regardless of whether they were married to the child's mother. It was the father's responsibility to negotiate an apprenticeship for his children, a strat-egy designed to provide the child with a livelihood and therefore relieve the community of the burden of caring for the child.

Since most of the enslaved women in the colony were of African descent and not protected by British law, their children—regardless of whether their fathers were of English or other European ancestry—also would not enjoy that protection. In Virginia, slavery evolved into a hard racial category.[16]

The change in the law encouraged promiscuity among male slave owners, their sons, and hired overseers, since the courts no longer held them respon-sible for children born from either their forced or mutually consensual liai-sons with enslaved women. The new laws transformed all children born to slave mothers and free fathers into slaves, and when their fathers also owned the mothers, the children's fathers evolved from men whom the courts were bound to hold responsible for the welfare of their children to men who now could treat their sons and daughters solely as personal property. Other col-onies quickly followed suit.

Throughout the seventeenth century, blacks, white servants, and indentures frequently worked side by side in the service of white elites and were
united by friendship, kinship, and shared grievances. Disrupting these relations became the focus of Virginia lawmakers: "By a series of acts, the assembly deliberately did what it could to foster the contempt of whites for blacks
and Indians. In 1670 it forbade free Negroes and Indians," though baptized,
to own Christian servants. In 1680 it prescribed thirty lashes on the bare back
"if any negroe or other slave shall presume to lift up his hand in opposition
against *any* christian." This was a particularly effective provision in that it
allowed servants to bully slaves without fear of retaliation, thus placing them
psychologically on par with masters.[17] Late seventeenth-century colonial
Virginia was the crucible for the consolidation of America's rules of race.

Slavery was constituted officially in the colony of Virginia by a declaration
of the House of Burgesses in 1670 that read, in part, "All servants not being
Christians imported into this colony by shipping shall be slaves for their
lives."[18] The Virginia General Assembly followed with its own legislation in
1705, which gave slave masters supreme latitude in dealing with any of their
slaves whom they deemed uncooperative:

> All servants imported and brought into this country and such be
> here bought and sold notwithstanding a conversion for Christianity
> afterward. . . . All Negro, mulatto and Indian slaves within this
> dominion . . . shall be held to be real estate. And if any slave resists his
> master, or owner, or other person, by his or her order, correcting such
> slave and shall happen to be killed in such correction . . . the master,
> owner, and every other person so giving correction, shall be free and
> acquit of all punishment and accusation for the same, as if such incident
> had never happened.[19]

By 1700, the American colonies' enslaved population had grown to 25,000
(slaves outnumbered whites in some of the southern colonies); by 1750
there were more than 100,000 enslaved Africans in Virginia alone. Chafing
from the limitations of freedoms they believed were owed them as British
citizens, white elites tightened control over their servants and indentures
and systematically maintained and intensified the slavery of blacks.

While the British slave trade transformed the New World into one of the
world's most profitable financial centers, many colonists resented their
economic dependence on Britain. Perhaps it was inevitable that a thriving
outpost on the far end of the earth, a place where men of relatively modest

means could own other men and control their labor, would seek to break free from the grips of the motherland, especially when those men were heavily indebted to London creditors. On the eve of the Revolutionary War, colonial merchants and planters owed British financiers £5 million.[20]

Expanding its global reach to establish and rule the American colonies was costly for Great Britain. War with France, waged on the American continent between 1754 and 1763, had left Britain deep in debt. A series of encroachments and aggressions, beginning with two measures designed to generate revenues, was passed the next year without the consent of American colonists—the Sugar Act, which levied additional taxes on sugar imported from the West Indies, and the Currency Act, which prohibited colonists from minting paper currency or bills of credit.[21]

The settlers needed to maintain good relations with Britain in order to have access to a range of goods that could not be produced in America because of the absence of large-scale domestic textile manufacturing and iron-works foundries. If free white colonists could harness and direct the labor of slaves without incurring substantial debts in the process, they could produce what they needed and sever their ties with England. Passing laws that effectively made blackness synonymous with "slave" status could guarantee that a much-needed workforce would be available to transform the country into a mighty engine for economic growth and bring the colonists closer to the day they could separate from England. The expedient step was taken rather than the ethical step.

The Townshend Acts of June 1767, a tax on essential British imports and assessments for the payment of the salaries of a customs board, consolidated the belief that war was inevitable. Thereafter, Britain's King George III exercised monarchical authority and installed royal troops in Massachusetts in October 1768 to protect British agents. The Boston Massacre occurred fifteen months later, in March 1770. Parliament's passage of the Tea Act of May 1773, granting the East India Company a monopoly on the tea trade in America, sparked the Boston Tea Party protest in December 1773.

Not long after, the thirteen colonies met at the Second Continental Congress, and George Washington was appointed head of the Continental army. The Battle of Bunker Hill commenced on July 17, 1775, and King George III officially declared that the colonies were in a state of rebellion against the Crown.

The momentum for revolution became feverish with the circulation of Thomas Paine's pamphlet *Common Sense*, which argued against reconciliation and made the case for separation of the colonies from the Crown.

By June 11, 1776, the Continental Congress had appointed five men to draft a declaration of independence.

The entrenchment of slavery was not without its opponents on both moral and practical grounds. Instead of taking the path chosen by the Quakers, the early colony of Georgia, and the British Court of King's Bench by outlawing the practice, the colonial elite privileged its own welfare above all else and set the nation on a racial collision course. As early as the seventeenth century, prominent northern colonists and Europeans were railing against the slave system in the Americas. In 1688, a group of Dutch and German Quakers living in present-day Philadelphia united to declare their antipathy toward the trade in humans by producing the Germantown Quaker Petition Against Slavery.[22]

When the British royal charter established the colony of Georgia in 1732, no mention was made of slavery, and three years later, it became the only British colony to outlaw the institution outright with the passage of "AN ACT for rendering the Colony of Georgia more Defencible by Prohibiting the Importation and use of Black Slaves or Negroes into the same." It was not moral outrage that motivated Gen. James Edward Oglethorpe to prohibit the practice; rather, he wanted to create a place for impoverished British immigrants to live and prosper without the competition of enslaved laborers whose owners' pricing systems undercut the wages that could be earned by white laborers.[23] Unfortunately, the ban only lasted fifteen years, from 1735 to 1750.[24]

In 1772, the noteworthy Somerset case was brought to the English Court of King's Bench led by Lord Chief Justice William Murray, First Earl of Mansfield. James Somerset, a formerly enslaved African, sued for his freedom after being relocated by his owner from the Massachusetts Bay Colony to England. His suit was undertaken by esteemed British scholar and outspoken abolitionist Granville Sharp. Sharp successfully argued the case on behalf of Somerset.

Sharp's brief was directed against Charles Stewart, the man who had purchased Somerset in the province of Massachusetts and, after bringing him to England, attempted to affirm his right to retain possession of Somerset. Sharp learned of Somerset's case in 1771, when the enslaved man ran away and managed to evade capture for fifty-six days before bounty hunters caught him and put him on a slave ship bound for the Caribbean, where he was to be sold. Somerset was declared a free man in 1772. The British High Court's decision effectively ended legal enslavement in England.[25]

The case against the institution of slavery across the British Empire then was taken up by the Anglican evangelical Thomas Clarkson, cofounder in 1787 of the Committee for Effecting the Abolition of the African Slave Trade and one of the more vocal critics who gave speeches and published articles educating the public about the brutal realities of the trade in human flesh and advocating the dissolution of the practice of slavery.

Two years earlier, in 1785, one of the leaders in America's fight for independence, John Jay, established the New York Manumission Society and founded the African Free School.[26] In 1791, William Wilberforce, another member of Clarkson's committee, drafted the first of several parliamentary bills calling for the abolition of slavery and became one of the most quoted antislavery spokespersons in Europe and America.[27]

The Declaration of Independence could have been a document affirming universal rights. To the extent that black people are construed as fully human, championing liberty and freedom for some—"We hold these truths to be self-evident, that all men are created equal"—while condemning blacks to eternal servitude is highly problematic. Republicanism affirmed the ascendancy of the colonial aristocracy while maintaining a fine line of control over the masses of poor whites, providing opportunities for some of them to obtain land and own slaves while assuring even the most impoverished whites that they could exercise dominance over blacks. But Thomas Jefferson's ascendancy as the primary author of the Declaration of Independence all but guaranteed that America's enslaved Africans and their descendants would remain human chattel for the foreseeable future.

Although Jefferson was only thirty-seven years old when the document was written and had spent relatively little time in political office, he had risen rapidly in the esteem of American statesmen like John Adams. Indeed, Adams's intervention was critical for Jefferson to receive the assignment to draft the Declaration.

In 1757, at the young age of fourteen, upon the death of his father, Peter Jefferson—tobacco planter, slaveholder, and surveyor of Albemarle County, Virginia—Thomas Jefferson inherited fifty slaves, 1,900 acres that comprised the Monticello estate, and his father's vast library. From his mother, Jane Randolph, the daughter of a ship's captain and planter, he inherited a position of respect and noblesse oblige within the Virginia aristocracy. By his twenty-ninth year, Jefferson's estate had grown to 5,000 acres he owned free and clear. In 1773, less than a year after Jefferson married the young widow Martha Wayles Skelton, her father died, bequeathing an estate to the couple that consisted of 135 slaves, 11,000 acres of land, and his debts, "consequently doubl[ing] the ease of our circumstances," according to Jefferson.[28]

Family lore had it that one of Thomas Jefferson's early memories was of "being carried on a pillow by a mounted slave" as a three-year-old when the family moved from his birthplace, Shadwell plantation, to Tuckahoe plantation. Indeed, a "slave labor force isolated from the rest of society by race and racism" created the world Jefferson inhabited.[29] As historian David McCullough has observed, "It was not just that slaves worked his fields; they cut his firewood, cooked and served his meals, washed and ironed his linen, brushed his suits, nursed his children, cleaned, scrubbed, polished, opened and closed doors for him, saddled his horse, turned down his bed, waited on him hand and foot from dawn to dusk."[30]

A distinguished student of the law during his time at the College of William and Mary, Jefferson, something of a polymath, enjoyed an auspicious career as an attorney. Virginia's elite families were among his many clients, and in 1769 he formally entered politics when the eligible Albemarle County, Virginia, voters elected him to the House of Burgesses.[31]

During his tenure as a burgess, Jefferson developed "the reputation of a *masterly* pen," John Adams wrote with admiration. After the circulation of his widely read, though ultimately rejected, tract, *A Summary View of the Rights of British America*—written in support of the Boston Tea Party activists who felt they were being taxed unfairly by the Crown, in violation of their rights as Englishmen and without the benefit of elected representation in Parliament ("taxation without representation")—his standing in the colonies grew exponentially.[32] In 1775, immediately after the commencement of the American Revolutionary War, he became a delegate to the Second Continental Congress. Adams would recommend him to serve on the five-man committee tasked with drafting the Declaration of Independence one year later.[33]

An early version of Jefferson's text of the Declaration simultaneously embraced two seemingly inconsistent ideas—both involving the fate of human property. On the one hand, the text emphatically condemned Britain's King George III for his complicity in forcing the horrors of the international slave trade on Americans. Jefferson seemed to argue that since the British had had no history of conflict with the peoples of Africa before the slave trade, whatever conflict evolved had been attributable to the African slave trade itself.

On the other hand, simultaneously, the text condemned the king for offering freedom to those very slaves when their service as royal troops was needed in order to put down the colonial rebellion. Britain was proposing, in effect, to use one troublesome population to control another.

He [the king of Britain] has waged cruel war against human nature itself, violating its most sacred rights of life & liberty in the persons of a distant people who never offended him, captivating & carrying them into slavery in another hemisphere, or to incur miserable death in their transportation thither. This piratical warfare, the opprobrium of *infidel* powers, is the warfare of the *CHRISTIAN* king of Great Britain. determined to keep open a market where MEN should be bought & sold, he has prostituted his negative for suppressing every legislative attempt to prohibit or to restrain this execrable commerce: and that this assemblage of horrors might want no fact of distinguished die, he is now exciting those very people to rise in arms among us, and to purchase that liberty of which he has deprived them, by murdering the people upon whom he also obtruded them; thus paying off former crimes committed against the *liberties* of one people, with crimes which he urges them to commit against the *lives* of another.[34]

Despite Jefferson's equivocation over the immorality of the *slave trade*, the republic could not have been formed with all thirteen colonies had slavery not been perpetuated. What Jefferson was unequivocal about was the necessity of maintaining *slavery*. Apparently, for Jefferson and his fellow planters, there was no inconsistency between decrying the slave trade and simultaneously calling for independence while upholding slavery.[35]

As mentioned, the 1772 British High Court decision in the Somerset case de facto ended the practice of slavery in England proper. White colonists in America became fearful that slavery might come to an end throughout all the British dominions. Their agitation for independence was so closely tied to their attachment to the slave system that historian Gerald Horne has argued that the American Revolution was a reactionary struggle fought by the colonists to *preserve* slavery.

Horne comments, "On the one hand, there is little doubt that 1776 represented a step forward with regard to the triumph over monarchy. The problem with 1776 was that it went on to establish . . . the first apartheid state."[36] Thus, the American Revolution stands in stark contrast to the aims of the Haitian Revolution that began fifteen years later. The American Revolution was fought, in large part, by a colonial elite to preserve their right to human property. The Haitian Revolution was fought, in large part, by the enslaved to liberate themselves from slavery.

Thus, the deep stain of injustice was imprinted on the nation from its very beginnings. At least one-third of the signers of the Declaration of

Independence and the entire Virginia delegation—of which Jefferson was a member—owned or had owned slaves. Apparently, the contradiction between pursuit of liberty for the colonists, while preserving a system of enslavement, did not strike the primary author of the Declaration as problematic.

Ultimately, the U.S. Constitution, adopted in 1787 at the end of the Revolutionary War, specified that the legal slave trade to the United States would end in 1808. This gave slaveholders a twenty-year window to further increase their "stock" by human reproduction rather than importation. By 1750, it already was the case that the majority of blacks living in North America had never known freedom.[37]

It also meant that slaveholders in the upper south potentially could profit by supplying enslaved persons to the states in the lower south.[38] Perhaps it is unsurprising that Jefferson himself said in 1820, "I consider a woman who brings a child every two years as more profitable than the best man of the farm. What she produces is an addition to the capital, while his labors disappear in mere consumption."[39]

In contrast, abolition of both the slave trade and slavery went hand in hand with the process of the formation of new republics in a number of Latin American countries. In 1821, Ecuador, Venezuela, Colombia, and Panama declared that the children of slave mothers would be free and set up a program of compensated emancipation. Soon thereafter, slavery was declared illegal in Chile (1823), Mexico (1829), Bolivia (1831), and Guatemala, then called the Federal Republic of Central America (1824).[40]

All of these acts of liberation took place in the nineteenth century; consequently, they could not have served as a precursor for the American Revolution, but their existence demonstrates that other countries were willing to free their enslaved populations in service of the pursuit of independence from colonial rule.

In 1775, as the inevitability of war became increasingly clear, the rebellious Americans could have agreed that all slaves who enlisted and joined the colonists' cause of freedom from Britain would be freed. If a major motivation for the war had not been the preservation of slavery, the American Revolution would have presented another occasion to bring slavery to an end, but instead, here was another lost opportunity. Both enslaved and free blacks served in the British Army and the Continental army and navy, and each military entity promised to pay black soldiers salaries equal to those of whites. However, there were overt racial distinctions in the rank enlisted men could attain.

Blacks serving under the rebellious colonists could not rise above the rank of corporal. These men's reasons for joining the military varied—some who were enslaved enlisted in hopes of being granted their freedom at the war's end. Many enslaved and free blacks aligned with the Continental forces, with white citizens, in hopes of gaining greater rights.

At least 25 percent of the New England regiments were black. For two months—March to May 1775—free and enslaved blacks eagerly were recruited to serve in the war effort; however, fear of eventual slave revolts and concerns that the slaves who had fought for the country's freedom would demand that they, too, be freed led their owners to push to make slaves ineligible for military service.

In November of that year, the British made an extraordinary declaration: all bondsmen who served under the Loyalist flag—combatants and noncombatants alike—would be granted their freedom at the cessation of the war.[41] Indeed, by 1785, about 3,000 former bondsmen and their families eventually would be emancipated and resettled in London, the Bahamas, and Nova Scotia at the expense of the British government, the first mass emancipation of enslaved Africans in British history.

Recognizing that Britain's comprehensive policy to free all enslaved men who had labored and fought to maintain the sovereign's authority would quickly result in a mass exodus of runaway slaves to British military camps, the rebels reversed themselves. Active reenlistment resumed of free and enslaved blacks who had supported the American cause during the first months of the war.

In February 1778, as the war dragged on, the Rhode Island Assembly took the extraordinary step of allowing "every able-bodied negro, mulatto, or Indian man slave" to join the military. In exchange for their assistance, a slave who had enlisted would "be immediately discharged from the service of his master or mistress, and be absolutely free." Owners were to be compensated for the loss of their slaves at a fair market rate. At least eighty-eight slaves and an estimated fifty freedmen served in the First Rhode Island Regiment; however, many were reenslaved by unscrupulous whites after the war's end.[42]

Adoption of the new nation's constitution in 1787 presented another opportunity for the country to abandon slavery. Instead, the preposterous "three-fifths compromise" became the mechanism that inscribed slavery in the republic. Under the compromise, three-fifths of a state's enslaved population could be counted in the calculations for direct taxes (which had formerly been tied to the reported value of a citizen's land without any calculation for human property) and apportionment for representatives and presidential electors.

Essentially, southern lawmakers agreed to a higher rate of taxation in exchange for an assurance of greater representation in Congress and the Electoral College. It was one of those perverse twists that defined the era: slaves could not vote, but because three-fifths of their enumerated population could be counted for representational purposes, their very existence made it possible for their owners to elect politicians who favored legislation to preserve the slave system.

Thomas Jefferson's influence was evident in the inclusion of language in the Constitution that limited the rights of blacks. Prior to the compromise, the south controlled a minority of the seats in the Continental Congress (five of thirteen), where each state controlled one vote. The compromise boosted southern influence significantly as, in Jefferson's redoubtable words, it altered the way votes were apportioned. Southerners, by far the largest slave owners, no longer would be taxed "in accord with their numbers and their wealth conjointly, while the northerners [are] taxed on numbers only."[43] a major concession to the slaveholders, the compromise boosted the south's political ascendancy; the south would control presidential elections from 1800 to 1850.

Despite the claims of some historians, uprisings by the enslaved against their condition were frequent. Grade school and college textbooks typically underreport or ignore outright the existence of these tumultuous events and the impact they had on whites' decisions to tighten surveillance and control over their black captives. Stanley Elkins's influential study of slavery in the United States, which compared the psychological impact of the plantation world with Nazi concentration camps, was predicated on the belief that enslaved blacks were comparatively passive in their response to the slavery system.[44]

Contrary to Elkins, *it was those in bondage themselves who were the first abolitionists*, their resistance dating from the point of forced transport to the Americas.[45] Historian Harvey Wish found documentary evidence of at least fifty-five slave insurrections aboard ships that took place between 1699 and 1845, despite the captives' enchained and unarmed status.[46] Once the slaves landed and were sold in North America, their resistance did not evaporate—far from it. Wish reported that "the eastern counties of Virginia, where the Negroes were rapidly outnumbering the whites, suffered from repeated scares in 1687, 1709, 1710, 1722, 1723, and 1730."[47]

One of the earliest fully realized rebellions of armed blacks in colonial America took place in New York City on April 6, 1712, when "an estimated 23 slaves . . . lit an outhouse on fire, hid themselves, and when the townspeople came to extinguish the blaze, attacked [killing] somewhere between five and nine whites before being subdued."[48] Rev. John Sharpe, chaplain to the queen's forces, described the black insurgents as having "plotted to destroy all the White[s] in order to obtain their freedom."[49]

The slaveholders' reaction was swift and brutal, including the gruesome killing of blacks who had not been involved in the planning or the execution of the revolt.[50] Some whites expressed astonishment at the rebellion, viewing black enslavement as a favor to the enslaved. For example, Judge Daniel Horsmanden, presiding over the trial of two of the alleged plotters in the 1712 revolt, was incensed that the Africans would reward the civilizing, altruistic generosity of their white owners with a violent assault:

> Gentlemen, the monstrous ingratitude of this black tribe, is what exceedingly aggravated their guilt. Their slavery among us is generally softened with great indulgence; they live without care, and are commonly better fed and clothed, and put to less labour, than the poor of most Christian countries. They are indeed slaves, but under the protection of the law, none can hurt them with impunity; they are really more happy in this place, than in the midst of the continual plunder, cruelty, and rapine of their native countries; but notwithstanding all the kindness and tenderness with which they have been treated among us, yet this is the second attempt of the same kind, that this brutish and bloody species of mankind have made within one age. . . . But I fear, gentlemen, that we shall never be quite safe, till that wicked race are under more restraint, or their number, greatly reduced within this city.[51]

Some of the most prominent attempted slave revolts were not realized, but knowledge of these attempts circulated. Word of the successful campaign in the French colony of Saint-Domingue (present-day Haiti) reached America's black and white populations.[52] Fought over a thirteen-year period between 1791 and 1804, the revolt resulted in a conservatively estimated casualty count of 25,000 white colonists, 100,000 British and French soldiers, and at least 100,000 black ex-slaves during the course of the revolt.[53] The lesson learned from Saint-Domingue was that the system of slavery was increasingly dangerous and untenable.[54]

Unlike in the United States, where slave revolts led to great violence and then were quashed, revolutions led by enslaved blacks in other parts of the

Americas brought about an end to slavery. A series of relentless insurrections in Jamaica culminated in 1831, with an eleven-day-long battle. Fourteen whites and over 500 blacks were killed, and property damages were estimated at £1.15 million.

Britain's response was groundbreaking: passage of the 1833 Slavery Abolition Act, which emancipated human chattel in the British colonies in the Americas. However, the law did not provide any compensation to the ex-slaves for their forced labor and for their trials, but it did provide £20 million in payments to the former slaveholders for their loss of human property.[55]

The outcome of the Haitian Revolution solidified the case for abolition of the British slave trade. The outcome of the Jamaican revolt solidified the case for abolition of slavery in the British colonies.

While it may not follow directly that some slave revolts were harbingers of emancipation, liberation for the enslaved in America was in the air. In 1800, the efforts of the literate enslaved artisan known as Gabriel Prosser to organize a rebellion and form a separate black nation in Virginia were thwarted.[56] Denmark Vesey, a free man of color and a literate and highly skilled worker like Prosser, plotted an insurgency in Charleston, South Carolina. It was undermined by black informants. Vesey and thirty-five co-conspirators were hanged for their actions.

The enslaved were in constant war against slavery. There were as many as 313 so-called slave actions, or revolts that involved ten or more enslaved persons engaged in collective struggle against their status.[57] Documented executions of enslaved persons that indicate the cause of hanging also are indicative of the scope of black resistance to slavery. In Virginia alone between 1801 and 1818, fourteen slaves were executed for participating in slave revolts, and another six were executed for acts of poisoning. It is unclear to what extent the large remaining number of enslaved men and women who were put to death for "murder" (four black women and forty black men) and "conspiracy to murder" (three black men) had directed their attempts against their owners or other slaveholders.[58]

The scope of the slaves' war against slavery was underestimated intentionally, in large part because slaveholders actively suppressed information about suspected or actual uprisings to avoid stirring their human property to new actions. Slaveholders literally conspired to keep warnings out of the newspapers of "supposed insurrections" as well as reports of insurrections that had been actualized. In addition, they placed fictitious stories in newspapers ranging from the somewhat plausible claim made during the War of 1812 that "British officers [were] selling Virginia slaves into the West Indies in order to discourage slaves from running off to British lines" to the preposterous claim in the *Mobile Press-Register* on June 14, 1861, "about horrific northern plans to abolish slavery by mass murder of the South's 4 million slaves."[59] The press became an instrument for silencing the history of the resistance of the enslaved to their enslavement.

Slaveholders even perpetuated a fiction affirming that their human livestock were well treated and happy, and they actively blocked southern antislavery sentiment from the public sphere.[60] Of course, it was difficult to reconcile their claims of slave contentment with their fervid advocacy of fugitive slave laws.[61] An exception to these false narratives can be found in the private journal of native Mississippian Sarah Katherine "Kate" Stone, whose chronicles of the Civil War began in 1861, when she was twenty years old. The diarist was the daughter of the widow Amanda Susan Ragan Stone, who managed a 1,260-acre cotton plantation, Brokenburn, and the 150 black laborers she enslaved.[62]

Early in the journal, published in 1955—many years after her death—Kate Stone recalled the idyllic and hopeful time before the lives of her family members were interrupted by the "white heat" of war: "The Negroes seemed as much ours as the land they lived on. The crop of 1861 would pay off all indebtedness, leaving a surplus, and hereafter we would have nothing to do but enjoy ourselves."[63]

Together with her sister and five brothers, Stone was looking forward to her first trip abroad, in summer 1862, a grand tour of Europe, an indulgence that had become fashionable with the southern elite. It was canceled in the tumult of the war. Two of her brothers would die in service to the Confederacy.

Writing from her home in Tallulah, Louisiana, in 1900, the author—now Kate Stone Holmes—revealed a very different view of the relationship her family had with the men, women, and children forced into labor at Brokenburn. She wrote: "Even under the best owners, it was a hard, hard life: to toil six days out of seven, week after week, month after month, year after year, as long as life lasted; to be absolutely under the control of someone until the last breath was drawn; to win but the bare necessities of life, no hope of more, no matter how hard the work, how long the toil; and to know nothing could change your lot. Obedience, revolt, submission, prayers all were in vain. Waking sometimes in the night as I grew older and thinking it all over, I would grow sick with the misery of it all."[64] Nevertheless, in 1902 she helped establish the Madison Infantry Chapter of the United Daughters of the Confederacy and was influential in the erection of a Confederate memorial in Tallulah.[65]

Historian Thavolia Glymph has used letters exchanged among female slave owners and the narratives gathered by employees of the Works Progress Administration from former slaves during the 1930s to demonstrate the barbarity exercised by slaveholders in plantation life to maintain order and control.[66] Of particular importance are the many ways in which enslaved black women's reproductive lives were commercialized by white women slave owners. White women's babies were nursed and nurtured by black enslaved women under strict compulsion, a coercion masked by the United Daughters of the Confederacy's mythology of the benign and loving "mammy."[67]

Of the fifteen people in the United States who owned more than 500 slaves in 1860, eight were South Carolina residents. "Abolitionists inside and outside [Charleston] had long admonished its wealthy [planters'] 'taste for extravagance and display.' The pursuit of refinement championed by Charleston's upper-class set against the wretchedness of slavery was an uncomfortable paradox for many visitors. [Scotland native Adam Hodgson] described the contradiction as a mixture of gaiety and splendor with misery and degradation."[68]

Occasionally, the slaveholders themselves made explicit the oppressive foundation of their social system. In 1829, reversing the conviction of John Mann for shooting an enslaved woman, Lydia, when she sought to escape from his whipping, North Carolina Supreme Court justice Thomas Ruffin authored an opinion that rendered "absolute" the master's power over the slave. Recognizing that no one submits to slavery out of loyalty and faithfulness, Ruffin wrote, "Such obedience is the consequence of *uncontrolled authority over the body*." There were to be no constraints on the command that owners could exercise over their human property.[69]

The appalling savagery of the abuse inflicted on their human property by their owners was reported in great detail by abolitionists Theodore Dwight Weld, his wife, Angelina Grimké Weld, and her sister, Sarah Grimké, in their 1839 publication, *American Slavery as It Is: Testimony of a Thousand Witnesses*.[70] These eyewitness accounts, including many from southern whites themselves, undermine the ubiquitous assumption that *every* southern white thought slavery was normal, acceptable, or desirable.

Weld and the Grimké sisters recorded a litany of horrors. These included an enslaved black being buried alive, the placement of the head of a recaptured runaway on a stake as a warning to others, perpetual overwork and deprivation of normal rest (fifteen- and sixteen-hour workdays), the whipping of an enslaved pregnant black woman so severe that her child was stillborn, and the forced separation of relatives, among many other privations.[71]

The Grimkés had been born into a prominent slaveholding family in South Carolina.[72] Their father, John Faucheraud Grimké, had held a number of public posts—mayor of Charleston, South Carolina, state legislator, and chief justice on the South Carolina Supreme Court for over thirty-five years—and was a fervent proponent of slavery who owned "hundreds of slaves."

Sarah, a self-taught legal and history scholar, broke with her family and moved to Philadelphia. There, she and her sister, Angelina, who soon followed, came under the influence of the Quaker Society and developed friendships with the city's black abolitionists Sarah Mapps Douglass, Amy Hester "Hetty" Reckless, and Charlotte Forten.[73]

The Grimkés became public intellectuals themselves and reached legendary status in 1836 with the publication of two bold tracts. Angelina's *Appeal to the Christian Women of the South* implored women to read everything they could about slavery, pray for its abolition, become vocal in their support for the institution's collapse, and act on their intentions. Sarah's *Epistle to the Clergy of the Southern States* argued that slavery was against the divine order. Instantly, the sisters became synonymous with the antislavery movement.[74]

The Grimkés' commitment to ending slavery and racial and gender discrimination had been unheard of in their circles of privilege. Radical even among abolitionists, their position was an affront to their colleagues' more cautious—and more widely acceptable—view: slavery is intolerable, but blacks should be denied political and social equality with whites. Equally noteworthy, they yoked women's rights to those of blacks. Audiences were persuaded by the stories Sarah and Angelina shared about growing up in a slaveholding family, witnessing violent assaults on blacks, and the many ways that the institution compromised whites morally and spiritually. Fighting to "extinguish" slavery, Angelina wrote, "is a cause worth dying for."[75]

While the Grimké sisters were outliers, they were not the only southern white abolitionists. Indeed, the scope of southern white abolitionism largely has been erased from the historical record. It has been estimated that in 1827 there were more than 100 antislavery societies in the south, at a time when there were less than half that number in the north. Admittedly, the majority of southern white abolitionists wanted the end of slavery to be accompanied by sending blacks "back to Africa" rather than integrating them fully into American life, but nonetheless they actively opposed slavery. But expanding violent intimidation by proslavery advocates drove these organizations out of existence and led many southern white abolitionists to migrate north, where many of them continued to support the antislavery movement.[76] Indeed, that is precisely the move the Grimké sisters made.

The existence of white southern abolitionism makes clear that all white southerners did not subscribe to the legitimacy of slavery. In fact, suppression of the white southern antislavery movement was accomplished by the threat of deadly coercion.

Nevertheless, the coalition between abolition and women's rights that was forged by female abolitionists, black and white, and Radical Republicans did not survive the passage of the Fourteenth Amendment.

"Co-agitators for life," Susan B. Anthony and Elizabeth Cady Stanton were vocal advocates for women's rights and occasional collaborators with Harriet Tubman, the U.S. Army's first female military raid commander, a Union spy, and the Underground Railroad's most famous conductor.[77] When Anthony and Stanton realized that white men were not willing to grant them suffrage along with black men, they essentially abandoned black political rights.

Stanton argued explicitly that the franchise be limited to "Anglo-Saxons," who she believed possessed "intelligence and education." Black women would be better off as the slaves of "an educated white man," she insisted, "than of a degraded, ignorant black one." And blacks were not the only people Stanton deemed unworthy of suffrage.[78]

Debate over the eventual place blacks should occupy in society was a luxury that could be undertaken by whites, but collectively, blacks saw only one direction to be taken. That direction was freedom from slavery and full citizenship.[79] When all was said and done, the slaveholders themselves were well aware of the intensity of the enslaved people's war on slavery, routinely referring among themselves to their fears of "servile insurrection."[80] This led, in America, to two contrasting responses to the slave revolts: make the institution even more punitive while increasing the extent of surveillance and control of the enslaved, or bring slavery to an end altogether. The second option could have been chosen immediately, but it took another thirty years after the publication of *American Slavery as It Is* before the carnage of slavery was ended.

Of course, individual states could have made the decision to abolish slavery at any point, and for a brief period during the 1830s, it appeared that a divided Virginia might lead the way among the southern states. From the time of the state's formation, the criteria for voter eligibility had created a rift among residents. The eastern part of the state, which included the Tidewater and Piedmont, was home to the majority of Virginia's planter class, who were, not coincidentally, its eligible voters by virtue of the fact that only white males who owned at least 100 acres of land or at least twenty-five acres and a house could vote.[81]

Slave resistance in the United States took multiple forms, including workplace sabotage, flight—significant and frequent enough to lead to the adoption of the Fugitive Slave Act of 1850—and armed revolts.[82] Resistance ranged from the failed insurrections planned by Prosser and Vesey in 1800 and 1822, respectively, to the actualized slave uprisings in Louisiana in 1811 and Virginia in 1831, the latter led by Nat Turner. The revolutionaries in Louisiana sought to take control of the New Orleans area and, like Prosser, to form a separate black nation, presumably similar to the one founded in Haiti.[83]

Nat Turner, who was literate, may have read and been inspired by a smuggled copy of David Walker's *Appeal to the Coloured Citizens of the World*. Walker, a free black who migrated from Wilmington, North Carolina, to Boston, was an uncompromising opponent of slavery. He penned his *Appeal* to make the case for abolition and the subsequent provision of farmable lands to blacks. Walker's *Appeal* prefigured the black pride and black power movements that came to full flower a century later. It also drew the wrath of many whites, including some abolitionists, because it called for armed black struggle for liberation in the event that whites did not voluntarily end slavery.[84]

Whether Turner was inspired directly by the *Appeal*, the insurgency he led certainly was viewed as the fulfillment of Walker's message. Armed resistance to slavery, begun at least 150 years earlier by the enslaved themselves, reached its culmination with the attempt of a band of abolitionists, led by John Brown, to seize the federal arsenal at Harpers Ferry, Virginia, in 1859.

The Turner Rebellion was also the realization of the worst fears of slaveholders about the consequences of enslaved blacks acquiring literacy. As early as 1740 in South Carolina, the colonial legislature established a £100 fine—an extraordinary sum at the time—as punishment for teaching a slave to write or employing an enslaved person as a "scribe."[85]

Shaken by the 1831 Nat Turner revolt, the Virginia General Assembly debated the efficacy of slavery. In his address to the House of Delegates in January 1832, Samuel McDowell Moore of Rockbridge County argued that the "monstrous consequences that arise from the existence of slavery could be alleviated by abolition. . . . The evils and the dangers arising from the continued existence of slavery among us had escaped the observation of all but those who had devoted their attention to that of the subject, yet recent events had opened the eyes of the whole people to the magnitudes of these events, and to the imminence of the danger that is pending over them." Moore concluded that as long as Virginians held fast to slavery, they "can never know [or enjoy] a degree of happiness, peace and freedom from apprehension."[86]

Instead of a precedent-setting state-level decision to emancipate resident slaves—precisely the position Latin American countries took during this period, one after another—the less affluent, non-slave-owning Virginians in the western part of the state elected to increase their social, political, and economic influence by splitting the state in two. Virginia seceded from the Union in 1861 with the Civil War in progress, after several years of sparring among special interest groups and months of fierce debate; in 1863, West Virginia seceded from the larger Confederate entity and aligned itself with the Union.

Less than a year after Turner's execution, North Carolina native, lawyer, politician, and jurist William Joseph Gaston, then a trustee of the University of North Carolina at Chapel Hill, gave the university's commencement speech urging graduates to defend the Constitution, preserve the Union, and put an end to slavery, "which, more than any other cause, keeps us back in the career of improvement." While copies of Gaston's powerful speech were circulated widely, publishers failed to mention that the author was a slaveholder (at the time of his death he owned over 200 enslaved blacks).[87]

Two years later, in his capacity as North Carolina Supreme Court justice, Gaston wrote the majority opinion in *State v. Negro Will*, in which it was determined that enslaved persons could defend themselves against unprovoked attacks at the hands of their owners and their owners' agents. Will, the defendant in the case, had been enslaved on James Smith Battle's Edgecombe County plantation when he was accused of murdering Battle's overseer, Richard Baxter. Will had made a farm implement with his own hands and rather than surrender it to the overseer, attempted to evade him on foot. Baxter pursued Will and shot him in the back. After Will was captured, he wounded the overseer mortally.

Battle, convinced that Will had been unjustly provoked, retained attorney Bartholomew Figures Moore—paying a fee of $1,000—to represent Will. The attorney, a Halifax County, North Carolina, native whose father had fought in the American Revolution, declared, "Absolute power is irresponsible power." Moore's argument inspired Gaston to conclude in his opinion of the case, "The prisoner is a human being degraded by slavery, but yet having organs, senses, dimensions, passions like our own."[88] The court ruled that Will had acted in self-defense and reduced the charges against him to felonious homicide. In 1838, Gaston also wrote the opinion in *State v. Manuel,* which declared that North Carolina's free blacks were citizens whose rights were protected by the state constitution. This ruling formed the basis of the dissenting opinions of Supreme Court justices Benjamin R. Curtis and John McLean in the Dred Scott case. In a peculiar twist, Curtis later served as chief counsel to President Andrew Johnson during his first impeachment trial.[89]

However, Gaston's rulings were rare exceptions, not harbingers of a new perspective on slavery and the rights of the enslaved on the part of the southern judicial system.[90] Moreover, the U.S. Supreme Court never wavered in its proslavery stance.

In particular, the Supreme Court's 1857 Dred Scott decision was another missed opportunity to put blacks on the road to equality. For more than two years, Scott, his wife, Hazel Robinson Scott, and their two daughters had lived with U.S. Army surgeon John Emerson, the man who enslaved them in Illinois and in the Northwest Territory (present-day Minnesota), where the institution was illegal.[91] Had Scott won his case and been granted freedom for himself, his wife, and their daughters, he would have attained the same rights and authority on behalf of his family as that of any white American man.

A decision in favor of Scott would not have eliminated slavery, but it would have mitigated some key aspects of the institution. Also, had the case been decided in Scott's favor, it would have rendered the Fugitive Slave Act unconstitutional. Passed by the U.S. Congress in 1850, the act proclaimed that any runaway slave who had escaped successfully to a slave-free state and was subsequently captured had to be returned to his or her owner.[92]

The lesson of these decisions seemed to be "Once a slave, always a slave." For Harriet Jacobs, the enslaved Edenton, North Carolina, native who had escaped to freedom in New York, the passage of the Fugitive Slave Act was a source of intense fear and anxiety. Though she lived in a slave-free state, Jacobs and her fellow freedmen were officially "as subject to slave laws as [they] had been in a slave state."[93]

Tensions were mounting in the weeks before the November 1860 presidential election. Potentially, the unity of the republic itself was at stake. For a number of years, debates over the extension of slavery had created great divisions and resulted in the steady erosion of black individual rights. By 1790, Delaware, Vermont, Maine, New Hampshire, New Jersey, Massachusetts,

New York, and Ohio were among the states that allowed free men of color to vote. But in 1807, New Jersey disenfranchised blacks for the next sixty-eight years. Every new state that joined the Union after 1819 denied blacks the right to vote. Free black males could vote in Pennsylvania until 1837; Maryland permitted them to exercise the franchise from the American Revolution until 1820; and in North Carolina and Tennessee, free black men retained the vote until the mid-1830s.[94]

The acquisition of new territories in the western part of the continent raised the persistent issue of whether newly formed states would enter the United States as slave or free. Again, to accommodate the existing slave states, further compromises were reached. The precedent-setting agreement was the Missouri Compromise of 1820, where one state—Missouri—was admitted to the United States as a slave state and another—Maine—was admitted as a free state. This maintained the uneasy balance at twelve states for each side.

By 1840, a succession of momentous events forced whites to contemplate the real cost of containing blacks and American Indians. These events included the Indian Removal Act (1830), the Nat Turner Rebellion (1831), the Seminole Wars (beginning in 1835), the Creek Wars (1836), the Trail of Tears (1838), and the *United States v. The Amistad* (1838) court case. Whites took steps that limited to four states free blacks' ability to vote on equal terms with whites. When the Confederate army lost the decisive April 1865 battle at Appomattox, Virginia, marking the end of the Civil War, free blacks still held the franchise in only five of the thirty-six states that constituted the United States at that time.

Despite the protestations of Republican Party leadership, many slaveholders believed that if Abraham Lincoln, former Illinois legislator and one-term member of the House of Representatives—well known for his antislavery views—were elected commander in chief, the system of slavery would be threatened. Adding to their uneasiness was the New York State ballot that included a suffrage amendment to eliminate a major roadblock to free black men's participation in the electoral process, a virtually prohibitive $250 property qualification. The requirement had been dropped for white males in 1821; five years later, only sixteen of New York's 12,500 free black males could meet the legal condition. New York's suffrage amendment resoundingly failed.

Blacks were not granted more comprehensive voting rights until the adoption of the Fifteenth Amendment to the U.S. Constitution during Reconstruction, and even it was far from ideal. Unlike an earlier draft that barred additional requirements for voters, the Fifteenth Amendment allowed individual states to establish a range of criteria like the nominally race-neutral literacy test.

Legislators may have argued that literacy requirements were universal and not race specific; however, the tests definitely had the effect of disproportionately excluding black male voters, since approximately 80 percent of blacks had not been taught to read or write during slavery times.[95] The restrictive conditions eligible voters were required to meet guaranteed that the absolute number of black voters was relatively small.

The story of America could have been one of inclusive democracy. But it was not. At key junctures, when America could have separated slavery from blackness or abolished slavery entirely, it hardened those distinctions and intensified the institution. The revolutionary period could have been characterized by efforts to free slaves who supported the rebellion. The Declaration of Independence and the U.S. Constitution could have been structured to eliminate slavery, and the Dred Scott decision could have given blacks the means by which to escape bondage and, importantly, some measure of authority over family life. Tragically, the creation of the new nation was fused with the system of slavery. The narrative of the nation's beginnings is captured well in Edmund Morgan's terse observation that "the rise of liberty and equality in America had been accompanied by the rise of slavery."[96]

Part 3

5

Alternatives to War and Slavery

> In the fall of 1861 Lincoln attempted an experiment with compensated emancipation in Delaware. He interested his friends there and urged them to propose it to the Delaware legislature. He went so far as to write a draft of the bill, which provided for gradual emancipation, and another which provided that the federal government would share the expenses of compensating masters for their slaves. Although these bills were much discussed, there was too much opposition to introduce them. —John Hope Franklin, *From Slavery to Freedom*, 1947

The nation did not have to go to war with itself to bring slavery to an end. In this chapter, we examine the abandoned plans the nation could have pursued to avoid civil war and stop American slavery.

By May 1860, during the third year of James Buchanan's presidency, sectional rancor over slavery was high. John Brown, a freedom fighter for abolition, had been executed five months earlier. Brown had led a band of twenty-one men, black and white, enslaved and free, on a raid of the federal arsenal at Harpers Ferry, and the attack was engraved on the nation's consciousness. Brown's actions, and those of his supporters, were animated by the Supreme Court's 1857 ruling in the Dred Scott case.[1]

The Court's decision excluded blacks from the American polity; blacks effectively were rendered stateless in the only country most of them had known. Consequently, they had no standing in courts of law. This thorough erasure of black rights, coupled with Congress's vote to let white residents of Kansas and Nebraska choose whether to make slavery legal within their respective territories, created a perfect storm for antislavery insurrection.

Nevertheless, for many Americans, the fact of whites owning black people seemed a natural part of life, as natural as breathing; few could have anticipated the drama that would unfold over the next five years. Indeed, in May 1860, a resolution adopted by the Thirty-Sixth U.S. Congress declared, "Neither Congress nor a local legislature can abolish [slavery].... The federal government is in duty bound to protect slave owners as well as the holders of other forms of property in the territories."[2]

Moreover, President Buchanan's own temporizing over slavery and the growing secessionist sentiment in the southern states only fueled the momentum toward division of the nation and the onset of war. While heated debates over "the Negro question" were growing increasingly common, and some political groups called for bringing the rights of blacks into closer conformity with the rights of all Americans, the antislavery advocates' position remained a minority stance. Indeed, Buchanan did not aid their efforts, deliberately making no attempt to declare the antislavery cause just and right.[3]

In general, as states rescinded restrictions on white male voters, they tightened eligibility requirements for black men while imposing additional constraints on their lives. The north was no exception in the repression of blacks.

For example, the *Christian Recorder* chronicled the jeers and insults blacks in Philadelphia enountered on a daily basis when they walked down the street. In 1862, Illinois voters amended their constitution in order to bar escaping slaves from settling within the state's boundaries; in 1863, Indiana passed a law making it illegal for all blacks to enter the state. Whites in Iowa's Johnson and Wapello Counties also sought to restrict black access to their state: "First by lawful means, and when that fails, we will drive them, together with such whites as may be engaged in bringing them in, out of the State or afford them 'hospitable graves.'"[4] A formerly enslaved individual in Milledgeville, Georgia, recalled, for example, how after 1854 the state's general assembly required free blacks at all times to be able to prove their status "by the clearest evidence."[5]

To the amazement of many, Abraham Lincoln won the presidency in November 1860. Lincoln, who was practically unknown beyond Illinois when he had won the Republican Party's nomination that spring, carried all of the northern states, as well as California and Oregon. While he captured just under 40 percent of the popular vote, Lincoln won a significant plurality in a field that included three other contestants. Although he won none of the states in the south, the ambitious statesman, whose political acumen and eloquent oratorical style had helped him garner a reputation as a savvy public servant with his colleagues and the press, won a landslide victory in the Electoral College.[6]

Lincoln's election did not translate into immediate gains for enslaved blacks. As a candidate he had become a symbol of the antislavery effort because of his staunch opposition to the expansion of legal servitude into the western territories. But the Republican Party leader was elected at a point when most whites did not support equal rights for blacks, and he, in particular, was concerned deeply about conserving a unified nation.

Therefore, while he appeared to view slavery as morally wrong, he moved with great caution—some saw him as equivocating—on the matter of abolition. As early as 1837, while serving in the Illinois House of Representatives, Lincoln publicly declared that slavery was "founded on both injustice and bad policy," but he was reluctant to ally himself with the abolitionist cause.[7]

During his inaugural address one month later, President Lincoln asserted that sectional discord would not devolve into violence and bloodshed. He vowed, "There shall be none, unless it is forced upon the national authority." While clearly concerned about the hardening of opinions about slavery, Lincoln continued to express hope for "a peaceful solution of the national troubles and the restoration of fraternal sympathies and affections."[8]

The president's peaceful solution was embodied in his long-standing support for gradual and compensated emancipation, a cautious approach that was anathema to many abolitionists. In the days following the confirmation of Lincoln's victory, the mood in the country was apprehensive. For several months, Lincoln had attempted to quell what he termed the "groundlessness of the pretended fears" that swirled around him. In an interview with a reporter, he declared, "We say to the southern disunionists, we won't go out of the Union, and you shan't."[9]

As the south's secession threats became palpable, several political groups, attempting to sway public opinion, floated the radical idea of compensated emancipation. In exchange for voluntarily freeing the men, women, and children they held in bondage, slaveholders would receive payments from the federal government approximating the free-market value of their human chattel.

But a commitment to the slave system dominated the opinions of legislative bodies in the seven southern cotton-producing states. Unimpressed with Lincoln's conciliatory compensated emancipation proposals and determined to retain ownership of their human property, they voted their perceived self-interest and made good on the promise of "disunion" that Lincoln feared.

In February 1861—before Lincoln took office—those same seven southern states seceded from the Union and formed the Confederacy. Their aim was "to create a nation of their own—a slave nation."[10] Initially, the Confederacy included South Carolina, Mississippi, Florida, Alabama, Georgia, Louisiana, and Texas.

On April 12, 1861, the American Civil War began when southern Confederates opened fire on a small squadron of troops based at Fort Sumter, a military outpost situated on an island near Charleston, South Carolina.[11]

Had the enslavers agreed to compensated emancipation, whether gradual or immediate, the vast human and financial costs of the war could have been prevented or at least greatly reduced. There was an alternative both to war and to the continuation of slavery. In 1849, when Abraham Lincoln was a member of the U.S. House of Representatives from Illinois's Seventh District and a member of the Whig Party, he had introduced a plan to enable the citizens of the District of Columbia to adopt compensated emancipation in the nation's capital by referendum.

Eligible male voters would decide the future of enslaved persons in the District.[12] The proposal called for the federal government to pay enslavers a market rate for each person they voluntarily manumitted, sparing them the financial burden of having to replace an essential workforce without capital. The proposition failed.

During the fall of 1861, when it became clear the war was going to be a protracted affair, Lincoln approached Delaware congressman George P. Fisher regarding a gradual course of compensated emancipation for the state's 1,798 slaves—nearly 92 percent of the state's 21,627 blacks were free—and offered the payment of an average of $500 per person with funds that had been approved by the Republican-majority Congress.[13] If a Union border state like Delaware adopted the measure, Lincoln reasoned, Missouri, Maryland, and Kentucky might be persuaded to follow suit and perhaps even the states that comprised the Confederacy as well. Lincoln was seeking at least one state to serve as a demonstration site for his plan to achieve emancipation.

Moreover, and possibly of greater significance in Lincoln's calculation, Delaware's economic base was diverse and included "mixed" farms—properties where wheat, corn, and oats were produced with equipment that was increasingly mechanized, as opposed to the slave-centered tobacco, cotton, rice, and indigo production that fueled the economies of the state's southern neighbors.

Delaware's enslaved blacks constituted only 3 percent of the state's population, the lowest proportion and lowest absolute number (1,798) in any of the slave-holding states. In contrast, Florida, with a slightly larger total population than Delaware at the time—140,424 persons, compared with Delaware's 112,218—had an enslaved population of 61,763, or 44 percent of the state's population. Missouri recorded the second lowest proportion of human chattel, with 9.7 percent; however, that proportion represented 114,931 persons. Patently, neither Florida nor Missouri were likely candidates to *lead* the country down the path to compensated emancipation. Delaware ultimately proved not to be a candidate either.[14]

That Delaware's economy was not strongly dependent on the institution was deemed a plus, and Congressman Fisher agreed to float the proposal.[15] He cosponsored a bill with Republican ally Nathaniel P. Smithers. However, they withdrew the plan after determining that while it would likely pass the Delaware Senate, the measure would fall one vote short in the state's House.[16] Slavery's seemingly inconsequential hold on the state was not sufficient even to bring the measure to a vote.

The message the Delaware General Assembly sent to President Lincoln—we reject compensated emancipation—reverberated throughout the south. Echoing the intractable stance of this northern outlier, southern leaders declared that, for them, slavery was not negotiable. Undeterred by this recalcitrance, northern abolitionists organized a well-advertised public lecture series consisting of twenty-two speeches held at the 2,000-seat-capacity Smithsonian Institution Building in Washington, D.C., over a four-month period. Lincoln and members of Congress were frequent attendees. The new popularity of the reenergized abolitionist viewpoint was largely a consequence of the realities of the war—mounting human casualties, economics, and determination to save the Union.

For many years, proslavery-majority legislatures, commonplace in the south, had been prevalent in the north. Declaring oneself an abolitionist during the early decades of the nineteenth century was tantamount to political suicide; advocates were roundly and publicly denounced. The tar of the "abolitionist" label could mean a loss of public support and severely limit a politician's ability to work with his colleagues, even behind the scenes. It certainly would undermine any political actor's credibility.[17] But, now, the abolitionists were no longer the laughingstock of the national media or the political arena; now they were beginning to look like wise sages who had crafted a plan to deliver the country from destruction.[18]

There were even declarations of abolitionist sentiment in the south.[19] Throughout the winter of 1861 and spring 1862, abolition spokespersons George B. Cheever, pastor of the Church of the Puritans in New York City, and Wendell Phillips, a lawyer and member of the American Anti-Slavery Society, were in great demand. Both men were invited to speak at the Pennsylvania General Assembly and at the U.S. House of Representatives on two occasions, and Phillips was granted a private audience with President Lincoln.[20] Many abolitionists understood that northerners, whatever their feelings about African Americans' civil rights, were coming to the realization that freeing the slaves was a "military necessity."[21] Each slave conscripted by the Union army was one fewer soldier allied with the Confederates.

There was also another benefit: engaging enslavers' former chattel in the battle to defeat them gave the Union cause a tremendous psychological advantage.

Abolitionists, seizing the day, redoubled their efforts and began to circulate petitions calling for the immediate end of slavery. William Lloyd Garrison urged the government to act with haste and use the "war-power" "to . . . enact . . . the total abolition of slavery throughout the country—liberating unconditionally the slaves of all who are rebels" and to provide "a fair pecuniary award" to the "loyal" emancipators so that the war could be brought to a "speedy and beneficent termination."[22]

Eventually, abolitionists concluded that slaveholders preferred to bet on the institution's staying power and a Confederate victory. Slaveholders took that gamble rather than liquidating their human holdings and receiving a payment from the federal government to shorten or avoid war altogether. When the antislavery advocates' strategy to appeal to their fellow white citizens to take the high ground and respect blacks as equals ultimately was rejected, the abolitionists forged a new argument. Since slaveholders were willing to destroy the Union in order to preserve their right to build and maintain their fortunes with human captives, abolitionists resolved to destroy the institution of slavery itself.

On April 16, 1862, Congress passed the District of Columbia Compensated Emancipation Act mandating fair market value for the enslaved belonging to the residents of the nation's capital. Finally, there was movement on the slave emancipation front. Lincoln signed the act, which resulted in the freeing of 3,185 persons at a cost of nearly $1 million, providing owners with a maximum of $300 (approximately $141,500 today, compounded from 1862 at 4 percent interest) per enslaved person.

This was "the first great step towards that righteousness which exalts a nation," Frederick Douglass wrote at the time.[23] "He who to-day fights for Emancipation, fights for his country and free Institutions, and he who fights for slavery, fights against his country and in favor of a slaveholding oligarchy." Douglass, together with many abolitionists, celebrated the victory, hoping that the southern states would soon initiate negotiations for similar terms: "Not only a staggering blow to slavery throughout the country, but a killing blow to the rebellion—and the beginning of the end for both," Douglass wrote.[24] "Kill slavery at the heart of the nation, and it will certainly die at the extremities."[25]

Buoyed by this unprecedented success, Lincoln began working on a proposal that would enable the U.S. Congress to offer monetary aid to slaveholders in the border states of Delaware, Kansas, Missouri, and Kentucky who maintained an allegiance to the Union, compensating them for lost labor. Insofar as slavery was a problem for the entire nation, the thinking went, the nation should bear the financial cost of dismantling it. But the plan was not adopted.

Douglass, apparently skeptical that the amounts offered the District of Columbia's slave owners would be sufficient to motivate slaveholders across the nation to surrender the institution without defeat in war, had floated a version of a compensated emancipation program in a February 1861 antislavery editorial in his periodical *Douglass' Monthly*. He appealed to a sense of fairness. The article laid out a concrete compensated emancipation proposal advocated by some abolitionists. The federal government was advised to set aside $240 million over a ten-year period to reimburse slaveholders in Texas, Louisiana, Maryland, Missouri, Arkansas, and Delaware with a payment of $400 per slave.[26]

Historian John Stauffer caustically surmised that southern slaveholders refused to liberate their slaves "because slaves generated far higher rates of return than stocks, bonds, or real estate. And it was hard to satisfy one's sexual lust on a stock certificate."[27]

If the slaveholders' human property was valued at more than $3 billion in 1860, the average slave would have been worth at least $750.[28] Compensation in the range of $300 to $500 per enslaved person might not have appeared worth it to the owners.[29] However, there is no evidence that they agreed to negotiate a price for a settlement or even to discuss such an arrangement.

The total financial cost of the war to the Union has been estimated at $6.1 billion. The Confederate financial cost has been estimated at $2.1 billion.[30] Relative to these financial costs of the war—entirely apart from the human cost in mortality and morbidity—a bill of $3 billion would have provided $750 in compensation for each enslaved African had slaveholders been willing to part with the slave system.

This solution would have been feasible for the federal government to meet, especially if the payments were staggered over a few years. The Civil War was fought over 1,336 days, from April 12, 1861, through May 13, 1865. If southerners had emancipated 3,000 enslaved blacks each day of the hostilities at a cost of $750 each, the total expenditure would have capped at $3 billion—$3.1 billion less than the Union outlay, and $5 billion less than the total financial expenses for both sides of the conflict.[31]

The southern states had a viable alternative to secession and war; they refused it.

Before the hostilities began, both houses of Congress had adopted a resolution favoring compensated emancipation; however, the initiative was turned away by the southern states. H. B. Metcalf observed, "The Southern States rejected the overtures of peace on any terms that did not recognize the independence of the Southern confederacy.... They spurned the proffered hand that was held out to them, and the world knows the result."[32]

On July 12, 1862, Lincoln met with congressmen from the slaveholding states in the Union (Kentucky, Maryland, Delaware, and Missouri) and asked them to each persuade their state to adopt compensated emancipation of the human captives within their boundaries. While discussions were held in each of the four states, none of the congressmen agreed to the proposal.[33] Two days later Lincoln sent a bill to Congress that would have allowed the Treasury to issue bonds at 6 percent interest to cover the expense of paying the slave owners compensation for emancipating their human property. The bill was never even brought forward for a vote.[34]

As late as February 3, 1865, during the Hampton Roads Conference, Lincoln, desperate to end the bloodshed, spoke to the vice president of the Confederacy, Alexander H. Stephens, about a "fair indemnity" that might pay slave owners $400 million for emancipation.[35] But this overture also was rejected.

Lincoln biographer Alexander Kelly McClure's commentary on this chain of events is telling:

> Strange as it may now seem, in view of the inevitable tendency of events at that time, these appeals of Lincoln were not only treated with contempt by those in rebellion, but the border states congressmen who had everything at stake, and who, in the end, were compelled to accept forcible emancipation without compensation, although themselves not directly involved in rebellion, made no substantial response to Lincoln's efforts to save their states and people. Thus did the South disregard repeated importunities to accept emancipation with payment for their slaves. During long, weary months, Lincoln had made temperate utterances on every possible occasion, and by every official act that could direct the attention of the country, he sought to attain the least violent solution of the slavery problem, only to find that they make no terms with the government.[36]

The immense human tragedy of the Civil War could have been avoided had some version of Lincoln's plan been adopted. But the choice was made by the patrons of the slave system to reject gradual and compensated emancipation in favor of what ultimately would become military emancipation.

Lincoln was not only an antislavery gradualist; he also was an early advocate of so-called repatriation, manumitting the enslaved and transporting them with already free blacks to Haiti and Liberia. Liberia, an American colonial outpost on the African continent, was created via conquest and expropriation by the United States, with the assistance of the Society for the Colonization of Free People of Color of America, for the purpose of black resettlement.

Indeed, one of the earliest black Utopian strategies devised by white Americans was to manumit and resettle former captives on the African continent. From the 1820s through the remainder of the first half of the nineteenth century, many white abolitionists in the north urged repatriation of emancipated blacks to the West African colony that would become the country of Liberia in 1848.

A combined total of just over 500 Africans seized from slave ships—regardless of their countries of origin—together with black American volunteers, were repatriated to Liberia between 1820 and 1847, when the colony issued an uncontested declaration of independence.[37]

The vast majority of blacks in America did not support the colonization movement. Indeed, historian Manisha Sinha has asserted that "black abolitionism [came] of age in the 1820s by opposing the American Colonization Society."[38] In 1862, in the midst of the Civil War, when Lincoln floated a trial balloon for repatriation, black abolitionist Frances Ellen Watkins Harper responded with her characteristic ferocity and rapier insight:

> Let the President be answered firmly and respectfully, not in the tones of supplication and entreaty, but of earnestness and decision, that while we admit the right of every man to choose his home, that we neither see the wisdom nor expediency of our self-exportation from a land which has been in large measure enriched by our toil for generations, till we have a birth-right on the soil, and the strongest claims on the nation for that justice and equity which has been withheld from us for ages— ages whose accumulated wrongs have dragged the present wars that overshadow our head.[39]

Blacks would stay and demand full justice in America.

6

Race and Racism during the Civil War

I am proud and happy to know that the black man is to strike a blow for liberty. —Harriet Ann Jacobs, *The Liberator*, 1863

There will be some black men who can remember that, with silent tongue, and clenched teeth, and steady eye, and well-poised bayonet, they have helped mankind onto this great consummation; while, I fear, there will be some white ones, unable to forget that, with malignant heart, and deceitful speech, they have strove to hinder it. —Abraham Lincoln letter to Hon. James C. Conkling, 1863

It is often said that the war will make an end to slavery. This is probable; but it is surer still that the overthrow of slavery will make an end of the war. —Charles Sumner, address to Massachusetts State Republican Convention, October 1, 1861.

The conditions of the Civil War itself created an opportunity for setting America on a different racial footing. There were rich possibilities reflected in the black economic development experiments undertaken before and during the war; we will explore those social experiments in chapter 7. For their part, blacks responded with a mass migration to Union lines and a willingness to do whatever was needed to assure victory. Their acts of valor and sacrifice provided a valuable stimulus to the Union effort.

However, well before victory was in hand, a negative trend was evident, including the following abuses and aggressions: draft protests violently directed at blacks, segregated regiments, denial of commissioned officer status for black military personnel, underpayment of black combatants and noncombatants alike, and discriminatory practices that characterized the work camps. The brutalities and indignities of slavery were not lifted for blacks during the Civil War, even under the umbrella of the Union army. Reaching Union lines did not guarantee former slaves insulation from exploitation. These developments are the subject of this chapter.

When Virginia seceded from the Union in April 1861, Union general Benjamin Franklin Butler classified it as a "foreign" power, which nullified any claim the state's citizens previously held under U.S. laws. This bold step paved the way for the seizure of all assets belonging to Virginia residents that had been used to gain an advantage over the Union forces, including human property, as "contrabands of war."[1]

Butler reasoned that the refugees from slavery, or "contrabands" as they came to be called, had sought asylum at Fort Monroe after having been pressed into service to support the Confederate military operation.[2] Imperfect though it was, the first black refugee camp had been created. The Fort Monroe camp is discussed in greater depth in chapter 7.

The contrabands had been tasked with digging trenches, building fortifications, hauling supplies, and working as teamsters for the Confederacy. Butler concluded, shrewdly, that because they were "chattel"—a type of movable property—they could be "confiscated."[3] They would then be reassigned to work on Union-run plantations or tasked with repairing railroads or unloading freight. Formerly the property of individual slaveholders, ex-slaves were freed from bondage only to become the de facto property of the federal government.

Lincoln concurred with Butler's judgment regarding the status of the contrabands, if not with Butler's rationale.[4] On August 6, 1861, Lincoln signed the First Confiscation Act, which authorized the seizure of all property used "in aid of the rebellion," but did not specify how the act was to be executed or whether the contrabands would remain slaves. This ambiguity led to multiple interpretations (and misinterpretations) by the Union's field commanders.[5]

Twenty-four days after the Confiscation Act became law, Gen. John C. Frémont, leader of the Union's Western Department, took a bold step. After he declared martial law—temporarily replacing all preexisting executive, legislative, and judicial branches of government with a military power—Frémont made the stunning announcement that all of Missouri's blacks enslaved by rebels now were free.[6]

Four slave states had not yet joined the Confederacy—Missouri, Delaware, Maryland, and Kentucky. Lincoln, concerned that those key states would bolt from the Union, revoked Frémont's order on September 11, 1861, and used the occasion to emphasize that the Confiscation Act pertained only to those slaves who had been employed directly in the aid of Confederate military forces. If Maryland had fallen to the Confederacy, the opposition would have succeeded in surrounding the nation's capital, and the loss of Kentucky, Lincoln's birth state, would have signaled an embarrassing political defeat.[7]

Five months after the hostilities setting off the war began, sacrifices on both sides were mounting. Once again, abolitionists sprang into action—soliciting contributions, making presentations at public forums, writing letters, and circulating petitions to their representatives and to the national press—in an effort to apply pressure on the president and to win support for slave emancipation. During this spell of optimism, they also began to pour money into schools for freedmen and to recruit teachers to relocate to the south to work in Union-protected classrooms.[8]

The cause of freedom had never known greater support. As historian James McPherson wrote about that moment, "Abolitionism had arrived."[9] Whether they justified freedom for the enslaved because the institution robbed blacks of their humanity and denied them human rights, because of a desire to liberate the slaves as spoils of war, or because they felt that freedom for the enslaved would save the Union, abolitionists and Radical Republicans were united in their determination to end the vile institution. In an effort to garner international support, they argued that the termination of slavery was both a moral and a "military necessity"—an essential condition for victory.[10]

Petitions advocating abolition bearing thousands of signatures were sent to Washington, D.C. Lincoln's views on black incorporation in the American polity were evolving, but he was not ready to declare unconditional emancipation. In his first annual address to Congress, on December 3, 1861, Lincoln continued to advocate compensated emancipation on a voluntary basis in the border states and to promote colonization of the former slaves. He reaffirmed his gratitude for the crucial support of "noble little Delaware," for Maryland's renewed loyalty demonstrated by its "seven regiments to the cause of the Union," for Kentucky's loyalty evidenced by its determination to be "decidedly and . . . unchangeably ranged on the side of the Union," and for "comparative quiet" in Missouri.[11]

But now it was Congress's turn to push against Lincoln's cautious position. Between December 1861 and January 1862, more than a dozen confiscation bills were introduced, authorizing expansion of the executive and legislative branches' power to free enslaved persons. Thaddeus Stevens, the Radical Republican representative from Pennsylvania, circulated a petition that would have made emancipation one of the "step[s] which [Congress and the president could use to] subdue the enemy." Owen Lovejoy (R-Ill.), who believed "liberty of all men was an inalienable gift from God," attempted to make it a punishable offense "for any officer or private of the Army or Navy to capture or return, or aid in the capture or return, of fugitive slaves."[12]

Less than a month after the passage of the District of Columbia Compensated Emancipation Act, on May 9, 1862, Lincoln was forced, once again, to disavow publicly the actions of one of his military leaders and to clarify his position on emancipation. Maj. Gen. David Hunter, commander of the Department of the South, had issued General Orders No. 11, freeing all of the slaves under his command.[13]

Hunter was an early advocate of arming the ex-slaves. When he acted on his beliefs and began to form a black Civil War militia, the national press, assuming that such a radical step could have been taken only on the order of the president himself, convulsed with the news.[14] Abolitionists also capitalized on the momentum by organizing a new round of action opposing slavery.[15] When Lincoln ordered Hunter to disband the black troops, he was pilloried by the northern press.

Determined to maintain the support of the states that had not seceded from the Union, Lincoln publicly denounced Hunter's actions. As discussed in chapter 5, on July 12, 1862, Lincoln convened a second meeting of the representatives of the border states at the White House to reconsider compensated emancipation. For the first time, several members of Congress voiced approval of Lincoln's proposal, but the majority overruled them.

The next week, Congress passed the Second Confiscation Act.[16] Frustrated but resolute, the president constructed the Emancipation Proclamation, which would take effect on January 1, 1863. The proclamation, announced on September 22, 1862, directed the Confederacy to surrender to the Union or face immediate and uncompensated manumission of its slaves. This gave the secessionists 100 days to reconsider their position and still receive compensation for their human property. Since none of the Confederate states took the deal, the proclamation became effective on New Year's Day 1863.

The Emancipation Proclamation freed all of the slaves in the eleven states engaged in the rebellion against the Union—approximately 4 million black people.[17] The proclamation simultaneously approved the enlistment of "suitable" former slaves into the U.S. Armed Forces, which included the army and navy, and ordered the executive branch to "recognize and maintain the freedom of" those persons emancipated.

Secretary of State William H. Seward had convinced Lincoln that deferring the proclamation until a significant Union military victory had been won would be viewed as a measure of continued strength. The September 17, 1862, Battle of Antietam, "the great and terrible day," provided that opportunity when Union general George McClellan delivered a major tactical victory in the campaign. Over 23,000 soldiers were killed, wounded, or missing in action by the end of the most brutal day of the Civil War. But the cruel siege of Antietam paved the way for the Emancipation Proclamation.[18]

Still facing uncertainty about prospects for a Union victory, Congress passed the Enrollment Act on March 3, 1863, the first compulsory wartime draft of American citizens. Sufficient numbers of white men had not come forward, and now that the war was explicitly about black freedom, many whites held blacks responsible for the draft. The act required every male citizen between the ages of twenty and forty-five to report to the board of enrollment for entry into the military by April 1. The term of service was a two-year minimum and three-year maximum.[19]

Recognition that slavery's demise now was part of the Union's mission reactivated the most virulent forms of anti-abolitionism in the north. Staunchly opposed Democratic organizations held rallies protesting both the war and emancipation and blamed the Republicans for their troubles.

New York's governor, Horatio Seymour, a "Peace Democrat" who wanted the Confederacy to negotiate with the Union, vowed to challenge the military draft in court on the basis that quotas for Democratic districts were greater than those for Republican districts. By midsummer, protests against army conscription and the legal option of avoiding military service—for men who could afford to pay a $300 commutation fee—led to a violent uprising in New York City that still ranks in terms of mortality as "the most destructive civil disturbance in all of American history."[20]

In an incendiary speech given nine days before the riots, at a July 4 rally, Seymour declared, "The bloody and treasonable and revolutionary doctrine of public necessity can be proclaimed by a mob as well as by a government."[21] The mayor's speech might have fallen on deaf ears if not for the dramatic demographic changes that had taken place in the city over the previous twenty years.

In New York, prior to 1840, black men primarily were employed as laborers in occupations ranging from "longshoremen, hod-carriers, brickmakers, whitewashers, coachmen, stablemen, porters, bootblacks, barbers, and waiters in hotels and restaurants"; black women found work as "domestic maids, cooks, scullions, laundresses and seamstresses"—all of which provided steady employment, if low wages.

In an era where blacks were tolerated as separate and unequal members of the community, and the occupations open to them were considered widely to be "colored jobs," whites did not challenge blacks for those work opportunities. During the middle of the decade, especially after Ireland's Great Famine of 1846–50, successive waves of immigrants, some 200,000 people—the majority of them unskilled laborers—made their way to New York City and began to compete for these same low-skilled jobs, which set the stage for conflict.[22]

Black and white longshoremen constantly clashed over job assignments. In 1863, when white longshoremen and riggers staged a strike, they were repulsed when the mayor "ordered the military under arms" at the behest of the freight owners. In an effort to secure stable living wages for their fellow laborers, the embattled strikers formed the whites-only Longshoremen's Benefit Society in 1853.

The white dockworkers staged violent attacks on 200 of their black rivals and the waterfront businesses that catered to them in 1855 and again in March 1863. In response to the white backlash, waterfront business owners, acting out of self-interest, implored the city to put down the agitators—using violence if necessary—and protect the black strikebreakers.[23] The second white assault on black longshoremen and their bosses, in March 1863, also was crushed by the police. But when white working-class New Yorkers organized a protest against the military draft on July 13, 1863, that involved the destruction of government property, white longshoremen saw their opportunity to exact revenge on black dockworkers.

Stinging from the realization that their white bosses and the police would not protect their economic interests, the Longshoremen's Association and other white labor unions resolved to exclude black men from the city's commercial employment. Leslie Harris provides a disturbing description of their actions:

> White workers enacted their desires to eradicate the working-class black male presence from the city. The Longshoreman's Association, a white labor union, patrolled the piers during the riots, insisting that "the colored people must and shall be driven to other parts of industry." But "other parts of industry," such as cartmen and hack drivers, not to mention skilled artisans, also sought to exclude black workers. The riots gave all [of] these workers license to physically remove blacks not only from worksites, but also from neighborhoods and leisure spaces. The rioters' actions also indicate the degree to which the sensational journalists and reformers of the 1840s and 1850s had achieved their goals of convincing whites, and particularly the Irish, that interracial socializing and marriage were evil and degrading practices. The riots unequivocally divided white workers from blacks. . . . Finally, and most simply, white workers asserted their superiority over blacks through the riots. The Civil War and the rise of the Republican Party and Lincoln to power indicated to New York's largely Democratic white workers a reversal of power in the nation; black labor competition indicated a reversal of fortunes in New York

City itself. White workers sought to remedy their upside-down world through mob violence.[24]

Fueled by the exhortations of the Democratic Party and by the anti-abolition wing of the local press, both playing on fears that the city would be inundated by freed blacks, the rioters—initially a militant but disciplined group of draft protesters—grew in number and morphed into a vicious, anti-emancipation, antiblack mob of white supremacists. The terrorists turned their murderous ferocity on the city's existing black population during a five-day rampage that stretched from July 13 to 17, leaving an estimated 119 dead, 2,000 injured, and hundreds homeless. Both the Democrats and the proslavery press had been warning that huge numbers of freed blacks would migrate from the south and would compete with the white (largely foreign born, disproportionately Irish) working class for jobs.[25]

Carrying signboards and chanting, "There goes a $300 man"—$300 being the commutation fee that exempted draftees from serving in the war—and "Down with the rich men! Down with property! Down with the police!" the swarm proceeded through the streets in pursuit of prominent military and governmental outposts—symbols of Republican Party rule—setting fire to the city's arsenal, the armory, the Ninth District provost marshal's office, two police stations, and the draft office located in a four-story building with family dwellings on the upper floors.[26]

The rabble, which reached an estimated total of 30,000 men, women, and youth, cut down telegraph wires to impede government agents' ability to communicate, destroyed firefighters' vehicles and killed their horses, pulled streetcars off their tracks, and made makeshift clubs from telegraph poles, train tracks, and fences. They armed themselves with "guns, pistols, axes, hatchets, crowbars, pitchforks, knives, [and] bludgeons," beat police superintendent John Kennedy bloody and unconscious, and vandalized abolitionist Horace Greeley's *New-York Tribune* office. They set fire to the home of Republican mayor George Opdyke, warehouses, stores, Fifth Avenue and Lexington Avenue homes, and other property belonging to affluent whites. Entire black neighborhoods were systematically burned to the ground.[27]

That a white riot of this magnitude could happen in a northern city was revealing. Because this melee was triggered by the Emancipation Proclamation, it was clear that support for preservation of the Union was hardly synonymous with the abolition of slavery.

With the vast majority of Union army troops still in Pennsylvania, where they had been dispatched to fight Gen. Robert E. Lee's troops at the Battle of Gettysburg, waged at the start of July, there was little in the way of police capacity to contain the rioters.[28] Not even the city's black orphanage was spared the rioters' wrath. The mob looted the Colored Orphan Asylum (COA) on Fifth Avenue between Forty-Second and Forty-Third Streets and "went professionally to work, in order to destroy the building, and, at the same time, to make appropriation of anything of value by which they might aggrandize themselves." They took tables and chairs, beds and mattresses, linens, clothing, cooking implements, and food before setting the building ablaze.

Established by three Quaker women to train and give tangible support to black children—at the age of twelve the boys were indentured as farmhands, the girls as domestic workers—the COA was a four-story building that included a school, a nursery, and a hospital and was home to 233 children. One little girl who hid under her bed was found and savagely beaten to death by the mob; the others escaped injury and sought refuge in the Thirty-Fifth Street Police Station, where they remained for four days before being removed to safety.[29]

For five hellish days, white supremacists harassed, assaulted, stabbed, mutilated, murdered, and dismembered black men and women: William Jones was hanged and burned on the docks, Charles Jackson was beaten and nearly drowned, and Jeremiah Robinson was bludgeoned to death and his body thrown into the river. William Williams, a sailor, died after whites "jump[ed] on his chest, plung[ed] a knife into him, [and] smash[ed] his body with stones" as the crowd jeered, pledging "vengeance" on the city's black population.

After white laborer George Glass kidnapped black coachman Abraham Franklin from his home and the mob dragged him through the streets, he was hanged from a lamppost "as the crowd cheered for Jefferson Davis." Franklin's corpse was then cut down, and a sixteen-year-old mobster, Patrick Butler, "dragged the body through the streets by its genitals." James Costello was "stomped, kicked, and stoned" while trying to escape gangs of white predators before he was hanged. The rioters were making a gruesome statement that they were not going to put their lives on the line to achieve black freedom.

When Governor Seymour declared New York City to be "in a state of insurrection," Mayor Opdyke telegraphed Secretary of War Edwin Stanton and pleaded with him to send Union troops, who arrived on July 15 from the grounds of the Battle of Gettysburg. For a day and a half, the 6,000 troops of the Seventh New York Regiment fought alongside the 152nd New York Volunteers and the New York State Militia to subdue the gangs of protestors.[30]

The fate of eleven black male victims was described in various media: their genitals and other body parts were "cut off for trophies" during what became known as New York's Civil War Draft Riot.[31] As was the case with Nat Turner's corpse three decades earlier, a number of blacks lynched by white supremacists during the New York Civil War Draft Riot were butchered and their body parts distributed among white families so they could have a keepsake, or souvenir, from the occasion. The spectacle informed such acts across the American south and west for the next 100 years.

Throughout the north, working-class whites were increasingly hostile to participation in the Union army. A white uprising against the Enrollment Act had occurred in Detroit even before the New York turmoil; indeed, virtually every state in the Union experienced some type of violent white protest against the draft.[32] In some cases white men found ways to evade the draft without paying the commutation fee at all. In Boston, where another anti-draft riot erupted a day after the violence in New York commenced, only 1 percent of the city's white men who were eligible for the draft actually joined the war effort.[33]

The antidraft riots were frequently transmuted into antiblack massacres. No indemnity ever was offered or paid to the families or relatives of those persons killed by the white rioters or to those who survived the assault. The lack of redress for the New York or Detroit riots foreshadowed the long-term failure to provide recompense for blacks subjected to white massacres well into the mid-twentieth century.

Nonetheless, the Union effort demanded the participation of all qualified men. So great was the need for military personnel, the federal government—and, not infrequently, state, city, and even county governments—offered enlistment fees or cash bounties to eligible men who volunteered before they were drafted into service. There were instances when volunteers collected more than $1,000. In some cases, soldiers who made a commitment could even choose the regiment in which they would serve.

Monitoring the bounty system proved to be difficult, and the scheme often led to abuses. There were numerous so-called bounty jumpers, who would enlist and collect their fee, desert before even joining their regiment, then reenlist in a different jurisdiction under an alias.[34] As northern white male resistance to military service grew, the inclusion and mobilization of black troops increasingly became vital to the Union cause.

After the first Confederate assault on Fort Sumter, Lincoln issued a call for 75,000 volunteers. Within thirty-six hours, black men residing in Boston, Philadelphia, and New York began to form militias and offer their services to the Union forces. Free blacks and refugees from slavery, all prepared to fight for freedom, made their way to the War Department's recruiting offices in comparable numbers.

Escaped slaves, gambling that they would not be sent back to their former masters, settled the question of gradual and compensated emancipation. Since their owners had refused to free them in exchange for a cash payment from the national government, the slaves would be their own liberators and join with the Union cause. The owners would receive no compensation.

Two months later, Lincoln called for 300,000 new troops. Union general George McClellan had suffered a major defeat at the hands of Gen. Robert E. Lee in Richmond. Few whites responded to the appeal.[35] Now an absolute necessity, the campaign for black recruits expanded exponentially. The Militia Act soon followed, which repealed the 1792 law prohibiting blacks from enlisting. The first five black regiments—all comprising residents of South Carolina—were mustered in August 1862.

That blacks could join the military and directly act to bring about an end to race-based slavery may have been the most remarkable aspect of the war. Arming former slaves and authorizing them to attack Confederate forces when, just a short time before, many of those new recruits had been the property of those same white Confederate enemies only heightened the significance of the war effort for African Americans. Motivated in part by patriotism, blacks were hopeful that their sacrifice would improve their chances for citizenship and equality and potentially put an end to slavery, even though emancipation was not yet part of the congressional discussions.

The original black battalion, the First South Carolina Volunteers, marched under the leadership of the charismatic Thomas Wentworth Higginson.[36] At various times, Harriet Tubman, the escaped slave, Underground Railroad conductor, and woman that revolutionary abolitionist John Brown introduced to antislavery advocate Wendell Phillips as "one of the best and bravest persons on this continent," provided support to the Volunteers as a nurse, cook, spy, and scout. She was also a member of the armed strategic team tasked with identifying opportunities to liberate enslaved blacks and that freed over 700, along the Combahee River in South Carolina, under the cover of "Lincoln's gun-boats come to set them free."[37]

The long-awaited declaration that confirmed the slaves' belief that the side of justice was with the north came January 1, 1863, when Lincoln, in his capacity as commander in chief of the armed services, executed the Emancipation Proclamation. The proclamation was, in Lincoln's words, "an act of justice" that asserted that "all persons held as slaves within any State or designated part of a State, the people whereof shall then be in rebellion against the United States, shall be then, thenceforward, and forever free; and the Executive Government of the United States, including the military and naval authority thereof, will recognize and maintain the freedom of such persons, and will do no act or acts to repress such persons, or any of them, in any efforts they may make for their actual freedom."[38]

Unlike the Confiscation Acts, which preceded it, the proclamation freed all slaves residing in areas controlled by the Confederacy, regardless of the political allegiances of their owners. Lincoln's Emancipation Proclamation made it clear that for the Union, the war, finally and unequivocally, was not only about the preservation of the United States but also about bringing an end to slavery.

Immediately after the proclamation, Massachusetts governor John Albion Andrew, hopeful that Lincoln would "recognize *all* men, even black men, as legally capable of loyalty" and establish a precedent for equal pay and opportunity in the military, approached Secretary of War Edwin Stanton about creating a black regiment with commissioned officers. Andrew was forced to settle for a promise that his state's black troops would receive pay equal to whites performing identical tasks and equal treatment—a concession no other governor had been able to extract—but he had to surrender on the commissioning of black officers.[39]

Black Massachusetts abolitionist George E. Stephens experienced the extremes of military treatment during the Civil War. In what is likely a rare case, he served in the U.S. Navy, where "[he and his fellow black sailors were] treated like [their white] mess-mates," and in the army, where "every pledge made [on] our enlistment has been broken and every promise remains unfulfilled." Stephens wrote further, "We are unprotected and there is no refuge and no appeal."[40] Stephens's commitment was shaken during events like the draft riots, but he continued to serve alongside other blacks who resolved to "do . . . our utmost to sustain the honor of our country's flag, to perpetuate if possible, those civil, social, and political liberties, they, who so malignantly hate us, have so fully enjoyed."[41]

Col. Robert Gould Shaw, the son of prominent white abolitionists and philanthropists, commanded the all-black Fifty-Fourth Regiment Massachusetts Volunteer Infantry, the first African American military unit from the north.[42] Shaw advised his troops to refuse their military salaries until the federal government agreed to pay them at the same rate as their white counterparts, as had been promised. The men worked for more than a year before Congress met their demands.[43]

While white public opinion was not yet ready to accept blacks in this elevated capacity, Harriet Jacobs was jubilant: "I am proud and happy to know that the black man is to strike a blow for liberty. I am rejoiced that Col. [Robert] Shaw heads the Massachusetts regiment, for I know he has a noble heart."[44]

Throughout the war, Jacobs used her celebrity to raise money to assist black contrabands living in Washington, D.C. She and her daughter Louisa Matilda Jacobs operated a school for former slaves in Alexandria, Virginia, from 1863 to 1865 with the meager funds the former slaves were able to contribute and the support of the New York Society of Friends.[45]

Clearly, black soldiers played a vital role in the Union victory. "The Fate of the Confederacy was sealed when Vicksburg fell," a proud Ulysses S. Grant wrote of the significance of the attack that took place May 18–July 4, 1863. "Much hard fighting was to be done afterwards and many precious lives were to be sacrificed; but the *morale* was with the supporters of the Union ever after."[46]

Black soldiers played no small part in that brutal and costly battle. "The bravery of the Blacks at Milliken's Bend," reported Assistant Secretary of War Charles A. Dana, "completely revolutionized the sentiment of the army with regard to the employment of Negro troops. I heard prominent officers, who formerly had sneered . . . at the idea of the Negroes fighting, express themselves after that, as heartily in favor of it."[47] Increasingly, Union officers were willing to affirm that the efforts of the black troops approximated those of whites. One could hope that their revelations would be amplified and that blacks' desires would be fulfilled in the aftermath of the war.

Five months earlier, after Grant's initial failed attempt to vanquish Confederate general John Clifford Pemberton's troops, Lincoln had let it be known that he wanted control of the Mississippi River.[48] Grant's triumphant command included 1,410 soldiers—1,250 of whom were African Americans from Louisiana and Mississippi—at the pivotal battle at Milliken's Bend, Louisiana.[49]

Black recruits also had been essential to the Union victory at Port Hudson, Louisiana, a key strategic outpost above Baton Rouge and Vicksburg along the Mississippi River. Capt. Robert F. Wilkinson described the valor of the 1,000 freedmen who fought side by side with whites in one of the war's first such engagements in a letter to his father: "One thing I am glad to say, is that the black troops at P. Hudson fought & acted superbly. The theory of negro inefficiency is, I am very thankful at last thoroughly Exploded by facts. We shall shortly have a splendid army of thousands of them."[50]

At that time, a *New York Times* editorial affirmed the black recruits' "great prowess" as "effectual supporters and defenders," from the testimony of Maj.

Gen. Nathaniel P. Banks, which it quoted extensively: "They were comparatively raw troops, and were yet subjected to the most awful ordeal. . . . The men, white or black, who will not flinch from that, will flinch from nothing. It is no longer possible to doubt the bravery and steadiness of the colored race, when rightly led."[51]

Despite widespread evidence of black troops' courage, discipline, and dependability in battle, arming former slaves—when only recently they had been forbidden to possess firearms—and authorizing them to attack Confederate forces remained controversial. Nevertheless, the War and Treasury Departments devoted a great deal of their resources to the black recruitment effort. In May 1863, the War Department opened the Bureau of Colored Troops, with George Luther Stearns, the master recruiter who had manned the Massachusetts Fifty-Fourth and Fifty-Fifth, at the head. In addition to the department's funds, Stearns raised $50,000 privately to support the operation.[52] But would the federal government's investment in black recruitment translate into real gains for blacks after the war's end?

Black abolitionists Frederick Douglass, Sojourner Truth, Charles Lenox Remond, William Wells Brown, John Mercer Langston, Henry Highland Garnet, and Martin Delany temporarily set aside their consternation over the unequal pay black troops and support staff would receive and rallied blacks to enlist; Truth's grandson and two of Douglass's three sons answered the call. Their presence introduced new life, commitment, and enthusiasm for the Union cause.[53] In Ohio, Rhode Island, Connecticut, and Pennsylvania, blacks served in the infantry and the artillery in addition to a variety of noncombat positions—carpenters, masons, waiters, cooks, scouts, spies, surgeons, nurses, teamsters, blacksmiths, steamboat pilots, longshoremen, guards, chaplains, and construction-team workers building and fortifying bridges, highways, and railroads.

The black troops did not disappoint. The Fifty-Fourth Massachusetts won commendations from many factions during the fierce July 1863 assault on the Confederate garrison at Fort Wagner, located on Morris Island along the Charleston, South Carolina, harbor.[54] Casualties on the Union side were high—two-thirds of the officers and at least half of the 600 men died in battle, including the regiment's leader, Col. Robert Gould Shaw.[55] One of the black soldiers in the regiment, Sgt. William H. Carney, was awarded the Medal of Honor.[56]

In a private letter that was published widely on August 26, 1863, Lincoln was critical of citizens who opposed emancipation, and he also took the opportunity to acknowledge and laud the black troops: "Some of the commanders of our armies in the field who have given us our most important successes, believe the emancipation policy, and the use of colored troops, constitute the heaviest blow yet dealt to the rebellion. . . . You say you will not fight to free negroes. Some of them seem willing to fight for you."[57]

The president was faced with a dilemma. For the first time, large numbers of blacks were engaging in activities identical to those of their white counterparts, including combat, and in some cases working side by side with them; they would have to be remunerated for their labor. How should black wages be determined? Should they receive what whites were paid? What would be the political and social repercussions of such a plan?

Presidential praise notwithstanding, equal pay for equal work was not forthcoming. With the lone exception of the promise Massachusetts's governor was able to extract from Secretary of War Edwin Stanton for his state's black troops, income inequality was built into the salary provisions of the Militia Act of July 1862 and continued even after the Bureau of Colored Troops was created.

By the time Congress had reversed the mandate of the Militia Act and determined that African American troops would receive equal pay to whites, three years had passed—1861 to 1864. In the intervening years, black American army privates' wages—routinely paid late and frequently not at all— were $10.00 per month ($3.00 of which was deducted to cover the cost of their clothing, for a net of $7.00), while their white counterparts received $13.00 per month plus an allotment of clothing or a cash allowance of $3.50, for a total of $16.50. A black soldier's pay was less than half of a white soldier's pay. Nor were blacks eligible for noncommissioned officer status or pay regardless of their record of valor or qualifications.[58] When the freedmen and their white allies pressed the case for equal pay, they often were rebuked and worse.[59]

In one stupefying example, Sgt. William Walker, an African American and a member of the Third South Carolina Volunteers, paid a high price for his insistence on equality. Walker instructed his men to lay down their arms in protest over their reduced salaries and unequal treatment, and in November 1863, he was court-martialed for mutiny and executed. Opponents of closing the income gap argued that a system of equal pay would be degrading to whites. When Frederick Douglass took the case to Lincoln, the president argued that until northern opinions on the matter changed, the lower wages were "a necessary concession to smooth the way to [blacks'] employment at all as soldiers."[60]

Blacks who made it to Union lines routinely faced alarming treatment at the hands of their "liberators." Indeed, it would be a gross understatement to say that the black recruits' lot was not an easy one. Racial discrimination was commonplace—even in the north—and the U.S. military was one of the worst offenders. After the Enrollment Act was passed, runaways were not guaranteed a warm welcome from Union troops. Many resented blacks' inclusion in the military, and others continued to doubt their ability—even after blacks proved to be reliable fighters once they received sufficient training and experience. Freedom from slavery did not mean freedom from discrimination.

For black troops, there was the added fear of capture by the Confederates; the threat of immediate execution, being sent back into slavery, or being impounded under intolerable conditions was a constant worry.[61] One of the most foreboding and reviled of the Confederate commanders was the glory-stoked Maj. Gen. Nathan Bedford Forrest. An intimidating figure, Forrest was heralded by his compatriots for his "unorthodox methods and slashing attacks."[62] On more than one occasion, by orchestrating chaos—destroying telegraph wires and intercepting supply lines while employing diversions—Forrest managed to dupe much larger Union forces into surrendering to him before the anticipated battle had commenced.

In April 1864, during the battle at Fort Pillow, Tennessee, located some sixty miles outside of Memphis, the Union forces were greatly outmanned. Throughout the spring Forrest had been raiding Union garrisons in western Tennessee and Kentucky in search of horses and supplies and hoping to capture Union prisoners. When he moved to take back Fort Pillow—the fortification had been established two years before as a Confederate outpost—Forrest's troops overwhelmed the Union soldiers, approximately 550 men, evenly divided racially between the black soldiers of the First Alabama Siege Regiment Colored Heavy Artillery, under the command of Lionel F. Booth, and white soldiers from the Thirteenth Tennessee Cavalry, commanded by Lt. Gen. William F. Bradford.[63] Forrest sent a messenger to deliver his terms for ending the skirmish, adding, "Should my demand be refused, I cannot be responsible for the fate of your command."

When the Union commander initially requested an hour to consider his options, Forrest, concerned that enemy reinforcements might well be approaching, revised his initial offer and narrowed the window for the Union officer to convey his decision to a mere twenty minutes. "If at the expiration of that time the fort is not surrendered," Forrest declared, "I shall assault it." Moments after the Union officer replied, "I will not surrender," Forrest gave the charge to his men and the horrible bloodbath began.[64]

While there are conflicting stories about when—and if—the Union forces surrendered to Forrest, there is little debate over the outcome.[65] At least 221 of the 557 Union forces were killed and another 128 were wounded—a combined 63 percent of the two companies—compared to 14 Confederate deaths and 86 Confederate wounded. Reports that Union soldiers had been shot while begging for mercy from a kneeling position and of the "indiscriminate slaughter" of men, women, and children of both races, some of whom were incinerated when the Confederates set the hospital tent on fire, were harder to refute. Black soldiers were killed disproportionately in battle or shortly thereafter. White Union soldiers were taken as hostages at triple the rate of black soldiers: 168 whites—or 60 percent of the 280 whites who had fought—compared with 58 blacks—or 20 percent of the 262 who had fought.

In a letter penned to his sisters not long after the battle, Achilles V. Clark, a soldier in the Confederate Twentieth Tennessee Cavalry who fought in the battle, provided a chilling testimony: "The slaughter was awful. Words cannot describe the scene. The poor, deluded, negroes would run up to our men, fall upon their knees, and with uplifted hands scream for mercy but they were ordered to their feet and then shot down. I, with several others, tried to stop the butchery, and at one time had partially succeeded, but General Forrest ordered them shot down like dogs and the carnage continued. Finally our men became sick of blood and the firing ceased."[66]

While the Fort Pillow massacre is evidence of the deep hostility some members of the Confederate military had for blacks and their supporters, blacks routinely also were subjected to callous and violent attacks at the hands of Union forces.[67] Squires Jackson escaped to Union lines in Wellborn, Florida, with the intention of signing up but changed his mind after seeing "wounded colored soldiers stretched out on the filthy ground" of a horse stable "and the feeble medical attention given them by the Federals." One of the wounded was a member of the celebrated Fifty-Fourth Massachusetts, the all-black unit that had waged the attack on Fort Wagner, South Carolina.[68]

Especially during the early years of the war, the contrabands were poorly trained for the battles they faced. William Sherman of Chaseville, Florida, who was formerly enslaved by Confederate president Jefferson Davis's nephew Jack Davis, recalled that many contrabands did not receive sufficient training for battle: "Those slaves who joined were trained about two days and then sent to the front. Due to lack of training they were soon killed."[69]

Union major general George Henry Thomas had little confidence in the ex-slaves' fighting ability initially. When the contrabands asked for weapons, he instructed his officers to give the blacks spades and shovels and put them to work digging trenches and repairing roads and breastworks. But by December 1864, when the Battle of Nashville approached, Thomas had become so impressed with the black recruits that he took eight black units with him into the conflict. Thomas's black troops scored a decisive win against the Confederate Army of Tennessee, which was under the command of Gen. John Bell Hood, and sustained minimal casualties.

An officer in the 100th U.S. Colored Infantry, who had surveyed the aftermath of the Tennessee battle, in which some 300 members of the 3,500 U.S. Colored Troops had died, noted, "Colored soldiers had again fought side by side with white troops; they had mingled together in the charge; they had supported each other; and they assisted each other from the field when wounded, and they lay side by side in death. The survivors rejoiced together over a hard fought field, won by common valor. . . . [But] that winter, an estimated one-out-of-every-six Contraband who had made it to the Nashville Union line—about 1,400 men, women and children—would die of exposure, disease, and starvation."[70]

Numerous decisive battles had been fought by predominantly white battalions early in the war—victories at South Mountain, Virginia, and Antietam in Maryland (also known as the Battle of Sharpsburg), both won at great human cost in 1862, are just two such events—but the infusion of black troops provided a vital boost to the Union effort.

In total, more than 180,000 black men—about 10 percent of the combined forces—had served the Union cause by the war's end in June 1865. Included in that number were 29,000 black Union marines, some 25 percent of the entire marine force.[71] The proportion of casualties among blacks engaged in combat far outstripped those of whites enlisted in the Union forces.[72] They had earned the esteem of their white Union military comrades and the grudging respect of many on the Confederate side. Another 200,000 blacks were employed by the government to plow entrenchments and build fortifications, care for horses and mules, work as longshoremen, build and operate railroads, and serve as waiters, cooks, and valets.

The Civil War had a tremendous effect on the country's economy, landscape, and social structure, and it claimed more lives than any conflict fought on American soil since the nation's founding. Once estimated at 618,222—including 360,222 on the Union side and 258,000 fighting for the Confederacy—the total number of deaths has been revised to 750,000.[73] The Union preserved, now it was possible for blacks to be granted full inclusion in American life with all of the rights and privileges previously afforded only to whites. Tragically, that possibility once again would be forestalled.

Part 4

7

Rehearsals for Freedom

Enslavement denied blacks the fruits of their two hundred years of backbreaking labor. They could not make or enforce contracts. Property rights of use, ownership, and management did not follow from their market participation in the labor force, but were systematically denied by the state. The slaveholding states did not confer legal status on black families; through inheritance, the family is one of the primary institutions of wealth transfer, but black slaves were excluded from intergenerational wealth transfer, one of the centerpieces of Anglo-American culture.
—Adrienne Davis, "The Case for U.S. Reparations," 2007

The Negroes organized themselves and, armed with rudimentary farming tools and seeds, flocked to the islands to begin spring planting. The Edisto people left St. Helena promptly, eager to return to their old homes as landowners. Other groups joined them from Georgia. "We shall build out cabins, and organize our town government for the maintenance of order and the settlement of all difficulties," said the Reverend Mr. Ulysses Houston, a Negro minister of Savannah, to an interested Northern correspondent. He was conducting a large party of Negroes to Skidaway Island and had laid his plans carefully. "He and his fellow colonists selected their lots, laid out a village, numbered their lots, put the numbers in a hat, and drew them out." The reporter was thrilled. "It was Plymouth colony repeating itself. They agreed if any others came to join them, they should have equal privileges. So blooms the Mayflower on the South Atlantic coast." —Willie Lee Rose, *Rehearsals for Reconstruction*, 1964

One sees that revolutions may go backward.
—Thomas Wentworth Higginson, *Army Life in a Black Regiment*, 1869

America's story is built on the idea of opportunity. If you work hard and persist, you will get ahead. For black people living in the mid-nineteenth century, however, there was at least one additional required condition: emancipation from slavery.

Immediately before and during the Civil War, anticipating the eventual coming of emancipation, many whites who supported abolition held the view that enslaved blacks would require preparation for freedom. The formerly enslaved would have to be trained to live as free Americans—with training provided by "enlightened" whites. Harriet Beecher Stowe, author of the 1852 best seller *Uncle Tom's Cabin*, advanced this notion four years later in her novel *Dred: A Tale of the Great Dismal Swamp* when her characters, the slave-owning siblings Edward and Anne Clayton, who were pro-abolition, set up a scheme to "bring a set of their own slaves out of barbarism" to prepare them for freedom.[1]

Of course, enslaved blacks already had developed their own plans and visions for life after slavery, and frequently black desires and white supporters' preferences came into collision—typically to the black disadvantage. The organizations and communities formed by blacks themselves were not predicated on the paternalism that characterized the "experiments" organized by whites.

A variety of preemancipation projects initiated by the federal government with blacks as farmers and piece-rate laborers also were treated as demonstrations. In addition, the inclusion of blacks in direct combat as salaried Union soldiers was initially conducted on an experimental basis.

Throughout the theater of rehearsals for freedom, blacks continued to be subjected to indignities and injustices. We document those experiences in this chapter as we continue to build our case for reparations.

At the point that the Emancipation Proclamation was issued, in January 1863, neither Abraham Lincoln nor Congress nor the federal government writ large had made any plans for the more than 3.5 million slaves residing in the states and territories still in rebellion. Even though they were engaged in the Union effort and would make a decisive contribution to the war's outcome, the contrabands—largely homeless—had no land, no jobs, no money, and no rights of citizenship.

Of the approximately 4.5 million African Americans living in the United States by 1860, an estimated 500,000 were free people of color. Some had been granted their freedom by their owners and some had been born free (that is, born to free mothers). Still others had asserted their right to freedom after a long residence as a fugitive in a free state. A small number of those free black Americans lived in intentional black communities—often communities established as experiments by white abolitionists who believed training ex-slaves to be productive citizens was a prerequisite for life in a majority-white society.[2]

In 1845, Sojourner Truth, a slave the first twenty-nine years of her life, launched a career as an orator and champion for women's rights and the abolition of slavery after having been radicalized by the experience of living for two years in an integrated commune, the Northampton Association of

Education and Industry in western Massachusetts.[3] It was there that she met abolitionist Frederick Douglass, the social reformer, author, orator, and publisher who had escaped to freedom on his third attempt; Wendell Phillips, a lawyer and member of the American Anti-Slavery Society; William Lloyd Garrison, founder and publisher of the abolitionist newspaper the *Liberator*; and David Ruggles, the freeborn African American writer, publisher, and bookstore owner who had aided Douglass's own escape to freedom.[4]

In 1846, Gerrit Smith, an eventual member of the Secret Committee of Six, which supported John Brown's efforts to initiate an antislavery insurrection in Virginia, donated 120,000 acres of land in 40-acre lots to 3,000 free blacks in the Adirondacks in upstate New York. Smith had two objectives. First, because New York state law mandated that blacks must own at least $250 in real estate to be eligible to vote, the apportionment of 40-acre lots was a mechanism for black enfranchisement. Second, Smith hoped to demonstrate that blacks could establish a prosperous and thriving agriculturally based community as a model for the postslavery world.[5]

This experimental commune, known as Timbuctoo, ended by 1855, primarily because the black settlers on the granted land had been northern urban dwellers with no experience in farming. The outcome probably would have been different had Smith had the capacity to distribute the land to freed southern blacks who had familiarity with agricultural labor.[6] A handful of whites manumitted their slaves—Samuel Gist, the British owner of a Virginia plantation, and John Randolph of Roanoke, Virginia, among them.[7] In 1826, Robert Wilson of South Carolina's York District consigned his slaves to the Nashoba Commune, which was established in 1825 in present-day Memphis, Tennessee, by social reformer and freethinker Frances Wright for the purpose of educating former slaves and resettling them in Haiti.[8]

Several black settlements were organized in Michigan, Illinois, Indiana, and Ohio (Brown and Mercer Counties), and in what are now the towns of Dresden, Lucan, Chatham, and Windsor in Canada's Ontario Province. While they found greater access to land, "economic independence, basic education, and community self-sufficiency" in their adopted country to the north and were not subjected to legal discrimination, black Canadians generally were relegated to low-paying, unskilled jobs. Indeed, they feared becoming too visibly successful lest they find themselves "mobbed or burned out" at the hands of their "white friends." They lived under the constant threat of kidnapping by bounty hunters whom American slave owners hired to return their runaway chattel to them.

Historians William H. Pease and Jane Pease reported on black Canadians who had appealed to Upper Canada's lieutenant governor, Sir Peregrine

Maitland, in 1828 to grant them a homestead they could secure as a "means of preventing the system of kidnapping which is now carried on through his Majesty's provinces by the Georgia and Virginia kidnappers from the southern states of America." The petitioners believed, once they were settled, that they could "become useful to our King and country." Pease and Pease estimated that between 1830 and 1860 approximately 60,000 blacks left the south and resettled in the north, and an additional 20,000 to 40,000 blacks migrated to Canada. They estimated the number of blacks living in intentional black communities during the forty-year period before the Civil War at 3,500 to 5,000 persons.[9]

At least as early as 1780, blacks pooled their resources and established organizations to provide a range of mutual aid and benefits to enslaved, free, and fugitive blacks, including "clothing, shelter, and emotional and physical sustenance."[10] They assisted members with medical care and burial expenses when no other support was available. Frequently, these mutual-aid and benefit societies grew out of communities of faith. The African American Methodist Episcopal Church, the country's first independent black church, founded the second African American mutual-aid society, the Philadelphia-based Free African Society.[11]

Black women, in particular, were a vital resource for the black community. With their own meager savings, and with funds solicited from sponsors, dues-paying members and members' networks of acquaintances, and raffles and special events, "black women established day nurseries, orphanages, homes for the aged and infirm, hospitals, cemeteries, night schools, and scholarship funds" in every major city. By 1830, more than 100 mutual-aid societies existed in Philadelphia; twenty-five years later, black membership in those organizations had grown to 9,762.[12] In a society where enslavement was legal, blacks did their utmost to envision and chart a course beyond slavery.

Throughout the Civil War, abolitionists championed a series of programs designed to alter America's racial divide: the immediate and universal end to slavery, enlistment of blacks in the Union army, creation of a federal agency that would help enslaved blacks make the transition to freedom, allocation of government funds for public schools open to freedmen, political equality in the form of the right to vote, and grants of confiscated and abandoned land to the distressed former slaves.

As early as July 1861, they urged creation of an "Executive Bureau" that would "care for and protect, and educate these four millions of new born freemen," but nearly four long years elapsed before the bill to enact the

Freedmen's Bureau was passed in March 1865.[13] New York attorney and statesman John Jay II wrote to Senator Charles Sumner to propose an agency that would "take charge of the blacks where our army lands in the Southern States, under rules & regulations to be prepared by the War Department."[14]

Abolitionists provided much of the early research that informed these deliberations. The Kansas Emancipation League (previously the Boston Emancipation League, founded in September 1861 by slavery opponents, former John Brown supporters, and other sympathetic Republicans) developed a questionnaire that was distributed to government administrators tasked with the contrabands' affairs and sought their assessment of the newly liberated blacks in their jurisdictions and the conditions to which they were subjected.[15] The replies of the eight supervisors who responded were published and circulated widely, making it possible for large numbers of Americans—especially northerners—to gain insights about these government emissaries' assessments of the freedmen's work ethic, honesty, sobriety, chastity, and religious observances.

While the majority of respondents reported that slaves were religious, some suggested that the institution of slavery itself had forced some enslaved people of whom they had acquaintance to resort to lying and stealing to survive. The American public learned that when black men were employed by the War Department they were paid less for their labor than whites who had executed identical tasks. They also learned that the supervisors believed their charges possessed the capacity to benefit from educational instruction and that the freedmen themselves were determined to obtain an education.[16] These findings added quantifiable data to the stories told by illiterate former slaves who had become featured orators at churches and public halls and to the eloquent writings and presentations of formally educated blacks.

Revolutionary abolitionist John Brown, also known as Capt. John Brown, did not countenance the notion that enslaved blacks needed preparation for emancipation. He timed his actions to liberate large numbers of enslaved blacks on October 17, 1859, to coincide with the critical harvesting season. Thus, freed runaways could join raiding parties or be connected to the Underground Railroad and guided to freedom in Canada. Brown's expectation was that they would build their new lives and communities without any special guidance from sympathetic whites.

When the Kansas-Nebraska Act passed in 1854, Brown, a Republican, had moved to the formerly Native American–controlled territories where, by congressional decree, the popular vote would determine slavery status. The Republican Party was founded in opposition to the expansion of slavery in the western states; Abraham Lincoln's subsequent election as president was the party's first national political success. Conflict broke out between the Kansas factions, and Brown and his sons killed five proslavery settlers, earning Brown the reputation of a madman and an outlaw.

But Karen Whitman has observed that the reputation is peculiar, because Brown's actions—motivated like Nat Turner's to achieve black liberation—did not approximate the insanity of the mortality wreaked in the Great War that would follow: "In *The Inner Civil War*, George M. Fredrickson describes John Brown as 'a narrow-minded and possibly insane religious fanatic.' This dismissal of Brown as a lunatic or, at best, a religious fanatic, is common among contemporary historians. It is ironic that the Civil War, which cost 600,000 lives, is today considered a 'reasonable' or at least 'understandable' event in our history, but John Brown's raid is disregarded as the bloody act of a 'madman.'"[17]

"I will raise a storm in this country that will not be stayed so long as there is a slave on its soil," Brown declared.[18] An interracial group of twenty-one men under his leadership raided the federal arsenal at Harpers Ferry, Virginia (now part of West Virginia). President Buchanan sent the U.S. Marines under Col. Robert E. Lee, with J. E. B. Stuart serving as a volunteer aide, to subdue the group. Seven members were captured; two of Brown's sons and eight other men were killed in battle. After a hasty trial, Brown was convicted of conspiracy, insurrection, and high treason.[19] He was hanged on December 2, 1859, leaving the following message in his last letter: "I . . . am now quite *certain* that the crimes of this *guilty*, *land*: *will* never be purged *away*; but with Blood. I had as I *now think: vainly* flattered myself that without very *much* bloodshed; it might be done."[20] The storm he had promised was on the immediate horizon.

As Union forces conquered Confederate strongholds and panicked plantation owners abandoned their estates, hundreds of former slaves—men, women and children—took advantage of the upheaval and made their way to Union military fortifications, many of them with little more than the clothes on their backs, a few tools, and foodstuffs. In his pathbreaking book *Black Reconstruction in America*, sociologist and historian W. E. B. Du Bois characterized as a general strike blacks' determination to escape from the plantations where they had been enslaved to the protection of the Union military and to antislavery communities in the north.[21]

Although the former slaves' exodus was not orchestrated by a single individual, organization, or political party—or motivated by the single imperative to bankrupt the planter class—countless livestock were left untended and hundreds of thousands of acres of cotton and food crops were left uncultivated, greatly devaluing those properties.[22] During the first twelve months of the war, President Lincoln took the view that Union forces could not liberate slaves that were located in former Confederate territory. Contrary to his orders, U.S. generals frequently enlisted slaves they encountered, creating great controversy.

That is precisely what happened at Fort Monroe in the Hampton, Virginia, area, where blacks seeking refuge were brought together to secure the town. Located at the southernmost tip of the Virginia peninsula, Fort Monroe was the earliest military fortification in the colony of Virginia. Across the shore from Old Point Comfort and Hampton Roads lies Jamestown, the first permanent English settlement, founded in 1607. The earliest known Africans at the settlement, "20 and odd Negroes," arrived at the colony in 1619, after first being enslaved by the Portuguese who were forced to surrender them to British pirates. Now, 242 years later, the descendants of those forced migrants were returning to that fateful site to liberate themselves.[23]

Running an army involves a thousand small and large complex tasks: the refugees poured into the camp and were set to work rebuilding bridges, artillery batteries, and fortifications that the Confederates had destroyed; they also undertook the labor-intensive construction of protective breastworks, parapets, earthen mounds, and trenches around the city.[24] This was the first federal project to engage blacks as workers that even contemplated paying them for their labor.[25]

However, living and working under Union control was no panacea. The range of indignities, injuries, acts of cruelty, undeserved punishments, and deprivations inflicted on the contrabands by the Union soldiers that directed their labors were legendary. One missionary observing abuses at Fort Monroe reported, "Officers take advantage of their ignorance in every way possible, and torment them like fiends, while the government retains them on its highways and public works, and the quartermaster refuses to pay them." Nevertheless, many of the ex-slaves recognized the experience for what it was, release from their former masters and a major step toward freedom for themselves and their families.[26]

Formerly enslaved blacks' expectations may have seemed fantastic to some, given what they had undergone; they could no longer be sold nor could their children be sold away from them, they could not be subjected to corporal punishment, and going forward, they could choose their employers and negotiate their wages. Millions of them had been subjected to brutal coercion over the course of their lives. The potential end of such violence had the effect of waking from a nightmare. A number of plans to endow blacks with an initial grubstake at reduced or no cost—land, tools, seeds—were enacted temporarily.

Toward the end of 1861, Lincoln introduced a government reparations plan to compensate blacks for their lifetime of enslavement. The ramifications of such a plan—financial and otherwise—would have been life changing. One of the more consequential schemes was the Port Royal Experiment, which ran for forty months (December 20, 1861, to March 3, 1865) *while the war raged.* It was predicated on the principle that newly freed men and women should have an opportunity to engage in homesteading on land vacated en masse by southern planters.

The land in question had become available as spoils of war. Northern forces led by fleet commander Samuel F. Du Pont had bombarded Fort Beauregard and Fort Walker, two strongholds on either side of the Port Royal Sound, South Carolina, on November 7, 1861, seven months after the Battle of Fort Sumter. The hostile encounter did not last long. Confederate troops hastily deserted their forts, and local plantation owners and other whites loyal to the south's cause, after gathering a few belongings and their house slaves, fled to the mainland.

The Union victory was significant on several counts: Beaufort was a major economic center and a secessionist stronghold; the sound was a valued commercial harbor; cotton plantations with crops in the ground stretched across a collection of islands; and critically, perhaps as many as 16,000 persons in the region had liberated themselves from their owners or had been left behind.[27]

Homeless, barely scratching out an existence, and near starvation, the refugees—initially deemed "contrabands of war"—were in a limbo state; they were neither slave nor free. What would be the outcome for the people the *New York Times* called "contraband property having legs to run away with, and intelligence to guide its flight"?[28] Without settling the legal status of the formerly enslaved, the Treasury Department initiated an experiment designed to dramatically improve the contrabands' financial status.

Conducted in the Sea Islands of South Carolina, under the auspices of the U.S. Army's Department of the South, the Port Royal Experiment was executed in phases. The first phase began December 20, 1861, when Secretary of the Treasury Salmon Chase sent Lt. Col. William H. Reynolds to take possession of all abandoned cotton fiber in the surrendered territory and sell it on the open market.

Many South Carolina cotton growers had shut down their export operations during the summer of 1861 in anticipation that Europe, the south's primary export site, would support them in the war effort. Europe did not come to their aid, and the stockpiled cotton was declared government property.[29] A cotton dealer before the war and an officer in the First Rhode Island Artillery, Reynolds had his work cut out for him. In the four Beaufort District parishes alone were the former homesteads of 939 property owners, whose plantations had included 883,048 acres of "improved land" and 33,339 human chattel. Federal agents discovered at least 2.5 million pounds of ginned cotton that had been stored before Union forces arrived.

A month after Reynolds began his work, Chase dispatched Edward Lillie Pierce to evaluate the likelihood that area slaves, once freed, could manage the plantations, become government wage workers, and engage in "useful citizenship."[30] Pierce was charged with presenting his findings in person in Washington. A Boston attorney and delegate to the 1860 Republican National Convention, Pierce had enlisted as a private in the Third Massachusetts Regiment and, from June to December 1861, had been part of the military detail at Fort Monroe. In his report to the secretary of the Treasury, Pierce revealed the state of South Carolina's astonishing demographics. Over 57 percent of South Carolina's population was black—the highest proportion of any state in the country. Beaufort County, where Port Royal was located, reported a population of 40,053, 83 percent of whom were black. Only seven other counties in the entire country were home to a higher percentage of blacks.[31]

The high black presence in South Carolina was attributable to the heavy exploitation of slave labor for the purpose of producing cotton, rice, tobacco, and indigo. After British markets for indigo declined in the 1790s, South Carolina planters began to grow more cotton, a move that proved prescient when, after *twelve years* of insurrection, the Saint-Domingue slave revolution succeeded and, in the process, extinguished the country's formerly thriving cotton and sugar industries.[32]

Cotton production in the United States received another dramatic boost when Eli Whitney invented the cotton gin in 1793–94, which made it possible to increase the amount of cotton one person could clean for market by fiftyfold. In 1795, South Carolina's exports were valued at $1,109,653. In 1801, 20 percent of the country's 40 million pounds of cotton was grown in South Carolina.[33]

Cotton crop yields quickly realized high profits. In his epic study *Empire of Cotton*, Sven Beckert comments, "As early as 1807 a Mississippi cotton plantation was said to return 22.5 percent annually on its investment."[34] With access to healthy plant stock and a near-endless supply of forced labor, a planter could invest in more land, buy more slaves, and achieve spectacular wealth. By 1860, South Carolina, together with Mississippi, Georgia, and Alabama, had become the largest producer of cotton in the world.

After conducting an investigation of 195 plantations abandoned by their Confederate owners and scattered across seventeen islands, Agent Pierce concluded that there were at least 4,000 blacks in dire need of support—out of the 8,000 residents of plantations and 12,000 in the towns and countryside—half to one-third of whom continued to work as field hands. Newly liberated, blacks, in groups of 20–38 people, managed the workload at most of the plantations in the area. The Coffin Point plantation was maintained by 260 blacks, however, while 130 blacks supported the Dr. Jenkins Place plantation, and 120 blacks kept the Eustis plantation going.[35]

Pierce questioned field hands and drivers alike about their skills and the type of work they had done; asked how they had been treated by their former owners; examined their housing—some of which he described as "tenements unfit for beasts, without floor or chimneys"—and material possessions, clothing, tools, furnishings, and livestock; and assessed their character and capacity to become "useful citizens."

He gathered details about crop production on seventeen plantations—the range of activities required during each month to bring in a large yield, how the labor was divided, and the cost of production. And he solicited the former slaves' desires for their futures. Many were destitute and suffering from diseases or malnutrition—their former masters had taken many of the livestock and portable foodstuffs with them (and the Union army also had seized livestock for the troops' consumption)—and they had not received their customary allocations of winter clothing.

A small percentage of the contrabands were on the government payroll: sixty-three workers were paid a total of $101.50 for tasks completed in November. But no remuneration was immediately forthcoming for the 127 laborers who were owed a total of $468.59 as of January 1863 or the 137 workers to whom slightly more was due a month later.[36]

Impressed with the potential of the Port Royal contrabands to become a paid force of agricultural workers, Pierce declared in his February 1862 report that "when properly organized, and with proper motives set before them, [the contrabands] will as freemen be as industrious as any race of men are likely to be in this climate."[37] The report gave Washington the evidence it needed to finance a new system of economic cooperation with the freed blacks of Port Royal, South Carolina, a system they believed could become a model for the country.

Edward L. Pierce, doubtless the Union's foremost authority on the Sea Islands plantations and contrabands, was appointed as the general superintendent at the former Confederate base and began phase two of the Port Royal Experiment. When he arrived in March 1862, nearly sixty grade-school teachers, superintendents, doctors, and ministers accompanied him. By mid-April, seventy-four men and nineteen women had been assigned to work in Beaufort, Port Royal Island, St. Helena, Lady's, Edisto, Hilton Head, Pinckney, Cat, Cane, Paris, and Daufuskie; 2,500 students received instruction on weekdays, one-third of whom were adults who came to class at the end of the workday. The federal government paid the housing expenses for these critical employees, and the National Freedmen's Relief Association of New York, the Education Commission of Boston, and the Port Royal Committee of Philadelphia paid their salaries.[38]

Pierce also supervised the cultivation of the Port Royal cotton crop. Blacks enrolled in the program were allocated one- and one-half-acre plots and, until November 1862, also received basic rations from the federal government—meat, bread, potatoes, and when it was available, rice, salt, coffee, and vinegar.[39] The freedmen told Pierce that an average acre of land would yield 133 pounds of cotton and that a single hand could cultivate five acres of cotton and corn combined.[40]

Despite having commenced six weeks after the growing season had begun, the contrabands cultivated "nearly 15,000 acres of cotton, corn, potatoes, and grain" and worked valiantly while receiving erratic payments for their efforts.[41] The government had agreed to purchase the farmers' raw cotton crop at the guaranteed price of one dollar per 400 pounds of cotton, but few had received payment for their crops.

Essentially a modest reparations plan, the federal government, in partnership with a network of private abolitionist organizations, provided rent-free housing in uninhabited domiciles and a free education to the freedmen and their children. These steps were unprecedented on two counts: (1) educating blacks had formerly been illegal, and free public education in the south did not yet exist, and (2) the government plan provided paid employment to the freedmen for a range of occupations from domestic servant and retail vendor to carpenter and water navigator, but primarily as field hands. The freedmen were to become cotton farmers in the service of the U.S. government and thereby join the ranks of "useful citizens" many believed to be an essential component of American society.

By one account, the government controlled approximately 76,775 acres in the sound.[42] At least 3,000 blacks were engaged in cotton farming on government-owned land by the spring of 1862.[43] While whites had allowed some slaves to negotiate payment for their labor on occasion, this would be a new experience for the majority of blacks. It is likely that knowing ahead of time—with a high degree of certainty—what one would be paid for one's labor also was novel.

"Here, within the protection of the arms of the United States, might a new experiment of tropical culture by free labor be tried," an editorial in the *National Anti-Slavery Standard* boasted. "Succeeding there, as succeed it must and would, how simple the process by which it might be extended wherever the arms of the nation may be predominant."[44] Would that the editorial's boast had proved prescient.

A host of difficulties weighed against the ex-slaves' success: the process of restoring fields of agricultural crops destroyed during military battles or neglected during the war was costly, the bulk of the nation's coveted cotton seeds had been sold overseas in Egyptian markets, and few had access to capital during what would become a national economic depression.

To make matters worse, the Union did not protect black Port Royal residents from rapacious whites who preyed upon the newly remunerated contrabands, nor did it eliminate raids directed by its own military forces. Among the marauding soldiers that thwarted the freedmen were the 100th New York Infantry and the Ninth New Jersey Volunteer Regiment, who as late as 1863 ransacked the colony, stole livestock and cash, assaulted black residents, and burned all of the cabins on the Dr. Jenkins Place plantation to the ground.[45]

What should have been a program of black wealth accumulation under the protection of the federal government was, instead, a shamefully executed program that coexisted with the constant threat of brutality, rife with irregular pay for the black laborers or no pay at all. The reaction to the experiment should have been anticipated. Never before had there been a recognition that the formerly enslaved should be the recipients of an economic boost. Nor had there been a realization that if they were to have a long-lasting shot at success, landownership—a primary source of wealth and an asset that could be passed on to the next generation—was essential.

The Port Royal Experiment was designed to demonstrate that unpaid enslaved labor could be converted successfully into fully free wage labor. Unfortunately, the transition was stunted by an absence of will to enable large numbers of black Americans to become landowners or decently paid wage laborers.

For the most part, abolitionists were united in their belief that all freedmen should have access to a formal education and that adult males be granted the right to vote. More controversial was the question of black economic independence. On one side of the divide were those who preferred a federal land redistribution program that would provide free or low-cost arable land to emancipated slaves. On the other side were proponents of large-scale sales of plantation lands to wealthy whites, whether northern sympathizers or former Confederates who now declared their loyalty to the Union. These white landowners then hired (or rehired) black field hands at prices set by the renewed racial aristocracy.

Edward Philbrick, head of the "Boston Concern," a consortium of northern investors that organized to take advantage of the government's land auctions, publicly identified as an abolitionist while contending that blacks were not ready for the responsibilities of landownership. For him, the Port Royal blacks "regarded their change of condition with fear and trembling, looking at the cotton-field as a life-long scene of unrequited toil, and hailing with delight the prospect of 'no more driver, no more cotton, no more lickin.'" Without the "benefit" of whites to drive and threaten them with the lash, the former slaves were unreliable farmworkers in his eyes. It was all well and good that blacks become an "industrious and useful laboring class," Philbrick said, but landownership—at least ownership achieved through a government program based on the premise that granting land to formerly enslaved blacks was one critical step to right the wrongs of slavery—was not in the country's best interest.[46]

Philbrick's group, not the ex-slaves, purchased nearly half of the 16,479 acres of Port Royal land auctioned by the government under the Direct Tax Act in 1863; the group bought it at the unbelievably low average price of less than one dollar per acre and cultivated cotton crops using laborers drawn from the freedmen's population who were supervised by several former federal plantation supervisors.[47] Philbrick exploited what was intended to be a land reform strategy and economic boost for the contrabands. His effrontery and crassness cost the formerly enslaved about 205 homesteads at forty acres apiece.

Of course, there was no presumption that the productivity of Philbrick and his white partners would be harmed by the opportunity to purchase large parcels of confiscated land at below-market prices. Freedmen, on the other hand, allegedly would be corrupted morally by such largesse, made soft and unsuitable for work.[48] Better for "Northern capital" to own the Sea Islands than for it "to be abandoned to the negroes and wild hogs."[49] There is no doubt that northern capital in the hands of Edward Philbrick turned a huge profit on the inexpensively purchased land from the cotton crop raised by the former slaves.[50] Philbrick's private correspondence and his public affairs lend grounds for skepticism about the sincerity of his philanthropic intentions.

The former slaves were paid by the "job system."[51] In principle, 16,000 black Port Royal farmers were eligible to purchase 40,000 acres of land at the rate of $1.25 per acre.[52] Claude F. Oubre reports that a single black collective purchased the land they were working, some 470 acres, at $7.00 per acre.[53] Although Lincoln instructed the Treasury Department to offer black families who had lived in the Sea Islands before the war forty-acre plots at $1.25 with 40 percent down (individuals over the age of twenty-one were eligible to purchase twenty acres), Secretary Chase delayed the sale and then allowed ineligible whites to purchase the majority of the land for an average of $11.00 per acre.[54]

Advocates of black landownership included a contributor to the *Liberator*, the antislavery newspaper, who wrote from Port Royal in January 1864: "If large sums of money can be made at cotton growing, why should not these [ex-slaves] who have served so long and painful an apprenticeship at this business, now that they should be attaining to their majority, bare their share of this business, and thus gather up for themselves some of the ordinary comforts of life, and use their surplus earnings to help on their civil, economical and educational interests?"[55]

Another Port Royal correspondent to the newspaper argued that blacks "be made proprietors of the soil in fee simple, as speedily as possible." The writers' urgings may have been informed by eyewitness accounts of the resistance local black farmers faced when they attempted to negotiate for fair competitive wages at a time when they were not allowed to pursue remedies through the court system: "It is going to make a mighty difference to the 'landless and homeless,' whether they are to get only the poor pittance of twenty-five or thirty cents per day and be thus kept dependent, or whether they shall receive four or five times this amount by planting on their own land. The conflict between capital and labor is as old as the world; but in this case the contest could never be more unequal."[56]

The Radicals within the Republican Party stood firm in their resolve and continued to support the reparations plan. Senator Charles Sumner affirmed, "Every head of a family [should] have a piece of land." In a February 1863 bill, he proposed that every black Union soldier receive ten acres.[57] The bill did not pass.

Soon thereafter, Congressman George Washington Julian (R-Ind.), chair of the House of Representatives Committee on Public Lands, in an appeal that anticipated the devastating poverty that would define the lives of the majority of black Americans for the next 100 years, argued for "an equitable homestead policy, parceling out the plantations of rebels in small farms for . . . the freedmen . . . instead of selling it in large tracts to speculators, and thus laying the foundation for a system of land monopoly in the South scarcely less to be deplored than slavery itself."[58]

Dismantling the large plantations and allocating blacks an endowment was the only possible route to black equality, declared abolitionist Wendell Phillips, charging that "the whole social system of the Gulf States is to be taken to pieces, every bit of it."[59]

There were two major motives, not mutually exclusive, that informed whites' opposition to black land acquisition: blatant self-interest—the overarching desire to take possession of the land for themselves—and a patronizing and paternalistic concern that blacks were incapable of making a go of it as economically independent landowners. The latter perspective disturbingly anticipated claims made today about black indolence and dysfunctional behaviors. Edward Philbrick, the Boston land speculator who invested heavily in Sea Islands properties, represented the confluence of both attitudes.

Nevertheless, thanks to the freedmen's skill and their excitement about receiving an honorable wage for their labors, the government's efforts to prevent the deterioration of the estates and save the Sea Islands cotton crop were enormously successful. But the Port Royal Experiment was plagued with the same income disparities blacks were experiencing in the military. Commonplace were late wage payments and wage payments in scrip or "tickets" that could be used only in privately run and unregulated plantation commissaries where the prices for goods had been raised to extreme levels.

And only a fraction of the freedmen were allowed to purchase land. Although Union officer William H. Reynolds acknowledged the "energetic men, who labor night and day" and "saved from destruction an immense amount [of cotton]," by January 1, 1862, he was pained to admit, "I am very sorry that the money which I asked for was not sent, as in consequence I have been compelled to break faith with the Negroes, for not being able to pay them as I had promised."[60]

Edward L. Pierce, the special agent of the Treasury who had produced the detailed report on the Port Royal colony's plantations, was planning to write a letter of complaint to his supervisor on May 13, 1862, to deplore the "repugnant" treatment of the contrabands by the Union army. Before he executed the letter, Pierce received an upsetting communication from Superintendent L. D. Phillips describing the strong-arm tactics the Union army had used, at the orders of Gen. Isaac Ingalls Stevens, to carry out the military directive to impress "every able-bodied negro between the ages of eighteen and forty-five capable of bearing arms" that had been working on the Dr. Pope plantation in St. Helena, South Carolina. "The plea of military necessity had been stretched to cover up many a mistake and some acts of criminal injustice," Phillips continued, "but never, in my judgment, did major-general fall into a sadder blunder and rarely has humanity been outraged by an act of more unfeeling barbarity."[61]

In his letter to Secretary Chase, Pierce indicated he had learned that Maj. Gen. David Hunter, without consulting Pierce or any of the superintendents working in direct contact with the contrabands, had gone against his word and given instructions that blacks would be enrolled "against their will." Some 500 men had been impressed using General Hunter's "mode of violent seizure and transportation . . . spreading dismay and fright." Pierce felt strongly that these tactics "should not be done with white men, least of all with blacks, who do not yet understand us, for whose benefit the war is not professed to be carried on, and who are still without a Government solemnly and publicly pledged to their protection."[62]

Pierce then wrote to Hunter directly to express his dismay at the unfortunate "recruiting service" approach the military's impressments of contrabands in Hilton Head was taking under Hunter's command:

> As those on this plantation were called in from the fields, the soldiers, under orders, and while on the steps of my headquarters, loaded their guns, so that the negroes might see what would take place in case they attempted to get away. This was done in the presence of the ladies here. Wives and children embraced the husband and father thus taken away, they knew not where, and whom, as they said, they should never see again. On some plantations the wailing and screaming were loud and the women threw themselves in despair on the ground. On some plantations the people took to the woods and were hunted up by the soldiers.[63]

Hunter thought it expedient to liberate the bondsmen for the specific purpose of adding them to the Union's fighting forces by any means necessary. Ultimately, his objective prevailed.

In June 1862, when the Port Royal Experiment was transferred from the Treasury to the War Department, Pierce was recommended to continue as the government's chief agent, but he declined the offer. Later, he was a candidate for the military governorship of South Carolina, but he was not appointed.

Pierce was replaced by Brig. Gen. Rufus Saxton, the son of transcendentalists and abolitionists and a graduate of West Point, where he had taught classes in artillery, military tactics and strategy, and army organization before the Civil War.[64] Saxton had served General Sherman as quartermaster during the Port Royal expedition that began in September 1861 and the planned invasion that took place that November.

In 1866, Saxton would testify before Congress's Joint Committee on Reconstruction about African Americans' suitability for military service and citizenship. When asked if he thought African Americans would be inclined to insurrection if they were given the same rights as whites, he responded, "I do not; and I think that is the only thing which will prevent difficulty. I think if the Negro is put in possession of all his rights as a citizen and as a man, he will be peaceful, orderly, and self-sustaining as any other man or class of men, and that he will rapidly advance."[65]

Saxton identified as an abolitionist and had proposed in 1862 that a congressionally authorized commission be created to "give the negroes a right in that [Sea Islands] soil to whose wealth they are destined to contribute so largely to save them from destitution, to enable them to take care of themselves, and prevent them from ever becoming a burden upon the country."[66]

While Saxton did not believe freedmen needed to be "taught" how to live as free men and women, the question was one of the key issues abolitionists and the military raised. Should ex-slaves be required to complete a guardianship or apprenticeship program before they could assume their place among free whites? One after another black spokespersons and a number of abolitionists argued that "equal laws *faithfully* administered" would suffice.[67]

However, the condition that would make freedom real for the former slaves was landownership. After all, Europe's serfs had not undergone any such training in order to earn their place in society when feudal practices were abandoned in the mid-fourteenth century. What the liberated serfs did have, though, was access to commonly held land where they could fish, graze their livestock, cut wood, grow crops, and collect water, at least until it was subject to enclosure over the course of several centuries and deemed the sole property of a few individuals. Would a modern-day equivalent be created for blacks?[68]

In March 1863, while the U.S. Direct Tax Commission was auctioning off confiscated and abandoned land, real progress began on the creation of a federal agency tasked with assisting the contrabands in their transition to freedom. Secretary of War Stanton designated the War Department's American Freedmen's Inquiry Commission to gather information to assess blacks' present condition and their capacity to live and thrive in a democratic society.[69] The commission's findings were to be made available for congressional review and action.

The three-man fact-finding team traveled across the Union-controlled areas of the South and conducted extensive interviews with blacks and whites, especially Union field officers. They sought to learn, firsthand, how blacks were faring and to understand what they would need to convert them from "contrabands"—fugitives from slavery—to free American citizens.

Over a twelve-month period, the men researched black American history and French and British emancipation strategies in the Caribbean, visited black encampments within Union lines and free black communities in New England and Canada, and analyzed the results of a questionnaire they devised to elicit input on the freedmen. Unlike the 1862 government study to assess enslaved blacks' readiness for emancipation, which sought responses only from army and Treasury Department agents and supervisors, their query was sent to a far-reaching public—abolitionists, military officers, politicians, ministers, freedmen aid society teachers, and freedmen themselves.

Key findings gleaned from the American Freedmen's Inquiry Commission study included the following: there was widespread poverty among the country's enslaved and free blacks, freedmen were desperately in need of emergency relief, the desire for remunerative work was paramount, and emancipation should not be a gradual process. The lessons of the West Indies confirmed that former slaves fared better and experienced fewer setbacks when unconditional freedom was granted. Almost uniformly, respondents underscored the necessity for arable land that could be purchased at *discounted* prices in order for the freedmen to make a livelihood and the importance of access to an education.[70]

Even with the mountain of conclusive data, the initial legislative bill providing for the Bureau of Refugees, Freedmen, and Abandoned Lands failed in December 1864.[71] A modified Freedmen's Bureau Bill was approved March 3, 1865, but its provision for land distribution to the formerly enslaved was not implemented with any force. A subsequent bill was vetoed by President Johnson.

In March 1863, when a single white consortium was allowed to purchase nearly 8,000 acres at the U.S. Direct Tax Commission auction—some with houses and other structures on the property—for an average of ninety-three cents per acre, African Americans managed to purchase 3,500 acres, including eighty houses in Beaufort, South Carolina, for forty to eighty dollars each.[72] That September, when government agents were to have earmarked another 16,529 acres for auction to black heads of household in parcels not to exceed twenty acres, an additional 24,000 acres also were made available in parcels of 320 acres, which would put them out of the reach of the average black family.

White speculators leaped at these opportunities knowing that they would reap a return on their investments quickly if they were able to hire experienced black field hands to work their crops. In theory, those black employees could demand competitive rates of pay now that they were free and their potential employers were dependent on their labors to develop their enterprises. However, given the unpredictability of these arrangements and the former slaves' knowledge of dozens of examples where their fellow freedmen had been threatened, injured, or killed for attempting to negotiate with whites, most preferred to work their own land even if it meant a long period of limited cash reserves.

In December 1863, when Lincoln recognized that the reparations plan was not working as he had intended and that wealthy whites, not black ex-slaves, were the primary beneficiaries of the government's land deals, he stipulated that prospective Port Royal land buyers had to meet the following criterion: six months' residency or the equivalent time spent cultivating land in the district. Absentee owners were barred from participation. Buyers could purchase a maximum of two twenty-acre tracts at the fixed price of $1.25 per acre. Blacks who were currently serving in the military could purchase one additional parcel.

A total of 40,000 acres were available for sale. At the time of the June 1864 census, Port Royal Island's black population was 9,443. Approximately 1,900 families were eligible to take advantage of the land auction.[73] Unfortunately, the government's tax agents ignored the new stipulations at that month's land sale and continued to constrain black buyers.

Despite many obstacles, the freedmen also sought formal education. Scores of one-room schoolhouses were built at this time, along with advanced institutions like Howard University in Washington, D.C. Founded in 1866 and named for the school's first president, Civil War general Oliver O. Howard, who had become the commissioner of the Freedmen's Bureau the previous year, the school was expanded under an 1867 U.S. charter.

Commenting on the barriers to education confronting blacks, General Howard observed: "The opposition to Negro education made itself felt everywhere in a combination not to allow the freedmen any room or building in which a school might be taught. In 1865, 1866, and 1877 mobs of the baser classes at intervals and in all parts of the South occasionally burned school buildings and churches used as schools, flogged teachers or drove them away, and in a number of instances murdered them."[74]

On April 9, 1865, the Confederate army lost the decisive battle at Appomattox, Virginia. It became the battle that marked the end of the Civil War. Six days later, Lincoln was assassinated. He died the next day, three months after Sherman's Special Field Orders No. 15, the orders that granted the formerly enslaved forty acres of land, went into effect. The Second Freedmen's Bureau Bill, which was drafted December 4, 1865, and authorized up to 3 million acres of land in five states for freedmen, was vetoed February 16, 1866, by Lincoln's successor, Andrew Johnson.[75] By 1865, free blacks held the franchise in only five of thirty-six states—Maine, Massachusetts, New Hampshire, Rhode Island, and Vermont—and could not force a referendum on the matter. With President Lincoln assassinated and the Freedmen's Bureau in disarray, what would become of the reparations plan?

If only the advice of Frederick Douglass had been heeded:

What shall be done with the Negro if emancipated? Deal justly with him. He is a human being, capable of judging between good and evil, right and wrong, liberty and slavery, and is as much a subject of law as any other man; therefore, deal justly with him. He is, like other men, sensible of the motives of reward and punishment. Give him wages for his work, and let hunger pinch him if he don't work. He knows the difference between fullness and famine, plenty and scarcity. "But will he work?" Why should he not? He is used to it. His hands are already hardened by toil, and he has no dreams of ever getting a living by any other means than by hard work. But would you turn them all loose? Certainly! We are no better than our Creator. He has turned them loose, and why should not we?[76]

8

Radicals and Rebels

We recognize the fact of the inferiority stamped upon that race of men by the Creator, and from the cradle to the grave, our Government, as a civil institution, marks that inferiority. —Jefferson Davis, "Reply in Senate to William H. Seward, 1860"

The whole fabric of southern society must be changed, and never can it be done if this opportunity is lost. Without this, this government can never be, as it never has been, a true republic. —Thaddeus Stevens, speech before U.S. House of Representatives, 1865

It would grant me much relief to learn your sons were engaged matrimonially to other white men if I was previously faced with the spectre of those same sons wedding negro women, slave or free, and siring negro sons that could presume to claim inheritance of your namesakes and property, or worse, equality with your purer grandchildren. —Jefferson Davis, U.S. Senate debate on legality of interracial marriages, 1860

And be it further enacted, That so soon as the military resistance to the United States shall have been suppressed in any such state, and the people thereof shall have sufficiently returned to their obedience to the constitution and the laws of the United States, the provisional governor shall direct the marshal of the United States, as speedily as may be, to name a sufficient number of deputies, and to enroll all white male citizens of the United States, resident in the state in their respective counties, and to request each one to take the oath to support the constitution of the United States, and in his enrolment to designate those who take and those who refuse to take that oath, which rolls shall be forthwith returned to the provisional governor; and if the persons taking that oath shall amount to a majority of the persons enrolled in the state, he shall, by proclamation, invite the loyal people of the state to elect delegates to a convention charged to declare the will of the people of the state relative to the reestablishment of a state government subject to, and in conformity with, the constitution of the United States. —Section 2 of the Wade-Davis Bill, 1864

We prefer, however, our system of industry, by which labor and capital are identified in interest, and capital, therefore, protects labor–by which our population doubles every twenty years–by which starvation is unknown, and abundance crowns the land–by which order is preserved by unpaid police, and the most fertile regions of the world, where the white man cannot labor, are brought into usefulness by the labor of the African, and the whole world is blessed by our own productions. All we demand of other peoples is, to be let alone, to work out our own high destinies. United together, and we must be the most independent, as we are the most important among the nations of the world. United together, and we require no other instrument to conquer peace, than our beneficent productions. United together, and we must be a great, free and prosperous people, whose renown must spread throughout the civilized world, and pass down, we trust, to the remotest ages. We ask you to join us, in forming a Confederacy of Slaveholding States. —Address of South Carolina legislature to the slaveholding states, 1860.

At least as early as 1862, the president and Republicans in Congress were developing plans in the event of a Union victory. They were considering not only the future of the enslaved community whose emancipation was anticipated but also the future of the Confederate rebels. Shortly before the war ended in 1865, it was clear that leniency toward the former Confederates could not be reconciled with the establishment of full citizenship for blacks, and the establishment of full citizenship for blacks would require punitive measures to be taken toward the ex-Confederates.

It would not be possible to both extend clemency to the rebels and achieve justice for blacks. Ultimately, the former path was chosen over the latter, thereby consolidating an arc of prolonged racial inequality in the postwar era.

It was the Radical Republicans who made the most deliberate and sustained commitment to including the formerly enslaved in, and excluding the rebels from, the national polity after the war's end. Their aims were not realized, but those aims had deep origins in the antislavery movement's growing recognition of the requirements for making blacks legally and functionally American citizens.

Although in 1840 it was unfathomable that anyone could have confidently predicted that the institution of slavery in the United States would end twenty-five years later, there were hopeful, undeniable signs that the public's attitude about the feasibility of maintaining human chattel was changing. As noted in chapter 5, although it was defeated, an 1839 resolution was introduced in the House of Representatives to abolish slavery in the District of Columbia and to compensate the slaveholders for the loss of their human property.[1] Ten years later, Representative Abraham Lincoln (Ill.-Whig) was a member of that body from Illinois's Seventh District when he introduced a

plan to establish compensated emancipation in the nation's capital by referendum. Eligible male voters would decide the fate of enslaved persons; that
proposition also failed.[2] Had it succeeded, local emancipation would have
been achieved by paying slaveholders the market price equivalent for their
human chattel.

In 1800, nine years before Lincoln was born, slavery was legalized in the District of Columbia, newly designated as the nation's capital. It was not a given
in 1800 that slavery would become legally inscribed there; the decision to
declare blacks to be human property in the nation's capital was contested.
During the ten years that it took to construct the building where the seat of
government was to be housed, an antislavery alternative could have been
implanted.

The decision of whether to legalize or outlaw slavery in the District was
Congress's to make. Benjamin Franklin submitted a petition to the First Congress to outlaw slavery and the slave trade in 1790, to "promote mercy and
justice toward this distressed Race." The request was discussed in both the
Senate and the House, but the measure was refused.

Southern elites were candid about their preferences and did not hesitate
to instruct their representatives on the subject. Before the vote in June 1790,
less than seven years after the end of the Revolutionary War, Henry "Light
Horse Harry" Lee III wrote to Congressman James Madison of Virginia to
voice sentiments that were later consonant with the motives for the formation of the Confederacy. Lee wrote to express his predisposition for disunion
(or secession) over abolition: "I had rather submit to all the hazards of war
and the loss of everything dear to me than to live under the rule of a fixed
insolent northern majority."[3]

Both the location of the capital and the acquiescence to the promulgation of slavery were the price the North paid to keep the southern elite in
the Union. The Compromise of 1790 would be the first of several "under-
standings" whose effect was to deprive blacks of their humanity and place
citizenship beyond their grasp.

Indeed, only after the capital was created and the federal government
permanently installed did Congress adopt the laws of the state of Maryland,
which had legalized slavery and Black Codes, discriminatory provisions
limiting the rights of black people.[4] By 1800, one in three District of Columbia residents was black, though less than 20 percent of the capital's black
population had free status. Slave markets operated openly in proximity to
the White House, and the spectacle of enslaved blacks chained in coffles

laboring on public-works projects was ubiquitous. In 1820 President James Monroe signed legislation, known as the Missouri Compromise, mentioned in chapter 4, preserving an equal number of slave and free states. This was another bow to the slaveholding south.

While these activities fueled the public slavery debate, events that transpired during the forty-year run-up to Lincoln's 1863 Emancipation Proclamation were pivotal. The scope of resistance on the part of the enslaved had been pronounced and constant both in the United States and in the Caribbean. Slaveholders in the United States and in the West Indies were linked closely, especially via intimate family ties, and they were in continuous communication about the levels of restiveness of their human captives.[5] Proslavery advocates in the United States, angered by the successful uprisings in Saint-Domingue (now present-day Haiti) earlier in the century, discussed in chapter 4, and in Jamaica in 1831–32, charged that those countries were being run disastrously under "Negro rule."[6]

In 1833, when the British Parliament adopted emancipation throughout the empire's dominions, it did not fall on deaf American ears. Many considered slavery's existence in the American capital an abomination—evidence of both a moral failing and hypocrisy. The same year the Slavery Abolition Act was passed in England, the American Anti-Slavery Society was founded on the belief that the institution was antithetical to the country's vaunted ideals of freedom, equality, and justice. "Slavery is contrary to the principles of natural justice, of our republican form of government," the society declared in its manifesto, and it "is endangering the peace, union, and liberties of the States."[7]

An 1836 broadside published by the American Anti-Slavery Society specifically targeted the persistence of the institution in the nation's capital. Illustrative of the dictum that a picture is worth a thousand words, the printed sheet pairs nine drawings with short captions that spell out the contradictions between the stated goals of the Declaration of Independence, the Constitution of the United States, the constitutions of the states, and the legality of slavery in the District of Columbia—all seemingly designed to shame the country into outlawing the institution.

By the mid-1830s, the U.S. Congress was receiving thousands of petitions to end slavery each year. In March 1836, at the urging of South Carolina senator John C. Calhoun and congressman Henry Pinckney, both legislative bodies passed "gag rules" banning the introduction of petitions or bills pertaining to slavery. When, in 1850, the Fugitive Slave Act was passed, it became illegal to assist runaway slaves anywhere in the United States. Critically, the law imposed fines of up to $1,000 (the rough equivalent of an incredible present value of $756,195, compounded from 1850 at 4 percent interest) and possible imprisonment of citizens if they did not return escaped slaves to their owners or if they refused to be deputized for this purpose.

After passage of the Fugitive Slave Act, slaveholders whose human chattel sought refuge in states where the institution was outlawed could demand that they be returned to them. Under the law, escaped slaves, like stray horses or cattle, were private property; consequently, they were to be returned to their owners.

Realizing the law's potential to pull free and escaped blacks into slavery and destroy their communities, abolitionists across the country sprang into action. Benjamin Franklin Roberts, who was born free, drafted and circulated flyers and posters from his printshop cautioning the "COLORED PEOPLE OF BOSTON . . . [who] value your LIBERTY, and *the Welfare of the Fugitives* among you" to avoid conversing with local "Watchmen and Police Officers" who were acting as "KIDNAPPERS AND Slave Catchers" on "the recent ORDER OF THE MAYOR & ALDERMEN."[8]

The Fugitive Slave Act indicated the depth of the difficulties confronting the abolition movement. It signaled the comprehensive nationalization of slavery by creating a legal obligation for fugitives to be restored to their owners, even from states where the practice of slavery was outlawed. Both the northern states and their citizens were forced to be complicit in the maintenance of slavery—or break the law.[9]

The Fugitive Slave Act was followed by the Kansas-Nebraska Act four years later. The latter authorized "popular sovereignty"—essentially, the will of the majority to determine whether the territory would allow or outlaw slavery. Both laws galvanized advocates on both sides as previous actions had not done. Many northern abolitionists boldly resisted the Fugitive Slave Act and came to the aid of escaped bondsmen. And in the proposed new states, political disagreements gave way to combat, escalating to protracted violence, particularly in the territory that became known as Bleeding Kansas.

Before passage of the two acts, the two main political parties were the Democrats—largely southerners—and the Whigs—largely northerners. Neither party survived the turmoil. The Democrats split into northern and southern factions, and the Whigs were replaced by a newly constituted antislavery Republican Party, emerging with Abraham Lincoln leading their ticket.

The history of the abolition movement made it clear that ending both slavery and black subjugation would not be achieved easily. One thing was certain: the slavery question was leading the country into dangerous waters. The depth of opposition to full black citizenship was so severe that the southern states made the decision to secede from the United States and go to war. Implacable enemies of black equality, it was wholly unlikely that the secessionists would submit to a postwar social order that gave blacks equal status.

Indeed, in 1861, the vice president of the Confederate States of America, Alexander Stephens, famously connected secession to the maintenance of slavery, an aim he explicitly predicated on a belief in black inferiority. We reproduce a lengthy portion of Stephens's speech because of its importance in clarifying the raison d'être for the formation of the Confederacy:

> Our new government is founded upon exactly the opposite idea [from the equality of the races]; its foundations are laid, its corner-stone rests upon the great truth, that the negro is not equal to the white man; that slavery—subordination to the superior race—is his natural and normal condition. This, our new government, is the first, in the history of the world, based upon this great physical, philosophical, and moral truth. This truth has been slow in the process of its development, like all other truths in the various departments of science. It has been so even amongst us. Many who hear me, perhaps, can recollect well, that this truth was not generally admitted, even within their day. The errors of the past generation still clung to many as late as twenty years ago. Those at the North, who still cling to these errors, with a zeal above knowledge, we justly denominate fanatics. All fanaticism springs from an aberration of the mind—from a defect in reasoning. It is a species of insanity. One of the most striking characteristics of insanity, in many instances, is forming correct conclusions from fancied or erroneous premises; so with the anti-slavery fanatics; their conclusions are right if their premises were. They assume that the negro is equal, and hence conclude that he is entitled to equal privileges and rights with the white man. If their premises were correct, their conclusions would be logical and just—but their premise being wrong, their whole argument fails. I recollect once of having heard a gentleman from one of the northern States, of great power and ability, announce in the House of Representatives, with imposing effect, that we of the South would be compelled, ultimately, to yield upon this subject of slavery, that it was as impossible to war successfully against a principle in politics, as it was in physics or mechanics. That the principle would ultimately

prevail. That we, in maintaining slavery as it exists with us, were warring against a principle, a principle founded in nature, the principle of the equality of men. The reply I made to him was, that upon his own grounds, we should, ultimately, succeed, and that he and his associates, in this crusade against our institutions, would ultimately fail. The truth announced, that it was as impossible to war successfully against a principle in politics as it was in physics and mechanics, I admitted; but told him that it was he, and those acting with him, who were warring against a principle. They were attempting to make things equal which the Creator had made unequal.[10]

Earlier, in an 1858 speech on the floor of the U.S. Senate, James Henry Hammond (D-S.C.) advanced the "mudsill theory," declaring that enslaved blacks were in the position that best suited their place in the natural social order:

In all social systems there must be a class to do the menial duties, to perform the drudgery of life. That is, a class requiring but a low order of intellect and but little skill. Its requisites are vigor, docility, fidelity. Such a class you must have, or you would not have that other class which leads progress, civilization, and refinement. It constitutes the very mud-sill of society and of political government; and you might as well attempt to build a house in the air, as to build either the one or the other, except on this mud-sill. Fortunately for the South, she found a race adapted to that purpose to her hand. A race inferior to her own, but eminently qualified in temper, in vigor, in docility, in capacity to stand the climate, to answer all her purposes. We use them for our purpose, and call them slaves.[11]

Hammond's mudsill theory was an elaborate echo of the position taken by the author of an 1856 editorial in the *Richmond Enquirer*. In a perfectly "Orwellian definition of liberty," the editorialist made the following terse statement, designating blacks to hold a position at the bottom of the American hierarchy to insure appropriate freedoms for whites: "In this country alone does perfect equality of civil and social privileges exist among the white population, and it exists solely because we have black slaves. . . . Freedom is not possible without slavery."[12]

While not invoking black inferiority at the time, Judah P. Benjamin, who served variously as attorney general, secretary of war, and secretary of state for the Confederacy, argued that the right to own slaves was sacrosanct. For Benjamin, that right in human property transcended any legislative action that might be taken by the U.S. Congress. In 1858, while he was still serving as U.S. senator from Louisiana, slightly less than three years before the state's secession, Benjamin made the following observation on the floor of the Senate:

> Slaves, if you please, are not property like other property in this: that you easily rob us of them; but as to the *right* in them, that man has to overthrow the whole history of the world, he has to overthrow every treatise on jurisprudence, he has to ignore the common sentiment of mankind, he has to repudiate the authority of all that is considered sacred with man, ere he can reach the conclusion that the person who owns a slave, in a country where slavery has been established for ages, has no other property in that slave than the mere title which is given by the statute law of the land where it is found.[13]

Later, when Benjamin struck a more defiant note in December 1860, on the eve of his exit from the U.S. Senate accompanying Louisiana's secession, his case for the southern cause was laced blatantly with the rhetoric of white supremacy:

> What may be the fate of this horrible contest, no man can tell, none pretend to foresee; but this much I will say: the fortunes of war may be adverse to our arms; you may carry desolation into our peaceful land, and with torch and fire you may set our cities in flames; you may even emulate the atrocities of those who, in the war of the Revolution, hounded on the blood-thirsty savage to attack upon the defenceless frontier; you may under the protection of your advancing armies, give shelter to the furious fanatics who desire, and profess to desire, nothing more than to add all the *horrors of a servile insurrection* to the calamities of civil war; you may do all this—and more, too, if more there be—but you never can subjugate us; you never can convert the free sons of the soil into vassals, paying tribute to your power; and *you never, never can degrade them to the level of an inferior and servile race.* Never! Never![14]

In an 1856 letter, Robert E. Lee, eventual Confederate general, described slavery as a "moral and political evil" but went on to argue that it was justified fully on the grounds of necessity. For Lee, slavery was an instrument for civilizing the African; whites generously were performing a difficult service for blacks by enslaving them:

> I think it however a greater evil to the white man than to the black race, & while my feelings are strongly enlisted in behalf of the latter, my

sympathies are more strong for the former. The blacks are immeasurably better off here than in Africa, morally, socially & physically. The painful discipline they are undergoing, is necessary for their instruction as a race, & I hope will prepare & lead them to better things. How long their subjugation may be necessary is known & ordered by a wise Merciful Providence. Their emancipation will sooner result from the mild & melting influence of Christianity, than the storms & tempests of fiery Controversy.[15]

Even after the war, Lee's attitude remained unchanged:

Nor did Lee's defeat lead to an embrace of racial egalitarianism. The war was not about slavery, Lee insisted later, but if it was about slavery, it was only out of Christian devotion that white southerners fought to keep blacks enslaved. Lee told a *New York Herald* reporter, in the midst of arguing in favor of somehow removing blacks from the South ("disposed of," in his words), "that unless some humane course is adopted, based on wisdom and Christian principles you do a gross wrong and injustice to the whole negro race in setting them free. And it is only this consideration that has led the wisdom, intelligence and Christianity of the South to support and defend the institution up to this time."[16]

After all, the southern states' motive for waging war to preserve black enslavement was transparent in the Constitution of the Confederate States of America, composed in 1861. The Confederate States Constitution made explicit the centrality and permanence of slavery to the secessionists' agenda. Article 1, section 9, of the document included the following absolute provision: "No bill of attainder, ex post facto law, or law denying or impairing the right of property in negro slaves shall be passed."[17] The forceful assertion of states' rights was merely instrumental to the determined effort to continue the system of slavery by the leaders of the states that had exited from the Union. Not only were the Confederate states determined to maintain slavery; they were determined to maintain *"negro slavery"*—and, hence, black subordination.

On April 11, 1865, shortly after Lee's surrender to Grant at Appomattox, the president delivered a speech at the White House in which he ventured the possibility of extending the right to vote to two groups of black freedmen who had served in the Union military during the war and, if the southern state legislatures approved, blacks who were literate. John Wilkes Booth, who assassinated Lincoln three days later, and his co-conspirator, Lewis Powell, were present.

Booth reportedly said to Powell at that moment, "That means nigger citizenship. Now, by God, I'll put him through. That is the last speech he will ever make."[18] Three days later, Booth killed Lincoln while the president was attending a play at Ford's Theatre in the nation's capital.

Lincoln may have underestimated the extent to which the Confederacy would refuse to accept defeat as a verdict condemning white supremacy. When he issued the dramatic Emancipation Proclamation, Lincoln also began to conceive a plan to reunite and rebuild the country, once the war ended, that would be largely conciliatory toward the Confederates.

In December 1863, the president had issued a generous "Proclamation of Amnesty and Reconstruction" that included three central provisions: (1) Confederate rebels who had not held elected or high positions of leadership would be granted full pardons, and their property, excluding human chattel, would be reinstated. Rebels who had held elected or high leadership positions still could petition for a presidential pardon on their own behalf. (2) All southern states that could demonstrate that at least 10 percent of eligible voters had pledged allegiance to the United States would be readmitted to the Union. (3) Once readmitted, the southern states would have to uphold the provisions of the Emancipation Proclamation and must affirm and protect the liberation of freedmen.[19]

The distinct difficulties in the case of the American Civil War come into focus when we compare the war with violent civil conflict in other locations. The Nigerian Civil War, which lasted from July 1967 to January 1970, took place a full century after the American Civil War. The Nigerian conflict was triggered by the Biafran secession; the U.S. Civil War was triggered by the Confederate secession.

When the Nigerian war ended, the winning side—the side seeking to preserve a unitary Nigeria and opposing the Biafran secession—took a surprisingly magnanimous stance toward the secessionists. This posture, which eased the transition to peacetime with minimal ongoing resistance from the secessionists, may have been a finer moment for Gen. Yakubu Gowon and the victors than the conduct of the war itself.[20]

Four years after the end of Nigeria's twentieth-century civil war, the U.S. State Department sponsored a convening of scholars, primarily from Nigeria and the United States, to compare the two nations' respective civil wars under the heading of the African History Professors Project. The academic phase of the conference was held at the University of Washington in Seattle in July 1974.

One of the major conclusions that emerged from the convening was the idea that the United States had much to learn from the aftermath of the Nigerian Civil War. Had the chronology been reversed, the scholars concluded, the welcoming and general nonpunitive posture of the winning side toward the rebel Biafran secessionists was, ostensibly, a position that would have served the United States well.[21]

But the comparison of the two civil wars and the lessons from the Nigerian conflict are limited. If anything, the north was far *too placatory* toward the southern secessionists in the United States. The American experience must be distinguished from Nigeria's because of the presence, in the United States, of an enslaved population *over whose status the war was fought.* Indeed, by readily adding their intelligence, determination, and bodies to the Union effort, former captives deeply affected the outcome of the war.

The problem was unique to the U.S. context. After preparing to accept sanctions that never materialized, the Confederates unleashed new—and largely unchallenged—assaults on the freedmen. "Reconciliation" would be enacted on their terms and would require smashing the rights and aspirations of black Americans. Rehabilitation of goodwill between the Union and the Confederacy necessitated accommodations made to the south that enabled the establishment of conditions now characterized as "neoslavery."[22]

The victorious north, improbably, granted major concessions to the traitorous Confederacy. The reunification of north and south, on conciliatory terms, meant reasserting the centrality of whiteness as the precondition for American citizenship, despite the language of the Reconstruction-era amendments to the U.S. Constitution.[23]

While Lincoln was not inclined to take a hard line against the secessionists, he was nonetheless willing to contemplate efforts to incorporate the emancipated slaves into full citizenship—two irreconcilable aims. After Lincoln's assassination, his successor, Andrew Johnson, brought the aims of the postwar period into harmony by taking the soft line against the secessionists and trampling black citizenship. He pursued a thoroughgoing accommodation both to the defeated Confederates and to white supremacy.

Much has been made of the fact that Johnson was no enthusiast for the southern planter aristocracy that led the formation of the Confederacy—he had opposed secession—but, perhaps, *too much.* Johnson's hostility toward blacks far outstripped his dislike for the southern elite. He became the key actor of obstruction for full black inclusion in the American polity. In fact, his actions sowed the seeds for the Jim Crow period that followed Reconstruction.[24]

The Radical wing of the Republican Party argued that, at minimum, the *leaders* of the states that had rebelled against the United States of America should be treated as traitors and punished accordingly. Moreover, the Radicals understood that black citizenship could not be achieved unless the secessionists were dealt with harshly. The nation's very existence had been placed on the brink of perdition by the Confederates' determination to safeguard slavery, and tomorrow's horizon remained in danger if they were not disciplined and contained by the Union.

Since the rebels continued to deny equal status for blacks—including resorting to guerilla tactics or renewed outright warfare—the Union would have needed to bear the burden of a durable military presence in the south until the safety and security of the newly freed men and women finally was secure.[25] Scott Malcomson has described "the white South" as already having "rounded on the freed-slave population *even before the war had ended* and soon passed Black Codes intended to keep all blacks, including those free prior to the war, in a subordinate position."[26]

At minimum, if the Union army was to be withdrawn from the south and black rights protected, it would have been necessary for blacks to be armed adequately to act in their own self-defense.

Although Abraham Lincoln was reluctant to do so, the logic of his own constitutional interpretation—that denied the southern states the right of secession—de facto designated the rebels as "traitors." This interpretation, advanced primarily by Daniel Webster and Lincoln himself, treated the Declaration of Independence as one of the core founding documents of the United States. This, in turn, enabled Webster and Lincoln to argue that national authority came from "the people," not "the states." National authority would be exercised by the federal government, and the states would function as subordinate administrative units.[27]

An exit from the Union would require the approval of "the people" represented by Congress. Of course, Congress had the authority to expel any state, but no state had the right to withdraw unilaterally from the Union.[28] Hence, the United States was not seen, as the rebels had it, as a "league of states"; for Lincoln, it was a league of "the people." Correspondingly, Lincoln never saw the states in rebellion as constituting "foreign soil." For him, they were always American soil, albeit under insurrection.[29]

At the emotive level, national pride should dominate sectional pride, and any accommodation to sectional pride would not mean surrender to sectional authority. The national government would have the final word on American policy, with no capacity for nullification on the part of a state government.

The Radicals in Lincoln's party had no compunction about labeling the rebels as traitors. The Radical Republicans were seeking a comprehensive "de-Confederatization" of the American south.[30] "Abolish—Yes! abolish everything on the face of the earth but this Union; free every slave—slay every traitor—burn every rebel mansion, if these things be necessary to preserve this temple of freedom to the world and to our posterity." This was the rallying cry Thaddeus Stevens, the conscience of the Radicals, raised during the speech he gave when he won renomination for his congressional seat in 1862.[31]

Stevens was joined by fellow Radical Republicans Senators Benjamin Wade (R-Ohio) and Ira Harris (R-N.Y.) and Representative Henry Winter Davis (R-Md.) in the drive to impose tougher eligibility requirements on the former Confederate states before they could be readmitted to the Union. The Wade-Davis Bill would have accomplished that goal and potentially eliminated the possibility that members of Confederate officialdom could assume political office during the postwar period.[32]

In the Radical Republicans' view, lifetime exclusion from the political process and a purging of the government, a procedure called "lustration," was a logical step to take after the "greatest difficulty the country had ever experienced . . . or was likely to experience."[33]

Given the horrendous crimes and injustices that had been committed by the secessionists, the bill's supporters reasoned, only drastic steps could reestablish the country's moral order and restore peace. The Wade-Davis Bill passed both the Senate and the House only to be "pocket vetoed" by Lincoln. Although Lincoln affirmed Wade-Davis as "one very proper plan for the loyal people of any state choosing to adopt it," Lincoln did not sign the bill, thereby killing it, and counseled tolerance and cooperation instead.[34]

The president continued to press his offer of compensated emancipation, even as the outcome of the war was becoming increasingly clear in the Union's favor. In February 1865, when the war approached its fourth full year, Lincoln and Secretary of State William Henry Seward met with Confederate vice president Alexander Hamilton Stephens in an attempt to come to an agreement on Confederate surrender (see chapter 5).

Lincoln's offer to minimize additional loss of life, by compensating the slaveholders for removing the shackles from their human captives if they would agree to an armistice, was rejected. Two months after Stephens met with Lincoln at the peace conference, Lee relinquished his command and surrendered, and the war finally ended. *But the Confederate president, Jefferson Davis, never surrendered.* As George Fletcher has noted, "[Davis] was so devoted to the cause that even after Lee's surrender on April 9, 1865, Davis remained defiant. He took his rump government into hiding in the Deep South and was not captured until May 11."[35]

In Thaddeus Stevens's view, only a "radical reorganization of Southern institutions, habits and manners" would bring about the transformation he and others had been advocating over the course of the previous twenty years.[36] During July 1861, in his capacity as chair of the House Ways and Means Committee, Stevens worked to secure passage of "An Act to Confiscate Property Used for Insurrectionary Purposes," which included the human chattel of leaders of the rebellion.

On September 7, 1865, he proposed that the government "confiscate all of the estate of every rebel belligerent whose estate was worth $10,000, or whose land exceeded two hundred acres" but counseled forgiveness for "the poor, ignorant, and [all who were] coerced" to support the Confederacy. Any remaining property could be sold to help defray the Union's war expenses. Stevens estimated that 90 percent of the south's white population would be absolved from this type of penalty under these terms.[37]

Confiscation of larger estates would provide the basis for a redistribution of land to freedmen. Stevens gauged a total of 465 million acres of land across the states forming the Confederacy. He proposed that the bulk of that land, 354 of the 394 million acres owned by elite whites, be sold to the highest bidder to create pensions for veterans, funds to reimburse the "loyal men North and South" for damages incurred during the rebellion. Stevens estimated the freedman population at 4 million (or approximately 1 million families consisting of four individuals) and proposed the government allocate each adult male forty acres for a total of 40 million acres. The remaining 71 million acres consisted of parcels of 200 or fewer acres and would remain in the hands of their prewar owners.[38]

Stevens was unequivocal in his belief that "the whole fabric of Southern society must be changed."[39] For Stevens, land redistribution to freedmen was a critical step in achieving that change—in making Reconstruction succeed. After all, they were released from bondage with virtually no monetary resources of their own, leading Stevens to issue the following stern warning in December 1865:

We have turned, or are about to turn, loose four million slaves without a hut to shelter them or a cent in their pockets. The infernal laws of slavery have prevented them from acquiring an education, understanding the common laws of contract, or of managing the ordinary business of life. This Congress is bound to provide for them until they can take care of themselves. If we do not furnish them with homesteads, and hedge them around with protective laws; if we leave them to the legislation of their late masters, we had better have left them in bondage.[40]

Land reform was a vital plank of the Radicals' vision for Reconstruction. Many also believed that courts-martial were appropriate for some rebels and, in Stevens's words, "could do justice according to law" while helping to "propitiate [pacify] the manes [souls] of our starved, murdered, slaughtered martyrs."[41]

For more than 150 years, American folklore has preserved the tenets of the federal government's promise of reparations to the former slaves: forty acres and a mule.[42] That promise was not a figment of the collective black imagination. Rather, it was the centerpiece of another, even bolder, federal plan. General Sherman's Special Field Orders No. 15 were the directives that first authorized the redistribution of the balance of the landholdings confiscated from or abandoned by Confederates who supported the south against the north during the war—an expanse reaching thirty miles inland from the South Carolina Sea Islands to Florida—to the freedmen.[43]

Sherman's plan had begun to take shape in January 1865—three months before the final battle of the Civil War was fought—when he and Secretary of War Edwin Stanton met in Savannah, Georgia, with twenty black leaders— ministers and church officers, primarily—to discuss the plight of the state's freedmen.[44] The leaders selected former slave and Granville County, North Carolina, native Rev. Garrison Frazier, sixty-seven years of age and a minister for thirty-five years, to be their spokesperson. He had managed to purchase his and his wife's freedom eight years earlier with $1,000 in silver and gold. When asked to define the institution of slavery and state his understanding of the Emancipation Proclamation that President Lincoln had issued January 1, 1863, Reverend Frazier replied: "Slavery is, receiving by irresistible power the work of another man, and not by his consent. The freedom, as I understand it, promised by the proclamation, is taking us from under the yoke of bondage, and placing us where we could reap the fruit of our own labor, take care of ourselves and assist the Government in maintaining our freedom."[45]

When asked how the freedmen proposed to provide a livelihood for themselves, Reverend Frazier responded: "The way we can best take care of ourselves is to have land, and turn it and till it by our own labor—that is, by the labor of the women and children and old men; and we can soon maintain ourselves and have something to spare. And to assist the Government, the young men should enlist in the service of the Government, and serve in such manner as they may be wanted. . . . We want to be placed on land until we are able to buy it and make it our own."[46]

When asked if he preferred to live among whites or solely among blacks, Reverend Frazier indicated that, while he could not speak for the other ministers, he preferred to live among blacks, "for there is a prejudice against us in the South that will take years to get over." When questioned separately, all but one of the ministers—freeborn Baltimore, Maryland, native James Lynch, twenty-six years of age—indicated that they would prefer to live among only other blacks.[47]

Reverend Frazier then gave an astute and nuanced assessment of the rationale Union and Confederate proponents had stated for the Civil War and their actions:

The war was commenced by the Rebels before [President Lincoln] came into office. The object of the war was not at first to give the slaves their freedom, but the sole object of the war was at first to bring the rebellious States back into the Union and their loyalty to the laws of the United States. Afterward, knowing the value set on the slaves by the Rebels, the President thought that his proclamation would stimulate them to lay down their arms, reduce them to obedience, and help to bring back the Rebel States; and their not doing so has now made the freedom of the slaves a part of the war.[48]

The day after his meeting with the ministers, on January 16, 1865, Sherman issued the directives, providing for the immediate settlement of some 18,000 former slave families on confiscated land that had been abandoned by slaveholders along the Atlantic Seaboard. Each family's allocation was to have been forty acres.

Sherman's Special Field Orders No. 15 allotted a continuous thirty-mile-wide band of confiscated land for the exclusive use of the previously enslaved. It stretched across the coast of South Carolina, beginning at Charleston, and extended through Georgia and down to the northern portions of Florida. The distance from "the islands from Charleston south, the abandoned rice-fields along the rivers for thirty miles back from the sea, [to] the country bordering the Saint Johns River, Fla." is 341 miles.[49]

The Florida allotment was bounded by the Atlantic coast and the Saint Johns River, about twenty miles west, which undulates through or runs alongside twelve counties, covering some ninety-five miles. By our calculations, some 1,900 square miles lie between the river and the ocean. Each of those square miles is made up of 640 acres, which means that in Florida alone more than 1,216,000 acres of land would have been available to freedmen.

This unparalleled federal land distribution would have made approximately 5.3 million acres of land in three states available to refugees from the war and to the formerly enslaved. In fact, 40,000 freedmen did settle on 400,000 acres of land.

There appears to be confusion in the historical literature regarding the total amount of land designated under Sherman's orders. Some sources have conflated the 400,000 acres actually settled temporarily by 40,000 freedmen with the much larger total amount specified.[50] *The 400,000-acre figure falls almost 5 million acres short of the full allocation under Special Field Orders No. 15.*

A complete allocation of the full acreage specified in Sherman's orders would have created a vast zone of land occupied by those formerly enslaved—a virtual coastal "Black Belt"—with a uniquely equal foundation for wealth accumulation among the formerly enslaved.[51] While, at least at the outset, this would have been a racially separate community, it would not have been an impoverished community. In fact, the fulfillment of the provision of forty acres and a mule would have demonstrated clearly that segregation and economic inequality are not intrinsically linked.[52] This was the precedent that might have sealed the case for the Radical Republicans' aims for Reconstruction. But, again, this was a critical fork in the American historical road where, once more, the wrong path was taken.

One of Andrew Johnson's first acts as president was to appoint Confederate apologist Francis Harrison Pierpont as Virginia's "counterfeit" governor. Then, in a move that left no doubt about his intentions, Johnson rebuffed the Radical Republicans' call for a special session of Congress to register displeasure with Pierpont's lenient treatment of ex-Confederates. When Congress finally met, frustrated Radical Republicans took steps to prevent the southern congressmen, who had been put into office by all-white electorates, from taking their seats.[53] The Radicals fully understood they would not be able to compel change in the southern political sphere if the unrepentant Confederates were allowed to participate in the legislative process.[54]

In addition to lustration, the extended exclusion of prominent Confederates from political involvement in the reconstructed south, several other actions were considered to alter the southern political landscape.[55] These included the prospect of the creation of tribunals to assess and assign penalties for participation in the secession and trials with the possibility of conviction and execution for officials in the Confederate government and military.

Plans also were considered to redraw state lines to dilute the relative voting strength of the white supremacists. In 1861, a proposal had been advanced to alter the borders of Maryland, Virginia, Delaware, and the District of Columbia. This plan would have divided Virginia roughly in half and assigned the disloyal region consisting of the state's major cities and its coastal zone to Maryland. The western part of the state, the section that was predominantly loyal to the Union, would have continued to have had the designation of "Virginia," and the state of Delaware would have been significantly extended to the south.[56]

This wartime plan, developed by Lincoln's first secretary of war, Simon Cameron, was intended to accomplish multiple goals. Dan Malouf observed that the plan was expected to have "1. Separated the loyalist western parts of Virginia, allowing them to be reintroduced to the Union as a northern state. 2. Punished eastern Virginia, the intellectual and economic heart of the Confederacy, by taking away its independence as a state. 3. Rewarded Maryland and Delaware for remaining in the Union. 4. Protected Washington [D.C.] from having a hostile territory directly across the Potomac."[57]

The Cameron plan suffered from a major weakness. According to Malouf,

In 1861, as Cameron was making this proposal, West Virginia *was already in the process* of splitting off from Virginia to become its own state. How, exactly, to draw its borders and what to call it was a perfectly reasonable question. The most doubtful part of this idea is the notion that new-and-bigger Maryland would be a safe northern state. Although Maryland never seceded, it was a slave state and its loyalty to the Union during the Civil War was *tenuous at best*. Adding the wealthy and populous parts of Virginia to Maryland seems more likely to have drawn Maryland towards the south than vice versa. Presumably that's why the deal would have required Maryland to free its slaves.[58]

Still, the 1861 plan indicates the scope of thought about steps that could have been taken to achieve de-Confederatization. Indeed, legal scholar Edward Rubin has speculated about an alternative configuration of the states that Congress might have adopted to transform the post–Civil War southern political terrain to dilute significantly the solidarity of the Confederate voter base.[59]

The southern racial terrain far too closely resembled its characteristics before the war. The failure of emancipation to produce black citizenship was not solely a matter of what was not done *for* blacks; it was also a matter of what was not done *to* the rebels. We are left only to speculate at what might have been if there had been a thoroughgoing de-Confederatization of the American south.

Lincoln's amnesty plan was designed to reestablish the brotherhood of the divided Union and to hasten the war's end. Johnson initially insisted that harsh punishment should be meted out to the ex-Confederate leaders. As vice president, Andrew Johnson had espoused antislavery views.[60] Less well known, however, was his harshly antiblack viewpoint. Johnson's complete disdain for black Americans would shape his approach to Reconstruction.

Reports detailing the extensive abuses blacks were suffering at the hands of ex-Confederates arrived at the White House by the mail-coach-load. From the convention halls of Louisiana came complaints from free men of color, who previously had enjoyed privileges unheard of in other parts of the south, that members of the planter class and affluent merchants were determined to hold exclusive power and refuse to co-govern with blacks.

Eleven black men from Alabama, who described victims of contract fraud and the absence of due process in the courts, concluded emphatically, "This is not the persuit [sic] of happiness."[61] Johnson's own emissary, Gen. Carl Schurz, the influential German American immigrant leader and journalist, brought back overwhelming evidence of widespread violence against blacks, the lack of accountability in local justice systems, and blacks' impoverished living conditions.

He and other northerners who had traveled across the south had come away with similar impressions. When they inquired about engaging newly freed black laborers, white southerners would counter that the visitors "do not understand the character of the negro." Blacks, they insisted, were undisciplined and would not work unless they were threatened with bodily harm. Even the "offer of more or less money" would not be a sufficient motivator, according to a Louisiana planter.[62]

Immediately after the surrender, when the ex-Confederates had been brought down by their defeat, there was a propitious moment. From fall 1865 to early 1866, many Americans—blacks and whites, northerners and southerners—expected significant penalties to be imposed on the states formerly in rebellion as a condition for their readmission to the Union.

When Whitelaw Reid traveled along the Atlantic coast and spoke with a cross-section of residents, including shopkeepers, black artisans, farmers and planters, Freedmen's Bureau agents and officers, and freedmen in urban and rural areas, and toured several cotton plantations, he observed, "It was manifest that if restoration of civil authority depended on negro suffrage it would be accepted." Schurz's report to Johnson concluded, "When the news of Lee's and [Joseph] Johnston's surrenders burst upon the Southern country, the general consternation was extreme. . . . The public mind was so despondent that if readmission at some future time, under whatever conditions had been promised, it would have been looked upon as a favor."[63] Here was the ideal moment to push forward for the full array of black rights.

But when Johnson opened the door for North Carolina to reorganize its state government without making provisions for blacks' political rights and followed that with pardons and paroles for "prominent, wealthy insurgents," ex-Confederate leaders, generals, and diplomats, southerners understood "the President was willing to concede to them more power than they had dared hope." Almost immediately after Johnson's proclamation was announced, white southerners' resistance to black voting and civil liberties began to harden. Gen. John W. Sprague wrote of the mood he observed in Little Rock, Arkansas, "Those who had returned from the rebel armies were the most quiet and orderly, it is not so now."[64] Increasingly, southern whites were observed treating freedmen with "cruelty and callousness."[65]

To many, it appeared that the Union was at risk of "losing the war during the peace." When black Union private Calvin Holly was assigned to the Freedmen's Bureau's Mississippi branch in December 1865, he wrote to bureau commissioner Gen. Oliver O. Howard that blacks there were "in a great many ways being outraged upon beyound humanity." He had observed women and children whose homes were "tourn down from over the[ir] heads," the bodies of two black women with their throats slit found along the road to Jackson, and a church that had been burned to the ground. "The Rebbles are going a bout in many places through the State and robbing the colered pe[o]ple of arms money and all they have and in many places killing."[66]

Private Holly advised General Howard of the need to act forcibly to restore order: "The safety of this country depenes upon giving the Colered man all the rights of the white man, and especially the Rebs, and let him know that [there] is power enough in the arm of the Government to give Justice, to all her loyal citizens." Holly and others believed that passing laws that would restore order and "give protection to the colered man and meet out Justice to traters in arms" would be the obvious and most effective course of action.[67]

The rights of the freedmen going forward were absent from Andrew Johnson's plan, and the former rebels were returning to power in record numbers with impunity. Lincoln's radical agenda for economic justice was cast aside. Seceded states were required to meet only four conditions: call a statewide convention, abolish slavery, nullify all secession ordinances, and repudiate—that is, make it illegal to pay—Confederate war debt with state funds.

South Carolina's choice for provisional governor was Benjamin F. Perry, a lawyer from Greenville and a Union conservative who had killed a nullificationist in a duel and subsequently served as a district court judge under the Confederacy.[68] As early as 1832, South Carolinians who opposed a series of federal tariffs advocated "nullification" on the ground that the tariffs violated state sovereignty and, as such, were unconstitutional and unenforceable. After the war, the state was not penalized when it refused to repudiate its war debt, and New Jersey, Delaware, Kentucky, and Mississippi rejected the Thirteenth Amendment outright.[69]

The Radical Republicans had thought Johnson's bar for readmission dangerously low. Now they would see the extent to which his hands-off policy provided a cover for a host of legal measures the formerly seceded states could enact to establish near-slavery conditions for blacks and erode the Republican Party's political power.

In his 1866 inaugural address, newly elected Texas governor, James W. Throckmorton, acknowledged that the state had "just emerged from the most terrible conflict known to modern times, with homes made dreary and desolate by the heavy hand of war." Publicly, Throckmorton struck a conciliatory tone, pledging to work to "insure exact justice to all classes of men, of every political faith, religious creed, race and color." While he recognized that the "changed relations, so suddenly brought about" would require "much thoughtful consideration," the governor appeared to accept those reforms not solely because they were inevitable but also, he said, because "it is a duty we owe alike to ourselves and to humanity, to enact laws that will secure the freed people the full protection of all the rights of person and property guaranteed them by our Amended Constitution."[70]

In fact, he was lenient with the former Confederates and turned a blind eye when Union generals Philip Sheridan, Joseph Barr Kiddoo, and Charles Griffin repeatedly implored him to provide adequate protection to blacks and Freedmen's Bureau agents located in the northern part of the state. By the time the members of Texas's Eleventh Legislature began their deliberations, there was "little tendency toward the justice and charity called for by Throckmorton." Legislators opted, instead, for the position of arch-secessionist senator Oran M. Roberts, who retaliated against members of the Union and restricted the activities of ex-slaves. When Throckmorton did nothing to counter these actions, Sheridan eventually would remove him from office.[71]

No longer "quiet and peaceable, disposed to submit to almost anything" after the war ended, whites in the Shenandoah Valley also had slowly begun to comprehend that there would be no consequences for secession, for the Civil War itself, or for the nation's loss of more than 600,000 lives. Once solemn and expecting no mercy from the government, southerners who had prepared to take their punishment were emboldened by their protection from imprisonment and displacement. Assurance that their fears would not be realized did not soften their positions on black rights. Quite the contrary, "the more lenient the government, the more arrogant they became." Indeed, many southerners "found . . . the policy of the President of the United States" very much to their liking.[72]

That Johnson had let his plan for readmitting the states that had been in rebellion collapse confounded even his assistant, Gen. Reuben D. Mussey. How had the administration lost not one but two chances to bring about radical change? "It seems to me that we had the opportunity when Lee surrendered and more than that when Lincoln was assassinated to make our own terms."[73]

It is indeed the case that even some of the highest-ranked ex-Confederates anticipated that giving blacks the vote and the right to own arable land was inevitable. The former secretary of the Confederacy, Christopher Memminger, said as much in his 1871 letter to Schurz: "I think you are right in saying that if we had originally adopted a different course as to the negroes, we would have escaped present difficulties. But if you will consider a moment, you will see that it was as impossible, as for us to have emancipated them before the war. The then President [Andrew Johnson] held up before us the hope of a 'white man's government,' and this led us to set aside negro suffrage."[74] Again, if ever there was a moment when the nation could have made a dramatic leap forward, it was in the days and months immediately after the war concluded.

President Johnson seemed to have been fantasizing in 1865 when he wired South Carolina governor Benjamin Perry, "I trust in God that restoration of the Union will not now be defeated, and all that has so far been well done thrown away. I still have faith that all will come out right yet."[75] While he claimed to be hoping for the best, Johnson actually was taking steps to hamstring the freedmen. The nullification of Sherman's order and the general denial of the confiscated and abandoned land that had been allocated to blacks along the Gulf coast made it abundantly clear to blacks and their allies that they could not expect any relief from the government.

Johnson's Reconstruction plan impeded the Radical Republicans' efforts to guarantee the rights of the ex-slaves, and it allowed ex-Confederates to regain control of the state governments. After repeated attempts to reverse Johnson's intractability failed, members of the Republican Party resolved to impeach the president. In February 1868, Johnson was impeached in the U.S. House of Representatives; however, he was acquitted of all charges because the Senate lacked the supermajority necessary for conviction. Though the president emerged from the hearings effectively powerless, he had already done irreparable damage to the nation's future.[76]

By far, the greatest protection for freedmen living in the south was afforded by the Union army. Beginning in 1867, during the period of Radical Reconstruction, two crucial measures were ratified despite substantial resistance from both the north and the south—the Fourteenth Amendment, which broadened the definition of citizenship and granted "equal protection" to former slaves, and the Fifteenth Amendment, which guaranteed that a citizen's right to vote could not be denied "on account of race, color, or previous condition of servitude." Troops stationed in each of the five military districts provided protection, and blacks voted in state and congressional elections for the first time in the nation's history.

Despite the optimism engendered by passage of the amendments, the period also saw rapid escalation of organized white supremacist savagery against the freedmen.[77] Many Radical Republicans looked to Johnson's successor, Ulysses S. Grant, for the kind of sustained change that would be necessary if blacks were to become full-fledged citizens.

Between 1870 and 1875, President Grant sent federal troops to put down the Ku Klux Klan and other white terrorist groups in North Carolina, South Carolina, Louisiana, and Vicksburg, Mississippi: The Republican Party carried Mississippi in 1874 but lost badly in August in Vicksburg, after the Democratic Party used intimidation, arson, and murder. Grant's evolving response to white vigilante violence aimed at suppressing blacks' civil rights is discussed in detail in chapter 9. "Violence had made it virtually impossible for Republicans to campaign or vote in large parts of Georgia." In Alabama, waves of white terrorism shut down the black vote. By 1871, Foner writes, "the Klan [had] devastated the Republican organization in many local communities," and activists were "scattered and beaten and run out." Hundreds of black-rights advocates were murdered. "They have no leaders up there—no leaders" in Union County, South Carolina, a freedman reported.[78]

As Scott Malcomson has observed, by the early 1870s, the die had been cast; white rule and terror were, indefinitely, on the horizon:

For a time it appeared that some Northern whites, particularly the radical Reconstructionists, would, in league with blacks, north and south, be able to force through a legal structure that would guarantee the basic civil rights of black people. . . . Blacks did indeed gain [formal] citizenship rights, against great resistance (and not only in the South).

They did not get much more, and in the course of the 1870s even the right to vote was steadily whittled away. Blacks were killed in large numbers after the war and would continue to be killed well into the twentieth century because of their skin color. Into the 1870s whites fought blacks in countless small battles, particularly at election time, [in order to] consolidate . . . white power.[79]

The Reconstruction era officially ended with the so-called Compromise of 1877. During the contested presidential election of 1876, only Florida and Louisiana, with significant numbers of black voters, and South Carolina, with a majority black population, remained under Republican control. Democratic candidate Samuel J. Tilden, who had received the majority of the popular vote and the uncontested electoral votes, abided by his party's decision to concede the race to Republican candidate Rutherford B. Hayes, in exchange for an agreement to grant the Democratic party control of the formerly seceded states. This compromise would return the ex-Confederates to congressional power for the first time since 1852 and, critically for black Americans, withdraw federal troops from the south without any provisions to arm the freedmen.

An ex-Confederate officer, reflecting on the ambitions of the resurrected Confederacy, characterized them thusly: "To defy the reconstructed State Governments, to treat them with contempt, and show that they have no real existence." Blacks and their white allies were left to fend for themselves as one massacre after another destroyed the Reconstruction leadership's ranks.[80]

After 1877, blacks were left fully exposed to white supremacist brutality and armed domination. The consequences were palpable in the enormous death toll resulting from white murders of blacks throughout the south. In 1895, black Civil War hero and postwar South Carolina congressional representative Robert Smalls (1875–87), reported that a stunning 53,000 blacks had been killed by white terrorists since the end of the war. This was equivalent to 1,766 murders annually, or five per day.[81] Reconstruction had been overthrown violently, and the promise of emancipation lay in the tragic ruins of reconciliation between the white north and the white south.

9

Seven Mystic Years (1866–1873)

It may be true that the law can't change the heart, but it can restrain the heartless. —Martin Luther King Jr., "Remaining Awake during a Revolution," 1968

For a brief period—for the seven mystic years that stretched between [Andrew] Johnson's "Swing Around the Circle" to the Panic of 1873, the majority of thinking Americans in the North believed in the equal manhood of Negroes. They acted accordingly with a thoroughness and clean-cut decision that no age which does not share that faith can in the slightest comprehend. . . . They simply recognized black folk as men. "The South called for war," said James Russell Lowell, "and we have given it to her. We will fix the terms of peace ourselves, and we will teach the South that Christ is disguised in a dusky race."

   Then came in 1873–1876 sudden and complete disillusion not at Negroes but at the world—at business, at work, at religion, at art. A bitter protest of Southern property reenforced Northern reaction; and while after long years the American world recovered in most matters, it has never quite understood why it could ever have thought that black men were altogether human. —W. E. B. Du Bois, *Black Reconstruction in America*, 1935

If any people have a divine right to these tropical lands, they are the slaves who have bought them, over and over, by their sweat and toil and blood, through centuries of oppression. . . . Had I the power I would give a free home on the forfeited land of rebels to every bondman in the insurrectionary districts. . . . Let the Government, which has so long connived at his oppression, now make sure to him a free homestead on the land of his oppressor. Let us deal justly with the African, and thereby lay claim to justice for ourselves. —George Washington Julian, "Homesteads for Soldiers on Lands of Rebels," 1864

No more auction block for me, no more, no more. Many thousand gone.
No more hundred lash for me, no more, no more . . .
No more peck o' corn for me, no more, no more . . .
No more pint o' salt, no more, no more . . .
No more mistress's call for me, no more, no more. Many thousand gone.
—Classic song of the enslaved

W. E. B. Du Bois coined the phrase "seven mystic years" to mark the all-too-brief period, from 1866 to 1873, when the Republican majority swept the midterm elections and erected a new scaffolding for the United States of America. In short order, the Radicals established the Bureau of Refugees, Freedmen, and Abandoned Lands and passed the Fourteenth and Fifteenth Amendments to the U.S. Constitution. Taken together with the Thirteenth Amendment, these Reconstruction Amendments recast blacks as American citizens with rights and protections previously available only to whites. It was an unprecedented moment in the nation's history, a moment when the federal government's political strategies and military aims were directed at ending the unequal status of blacks.

However, President Lincoln did not live to see these changes take place. His successor, Andrew Johnson, put forth his own Reconstruction plan and, once again, changed the course of history, diverting it back to the familiar path of racial inequality.

The election of avowed antislavery advocate Abraham Lincoln in 1860 as chief executive of the republic, coupled with the Republican Party's dominance in the U.S. House and Senate, fueled the fire of secession in the slaveholding states. At that point, apart from Connecticut, every New England state had granted black Americans equal suffrage with whites. For many southerners, the right to enslave black people was both a pocketbook issue and a matter of stubborn principle. For them, the assumption that all men, black or white, stood on equal footing was "fundamentally wrong."[1]

Voicing a sentiment echoed across the south, Mississippi's Confederate States of America delegation wrote, "Our position is thoroughly identified with the institution of slavery—the greatest material interest of the world. Its labor supplies the product which constitutes by far the largest and most important portions of commerce of the earth."[2] The declarations of President Lincoln and Radical members of the Republican Party to the contrary, the widely held belief that slavery was not only natural but essential was not to be dislodged easily.

As war casualties mounted on both sides, Lincoln began to lay groundwork for rebuilding formerly Confederate-controlled southern states that had been reconquered by Union forces. Readmission to the Union would not be automatic or without political costs. The multistep proclamation Lincoln introduced in December 1863 to bring the eleven states in secession back into the Union required those states to demonstrate a dramatic change in their political posture, and critically, it required them to outlaw slavery.

Pardons, with some exceptions, would be extended to all Confederates who would swear their allegiance to the Union. Only after a Union-controlled state affirmed that 10 percent of its eligible voters during the 1860 election had taken the loyalty oath could it hold a constitutional convention and organize a state government. Chief among the states' mandates was the abolition of slavery; however, the demands, at that stage, did not include black suffrage. Once these criteria were met, the states in compliance would be recognized by the chief executive and readmitted to the Union.

Arkansas had much to gain from the process. The state had wrestled with the question of secession in statewide conventions, held in February and May 1861, before formally joining the insurgency and, subsequently, had suffered major losses at the Battle of Helena and the Battle of Little Rock in July and September 1863, respectively.[3] The state took a major step toward rejoining the Union in April 1864, when wealthy paper manufacturer Isaac Murphy, the lone dissenter in Arkansas's call for secession, was elected governor with Lincoln's approval.[4]

The Civil War upended America's social order. When the war ended in 1865, the nation had prevailed over the individual states as the supreme governing body, paving the way for the country's 4 million newly liberated enslaved persons to join the ranks of free blacks—the latter some 500,000 people in 1860. The war had altered the nation's path, but tomorrow's contours were not clear. Lincoln's aims for Reconstruction were evolving and the political process now had two fundamental goals: the democratization of the political process by inclusion of the ex-slaves and the provision of economic opportunities for the freedmen to own land.

Although he had authorized the Port Royal Experiment in South Carolina, which provided a trial for black landholding, Lincoln was silent about a distribution of land to the freedmen in his final address. Still, he had not reversed General Sherman's order allocating land to ex-slaves along the Atlantic coast (discussed in detail in chapter 8), and he did not speak negatively about such a policy.

Regardless, heretofore no chief executive of the United States had affirmed any rights of black Americans. Politicians wasted no time voicing reactions to this unprecedented directive, ranging from jubilant support to raging damnation. But apart from the short "seven mystic years" of Reconstruction, from the date of Lincoln's murder until the passage of the Voting Rights Act a century later in 1965, his plan would be ignored.[5]

Part of the failure to carry out Lincoln's proposal was the lack of a united front within the Republican Party. The wing of the Republican Party that was committed to legal rights for blacks, known as the Radical Republicans, had thought Lincoln's Proclamation of Amnesty and Reconstruction dangerously lenient and that it undermined the sacrifices northerners had made to preserve the Union.

In 1861, Congressman Thaddeus Stevens, a Pennsylvania Whig turned Know-Nothing and eventual Republican, together with other members of the party's Radical faction, fought to secure passage of an act to confiscate the property of affluent rebels—including enslaved persons—and advocated legislation to emancipate those enslaved and to redistribute "not more than forty acres" of confiscated Confederate land to each family of freed slaves. Importantly, the Radical Republicans authorized the creation of the Freemen's Bureau while imploring Lincoln to execute "a more vigorous prosecution of the war."[6]

Southern Democrats were incredulous and incensed by the president's call for new governmental leadership in the seceded states and by his support for the freedmen—4 million of whom lived in the south. Deep in debt, their coerced labor system and way of life shattered, many former Confederates ignored the president's mandate and focused instead on reestablishing the old regime. Shared governance with blacks was not on their agenda.

Andrew Johnson's political career began in 1829, when he was elected one of the town aldermen of Greeneville, Tennessee. A gifted orator, he became known on the larger Tennessee stage in 1831, when he addressed the state convention after the Nat Turner Rebellion and argued successfully that the rights of free blacks should be curtailed further. While Johnson was an avowed friend of small farmers and merchants, he was no champion of black rights, nor did he support antislavery legislation. He was elected to the U.S. Senate after serving as governor of Tennessee from 1853 to 1857.

The Civil War had a profound effect on Johnson, temporarily moving him toward the ideals of the Republican Party. He broke with the Democrats when Tennessee seceded from the Union in 1861, and he became the lone southern senator to refuse to join the Confederacy.[7]

By winter's end 1862, Union forces had recaptured many former Confederate strongholds. Lincoln, determined to retain control of the south, appointed military governors to fill the leadership void left by the fleeing rebels, and in March 1862, against the advice of several leading Republicans, Johnson became the first to receive an assignment.

Later, several Republicans opposed Johnson's nomination as Lincoln's vice president. Among the more prominent was Robert Jefferson Breckinridge, Presbyterian minister, education czar from Kentucky, and the presiding officer at the National Union Party's 1864 convention in Baltimore.

Breckinridge was an outlier in his family, a slaveholder who came to oppose slavery, unlike several of his relatives, including John C. Breckinridge, a one-time U.S. vice president who subsequently served as the last secretary of war for the Confederacy.[8]

Republicans changed the political organization's name to the Union Party on the national ticket to signal its intention to preserve a coalition that also included abolitionists, Whigs, and American Know-Nothings.[9] Another opponent was Thaddeus Stevens, the fiery leader of the House of Representatives from Pennsylvania's Ninth District, who warned the party that embracing a man from "one of those damned rebel provinces" was a mistake. The convention did not put black suffrage in its platform.[10]

Lincoln's sustained confidence in Johnson may have been borne of the latter's performance as Tennessee's provisional chief executive. Johnson operated with an iron fist even as Confederate forces relentlessly attacked the state by "raiding, cutting rail lines, blowing up bridges and railroad tunnels" and by interrupting Federal correspondence. During the three years he served in this interim capacity, Johnson unseated state officials who continued to push for secession; shuttered newspapers hostile to the Union; arrested critics of the president, including Nashville mayor Richard B. Cheatham, ex-governor Neill S. Brown, and several ministers; and heavily taxed the planter class—even as his own property, including his slaves, was confiscated.[11]

Lincoln's appointee never wavered in his loyalty toward the Union, but he was not a supporter of black rights. Early in his term, when told that northern Unionists opposed slavery because it unjustly robbed the bondsmen and bondswomen of their rights, Johnson countered angrily, "Damn the negroes! I am fighting these traitorous aristocrats, their masters." He added, "I believe slaves should be in subordination and I will live and die so believing."[12]

However, that summer, he modified his stance, saying, "I believe indeed that the Union is the only protection of slavery—its sole guarantee. . . . But if you persist in forcing the issue of slavery against the Government, I say in the face of Heaven, 'Give me my Government and let the negroes go!'"[13] Two years later, despite concerns about Johnson's lack of decisiveness regarding black rights and his prior Democratic Party affiliation, delegates at the National Union Party convention overwhelmingly supported his nomination as Lincoln's running mate.

Vice presidential candidate Johnson's verbal support of black rights was never stronger than in a speech he made one month before the 1864 national election to "[address] a torchlight crowd of blacks in Nashville,

Tennessee." The Emancipation Proclamation, he said, possibly with calculated dishonesty, "left [many of you] in bondage. . . . I, Andrew Johnson, do hereby proclaim freedom to every man in Tennessee!" He added, "I invoke the colored people to be orderly and law-abiding, but at the same time let them assert their rights, and if traitors and ruffians attack them, while in the discharge of their duties, let them defend themselves as all men have a right to do." Referring to himself as the biblical Moses, candidate Johnson told those assembled, "I will . . . lead you through the Red Sea of war and bondage to a fairer future of liberty and peace. . . . I speak now as one who feels the world his country, and all who love equal rights his friends."[14]

The defeated Confederate states' responses to the Reconstruction mandate varied greatly. In January 1865, Congress formally abolished slavery with the passage of the Thirteenth Amendment. In the interim, the federal government opened the Bureau of Refugees, Freedmen, and Abandoned Lands in March 1865—scheduled to be in existence for one year—headed by Union army general Oliver O. Howard. The bureau's assignment was to assist black and white refugees.

A month later, while the country was still trying to make sense of the epic changes that had taken place, Lincoln, in what would prove to be his last address, praised the electorate of the "heretofore slave state" of Louisiana for taking a brave and unprecedented stand and "giving the benefit of public schools equally to black and white, and empowering the Legislature to confer the elective franchise upon the colored man."[15] Thus, the standards for readmission to the Union now also included authorizing the state legislature to give the vote to black men in local, gubernatorial, and congressional elections, to hold free elections, and to provide equal access to public education for black and white children.[16]

In the wake of relentlessly contested battles fought across the south lay vast stretches of cratered fields, walls, and fences; demolished bridges, canals, and loading docks; pulverized lumber mills and factories, homes, farm buildings, and machinery; and ravaged livestock. Agricultural production was reduced severely, not least because the centuries-old plantation labor system had vanished abruptly. Black men—mostly from the south—accounted for some 40,000 of the 365,000 Union dead, and nearly 300,000 whites had died for the Confederate cause.

Now that slavery had ended, whites would be obliged to negotiate wages with blacks, a process many resented. One correspondent from a prosperous Georgia family, Fanny Andrews, wrote, "It seems humiliating to be compelled to bargain and haggle with our own servants about wages."[17]

How was the south to pick up the pieces and knit together a new social and economic fabric that would put it on the path to recovery?

Throughout 1865, there was tremendous disagreement about what rights, if any, would be granted to blacks. At stake was the extent to which southern white elected officials could be forced to accept federal Reconstruction reform measures and to govern jointly with blacks. Now no longer the property of whites, the freedmen had been emancipated by law. The ratification of the Thirteenth Amendment in January 1865 had blocked whites' ability to continue to compel blacks to provide them with unpaid labor. Nor could black freedom of movement be policed in the direct ways it had been under slavery. These were profound changes that had huge repercussions on the daily lives and fortunes of both blacks and whites.

During the brief window of Republican domination of southern state legislatures, blacks exercised a profound influence on public policy. Reconstruction-era legislatures introduced public funding for schooling and the goal of access to schooling for all, authorized the use of public funds for infrastructure development, established fairer systems of taxation, and promoted the general rebuilding of the devastated landscape in the south. Their mission, effectively, was to create a public sector in the southern states. Nevertheless, the story of Reconstruction has been reduced to a story of exceptional corruption and black "misrule" by proponents of the "Lost Cause."[18]

These slavery apologists perverted the record of Reconstruction and the Civil War to bury the white terror campaign and accompanying rivers of black blood. Lost Cause organizations like the United Daughters of the Confederacy (UDC) have ensured that the murderous actions of the "redeemers" and the Confederacy's cause are portrayed as a matter of principled heroism.

The project of producing *dismemory*—organized and systematic efforts to manipulate and distort the nation's history—began immediately after the cessation of the Civil War. As early as 1866, the term "Lost Cause" first appeared in the title of *The Lost Cause: A New Southern History of the War of the Confederates* by popular *Richmond Examiner* war editor Edward A. Pollard.[19] Reputedly, in April 1865, Confederate major Sidney Alroy Jonas penned the poem "Something Too Good to Be Lost" on the back of a $500 Confederate note. The poem, essentially a paean to the travails of Confederate finances, was written shortly before Jonas's discharge after Gen. Joseph Johnston surrendered to General Sherman at Bennett Place in Durham, North Carolina. In 1872, Jonas's poem was accessioned by the Library of Congress on a plaque titled "The Lost Cause."[20]

Plessy v. Ferguson, the 1896 U.S. Supreme Court decision affirming the legality of separate public spaces and conveyances for blacks and whites as long as those accommodations are equal in quality, appears to have motivated the largest sustained spike of activities.[21] The 1900–1920 wave of dismemory projects included erecting Confederate monuments, many of them placed on courthouse grounds; naming schools, streets, and military bases after rebel officers; and lobbying for Confederate holidays. Seven states, including North Carolina, honor the rebel defeat today. More than 1,500 Confederate monuments existed in the United States in 2016; the top six states were Virginia (223), Texas (178), Georgia (174), North Carolina (140), Mississippi (131), and South Carolina (112).[22]

The facts of enslavement, the early and sustained efforts of black abolitionists, and even the voices of dissenting whites were suppressed in favor of the discriminatory policies of the UDC's persistent and ongoing efforts not only to erect monuments and historical markers to the Lost Cause but to conduct genealogical research to document the lives of Confederate Civil War veterans and to lobby states to build archives that would become repositories for the men's stories.

Related key tactics, practiced to the present, included the manufacturing of false textbook narratives about the incompetence of Reconstruction-era southern state governments—when black political influence held sway—and the sanitization of the central role of human enslavement as a cause of the Civil War. The "revisionist" history phase of the dismemory project came into full flower in the 1890s:

> Many white southerners sought to impart the proper lessons within the privacy of their own homes. By the end of the nineteenth century, Charlestonian Mary Esther Huger had become frustrated by her granddaughter's ignorance of the conflict between North and South. "She had never any reason given for the civil war, except that the Southerners had Negro slaves, & the Northerners thought they ought to be made free," explained Huger. So she wrote her own narrative of the Civil War. Others made a point of directing Lost Cause appeals directly to the southern youth. "My young friends who have grown up since the war, educated from modern histories (so called) I commend this especially to you," proclaimed Cornelius Irvine Walker in his 1900 Memorial Day address at Magnolia Cemetery [in Charleston, South Carolina]. Walker believed that it was older southerners' duty to preserve the memory of Confederate heroes and martyrs for the benefit of "the younger generation, who

should be taught that their fathers fought a good fight, in a pure cause, and fought it well."[23]

Historian Jacquelyn Dowd Hall describes how affluent white women pressured school districts to replace their history textbooks with pro-Confederacy tomes written by authors sanctioned by the UDC. The UDC approved textbooks that romanticized the cause of the Confederacy, depicted blacks as servile happy-go-lucky creatures whose highest aspiration was doing the bidding of their "owners," and omitted the voices of whites who were critical of the Lost Cause narratives.[24] Charles Dew, who was born in 1937 and is the author of the fascinating and disturbing memoir *The Making of a Racist*, writes about being given a copy of *The Confederate First Reader* when he was a child and being quizzed about its contents and significance.[25]

Catherine Bishir has made the following keen observation on the deliberate and calculated nature of Lost Cause memorialization: "By putting in permanent public form a single version of the past, the creators of these monuments laid lasting claim to their definition of the past and set the terms by which they meant to shape the future."[26] They sought, with great success, to ensure that the memory of the Confederacy and its leadership was an object of veneration instead of an object of shame.

At the federal level, the Freedmen's Bureau, as the government's relief agency came to be called, was operated by the War Department and tasked with shepherding the formerly enslaved to freedom on a fast track. The bureau was charged with providing food, clothing, and fuel to those in need within Union lines and with the "control of all subjects relating to refugees and freedmen." A key strategy for black economic prosperity involved grants to "loyal refugees and freedmen," forty-acre grants drawn from land that came into the possession of the U.S. government via desertion by their former owners, appropriation, or direct purchase.[27]

Receiving a land allotment and gaining the use of a mule—highly valued agricultural livestock championed for its versatility and hardiness—in the aftermath of the Civil War would have dramatically reversed black asset poverty and reduced blacks' economic vulnerability across generations. No such grant would be made to the formerly enslaved.

The vision of an enfranchised landholding black citizenry was more than the southern white majority could bear. Not only were the freedmen denied the total allotment of land specified under Sherman's Special Field Orders No. 15; they were not permitted to retain the initial Sea Islands acreage, which would have been the first step toward delivery of a land grant.

The ex-slaves explicitly linked access to land with freedom and even expressed their willingness to pay whatever amount the government demanded to preserve ownership of their respective forty acres.[28] Nevertheless, President Johnson dispatched Gen. Oliver O. Howard, commissioner of the Freedmen's Bureau, to the region to inform the ex-slaves that the land was to be returned to the former slaveholders. Howard, a dedicated advocate for the well-being of formerly enslaved blacks, had done his best to resist restoration of the land to its previous owners; now he was charged with undertaking a task that he later described as one of the worst missions he ever had to conduct in his lifetime.[29] The restoration of the coastal zone lands to their former owners fueled a momentum that led the families of the major slaveholders to nearly recover their wealth within a generation.[30]

When the Radical Republicans succeeded in having a revised Freedmen's Bureau Bill approved March 3, 1865, it included an unenforced provision for land allocation that appears to have its precedent in the language of Sherman's Special Field Orders No. 15. The Freedmen's Bureau Bill read, in part:

> And be it further enacted, That the commissioner, under the direction of the President, shall have authority to set apart, for the use of loyal refugees and freedmen, such tracts of land within the insurrectionary states as shall have been abandoned, or to which the United States shall have acquired title by confiscation or sale, or otherwise, and to every male citizen, whether refugee or freedman, as aforesaid, there shall be assigned not more than forty acres of such land, and the person to whom it was so assigned shall be protected in the use and enjoyment of the land for the term of three years at an annual rent not exceeding six per centum upon the value of such land, as it was appraised by the state authorities in the year eighteen hundred and sixty, for the purpose of taxation, and in case no such appraisal can be found, then the rental shall be based upon the estimated value of the land in said year, to be ascertained in such manner as the commissioner may by regulation prescribe. At the end of said term, or at any time during said term, the occupants of any parcels so assigned may purchase the land and receive such title thereto as the United States can convey, upon paying therefore the value of the land, as ascertained and fixed for the purpose of determining the annual rent aforesaid.[31]

The battle over the possession of land in the war-torn southern states was fierce. Wealthy whites had lost their property—land and human chattel—and the control of their government. In the ensuing chaos when so much was unsettled, all strata of whites were eager to exact punishment for the war's outcome; the freedmen were an easy and obvious target. White supremacists in the former Confederate states lost no time in mobilizing both legal and extralegal efforts aimed at curbing black rights and protecting their own self-interest.

While Lincoln was alive, Congress had sought to extend and strengthen the president's Reconstruction plan without success. In February 1864, the Republican-led Congress passed the Wade-Davis Bill, which introduced an ironclad loyalty oath and would have raised the minimum number of eligible white voters required to take the oath from Lincoln's 10 percent to 50 percent before the state could rejoin the Union. The bill also would have given blacks the right to vote. Vice President Johnson's endorsement of Lincoln's decision to let the Wade-Davis Bill die may have been another foreshadowing of his preference for the Confederates over the freedmen.

Vice President Johnson had entreated Lincoln to punish the rebels. In a speech given after the fall of Richmond, which signaled the end of the war, he sounded like a Radical Republican when he said, "I would arrest the [high-ranking Confederates]; I would try them; I would convict them." Johnson seemed to recognize, fleetingly, the need for what we call de-Confederatization: "Death is too easily a punishment. . . . Treason must be made odious, and traitors must be punished and impoverished, their social power broken; . . . they must be made to feel the penalty of their crimes."[32] But within one month of his swearing-in ceremony, President Johnson— largely acting independently of Congress—implemented a fundamentally divergent Reconstruction plan, calling for the elimination of the loyalty oath quota and weakening the states' obligation to protect the new, liberated status of the ex-slaves.

In an affront to the Radical Republicans, Johnson announced his intention to restore all but the highest civil and diplomatic officers of the Confederacy to the Union. He also asserted explicitly that states' rights trumped congressional authority, thereby entrusting the question of black suffrage to the individual states and to the executive office, and affirmed that white supremacy must be upheld.[33] "This is a country for white men," Johnson wrote to Governor Thomas C. Fletcher of Missouri, "and by God, as long as I am President, it shall be a government for white men."[34]

Over the next eight months, when Congress was not in session, Johnson installed provisional governors in eight of the former Confederate states and authorized them to hold constitutional conventions, conduct public elections, and ratify the Thirteenth Amendment to the Constitution.[35] Then, toward the end of the summer of 1866, Johnson conducted a national tour called Swing Around the Circle to tout his plan, thinking Republican voters would side with him. His miscalculation resulted in a loss of political power within the party and set the stage for his impeachment trial.[36]

Johnson let the south's provisional governors know he would not interfere with their efforts to make white supremacy the centerpiece of their political structure. He declined to challenge the Black Codes' statutes, and he refused to compel southern whites to accept former slaves as citizens. Johnson also was willing to grant amnesty to former Confederate officers on extremely lenient terms. By May 1865, he had freed virtually all persons who had been charged with treason by military tribunals: "A presidential Proclamation of Authority offered pardons to all who had participated, directly or indirectly, in 'the existing rebellion,' with full restitution of property rights—except of course slaves—on the taking of an oath by such people that they would 'henceforth' support and defend the Constitution and abide by the laws of the reunited land."[37]

He began to roll out amnesty proclamations to the states, beginning with North Carolina and Mississippi, in May and June 1865, respectively. Further, in a move calculated to appeal to his working-class constituents, Johnson also called for the seizure of former rebels' taxable property valued at or above $20,000 and redistribution of that property to small-scale white farmers, artisans, and merchants.

Johnson's amnesty declaration rendered section 4 of the Freedmen's Bureau Act of 1865 null and void, making it impossible for ex-slaves and loyal white refugees to rent up to forty acres with an option to purchase the land and then receive the title. He accepted rebel requests for the restoration of their seized property.

Apart from the abolition of slavery, Johnson's plan for Reconstruction made absolutely no provisions for blacks. Across the south, elected officials interpreted his liberal Confederate pardon policy—and the plan's glaring absence of language affirming blacks' right to vote, own land, educate their children, and engage in labor contracts of their choosing—to mean blacks had no rights that whites need respect. In essence, Johnson had executed a full restoration of the principles that prevailed at the time of the Dred Scott decision.[38]

By September 1865, Johnson had decreed that fourteen classes of Confederates—eight more than Lincoln had privileged—were now eligible for amnesty, including "high military, civil, and judicial officers of the

Confederacy, officers who had surrendered their commissions in the armed forces of the United States, war criminals, commerce raiders, and those with taxable property of more than $20,000." Essentially reversing his own policy, the president promised mercy and affirmed that pardons for all others would be "liberally extended."[39]

Throughout the fall, the southern states met in constitutional conventions presided over by ex-Confederates, and by the end of the year, the Union military presence had been diminished from a high of 1 million in May 1865 to 152,000 men, acutely reducing the only significant security that blacks had possessed.

In 1867, Johnson reduced the number of excluded categories from fourteen to three. On July 4, 1868, he proclaimed amnesty for all former rebels except the 300 or so who were currently standing trial or facing potential indictment for treason or other felonies. *Then, on Christmas Day 1868, Johnson granted a universal pardon to the entire Confederacy.*

Instead of Radical Reconstruction's enforced limitations on ex-Confederates, Andrew Johnson progressively issued a blanket pardon to all rebels and restored all of their property (except slaves). Indeed, Johnson even abrogated Lincoln's 10 percent loyalty rule as a precondition for Confederate amnesty. Few trials were held and those that were conducted generally were held to address evidence of wartime atrocities but not treason. In Jefferson Davis's case, a jury was impaneled, but the trial never was held. Unlike Davis, Robert E. Lee did take the amnesty oath, on October 2, 1865, the very day he was inaugurated as president of Washington College—present-day Washington and Lee University—in Lexington, Virginia.

White mayhem ruled. In Richmond, Virginia, the owner of a "shaving emporium" reported that a "drunken white man assault[ed] a colored boy" in the street. Initially, the boy did not attempt to defend himself; eventually he fought off his attacker and stepped away from the scene only to be "arrested and strung up by his arms in front of the Exchange Hotel." The proprietor who witnessed the attack convinced the local police to release the boy, only to be assaulted himself by two U.S. soldiers while "talking in the street" with a U.S. Army chaplain.

In another instance, Albert Brooks had purchased his freedom and entered a business partnership with James Turner before emancipation. Together the Richmond, Virginia, businessmen owned a livery and hack stable valued at $10,000. During the war, rebel forces had impressed twenty-one of the concern's twenty-two horses and destroyed seven of their ten hacks.

When the Federal army came to restore the city to Union control, the partners were instructed to "appl[y] to the Military Authorities for permission to carry on their business."

Brooks and Turner "took the oath of allegiance[,] paid $12.50 each for a license to run five hacks and received 'protection' papers." Not long thereafter, Brooks recounted, "one of Mayor Major's [*sic*: Mayo's] old policemen, who had known all about me and my business for many years called at my stable and asks me if I had a pass. I showed him all my papers. He said they were no account[.] I must have a pass, and that I must come along with him and go to jail—all niggers that did not have a paper from their master, showing that they were employed, must be taken to jail and hired out for $5.00 per month."

At the time of his arrest, Brooks and his partner employed four men who were paid thirty-five dollars each per month. Harassment of this type, the police officer told Brooks, was a natural consequence of the war: "Your Yankee friends, who pretended they was agoing to set all the niggers free—we always told you they was the meanest men in the world, and that it would be a great deal worse for you when they come."[40]

Navigating the new social order was an all but impossible task for the freedmen. Generally, no authority provided protection or recourse.

In July 1866, two months after martial law was lifted, a full-scale riot broke out in New Orleans when a group of Radical Republicans, led by Judge R. K. Howell and Anthony Paul Dostie, organized a constitutional convention with the goal of granting black suffrage and eliminating the most pernicious Black Codes devised by the delegates of the 1864 assembly. Before the initial convention, the *gens de couleur*, free people of mixed Haitian, African, and French descent who were educated property owners, had enjoyed some freedom of movement. Unlike enslaved blacks and other free black residents, the *gens de couleur* had not been subjected to "curfews and restrictions on travel." Now those rights had been extinguished.

Inspired by the 1864 constitutional convention's suppression of black voting rights, New Orleans's white supremacists orchestrated the egregious reelection of the city's Confederate mayor, John T. Monroe. Tensions were high across the region, but the presence of Federal troops prevented them from erupting. However, when the military was withdrawn, there were no checks on white bedlam.

Gen. Philip H. Sheridan said that three days before the riot, "a very large number of colored people marched in procession . . . and were addressed from the steps of the City Hall by Dr. Dostie, ex-Gov. Hahn, and others."[41] Dostie urged the crowd to be prepared to take armed action should they be attacked by whites. On July 30, 1866, the convention recessed, "the timid members absenting themselves, because of the tone of the general public was ominous of trouble." Outside, the group merged with "a procession of say 60 to 130 colored men [and] marched up Burgundy Street and across Canal Street, toward the Convention, carrying an American flag."[42]

Encircled by hostile whites, the marchers—and other blacks in the vicinity as well as passengers on nearby cable cars—were attacked by gunfire, with the police also firing, inflicting mortal wounds on persons who had been taken into custody as prisoners. The black marchers, thought to have "had about one pistol to every ten men, and canes and clubs in addition," appear to have been greatly outnumbered and outgunned.[43] Sheridan later said of the event, "It was no riot; it was an absolute massacre by the police, which was not excelled in murderous cruelty by that of Fort Pillow. It was a murder which the mayor and police of this city perpetrated without the shadow of necessity. Furthermore, I believe it was premeditated, and every indication points to this."[44]

It is estimated that 238 people were killed, including at least 200 black Union veterans—some of whom were among the forty convention delegates who died at the hands of the mob.[45] Dostie, the white Radical Republican who deigned to fight for black rights, was one of the first to be attacked. Unarmed, he was shot during the riot, and when presumed dead, he was thrown into a cart with other victims of the massacre. Eventually Dostie was taken to a hospital, where he died six days later.[46]

In October 1866, a Tennessee Freedmen's Bureau agent reported that Union supporters north of Nashville, in Sumner and Robertson Counties, were assaulted by "numerous and revolting outrages." Overpowered, the victims were unable to defend themselves, and "the civil authorities either will not, or dare not attempt to bring the ruffians to justice."[47]

Over a two-week period in Saint Landry Parish, Louisiana, in 1868, an estimated 250 people were killed by organized white terror squads. The victims were overwhelmingly black, and the objective of the murder campaign was, once again, to exclude Republican voters from participating in the electoral process. The white perpetrators were members of the Knights of the White Camelia, an Italian "fraternal" group known as the Innocents, and the Seymour Knights. Three thousand white men, out of an overall 14,000 whites in the parish, were members of the Knights of the White Camelia alone. The murder campaign was grimly effective. Not a single Republican vote was cast in Saint Landry Parish, despite the fact that the Republican presidential nominee, Ulysses S. Grant, prevailed in the national vote.[48]

Throughout the Reconstruction era, legions of white paramilitary groups organized to intimidate freedmen and members of the Republican Party. When the threat of violence was not sufficient to suppress associations that organized blacks and to keep black constituents away from the polls, the Red Shirts, Ku Klux Klan, Knights of the White Camelia, White Leagues, White Shirts, and the White Brotherhood destroyed property belonging to the opposition, while maiming and killing them in cold blood.[49] Working customarily at the behest of a white landowning elite that also controlled the local constabulary and, not infrequently, side by side with white "planters, merchants, lawyers, and even ministers," these illegal enforcers could operate largely as they pleased, knowing that no governmental power would police their actions.

"Emanuel Fortune [was] driven from Jackson County, Florida, by the Klan," whose "object . . . it is to kill out the leading men on the republican party . . . men who have taken a prominent stand." At least 10 percent of the black delegates to the constitutional conventions "became victims of violence during Reconstruction, including seven actually murdered."[50] White Republicans who stood in solidarity with blacks fighting for their rights were not spared either. Among the casualties was North Carolina's white state senator John W. Stephens, who was assassinated in 1870.[51] The marauders were wildly successful, and all-white, largely ex-Confederate-affiliated fields of candidates were elected. Once they ascended to power, they proceeded to adopt Black Codes, dozens of extensive and repressive interlocking laws designed to control blacks' mobility and limit their access to competitive and desirable work opportunities. With the creation of these oppressive measures, a rejuvenated white elite began to fashion the postwar south in the image of the prewar south.

In 1864, before the Civil War ended, Louisiana became the first state to accept Lincoln's Reconstruction plan, revise its constitution, and abolish slavery (effective in thirteen parishes controlled by the Union, out of a total of forty-seven). Legislators there had authorized—but not granted—the vote to black men who had fought in the Civil War on the Union side, owned property, or were literate. But they had also passed scores of odious measures that broadened the scope of vagrancy and contract laws and stiffened the penalties for conviction.

While those laws, as written, did not appear to apply specifically to blacks, they functioned, as one historian observed, like the Sword of Damocles, a powerful weapon hanging over the heads of the freedmen that could be deployed at any time.[52] Louisiana's new restrictions were overwhelmingly enforced against blacks, resulting in their arrests for minor infractions. If convicted and unable to pay the fines, blacks then were made "available to the agricultural interests of the state" as forced laborers.

The Georgia General Assembly's October 1865 decision to exclude blacks from its constitutional convention was typical of the southern states. Only white men who had taken the loyalty oath, accepting the U.S. Constitution and all federal laws, could participate. The all-white delegation drafted a new state constitution; ratified the Thirteenth Amendment to the U.S. Constitution, which abolished slavery and involuntary servitude except as punishment for a crime; and nullified (rather than repealed, as required by Johnson's plan) the Ordinance of Secession—itself an act of defiance for which the legislators were not sanctioned. Encouraged by the lack of consequences for these actions, the Georgia delegates launched a wave of white nationalism, marked by the election of a host of ex-Confederates to state government and the election of the vice president of the Confederacy and a Confederate senator to the U.S. Senate.[53]

Georgia's Black Codes were not quite as draconian as those of its sister states, because they provided blacks token access to the courts and allowed them to buy and rent property. But when Charles J. Jenkins, a former Whig who was elected to the governorship after the war, petitioned the state legislature to revise its Black Codes and allow blacks to testify in court, the body responded by "limiting that opportunity to civil cases in which the defendant was black or those that concerned an infringement of a black's rights to person or property."[54] While more accommodating in some ways, Georgia did not enfranchise black men, and it sought to permanently reduce blacks to the status of noncitizens.

Before reversing himself in 1868, Texas's provisional governor, Andrew Jackson Hamilton, struck a more conciliatory tone. In his July 1865 proclamation, "To the People of Texas," Hamilton declared: "If the rebellion is conquered, slavery is dead—one is as much a fact as the other. The negroes are not only free, but I beg to assure my fellow-citizens that the government will protect them in their freedom."

Hamilton also issued a warning to those who sought to force freedmen into labor contracts that resembled conditions of bondage: "Let it be understood that . . . those interested in securing [ex-slaves'] labor to prevent them from hiring to persons who will pay the best price for such labor, and to ostracize in society those who oppose such . . . will meet with no favor at the hands of the people or Government of the United States." Hamilton feared that such violations could have far-reaching negative consequences for Texas, namely, "if the negro is characterized or treated as less than a free-man, our Senators and Representatives will seek in vain admission to the halls of Congress."

Governor Hamilton eventually rejected Johnson's Reconstruction plan outright and aligned himself with the Radical Republicans and the campaign for black suffrage. His fellow Texas Republican lawmakers did not share his views. When the state's constitutional convention met a year later, in 1866, it ushered in a host of restrictive measures over his objections.[55]

In the eyes of observer Samuel C. Sloan, a Freedmen's Bureau agent who was installed at the Millican (Brazos County), Texas, office on August 4, 1866, the labor, vagrancy, and apprenticeship legislation that followed effectively "enslave[d] the rising generation" of freedmen in "worse conditions" of bondage "than they have ever been." Blacks who deigned to challenge their employers' account of their earnings or who voiced complaints about physical abuses inflicted by their employers were also likely to be targeted by white vigilantes. Sloan believed that a "practical application" of the law would result in "an intolerable system of oppression and revive African Slavery under another name and with increased horrors."[56]

Black Texas parents were denied the right to supervise their children in their own homes, and they were prevented from seeking better opportunities for their children to receive education and training as apprentices if their children had been bound to whites before the war. North Carolina's Black Codes dictated, "The former masters of . . . apprentices [of color], when they shall be regarded as suitable persons by the court, shall be entitled to have such apprentices bound to them, in preference to other persons."[57] Black parents had no power to challenge the control the courts conveyed upon whites to whom their children were apprenticed. Physical punishment was routine and the Black Codes gave whites "power to inflict such moderate corporeal chastisement as may be necessary and proper."[58]

Black parents had to be constantly vigilant to protect their children. Sheriffs, justices of the peace, and other civil officers were authorized to round up black minors they deemed "indigent or vagrant" or "whose parent or parents have not the means, or who refuse to support said minors," and to apprentice them, without their parent's consent or knowledge, to "some suitable or competent person, on such terms as the Court may direct."[59]

Tragically, these kinds of practices were not the most vile. In his report to the state's Freedmen's Bureau headquarters in Galveston, Texas, Sloan indicated that between December 8, 1865, and September 15, 1866, six freedmen—including a father and his son—and one freedwoman had been victims of white "cold blood murder." One of the men, "Seaton, a freedman under contract with a Mr. Goggan of Burleson Co.," had been abducted in the night "by a party of armed men (citizens)" while in the custody of the civil authorities. Sloan was worried about his own safety and for that of the other officers and soldiers in his district: "The feeling is becoming more cynical toward 'Yankees' as they are termed daily. It will be dangerous to attempt to remain after troops are withdrawn from the community."[60] Given agent Sloan's level of concern about the safety of the Union officers—who were armed—there is no doubt about the degree of danger that would befall the freedmen once federal troops exited the south.

In September 1865, the Freedmen's Bureau national chief, Gen. Oliver O. Howard, had characterized Texas's political climate as "seem[ing] at the time . . . to be the post of greatest peril."[61] Howard recalled that little had changed a year later, when the state's bureau commander, Gen. Joseph B. Kiddoo, "found little respect for any law in the northeast counties." The Texas legislature had not ratified the "Civil-Rights-Law"; consequently, freedmen could not yet testify in courts of law. Kiddoo's "chief troubles," said Howard, were the white supremacists that thwarted the Texas bureau chief's "efforts to protect [the freedmen] from violence." His plan to "entreat . . . more troops for those remoter districts where the greater number of outrages occurred" was only minimally successful.[62]

By the election campaign of 1868, the first election in which black Texans could vote, the manslaughter counts that had troubled General Howard immediately after the end of the war were dwarfed by a factor of at least thirty-two. "The negroes never recovered from the election murders of 1868," Maj. James McCleery, Texas's state superintendent of education, later reported. By his account, "there had been in nine parishes two hundred and twenty-seven (227) freedmen and Union white men (freedmen mostly) killed outright, and sixty eight (68) wounded by gun shots or maltreated; that is, this was the number of officially discovered and sworn to; but there are many who had disappeared whose fate was not known." The bureau officer added, "All this has had a terrible effect on these (colored) people, unnerving and discouraging them in all respects."[63]

Unfortunately for the freedmen, the steps recommended by Governor Hamilton never were implemented. Instead, resolute white extremists fortified by Johnson's accommodating posture toward the former Confederates resumed power in Texas and ushered in race-specific laws similar to the measures enacted in North Carolina. Stunning in their scope and punitive capacity, the Black Codes were like a vise that effectively tightened the controls on where and how blacks lived and worked. The aim was not just to send a message to the freedmen but to signal to Congress that the states formerly in rebellion had reclaimed their power and a new legitimacy. By turning the clock back to the pre–Civil War period, the rebels signified that they did not fear federal disciplinary measures.

In his December 1866 report detailing outrages committed against blacks who had been loyal to the Union, Col. Eliphate Whittlesey, the assistant commissioner of the Freedmen's Bureau in North Carolina, declared that there was no safe haven for freedmen in the rebel states: "It is evident all over the South that the colored race cannot be safely left in the hands of the late masters or the Southern people. Just as sure as that is done, such oppressive laws will be enacted that the blacks will be driven to desperation and the scenes lately witnessed in Jamaica will be reenacted in many sections of our own country."[64]

Confident that they could seize near-absolute control of the formerly enslaved, white lawmakers in the former Confederacy required freedmen to work for their former masters and deprived them of the right to negotiate their wages and working conditions, initiate or break a contract, or bargain collectively. The operation of the Black Codes signaled the death of blacks' hope for economic independence.

Informed by the unrest in Jamaica, legislators across the south enacted Black Codes denying freedmen the right to purchase and carry firearms. In that respect, the Black Codes were modeled directly on slave codes but with even more severe penalties. The earliest example, Virginia's 1705 colonial government's "Act concerning Servants and Slaves," declared that

> no slave go armed with gun, sword, club, staff, or other weapon, nor
> go from off the plantation and seat of land where such slave shall be
> appointed to live, without a certificate of leave in writing, for so doing,
> from his or her master, mistress, or overseer: And if any slave shall be
> found offending herein, it shall be lawful for any person or persons
> to apprehend and deliver such slave to the next constable or head-
> borough, who is hereby enjoined and required, without further order
> or warrant, to give such slave twenty lashes on his or her bare back, well
> laid on, and so send him or her home."[65]

In 1833, less than fifteen years after Alabama was granted statehood, it passed slave codes that read, in part, "No slave shall keep or carry any gun, powder, shot, club, or other weapon whatsoever, offensive or defensive, except the tools given to him to work with, unless he is ordered by his master or mistress, or overseer, to carry the said articles from one place to another." Any such "gun, weapon, or ammunition found in the possession or custody of any slave, may be seized by any person." Offenders "shall receive, by order of [the justice of the peace], any number of lashes not exceeding thirty-nine, on his bare back, for every such offence."[66]

Alabama's Black Codes, ratified in 1866, after slavery had been abolished, made it "unlawful for any freedmen, mulatto, or free person of color . . . to own fire-arms, or carry . . . a pistol or other deadly weapon," punished by a fine of $100 or three months' imprisonment instead of the lash. Significantly, Alabama also made it illegal for "any person to sell, give, or lend fire arms or ammunition of any description whatever" to blacks, "under penalty of not less than $50 not more than $100 at the discretion of the jury."[67]

Catherine Bishir has speculated that in North Carolina and throughout the south, the "leniency . . . and paternalistic protections" some whites had extended to blacks when they were enslaved were withdrawn after emancipation. Accepting that blacks were no longer enslaved was one thing. Granting them citizen rights was not just unconscionable but "revolutionary and destructive."[68] In the white mind, any advantage for blacks meant a loss of advantage for whites. The Black Codes were intended to control every aspect of black life.

South Carolina and Mississippi—the states whose prewar black populations had ranked first and second in the nation, respectively, and not coincidentally, the first states to secede from the Union—both enacted extreme versions of the Black Codes. South Carolina's legislature took an obsessive interest in the whereabouts of its black residents, requiring "migra[nts]" intending to set up "reside[nce] in this state" to "enter into a bond with two freeholders as sureties" within twenty days of their arrival. Blacks were to be actively engaged in gainful work from "sunrise to sunset"—preferably under the supervision of white "masters"—and never to be "idle" lest they become "vagrants." Vagrancy was a crime that could result in fines, imprisonment, or being "leased" to anyone who would pay any accrued fines.

Furthermore, South Carolina lawmakers passed a litany of laws governing "Master and Apprentice" relationships. In one of over a dozen measures, black children as young as two years old could be bound out to learn a trade or service by the district judge if their parents were said to reside in another district or presumed to be "paupers, or . . . not teaching the[ir children] habits of industry or honesty or are persons of notoriously bad character, or are vagrants." Black children who had reached the age of ten years, whose parents did not live in the "district," could be "contract[ed] for labor or service for one year or less."[69]

The apprentice laws were of particular concern for black parents. Less than three years after the Emancipation Proclamation, blacks found themselves once again confronting the possibility of their children being sold away and forced to work at unpaid labor.

White South Carolinians who employed blacks were given near-complete control over those laborers by law. If, for example, their black hires were alleged to have committed "any acts or things . . . declared to be causes for the discharge of a servant, or for any breach of contract or duty . . . instead of discharging the servant, the master may complain to the District Judge or one of the Magistrates . . . to inflict, or cause to be inflicted, on the servant, suitable corporal punishment, or impose upon him such pecuniary fine as may be thought fit, and immediately to remand him to his work; which fine shall be deducted from his wages, if not otherwise paid."[70] The fine would include the cost of the time and effort of the district employee whose job it was to beat the freedman. Douglas Blackmon notes that across the south during the decades following the Civil War, "county sheriffs and their deputies received no salaries." They were remunerated from "specific fees charged to those who voluntarily or involuntarily came into the court system."[71] And since freedmen could not bring testimony independently against whites in a court of law, they would be at the mercy of the state's legal system.

Opportunities for blacks to improve their standard of living were severely limited. Blacks who were thought to possess the necessary skills, fitness, and "good moral character" by the residing district judge—and who also could pay an annual licensure fee of $100—might be allowed to "pursue or practice the art, trade or business of an artisan, mechanic or shopkeeper, or any other trade, employment or business (besides that of husbandry, or that of a servant under a contract for services or labor) on his own account and for his own benefit, or in partnership with a white person." An individual in possession of a hard-won license that later was said to have been obtained fraudulently was subject to a fine of "double the amount of the license: one half whereof shall go to the informer, who shall be a competent witness." Field laborer and cultivator and producer of edible crops and animals were the occupations whites preferred for blacks.[72]

Preventing black laborers from improving their pay and work conditions through negotiation with an employer or seeking alternate employment was another goal of the Black Codes. Entire sections of the Black Codes were devoted to punishment for "enticements," efforts made by any citizen to inform a black person bound by a labor contract about a job with better pay, reduced work hours, or better working conditions. "Any person who shall deprive a master of the service of his servant, by enticing him away, or by harboring and detaining him, knowing him to be a servant," could be liable, upon conviction, to a fine starting at $2,200 and "imprisonment or hard labor, at the discretion of the Court, not exceeding sixty days; and, also to an action by the master to recover damages for loss of services."[73]

Mississippi's legislature required all blacks eighteen years of age or older to present written proof of employment by January, four weeks after the lawmakers ratified their state's Black Codes, and every January thereafter or risk being fined fifty dollars. Blacks in the employ of whites were expected to be available and virtually on call. Other work to be "exacted"—in addition to the daily labor scheduled six days a week, every week, from "sunrise to sunset"—included "work at night, and outdoor work in inclement weather" or "in case of necessity" and "on Sunday . . . to take care of the premises, or animals thereupon, or for work of daily necessity, or on unusual occasions."

It was a criminal offense for blacks in Mississippi to negotiate contracts for their labor on their own terms. Before a black person could agree to a labor contract of a month or more in duration, she or he was required to first engage "a beat, city or county officer, or two disinterested white persons of the county in which the labor is to be performed." Once engaged, the white monitors were instructed to read the contract aloud and to store a copy of the document for verification.

In addition, any black laborer who "quit the service of his employer before the expiration of his term of service, without good cause," was made to forfeit his wages earned during that year. Self-appointed "civil officer[s]" who suspected that "any freedman, free negro, or mulatto" had "quit the service of his or her employer before the expiration of his or her term of service without good cause" could "arrest and carry [him or her] back" to their employer and collect a bounty of "the sum of five dollars."[74]

Across the south, these slyly crafted laws provided financial inducements to whites to actively police black citizens and even to fabricate offenses, the very definition of a moral hazard problem. Essentially, dishonest white "witnesses" could assert that blacks engaged in criminal behavior based on these laws and could receive pecuniary rewards for having done so, regardless of the veracity of the charge. The law created an incentive for whites to lie.

Blacks in South Carolina often found themselves in a double bind. Unsafe working conditions were not sufficient grounds for leaving an employer. Nor was being paid less than you were owed. At the same time, however, blacks were required to protect the interests of their white employers. Any master that perceived a danger to his "person, family, premises or property," or to the "person or property of any servant on [his] premises," was empowered to "command his servants to aid him in the defense" of said property.[75]

Scores of states actively engaged in policing blacks for "idleness" and "vagrancy," a catchall legal term as old as American slavery itself that encompassed acts determined to be "public grievances [that] must be punished as crimes." The Mississippi Black Codes defined the term "vagrant" broadly enough to include practically every black resident. The term incorporated

all rogues and vagabonds, idle and dissipated persons, beggars, jugglers, or persons practicing unlawful games or plays, runaways, common drunkards, common night-walkers, pilferers, lewd, wanton, or lascivious persons, in speech or behavior, common railers and brawlers, persons who neglect their calling or employment, misspend what they earn, or do not provide for the support of themselves or their families, or dependents, and all other idle and disorderly persons, including all who neglect all lawful business, habitually misspend their time by frequenting houses of ill-fame, gaming-houses, or tippling shops to be criminals liable to punishment, upon conviction, of a fine not exceeding one hundred dollars, with all accruing costs, and [imprisonment] at the discretion of the court, not exceeding ten days.[76]

The laws also gave all whites police authority over blacks, regardless of whether the white person held an official position. Town watchmen were tasked with patrolling blacks and were empowered to make arrests if they encountered a freedman whose labor activities did not meet their criteria for "work" or if they chanced upon an ex-slave they believed to be indigent. White vigilantes also were permitted to accost blacks who *were actively engaged in allowable work activities* and to demand that they provide written proof of employment with a white "master." Blacks who were unable to produce the required documentation could be forced into labor, at the will of the court, until the fine and the accumulated fees for any related "services" assessed by every officer or bureaucrat in the chain had been paid.[77] Measures of this type made it nearly impossible for blacks to develop their own farms or business enterprises.

South Carolina gave whites latitude to run their enterprises as they saw fit, largely without having to take the needs or desires of their black laborers into account. The Black Codes affirmed the right of a "master" to inflict corporal punishment on "moderately correct servants who have made contracts, and are under eighteen years of age." In every instance, masters' rights trumped those of blacks. Blacks who felt compelled to leave an exploitative employer may have survived with their dignity intact, but they paid a heavy price. The law was not on their side: "When the servant shall depart from the service of the master without good cause, he shall forfeit the wages due to him."[78]

Florida's Black Code made the freedmen's "willful disobedience, wanton impudence, and [even] disrespect to [his] employer" a crime. Blacks who broke labor contracts could be whipped, placed in the pillory, and sold for up to one year's labor, while whites who violated contracts faced only the threat of civil suits. Historian Joe M. Richardson wrote, "A Union chaplain concluded that [white] Floridians had 'so long and so selfishly' regarded the Negro 'as created to be their slave—only that and nothing more—that their minds are cast in that mold.' . . . A school teacher quoted a planter as saying after emancipation that a Negro 'would still be their slave in some way.'"[79]

Whites wanted to keep blacks confined physically, economically, and politically. Blacks' ability to discuss their plight, challenge authority, or organize politically was thwarted by a range of laws designed to silence black insistence on full citizenship. Mississippi forbade its black populace to engage in a broad range of activities where critical discourse might take place. Serious consequences awaited blacks alleged to have participated in "riots, routs . . . trespasses, malicious mischief . . . seditious speeches, *insulting gestures*, language, or acts . . . disturbance of the peace, exercising the function of a minister of the Gospel without a license from some regularly organized church, . . . or committing any other misdemeanor. . . . [They could] be fined not less than ten dollars, and not more than one hundred dollars, and may be imprisoned at the discretion of the court, not exceeding thirty days."[80]

The ease with which white southern legislators created the Black Codes, the willingness of the courts to approve them, and the enthusiasm of myriad county- and city-level government agents—sheriffs, constables (police officers), mayors, justices of the peace, and vigilantes—to enforce them all left a brutal mark on the everyday lives of freedmen.

Blacks with scarce resources and no insulation from white hostility lived in constant danger. In his testimony before Congress in 1865, Col. Samuel Thomas, assistant commissioner of the Freedmen's Bureau in Mississippi, shared his observations of the treatment blacks in the state routinely received at the hands of whites:

Wherever I go—the street, the shop, the house, or the steamboat—I hear the people talk in such a way as to indicate that they are yet unable to conceive of the Negro as possessing any rights at all. Men who are honorable in their dealings with their white neighbors will cheat a Negro without feeling a single twinge of their honor. To kill a Negro they do not deem murder; to debauch a Negro woman they do not think fornication; to take the property away from a Negro they do not consider robbery. The people boast that when they get freedmen affairs in their own hands, to use their own classic expression, "the niggers will catch hell."

The reason of all this is simple and manifest. The whites esteem the blacks their property by natural right, and however much they may admit that the individual relations of masters and slaves have been destroyed by the war and the President's emancipation proclamation, they still have an ingrained feeling that the blacks at large belong to the whites at large, and whenever opportunity serves they treat the colored people just as their profit, caprice or passion may dictate.[81]

Although the federal government had determined that black labor no longer could be obtained free of charge, states could create mechanisms to enable white employers to retain access to black workers and to force them to toil at their will, while simultaneously pushing blacks' wages below a livable standard.

Indeed, freedmen already faced fierce opposition from white planters to pay them in cash for their labor immediately at the end of the Civil War. The consequences reinforced the subordination of blacks that did not cease with the end of slavery.

The following account, reported here in some detail, was made in 1866 by Gens. James Barrett Steedman and J. S. Fullerton, the commissioners who President Andrew Johnson had authorized to report on the condition of the Freedmen's Bureau in the southern states: "The freedmen who still remain on the [Sea] [I]slands on the coast of South Carolina, which have been and still are . . . under the exclusive control of the Bureau, are in destitute circumstances." Blacks who had "raised good crops, and could easily have reimbursed the Government for the supplies provided for them . . . were swindled out of all they made by a gang of white sharpers who, pretending to be their Friends . . . set up stores" with the goal of "plunder[ing] these poor creatures of their hard earnings." Indeed, Steedman and Fullerton found that the actions of some of the agents of the Freedmen's Bureau hardly was beyond reproach:

A delegation of freedmen subsequently called on us and stated that in addition to the two plantations General Bly [subassistant commissioner of the Freedmen's Bureau] was cultivating on Government-account, he was also planting on his own account the farms of Robert Joiner and A. M. Hunt. This delegation further stated that twenty-nine colored persons, men, women, and children, suffering from the small-pox, were crowded into one room, about twenty feet by twenty-four in size, and placed on the bare floor, with no bedding, while their only covering was the blankets they had brought with them. These poor creatures were left in this condition several days, some of them delirious, with only one black woman to attend them, and without any nourishment but meat and bread. A number of respectable old colored people, attacked with the small-pox, were taken from their comfortable homes and placed in this room to die of neglect. One of this delegation assured us that he called to see General Bly on several different days to inform him of the suffering condition of the freedmen in the small-pox hospital, and was told on each occasion that the General could not be seen, as he was absent tending to his plantations. . . .

We have examined a contract between a planter and a freedman, which is on file in General Bly's office. . . . If this contract is to be regarded as evidence of the condition of the freedmen under the charge of General Bly, they are certainly very little better off than they were under slavery.[82]

Among the many such operations on Edisto and Wadmalaw Islands was the store "on the farm rented and cultivated by a Mr. Underwood, of Boston, Massachusetts," where blacks worked

by the task, which is precisely the same manner in which their former owners worked them. The price per task is fifty cents, which, if paid in money or its equivalent, would be fair wages; but, in lieu of money, tickets were given them, on which was printed, "Good for __ in provisions at our store." These tickets were taken up by the storekeeper, with corn at $3 per bushel, and other articles at similar exorbitant prices. There was no meat at the shop. The freed people gathered around us while we were there, and complained bitterly of their treatment, stating with the wages paid them they were unable to earn enough to buy, at the prices charged, their necessary subsistence. If these freedmen were paid in money for their labor they could escape the extortions of the shopkeeper, but with the tickets issued to them they are compelled to pay the prices charged and take whatever the shopkeeper sees fit to give them. Competition, which would greatly reduce the price of provisions, is prevented, at least on this plantation by military orders. Mr. Tolls, on an adjacent plantation, was selling corn to these people at $2 per bushel, and taking Underwood tickets in payment, but he was compelled to desist by special order.[83]

The era of "private bondage" had ended, but it was rapidly being replaced by a different invidious harm: public subjugation. The new reality blacks found themselves in was captured well by novelist and New Orleans *Picayune* reporter George Washington Cable, in historian Allen W. Trelease's valuable and engrossing *White Terror: The Ku Klux Klan Conspiracy and Southern Reconstruction*. "The ex-slave was not a free man; he was only a free Negro."[84] No longer enslaved by a single white master, Trelease surmised, "[blacks] were now the slave of every white man."[85] Now, without even the protection of their former enslavers, blacks could be subject to the accusations and whims of all whites, even white children.

"Presidential Reconstruction" was the name given to the measures Andrew Johnson promoted under the aegis of his cabinet, without congressional approval, between May and December 1865. By omitting protections for blacks and opening the door for the insurrectionists to return to their homes and elected offices they had held before the Civil War, the president's plan let southern states gain readmission to the Union and usher in legislation that restored the major features of the slave regime. Radical Republicans caustically dubbed Johnson's project a plan for restoration—restoration of comprehensive white supremacy in the south. In eight short months, Johnson had effectively crushed black ambitions for the world they envisioned after slavery.

By the end of 1865, Lincoln's successor had appointed provisional governors for every former insurrectionist state, and, apart from Texas, each of those states had been readmitted to the Union.

Johnson's dilution of Lincoln's plan was not taken lightly, and the Republicans lost no time in publicly denouncing the new president's proclamation. When the southern states moved decisively to reinstall Confederate officers and pass the Black Codes—laws designed to catapult the region back toward the antebellum period—the Radical Republicans stepped in, rejected Johnson's plan and refused to seat the ex-Confederate legislators. Insistence on full legal and political equality for black Americans was at the forefront of their movement.

After it became clear that the Republican Party, dominated by the Radicals, was determined to enfranchise black men and to extend them all rights of citizenship, Johnson broke forcefully with the Republican majority. He vetoed the second Freedmen's Bureau Bill on February 19, 1866, in large part because he had no investment in black American postwar success. He saw no need to commit government resources to support or protect freedmen during the period of national reunification. He also maintained, disingenuously, that "there is no part of our country in which the authority of the United States is disputed . . . and . . . the country has entered or is returning to a state of peace and industry," because "the rebellion is in fact at an end."[86] In fact, what was coming to a premature end was Reconstruction.

Johnson's objectives were to diminish the Freedmen's Bureau's authority, to block the allocation of property to the formerly enslaved, to derail the establishment of military courts in the southern states charged with protecting freedmen's rights, and to halt the inauguration of public schools. One month after vetoing the Freedmen's Bureau Bill, Johnson rejected the Civil Rights Act of 1866, which defined U.S. citizenship and provided equal protection to all persons born on American soil. When the legislature convened in December, it wasted no time in overriding Johnson's veto. However, he would continue to clash with the majority congressional Reconstruction coalition for the duration of his presidency.

After Johnson's veto, a succeeding Freedmen's Bureau Bill ultimately passed in Congress in July and mandated that blacks receive "any of the civil rights or immunities belonging to white persons, including the right to . . . inherit, purchase, lease, sell, hold and convey real and personal property, and to have full and equal benefit of all laws and proceedings for the security of person and estate, including the constitutional right of bearing arms."[87]

Thaddeus Stevens, convinced that Reconstruction could be achieved only through legislative action, wrote Johnson to object to the president's insistence that the executive branch was incapable of actions that would "revolutionize Southern institutions, habits, and manners . . . [break] up [those] foundations and rela[y] them," lest "all our blood and treasure have been spent in vain."[88]

Like Congressman George W. Julian, chair of the House Committee on Public Lands, who advocated "government, the strong arm or power, outstretched from the central authority here in Washington," many Republicans understood that it would take time for southerners to govern willingly in partnership with blacks. Change was possible, but it would require deliberate action and sustained federal intervention. In time, the Republicans believed, biases would soften and new ways of thinking would emerge, paving the way for "Northern capital and labor, Northern energy and enterprise," to breathe new life into the south and to create a "Christian civilization and living democracy."[89] More practically, federal troops were to be stationed across the former states of the Confederacy to preserve order and to protect the rights of the formerly enslaved.

A report from Washington found Republican leaders to be "fully settled" on three key issues: all existing southern governments should be replaced, "rebels" should not be allowed to take public office, and "negroes should vote."[90] The 1867 Reconstruction Acts, passed over Andrew Johnson's veto, reorganized ten former Confederate states into five military districts: Virginia; North and South Carolina; Alabama, Georgia, and Florida; Arkansas and Mississippi; and Texas and Louisiana. Tennessee was readmitted to the Union in July 1866 and was therefore exempt from federal control.

These congressional acts validated the black male vote and simultaneously disenfranchised thousands of former rebel leaders. For the first time, there were Republican-dominated state legislatures across the south, and equally significant, blacks were elected to a host of city, county, state, and national offices. Historians Harold Holzer and Norton Garfinkle report that between 1868 and 1876, when federal troops maintained order in the south, "the turnout of potential white and black voters rose to 67 percent." But over the next fourteen years, voting requirements became so restrictive that "the almost exclusively white voter turnout in the southeastern states represented only 39 percent of the total potential white and black voters." This is compared to a greater than 75 percent participation rate among eligible voters in the north and west.[91]

When Congress passed the Fourteenth Amendment, it defined citizenship to include all people born in or naturalized in the United States, including, most notably, the formerly enslaved. It also strengthened the federal government's ability to protect the rights of American citizens. Beginning in 1866, with the decisive Republican victory in both the U.S. House and Senate, the Republicans used their two-thirds majority to override President Andrew Johnson's vetoes and proceeded to expand the authority of the Freedmen's Bureau, under the protection of the army, throughout the south.

One effect of the Fourteenth Amendment was the elimination of the provision of the U.S. Constitution that required enslaved blacks to be counted as three-fifths of a white inhabitant in the determination of congressional representation.[92] If blacks in the southern states could vote, the Republicans reasoned, they could offset the Democratic Party bloc. The Democrats fully understood this and were determined to use all means—legal, extralegal, and illegal—to prevent it from happening.

While Civil War historians often focus their attention on the win/loss column in the theater of war, another set of playing fields was emerging that defined the terms of engagement between whites and blacks after the war ended. The new battlefields were the southern state legislatures and the city streets. Relieved that losing the war did not mean having a host of punitive measures imposed upon them by the federal government, southern white leaders defiantly opposed all mandates to share governance in collaboration with blacks and passed laws that would effectively kneecap freedmen far into the future.

Before the war ended, President Lincoln had selected Union-occupied Louisiana, a Confederate state then under the command of Gen. Nathaniel Banks, to put his Reconstruction plan to the test. Had Lincoln's plan succeeded, Louisiana would have been the first state where blacks and whites loyal to the Union shared governance. After Banks administered the loyalty oath to 12,000 of the state's voters, Lincoln granted them a presidential pardon. Elections were held to choose constitutional convention delegates.

Duly elected, the delegates drafted a new constitution stipulating the abolition of slavery; allowing the state legislature to authorize voting rights for black men who had fought for the Union, owned property, or were literate; and disenfranchising ex-Confederates who refused to take the loyalty oath. The new constitution also enabled the legislature to create free public schools without any mention of race. But it did not authorize an immediate statewide election.

Louisiana's postwar governor was James Madison Wells, an ardent Union supporter and Whig turned Democrat who owned several plantations and had enslaved over 100 Africans before embracing progressive ideals during the Civil War and aligning himself with the Radical Republican cause. Whether Wells's radicalization was authentic or a ruse is not clear.

What is clear is that the exclusion of blacks from the voting process crushed the Republican Party in Louisiana. In an ill-conceived, if not disingenuous, effort to control the state, Wells began appointing members of Louisiana's former aristocracy to public offices. If he had a strategy for radicalizing these former rebels and turning them into advocates for black suffrage and the abolition of the Black Codes, it was not successful. With no interference from President Johnson and no quid pro quo from the governor, the state's newly elected legislators—predominantly Confederates—continued to refuse to confer blacks their voting rights.

On December 21, 1865, fifteen days after the states ratified the Thirteenth Amendment and quashed slavery (except as punishment for a crime), Louisiana passed devastatingly repressive Black Codes that approximated its colonial era Code Noir of 1724.[93] Three months later, New Orleans's "Confederate mayor," John T. Monroe, was reelected over the veto of Governor Wells. In May 1866, the Union army—first deployed in Louisiana in 1862 to impose martial law—was withdrawn. This was a decision that organized gangs of white supremacists correctly interpreted to mean that the rapes, beatings, and murders they inflicted upon blacks and white Republicans would go unpunished.

When Wells announced plans to reassemble the constitutional convention of 1864 with the intention of enfranchising blacks, denying rebels the vote, and establishing a new state government, the Confederates denounced the governor and vowed to break the state's Radical Republicans.

Before the Confederates in Louisiana could deliver on their promise, however, white riots broke out in Memphis. On May 1, 1866, when an argument between black Union veterans and white police officers escalated, rioting stretched over three days, culminating in the deaths of thirty-four blacks and two white police officers. White rioters strategically looted and pillaged businesses belonging to blacks deemed too successful or insufficiently subservient; incinerated the homes of black veterans—ninety in all—four churches, and nine schools; and raped five black women.[94]

Two months after the Memphis riot, the Louisiana state legislature reconvened in New Orleans as Governor Wells had planned. When Democratic members attempted to take their seats before the election results had been confirmed, federal troops, hoisting bayonets, intervened and marched them out of the hall. But, as the chronology of events described here and above makes clear, the ex-Confederates had no intention of accepting the eradication of their power:

> On the appointed day, July 30, only twenty-five delegates in fact assembled, soon joined by a procession of some 200 black supporters, mostly former soldiers. Fighting broke out in the streets, police converged on the area, and the scene quickly degenerated into what Gen. Philip H. Sheridan later called "an absolute massacre" with blacks assaulted indiscriminately and the delegates and their supporters besieged in the convention hall and shot down when they fled, despite posting white flags of surrender. By the time federal troops arrived, thirty-four blacks and three white Radicals had been killed, and well over 100 persons injured. [Cyrus Hamlin, t]he son of former Vice President Hannibal Hamlin, a veteran of the Civil War, wrote that "the wholesale slaughter and the little regard paid to human life I witnessed here" surpassed anything that he had seen on the battlefield.[95]

The massacres of blacks and Republicans in Memphis and New Orleans by an array of Democratic "clubs"—the Innocents, the Red Shirts, the White League, and the Knights of the White Camelia, among them—swayed northern public opinion and tilted the Republican Party toward the Radicals, setting the stage for a host of Republican political victories in the 1866 congressional elections. Widely criticized by Republicans for his failure to protect the convention delegates and their supporters, Governor Wells was removed from office.

Louisiana passed a new state constitution granting blacks unprecedented citizenship rights and elected a Republican governor, Henry Clay Warmoth, and a black lieutenant governor, Oscar J. Dunn, who immediately reorganized and armed the metropolitan police force.[96] Unable to overturn Louisiana's new government, ex-Confederates within the Democratic Party focused their attention on the 1868 presidential election and rededicated themselves to organizing political militias that intimidated and terrorized Republican voters across the state with impunity.

Body counts among Republican political organizers escalated in the days and weeks preceding local elections. In Lafayette County, Arkansas, during the run-up to the 1868 presidential vote, the Ku Klux Klan recruited over 100 men "for the avowed object of killing Union men, of both colors, who would not join democratic clubs and vote their ticket. Some ten to fifteen colored men were shot down for this cause." Mississippi's Klan activity was concentrated in a two-county-wide band "extending down the Alabama border as far as Meridian."[97]

When Ulysses S. Grant was elected president of the United States in 1868, many Republicans hoped that the popular commanding Union army general and American hero would unify the north and the south, implement congressional Reconstruction, and steer the country out of the depression. Blacks expected him to enforce the laws that would transform them into fully realized American citizens.[98] White elites, on the other hand, looked to Grant to pave the road for the restoration of the ex-Confederates, make the south safe for investors, and pursue what they believed were their shared fiscally "conservative and commercial interests."[99]

By many accounts, Grant was a man of integrity and courage who displayed the nerve for battle and the ability to lead and motivate others in the face of great odds. But observers also noted that he was neither a skilled politician nor a good judge of character, shortcomings that would prove disastrous during his presidency.[100] His predecessor, Andrew Johnson, had waged bitter fights with Congress, lost the support of the public, and had been impeached—although not convicted. Still, Johnson had succeeded in obstructing Reconstruction. Would Grant's presidency be another lost opportunity to democratize America?

Grant inherited a divided and extremely volatile electorate. Ex-Confederates had begun to contest the national political hegemony, and violent outbreaks with high black casualty rates had become horrifyingly common. Democrats were not prepared to let the past remain in the past, nor were they willing to allow blacks to govern. And Republicans were anything but unanimous regarding their support for black rights.

When Democrats "fired into a Republican political procession" in New Orleans on September 22, 1868, the membership of the city's branch of the Knights of the White Camelia was an estimated 15,000, just under half of the white male population. Over the next three days, armed white insurgents in New Orleans proper and in the suburban Saint Bernard Parish determined to "drive[e] out white Republicans and [shoot] down troublesome Negroes. . . . At least thirty-eight persons had lost their lives." By the November election day, another sixty-three blacks had been murdered in Jefferson Parish.[101]

Blacks, white Republicans, and their allies had confidence in Grant's election, expecting it would bring about an end to white paramilitary group attacks. In fact, terror attacks became commonplace. The number of black Floridians murdered by whites was astounding. Florida's secretary of state, Jonathan Gibbs, also raised the alarm about the level of white violence in the state, "I am certain I have understated the matter. . . . I [have noted] one hundred and fifty-three murders in Jackson County" alone between 1868 and 1871, the years when he held the office.[102]

When Senator William McKendrik Robbins (D-N.C.) made his argument for white supremacy in Raleigh in July 1868, Ku Klux Klan night riders "raged in many Piedmont and eastern North Carolina Counties."[103] In October 1870, white raiders attacked a Republican campaign assembly in Eutaw, Alabama, killing four blacks and wounding fifty-four. That same month, when a Republican majority was declared victorious in South Carolina's Piedmont cotton belt, white mobs scoured the Laurensville countryside in a "negro chase" and drove "150 freedmen from their homes and [committed] thirteen murders . . . including a newly elected white probate judge, a black legislator, and others 'known and prominent as connected with politics.'"

In February 1871, Jack Dupree, a Mississippi Republican club president who lived in Monroe County, "was beaten severely, then taken to a wood several miles away, beaten again, and disemboweled."[104] Klansmen and the White Rose Society murdered black Republicans in Mississippi's Alcorn and Noxubee Counties and in Monroe County, Arkansas.[105] Then, in March 1871, in Meridian, Mississippi, gunshots interrupted the courthouse proceedings for three black activists who were said to have given "incendiary" speeches, setting off a riot that ended with the removal of the Republican mayor and the deaths of an estimated thirty blacks, including "all the leading colored men of the town with one or two exceptions" being "murdered in cold blood."[106]

Black men in Mississippi, many of them affiliated with the Republican Party, had been exercising their right to vote since 1867. The election campaign of 1874 provided Democrats with the first opportunity to put a permanent end to black suffrage. During the August 1874 Vicksburg municipal elections, white "armed gangs" calling themselves the "People's or White Man's party" took to the streets and tyrannized enough black voters to unseat the city's elected Republican officials. Following that coup d'état, plantation owners in nearby rural areas "formed White League clubs" with the goal of weeding out "all bad and leading negroes . . . and controlling more strictly our tenants and other hands."[107]

In December of that year, after a tsunami of Democratic victories in the north, white supremacists openly declared war on blacks and the party of Lincoln. Vicksburg was again the site of atrocities perpetrated by militant whites. After demanding that black sheriff Peter Crosby and his board of supervisors vacate their offices, former rebels launched what became known as the Vicksburg massacre, "*murdering perhaps 300 blacks*." In Yazoo County, insurrectionists forced Sheriff Albert T. Morgan to leave the area. Morgan, who was married to a black woman, had played a critical role helping about 300 black families purchase real estate, and he had overseen the growth of the county's school system "all without corruption and only a slight increase in taxes." Members of a white "military company" murdered state senator Charles Caldwell in Clinton, Mississippi, and approximately thirty blacks, including his brother, Sam.[108]

Grant's initial response to governors from Louisiana, Mississippi, and South Carolina requesting assistance quelling insurrections was to send in federal troops. The president was instrumental in the passage of the Enforcement Act of 1871, legislation making it a criminal offense for groups to "conspire together to overthrow or to put down, or to destroy by force, the government of the United States" or to "oppose by force the authority of the government of the United States." In addition, any acts against government officers "so as to molest, hinder, or impede" them during the course of their duties, including "go[ing] in disguise upon the public highway or upon the premise of another for the purpose of . . . depriving any person or class of persons of the equal protection of the laws," were hereby illegal and punishable by a fine and likely imprisonment. The measure made it possible to prosecute members of the Ku Klux Klan and temporarily drove the terrorist group underground.[109]

Over time, however, Grant adopted a policy of conciliation toward the southern elites and relied more on local governments to police insurgents. He also may have taken the temperature of white northerners, many of whom were wearied by endless rounds of horrifying news from the south and had begun to refocus their energies on their personal financial agendas, leaving black Americans to protect themselves as best they could.

While Grant and the Radical Republicans were fighting to maintain control of the south and white butchers were escalating physical assaults on Unionists, the Republican Party was also coping with the Panic of 1873, a financial crisis that affected the United States and Europe and triggered an international depression. Democrats, recognizing the impotence of Grant and his party—in fact, the crisis would last six years—capitalized on the chaos and took the U.S. House. It was their first major victory since prewar times. Mississippi's governor, Adelbert Ames, pleaded for Grant to provide protection from the federal government, but this fell on deaf ears. Grant's refusal was the first nail in the coffin of Mississippi's freedmen and the state's Republican Party. He justified his position in a letter to Attorney General Edwards Pierrepont, written September 13, 1875: "The whole public are tired out with these annual autumnal outbreaks in the South."[110]

Resigned to ceding control of the south to ex-Confederates, Grant found himself at the center of another losing battle: the groundswell of patronage and embezzlement charges lodged at high-ranking officials in his administration. On numerous occasions, Grant had been outmaneuvered by robber barons, who were transforming the country into an industrial and financial powerhouse, further enriching themselves in the process. Several government officials were accused of accepting bribes in exchange for lucrative infrastructure contracts for the expansion of railroad lines, mining, and steel manufacturing and for sanctioning the proliferation of banks across the entire country. One of the scandals that had dire consequences for the freedmen was the dissolution of the Freedman's Saving and Trust Company, also known as the Freedman's Bank.

Chartered—but not insured—by Congress in 1865, the financial institution was established to provide a safe repository for the assets the formerly enslaved and their descendants had accumulated. To increase the freedmen's confidence, white bank tellers and branch advisory board members were replaced with blacks. Unfortunately, fraud and embezzlement at the hands of the bank's majority-white upper management and board of trustees, coupled with the Panic of 1873, led to the bank's closure, leaving more than 61,144 depositors unable to retrieve accounts valued at $2,993,790.68.[111]

In 1874, a decade after Lincoln had launched his doomed Reconstruction plan in Louisiana, the state remained a battleground. In August of that year, racial animosity initiated by whites in Coushatta, in Red River Parish, claimed the lives of six white Republicans and as many as thirty blacks.

With Grant's growing indifference to southern Republicans, Democratic Party marauders exercised unchecked domination of black Americans. In his characterization of the 1868 election campaign, historian Eric Foner wrote, "Violence, an intrinsic part of the process of social change since 1865, now directly entered electoral politics." Among the politicians who were murdered during the run-up to the election were Arkansas congressman James M. Hinds—the first U.S. congressman assassinated in office—three members of the South Carolina legislature, and several men who had served in constitutional conventions.[112] In Arkansas in 1874, when civil disorder led to white riots, the president's inaction—by then routine—made clear his decision to wash his hands of his party's Radicals once and for all.[113]

The Mississippi election campaign of 1875—the first year disenfranchised ex-Confederates could vote—"united the white population as never before." White elites rallied their race across all social classes. The Red Shirts, the military arm of the Democratic Party, extended the mission of the Klan. The deadly assassins operated in the open and without fear of sanction and succeeded in delivering landslide Democratic victories.[114]

The advent of the 1876 election season could not come soon enough for the Grant administration. Disgraced and enveloped in scandal, the president had squandered much of the political capital—not to mention the ideological high ground—that had ushered him into office in 1866. No longer championing black citizenship, Grant and the Republican Party permitted the sword to be put to Reconstruction when Republican Rutherford B. Hayes was deemed the victor in the disputed election. Initially, it appeared that Samuel J. Tilden, the Democrat, had won. However, the Republicans alleged there had been sufficient incidents of voter fraud and violent attacks of blacks and Republicans in South Carolina, Louisiana, and Florida to call Tilden's victory into question.

Congress appointed an electoral commission to investigate the election results and declared Hayes the winner. What was not immediately apparent to the American people at large, though, were the terms of the Republican victory. In exchange for the presidency, the Republican Party had agreed to withdraw federal troops from Florida, Louisiana, and South Carolina, abandoning forever southern blacks and white Republicans.

Soon, the Supreme Court eroded and even reversed the legal measures designed to protect blacks' rights. Chief among the changes were the diminution of the Civil Rights Act of 1875, which granted every U.S. citizen "full and equal enjoyment" of public accommodations and facilities regardless of race, color, or creed, and of the Enforcement Acts of 1870 and 1871, which protected blacks' right to vote, hold public office, testify against whites in a court of law, serve on juries, and receive equal protections under the law. These modifications effectively nullified the Fifteenth Amendment and provided the legal cover and sanction for the Ku Klux Klan's full-on intimidation of blacks and Republicans.

One by one, the southern states fell back into Democratic Party hands—Virginia and Tennessee in 1869, North Carolina in 1870, and Georgia in 1871. Many Republicans caved to the pressure exerted by the self-proclaimed "redeemers," who openly thwarted black voters with violence and intimidation. Some Republicans even denounced their party and joined forces with the Democrats. Texas became Democratic controlled in 1873 and Alabama and Arkansas in 1874.

As W. E. B. Du Bois observed only seven years after Andrew Johnson's notorious 1866 Swing Around the Circle, northern whites' appetite for vigilant support of black citizenship was already in eclipse. The "seven mystic years" had ended. The nation paid the price demanded by southern whites for reconciliation: the renewed subjugation of blacks. America has suffered the consequences ever since.

Part 5

10

Sins of the Sons and Daughters

The Negro was . . . in America to stay. What was to be done with him? Charles Sumner, the Massachusetts senator, had an answer: Give him the ballot, and treat him like a man. Thaddeus Stevens, the Pennsylvania Congressman, had an answer: Give him 40 acres, and treat him like a man. —Lerone Bennett Jr., "Black Power in Dixie," 1962

The tragedy of Reconstruction is the failure of the black masses to acquire land, since without the economic security provided by land ownership the freedmen were soon deprived of the political and civil rights they had won. —Claude F. Oubre, *Forty Acres and a Mule*, 1978

Race riots resulting in real property takings, like race riots themselves, are not as rare as they might seem. Quite a few incidents are infamous, but many others are relatively unknown, buried by decades of fear and secrecy. Although they occurred in different places, and different events were blamed as triggers, common threads exist among them. Generally, the takings happened after there had been substantial accumulation of wealth in the black communities. The black citizens typically fled from their communities under threat of death, too afraid to return; their aggressors either seized their property without compensation or gave them insignificant compensation. As with Ocoee [Florida], white representatives were sometimes appointed to execute the estates of those who died in the riot. —Melissa Fussell, "Dead Men Bring No Claims," 2015–16

The article by Ta-Nehisi Coates in the June 2014 issue of the *Atlantic* resurrected the national conversation over reparations for black Americans. One of the most impressive aspects of Coates's article is his insistence that the events and conditions during the antebellum period are far from the only basis for reparations.[1] A focus on the indignities and atrocities heaped upon black people after slavery provides at least as strong a case for black reparations as slavery itself.[2] In this chapter, we enumerate the abuses blacks experienced in the United States from the end of Reconstruction through the Jim Crow years.

The first indictment must be the failure to fulfill the promise of the grant of forty acres and a mule to families who had been enslaved. Had that promise been kept—had ex-slaves been given a substantial endowment in southern real estate—it is likely that there would be no need for reparations to be under consideration now. If the forty acres had been allocated roughly to families of four, each ex-slave would have received ten acres of land. Since there were approximately 4 million freedmen, a total of 40 million acres of land should have been allocated to formerly enslaved blacks.

The scale of the largest southern plantations was enormous. The Cameron-Bennehan plantation in North Carolina spanned forty-seven square miles, or 30,000 acres.[3] Paul Cameron, the owner of the plantation, claimed at the peak of his enterprise to have owned 1,900 human beings.[4] That total would have constituted approximately 475 families. If his full estate had been divided evenly among the number of families Cameron held in bondage, each family would have received more than *sixty* acres of land.

While forty acres was small compared to the scale of many American slave plantations, it would have been a substantial allotment. In 2013, the median American home was located on 8,596 square feet of land, or 0.2 acres.[5] Therefore, an average of 200 residences could have been built on a typical tract of land that should have been distributed to ex-slaves. It would have made it possible for descendants of the enslaved, in addition to farming it themselves, to have sold significant property at a high price to developers, to have become developers themselves, or to have created other, innovative commercial uses for their property.

While the allocation of forty acres never happened, black American farmers managed to amass 15 million acres of land by dint of their own efforts by 1910—still less than half of the amount ex-slaves should have received during Reconstruction but not insubstantial.[6] This was the peak of landownership by black farmers in the United States, with 218,000 farmers full or partial owners. However, by 1997, black farm landownership had diminished to a mere 2.4 million acres.[7] Today, the top five white landowners in the United States own more land than the whole of black America; Ted Turner alone owns more than the equivalent of one-quarter of the entire acreage of land in the possession of black Americans.[8]

The record of black land loss generally has not been one of voluntary sales at market prices: "The land African Americans lost over the 20th century was taken in some form, and not sold freely."[9] In many instances black land literally was seized in the climate of white terror. A meticulously researched three-part series released by the Associated Press in December 2001, titled "Torn from the Land," chronicled the violence and injustice African Americans in the south suffered in an effort to become and remain landowners. The journalists analyzed transcripts from more than 1,000 interviews and examined numerous public records. They found 107 documented land takings in thirteen states in the south and along the border between the north and the south.

A close look at these documented cases reveals that more than 24,000 acres of farm and timberland were seized, including smaller properties like stores and city lots.[10] Further, over half (fifty-seven) of the documented cases were violent land takings, and the others involved trickery and legal manipulation. Murders of African American landowners, for the purpose of appropriating their property, and coerced public sale of family land resulted in a rapid decline in black American landownership in the twentieth century. The trajectory of black land loss has continued in the twenty-first century.[11]

Seizure of black-owned land finds its origins at the close of the Reconstruction era. In just one example, investigative reporters at the Associated Press used county records to chronicle the events leading up to ex-slave Robert Gleed's colossal loss of land, homestead, and business enterprise. In 1855, when he was about seventeen years old, Gleed eluded his Virginia enslaver and established himself in Columbus, Mississippi, only to be apprehended when he could not produce his "freedom papers." When he refused to say who "owned" him, Gleed was sold to a John Miller.

Like other blacks in the area, Gleed prospered in the years after the war under the protection of the U.S. Army. Literate and active in local politics, Gleed caught the attention of the state's military governor, who appointed him to the Columbus City Council (1867–72), and he made a successful bid for state senator in 1869, serving two terms. In 1875, he ran for sheriff of Lowndes County, Mississippi, by which point registered black voters, Republicans mostly, outnumbered white voters, who largely were aligned with the Democratic Party—3,800 to 1,250. A highly visible and much sought-after adviser, Gleed held the positions of president of the Mercantile Land and Banking Company and head of the county chamber of commerce, and he owned 250 acres of arable land, three city lots, and a general store.[12]

The night before the 1875 election, "a mob of whites attacked a parade of his supporters. Four blacks were killed, one on the sidewalk in front of Gleed's store." Whites set fires across the county, broke into Gleed's unoccupied house, destroyed his furnishings with gunfire, and shredded his wife's clothes. Gleed owed his life to a white friend who hid him in his well.[13]

The next day, the Democratic candidate for sheriff, a white man, won the election. Gleed and his family fled to Paris, Texas, abandoning their property. County records reveal that not long afterward, two Columbus whites claimed Gleed owed them money and foreclosed on his property. A Toby W. Johnston "liquidated the store and stock[,] pocketing $941." City councilman Bernard G. Hendrick took possession of 215 acres of Gleed's land to satisfy a supposed $125 debt. Hendrick also purchased the fleeing man's house and adjoining lot for "$11 at auction" and took possession of all remaining properties after paying $500.[14]

Curious about this civic leader's reversal of fortune, we searched for additional information about Robert Gleed. We learned he had testified at the so-called Ku Klux Klan hearings convened by the Joint Select Committee to Inquire into the Condition of Affairs in the Late Insurrectionary States in 1872, an action that only intensified the dangerous attention he received from the Klan. The testimonies recorded by the committee, from witnesses in six states, comprise thirteen volumes and 7,815 pages.[15]

In his June 1872 testimony, Gleed recounted incidents in which blacks were attacked by gangs of white men. He described his own efforts to have Democrats who opposed the Klan bill tone down their antiblack rhetoric. He expressed horror upon seeing his own name and that of several other Republican Party members mentioned in a Eutaw, Alabama, newspaper article, together with the charge that they "should not be allowed to breathe the air" and instructions to readers: "We must kill or drive away the leading negroes, or the intelligent negroes, and only let the humble and submissive remain among us."[16]

Gleed gave extensive testimony and made known that he had received a "Ku-Klux notice," signed "KKK," the previous year. "The character of the notice was that my behavior would not be long tolerated . . . that I had to change my course, or they would visit me on the first bloody moon." He related the deaths of a Mr. "Mason, that was killed by persons in disguise," some "fifty in the gang that killed him," and Dick Malone, who was killed in Noxubee County by masked assassins. A man named Jacob Hicks had been whipped the previous spring, and an unnamed man who was "whipped almost to death" and came "very near to losing his crop from the whipping" had refused to identify his attackers to the grand jury "for fear of personal violence." A "colored woman taken [away from] Buttahatchie, on Mr. Herring's plantation," was beaten severely. Her crime? "They said she and Mrs. Herring a few days prior to the whipping had had some words." Gleed told of the destruction of all but one of the county schools for black youth: "The schools in the northern portion, northeastern portion, and northwestern portion of the county have been broken up" so much that "they could not get anybody to teach them up there, for fear of their lives, either white or colored."[17]

In the northern and eastern quadrants of Monroe County, "from March until about the 1st of July, there was a great deal of disturbance," and blacks were "leaving home altogether, and squads moving off to Louisiana. . . . Whole families moved . . . on account of the murdering." Realizing that no justice, protection, or fair treatment was forthcoming, blacks began to leave Monroe County en masse.[18]

"What is the trouble in bringing the . . . [murderers] to justice?" the committee asked. Gleed responded, "The trouble seems to be that there is sufficient influence in their favor—enough men in the organization . . . to get on the different departments of the judiciary, on the grand jury, and on the petit jury, one place and another—to keep any bill from being brought; and first they terrify parties so they are afraid to report them."[19]

When the Joint Select Committee chairman, John Scott, instructed him to "state what, from your best information, seems to be the purpose of these outrages, if there was any general purpose," Gleed responded emphatically:

Well, sir, we have thought . . . the purpose of the organization . . . have been to remand the colored men of the country to as near a position of servitude as possible, and destroy the republican party if possible; it has been, in other words, political. We believe it had two objects, one was political, and the other was to hold the black man in subjection to the white man, and to have white supremacy in the South; that has been the tendency; and then we have evidence of it from the parties who have sworn and bound themselves together under oaths, that is, in clubs, to do all they can from year to year, and from month to month, as long as they live, to establish white supremacy in Mississippi, and the disenfranchisement of the black man.[20]

Blacks and white Republicans were executed summarily at the whim of white vigilantes. A congressional investigation in 1871 revealed that their murders often were followed by the tarring of their reputations—as if to justify the killings.[21] This closely parallels the contemporary defamation of the dead that follows police executions of unarmed blacks.[22] For example, W. H. Humphries, in testimony during the minority Democratic Party's portion of the hearings, consistently sought to undermine Gleed's credibility and implied that Gleed had been susceptible to bribery. However, Humphries never challenged Gleed's account of the atrocities perpetrated by white terrorists.[23]

The legal scholar Melissa Fussell has observed that the white riot in Ocoee, Florida, after the lynching of Jule Perry, a black man who had had the temerity to try to vote on Election Day 1920, immediately resulted in white appropriation of black property under official sanction:

A committee of white Ocoee residents, together with the local court, distributed black residents' property to white citizens in the aftermath; the victims were uncompensated for the most part although some received a few dollars. Congress endorsed the actions of the Ocoee government and white citizens after the fact, commending them for upholding "law and order." Cruelly, the black cemetery in Ocoee— abandoned for eighty years after the riot—is located in a subdivision off Bluford Avenue, named for Captain Sims, who took ownership of Perry's land. Adding insult to injury, every year the Ocoee government throws a festival celebrating the town's founders: former slave owners J. D. Starke and Captain Sims himself. In 2014, the city of Ocoee paid $302,000 to celebrate the founders.[24]

Despite white officialdom's complicity, Fussell argues that property takings of this type are a clear violation of the Fifth Amendment to the U.S. Constitution. The Fifth Amendment deems illegal the seizure of private property "by the government without just compensation." Indeed, Fussell adds, "The Supreme Court has held that outright seizure of property is unnecessary to support a takings claim for compensation; it is enough if 'the government authorizes a compelled physical invasion of property.'"[25] This legal interpretation has never been applied or executed to benefit the black victims of the Ocoee land takings or their descendants.

The failure to grant ex-slaves an initial stake in American property ownership and the subsequent land taking from blacks has contributed to the comprehensive denial of black wealth accumulation.[27] Apart from the barriers to landownership, black home ownership was restricted throughout the twentieth century by discriminatory redlining, differential access to government finance for home mortgages, and, most recently, by the subprime mortgage crisis induced by the banking system's loan-pushing schemes.[28]

Another brutal, and yet uncompensated, instance of violent white seizure of black-owned land took place in Mississippi in the 1940s. A black minister, Isaac Simmons, and his family owned 270 acres of land in Amite County, apparently since 1887. As he began to prosper from the sale of produce and wood from his property—and after rumors began to circulate that there might be oil on his land—six white men approached him and ordered him to stop his logging activities. When he sought legal help to deal with their pressure, the six men returned and tortured and murdered him, drove his family off the land, and took control of it. Only one of the six came to trial, and he was acquitted by an all-white jury.[26]

Not only were blacks not given the promised forty acres and a mule after the Civil War, but a white terror campaign that included assassinations of black political leaders, freedmen, and their white allies throughout the south prevented blacks from exercising their right to vote and holding official positions. Black elected leaders were tortured and killed, and a host of impediments was established for black voters. The net effect was the exclusion of blacks from the policy-making process, inclusive of policies that might have supported and protected black wealth accumulation and social participation.

In 1897, in Hogansville, Georgia, whites "were so enraged over having a Negro postmaster that they tried to assassinate him. Failing in that they burned his post office."[29] Thirty years earlier, in 1868, Benjamin F. Randolph—a black state senator and prominent delegate to the post–Civil War South Carolina constitutional convention, a staunch advocate of black suffrage and education, and the publisher and coeditor of the Charleston *Advocate*, a newspaper for freedmen—was executed by the Ku Klux Klan at a train depot in Hodges, South Carolina.

The Klan executed white North Carolina state senator John W. Stephens in a courthouse in Yanceyville in 1870; Stephens had been a member of the Republican Party and the Union League. A former Confederate, Stephens's efforts to organize blacks in Caswell County, North Carolina, inflamed white supremacists. White disdain for black life and black political rights produced the conditions for an intense and systematic level of white racist political violence throughout the states of the former Confederacy. This was particularly true in Louisiana, Florida, South Carolina, and Mississippi, the states where Republican Party dominance persisted as late as 1874, almost a decade after the end of the war.

After 1873, terrorist white supremacy organizations, especially the Ku Klux Klan and the Red Shirts, pursued their goal of restoring the old racial hierarchy. Intimidation of black voters with gun and noose became the norm. As Lerone Bennett Jr. recounted: "In the big three (Miss., S.C., La.), Negro voters were so deeply entrenched that nothing short of a full-scale revolution could dislodge them. Southern Democrats were up to the demands of the hour. The white population organized for war. The Negro population, at the same time, was systematically disarmed. By hook and crook, on any and every pretext, the homes of Negroes were searched and arms were systematically appropriated."[30]

The scope of white voting manipulation during the period was so extreme that had there been an international election-monitoring team present, its report would have been a devastating indictment of the process. Again Bennett wrote:

> Polling places were located in bayous and on islands, in barns and in fodder houses. Armed white men were stationed on the roads leading to the polls "to prevent Negroes from seizing arms." In one Louisiana county, the polling places were located in an isolated wilderness. The whites gathered at the white church and were told, in whispers, how to reach the polls. In another county, the polls opened in the dark of the morning and whites voted by the light of a candle. When the Negro voters showed up, the polls were closed for the day. In Mississippi, white men from Alabama and Louisiana streamed across the state lines and voted early and often. In South Carolina, "citizens" came from North Carolina and Georgia.[31]

Guy B. Johnson, a founder of historical sociology, seeking to characterize the era accurately declared, "Reconstruction was in a sense a prolonged race riot." Johnson reported that Gen. Philip Sheridan estimated that 3,500 blacks were killed in the south in the decade after emancipation. Johnson's personal estimate, which he described as "conservative," was 5,000 during Reconstruction.[32]

By 1876, when federal troops were removed entirely from the southern states, blacks were faced with doom. With rare exception, the right to vote was quashed for blacks, leading Bennett to conclude, "Soon the Civil War would be sucked of all meaning and would become an agency of reconciliation between the North and the South."[33]

Benjamin Butler figured in the passage of the Civil Rights Act of 1875, which was coauthored by John Mercer Langston—the founder of the Howard University School of Law—and Senator Charles Sumner from Massachusetts. Sumner and Butler introduced the measure, and it became the last successful legislative action of Ulysses S. Grant's presidency.

The act made it illegal to exclude blacks from jury service and granted them equal rights to public transportation and public accommodations (hotels, restaurants, retail stores, rental properties, educational institutions, recreation facilities, and service centers). The federal government's failure to enforce the Civil Rights Act of 1875 and the U.S. Supreme Court's decision to overturn the measure in 1883 consolidated the legal basis for the Jim Crow regime.[34]

Preceded by the adoption of the Black Codes, laws that limited black mobility and black legal rights, discussed in detail in chapter 9, the Jim Crow regime of sanctioned segregation had spread across the south and many parts of the north by 1880.[35] White supremacists had regained control of most of the legislatures in the former states of the Confederacy. Local whites determined which rights blacks would be allowed to exercise, regardless of the letter of the law.

An additional example is provided by the lawyer and author Bryan Stevenson. Writing about the 1880 Supreme Court ruling in *Strauder v. West Virginia*, Stevenson noted, "Excluding black people from jury service was unconstitutional, but juries remained all-white for decades afterward."[36] *Strauder* was one of the rare nineteenth-century cases where a Supreme Court decision outwardly favored the rights of blacks; the Court ruled that barring blacks from serving on juries solely because of their race was a violation of the equal protection clause in the Fourteenth Amendment. Clearly the decision did not lead to widespread empaneling of black jurors.

Thirteen years after the *Strauder* decision, when the *Plessy v. Ferguson* case was brought before the Supreme Court in 1896, the justices, in a perverse interpretation of the Fourteenth Amendment, found that the provision for "separate but equal" treatment met the test for "equal protection under the law." Under the "separate but equal" doctrine, blacks constitutionally could be segregated in individual railway cars (and eventually schools, theaters, restaurants, and restrooms) if those vehicles and structures were "equal" to those designated for whites. In general, the accommodations for blacks were grossly inferior to those of whites, so this condition rarely, if ever, was met. These institutions were integral to blacks' daily lives. That they were second- or third-rate, even after the passage of the Reconstruction Amendments, signaled that blacks still were being denied citizenship. The system of American apartheid, reinforced under *Plessy*, was not to be deemed officially illegal until the passage of the Civil Rights Act of 1964.

Political intimidation, economic exclusion, and the erasure of communities where blacks had attained some measure of affluence were the customary aims of a wave of massacres conducted by whites from the 1870s well into the 1940s. Among the very earliest in the post–Civil War period were the Memphis riot of 1866 and the brutal attacks conducted by the White League in Colfax (1873) and Coushatta (1874) in Louisiana. A white riot in Danville, Virginia, took place in 1883, followed by even more destructive bloodbaths in Thibodaux, Louisiana, and Wilmington, North Carolina. In Thibodaux, an 1887 strike taken primarily by blacks working in sugar fields, gave white vigilantes the opportunity to take deadly action against unarmed blacks, resulting in the murder of at least thirty-five blacks and perhaps as many as 300.[37]

Two years after the *Plessy* decision, a mass murder took place in the Greenwood County town of Phoenix, South Carolina. The Phoenix massacre began when a white Republican, Thomas Tolbert, set up a stand in front of the polling station at the Watson and Lake general store and attempted to get black men on the county's voter rolls. When a group of white Democrats forcibly sought to make Tolbert stop, a fight ensued and the local Democratic Party boss, J. I. "Bose" Ethridge, was killed when shots rang out. Although the original source of the gunfire remains unknown, the consequences were tragically predictable:

The Democrats retaliated by opening fire on the crowd of African American men gathered outside the store; Thomas Tolbert was shot in the neck, arms, and side, but he survived.

White retribution was swift and severe. In the days that followed, between six hundred and one thousand white men gathered in Phoenix, where they burned the Tolberts' homes and forced the Republicans into exile. Several local black men were not so fortunate; four were lynched outside of Rehoboth Church. Over the next several days the white mob killed at least eight black men, though the exact number is not known. No one was ever charged with any of these murders. The Phoenix Riot is usually overshadowed in larger historical narratives by the Wilmington, North Carolina, race riot that began on November 10, 1898, and resulted in the triumph of Democrats over Republicans and Populists in North Carolina's government. The Phoenix Riot occurred in an area that was already under Democratic control. [Thomas Tolbert's brother] Robert Red Tolbert, the Republican, lost the 1898 election to Democrat A. C. Latimer by a 996 to 107 margin [despite the fact that blacks were a numerical majority in the country].[38]

A mere two days later, the Wilmington massacre was under way. Planned and systematically encouraged by white supremacist agitation, the goal of the white conspirators was to overthrow the Republican elected municipal government. The plotters were drawn from the "best class" of the city's whites, most visibly including Alfred Waddell, a former Confederate army colonel, who installed himself as mayor after the uprising.

In each case, local police forces were implicated as agents of exterminatory onslaughts directed against blacks.

White supremacists who fomented the Atlanta riot that took place in September 1906 and led to dozens of black deaths modeled their vigilante assault after the tactics pursued by the conspirators in Wilmington.[39] In 1917, East Saint Louis, Illinois, was engulfed by white destruction, and in the aftermath of World War I and the Bolshevik Revolution, the grisly Red Summer of 1919 witnessed homicidal white assaults on black communities in dozens of towns and cities, including Elaine, Arkansas; Chicago, Illinois; Washington, D.C.; Longview, Texas; Norfolk, Virginia; Omaha, Nebraska; Charleston, South Carolina; Indianapolis, Indiana; and Bisbee, Arizona.[40]

The horrific 1921 massacre in Tulsa, Oklahoma, razed the prosperous black Greenwood community—a so-called Black Wall Street—and included the dropping of incendiary devices on black homes and businesses from decommissioned military planes.[41] The white riot depicted in the 1997 film *Rosewood* took place in 1923 in a small town of the same name in Florida, but the white violence in Rosewood was only one of many instances in the bloody state in the first two decades of the twentieth century. Perhaps the most savage in Florida was the Ocoee massacre, a white supremacist response, mentioned above, to the determined efforts of blacks to exercise their right to vote; at least fifty black people were killed in a single day.[42]

Often, white soldiers killed black soldiers on military bases with impunity; the assaults intensified when black soldiers responded by defending themselves.[43] During World War II, white rioters even drove black workers out of *segregated* employment on naval shipyards.[44] Antiblack riots continued throughout the war and beyond, including in Detroit in 1943 and Fernwood Park in Chicago in 1947.[45]

The cumulative toll of black deaths from white massacres is difficult to estimate. Between the end of Reconstruction and the beginning of the 1950s, the lower-bound estimate is 700, while the upper-bound estimate exceeds 1,500 persons. The uncertainty is attributable to the failure of public officials to have any concern about recording black mortality accurately, another sign of the depth of worthlessness assigned to black lives in American society.[46]

Throughout the twentieth century, America also was characterized by a long and extensive lynching trail—a pathway of extralegal executions of blacks. One obvious consequence was the frequent elimination of a family's breadwinner. The most recent estimates place the number of blacks murdered in this fashion by white gangs and mobs between 1877 and 1950 at close to 4,000 in Alabama, Arkansas, Florida, Georgia, Kentucky, Louisiana, Mississippi, North Carolina, South Carolina, Tennessee, Texas, and Virginia.[47] Moreover, lynchings often were associated directly with the expropriation of black-owned land, and the threat of lynching created a climate of intimidation to promote black subordination.[48]

Kentucky, the only state among the twelve where enslaved persons had represented less than 25 percent of the overall population, was the only state among these that did not secede from the Union. The estimated numbers of lynchings in the twelve states do not include approximately 300 more that took place outside of the south. But these numbers are dwarfed by South Carolina congressman Robert Smalls's calculation discussed at the end of chapter 8—a calculation increasingly viewed as accurate—that 53,000 blacks were murdered by whites from 1865 to 1895 alone.[49]

Although there are still numerous instances of extrajudicial executions conducted by private citizens, today's lynching trail is dominated by police killings of unarmed black men and women.[50] Among the approximately 1,000 persons now killed by the police each year, one-quarter are black Americans, a proportion far greater than their presence in the overall population. This annual level of black executions virtually exceeds the number of lynchings in any year of the first half of the twentieth century.[51] A common attribute of all of these murders is the failure to convict the perpetrators of the crimes; rarely are they even prosecuted. Indeed, there is a sustained pattern of failures to prosecute perpetrators—whether or not the murder was carried out by the police—from the clandestine murder of Emmett Till to the open execution of Michael Brown on a street in Ferguson, Missouri.

11

Beyond Jim Crow

Contract sellers became rich. North Lawndale became a ghetto. Clyde
Ross still lives there. He still owns his home. He is 91, and the emblems of
survival are all around him—awards for service in his community, pictures
of his children in cap and gown. But when I asked him about his home in
North Lawndale, I heard only anarchy.

"We were ashamed. We did not want anyone to know that we were
that ignorant," Ross told me. He was sitting at his dining-room table. His
glasses were as thick as his Clarksdale drawl. "I'd come out of Mississippi
where there was one mess, and come up here and got in another mess. So
how dumb am I? I didn't want anyone to know how dumb I was.

"When I found myself caught up in it [the contract-buying scam], I said,
'How? I just left this mess. I just left no laws. And no regard. And then I
come here and get cheated wide open.' I would probably want to do some
harm to some people, you know, if I had been violent like some of us. I
thought, 'Man, I got caught up in this stuff. I can't even take care of my
kids. I didn't have enough for my kids.' You could fall through the cracks
easy fighting these white people. And no law." —Ta-Nehisi Coates, "The
Case for Reparations," 2014

The chickens of the tragic failure of Southern leadership are still coming
home to roost. —Samuel DuBois Cook, "Political Movements and
Organizations," 1964

The message of the Black Lives Matter movement encapsulates the racialized
injuries of the 150 years since the end of legal American slavery. The movement's message alerts us to the many ways in which black life has been devalued and unprotected so thoroughly in the United States. The discount rate
on black humanity has been enormous. A variety of metrics indicate that,
even after the end of Jim Crow, black lives are routinely assigned a worth
approximately 30 percent that of white lives.

There are a number of ways in which numerical estimates can be placed
on the differential value assigned to black versus white lives in the United
States. For example, as early as the 1840s, New York Life typically insured
whites for anywhere from $1,000 to $5,000, while enslaved blacks typically

were insured on behalf of their owners for no more than $400 and sometimes for as little as $200.[1] It has been estimated that in 1928 there was one hospital bed for every 139 white Americans but only one for every 1,941 black Americans, indicating that the average black life was worth only 7 percent of the average white life.[2]

During the Jim Crow years, when the dual system of schooling operated, the gap in per pupil expenditures provides a powerful index of the magnitude of the discount rate on black lives. For example, in 1939–40, per-pupil expenditures for white students in most of the southern states were three times more than they were for black students, suggesting that a young black life was worth about 30 percent of a young white life. In Mississippi, per-pupil expenditures were seven times greater, suggesting that in Mississippi at that time, a young black life was worth 15 percent of a young white life.[3] In Alabama in 1912, a cluster of counties spent thirty-two cents on black students' education per every fifteen dollars spent on white students' education, implying that a white youth's life was deemed to be worth an incredible 4,700 percent more than a black youth's life.[4]

Today the estimated difference in spending per black and white student is reduced substantially, although a 13 percent gap remains.[5] Unfortunately, the narrowing of the spending gap disguises a profound racial gap in curriculum and instruction in a world of desegregated schools.

The disparity in the rate of placement of black students in gifted and talented programs provides a marked indicator of the devaluation of black youth in the nation's educational system. Black and Latinx students constitute 40 percent of America's public school students but only 26 percent of the students enrolled in gifted and talented programs. The average black child is "66 percent less likely to be referred for gifted math and reading than their white classmates."[6] The gross underrepresentation of black children and overrepresentation of white children in gifted education suggests that black youth are being assigned a value of less than 40 percent of the worth of a white child in the nation's schools.

Moreover, the gap in the rates at which blacks and whites are killed in police shootings delivers another contemporary message on the devaluation of black lives, similar to some estimated magnitudes under legal segregation. For example, black men are killed by the police at three times the rate of white men each year. This would imply that black men's lives are worth one-third of white men's lives.[7] Discriminatory wage penalties, differential exposure of black children to lead poisoning, and the far greater use of black bodies for medical experimentation afford additional avenues for estimating how heavy the discount rate continues to be on black lives.

This chapter provides a grim and extensive (albeit incomplete) catalog of the damages visited upon blacks *into the present moment*, indicative of a permanent markdown on the worth of black lives.

In addition to the sheer ascription of worthlessness to black lives, several mechanisms have been developed to sustain wealth stripping from blacks. One of these was the so-called contract-buying scheme, which was particularly notorious in mid-twentieth-century Chicago. "Contract selling" for homes, now undergoing an unfortunate revival, involves the following arrangements: "In this model, buyers shut out from conventional lending are offered an alternative: They can make monthly payments on a home directly to the seller, instead of a bank, with the promise of receiving the deed only once the property is entirely paid off, 20 or 30 years down the road. In the meantime they have few of the legal protections of a typical home buyer but all of the responsibilities of one. They don't build equity with time. They can be easily evicted. And if that happens, they lose all of their investment."[8]

Members of black households, highly motivated to become homeowners, were most likely to be exposed to the scam because of their discriminatory exclusion from standard borrowing options. In his feature article in the *Atlantic* on black reparations, Ta-Nehisi Coates devoted special attention to the contract-buying scheme in Chicago, demonstrating how it enabled white realtors to defraud thousands of black families of homes they were led to believe they owned.[9] The ongoing destruction of comparatively affluent black communities no longer is achieved primarily via white riots or outright fraud but by somewhat more subtle mechanisms—first, by urban renewal and, second, by gentrification. Both processes have been described sarcastically as "Negro removal." Both processes are traumatic for their victims.

Black districts produced under the constraints imposed by white preferences for residential segregation often developed stable, middle-income communities and black-owned business sectors. Nevertheless, these Jim Crow neighborhoods still have been subjected to demolition. "Negro removal" demonstrates that the precise nature of the processes producing racial inequality change over time, but more than a half century after the passage of the Civil Rights Act of 1964, those processes still operate specifically to undermine opportunity and well-being for black Americans.

For example, in 1953 Memphis, the middle-income, black Lauderdale–Vance Avenue community was declared a "slum" to justify demolition, including the symbolically significant burning of the former home of a prominent black community leader, Robert Church, at 384 South Lauderdale Street.[10] The community's residents had protested the decision to no avail: "Residents beseeched Senator McKellar, their onetime neighbor and a conduit of federal authority, not to 'wreck this whole section of the city' as one letter put it. 'The home owners are sick and distressed beyond measure.' They wrote that they had toiled for years to pay off their mortgages and fix up their properties, and they'd succeeded in making this the best neighborhood for blacks in Memphis. Their community was more valuable than any relocation funds the city might provide. One of [E. H. 'Boss'] Crump's leading black organizers, the Reverend T. O. Fuller, protested that he'd lose his home, workplace, and church."[11]

Their grievances were ignored. The Memphis Housing Authority—established in the mid-1930s, part of the wave of local authorities begun under Roosevelt's New Deal—leveled a forty-six-acre area and replaced the single-family homes with a low-rise, 900-unit public housing complex.[12]

The black population of Tulsa, Oklahoma, had witnessed the destruction of its prosperous Greenwood community in the white rampage in 1921. In subsequent years, the community saw significant progress in rebuilding the black business district that had been erased during the white riot, only to witness that progress wiped away, beginning in 1967, by an urban renewal program that destroyed the resurrection effort in the former black stronghold.[13] Thus, the Greenwood community in Tulsa was subjected to *both* a white massacre and a "slum clearance," approximately half a century apart.[14]

The federal interstate highway program was deployed to situate new freeways through the heart of black communities, disrupting established neighborhoods, displacing residents, and destroying black-owned business districts. Raymond Mohl's 2002 report for the Poverty and Race Research Action Council identified city after city—in the north and south, east and west—where black communities were shattered by the location and construction of federal highways in their midst.[15] As Mohl observed: "Highway builders rarely mentioned African Americans specifically in their discussions about clearing out blight and slums. In fact, when these ideas first began to receive currency in the late 1930s the nation's largest cities had not yet received the full force of the massive wartime and postwar migration of southern blacks. But that changed dramatically in the 1940s and after. By that time, when the highwaymen talked about clearing out central-city blight, everyone knew what they meant."[16]

The goal was clear to most, even if it was rarely stated directly. Actions and policies made intentions transparent—and the visible consequences of the highways the highwaymen built are the best evidence of their desired objective. As one former federal highway official conceded in a 1972 interview, the urban interstates gave city officials "a good opportunity to get rid of the local niggertown."[17]

In the case of Miami, Florida,

> state highway planners and local officials deliberately routed Interstate-95 directly through the inner-city black community of Overtown. An alternative route utilizing an abandoned railroad corridor was rejected, as the highway planners noted, to provide "ample room for the future expansion of the central business district in a westerly direction," a goal of the local business elite since the 1930s. Even before the expressway was built, and in the absence of any relocation planning, some in Miami's white and black press asked: "What about the Negroes Uprooted by Expressway?" The question remained unanswered, and when the downtown leg of the expressway was completed in the mid-1960s, it tore through the center of Overtown, wiping out massive amounts of housing as well as Overtown's main business district, the commercial and cultural heart of black Miami. One massive expressway interchange took up twenty square blocks of densely settled land and destroyed the housing of about 10,000 people. By the end of the 1960s, Overtown had become an urban wasteland dominated by the physical presence of the expressway. Little remained of the neighborhood to recall its days as a thriving center of black community life, when it was known as the Harlem of the South.[18]

Anthony Foxx, the secretary of transportation during the second term of the Obama administration, grew up in Charlotte, North Carolina, where he also served as mayor. There, the black community known as Brooklyn was "eviscerated" by the interstate highway system; today, Brooklyn no longer exists.[19] Foxx estimates that throughout the United States during the first twenty years of installation of the interstate highway system, 475,000 families and more than a million citizens were displaced. These, overwhelmingly, were residents of black communities.[20]

In some cities, municipal authorities bore the responsibility for introducing new roadways that performed the same function—getting rid of "the local niggertown." For example, in Durham, North Carolina, the flourishing black business district, Hayti, was erased by two major road construction projects. First, in the late 1950s, the Durham Redevelopment Commission conceived and executed a plan to run an east-west expressway (US 15-501) through the center of the area. Still active in the 1960s, the commission planned a second thoroughfare, the Durham Freeway (NC 147), which crossed the expressway, displacing even more black enterprise and destroying Hayti.[21]

While urban renewal constituted a process of "Negro removal" engineered by the public sector, gentrification constitutes a process of "Negro removal" engineered by the private sector, frequently with public sector support. Gentrification principally involves the displacement of low- and moderate-income blacks by affluent whites from neighborhoods where blacks have lived for generations.

In many instances, whites are "reclaiming" America's inner cities. This process frequently is coupled with the demolition of the high-rise public-housing buildings that were built after the leveling of black-owned single-detached homes, the substitution of public and low-income housing with "mixed-income" housing, and the continued designation of predominantly black communities as areas that require economic renewal and development. In short, the black population literally is pushed out of their homes and neighborhoods.

Dallas, Texas, provides a paradigmatic example of the reversal of the original "urban redevelopment" project, a reversal that now promotes the comprehensive whitening of once all-black communities. The "A New Dallas" plan proposes to tear down the highway that once was built through the heart of a black business district to reopen the land to commercial and residential use, but it promises to bring a very different population into the area than the one that had developed a community there in the past.[22]

Another Brooklyn—Brooklyn, New York—provides a dramatic example of the various dimensions of the private-public collaboration that makes gentrification happen. Between 2000 and 2010 it is estimated that Brooklyn lost 50,000 black residents, while its white population increased by 37,000. Blacks faced with foreclosure and/or job loss during the Great Recession were enticed into turning over their deeds to white developers and surrendering their rent-controlled apartments for comparatively small sums of money.

The dilution of rent regulation in New York City also has contributed to the push-out effect; an empty apartment no longer is subject to rent control. Once a rent-controlled apartment is vacated, the landlord is free to increase the rent. Moreover, an apartment is no longer subject to rent regulation once the rent exceeds $2,700 per month, making that source of housing unaffordable for scores of black Brooklyn residents.

While the city steadily deregulates rental housing prices, its 421a program ostensibly provides incentives for developers to build mixed-income housing in Brooklyn. Instead, the program has been manipulated to provide a 95 percent tax abatement for a developer building a $100 million condominium in Manhattan. Furthermore, as the neighborhoods change, the composition of local juries also changes, making it more difficult for black plaintiffs to bring suits against landlords and for developers to preserve access to their homes.[23]

Of course, it is ironic that these same black communities that have been or are now being dismantled were initially products of the forces of segregation, both legal and informal. Now that the areas where black residents have lived are deemed commercially useful to developers, newer forces of segregation are leading to the dispersal of those communities. Their segregated status merely is being transformed from predominantly black to predominantly white neighborhoods.

The historical record is clear: "Black people who had money to buy and develop properties were prevented from doing so by redlining which prevented mortgages, bank loans and even insurance from being utilized in black neighborhoods across the country. Urban areas had large black populations because white people fled. White people left to get away from black people and capital paved the road to the suburbs. The tide is now turning because there is once again money to be made in the cities."[24] In 2018, a study conducted in Harris County in Houston, Texas, found that the values of homes in black neighborhoods continue to depreciate relative to white-owned homes, regardless of the safety and amenity characteristics of the black neighborhoods or the characteristics of the residential structures.[25] Nationally, a Brookings study found that the average home in a predominantly black neighborhood is undervalued by $48,000, corresponding to a $156 billion total loss in equity.[26]

Segregation in the public sphere has taken many forms: separate water fountains, separate train cars, separate waiting rooms, separate seats on city buses and in theaters, separate toilets (when blacks were given access to public toilets at all), separate physical spaces with black spaces marked and designated as inferior, and even "Negro days" at state fairs, city parks, or downtown shops. There were even "sundown" towns, municipalities where blacks might be welcome to work during the day—at least in menial jobs—but were not welcome after sunset. These all are examples of microaggressions, indignities that erode the human spirit without overtly damaging life or limb, directed with laser-like precision against blacks.[27] Of course, blacks who transgressed these segregated public spaces frequently did find both life and limb in danger.

Another profound dimension of the devaluation of black lives that was a direct product of public segregation was the maintenance of separate *and unequal* schools. The formal structure of Jim Crow schooling did not end until 1954, with the U.S. Supreme Court's *Brown v. Board of Education* decision. The court's decision triggered the pursuit of "massive resistance" by the states of the old Confederacy. Consequently, genuine school desegregation did not get under way until the early 1970s.

In the 1950s, to resist school desegregation—and desegregation in general—in conjunction with the rejuvenation of the Ku Klux Klan, the "best class" of white southerners formed White Citizens' Councils throughout the former insurrectional states. As Samuel DuBois Cook observed, the councils were dominated by "responsible citizens—bankers, businessmen, public officials and other politicians, doctors, lawyers, and other members of upper and middle classes."[28] While the councils also included "farmers, laborers, and similar 'God-fearing' ordinary people," in seeking "respectability" and a "good public image," the councils genuinely represented southern white-establishment sentiment.[29]

The councils attacked all facets of desegregation efforts by mobilizing a movement designed to defend an apartheid status quo. An important dimension of this attack was the erection of tried-and-true obstacles to black voter participation. Those established techniques to suppress the black vote—intimidation, purges of black voters from the rolls, and absurdly restrictive voter eligibility standards—had their effect, despite intensive efforts by civil rights activists to register black voters; as late as 1960 an estimated 1,414,052 blacks were registered to vote, "about one-fourth of the potential."[30]

From the mid-1950s to the mid-1970s, the council controlled politics in Mississippi. In 1962, when Robert Moses and his fellow volunteers from the Student Nonviolent Coordinating Committee (SNCC), together with the Council of Federated Organizations, attempted to register blacks to vote, they discovered the council was behind state legislation that required election administrators to publish the names of new applicants in the local newspaper. In addition, existing voters were permitted to object to the "moral character" of applicants. SNCC's efforts were thwarted further when, in the midst of a famine, federal food surpluses were shut off in two adjacent Mississippi counties—Sunflower County, home of cotton plantation owner and arch-conservative U.S. senator James O. Eastland, and Leflore County, home to the White Citizens' Council headquarters and the place Emmett Till was lynched in 1955. "In LeFlore [*sic*], the cut off stopped food relief to some 22,000 people—nearly half of the county population, mostly Negroes, fully a third of them [having] an income less than $500."[31]

While we often think of the civil rights movement as a mid-twentieth-century phenomenon with a small cast of heroes, blacks' mobilization to obtain human rights dates from their earliest forced migration to the United States. White retaliation against those efforts also is long-standing.

Soon after its inception in 1844, Greenwood, Mississippi, founded at the height of the international demand for cotton, became a cotton-production capital with the aid of the domestic slave trade and the forced migration of blacks to the region. With enslaved blacks outnumbering whites three to one, whites in Greenwood legislated repressive and far-reaching measures policing black lives, cementing the city as the symbolic heart of Mississippi defiance.[32]

During Reconstruction, the seven mystic years when the tables were turned and black men were enfranchised, the state's first two black senators, Blanche K. Bruce and Hiram Revels, were elected. In 1890, long after federal troops providing protection to blacks and their supporters had been recalled—and less than a decade after Bruce left his Senate seat to accept a position as register of the Treasury—Mississippi adopted a new constitution and effectively denied the vote to its black residents.[33] Black political activism moved underground. Always simmering, the movement grew more heated after each of the world wars, when black military men who had served the country and defended foreign allies returned to the United States only to find their own rights unchanged.

White newspapers fanned the fires for hostile whites. "Political dominions of the white race are threatened by the education of the Negro," was the rallying cry of *Greenwood Enterprise* editor James K. Vardaman (1890–96). His gubernatorial election campaign promise to remove the black vote and restore the "absolute domination by the white race" won him the support of the white working poor, owners of small farms, and factory workers.[34] During his first year as governor, Vardaman closed the state's black public schools.

By 1906, white Mississippians had long engaged in violent retribution against blacks seeking higher wages, better working conditions, the right to vote, education for their children, or, merely, respectful treatment from whites in their daily lives. In December of that year, when a disagreement between a Mobile & Ohio train conductor and a black passenger resulted in two blacks being mortally shot and a third injured—he was later lynched by a mob—white riots broke out in Wahalak and Scooba, Mississippi, in Kemper County, and at least twelve other blacks and two whites were killed.

In 1952, at a rally organized by the Regional Council of Negro Leadership in the all-black Delta town of Mound Bayou, Mississippi, residents were encouraged to register to vote.[35] At the time, fewer than 6 percent of eligible blacks in the state had succeeded in doing so, some 17,000 people, compared to 90 percent of eligible whites. Three years later, the number of registered blacks was cut in half after the state adopted new registration criteria.[36] Rev. George Washington Lee was the first known black man to register to vote in Humphrey County. He and Gus Courts, from Leflore County, were grocers in an area where no blacks had voted since Reconstruction. They organized a chapter of the National Association for the Advancement of Colored People (NAACP) in 1953 in the town of Belzoni, advocated for school equality, and succeeded in getting nearly ninety blacks to register to vote. Area municipalities responded by placing an additional demand on black voters, the payment of a poll tax. When the local sheriff refused to allow the black registrants to pay the tax, Courts and Lee sued him, greatly escalating tensions in the region.[37]

In May 1954, when the landmark civil rights case *Brown v. Board of Education of Topeka* passed, making the segregation of public schools unconstitutional, white supremacists redoubled their efforts to stamp out black activism in the Delta. While at least a dozen activists were driven out of their homes, Courts and Lee were undeterred and organized a rally in Mound Bayou in April 1955, where more than 7,000 people heard Reverend Lee's impassioned speech. "Pray you can make it through this hell," he urged. On two occasions that month the windows of cars and businesses owned by black residents who had paid their poll tax were broken, and notes were left on the premises warning, "This is just a token of what will happen to you."[38]

On May 7, 1955, Reverend Lee was assassinated by white terrorists.[39] Members of the white business elite began to pressure Courts to hand over the NAACP membership lists. Over the next six months, Courts bravely continued his work and registered another twenty-two black voters.

Four months later, Emmett Till, a fourteen-year-old boy from Chicago who came to Mississippi in the summer of 1955 to visit his uncle Moses Wright and earn money picking cotton, was murdered by the husband and the half brother of a white woman Till is said to have insulted.

Members of the white business elite then launched a full-on effort to bankrupt Courts's store: "Bankers refused him credit [and rebuffed his offer of cash], wholesalers denied him service, his landlord tripled the rent, a local gas station refused to sell him fuel, and whites warned blacks not to shop at his grocery."[40] New suppliers from Memphis and other centers of commerce enabled him to keep his doors open for a time. Eventually, he reached out to the NAACP for financial support. Then, in November, Courts was shot in the abdomen and one arm while standing in front of his Belzoni store. His insistence that he be taken to a black-run hospital in Mound Bayou, some ninety miles away, may have saved his life.

In 1961, efforts to educate blacks in Mississippi about their right to vote and to assist them with the registration process were met with fierce white opposition. That August, the assistant director of SNCC, Robert Moses, was arrested while accompanying three residents to the registrar's office, and he was attacked two weeks later when he attempted to bring two more residents to the office.

After the national press reported that armed whites had broken into a registration office, U.S. attorney general Robert Kennedy promised federal troops would be sent in to protect the volunteers. "They notified the FBI and were told an agent was on his way. None came." Kennedy had realized that "only something tantamount to a military occupation could protect the workers."[41] This was a commitment that he and his brother, President John F. Kennedy, were unwilling to make.

SNCC, based in Atlanta, sent fieldworkers to the Mississippi Delta to prepare blacks for the multitude of literacy tests they would need to pass in order to vote. These efforts were met with brutal resistance. "In Amit [*sic*: Amite] County, a SNCC worker was beaten in Liberty by the cousin of the sheriff. The Waltham County registrar pistol-whipped another SNCC worker."[42] Herbert Lee, who worked with Moses on the voter registration campaign, was murdered by state legislator Edward Hurst in September 1961 in Liberty, Mississippi. Louis Allen, who witnessed the murder, was killed in January 1964, just as he was about to leave for the north after enduring more than two years of intimidation and threats on his life. No one was convicted for either murder.

The summer of 1963, Freedom Summer, when young black civil rights workers and over 1,000 white volunteers came to Mississippi to make a dramatic push for voter registration, led to the murders of civil rights workers Michael Schwerner, James Chaney, Andrew Goodman, and at least five others. Medgar Evers, the state's operations director for the NAACP, was assassinated in the front yard of his home on June 12, 1963.

The NAACP had been active in Louisiana as early as 1915, and entities like Louisiana's League for the Preservation of Constitutional Rights and the People's Defense League paved the way for the activism of the 1950s and 1960s. Blacks in Madison Parish won the right to vote in 1963 on grounds that it was unlawful for all black residents to be barred from the franchise, but the fight dated as early as 1947, when Moses Williams, Zelma Wyche, Harrison Brown, and others first attempted to register to vote and began to agitate for black rights. For years, Madison sheriff Clifton Hester had threatened and intimidated organizers, and he succeeded in thwarting several early legal cases.

In October 1963, New Orleans police raided the offices of the Southern Conference Education Fund, confiscated documents, and followed up with searches of the homes of James Dombrowski, executive director, Ben Smith, treasurer, and Bruce Walzer, Smith's law partner, each of whom was arrested and jailed on charges of subversion. The fund's records were delivered to the Senate Internal Security Subcommittee, then chaired by ultra-white supremacist Mississippi senator and planter James O. Eastland.

In Alabama, blacks' efforts to gain their long-denied rights to full citizenship were frequently met with bomb attacks. An explosive device destroyed the porch and part of the front parlor of Martin Luther King Jr.'s home in Montgomery on January 30, 1956, while he was serving as pastor of the Dexter Avenue Baptist Church.[43]

The city of Birmingham, Alabama, came to be known as "Bombingham." The reign of white terror in Birmingham came to a head with the bombing of the Sixteenth Street Baptist Church that killed four young girls, Addie Mae Collins, Denise McNair, Carole Robertson, and Cynthia Wesley, all under fifteen years of age. In the immediate aftermath, thirteen-year-old Virgil Lamar Ware was shot to death by white teenagers who had attended a segregationist rally that followed the bomb blast at the church.[44]

Two strategies that animated the Confederate secession—"interposition" and "nullification"—were reactivated by the White Citizens' Councils and their allies to stall school desegregation.[45] The exclusion of black voters enabled whites to control local school boards and keep their schools white and better financed. Ultimately, school desegregation in the south was delayed for close to twenty years after the *Brown* decision.

The dual school system had ensured racial differences in the quality of school facilities, in teacher compensation per pupil, and in the quality of instructional materials. The magnitude of these disparities was first documented carefully by Horace Mann Bond in his classic study *The Education of the Negro in the American Social Order*, where he detailed the widespread practice of paying black teachers significantly less than white teachers; frequently under the dual system, black teachers' salaries were 60 percent or less of white teachers' salaries.[46]

These huge disparities in teacher pay could not be fully explained by differences in teacher training. Economic historian Robert Margo has estimated that both in 1910 and 1940, about 80 percent of the difference in black and white teacher pay was sheerly based on racial differences, with compensation established on pay schedules by local, white-dominated school boards.[47] This was out-and-out discrimination.

School segregation provided an avenue for the systematic fulfillment of the desire expressed by Reconstruction-era white supremacist President

Andrew Johnson to "uplift the Negro" while fixing an eternal educational gap between blacks and whites: "[Johnson made] his racial views perfectly clear to Benjamin B. French, the commissioner of public buildings. 'Everyone would, and *must* admit,' he explained to French in the fall of 1865, 'that the white race was superior to the black, and that while we ought to do our best to bring them . . . up to our present level, that, in doing so, we should, at the same time raise our own intellectual status *so that the relative position of the two races would be the same.*'"[48]

Johnson's nineteenth-century objective of designing a system of relatively inferior education for blacks has been maintained in the post–*Brown v. Board of Education* era. De facto segregation of schools attributable to school assignment plans and residential segregation, coupled with grossly unequal allocations of resources to predominantly black schools, has continued to the present day in many urban areas.[49]

At least as pernicious are arrangements that generate *within-school* segregation, resulting in the assignment of black students to the least challenging and engaging curricula and instruction. Racialized tracking is the culprit. Indeed, teachers, particularly white teachers, who function as the primary gatekeepers in gifted and talented identification, are less likely to refer black students for gifted programs than white students with similar levels of academic achievement.[50]

Not only do black Americans have reduced opportunities to obtain quality education; they also receive less of a payoff for any credential they earn. The persistence of wage and employment discrimination and racial wealth inequality ensures that America's dice are loaded against blacks in two ways. As we noted in chapter 2, at each level of educational attainment blacks have an unemployment rate two times that of whites. Blacks with some college education or an associate's degree frequently have a higher unemployment rate than whites who never finished high school.[51] Job prospects for recent black college graduates, including those with degrees in engineering, remain comparatively grim.[52]

The disregard for black lives evidenced by antiblack riots, lynchings, neighborhood devastation, and inferior education is also apparent in the process that Douglas Blackmon has called "black reenslavement." During the first half of the twentieth century, many blacks who were charged with a crime found themselves entrapped in a prison bondage system. They were placed in forced labor camps where their work was imposed by local governments, or they were leased to private businesses or individuals, without receiving any compensation.

The harsh and often dangerous conditions of the labor camps and the imprecise nature of the length of their sentences meant that prospects for survival and release were dim. Individuals often disappeared into the labor camps without any notification of family or friends from whom they had gone missing. Frequently, those reenslaved were not guilty of any crime whatsoever and certainly not of crimes of a sufficient magnitude to justify reenslavement:

> Instead of thousands of true thieves and thugs drawn into the system over decades, the records demonstrate the capture and imprisonment of thousands of random indigent citizens, almost always under the thinnest chimera of probable cause or judicial process. The total number of workers caught in this net had to have totaled more than a hundred thousand and perhaps more than twice that figure. Instead of evidence showing black crime waves, the original records of county jails indicated thousands of arrests for inconsequential charges or for violation of laws specifically written to intimidate blacks—changing employers without permission, vagrancy, riding freight cars without a ticket, engaging in sexual activity, or loud talk—with white women. Repeatedly, the timing and scale of surges in arrests appeared more attuned to rises and dips in the need for cheap labor than any demonstrable acts of crime. Hundreds of forced labor camps came to exist, scattered throughout the South—operated by state and county governments, large corporations, small-time entrepreneurs, and provincial farmers. These bulging slave centers became a primary weapon of suppression of black aspirations. Where mob violence or the Ku Klux Klan terrorized black citizens periodically, the return of forced labor as a fixture in black life ground pervasively into the daily lives of far more African Americans. And the record is replete with episodes in which public leaders faced a true choice between a path toward complete racial repression or some degree of modest civil equality, and emphatically chose the former. These were not unavoidable events, driven by invisible forces of tradition and history.[53]

The forced-labor system put many black lives and the well-being of many black families in jeopardy. Blackmon's research uncovered private prison contractors, predatory "labor agents" whose job, as early as 1863, was to supply companies like Shelby Iron Works with "as many mules as possible, and the feed corn to feed both the four-legged and two-legged creatures."[54]

From 1878 to 1883, business partners and former Confederate officers Edward H. Cunningham and Littleberry Ellis, owners of sugarcane plantations in close proximity to Galveston, Texas, and of the Imperial Sugar Company, leased the state's entire prison population to work their fields. The Imperial Sugar Company, based in Sugar Land, Texas, laid the foundation for the long-term affluence of white residents of the small city, now one of the wealthiest in the state.[55]

By 1880, when Cunningham was paying the state $3.01 per month for each of the 365 convicts he leased, he was said to be "one of the wealthiest men in the state."[56] The abominable conditions of work and the high mortality rates the convict laborers suffered demonstrated clearly that the horrors of southern plantation agriculture continued after slavery ended.

Today, the United States has the "highest rate of incarceration in the world, dwarfing the rates of nearly every developed country, even surpassing those in highly repressive regimes like Russia, China and Iran," observes the legal scholar Michelle Alexander.[57] Those numbers are driven primarily by the overincarceration of black Americans.

Convict-made goods are a major revenue source in many states. Other states borrow another page from nineteenth-century systems of policing blacks: targeting black Americans for arrest and then hitting them with a barrage of fees and fines.

Alexander, speaking about black Americans and the role of the criminal justice system in Ferguson, Missouri, said, "Poor people, particularly poor folks of color are targeted by our criminal justice system, arrested for extremely minor offences—the very sorts of crimes that occur with equal frequency in middle class communities or on college campuses, but go largely ignored—targeted, arrested or cited and then saddled with fines and fees that are nearly impossible for them to pay back. Then warrants are issued for their arrest for failure to appear in court or to pay back their fees or fines in a timely manner, leading then into a system from which they have little hope of ever truly escaping. . . . We can look back at history and see this is not the first time we've done something like this."[58]

Black life was so devalued in the nineteenth century that there was little hesitation about using blacks as objects of nonconsensual medical experimentation. As early as the 1840s, Alabama physician J. Marion Sims used enslaved black women as involuntary subjects—without anesthesia—for his efforts to develop gynecological instruments. Known by his admirers as "the father of gynecology," Sims felt no compunction in reducing black women to the status of laboratory animals.[59]

The use of black bodies for medical experiments without informed consent continued deep into the twentieth century. Perhaps the most notorious example is the Tuskegee experiment, in which black men were left untreated for syphilis for forty years (1932–72) so that investigators could "observe" the progression of the disease.[60] A "litany of medical misdeeds" directed against black Americans in the twentieth century has been cataloged by sociologist Alondra Nelson:

> In 1945, Ebb Cade, an African American trucker being treated for injuries received in an accident in Tennessee, was surreptitiously placed without his consent into a radiation experiment sponsored by the U.S. Atomic Energy Commission. Black Floridians were deliberately exposed to swarms of mosquitoes carrying yellow fever and other diseases in experiments conducted by the Army and the CIA in the early 1950s. Throughout the 1950s and '60s, black inmates at Philadelphia's Holmesburg Prison were used as research subjects by a University of Pennsylvania dermatologist testing pharmaceuticals and personal hygiene products; some of these subjects report pain and disfiguration even now. During the 1960s and '70s, black boys were subjected to sometimes paralyzing neurosurgery by a University of Mississippi researcher who believed brain pathology to be the root of the children's supposed hyperactive behavior. In the 1990s, African American youths in New York were injected with Fenfluramine—half of the deadly, discontinued weight loss drug Fen-Phen—by Columbia researchers investigating a hypothesis about the genetic origins of violence.[61]

Black lives were put at risk and destroyed by medical experimentation that, again, involved no hint of informed consent. Perhaps the most glaring example was the extensive use in the medical field of the HeLa cells of the late Henrietta Lacks without her family's or her own knowledge and agreement.[62] Lacks's unusual cells that could be kept alive and had the capacity to grow in number proved to be a remarkable boon for biomedical researchers, but neither Lacks nor her relatives had ever given permission for their use in this fashion.

Black families' reproduction has also been prevented by involuntary sterilizations—both officially under state eugenics programs and unofficially by coercive physicians who insisted on tying the tubes of black women after they had given birth. Some physicians seized upon the opportunity to perform hysterectomies on black patients when the women were admitted to hospital for other, nonobstetrical reasons. Eugenic sterilization programs were adopted in thirty states and resulted in the sterilization of upward of 60,000 persons between the 1930s and 1970s.[63] In particular, the states of California and North Carolina disproportionately sterilized their black residents.[64]

In the 1960s and 1970s, the use of involuntary sterilization to curb black fertility also was evident in a pattern of physicians denying black female welfare recipients medical services unless they agreed to have their "tubes tied":

> The pill gave black women greater control over reproduction than ever before. Why should this seemingly positive development be so controversial? One reason is the role white-dominated birth control programs played in furthering racial injustice. As black Americans agitated for their civil rights, the white backlash included reproductive regulation. The pill was introduced at a time when scientists such as Arthur Jensen and William Shockley were promoting genetic explanations of racial differences in intelligence-test scores. During the 1960s and 1970s, thousands of poor black women were coercively sterilized under federally funded programs. Women were threatened with termination of welfare benefits or denial of medical care if they didn't "consent" to the procedure. Southern blacks claimed that black women were routinely sterilized without their consent and for no valid medical reason—a practice so widespread it was called a "Mississippi appendectomy." Teaching hospitals in the North also performed unnecessary hysterectomies on poor black women as practice for their medical residents. During this period, state legislators considered a rash of punitive sterilization bills aimed at the growing number of blacks receiving public assistance.[65]

The health of black people is consistently put in greater jeopardy than the health of white people. Blacks are far likelier than whites to live in communities located near hazardous-waste sites and to suffer from nitrogen dioxide exposure and two times more likely to lack potable water and sanitation.[66] A recent dramatic example of black vulnerability to environmental hazards is the poisoned tap water crisis in Flint, Michigan, where, "when sour-smelling, discolored water came out of Flint residents' pipes in the spring of 2014, their complaints went ignored for nearly two years."[67]

In some cases, environmental damage done by heavily polluting corporations destroys black lives and drives residents out of long-standing black towns. One of the most glaring examples is the series of cancer-related deaths and community destruction wrought by the location of Axiall's and Sasol's chemical plants in Mossville, Louisiana, a process begun in the 1990s. Mossville, a black town established more than 225 years ago by persons formerly enslaved, now no longer exists.[68]

And for black communities subjected to environmental hazards, redress is rarely forthcoming: "The complaints of black and poor communities usually go ignored. The Environmental Protection Agency . . . has . . . denied 95 percent of the civil rights claims brought by communities of color against polluters, and it has never once made a formal finding of a civil-rights violation."[69] Indeed, the evidence presented in part 5 of this book has demonstrated that black lives *have not mattered* in the United States since the end of slavery. American society has marked down the value of black well-being for a century and a half. We have documented many aspects of the devaluation of black lives in this chapter. Setting aside the evil of slavery itself, the catalog of injustices listed here is sufficient to make the case for reparations.

When the United Nations' Working Group of Experts on People of African Descent issued its dramatic report calling for reparations for black Americans in 2016, the group emphasized current injustices as well as enslavement and its long-term effects. As the *Washington Post* reported: "In particular, the legacy of colonial history, enslavement, racial subordination and segregation, racial terrorism and racial inequality in the United States remains a serious challenge, as there has been no real commitment to reparations and to truth and reconciliation for people of African descent. Contemporary police killings and the trauma that they create are reminiscent of the past racial terror of lynching." Citing the previous year's spate of police officers killing unarmed African American men, the panel warned against "impunity for state violence," which has created, in the panelists' words, a "human rights crisis" that "must be addressed as a matter of urgency."[70]

Part 6

12

Criticisms and Responses

Reparations-induced resentment toward blacks by non-blacks, in fact, would increase. Blacks would claim that the solution is even more reparations. And the vicious cycle would continue. —Peter Flaherty and John Carlisle, "The Case against Slavery Reparations," 2004

It is true that there are no living former American slaves, but every African American has either directly or indirectly experienced racial discrimination or has been indirectly influenced by it. The failure to treat reparations as a legitimate issue acknowledges that America is far from being a "color-blind" society. . . . Reparations could be the beginning of a true revolution in values. —Charles P. Henry, *Long Overdue*, 2007

[The] story [of more than 6,000 black Union soldiers from North Carolina who participated in the Civil War] needs to be told like any other North Carolina story. . . . It's not just a story about Confederate bravery, defending homeland. I'm a Southerner, and this is my heritage too. When I'm telling the story, I'm just telling it from a different end of the gun.
—Malcolm Beech quoted in the *Winston-Salem Journal*, 2015

If you stick a knife in my back 9 inches and pull it out 6 inches, that's not progress. If you pull it all the way out, that's not progress. The progress comes from healing the wound that the blow made. They haven't even begun to pull the knife out. . . . They won't even admit the knife is there.
—Malcolm X, interview, 1964

Over the past fifteen years, when we have been invited to make presentations at public libraries and historic sites, on college campuses, and before civic organizations across the United States, Canada, and India, we have received a wide variety of comments and criticisms about our proposals. During this time, audiences' receptiveness to the idea of reparations for African Americans and the content of their queries have shifted dramatically. Comments such as "Reparations will never happen!" and "How can you propose such a preposterous thing?" have now become "How would you do it?" and "Who are the people that are working to make this happen?"

Most important, audiences gradually have shifted from challenging the legitimacy of reparations to asking questions about the logistics of a reparations plan. Noah Millman, at the time a senior editor with the *American Conservative*, actually conceded both the moral case for and the feasibility of black reparations but argued, instead, that he had a lingering "practical" concern that "reparations are not intended, nor should they be expected, to redress the socioeconomic inequalities associated with race . . . [and] the push for reparations might well stiffen opposition to other programs designed to address those disparities."[1] However, the core reason that a comprehensive plan for reparations is needed is that the "other programs" have not been up to the task of eliminating "those disparities." The objective of a reparations project is precisely "to redress the socioeconomic inequalities associated with race."

Moreover, in our estimation, the climate for the acceptance of a reparations program has never been better. We have read excellent scholarship on the subject, but no single existing document addresses all of the critiques we have encountered. In this chapter, we examine the most frequently voiced criticisms of reparations from both lay and academic audiences. Each of the responses we have developed helps make our case for the necessity and practicality of reparations. We present the most frequently articulated concerns here.[2]

"It was so long ago; there is no reason to keep bringing up slavery."

Few institutions have shaped America's present condition like slavery. Formative and powerful, slavery's hold on our psyches is continually reinforced, in part by the circulation of visual images and verbal descriptions of the subjugation and the habitual violence that was forced upon African Americans during that period. Slavery was outlawed 150 years ago. The republic itself was created a mere eighty-nine years before that.

Consider, also, the 120 natives of the West African country of Dahomey, present-day Benin, who were smuggled into the United States in 1860 and then sold into slavery in Mobile, Alabama, more than fifty years after the importation of new slaves to the country had been outlawed. One of the captives was a nineteen-year-old, Oluale Kossola—later known as Cudjo Lewis. Interviewed by anthropologist Zora Neale Hurston in 1927, he described the horrors of his abduction and the Middle Passage. One of this country's last known human chattel, Kossola died in 1935, a mere eighty-five years ago.[3]

New scholarship has emerged about another hostage on that ship, a girl named Redoshi. She was twelve years old when the whites who bought and enslaved her in Alabama changed her name to "Sally Smith." Redoshi died in 1937.[4]

Slavery is not so distant when you consider that, as of this writing, there are living Americans whose parents, grandparents, or great-grandparents were enslaved. Martha Burdette, education curator for the Cameron Art Museum in Wilmington, North Carolina, speaking about Civil War battle reenactments, has observed: "It's the ancestor thing. . . . It's close enough in history that almost everybody knows of someone in their family line who participated in some way in the Civil War. It's something they have a personal attachment to."[5]

More than half a century after slavery ended, whites holding positions of authority continued to exert power over blacks. Blacks no longer could be bought and sold like livestock, but they did not enjoy an easy coexistence with whites, and their lives and livelihoods could be subjected to harm at any time.

Sebrone Jones King, a man with a prodigious intellect and a keen survival instinct, emerged from the shadow of slavery only to find that his successful lumber business made him a target for whites, who resented his prosperity and tried to thwart him at every turn. When a white railroad station dispatcher in Kilgore, Texas, refused to allow King's hired hands to load his milled timber onto the train for delivery to a buyer in 1924, King confronted the dispatcher. The men argued and the dispatcher told King he would kill him if he continued to press his case. King is said to have replied, "Well, you'd better kill me quick, because if you don't, I'll shoot and kill *you* before I hit the ground." The dispatcher did not act on his threat.

Born in east Texas on January 14, 1865—about 150 years ago—nearly a year before slavery was declared illegal in December 1865 with the ratification of the Thirteenth Amendment to the Constitution, King conferred with his parents and siblings after the altercation with the dispatcher. He decided his best option was to pull up stakes and move his young family to Boley, Oklahoma, one of that state's all-black towns.

King's daughter, Hortense McClinton, was five years old when the family moved to Boley. In 1966, McClinton became the first black faculty member hired by the University of North Carolina at Chapel Hill; she taught in the School of Social Work. *Vigorous, lively, and vital at 101 years of age, she recently urged us to finish this book. McClinton, the daughter of a slave, is one generation removed from slavery.*[6]

McClinton's family history is extraordinary, but there are other black Americans for whom—when one takes a generational perspective—slavery is not so distant. If a new generation comes into existence approximately every thirty years, the youngest cohort is the fifth generation born *since the end* of American slavery. Put another way: today's black twenty- and thirtysomethings typically are the great-great-great-grandchildren of enslaved ancestors. Our cursory inquiries produced over a dozen families for whom the generational distance is much smaller.[7]

Many black Americans are only three generations removed from slavery. Pamela Footman, a chemist living in Durham, North Carolina, was born in 1959. Her mother's grandfather, Essex Shaw, was born in slavery in Duplin County, North Carolina. Footman's daughter, Alison, now in her early twenties, is part of the fourth generation born after slavery ended. Footman relates a tragic family history of dispossession, disinheritance, and even murder. In Footman family lore, her father, John Wallace Footman, had an uncle, Wallace Roby, who was lynched by the Klan in the 1920s.

Bryan A. Stevenson, born in 1959, is a professor of law at New York University, the founder and executive director of the Equal Justice Initiative, the author of *Just Mercy: A Story of Justice and Redemption* (2014), and the great-grandson of slaves. Two of Stevenson's great-grandparents—his mother's maternal grandparents—John and Mary Baylor, were born into slavery in Virginia in the late 1840s and early 1850s, respectively.[8]

One of the coauthors of this book, Kirsten Mullen, is also in the third generation born after slavery times. Her mother's maternal grandfather, Walker Tolliver, was enslaved at the time of his birth in 1854 and was eleven years old when slavery ended.

Kelly Elaine Navies, an oral history specialist at the Smithsonian's National Museum of African American History and Culture, has been conducting research on "a maternal ancestor [her] mother had been telling [her] about all [her] life," Elizabeth Gudger Stevens (1850 or 1854–1956). Stevens and her parents, Sam and Ann "Annie" Penland Gudger, were born into slavery. Navies's mother, Constance Elaine Gregory Navies Edwards, a member of the third generation born after slavery was outlawed, remembered meeting her grandmother in Asheville, North Carolina, when she was a child.[9]

Similarly, Kenneth Lewis, an attorney who was a 2010 candidate for U.S. senator from North Carolina, is a member of the third generation born after the end of slavery; his children are in the fourth. Lewis's grandmother Amelia Stewart Winstead was born June 10, 1893, and died in December 1993. She was born on a plantation in Person County, North Carolina, where her mother had been enslaved.

Winstead's mother died prematurely, and Winstead was raised by several relatives who Lewis believes also had been enslaved. Lewis says his mother's paternal grandfather had also been a human captive and that his mother knew him and remembers Sunday suppers at his home. Remarkably, Lewis's own mother has shared Sunday suppers with both her grandfather, who had been a slave, and her grandchildren, the youngest of whom were born in 2000 and 2011. Lewis concludes, "The hand that touches slavery, touches us today."[10]

Regardless, the injustice of slavery—with its ferocious cruelty—is hardly the sole basis for reparations. There is no doubt that slavery's aftermath is responsible for a host of significant and injurious long-term repercussions that contribute to racial inequality in America today. For example, the failure to fulfill the promise of forty acres and a mule immediately after the Civil War has had a major impact, extending to the creation and perpetuation of current racial wealth differentials. These inequalities were discussed in chapter 2.

In part 5 of this book, we argued that the systematic abuses blacks were subjected to during the Jim Crow period, coupled with exposure to ongoing discrimination and brutality in the present moment, have produced even more devastating and direct effects on the status of blacks in America today. These events are extended products of the initial abuse of slavery.

America's public narrative of continued progress frequently has meant sloughing off the ugly parts of our past and present. The Civil War and Reconstruction are the most pivotal events of our nation's collective history. The presumption of America's moral superiority over other countries presumes that the nation has no debt to pay for the injustices in its own past.

Another key consideration: legal segregation in the United States ended only about fifty years ago. William Darity Sr., the late father of one of the coauthors of this book, lived close to half his life under the Jim Crow regime. If we treat legal segregation as formally ending with the passage of the Civil Rights Act of 1964, both of the coauthors of this book spent the first decade of their lives under formal American apartheid. *Black baby boomers are the living victims of the Jim Crow era.*

Of course, if the institution of a reparations program is delayed long enough—if the "delay until death" tactic is deployed—soon there will be few living victims of Jim Crow. But the failure to pay a debt in a timely fashion does not extinguish the obligation, particularly since the consequences of past injustices continue to be visited upon the descendants of the direct victims. A national act of procrastination does not eliminate the debt.[11]

"Wouldn't black reparations only create more animosity between the races?"

We know there is resistance to reparations. But failure to adopt a reparations program now would mean another missed opportunity to remake this country. Colonial officials in Virginia had already begun the process of creating separate laws for blacks and whites to the detriment of blacks by the late seventeenth century. Those distinctions, although no longer codified, persist to the present day.

We believe that Congress, not the judiciary, should enact the reparations program. Congress alone has the power to oversee the initiative at the needed scale to appropriate the necessary funds and to ensure that the mandate is carried out.

In order for reparations to be adopted, white America must come to terms with its false beliefs about "black behavior" and with the sanitized and inaccurate version of the nation's history. The majority of the populace also must accept national responsibility for the damages inflicted on black people. Therefore, not only would white animosity toward blacks need to decrease significantly for legislative action to take place and for a reparations program to become a reality, but such animosity actually would need to be converted into support. Only after this work has been done can reparations be achieved. When the nation is ready to be transformed, Congress can legislate a reparations program.

"Demands for reparations should be directed at the African countries, since some Africans sold other Africans into slavery."

But the United States is where ancestors of most of today's black Americans were forced into slavery. It was the demand in the Americas for enslaved labor that motivated the creation of the supply pipelines of captive emigrants on the African continent. Furthermore, from the beginning of the trade, there was significant African opposition to the slave trade. A notable example was Queen Nzinga's armed resistance, from 1627 until her death in 1663, to Portuguese incursions into present-day Angola for the purpose of procuring enslaved Africans.[12]

The African struggle against the slave trade failed—might prevailed over right—leaving many Africans with a prisoner's dilemma: either engage in the sale of other Africans or be the object of sale yourself. Finally, we cannot overemphasize the point that the postslavery harms—the Jim Crow regime and ongoing discrimination—were not associated with practices on the African continent. If anything, practices of segregation and discrimination on the continent of Africa, particularly in the cases of southern Africa's Republic of Rhodesia (now the Republic of Zimbabwe) and South Africa, *were modeled after the U.S. system of legal segregation.*

"Groups who bear no responsibility for slavery will be compelled to foot the bill, particularly groups who immigrated to the United States long after slavery was over."

First, *voluntary* immigrants to the United States have chosen to migrate to a country with this national history. Frequently, what appeals to recent immigrants about life in the United States is the high degree of economic development produced, in significant part, by the exploitation of black labor both under slavery and thereafter.

Second, this argument against reparations presumes, once again, that the case for reparations depends exclusively on the injustice of slavery. Voluntary immigrants arriving in the United States from the 1880s to the present, especially white and Asian immigrants, have benefited from America's Jim Crow regime and its established and ongoing racial hierarchy, including the perverse advantages associated with Asian Americans being marked as "model minorities."[13]

Third, and perhaps most important, black reparations is a debt that must be borne by all Americans, not specific individuals or social groups that carry a special burden of guilt or shame. Indeed, from our perspective, reparations for black Americans are an obligation that need not be linked to guilt or shame but driven by recognition of the need for national redemption. It is the federal government that should implement reparations via congressional legislation.

"Didn't white America (or America in general) already pay its debt for slavery in blood by waging the Civil War, which resulted in emancipation?"

This is a puzzling question. If the dissolution of a patently unjust system of social organization is financially disastrous for the perpetrators, does it follow that the victims of that system are owed nothing for the harms they have suffered? Malcolm X made the following apposite comment about the peculiar morality embodied in this question: "If you stick a knife in my back nine inches and pull it out six inches, there's no progress. If you pull it all the way out that's not progress. Progress is healing the wound that the blow made. And they haven't even pulled the knife out much less healed the wound. They won't even admit the knife is there."[14] Suppose that you are forced to work for me. Suppose further that I also deprive you of your freedom and your earnings. In addition, I profit from having done so. Then, finally suppose that, after some time—decades, perhaps—I am made to or choose to cease this practice, but I retain all profits accrued up to this point and you have nothing. Is that justice? We think not.

Recompense for a grievous injustice is not achieved merely by ending the practice. It requires some form of payment or compensation for the damage or injury—in this case, for the years of unremunerated labor, economic subjugation, and deprivation of rights. Still outstanding is the debt owed to those who were subjected to this inimical abuse and the debt to their descendants, who continue to experience the effects of past and ongoing injustices.

Furthermore, slave emancipation did not require a great war to be fought. There was a viable alternative to armed conflict that could have ended slavery which the white male electorate would not accept. That alternative, which we have discussed in depth in chapter 5, was compensated emancipation. If slaveholders had only agreed to such a scheme after the war had begun, the conflict would not have lasted as long, and the horrendous casualty count could have been far lower.

A final critical observation must be made in response to this specific challenge to the case for reparations: enslaved blacks bore massive costs themselves to support the Union war effort, beginning with their mass exodus from plantations to join the Union lines, followed by their own participation as soldiers in the Union army. To characterize emancipation as a gift delivered to the country's slaves by well-meaning whites ignores the high price in loss of life, pressure, and danger that enslaved African bondsmen endured to free themselves.

Indeed, by 1863, in the aftermath of the Emancipation Proclamation, white northerners' reluctance to serve in the war effort had become so pronounced that the black military contribution was essential to the Union's survival. About 180,000 black soldiers participated in the U.S. Army—10 percent of all the soldiers who served the Union—during the Civil War. Approximately one-third of them lost their lives. Black determination in the pursuit of black freedom exacted a great toll. The termination of slavery was a consequence of great acts of sacrifice on the parts of black and white Americans. It was not simply a "gift" that white America bequeathed to black America.

"Blacks already have received reparations in the form of an abundance of welfare monies and funds from other social programs."

Ironically, when those social programs were first introduced in the 1930s, they were structured to *exclude* blacks from their benefits.[15] Blacks did not get full access to the nation's social safety net until 1965, three decades later. Moreover, America's social programs were never black-specific initiatives; in fact, excluding benefits from agricultural and domestic household workers— when the majority of blacks were employed in those occupations—was one of the conditions congressmen from the southern states exacted in exchange for their support. Preventing these workers from educational opportunities and higher-paying jobs protected the southern "way of life." It has also never been true that the majority of recipients of federal benefits are black.

Political scientist Ira Katznelson has observed that the "white-targeted nature of extensive federal legislation before 1965 has largely been ignored by policy analysts."[16] In the following account, Katznelson details the extent to which federal policy provided a unilateral boost to economic security for whites for at least three decades:

> But most blacks were left out. The damage to racial equity caused by each program was immense. Taken together, the effects of these public laws were devastating. Social Security, from which the majority of blacks were excluded until well into the 1950s, quickly became the country's most important social legislation. The labor laws of the New Deal and Fair Deal created a framework of protection for tens of millions of workers who secured minimum wages, maximum hours, and the right to join industrial as well as craft unions. African Americans who worked on the land or as domestics—the great majority—lacked these protections. When unions made inroads in the South, where most blacks lived, moreover, Congress changed the rules of the game to make organizing much more difficult. Perhaps most surprising and most important, the treatment of veterans after the war, despite the universal eligibility for the benefits offered by the GI Bill (supposed to give assistance to all returning soldiers, regardless of colour), perpetuated the blatant racism that had marked the affairs of a still-segregated military service during the war itself. Southern members of Congress used occupational exclusions and took advantage of American federalism (the "state rights" principle) to ensure that their region's racial order would not be disturbed by national policies. Benefits for veterans were administered locally and the GI Bill was adapted to "the southern way of life" by accommodating to segregation in higher education, to the job ceilings local officials imposed on returning black soldiers who came home from a segregated army, and to an unwillingness to offer loans to blacks even when they were insured by the federal government. Of the 3,229 GI Bill–guaranteed home, business, and farm loans made in 1947 in Mississippi, for example, only two were offered to black veterans. At no other time in American history has so much money and so many resources been put at the service of the

generation completing education, entering the work force, and forming families. Comparatively little of this largesse was available to black veterans. With these policies, the Gordian Knot binding race to class tightened.[17]

This extreme disparity in Mississippi was virtually preordained. Representative John Elliott Rankin (D-Miss.), who served sixteen terms, was a principal architect of the GI Bill's exclusion of black beneficiaries. Rankin demanded that the bill be "a matter of local control and states' rights." Counselors from the Veterans Administration "guided" black veterans toward vocational and trade schools rather than colleges and universities. Furthermore, "counselors didn't merely discourage black veterans. They just said no. No to home loans. No to job placement, except for the most menial positions. And no to college, except for historically black colleges, maintaining the sham of 'separate but equal.'"[18]

Finally, eligibility for benefits is means tested: only families or individuals living below the poverty line are deemed eligible for support. America's solution to this problem does not prevent people from falling into poverty; rather, it provides them with limited assistance only after they have already become poor. Moreover, these programs do not address—nor were they intended to address—the group-specific injustice directed at black Americans across the span of the nation's history.

"Blacks already have received reparations from affirmative action programs."

The way it has been practiced in the United States, affirmative action has never been a form of reparations. It has served, instead, as an antidiscrimination measure, a mechanism for including a group that otherwise would be excluded unjustly from preferred positions "despite their qualifications and merit." It complements the presence of other antidiscrimination laws that invariably require legal action to be brought against perpetrators of acts of racialized exclusion. It has produced some positive effects, but it is not an ideal remedy. Basically, affirmative action has been used "to desegregate elites," chiefly in employment, university admissions, and government procurement. In the best of circumstances, it can open a door for a qualified entrant, but it cannot guarantee equal treatment.[19]

It may be useful to examine the limitations of affirmative action as an instrument for racial transformation, a core objective of black reparations. These limitations include the following: While affirmative action may provide entry into excluded spaces, it does not require those affected institutions to guarantee that the entrants experience safety, acceptance, and or good-will in the environment where they newly have gained access. Affirmative action affords no direct impact on racial income inequality, nor are affected institutions required to eliminate those disparities. Affirmative action offers no significant impact, direct or indirect, on wealth inequality. Affected institutions are under no obligation to reduce or eliminate wealth disparities.

Affirmative action cannot affect the total number of preferred positions available; in some cases, while the share of members from an excluded group with access to the preferred positions goes up, the absolute total held by members of the excluded group could decline—or stay relatively unchanged. Affected institutions are not obligated to create preferred positions for all eligible candidates.

Insofar as discrimination persists, affirmative action, while useful, clearly has not been sufficiently effective to eliminate it. At its heart, affirmative action was not designed or intended to be a program of reparations, regardless of how it was perceived at the time of its introduction. Affirmative action can get you through the door, but it does not provide you with restitution for having been kept out of the door in the past, nor does it assure that you will receive fair treatment after getting through the door.

Affirmative action is a specific type of antidiscrimination measure intended to include persons from social groups who otherwise would be excluded due to biased selection processes. Insofar as it actually reduces discrimination and its effects, it does not compensate for past or ongoing discrimination or the continuing effects of either. In general, stopping an unjust practice is not compensation for the unjust practice. Otherwise, one could take the position, incorrectly, that Japanese Americans received de facto reparations merely by being released from internment camps and that there was no reason to provide them with any further restitution.

Finally, on at least two occasions pundits have recommended the provision of a reparations-style monetary payment to black Americans in exchange for the elimination of affirmative action policies. The most recent version of this Faustian bargain has been advanced by Ross Douthat, who has proposed a $10,000 payment to each African American in exchange for the termination of affirmative action policies.[20] Close to two decades earlier, in 2001, Charles Krauthammer recommended a similar deal with the prince of darkness but for a slightly higher amount of money ($50,000 per family of four).[21]

As we demonstrate in chapter 13, these are extremely low amounts to meet the debt owed to black America.[22] And the ante seems to have declined for blacks to consent to the eradication of affirmative action.

"Why should blacks receive reparations when other groups have strong claims and are not asking for much?"

The objective of *From Here to Equality* is to make the case for reparations for black Americans. We have no doubt that other groups may have legitimate claims, and we urge them to bring forward their cases. The existence of other communities deserving reparations does not, in any way, constitute a denial of the obligation to black America. Nor does the magnitude of the expenditure determine its legitimacy. There is at least one other group that potentially could make a far more costly claim on the American government than black Americans: Native Americans could reclaim virtually all of the land area of the United States if they brought forward their case for reparations.

We pose, instead, an inversion of the question advanced here: "Why should blacks have to continue to wait for the debt owed to them to be paid?"

Furthermore, the potential magnitude of the demand for reparations claimed by other victimized groups—whether more or less than the amount necessary to meet the black reparations claim—is irrelevant to the principle of the provision of just compensation.

"Reparations paid to Japanese Americans and Holocaust victims were made to direct victims and/or their immediate families; therefore, these are not precedents for black reparations for slavery."

We reiterate that, absolutely, there still are living victims of legal segregation and ongoing discrimination in the United States. And not all payments were made exclusively to individuals and their families in either the case of Japanese American reparations or that of compensation for the genocide of the Holocaust. Any society can delay the provision of reparations until all of its direct victims have died. Delay should not absolve the community of the debt, particularly if the impact of the injustice has long-term intergenerational effects. The shackles of history are long-standing and must be removed.

The Civil Liberties Act of 1988, the enabling legislation for restitution for Japanese Americans subjected to internment during World War II, included a provision for the establishment of a public education fund to inform Americans about this injustice and to prevent its reoccurrence. German compensation for victims of the Holocaust included payments made to the state of Israel to aid in its development and consolidation, and, in fact, payments have been made to *heirs and descendants* of direct victims. In fact, the U.S. government has even made payments to citizens who are Holocaust victims and relatives of victims, despite the fact that, in this instance, the U.S. government was not the perpetrator.

"Reparations demean the memory of the victims who cannot speak for themselves."

Direct victims of Jim Crow and ongoing discrimination, which include the authors of this volume, *still* can speak for themselves. And the direct victims of slavery also spoke for themselves. Reconsider the conversation described in chapter 8 between General Sherman and Secretary of War Edwin Stanton and the spokesperson for a group of free black community leaders that took place in Savannah, Georgia, on January 12, 1865—a conversation in which African Americans were asked to imagine their new lives in the south. That discussion was a prelude to Sherman's Special Field Orders No. 15, which provided families of ex-slaves with forty acres of land along the South Carolina, Georgia, and Florida coasts.

At the core of the men's visions for their future was a desire to become self-sufficient, "to have land and turn it and till it by [our own] labor . . . until we are able to buy it and make it our own." The leaders also expressed their willingness "to assist the Government," insisting that "the young men should enlist in the service of the Government, and serve in such manner as they may be wanted." Keenly aware of the "prejudice against us in the South that will take years to get over," they also requested that they be allowed to live apart from whites—"to live by ourselves."[23]

Participants in two freedmen's conventions, one in Georgia and one in North Carolina, also gave voice to the dreams and aspirations of those once held as human property. They wanted education, they wanted the vote, they wanted protection from attacks and assaults from whites, they wanted to know that their children could not be taken from them, they wanted to be left alone to build their own lives and communities, and *they wanted land.*[24]

When 3,000 freedmen gathered in Mississippi that same year to learn the Freedmen's Bureau's plans for establishing schools for them and their children, "their joy knew no bounds." Many shared the desire of the ex-slave who was enrolled in a Mississippi school and wanted "to learn to cipher so I can do business."[25]

Tragically, President Andrew Johnson ordered the land allocated under Special Field Orders No. 15 restored to the former slaveholders. Indeed, the freedmen's desires for land, schools and education, and freedom to live their lives alone in peace went unfulfilled.

Given the unmet desires of the freedmen—as well as of now-deceased blacks who lived under Jim Crow—the provision of reparations to their descendants will *honor* their memory. In the case of the September 11, 2001, attacks, the federal government provided payments to the victims' families. Why, then, when it comes to the case of black reparations, is there a double standard? The American legal and political systems have a long-standing tradition of placing a dollar value on both emotional and physical suffering.

"Dwelling on slavery and pursuing reparations perpetuates a crippling psychology of victimization among blacks."

What really cripples black Americans is racism, not an alleged victimization mentality. Racism exposes blacks to both micro- and macroaggressions. Microaggressions range from insults and jokes depicting people of color as scofflaws or as stupid or incompetent to the experience of being physically present but excluded from a conversation and hearing racial slurs and innuendos. Macroaggressions range from racial profiling and public humiliation to physical violence that threatens life and limb.

The denial of wealth is far from a purely psychological phenomenon. Actually, despite the extent to which they have been subjected to assaults, black Americans display a remarkable degree of resilience and motivation. Consider educational attainment. We provided evidence in chapter 2 indicating that, after taking into account family socioeconomic position, blacks pursue higher education at rates significantly higher than whites.[26] In general, victims of trauma have healthier outcomes when their harm is recognized and awarded restitution.[27] It is no different for victims of racism. Acknowledgment and compensation for the harms they have endured are essential for them to "get over it."

Finally, acceptance of reparations payments is not mandatory. If any eligible recipient feels burdened by grants of restitution because it "inscribes" their victim status, they certainly will be free to refuse the payments, allowing the funds to go instead to others who do not share that sense of burden.

"When all is said and done, today's blacks are better off having had their ancestors enslaved here. Very few of them would opt to return to Africa rather than stay in the United States."

It is hard to believe that any person would suggest that blacks—or any group of people, for that matter—are better off by having been enslaved. This peculiar argument entirely overlooks the range of intergenerational harms attendant to slavery as a starting point for the racial inequalities that persist to this day. It is irrelevant whether living black Americans would prefer to live in the present-day United States or in one of the countries of the African continent, because living black Americans' ancestors did not come to America by choice.

Nor did they *choose* to do so by being enslaved. Nor did subsequent generations *choose* to be oppressed by the Jim Crow regime and sustained racism. Furthermore, as we have demonstrated in chapter 3, the United States would not have developed economically in the way that it did without the coerced exploitation of black labor. The fundamental issue for black citizens today is the unequal and inequitable quality of black lives vis-à-vis those of white citizens in the United States. Indeed, there is much to admire in black Americans' long-standing desire to stay in the country and struggle for full citizenship instead of leaving for sites—whether on the African continent or elsewhere—where they may not encounter the same degree of racism.

Of course, as we have noted above, numerous efforts led by whites were organized to repatriate blacks during the nineteenth century. The American Colonization Society, founded in 1816, transported over 20,000 American slaves to the African continent, 13,000 of them to Liberia. Two Virginians, the Reverends Moses Tichnell and Samuel R. Houston, subscribed to the send-them-back-to-Africa solution, freed their slaves, and financed their passage to Liberia in 1855–56.

One of the more notable black advocates of repatriation was Marcus Garvey, whose Universal Negro Improvement Association was formed in August 1914. Despite the organization's visibility and renown, only small numbers of black Americans actually repatriated to countries on the African continent. They also have not migrated in large numbers to any other countries, including those that have a higher standard of living than the United States.[28] Black Americans have as strong a claim (or stronger) to America as other citizens; they have a particularly strong claim to a *just* America.

"Black reparations, unfairly, will ignore the parallel plight of the white poor."

Political scientist Cedric Johnson has argued against black reparations because, in his view, they neglect the equivalent plight of low-income whites.[29] While poverty in general in the United States unequivocally merits renewed and concerted attention, by collapsing blacks and whites into a single, homogeneous oppressed working class, Johnson ignores critical differences in the historical specificity of the circumstances that have produced each community and key differences in the substantive status of each community. Only black American descendants of persons enslaved in the United States have a claim to the debt that never was paid to their ancestors upon emancipation, the forty-acre land grants.

Material conditions are not the same for "working class" blacks and whites. Low-income whites are beneficiaries of racial privilege despite their comparatively deprived status. Indeed, "whites of all social classes and education levels have a much lower likelihood of exposure to unemployment; rarely become as asset-poor as blacks; experience better health outcomes and greater safety in encounters with the police and criminal justice system; and, of course, are not subjected to racial micro-aggressions that erode emotional well-being and self-efficacy."[30]

To elaborate, with respect to asset poverty, it is noteworthy that the median net worth of whites in the bottom 20 percent of the nation's income distribution is higher than the median net worth of *all* black Americans.[31] With respect to health outcomes, at every level of education black women's infant mortality rate exceeds that of white women, and black women with advanced degrees have higher infant mortality rates than white women who never finished high school.[32] With respect to safety in encounters with the police, not only are blacks far more likely to have fatal encounters, but they also are far more subject to harassment associated with police stops, especially while driving.[33] Being black and white in America is not the same experience, regardless of social class.

"Regardless, there is no way to pay enough to compensate for the evil of slavery."

Frederick Douglass would have agreed that it is unlikely that there is anything that could be done that would mitigate the harms inflicted on blacks by enslavement. In 1894, the final year of his life, Douglass made the following observation:

> People who live now, and talk of doing too much for the Negro . . .
> forget that for these terrible wrongs there is, in truth, no redress and
> no adequate compensation. The enslaved and battered millions have
> come, suffered, died and gone with all their moral and physical wounds
> into Eternity. To them no recompense can be made. If the American
> people could put a school house in every valley; a church on every
> hill top in the South and supply them with a teacher and preacher
> respectively and welcome the descendants of the former slaves to all the
> moral and intellectual benefits of the one and other . . . such a sacrifice
> would not compensate their children for the terrible wrong done to
> their fathers and mothers.[34]

But Douglass did not conclude from this that no steps toward justice should be made. Quite the contrary, he argued that white America could never do enough to repay "the Negro" but by all means should do as much as possible. In addition to public education and mandatory attendance laws for all children, he advocated a program of land acquisition specifically for freedmen and their progeny.[35]

The fact that full amends cannot be made for a grievous injustice does not mean significant recompense should not be made. Although the long-overdue bill will not match the price paid by the victims, the bill must be paid.

13

A Program of Black Reparations

Something that is often missing from "reparations talk" is a specific plan for repairing past tragedies. —Alfred Brophy, "Considering Reparations for the Dred Scott Case," 2010

The speeches of Stevens and other radical leaders, in pamphlet form, along with the Bureau laws and regulations, the homestead laws and the Confiscation Acts, were sown thickly over the South; and the Bureau agents, the missionaries and the teachers, taking the cue from these, encouraged the belief in the "forty acres and a mule." The negroes were told that since their labor had produced the property of the South, they ought at least to share it. Lincoln's second inaugural message suggests the same thought in regard to the origin of Southern property. Probably this belief that the property of the South was due to uncompensated negro labor was held by many Northerners and inclined them to favor a proposition to confiscate land. —Walter Fleming, "Forty Acres and a Mule," 1906

[Pappy said:] "It's victory. . . . It's freedom. Now we'es gwine be free." . . . It seem like it tuck a long time for freedom to come. Everything jest kept on like it was. We heard that lots of slaves was getting land and some mules to setup for themselves. I never knowed any what got land or mules or nothing. —From an interview with ex-slave Mittie Freeman, 1938

In this chapter we present the "something that is often missing from 'reparations talk'": a detailed program of reparations for black Americans. We begin by calling upon the U.S. Congress to assert leadership and authorize payments to be made by the U.S. government. Many atrocities, indignities, and micro- and macroaggressions have occurred in the well of American racism.

In numerous instances particular individuals or institutions can be identified as the perpetrators. Examples include Georgetown University's participation in the sale of 272 "head" of human property to sugar plantations in Louisiana to aid the institution's financial survival in 1838. But actions like that taken by Georgetown's leadership at that time occurred in a context of state-sanctioned white supremacy.

While it makes complete sense to seek recompense from clearly identified perpetrators, when the entire political order is complicit, it is not sufficient to bill individual perpetrators. Laissez-faire or *piecemeal reparations* may assuage individual guilt but cannot meet the collective national obligation. The invoice for reparations must go to the nation's government.[1] The U.S. government, as the federal authority, bears responsibility for sanctioning, maintaining, and enabling slavery, legal segregation, and continued racial inequality.

Specifically, the invoice should go directly to the U.S. Congress, the legislative branch of the national government. Jurisdiction over the matter of black reparations should be removed from the judicial system for three fundamental reasons: (1) Lawsuits brought against corporations, colleges, and universities for their participation in slavery are unlikely to succeed because slavery was legal at the time that they engaged in the practice. Their activities were undoubtedly immoral, but they were not illegal at the time. (2) In order to sue the U.S. government for reparations for the continuation of racial violence and discrimination in the post–Civil Rights legislation era, one would have to establish that U.S. government agencies knowingly and intentionally did not enforce the new laws. This would require an effort of Xena-esque proportions. (3) The courts do not have the capacity to implement or enforce any legal mandate they might hand down for black reparations.

As the Supreme Court's school desegregation decisions demonstrate, legal mandates without broad popular support will be blocked and deflected.[2] If popular support is a prerequisite for success in obtaining black reparations, then it is best to develop that support and push Congress to vote for a substantive program of black reparations.

Given its traditional connection to these issues, the legislative branch can lay the groundwork for the design of a reparations program, first by establishing a commission that can investigate the history of racial injustice in the United States. This would be a commission similar to the one Congress created to investigate the circumstances of the mass incarceration of Japanese Americans during World War II, the Commission on Wartime Relocation and Internment of Civilians.[3]

The report, produced by a commission that does a thorough analysis and constructs an official statement of the record of American racial injustice, can be a valuable instrument in widening public support for the reparations project.[4] Congressional approval of H.R. 40—originally developed by former representative John Conyers and now managed by Representative Sheila Jackson Lee to establish a congressional commission to investigate slavery and its multigenerational effects and assess the feasibility of recompense—could be an important step on the road to reparations.

The current legislation calls for it to be known as the Commission to Study and Develop Proposals for Reparations for African-Americans.

Again, whether such a commission is established via congressional action or presidential fiat, it is imperative that the appointees make an authentic commitment to developing a comprehensive program of reparations and that the commission have an eighteen-month deadline to issue its report.

We advance two criteria to determine eligibility for a black reparations program. First, U.S. citizens would need to establish that they had at least one ancestor who was enslaved in the United States after the formation of the republic. Second, they would have to prove that they self-identified as "black," "Negro," "Afro-American," or "African American" *at least twelve years before* the enactment of the reparations program or the establishment of a congressional or presidential commission "to study and develop reparations for African Americans"—whichever comes first. The first criterion, of course, could produce lucrative opportunities for private genealogists, but these investigations also could be facilitated by an arm of the professional (civil service) staff specializing in genealogical research for the agency that administers the reparations program.

The internet and the possibility of sharing information on dedicated websites also can facilitate the genealogical research that can assist individuals in establishing that they are descended from an enslaved ancestor (or several). For example, in the aftermath of its revelations, Georgetown University created the Georgetown Slavery Archive, and an independent organization founded the Georgetown Memory Project, websites used to identify descendants of the persons who were sold by the school.[5] As the Georgetown case indicates, researchers can start with the archived list of persons sold by the university to locate their living descendants. Alternatively, individuals can go backward in time to reconstruct their family tree to identify their enslaved ancestor(s), especially using census records.

The detective-like archival procedures displayed on recent television programs like the TLC network's *Who Do You Think You Are?* and PBS's *Finding Your Roots* also can provide templates for conducting the genealogical research that would be needed for the reparations program.[6] The archives of the Church of Jesus Christ of Latter-day Saints (Mormons) also afford a valuable database that could be helpful in the construction of any individual's ancestral history.[7]

Furthermore, if a black American has an ancestor who appears in the 1870 or 1880 U.S. Census and was old enough to have been alive before the

Civil War but is not present in the 1860 U.S. Census, it is reasonable to conclude that this ancestor was enslaved—since the censuses typically *did not enumerate enslaved persons by name*, even in the separate slave censuses taken in 1850 and 1860.

Still, those slave schedules may be helpful in genealogical research insofar as, in some instances, the first name of the enslaved person is indicated under the owners' names. More important, if individuals believe they have an ancestor who was enslaved by a particular owner, they can check the slave schedules to find the age and gender of each person he or she owned. This preliminary research can inform the examination of other documents that may be more specific in identifying the persons owned by the slaveholder in question: wills, deeds, estate records, or court records.[8]

With respect to the second criterion, any official government-issued document that indicates the individual's race would provide acceptable proof of racial identity. Everyone also has the right to make public their responses to any U.S. Census question; specifically, one's self-identification as black in response to the race question—*before the existence of a reparations commission or reparations program makes it advantageous to do so*—also would establish eligibility.

How much should be paid for black reparations? What is the size of the bill? It is customary, in the American court system, to assign monetary values for damages to human lives. Monetary damages for the collective injuries inflicted on black lives are long overdue.

Several strategies have been advanced for calculating the monetary value of a reparations bill. For those researchers committed to slavery as the basis for black reparations, a number of approaches have been proposed. Most of these approaches require a present-value calculation for unpaid wages, the purchase prices of the human property, or the land promised to the formerly enslaved. These present-value estimates are generated by increasing earlier values at compound interest. In the estimates that follow, we typically employ three interest rates—4, 5, and 6 percent—to accommodate varying measures of the rates of return on foregone or lost income and the rate of inflation.[9]

A method introduced by economic historians Roger Ransom and Richard Sutch uses the concept of slave exploitation to construct their estimate. They defined slave exploitation as the difference between the value of what was produced by enslaved Africans and the value of what was given to them for maintenance in the form of food, shelter, or other consumption items. In short, Ransom and Sutch sought to calculate the pure profit of the slave system to measure an appropriate bill for reparations. Their estimate over the interval of 1806 to 1860 compounded to 1983 came to $3.4 billion.[10]

Compounding to 2018 at 4, 5, and 6 percent interest rates, their estimate now would amount to $14 billion, $19.7 billion, and $27.7 billion, respectively. The researchers' method of estimation is problematic for at least three reasons: it excludes the profits from slavery during the first thirty years of the nation's existence; profits from the slave trade are not taken into account; and astonishingly, those enslaved are charged with the maintenance expenses of their own coerced labor. The result is the lowest bill for black reparations among those we examine here.

Economist Larry Neal's procedure also charges the enslaved for their own maintenance expenses but is slightly different from the Ransom and Sutch method. Neal subtracts slave owners' average expenditure for the maintenance of each of their enslaved Africans from the wage paid to nonenslaved laborers in the interval between 1620 and 1840. Neal's estimate comes to $1.4 trillion when compounded to 1983.[11] By 2019, at each of the three interest rates we deploy here, present values are $5.7 trillion, $8.1 trillion, and $11.4 trillion, respectively.

Note that Neal's estimate includes 156 years before 1776, or 164 years before 1783—his starting point appears to be the year after the first enslaved Africans were known to have been imported to colonial America—and omits the twenty years immediately before the Civil War. It also is important to take into account the extent to which the availability of enslaved laborers reduced market wage rates.

If blacks had not been captured and forcibly installed in the United States, there would have been a smaller pool of laborers and, correspondingly, higher wages. Consequently, the hypothetical wage that would have been earned by an African who migrated voluntarily to the United States would have been greater than the rate Neal used in his study.

Thomas Craemer has generated a provocative set of estimates of the slavery bill for black reparations by multiplying the prevailing average market wage by the number of hours "worked" by those enslaved over the interval of 1776 to 1865. Craemer assumes that each full twenty-four-hour day was stolen from the enslaved.

Using a 3 percent interest rate, by 2015 he estimates that the present value of U.S. chattel labor reaches $14.2 trillion.[12] Using Craemer's interest rate, the 2019 present value amounts to $15.7 trillion. At each of the three interest rates we use, the current values are $16.4 trillion, $17 trillion, and $17.7 trillion, respectively.

Unlike either Ransom and Sutch or Neal, Craemer does not deduct slave maintenance costs from his bill, but again, despite the higher levels of his upper-bound estimate, his reliance on the market wage for nonslave labor yields a lower calculation than the hypothetical non-slave-labor wage that would have prevailed in the absence of captive enslaved Africans.

A different estimate of the bill for reparations from slavery has been produced by James Marketti using the idea of income diverted from enslaved persons. He derived a cumulative figure of $2.1 trillion as of 1983.[13] Again, using our three interest rates, the 2018 present value amounts to $8.6 trillion, $12.1 trillion, and $17.1 trillion, respectively. The upper-bound estimate in Marketti's procedure is comparable to the upper-bound estimate in Craemer's study.

An alternative estimate is reached by calculating the present value of the wealth held in property in enslaved persons. On December 31, 1860, Judah P. Benjamin, who ultimately served in three different capacities in Jefferson Davis's Confederate cabinet, said, "Our slaves . . . directly and indirectly involve a value of more than four thousand million dollars."[14] Four billion dollars in 1860 compounds to $2 trillion, $9.3 trillion, and a whopping $42.2 trillion by 2019, at 4, 5, and 6 percent interest, respectively. With approximately 40 million black Americans in the United States today, the *per capita* amounts would come to about $50,000, $232,500, and $1,050,000 at each of those interest rates.

The estimates based on Benjamin's $4 billion valuation of slaves as property in 1860 would, in principle, involve the transfer of that entire amount in present dollars to the descendants of the enslaved. Nevertheless, all of these estimates have been made without incorporating the physical and emotional harms of slavery, the inherently coercive nature of the system, the denial of the ability to acquire property and some degree of autonomy, or the denial of control over one's own family life. So, as large as these estimates seem, they can be viewed, legitimately, as *underestimates*.

Another possibility is to focus on the land distribution that was promised—but never made—to the ex-slaves. The size of black reparations might be gauged by calculating the present value of the unfulfilled commitment of forty acres and a mule made to the formerly enslaved. We will focus here exclusively on the land allocation, although the mule as a stand-in for an array of farm implements and equipment is not to be dismissed. Furthermore, there were proposals afoot to provide larger plots of land or the forty acres with a "furnished cottage."[15]

Anuradha Mittal and Joan Powell conservatively report that the price of an acre of land in the United States in 1865 was about ten dollars.[16] In the typical plan, forty acres were to be allocated to all heads of household, male or female, and all other adult males among the freedmen.[17] If 4 million enslaved persons had gained emancipation by 1865, and the allocation rule meant that roughly forty acres would go to families of four, each formerly enslaved individual would have been allocated about ten acres.[18] This, in turn, would have implied a total distribution of at least 40 million acres of land.

At $10 per acre, the total value of the projected distribution of land to the freedmen would have been $400 million in 1865.[19] The present value of that sum compounded to the present at each of the three interest rates would be $168 billion, $733.2 billion, and $3.1 trillion, respectively. Obviously the bill would be considerably higher if the conditions of the Southern Homestead Act, which provided for eighty acres of land to be sold to freedmen at $5 total, is treated as the unfulfilled debt that must be paid.

At the time of emancipation, some observers interpreted *each* of the freedmen as being eligible to receive forty acres of land as an allocation.[20] Indeed, such an allocation would have been equivalent to the average size of land grants given to white families under the Homestead Acts between 1868 and 1934, which we reported in chapter 2 was 160 acres, or forty acres per member of a family of four. This larger allocation would have led to a much higher total value of the land to be distributed to freedmen after the war—amounting to $1.6 billion in 1865. Compounded to 2019 at 4 percent interest, the present value is $671 billion; at 5 percent interest, it is $2.9 trillion; and at 6 percent interest, it is $12.6 trillion.

Again, assuming there are approximately 40 million persons eligible for reparations, Craemer's original estimate at its 2019 value implies that the amount of reparations per person would be $392,500. If, instead, we base the amount of the reparations fund exclusively on the most conservative size of the plots of land that were to be delivered to ex-slaves—ten acres per person—each eligible recipient would receive payments of about $4,200, $18,245, or $74,500, depending on the interest rate.[21] At the other extreme, if forty acres were to be allocated to *each* freedman—amounts consistent with the grants to beneficiaries of the Homestead Acts—the approximate per person amounts due to today's African Americans are $16,800, $74,500, or $315,000, again contingent on the interest rate.

Other estimates of the reparations bill based on more recent economic injustices have been developed by concentrating on social penalties blacks incurred after slavery and well into the twentieth century. For example, Bernadette Chachere and Gerald Udinsky estimated the monetary benefits to whites gained from employment discrimination in the interval of 1929–69. By assuming that 40 percent of the black-white income gap was due to discrimination in the labor market, they concluded that gains to whites amounted to $1.6 trillion by the mid-1980s.[22]

Since the charge frequently is made that social transfer programs, including Social Security, Medicare, Medicaid, unemployment insurance, and other welfare programs—although not targeted specifically at blacks—already constitute reparations (see chapter 12), David Swinton subtracted the *total* cost of social transfer programs from the Chachere and Udinsky estimate over the same time span. He found that by the mid-1980s, there would still remain a $500 billion net benefit to whites from employment discrimination.[23] Therefore, even if *all* social transfer payments were taken into account, there was still a significant financial gain for whites from labor market discrimination alone.

A technique for estimating the reparations bill proposed by Boris Bittker is to calculate the difference between black and white per capita incomes. In 2017, the U.S. Census Bureau's Current Population Survey reported that mean per capita income for whites *fifteen years of age and over* was $49,609 and $36,636 for blacks in the same age range.[24] This would constitute a basis for a payment of $15,973 to each black American fifteen years of age and older.

However, as we indicated in chapter 2, we view wealth, or net worth, as a more powerful measure of economic well-being than income. *Indeed, we view the racial wealth gap as the most robust indicator of the cumulative economic effects of white supremacy in the United States.* The gap in mean household wealth by race derived from the 2016 Survey of Consumer Finances was about $795,000.[25] If the average black household consists of 3.31 persons, the mean shortfall in wealth for individual black Americans would have been approximately $240,000.

Multiplying $795,000 by the U.S. Census Bureau's estimate of about 10 million black households yields an estimate of a total reparations bill of $7.95 trillion. While the median is a more useful measure for calculating typical differences in wealth between blacks and whites because it is not affected by outlier values, the mean is the appropriate target measure for calculating the sum required *to eliminate the racial wealth gap*.[26] The wealth held by "outliers"—and more generally, whites in the upper two quintiles of the wealth distribution—must be taken into account when gauging the magnitude of the owed debt.[27]

Another route for arriving at a similar estimate of the magnitude of a reparations bill that centers on eliminating the racial wealth gap is to calculate the amount needed to give eligible black Americans a share of the nation's wealth comparable to their share in the nation's population. The eligible black population constitutes approximately 13 percent of the American community. The nation's total household wealth reached $107 trillion by the second quarter of 2018.[28] Thirteen percent of that figure amounts to $13.91 trillion. If, as an upper bound, black Americans are currently estimated to hold 3 percent of the nation's wealth, that amounts to $3.21 trillion. To eliminate the difference will require a reparations outlay of $10.7 trillion, or an average outlay of approximately $267,000 per person for 40 million eligible black descendants of American slavery.

Since racial disparities in income and net worth have persisted over many, many years, Bittker proposed that payouts of this size should be made over a number of years, somewhat arbitrarily suggesting two decades. If a disparity still persists after the initial commitment based on the prevailing wealth gap has been met, additional funds should be distributed to ensure that the gulf is spanned.

We have introduced several compelling calculations for monetary restitution. These include the estimates advanced by Ransom and Sutch, Neal, Craemer, and Marketti; several estimates anchored on the present value of land that was promised to the ex-slaves; an estimate based on the monetary value of enslaved people to their owners on the eve of emancipation; estimates based on the postslavery costs of discrimination; and an estimate moored to the racial wealth gap. Monetary restitution is necessary because the failure to provide ex-slaves with an initial outlay of property in land and the repercussions on black wealth and economic well-being redound to the present.

However, since today's differential in wealth captures the cumulative effects of racism on living black descendants of American slavery, we propose mobilizing national resources to eradicate the racial wealth gap. The magnitude of ongoing shortfalls in wealth for blacks vis-à-vis whites provides the most sensible foundation for the complete monetary portion of the bill for reparations.[29]

Outlays under the reparations program can take multiple forms under an arrangement that can be called a "portfolio of reparations": "[The sum of reparations payments] could partly take the form of a direct payout to eligible recipients. The payout need not take place in one lump sum but could be allocated over time. For example, German government payments to victims of the Nazi holocaust often have taken the form of $100 monthly checks. Reparations also could take the form of 'establishment of a trust fund to which eligible blacks could apply for grants for various asset-building projects, including homeownership, additional education, or start-up funds for self-employment,' or even vouchers for the purchase of financial assets."[30] An additional possibility is the use of the reparations fund to assist in developing endowments for historically black colleges and universities, which, despite their important role in the provision of higher education for black Americans, face steep financial challenges. Regardless, all uses of the funds must be directed at eliminating the racial wealth gap.[31]

Institution building as a use of reparations funds has a precedent in the reparations program developed by the German government in the aftermath of the Nazi Holocaust. In addition to payments made to individual victims and the relatives of victims, funds were given to the state of Israel to aid its economic development and financial stability. While a personal check or its equivalent need not be the only form in which the program makes payments, both the symbolism and the autonomy it conveys will be a key dimension of a black reparations program. *For both symbolic and substantive reasons*, an effective program of restitution must include direct payments to eligible recipients.

There are many effective options for financing a program of black reparations, even a program that would require a combined expenditure as large as $15 to $20 trillion. Obviously, lesser amounts would be managed more readily. For instance, even the full payout in 2016 based on our preferred standard—the racial gap in per capita wealth—would have amounted to less than half of the total national income.

Sequencing the payments over a series of years would increase the prospect of financing the reparations program by conventional means—the issue of new money, additional government borrowing, or even additional taxes—although, in principle, as we will show below, restitution could be financed without even altering tax rates.[32] With a staggered scheme of outlays, amounts must be adjusted for any inflation that takes place after the first round of payments. The aim should be at least to eliminate the racial wealth gap within a decade.

Two additional mechanisms for funding reparations merit consideration. First, historians V. P. Franklin and Mary Frances Berry have called for a "reparations superfund" that would pool government funding with contributions made by institutions and organizations that benefited from slavery, Jim Crow, and the continued subordination of black Americans.[33] With the superfund administered by a federal agency and seeded with government funds, Berry proposes other revenue sources, including "monies [that] could come from institutions and corporations that profited from slave labor; additional funds could come from banks and insurance companies that had been guilty of racial discriminatory practices, such as redlining and predatory financial lending."[34]

The superfund strategy would meld public and private responsibility for American racial injustice in funding a program of black reparations. However, we view public responsibility as paramount, since the federal government established and maintained the legal structure and pattern of enforcement that enabled private actors to engage in racist practices with impunity.

Second, as journalist Matthew Yglesias has proposed, *Congress could direct the Federal Reserve to fund black reparations either in part or in total.*[35] Given the overnight transfer of $1 trillion of funds from the Federal Reserve to investment banks during the Great Recession and monthly outlays of $45 to $55 billion to conduct "quantitative easing," there can be no doubt that the Fed has vast capacity to provide the funds required for a properly designed and financed reparations program, particularly if the funds are disbursed over the course of three to five years. The Fed certainly could manage an annual outlay of $1 to $1.5 trillion without any difficulty—and this funding mechanism would not have to affect tax rates for any American. Moreover, the Federal Reserve is a *public bank* charged with conducting a public responsibility.

Some have cautioned that releasing sums of this size could lead to excessive inflation. Indeed, the inflation risk truly is the major barrier to any big increase in federal expenditures.[36] Attenuation of the inflation risk will depend on the extent to which new resources in the hands of black Americans stimulate greater overall employment and production in the U.S. economy. But another way to mitigate prospects of excessive inflation would be to prevent an uncontrolled jump in consumption expenditures by distributing portions of the reparations payments as less-liquid assets.

In addition to staggering the disbursements from the total commitment, trust funds and endowments could be set up on behalf of those eligible for the program that could not be used until a later date, particularly for younger recipients. Another related option would be to give recipients full discretion in the use of the annual interest on their trust accounts but require trustee judgment on any use they might propose for asset building and/or well-being enhancement by utilizing the principal. So, for example, if in the process of closing the racial wealth gap, each eligible recipient was given a trust account of $250,000, normal interest earnings would generate an average annual discretionary fund of approximately $12,000 given a stable level of the principal.

A twelve-member reparations supervisory board will be established, *elected by all those with established eligibility for the reparations program*, with its own paid professional staff. The supervisors will select the team to serve as trust account managers (or *trustees*), who will determine which proposed projects justify use of the principal on an account. Board membership will be a full-time job to be held over a three-year term and compensated at the amount of at least $200,000 in 2019 dollars.

Board members will not be able to serve consecutive terms, although they will be able to stand for reelection after sitting out a term. Elections to the board will take place successively—four members will be elected each year—to ensure that there always will be members on the board with previous experience and historical memory. By the third year, the Reparations Supervisory Board will reach its full complement of twelve members, and at the end of that year the first wave of elected members will cycle off the board.

To the extent that additional government spending can be metered to contain inflation risk, the program also could be funded by sheer deficit spending, again requiring no change in tax rates. If black reparations provide a growth stimulus to the overall American economy, they could generate the tax revenues to fund the program after it is put into effect. Instead of "pay as you go," the operative regime would be one where you "go" first and pay later.[37] Regardless of the procedure, if the payments are made over time, their value must be maintained by use of appropriate cost-of-living adjustments to account for any general increase in prices.

An additional concern is the prospect that a uniform payout to all eligible black Americans could aggravate intraracial wealth inequality within the African American community. One strategy to generate a more equitable distribution of the reparations funds is to designate a portion of the funds for competitive application, with priority given to those applicants with lower current wealth or income positions. Applications might include proposals to launch a new business enterprise or pursue the development of a new invention. Again, the professional trustee team, appointed by the elected Reparations Supervisory Board, can judge which proposals merit funding.

In addition to the functions performed by the board, a National Reparations Bureau (NRB) will be established as the civil service agency responsible for day-to-day management and execution of the program.[38] The NRB will work closely with the General Accounting Office to ensure the financial fidelity of the black reparations program. The reparations agency's staff will provide recipients, on an ongoing basis, with information about scams and fraudulent schemes directed against them as well as other matters relevant to successful personal management of their resources.[39]

The agency also will develop a financial management curriculum to be made available to all students and adults via public schools and other voluntary organizations, like communities of faith, starting before the inauguration of the reparations program. This will ensure that all recipients can receive pre-reparations preparation for managing their new portfolios.

In addition, the NRB will facilitate reparations recipients' engagement in participatory research and monitoring of the program themselves.[40] There will be a highly accessible and user-friendly website where participants (and potential participants) in the reparations program can report verifiable past and ongoing instances of racial injustice to maintain a complete public record, report internal abuses within the reparations program itself, and seek additional assistance validating claims about their ancestry that will enable them to establish eligibility for reparations.

Further, the NRB will be charged with implementing a concerted education effort to document, preserve, and communicate America's history of racial injustice—the conditions that led to the adoption of a reparations program—and the impact of the reparations program on African American well-being and the nation as a whole.

The intensive phase of the public education effort should last for a minimum of three generations, or ninety years. As was the case with the National Holocaust Museum's "Never Forget" campaign, it is vital that America's racial history be put at the fore of the conversations Americans have about the nation's past, present, and future. Therefore, beyond the intensive phase, the educational dimension of the reparations program should continue in perpetuity.

The reparations agency can promote age-appropriate textbooks and lesson plans designed to be used at all levels of public school.[41] In addition, the agency can devote resources to support educators, historians, and artists in developing plays, music, visual art, video games, board games, documentary films, feature films, and new biographies and research studies that bring greater accuracy and depth to America's racial history.

With the support of the NRB, the National Museum of African American History and Culture, the National Register of Historic Places, state historic sites, plantations and Civil War battle sites all can contribute to a transformative national process of reinterpretation and learning. Dissemination of the most up-to-date knowledge and scholarship on race, history, and reparations can take place via social media as well as traditional media (print journalism, television, radio—especially public television and public radio).

New plaques or markers can be installed that commemorate persons who were heroes of the struggle for racial equality and justice and commemorate victims of lynchings or riots conducted by white supremacists. New markers also can be installed at sites where there are statues of or buildings named after iconic figures from the Confederacy and the Lost Cause movement to provide descriptions of these figures' activities in the secession movement and/or white terror campaigns to eliminate black political participation after the Civil War. New national holidays can be adopted; for example, an Emancipation Day commemorating the Emancipation Proclamation and the Thirteenth Amendment to the U.S. Constitution would be fitting.

The work of national memory and national consciousness is an essential component of an effective program of black reparations.

Reparations will directly confront the particular structures of injustice that have freighted the lives of black Americans since the founding of the United States. A key question is how we create the political conditions that will lead the U.S. Congress to enact a program of black reparations. Mari J. Matsuda contends that a high degree of solidarity in support of the program from the community that has been subjected to the deep injustice is necessary for a reparations program to become a reality.[42] Thus, Matsuda's perspective suggests that it is just as important to consolidate support for a reparations program within the black community as it is to build support from outside of it.

A number of whites descended from slave owners have asked us what they should do as acts of atonement. Our response has been to encourage them to build a lobbying organization to advocate, forcefully, for reparations for black Americans. Such an organization should be developed with the support of the colleges and universities discussed in chapter 3 that had explicit ties to slavery and the slave trade.

Student activists on college and university campuses—who increasingly are working to uncover the deep connection of many of their institutions to slavery, to the veneration of the Confederacy, and to the "scientific" perpetuation of ideas of black cognitive and cultural inferiority—can take on a new challenge. Instead of seeking *piecemeal reparations* from their institutions on a one-by-one basis, activists should push these institutions to join the lobbying effort for congressional approval of black reparations.

It will be far more useful for colleges and universities to become sponsors of a national effort for reparations than for them to individually address reparations claims among their immediate constituents. Joining the charge in a national campaign for reparations would give these institutions an excellent opportunity to demonstrate both a recognition of their own complicity and the importance of mobilizing their considerable resources to compensate for the harms.[43]

Of course, our hope is that this book will play a role in encouraging more Americans to recognize that black reparations are not only morally justified but practicable. We hope that the book will not only widen support for reparations among all Americans but also deepen support and intensify the championing of reparations among black Americans themselves.

A single book is unlikely to make a social movement, but the potential exists to mobilize growing support for reparations from a variety of activist efforts under way now. The indignation of Moral Mondays activism in North Carolina, the passion of the Black Lives Matter movement, the rise of the #ADOS movement, and the values and imagination shown by growing numbers of young Americans all point toward a groundswell of support for social justice that can energize the push for black reparations.[44]

We seek a new tomorrow that will enable the nation to realize the long-unfulfilled dreams of the freedmen. Reparations for black America, finally, will open the door to that new tomorrow. At last, reparations will move America from here to equality.

With Gratitude

It is a pleasure to recall the many people who have made this book possible.

We happily credit Richard F. America for inviting William "Sandy" Darity Jr. to write an introductory essay on black reparations for Dick's edited volume *The Wealth of Races: The Present Value of Benefits from Past Injustices* (1990). This task gave Sandy a chance to consolidate his thinking about redress for racial oppression and launched him on his path toward this project with A. Kirsten Mullen. We also thank Mary Frances Berry, author of the superb biography *My Face Is Black Is True: Callie House and the Struggle for Ex-Slave Reparations* (2005), a book that motivated us to press on and bring *From Here to Equality* to completion. Bernard Anderson's sustained commitment to bold, transformative policies to achieve equity and racial justice in America also has been an inspiration.

We are delighted to acknowledge the good folks at the University of North Carolina Press: Sian Hunter reached out to us and convinced us to tackle the project; David "Carlos" Perry embraced and helped shape it; Joseph Parsons was an enthusiastic supporter and cheerleader when a coauthor began to make tentative steps to engage with the Twitterverse; and Mark Simpson-Vos, the Wyndham Robertson Editorial Director, with assistance from Associate Editor Jessica Newman, shepherded *From Here to Equality* through to conclusion with an expert helping hand. Finally, we also thank Managing Editor Mary Caviness for the care and sensitivity given to copyediting and production of the book.

Our heartfelt esteem extends to Sandy's colleagues and students at Duke University, the University of North Carolina at Chapel Hill (UNC–Chapel Hill), and the University of Texas at Austin. A particular note of thanks goes to former students who have contributed directly to the literature on black reparations, Dania Frank Francis, Bidisha Lahiri, Tressie McMillan Cottom, and Kellin Stanfield.

A very special nod to Sandy's most sustained coauthors, collaborators, and co-conspirators over the many years: Samuel L. Myers Jr., Darrick Hamilton, Ashwini Deshpande, Arthur Goldsmith, Rhonda V. Sharpe, Michael Syron Lawlor, Bobbie Horn, James Kenneth Galbraith, Arjumand Siddiqi, Patrick Mason, Sukhadeo Thorat, Alan Aja, Anne E. Price, Tod Hamilton,

Timothy Diette, and Allin Cottrell. We also want to recognize Thomas Crae-mer and Trevon Logan for their yeoman's efforts to build multiple paths toward calculating the magnitude of the reparations owed to black descen-dants of American slavery, and the late Jewell Crawford Mazique, whose skepticism and scholarship made us rethink the transformative power of reparations. We also thank the many others who have worked with Sandy, too numerous to name, and ask them to accept our apology for not being included here.

This book also is a product of the support that Sandy has received from his team at the Samuel DuBois Cook Center on Social Equity (Cook Cen-ter) at Duke University. Profound thanks must go to Gwendolyn Wright and JoAnn Oneal, who have been critical staff members at the center since its inception in 2015. During their tenure at the center, Khaing Zaw and Mark Paul made substantial contributions to research activity on racial wealth inequality. Keisha Bentley-Edwards, now associate research director at the center, has advanced the research program, extending its reach to health disparities.

Many thanks to the friends who checked in with us regularly over the past six years and urged us to persevere—we are beholden to our "street team" for their wisdom and good cheer: Cynthia Biggers, Miriam Jiménez Róman, Bridgette Lacy, Wilma Liverpool, Danita Mason-Hogans and Cory Hogans, Juliet Monique McAfee McBride, Jessica Lundy McBride, and Anne Lundy. An armful of gratitude to Cindy, who was always eager to hear news of mile-stones, sympathetic at setbacks, and ready to enjoy a good laugh.

Harryette Mullen has been a tireless champion of this book (and her sis-ter, Kirsten) through thick and thin. She has conducted exhaustive research on the Mullen and Darity family trees. Dr. Avis Ann Mullen shared her mem-ories, offered context and suggestions for framing the history, encouraged her friends to attend our presentations, made frequent airport runs, gra-ciously took us into her home, and supported our writing in countless ways. Mom, your love and care for us means more than words can ever say.

Sandy's sister, Janki Darity, also was a great source of encouragement as the book evolved and a great source of comfort when she and Sandy lost their father in 2015.

For guidance in the early stages, when *From Here to Equality* was purely an idea, credit is due to Wendy Belcher, Michele Bowen, David Cecelski, William "Bill" Ferris, Scott Lubeck, and Harryette Mullen. We thank Lacy Ward Jr., then director of the Robert Russa Moton Museum in Farmville, Virginia, for bringing us up to speed on the desegregation of the Prince Edward County Public Schools. We are especially beholden to

Gia Peebles, whose early, thoughtful critique led us to rethink our approach to the entire project.

We are deeply indebted to Pamela Footman, Kenneth Lewis, Hortense McClinton, Kelly Elaine Navies, and Bryan A. Stevenson for entrusting us with stories of the enslaved members of their families.

In addition, we are obliged for Sandy's receipt of a yearlong fellowship at the Center for Advanced Study in the Behavioral Sciences (CASBS) at Stanford University, where the initial writing began, also supported, in part, by Duke University. During that year, Kirsten received support from the Community Folklife Documentation Institute of the North Carolina Arts Council. There we were assisted by the librarians extraordinaire Tricia Soto and Amanda Thomas and tech wizard Ravi Shivanna. We were nourished by the appetizing and healthful cuisine prepared each weekday by CASBS's chef, Susan Beach.

Sandy's subsequent fellowship at the Russell Sage Foundation, under Sheldon Danziger's leadership, greatly facilitated development of the book. The efforts of research librarian Katie Winograd and information services assistant Danielle Georges expanded our access to valuable scholarly material. Suzanne Nichols, James Wilson, Claire Gabriel, Aixa Cintrón Vélez, Jimmy Begland, and Mitch Dorfman were great sources of guidance and friendship. Chef Jacqueline Cholmondeley provided delectable gourmet fare each weekday, which we remember with fondness and admiration.

While we conducted the research, we were fortunate to share our ideas with audiences at the Durham (North Carolina) County Library, Durham Sunshine Rotary, the Association for the Study of African American Life and History, the University of Virginia-Charlottesville, Duke University, Middlebury College, the New School, Chicago State University, the University of Illinois at Chicago, the University of South Carolina–Columbia, Cornell University, Tulane University School of Law, the Centenary meeting of the Indian Economic Association (Acharya Nagarjuna University, Andhra Pradesh, India), the National Economic Association, the Angela Project of the Cooperative Baptist Fellowship and the Progressive National Baptist Convention, the Black Communities Conference of the Institute of African American Research at UNC–Chapel Hill, the Southern Economic Association, and the American Economic Association.

A special thanks to Rep. William Lacy Clay (D-Miss.), his chief of staff, Yvette Cravins, and his legislative director, Erica Powell, for holding a panel at the 2019 Congressional Black Caucus Annual Legislative Conference on the black-white wealth gap and potential remedies, including reparations.

The research on this book has been made much easier by the expert staff at the Durham County Public Library. We greatly appreciate the assistance of Interlibrary Loan Service coordinator Patrick Holt, who was patient with our overlong borrowings. Research tools like Documenting the American South, the digital portal of the University Library at UNC–Chapel Hill; the Internet Archive, the digital library of internet sites and other cultural artifacts; the extraordinary Black Past: Remembered and Reclaimed website (BlackPast.org), and the Congressional Record (Congress.gov) have been indispensable.

For their early and constant support, we recognize Gann Herman, Leoneda Inge, and Katherine Roberts, members of Kirsten's writing circle, for their thoughtful and sensitive readings of several chapters of the book and valuable suggestions for improvement that helped to make the writing experience and this book richer. Circle members' questions motivated the addition of two chapters. Gann's keen editorial eye throughout is deeply appreciated. Lew Myers, an ardent supporter of reparations, read an early draft in its entirety and urged us on with grace and enthusiasm.

Generous family members and friends, including Zachary Fisher, Billy D. Lee, Susie Ruth Powell, and Mel Williams, have done us the great favor of reading a portion of this manuscript and providing suggestions that have improved the work. The comments of two anonymous readers for the University of North Carolina Press led us to sharpen and reframe the text.

We wish to thank our wise friend, community organizer, civil rights worker, and folklorist Worth Long for reminding us to include the music.

Hats off to Lauren Brook Parker for locating photographs and keeping us organized early on.

Plaudits and affection to Karen Maloney, managing editor at Cambridge University Press, who, prompted by Sandy's inaugural efforts to develop the field of stratification economics, urged him to design and serve as the series editor for Cambridge Studies in Stratification Economics: Economics and Social Identity.

We also must gratefully recognize a number of print media journalists who have interviewed us or solicited articles from us and print media outlets that have featured our work on black reparations. These include Valerie Russ (*Philadelphia Inquirer*), Natasha S. Alford (*The Grio*), Lottie L. Joiner (*The Crisis*), Edwin Rios (*Mother Jones*), Nikole Hannah-Jones (*New York Times*), Trymaine Lee, George Pierpoint (*BBC News*), Kia Gregory (*Politico*), Jarrell Dillard (*Bloomberg News*), Cynthia Greenlee (*Durham Herald Sun*), Osha Gray Davidson, Alan Greenblatt (*CQ Magazine*), and Jacob Schlesinger (*Wall*

Street Journal). Douglas Clement's interview with Sandy for the publication of the Federal Reserve Banks of Minneapolis *The Region* was unique in its wide-ranging coverage of his research portfolio. Special regards to Lucas Hubbard for writing an in-depth profile of Sandy for *Duke Magazine* that included a detailed discussion of the work on black reparations and stratification economics.

Thank you also to the hosts of radio and television programs, podcasts, and websites that generously featured our ideas and/or gave us air time. We salute Frank Stasio (*The State of Things*, WUNC), Tanzina Vega (*The Takeaway*, WNYC), Todd Zwillich (*1A*, WAMU), April Dawson and Irving Joyner (*The Legal Eagle*, WNCU), Christine Nguyen (*THINK*, NBC News), Noel King (*Morning Edition*, NPR), Pedro Gatos (*Bringing Light into Darkness*, KOOP), Antonio Moore (*Tonetalks*), Yvette Carnell (*Breaking Brown*), Steve Grumbine (*Real Progressive Economics*), Pedro Echeverria (*Washington Journal*, C-SPAN), Chris Miller (*Charlotte Talks*, WFAE), Tim Pulliam (ABC-11), Ezra Klein (*The Ezra Klein Show*), Brian Lehrer (*The Brian Lehrer Show*, WNYC), George Brown and Maria Sanchez (*Shadow Politics*, BBS), Tommy Tucker (*First News*, WWL), Meghna Chakrabarti (*On Point*, WBUR), Alondra Nelson (*New Yorker Radio Hour*, WNYC), Mina Kim (*Forum*, KQED), Christina Edmondson, Michelle Higgins, and Ekemini Uwan (*Truth's Table*), Ranjani Chakaraborty (Vox), Paul Solman (*PBS Newshour*), Amirah Lawson, Kanita Sturdivant, Nobly Rogue, Kaliq Ray, and Valerie Regis (*Black American D.O.S. Caucus*), Dathon O'Banion, Denise Young, Brian Roberts, and Otis L. Griffin (*Mind on Freedom*), and Bill Hendrickson (WCOM).

Finally, we are supremely thankful for all who listened to us talk about this project and voiced their comments and questions.

Much appreciation for you all.

A. Kirsten Mullen and William A. Darity Jr.
Durham, North Carolina
January 2020

Appendix 1: Reparations Coordinating Committee

Other members of the Reparations Coordinating Committee between 2000 and 2002 were Randall Robinson, president of TransAfrica and author of the influential and controversial book *The Debt: What America Owes to Blacks*, which ignited considerable public discussion on reparations when it first appeared in print; Willie Gary, a trial lawyer who won a $500 million judgment against the Loewen Group, the world's largest funeral home operator; the late J. L. Chestnut Jr., a tireless civil rights attorney who was present at the March 7, 1965, assault called Bloody Sunday, when police beat an estimated 600 peaceful, unarmed demonstrators with nightsticks on the Edmund Pettus Bridge in Selma, Alabama, to prevent them from marching to Montgomery; the late Johnnie Cochran, a civil rights attorney who had won millions of dollars in awards to compensate African American victims of police brutality in California; Dennis C. Sweet III and Richard Scruggs, who won a $400 million settlement in the fen-phen drug case; Alexander Pires, a Washington, D.C., attorney who won a $1 billion settlement from the U.S. Department of Agriculture brought on behalf of 400 black farmers in 1999; James Lloyd, an attorney and member of the Oklahoma Commission to Study the Tulsa Riot of 1921; Alfred Brophy, a law professor then at the University of Alabama at Tuscaloosa and author of *Reconstructing the Dreamland: The Tulsa Riot of 1921, Race, Reparations and Reconciliation*; Michele Roberts of the Public Defender Service; Kimberly Ellis, then a doctoral candidate in American studies at Purdue University, whose dissertation was called "Literary Responses to the Tulsa Race Riot of 1921"; Suzette Malveaux, then a class-action-litigation specialist who had argued before the U.S. Supreme Court; Eric J. Miller, a Charles Hamilton Houston Fellow at Harvard Law School; Sharon Cole, an attorney; James Goodwin, an Oklahoma attorney; Johnnetta Cole, president of Bennett College; Cornel West, a professor at Harvard at the time; Richard F. America of Georgetown University; and the late Manning Marable of the Institute for African American Studies at Columbia University. Other prominent activists in the movement during the mid- to late 1990s included the late political scientist Dr. Ronald Walters of the University of Maryland at College Park and James Comer, a professor of psychiatry at Yale University School of Medicine.

Appendix 2: Horrors of Slavery

What follows is a sample of the testimonials from *American Slavery as It Is*, describing the savagery imposed on the enslaved.

> The slaves are often tortured by iron collars, with long prongs or "horns" and sometimes bells attached to them—they are made to wear chains, handcuffs, fetters, iron clogs, bars, rings, and bands of iron upon their limbs, iron masks upon their faces, iron gags in their mouths, &c.[1]

John M. Nelson, Esq., a native of Virginia, now a highly respected citizen of Highland county, Ohio, and member of the Presbyterian Church in Hillsborough, in a recent letter states the following: "In Staunton, Va., at the house of Mr. Robert M'Dowell, a merchant of that place, I once saw a colored woman, of intelligent and dignified appearance, who appeared to be attending to the business of the house, with an *iron collar* around her neck, with horns or prongs extending out on either side, and up, until they met at something like a foot above her head, at which point there was a bell attached. This *yoke*, as they called it, I understood was to prevent her from running away, or to punish her for having done so. I had frequently seen *men* with iron collars, but this was the first instance that I recollect to have seen a *female* thus degraded."[2]

Col. Elijah Wellsworth, of Richfield, Ohio, gives the following testimony:—"Eight or ten years ago I was in Putnam county, in the state of Georgia, at a Mr. Slaughter's, the father of my brother's wife. A negro, that belonged to Mr. Walker, (I believe,) was accused of stealing a pedlar's trunk. The negro denied, but, without ceremony, was lashed to a tree—the whipping commenced—six or eight men took turns—the poor fellow begged for mercy, but without effect, until he was literally *cut to pieces, from his shoulders to his hips*, and covered with a gore of blood. When he said the trunk was in a stack of fodder, he was unlashed. They proceeded to the stack, but found no trunk. They asked the poor fellow, what he lied about it for; he said, 'Lord, Massa, to keep from being whipped to death; I know nothing about the trunk.' They commenced the whipping with redoubled vigor, until I really supposed he would be whipped to death on the spot; and such shrieks and crying for mercy!—Again he acknowledged, and again they were defeated in finding, and the same reason given as before. Some were for whipping again, others thought he would not survive another, and they ceased. About two months after, the trunk was found, and it was then ascertained who the thief was: and the poor fellow, after being nearly beat to death, and twice made to lie about it, was as innocent as I was."

Narrative of Reverend Horace Moulton:

It is very common for masters to say to the overseers or drivers, "put it on to them," "don't spare that fellow," "give that scoundrel one hundred lashes," &c. Whipping the women when in delicate circumstances, as they sometimes do, without any regard to their entreaties or the entreaties of their nearest friends, is truly barbarous. If negroes could testify, they would tell you of instances of women being whipped until they have miscarried at the whipping-post. I heard of such things at the south—they are undoubtedly facts. Children are whipped unmercifully for the smallest offences, and that before their mothers. A large proportion of the blacks have their shoulders, backs, and arms all scarred up, and not a few of them have had their heads laid open with clubs, stones, and brick-bats, and with the butt-end of whips and canes—some have had their jaws broken, others their teeth knocked in or out; while others have had their ears cropped and the sides of their cheeks gashed out. Some of the poor creatures have lost the sight of one of their eyes by the careless blows of the whipper, or by some other violence.

Testimony of Mr. William Poe:

A captain in the United States' Navy, who married a daughter of the collector of the port of Richmond, and resided there, became offended with his negro boy, took him into the meat house, put him upon a stool, crossed his hands before him, tied a rope to them, threw it over a joist in the building, drew the boy up so that he could just stand on the stool with his toes, and kept him in that position, flogging him severely at intervals, until the boy became so exhausted that he reeled off the stool, and swung by his hands until he died. The master was tried and acquitted.

In a letter dated St. Helena Island, S.C., Dec. 3, 1832. Mr. G. writes,

"If a slave here complains to his master, that his task is too great, his master at once calls him a scoundrel and tells him it is only because he has not enough to do, and orders the driver to increase his task, however unable he may be for the performance of it. I saw TWENTY-SEVEN *whipped at one time* just because they did not do more, when the poor creatures were so tired that they could scarcely drag one foot after the other."[3]

Appendix 3: Narratives of Emancipation

E. Franklin Frazier detailed two narratives of formerly enslaved blacks' reactions upon learning that they had been emancipated:

> One ex-slave recalled that the announcement [of emancipation] sounded "like Greek" to him when his mother whispered, "Son, we have been slaves all our lives, and now Mr. Abe Lincoln done set us free, and say we can go anywhere we please in this country, without getting a pass from Marse Cage like we used to have to do." A Negro minister tells the following story of the announcement of freedom on the plantation where his grandfather held a responsible position:
>
> The slaves were in the fields chopping the cotton and chanting the rhythm of the day as a testimony to the drowsy overseer that they were doing his bidding. "Massah" Ridley was on the porch of the "big house" fast asleep. The Yankees had ridden up to the mansion and the horses put their hoofs on the low and unrailed porch as if at home. Doctor Ridley awakened quickly, surprised, startled, bewildered, perplexed, a riot of color. Some words passed between the parties, and then one of the soldiers took something from his pocket and read it. By this time "Missus" Ridley had come from the house. She too heard the story and saw her husband's eyes suffused with tears but said not a word. Doctor Ridley was trying hard to keep the tears back. He summoned Miles and spoke slowly with a tear in his voice: "Miles, call all the niggers together."
>
> The slaves did not know the meaning of Miles' news to them, although they had heard rumors that they should sometime be free. Few could read, and none had access to newspapers. As they left the field they wondered who was to be whipped or who was to be sold or what orders were to be given. Half-startled, half-afraid, they wended their way through the fields in one silent mass of praying creatures. On seeing the Yankees they started back, but "Massah" Ridley beckoned.
>
> The master was weeping bitterly. Finally he sobbed, "I called together, Miles—" then he stopped. His words were stifled with a sob.

The slaves were awe-stricken; they had never seen a white man cry. Only slaves had tears, they thought. All eyes were fastened on Doctor Ridley. He was saying something. "All you niggers—all you niggers are free as I am." The surprise was shocking, but in an instant in his usual harsh voice he added: "But there ain't going to be any rejoicing here. Stay here until the crop is made, and I'll give you provisions. Go back to work."

But the slaves did rejoice and loudly, too. Some cried; some jumped up and cracked their heels. Charlotte took her younger children in her arms and shouted all over the plantation: "Chillun, didn't I tell you God 'ould answer our prayer?"[1]

Appendix 4: Memories of the Fifty-Fourth

The Fifty-Fourth Massachusetts was memorialized in *Glory* (1989), the Academy Award–winning film account of the Civil War, which is based in part on the personal correspondence of the regiment's commander, Col. Robert Gould Shaw, and told from his point of view.[1] The National Park Service maintains a bas relief bronze monument to the north's first black infantry, *Robert Gould Shaw and the 54th Regiment Memorial*, created by artist Augustus Saint-Gaudens and located across the street from the Massachusetts State House in Boston.[2]

Earlier, *The Storming of Fort Wagner*, a commercially successful 1890 lithograph published by the Chicago-based firm Kurz and Allison, depicted the horrific South Carolina military engagement and became one of at least five chromolithographs depicting battle scenes featuring black Civil War soldiers. Rendered with varying degrees of accuracy, the Civil War print series was informed by archival research and interviews with veterans. Founded in 1880 by Louis Kurz, who had fought in the war, and Austrian native Allison (whose first name is variously recorded as Alexander or William), the Kurz and Allison firm was among the few publishing companies that portrayed nonstereotypical images of black Civil War troops in collectible formats (paper size twenty-six by twenty inches and image size twenty-four by nineteen inches).

In direct contrast to their competitors—printmaking companies like Currier and Ives, for instance—Kurz and Allison portrayed black troops and civilians aiding the Union war effort as brave, dignified, dedicated, disciplined, and heroic. *The Storming of Fort Wagner*, rendered from the vantage point of the Union forces, shows black soldiers of the Fifty-Fourth Massachusetts Volunteer Infantry Regiment with the harbor at their backs early in their attack on the Confederate-held fort. Dressed in complementary shades of Union blue and commanded by Col. Robert Gould Shaw, whose sword is raised as he shouts a command, the men advance with the U.S. flag held high and charge into the flanks of Confederate soldiers.[3]

Appendix 5: More Rehearsals for Freedom

Roanoke, Virginia, planter John Randolph directed his executors to manumit his slaves upon his death and to purchase between 2,000 and 4,000 acres of land for the creation of a settlement for their use. He also specified that they be furnished with "necessary cabins, clothes and utensils." Some 3,200 acres of land were purchased in Mercer County, Ohio, in 1846 for the use of the emancipated slaves.

Mercer County was already home to Carthagena—the name is derived from the ancient African city of Carthage—one of the country's few successful, if short-lived, black settlements. Carthagena was founded in 1836 by Augustus Wattles, a Quaker and Underground Railroad conductor who had operated a Cincinnati school for blacks from 1834 to 1836, which had an enrollment of 200 students at its peak. With the assistance of groups like the Emlen Institution for the Benefit of Children of African and Indian Descent, Wattles purchased 30,000 acres of arable land in Mercer County that he deeded to the black settlers and opened a school for boys—one of twenty-five such institutions across the state. When local whites discovered that a second wave of blacks was relocating to Mercer County, they resolved that they would "not live among negroes," formed an armed militia, and drove the blacks from their land under the threat of violence. Ultimately, both communities were dispersed; consequently, the Randolph ex-slaves benefited minimally from their former owner's benevolence.[1]

Most unusual was Samuel Gist, a London attorney and banker who owned and lived on his Hanover County, Virginia, plantation before 1757. The ideal subject of a biography, he was born in England, the son of David Gist, and he was orphaned at an early age and educated at Queen Elizabeth's Hospital. By 1739, he had made his way to Virginia, where he was indentured to shopkeeper John Smith. When Smith died, Gist married Smith's widow, acquired the family fortune, and became engaged in several commercial enterprises: he exported tobacco to London, was an early investor in the stock exchange and the Dismal Swamp Company, and insured ships during the American Revolution.

By 1782, he had returned to England and granted his property, which included seventy-two slaves, to his daughter Mary, wife of William Anderson, also of Hanover County. At the time of his death in 1815, Gist provided in his will for the manumission of the 500, and possibly 1,000, enslaved people he owned and indicated that they and their heirs should receive support from the sale of his plantation. His executor purchased what turned out to be "swampy and untillable" land in Brown County, Ohio, for one group of Gist's former slaves and, after driving them "like cattle" and "march[ing them] to Ohio," neglected to provide any material support for them and abandoned them to ruin. The ex-slaves that were settled in Ohio's Adams and Highland Counties fared better. Descendants of the Highland County "Gist Settlements" were still living on the land well into the twentieth century.[2]

Appendix 6: Jefferson Davis and the Haitian Revolution

Jefferson Davis made the following remarks before the U.S. Congress in 1850 on the implications of the insurrection of the enslaved in Saint-Domingue:

> They see that the slaves in their present condition in the South are comfortable and happy; they see them advancing in intelligence; they see the kindest relations existing between them and their masters; they see them provided for in age and sickness, in infancy and in disability; they see them in useful employment, restrained from the vicious indulgences to which their inferior nature inclines them; they see our penitentiaries never filled, and our poor-houses usually empty. Let them turn to the other hand, and they see the same race in a state of freedom in the North; but instead of the comfort and kindness they receive at the South, instead of being happy and useful, they are, with few exceptions, miserable, degraded, filling the penitentiaries and poor-houses, objects of scorn, excluded in some places from the schools, and deprived of many other privileges and benefits which attach to the white men among whom they live. And yet, they insist that elsewhere an institution which has proved beneficial to this race shall be abolished, that it may be substituted by a state of things which is fraught with so many evils to the race which they claim to be the object of the solicitude! *Do they find in the history of St. Domingo, and in the present condition of Jamaica, under the recent experiments which have been made upon the institution of slavery in the liberation of the blacks, before God, in his wisdom designed it should be done—do they there find anything to stimulate them to further exertions in the cause of abolition? Or should they not find there satisfactory evidence that their past course was founded in error?*[1]

Appendix 7: The Death of Freedman's Bank

The financial crisis began in Europe, reached U.S. shores during the fall of 1873, and triggered a national depression. Chief among the causes of the economic reversal was the collapse of Jay Cooke and Company, a major investment bank. The company backed the Northern Pacific Railroad and the bulk of the government's wartime loans, and it was a major player in the country's rapidly growing, but little understood, securities market.

Eric Foner's *Reconstruction* provides details on the web of business dealings Jay Cooke, "the financier of the Civil War," had with elected officials and members of the Republican Party.[1] The Freedman's Bank, "organized and controlled by white friends of the Negro ostensibly for his benefit," was one of many financial institutions that was brought down by short-sighted and ill-conceived lending practices. Blacks were "induced to believe that the bank was a government institution or that at least the government was responsible for their funds." Depositors' passbook covers featured images of President Lincoln, General Grant, and Gen. Oliver O. Howard, and the American flag was prominently draped over the banks.

Several bank trustees who also sat on the boards of financial institutions "unloaded some of [their institutions'] bad loans upon the Freedman's Bank. Others—[Henry David] Cooke, [D. L.] Eaton, [W. S.] Huntington, [George W.] Balloch, and [Zalmon] Richards—were connected with firms that borrowed large sums, notwithstanding the fact that officials of the bank were prohibited by law from borrowing from it, directly or indirectly. . . . There was hardly an officer after 1871 who was not connected with some outside interest that borrowed from the bank."[2]

In one example of a conflict of interest and unwise use of Freedman's Bank funds, bank trustee Henry D. Cooke, a financier and railroad executive who also had an interest in Jay Cooke and Company and sat on the board of the Seneca Sandstone Company, advocated for the Seneca Sandstone Company to receive an unsecured loan. Unable to collect revenues it was due after the Panic of 1873 took hold, Seneca Sandstone Company defaulted on its loan to the Freedman's Bank, pushing the institution into bankruptcy.[3]

Notes

INTRODUCTION

1. Similar policies were practiced both in the United States with the parallel placement of American Indian children in off-reservation boarding schools and in Australia with the removal of Aboriginal and Torres Strait Islander children from their families to be placed with white families. The latter are known as "stolen generations," and the provincial government of New South Wales has made some provisions for reparations for the victims and their families; see "The Stolen Generations: the Forcible Removal of Indigenous Children from their Families," *Australians Together*, https://australianstogether.org.au/discover/australian-history/stolen-generations. No reparations have been provided for the equivalent stolen generations in the United States.

2. While the prospect of receiving land and a farm animal made the freedmen targets of swindlers and scam artists, West Virginia University historian Walter Fleming declared unambiguously that "the expectations of the blacks were justified by the policies of the Government and the actions of its agents." See Walter Fleming, "'Forty Acres and a Mule,'" *North American Review* 182, no. 594 (May 1906): 721.

3. The necessity of forgiveness on the part of the victims to complete the process of atonement is thoroughly elaborated in Roy Brooks's "atonement model." See Roy L. Brooks, *Atonement and Forgiveness: A New Model for Black Reparations* (Berkeley: University of California Press, 2004). See also Kirsten Mullen and William Darity Jr., "The Big Payback," Root, July 1, 2008, https://www.theroot.com/the-big-payback-1790899972.

4. We thank Zachary Fisher of Durham, North Carolina, for this observation.

5. Boris Bittker, *The Case for Black Reparations* (Boston: Beacon Press, 1972); Brooks, *Atonement and Forgiveness*.

6. Joe R. Feagin, "Documenting the Costs of Slavery, Segregation, and Contemporary Racism: Why Reparations Are in Order for African Americans," *Harvard Black-Letter Law Journal* 20 (2004): 49–81.

CHAPTER 1

1. Please see the extended discussion in chapters 7 and 8 in part 4 below. From the earliest days of the republic, black captives were risking life and limb to escape bondage. In 1792, for at least a month, "Negro lad" Phil, about twenty years old, eluded bounty hunters despite the thirty-dollar reward owner Robert Pearce offered for his return. "Negro man" Hark, last seen in Kent County, Maryland, reclaimed his freedom for at least four months from Peregrine Lethrbury, a member of the Maryland General Assembly's 1777–78 House of Delegates. See "Run Away . . ." and "Thirty Dollars

Reward," *Gazette of the United States,* June 30, 1792, https://chroniclingamerica.loc .gov/lccn/sn83030483/1792-06-30/ed-1/seq-1.

2. "Newspaper Account of a Meeting between Black Religious Leaders and Union Military Authorities," Freedmen and Southern Society Project, http://www.history .umd.edu/Freedmen/savmtg.htm. See also "Minutes of an Interview between the Colored Ministers and Church Officers at Savannah with the Secretary of War and Major-Gen. Sherman," *New-York Tribune,* February 13, 1865.

3. Frederick Douglass, "Letter to Harriet Beecher Stowe," in *Negro Social and Political Thought 1850–1920,* ed. Howard Brotz (New York: Basic Books, 1966), 222–23.

4. "Speech of Frederick Douglass at the 1876 Republican National Convention," Frederick Douglass in Washington, D.C.: The Lion of Anacostia (website), May 16, 2016, https://thelionofanacostia.wordpress.com/2016/05/16/speech-of-frederick -douglass-at-the-1876-republican-national-convention. The beneficial effects of the land grants to the former serfs are elaborated in Stephen L. Hoch, "Did Russia's Serfs Really Pay Too Much for Too Little Land? Statistical Anomalies and Long-Tailed Distributions," *Slavic Review* 63, no. 2 (Summer 2004): 247–74. The author's answer to the question in the title is no.

5. Frederick Douglass, "Extract from a Speech Delivered at Elmira, N.Y., August 1, 1880," in *The Life and Times of Frederick Douglass from 1817 to 1882* (1881; London: Forgotten Books, 2018), 612.

6. "Address of Hon. Fred. Douglass," in *National Convention of Colored Men at Louisville, Kentucky, September 24, 1883* (Louisville: Courier-Journal Job, 1883), 7.

7. See esp. Mary Frances Berry, *My Face Is Black Is True: Callie House and the Struggle for Ex-slave Reparations* (New York: Alfred A. Knopf, 2005); and James Turner, "Callie House: The Pursuit of Reparations as a Means of Social Justice," *Journal of African-American History* 91, no. 3 (Summer 2006): 305–10. Prior to House's efforts, in the early 1880s, the peripatetic rogue John Wayne Niles, formed the Indemnity Party and lobbied Congress for the provision of substantial tracts of western lands for black settlement. His party may have reached a membership upwards of 2000 people, his petition to Congress was quashed, and "in 1884 he simply disappeared from the pages of history." Charlotte Hinger, "John Wayne Niles (1842–?)," BlackPast, July 14, 2014, https://www.blackpast.org/vignette_aahw/niles-john-wayne-1842.

8. Mary Frances Berry, interview by Juan Williams, *After Words,* C-SPAN, October 17, 2005, https://www.c-span.org/video/?189393-1/after-words-mary-frances -berry&start=146.

9. H.R. 11119 was introduced by Nebraska representative William J. Connell in the Fifty-First Congress, in 1890. Walter R. Vaughan's Justice Party founded the National Ex-Slaves Pension Club Association of the United States. Miranda Booker Perry, "No Pensions for Ex-slaves: How Federal Agencies Suppressed Movement to Aid Freedpeople," *Prologue Magazine,* Summer 2010, http://www.archives.gov/publications /prologue/2010/summer/slave-pension.html.

10. Vaughan's reasoning was an exact expression of the principles of Keynesian economics. The transfer of funds to blacks would function as an economic stimulus to the southern economy through black consumption spending. Rep. William J. Connell (D-Neb.) introduced the bill, H.R. 11119, in the Fifty-First Congress (1889–91).

It did not pass. See Charles P. Henry, *Long Overdue: The Politics of Racial Reparations* (New York: New York University Press, 2007), 46. See also Committee on House Administration of the U.S. House of Representatives, *Black Americans in Congress 1870–2007* (Washington, D.C.: Government Printing Office, 2008). Stefan Richards recently made a case similar to Vaughan's for reparations payments for slavery to be made by the European imperial nations to their former colonies in the Caribbean. Richards has argued that a major transfer of funds to the Caribbean nations would have beneficial effects on economic growth. See Stefan Richards, "On the Impact of Reparations for Slavery on Growth and Sustainable Development: Can Reparations Buy Growth?," Institute of the Black World 21st Century, April 24, 2017, http://ibw21 .org/docs/The_Economic_Impact_of_Reparations.pdf.

11. Miranda Booker Perry, preparer, *Correspondence and Case Files of the Bureau of Pensions Pertaining to the Ex-slave Pension Movement, 1892–1922* (Washington, D.C.: National Archives and Records Administration, 2006), www.archives.gov/research /microfilm/m2110.pdf.

12. See Act to Grant Pensions, Public Act No. 17-166, 2d Sess., 37 Stat. 566 (1862).

13. Roy Finkenbine has argued that the first recorded instance of a reparations claim of this type occurred in 1783 when a formerly enslaved, elderly woman known as Belinda petitioned the Massachusetts state legislature for a pension for her invalid daughter and for herself. Belinda's efforts were partially successful. Finkenbine also identifies several early nineteenth-century white abolitionist advocates of reparations for the enslaved upon emancipation, including Timothy Dwight, then president of Yale, in 1810 and Hosea Easton in 1837. See Roy E. Finkenbine, "Belinda's Petition: Reparations for Slavery in Revolutionary Massachusetts," *William and Mary Quarterly* 64, no. 1 (January 2007): 95–104.

14. For Mary Frances Berry's estimate of the number of ex-slaves living in 1899, see Mary Frances Berry, "Reparations for Freedmen: 1890–1916; Fraudulent Practices or Justice Deferred?," *Journal of Negro History*, no. 57 (July 1972): 219–30; and Berry, *My Face*, 148. Federal prosecutors, in their indictment of House in 1916, cited a membership figure of 300,000 for House's association; Berry, *My Face*, 253–54n2. For Berry's own estimate of the association's membership in 1900, see Berry, *My Face*, 7. Berry was a panelist on the New York Historical Society's panel "The Legacy of Slavery" in January 2006, on the occasion of the organization's exhibition *Slavery in New York*, where she reintroduced her estimates of the ex-slave population in 1899. The pension plan proposed by House provided a graduated one-time payment to all former slaves over the age of fifty, with slaves seventy years of age and older receiving the maximum payment of $500 plus a monthly pension of fifteen dollars for the rest of their lives; ex-slaves who were under fifty years of age would not receive a lump payment but would be eligible to receive a four-dollar-a-month pension for the rest of their lives. The proposal was modeled after the plan the U.S. government had developed for veterans, particularly Civil War veterans.

15. "Southern Cotton Tax," Johnson v. McAdoo, 45 App. D.C. 440, 1916.

16. Perry, "No Pensions for Ex-slaves."

17. Garvey and the Universal Negro Improvement Association also were brought down by mail fraud charges.

18. James Weldon Johnson, prolific author, black rights activist, and eventual member of the Harlem Renaissance, was a field secretary in charge of organizing peaceful protests for the National Association for the Advancement of Colored People in opposition to the riots when he coined the term.

19. See Chicago Commission on Race Relations, *The Negro in Chicago: A Study of Race Relations and a Race Riot* (Chicago: University of Chicago Press, 1922). The commission's report was unique insofar as it investigated both the condition of blacks in Chicago and the white riot simultaneously. In contrast, projects like W. E. B. Du Bois's *The Philadelphia Negro: A Social Study* (Philadelphia: University of Pennsylvania Press, 1899) focused exclusively on the economic and social conditions of blacks in that city; *Philadelphia Negro* was not also a study of white violence.

20. Chicago Commission on Race Relations, *Negro in Chicago*, 656. None of the commission's recommendations involved recompense for the African American victims of the Chicago riot.

21. She later attended the Million Man March in Washington, D.C., in 1995. See William Darity Jr., "Reparations," in Jack Salzman, David Lionel Smith, and Cornel West, eds., *Encyclopedia of African American History and Culture* (New York: Simon and Schuster, 1996), 4:2315–18.

22. Berry, *My Face*, 237.

23. Wikipedia, s.v. "Queen Mother Moore," http://en.wikipedia.org/wiki/Queen _Mother_Moore.

24. The working group grew out of the World Conference Against Racism, Racial Discrimination, Xenophobia, and Related Intolerance, which took place in Durban, South Africa, in 2001. Its directive was to "study . . . racial discrimination faced by people of African descent living in the diaspora" and "make proposals (designed) to eliminat[e it]." The urgency of the events of September 11, 2001, sidelined the working group's efforts for nearly seven years from the time it received its mandate from the UN Human Rights Council. See Office of the High Commissioner for Human Rights, "Statement to the Media by the United Nations' Working Group of Experts on People of African Descent, on the Conclusion of Its Official Visit to USA 19–29 January 2016," news release, January 29, 2016, https://www.ohchr.org/EN/NewsEvents/Pages /DisplayNews.aspx?NewsID=17000.

25. Terry Bisson's work in speculative fiction imagines an alternative history where militant abolitionist John Brown conducts a successful raid at Harpers Ferry, enabling him to arm enslaved insurgents. The slave revolt ultimately ends in their victory, leading to the formation of a black independent nation in the southeastern United States that he calls, tellingly, Nova Africa. See Terry Bisson, *Fire on the Mountain* (Oakland, Calif.: PM Press, 1988).

26. For a valuable biography of Robert Williams, see Timothy Tyson, *Radio Free Dixie: Robert F. Williams and the Roots of Black Power* (Chapel Hill: University of North Carolina Press, 1999). Williams himself was the author of a book that was a direct repudiation of limiting black resistance to nonviolent methods; see Robert F. Williams, *Negroes with Guns* (New York: Marzani and Munsell, 1962).

27. Quintin Schwartz, "Robert F. Williams: The Black Power Leader from Afar," Black Power in American Memory, April 19, 2017, http://blackpower.web.unc

.edu/2017/04/robert-f-williams-the-black-power-leader-from-afar; *"Negroes With Guns*: Rob Williams and Black Power,"* Independent Lens,* http://www.pbs.org /independentlens/negroeswithguns/rob.html.

28. Malcolm X, "The Race Problem" (speech, Michigan State University, East Lansing, Mich., January 23, 1963), Speeches and Interviews: The Autobiography of Malcolm X, http://ccnmtl.columbia.edu/projects/mmt/mxp/speeches/mxt24.html. We thank Howard Machtinger for alerting us to this speech.

29. "The Black Manifesto at the Riverside Church," The Riverside Church in the City of New York, https://www.trcnyc.org/blackmanifesto.

30. Browne was the first economist to advance a systematic argument for black reparations. See, for example, Robert S. Browne, "The Economic Case for Reparations to Black America,"* American Economic Review* 62, no. 1/2 (March 1972): 39–46.

31. See D. L. Chandler, "Little Known Black History Fact: James Forman's Black Manifesto," BlackAmericaWeb, May 27, 2015, https://blackamericaweb .com/2015/05/27/little-known-black-history-fact-james-formans-black-manifesto. The Black Economic Research Center's publication, the *Review of Black Political Economy,* continues to be published under the auspices of the National Economic Association.

32. We thank documentary filmmaker Macky Alston for sharing this information with us.

33. Numerous artists have made contributions to reparations advocacy. In 1965 Oscar Brown Jr. asked in a live performance in Washington, D.C., in an open letter to the president, "When do I get my forty acres and a mule?" In 1970, Gil Scott-Heron recorded "Who'll Pay Reparations on My Soul?" Perhaps best known is the Staple Singers' 1970 recording of "When Will We Be Paid (For the Work We've Done)?" Prince's powerful cover of the same song, recorded in either 1999 or 2000, was accompanied by a video that opened with the following text: "Reparations: the making of amends for a wrong one has done by paying money to those who have been wronged." On her 2010 album *My Soul,* singer Leela James issued a demand for "forty acres and a mule" in her song "I Want It All." A remarkable compendium of reparations-themed works from visual artists in New Orleans is presented in a volume depicting the Luciano Benetton collection; see Diego Cortez, ed., *Reparation: Contemporary Artists from New Orleans* (Treviso, Italy: Fabrica, 2014). The authors thank Diego Cortez for the gift of this beautiful publication.

34. See N'COBRA website, https://www.ncobraonline.org. An allied organization, the National African American Reparations Commission, emerged in 2015 with a ten-point plan for restitution. An important ambiguity in the commission's plan is who specifically should be eligible for reparations. Correspondingly, this vagueness means the ten-point plan excludes provisions for direct payments to eligible recipients; see "National African American Reparations Commission," Institute of the Black World 21st Century, https://ibw21.org/initiatives /national-african-american-reparations-commission.

35. Originally, the proposed commission was to comprise seven members, three each to be selected by the U.S. president and the Speaker of the House of Representatives and one by the president pro tempore of the Senate.

36. John Conyers, "My Reparations Bill—HR40," IBW21.ORG, October 3, 2013. https://ibw21.org/commentary/my-reparations-bill-hr-40.

37. Ed Bradley, host of the CBS news program *60 Minutes*, whose family hailed from Rosewood, "reported that about forty people were killed." And "Fred Kirkland, the white man . . . whose relatives were present during the massacre told investigators that there was a well where thirty-five women and children were dropped a couple days after the attack on the [prominent black] Carrier [family] house." Both accounts are in Marvin Dunn, *The Beast in Florida: A History of Anti-black Violence* (Gainesville: University Press of Florida, 2013), 116.

38. David R. Colburn, "Rosewood and America in the Early Twentieth Century," *Florida Historical Quarterly* 76, no. 2 (Fall 1997): 175–92; David Chalmers, "The Ku Klux Klan in the Sunshine State," *Florida Historical Quarterly* 42, no. 3 (January 1964): 209–15.

39. Paul Ortiz, "Ocoee, Florida: Remembering 'the Single Bloodiest Day in Modern U.S. Political History,'" *Facing South*, May 14, 2010, https://www.facingsouth .org/2010/05/ocoee-florida-remembering-the-single-bloodiest-day-in-modern -us-political-history.html.

40. The Rosewood case was brought to the nation's attention when journalist Gary Moore published an article about the massacre. Gary Moore, "Rosewood Massacre," *St. Petersburg Times*, July 25, 1982, http://www.tampabay.com/data/2018/06/06 /from-the-archives-the-original-story-of-the-rosewood-massacre. It was Moore who, in 1982, took the story to CBS's *60 Minutes*, which followed up with its own investigation in 1983. Moore went on to write *Rosewood: The Full Story* (n.p.: Manantial Press, 2015). His research informed the feature film *Rosewood* (1997), directed by John Singleton.

41. David R. Colburn, "Rosewood and America in the Early Twentieth Century," Florida Historical Quarterly 76, no. 2 (Fall 1997): 175–92. "Ku Klux Klan in Gainesville Gave New Year Parade," *Florida Times-Union*, January 3, 1923.

42. "Florida Urged to Compensate Victims of Racial Attack in '23," *New York Times*, March 22, 1994, http://www.nytimes.com/1994/03/22/us/florida-urged-to -compensate-victims-of-racial-attack-in-23.html. See also Michael D'Orso, *Like Judgment Day: The Ruin and Redemption of a Town Called Rosewood* (Berkeley, Calif.: Berkeley Publishing, 1996), 256–57.

43. Rosewood Family Scholarship Fund, Rule 6A-20.027, Florida Department of Education.

44. Sharon LaFraniere, "U.S. Opens Spigot after Farmers Claim Discrimination," *New York Times*, April 25, 2013, http://www.amren.com/news/2013/04/u-s -opens-spigot-after-farmers-claim-discrimination.

45. Sam Robinson, "Settlement Payments for Black Farmers in Years-Old Lawsuit Now Released," Midwest Center for Investigative Reporting, February 18, 2014, http://investigatemidwest.org/2014/02/18/settlement-payments-for-black-farmers -in-years-old-lawsuit-now-released.

46. The Oklahoma legislature set aside $50,000 for consultants and administrative costs for the commission.

47. A. G. Sulzberger, "As Survivors Dwindle, Tulsa Confronts Past," *New York Times*, June 19, 2011, http://www.nytimes.com/2011/06/20/us/20tulsa.html.

48. John Hope Franklin also recommended another scholar, historian and Tulsa native Scott Ellsworth, to the commission; Ellsworth also became a consultant.

49. Social Sciences Department chair Dr. Sheila Flemming was the architect of the Bethune-Cookman program. Bethune-Cookman College is also the repository of a permanent exhibition on the Rosewood, Florida, massacre of 1923.

50. *Tulsa Race Riot: A Report by the Oklahoma Commission to Study the Tulsa Race Riot of 1921* (Oklahoma City: Oklahoma Commission to Study the Tulsa Race Riot, 2001), http://www.okhistory.org/research/forms/freport.pdf. This was an extensively researched 175-page report replete with photographs, maps, and public meeting notices. See also Barbara Palmer, "Stanford Alumnus Seeks Reparations for Survivors of Deadly 1921 Tulsa Race Riot," *Stanford Report*, February 16, 2005, https://news.stanford.edu/news/2005/february16/tulsa-021605.html.

51. For a complete listing of the members of the Reparations Coordinating Committee please see appendix 1.

52. *Before They Die! A Documentary about the Tulsa Race Riot Survivors* (website), https://beforetheydie.wordpress.com.

53. The classic study of North Carolina's Fusion politics is in Helen C. Edmonds, *The Negro and Fusion Politics in North Carolina, 1894–1901* (Chapel Hill: University of North Carolina Press, 1951). While some have suggested that the 1898 white riot in Wilmington was the nation's first and last municipal coup d'état, events in post–Civil War Louisiana, especially in Coushatta in August 1874, indicate that elected local governments were overthrown by white terrorists in other locations. A similar overthrow of Republican Party elected officials took place in December 1874 in Vicksburg, Mississippi. Daniel Russell was North Carolina's only Republican governor until 1973.

54. The proclamation of the restoration of white rule has been attributed to Democratic Party leader Furnifold Simmons, who was elected to the U.S. House of Representatives in 1886. He was defeated by black Republican Henry Plummer Cheatham in 1888. Cheatham was the first of five known African Americans from the states of the former Confederacy to hold office in Congress in the last decade of the nineteenth century; after Cheatham's loss in 1892, no blacks were elected from the south until 1972.

55. It frequently was the case that the architects and executioners of antiblack terrorist campaigns emerged from the "best class" of white men. For example, consider the testimony of Richard B. Carpenter, a South Carolina judge and a Reform (Democratic) Party candidate for governor, before congressional investigators about Klan violence that had taken place in his state in 1870 and 1871. Carpenter said that "a great many" of the terrorists were "very respectable men in the neighborhood where they lived, and not confined to a low or desperate class of people." He went on to say that, contrary to the claims made by others, "a great many respectable and well-meaning men were engaged [in armed violence]," and "respectable people, people of substance, not only approved of it, but actually participated in it." See "The Ku-Klux Reign of Terror: Synopsis of a Portion of the Testimony Taken by the

Congressional Investigating Committee. No. 5. [n. p. 1872]," Printed Ephemera Collection, portfolio 237, folder 8, Library of Congress, https://www.loc.gov/resource /rbpe.23700800/?st=text.

56. Oliver H. Orr, *Charles Brantley Aycock* (Chapel Hill: University of North Carolina Press, 1961), 135–36.

57. Charles Brantley Aycock, "The Keynote of the Amendment Campaign: Speech Accepting the Nomination for Governor," in R. D. W. Connor and Clarence Poe, eds., *The Life and Speeches of Charles B. Aycock* (Garden City, N.Y.: Doubleday, Page, 1912), 218–19. The relevant amendments to the state constitution to which Aycock refers in the context of disenfranchising voters are part of what is popularly known as the "grandfather clause," a state constitutional provision adopted specifically to exclude blacks from the voter rolls and a poll tax, which would reinforce black exclusion.

58. William Sturkey, "Carr Was Indeed Much More Than Silent Sam," *Herald-Sun* (Durham, N.C.), October 31, 2017, https://www.heraldsun.com/opinion/article 181567401.html. See also Orr, *Charles Brantley Aycock*, 184; and "Julian S. Carr and the Carr Building," Duke University Archives, https://library.duke.edu/rubenstein /uarchives/history/faqs/carr.

59. Transcript of Julian Carr Speech, August 2, 1900, Addresses, folder 21, scan 137, p. 4, Julian Shakespeare Carr Papers, 1892–1923, Southern Historical Collection, Louis Round Wilson Library Special Collections, University of North Carolina at Chapel Hill.

60. Verna Williams, "Reading, Writing, and Reparations: Systemic Education Reform as a Matter of Justice" (paper presented at the "Does Reparations Have a Future?" conference, Carter G. Woodson Institute, University of Virginia, Charlottesville, Va., March 21–23, 2013).

61. "School choice" and voucher programs came onto the American policy scene courtesy of the massive resistance movement. See Nancy MacLean, "Neo-Confederacy against the New Deal: The Regional Utopia of the Modern American Right," in Joseph Crespino and Matthew Lassiter, eds., *The Myth of Southern Exceptionalism* (New York: Oxford University Press, 2010), 308–30. See also MacLean's excellent, more recent *Democracy in Chains: The Deep History of the Radical Right's Stealth Plan for America* (New York: Random House, 2017).

62. James Cox, "Corporations Challenged by Reparations Activists," *USA Today*, February 21, 2002, http://usatoday30.usatoday.com/money/general/2002/02/21 /slave-reparations.htm. See also Tamar Lewin, "Calls for Slavery Restitution Getting Louder," *New York Times*, June 4, 2001, http://www.nytimes.com/2001/06/04/us /calls-for-slavery-restitution-getting-louder.html.

63. Many captives did not survive the Middle Passage. The owners were eager to insure themselves against losses associated with both seagoing deaths and insurrections of enslaved persons on the vessels. A typical entry from the archives of the American International Group partner London Assurance reads as follows: "Captain Richard Pinnell [director 1726–38] 30th August, 1733 on the Mary Snow and Goods, both or either, according to the Assured's interest, at and from London to the Coast of Africa and at and from thence to her port of discharge in the British West Indies.

Warranted sheathed, and free from all damage by prohibited trade, and free from the death of Slaves either Natural, Violent, or Voluntary. £800." The following entry appears in the underwriting record dated June 15, 1728: "Henry Neale, Esq. [director 1720–47], on 50 negroes in the Benedicta Brigantina (Arthur Reymond, Captain) at and from Gambia to Virginia. The Assured doth hereby agree to warrant the ship sheathed, to take on himself all Averages arising by Death and Insurrection of negroes, and all loss or damage by prohibited trade. £500 @ 3%.Ten pounds a head!" Anita Rupprecht, "Excessive Memories: Slavery, Insurance, and Resistance," *History Workshop Journal* 64 (Autumn 2007): 17.

A London Assurance policy with similar language was submitted by the corporation for counsel's opinion in 1729:

> A policy of insurance was made on Ship and Goods at and from London to the Coast of Africa and thence to Carolina upon interest with the following Warranty: The Assured hath agreed to warrant the ship sheathed, to take upon himself all Averages arising by Death and Insurrection of Negroes and all Loss and Damage by prohibited trade. The ship proceeded to Africa, and the Master disposed of the outward-bound cargo in purchasing Negroes, a few Elephant's teeth, and some Gold Dust, and having finished the trade there, departed for Carolina, but before he got off the Coast, the Negroes made an insurrection, killed two of the mariners, and the Ship taking fire, the Master and rest of the mariners quitted her and got away in the boat, the Negroes ran the ship ashore and made their escape by leaping overboard and swimming to land, as is supposed, and the Ship was beat to pieces and totally lost with other goods on board ("Royal London Assurance Company," Quote.org, https://quote.org /quotes/details?id=dSLGH-10v-mLfELyAnQ-gAAJk69RedA7ubUjIEvr7Lw).

64. "Slavery Era Insurance Registry," California Department of Insurance, http:// www.insurance.ca.gov/01-consumers/150-other-prog/10-seir;

65. American International Group also provided a list of the names of slaves and slaveholders culled from U.S. Life Insurance bound registries. However, not all insurers chartered in the eighteenth and early nineteenth centuries insured slaves. The company Providence Washington, which celebrated its 200th anniversary in 1999, informed its initial 2,623 shareholders "that no insurance is to be made on behalf of this company upon any vessel, or property laden therein, for the purpose of carrying on the Slave Trade." "Slavery Era Insurance Registry."

66. David Horowitz, *Uncivil Wars: The Controversy over Reparations for Slavery* (San Francisco: Encounter Books, 2002), 12–16.

67. James Cox, "Reparations Gain Legal, Academic Interest," *USA Today*, March 24, 2002, http://usatoday30.usatoday.com/money/general/2002/03/25/reparations -sidebar.htm. See also "Slave Policies Reported to Illinois Division of Insurance." https://insurance.illinois.gov/Consumer/SlaveryInformation/SlavePolicies Reports.pdf.

68. Deadria Farmer-Paellmann, the main plaintiff in the lawsuit filed in federal court in Brooklyn seeking billions of dollars in reparations, named FleetBoston

Financial, the railroad firm CSX, and Aetna insurance company and cited their unjust profits from the slave trade. Filed in the U.S. District Court for the Eastern District of New York, the class-action suit was titled *Deadria Farmer-Paellmann, On behalf of herself and other persons similarly situated heirs of African-Americans v. FleetBoston Financial Corporation, Aetna Inc., CSX, and other unnamed defendants that profited from slavery and the slave trade.* It was referred to as the "New York / Class Action Complaint American Slavery Case–March 26, 2002 heirs of African-Americans." James Cox, "Insurance Firms Issued Slave Policies," *USA Today*, February 21, 2002, https://www.economicsvoodoo.com/wp-content/uploads/2002-02-21 -Insurance-firms-issued-slave-policies-Rothschild-Harrimans-JP-Morgans-etc -_-USA-Today.pdf.

69. "Slave Policies Reported to Illinois Division of Insurance."

70. Anna Galan, "Activist Addresses Slavery, Prisons," *Stanford Daily News*, February 11, 2002.

71. Associated Press, "North Carolina Senate Apologizes for Slavery," NBC News, April 5, 2007, http://www.nbcnews.com/id/17967662/ns/us_news-life/t/north -carolina-senate-apologizes-slavery.

72. Res. 2007–21, General Assembly of N.C. Sess. 2007, https://www.ncleg.net /Sessions/2007/Bills/Senate/PDF/S1557v3.pdf.

73. Ta-Nehisi Coates, "The Case for Reparations," *Atlantic*, June 2014, https://www .theatlantic.com/magazine/archive/2014/06/the-case-for-reparations/361631.

74. Eugene Scott, "What Obama Actually Said in His Rejection of Reparations," *Washington Post*, July 9, 2019, https://www.washingtonpost.com/politics/2019/07/09 /what-obama-actually-said-his-rejection-reparations.

75. Errol Louis, "Why Americans Think Trump Is a Racist," CNN Opinion, March 2, 2018, https://www.cnn.com/2018/03/02/opinions/why-americans-think-trump -is-a-racist-louis/index.html.

76. Hildegade Manzvanzvike, "'If Black Lives Matter, Go Back to Africa,'" *Herald (Harare, Zimbabwe)*, September 2, 2015, https://www.herald.co.zw/if -black-lives-matter-go-back-to-africa.

77. Tom Jacobs, "Research Finds That Racism, Sexism, and Status Fears Drove Trump Voters," *Pacific Standard*, April 24, 2018, https://psmag.com/news /research-finds-that-racism-sexism-and-status-fears-drove-trump-voters.

78. Roderick Graham, "Reflections on the ADOS Movement," Medium, March 3, 2019, https://medium.com/@roderickshawngraham/reflections-on-the-ados -movement-a8f0355c7275.

79. Bruce C. T. Wright, "Where All the Presidential Candidates Stand on Reparations, in Their Own Words," Newsone, April 13, 2019, https://newsone.com /playlist/2020-presidential-candidates-reparations/item/12. The maximum amount of the black reparations fund specified by Williamson was $500 billion. We demonstrate in chapter 13 that sum falls far short of any reasonable bill.

80. Wright.

81. Adam Harris, "Everyone Wants to Talk about Reparations: But for How Long?," *Atlantic*, June 19, 2019, https://www.theatlantic.com/politics/archive/2019/06/house -committee-explores-bill-study-reparations/592096.

CHAPTER 2

1. Pew Research Center, "On Views of Race and Inequality, Blacks and White Are Worlds Apart," Social and Demographic Trends, June 27, 2016, https://www.pewsocialtrends.org/2016/06/27/on-views-of-race-and-inequality-blacks-and-whites-are-worlds-apart.

2. Pew Research Center, 4–6.

3. Pew Research Center, 10.

4. Pew Research Center, 10. The report cautions that "white responses to [the work motivation] item may have been affected, at least in part, by social desirability bias. In this case, 35% of whites who believed they were speaking with a white interviewer said lack of motivation is a major reason blacks may have a harder time getting ahead; about one-in-five (21%) of whites who believed their interviewer was black gave this answer."

5. Pew Research Center, 11. A still more recent study demonstrates that both blacks and whites misperceive the degree of racial economic inequality in the United States, grossly underestimating the magnitude of the differentials in earnings, income, and wealth. Michael Kraus, Julian Rucker, and Jennifer Richeson, "Americans Misperceive Racial Economic Equality," *PNAS Early Edition*, 2017, http://www.pnas.org/content/early/2017/09/12/1707719114.

6. Economists across a surprisingly wide span of ideological stripes have succumbed to culturally based explanations for racial disparities in the United States. These include progressives such as George Akerlof and Rachel Kranton; neoliberals such as Glenn Loury, David Austen-Smith, and Roland Fryer; and right-wing libertarians such as Thomas Sowell and Walter Williams.

7. Darrick Hamilton and William Darity Jr., "The Political Economy of Education, Financial Literacy, and the Racial Wealth Gap," *Federal Reserve Bank of St. Louis Review* 99, no. 1 (First Quarter 2017): 59–76; italics in the original.

8. Lisa J. Deitling, Joanne W. Hsu, Lindsay Jacobs, Kevin B. Moore, and Jeffrey P. Thompson, "Recent Trends in Wealth-Holding by Race and Ethnicity: Evidence from the Survey of Consumer Finances," with assistance from Elizabeth Llanes, FEDS Notes, September 27, 2017, https://www.federalreserve.gov/econres/notes/feds-notes/recent-trends-in-wealth-holding-by-race-and-ethnicity-evidence-from-the-survey-of-consumer-finances-20170927.htm. The median is the value or amount at the middle of the frequency distribution. In this case, half of the households would lie above it and half below it.

9. The gap calculated from the Survey of Consumer Finances, which oversamples persons at the upper end of the income distribution, is a more conservative estimate relative to other sources. For example, estimates from the 2014 Survey of Income and Program Participation, which oversamples persons at the lower end of the income distribution, yield an estimate closer to black households holding seven cents in net worth per every dollar held by white households.

10. Rakesh Kochhar and Richard Fry, "Wealth Inequality Has Widened along Racial, Ethnic Lines since the Great Recession," Fact Tank, Pew Research Center, December 12, 2014, http://www.pewresearch.org/fact-tank/2014/12/12/racial-wealth-gaps-great-recession.

11. Melany De La Cruz-Viesca, Zhenxiang Chen, Paul M. Ong, Darrick Hamilton, and William A. Darity Jr., *The Color of Wealth in Los Angeles* (San Francisco: Federal Reserve Bank of San Francisco; Durham, N.C.: Duke University; New York: New School; Los Angeles: University of California at Los Angeles; Oakland, Calif.: Insight Center for Community Economic Development, 2016), 33, 40, https://www.researchgate.net/publication/301487531_The_Color_of_Wealth_in_Los_Angeles.

12. De La Cruz-Viesca et al., 29.

13. William Darity Jr., Darrick Hamilton, Mark Paul, Alan Aja, Anne Price, Antonio Moore, and Caterina Chiopris, *What We Get Wrong about Closing the Racial Wealth Gap* (Durham, N.C.: Samuel DuBois Cook Center on Social Equity, Duke University; Oakland, Calif.: Insight Center for Community Economic Development, 2018), https://socialequity.duke.edu/sites/socialequity.duke.edu/files/site-images/FINAL%20COMPLETE%20REPORT_.pdf.

14. Kochhar and Fry, "Wealth Inequality Has Widened."

15. Darity et al., *What We Get Wrong.*

16. For the most recent studies that present documentation about the absence of any significant difference in black and white saving behavior after controlling for household income, see Mariela Dal Borgo, "Ethnic and Racial Disparities in Saving Behavior," *Journal of Economic Inequality*, no. 17 (2019): 253–83; and Amy Traub, Laura Sullivan, Tatjana Meschede, and Thomas Shapiro, *The Asset Value of Whiteness: Understanding the Racial Wealth Gap* (New York: Demos; Waltham, Mass.: Institute for Assets and Social Policy, 2017), http://www.demos.org/sites/default/files/publications/Asset%20Value%20of%20Whiteness.pdf. See also Maury Gittleman and Edward N. Wolff, "Racial Differences in Patterns of Wealth Accumulation," *Journal of Human Resources* 39, no. 1 (2004): 193–227; and Ngina S. Chiteji and Darrick Hamilton, "Family Connections and the Black-White Wealth Gap among Middle-Class Families," *Review of Black Political Economy* 30, no. 1 (Summer 2002): 9–28.

17. Traub et al., *Asset Value of Whiteness*, 7–8.

18. Khaing Zaw, Jhumpa Bhattacharya, Anne Price, Darrick Hamilton, and William Darity Jr., *Women, Race and Wealth* (Durham, N.C.: Samuel DuBois Cook Center on Social Equity, Duke University; Oakland, Calif.: Insight Center for Community Economic Development, 2017), https://www.insightcced.org/wp-content/uploads/2017/01/January2017_ResearchBriefSeries_WomenRaceWealth-Volume1-Pages-1.pdf.

19. Zaw et al.

20. "Racial Wealth Divide Snapshot: Women and the Racial Wealth Divide," Prosperity Now, March 29, 2018, https://prosperitynow.org/blog/racial-wealth-divide-snapshot-women-and-racial-wealth-divide.

21. See Patrick L. Mason, "Race, Culture, and Skill: Interracial Wage Differentials among African Americans, Latinos, and Whites," *Review of Black Political Economy* 25, no. 3 (Winter 1997): 5–39; William Mangino, "Race to College: The 'Reverse Gap,'" *Race and Social Problems, no.* 2 (December 2010): 164–78; William Mangino, "Why Do Whites and the Rich Have Less Need for Education?," *American Journal of Economics and Sociology* 71, no. 3 (July 2012): 562–602; and William Mangino, "The Negative

Effects of Privilege on Educational Attainment: Gender, Race, Class, and the Bachelor's Degree," *Social Science Quarterly* 95, no. 3 (September 2014): 760–84.

22. A quintile is a 20 percent segment of a sample ranked from bottom to top.

23. Darity et al. (*What We Get Wrong*, 9) use data from the Survey of Income and Program Participation from 2014 to obtain their findings. Traub et al. (*Asset Value of Whiteness*) generate similar results using data from the 2013 Survey of Consumer Finances.

24. Raj Chetty, Nathaniel Hendren, Maggie R. Jones, and Sonya Porter, "Race and Economic Opportunity in the United States: An Intergenerational Perspective" (Working Paper No. 24441, National Bureau of Economic Research, Cambridge, Mass., March 2018), https://www.nber.org/papers/w24441.

25. Dylan Matthews, "The Massive New Study on Race and Economic Mobility, Explained," Vox, March 21, 2018, https://www.vox.com/policy-and-politics/2018/3/21/17139300/economic-mobility-study-race-black-white-women-men-incarceration-income-chetty-hendren-jones-porter.

26. Fabian Pfeffer and Alexandra Killewald, "Intergenerational Wealth Mobility and Racial Inequality," *Socius: Sociological Research for a Dynamic World* 5 (2019): 1–2.

27. Catherine W. Bishir, *Crafting Lives: African American Artisans in New Bern, North Carolina, 1770–1900* (Chapel Hill: University of North Carolina Press, 2013), 52.

28. Theodore Dwight Weld, Angelina Grimké Weld, and Sarah Grimké, *American Slavery as It Is: Testimony of a Thousand Witnesses* (New York: American Anti-Slavery Society, 1839); first emphasis added. See also Weld, Weld, and Grimké, electronic edition, http://docsouth.unc.edu/neh/weld/weld.html#p14. In another example, the enslaved blacks Griffin, Granville, and Rachael "belonged to [Mary A. Maverick], a gift of my Mother." Maverick was the wife of Samuel Maverick, a signer of the Texas Declaration of Independence. When she learned that her husband was being marched to prison in Perote, Mexico, after his capture by French Mexican general Adrián Woll during the conflict between Mexico and the Republic of Texas, Mary Maverick sent Griffin to be by her spouse's side with instructions to provide assistance to him as he was able. Griffin was killed at the Battle of Salado Creek in 1842, supporting Samuel Maverick. Samuel lived to oppose secession briefly before becoming an advocate and an administrator in the Confederate government. Mary Maverick's gift to her husband of the protection of her enslaved human chattel Griffin saved Samuel Maverick's life. See Neel Lane, "A Maverick Speaks: Tear That Confederate Statue Down," *Express-News* (San Antonio, Tex.), August 26, 2017. Special thanks to Janice S. Lawlor and Michael Syron Lawlor for sharing this article with us. See also Mary A. Maverick and George Madison Maverick, Mary Rowena Maverick, ed., *Memoirs of Mary A. Maverick* (San Antonio, Tex.: Alamo, 1874), 22, 92–94, 99–100, https://archive.org/details/memoirsmaryamavoomavegoog; and Joseph Milton Nance, "Woll, Adrián," Texas State Historical Association, June 15, 2010, http://www.tshaonline.org/handbook/online/articles/fwo03.

29. Fabian Pfeffer and Alexandra Killewald, "Generations of Advantage: Multigenerational Correlations in Family Wealth," *Social Forces* 96, no. 4 (June 2018): 1411–41.

30. Pfeffer and Killewald, 1411–41.

31. Laura Feiveson and John Sabelhaus, "How Does Intergenerational Wealth Transmission Affect Wealth Concentration?," FEDS Notes, June 1, 2018, https://www.federalreserve.gov/econres/notes/feds-notes/how-does-intergenerational-wealth-transmission-affect-wealth-concentration-20180601.htm.

32. A study produced by economists at the Federal Reserve Bank of Cleveland diminishes the importance of intergenerational transmission effects and overstates the effects of savings from current income by limiting the cross-generation effects exclusively to inheritances. This, in turn, omits in vivo transfers or gifts that can be important not only because of their amounts but also because of their *timing*. For example, if parents help a young couple with the down payment for the purchase of a home, the amount and timing of that gift can have a profound effect on the couple's economic well-being across their remaining years—and for *their* children. The Cleveland Fed study is Dionissi Aliprantis and Daniel R. Carroll, "What Is behind the Persistence of the Racial Wealth Gap?," *Economic Commentary* 2019, no. 3 (February 28, 2019), https://www.clevelandfed.org/newsroom-and-events/publications/economic-commentary/2019-economic-commentaries/ec-201903-what-is-behind-the-persistence-of-the-racial-wealth-gap.aspx.

33. Jennifer Mueller, "The Social Reproduction of Systemic Racial Inequality" (PhD diss., Texas A&M University, 2013).

34. Keri Leigh Merritt, "Land and the Roots of African-American Poverty," Aeon, March 11, 2016, http://aeon.co/ideas//land-and-the-roots-of-african-american-poverty.

35. Merritt.

36. Janell Hazelwood, "BE 100s: Nation's Top Black-Owned Businesses by the Numbers," *Black Enterprise*, June 27, 2014, http://www.blackenterprise.com/small-business/be-100s-nations-top-black-owned-businesses-by-the-numbers.

37. Fortune 500 Business Rankings (2019), *Fortune*, http://beta.fortune.com/fortune500/list.

38. Mehrsa Baradaran provides a devastating analysis of the limitations of a specific type of black entrepreneurship, banking, as a route to closing the racial wealth gap. Mehrsa Baradaran, *The Color of Money: Black Banks and the Racial Wealth Gap* (Cambridge, Mass.: Harvard University Press, 2017).

39. David Blanchflower and Andrew Oswald, "What Makes an Entrepreneur?," *Journal of Labor Economics* 16, no. 1 (January 1998): 26–60.

40. Certainly not from family assets. See National Longitudinal Surveys of Youth from 1966 to 1981 and Current Population Surveys from 1968 to 1987, as referenced in David G. Blanchflower, Phillip B. Levine, and David J. Zimmerman, "Discrimination in the Small-Business Credit Market," *Review of Economics and Statistics* 85, no. 4 (November 2003): 930–43. As early as 1995, Timothy Bates estimated that even highly educated individuals would require $100,000 in personal wealth to have reasonable prospects of business success upon entry; see Timothy Bates, "Self-Employment Entry across Industry Groups," *Journal of Business Venturing* 10, no. 2 (March 1995): 143–56.

41. Blanchflower, Levine, and Zimmerman, "Discrimination," 942–43. They used data from the 1993 National Survey of Small Business Finances. Creditworthiness

was assessed based on whether loan applicants had sought bankruptcy protection in the previous seven years or whether the firm had been delinquent on personal obligations for more than sixty days or had legal judgments against the principals in the previous three years. With these criteria, blacks were twice as likely to be denied loans for their enterprises (65.9 percent versus 26.9 percent for whites).

42. In 1968, 2 percent of black households and 5 percent of white households had incomes above $100,000 measured in 2008 dollars. By 2008, the percentage of black households with such an income was closer to 6 percent, while it was closer to 13 percent for white households. U.S. Census Bureau, "Income, Poverty, and Health Insurance Coverage in the United States: 2009," issued September 2010, https://www.census.gov/prod/2010pubs/p60-238.pdf. Although the proportions fell for both groups during the Great Recession, the approximate white-to-black two-to-one ratio continues to hold. "Distribution of Household Income by Race, 1975–2014," Infoplease, https://www.infoplease.com/business-finance/poverty-and-income/distribution-household-income-race.

43. Stephen Perlberg, "American Median Incomes by Race Since 1967," *Business Insider*, September 17, 2013, http://www.businessinsider.com/heres-median-income-in-the-us-by-race-2013-9.

44. U.S. Census Bureau, "Income." Per capita income was $18,406 for non-Hispanic blacks and $31,313 for non-Hispanic whites, for a black-to-white ratio of about 58 percent in 1968. By 2015, black per capita income was an estimated $20,277 while white per capita income was an estimated $32,910, yielding a ratio of about 63 percent. The data for these estimates was drawn from the U.S. Census Bureau's American Community Survey. See Wikipedia, s.v. "List of Ethnic Groups in the United States by Per Capita Income," https://en.wikipedia.org/wiki/List_of_ethnic_groups_in_the_United_States_by_per_capita_income.

45. David R. Roediger, *Working toward Whiteness: How America's Immigrants Became White; The Strange Journey from Ellis Island to the Suburbs* (New York: Basic Books, 2005).

46. William Darity Jr., Jason Dietrich, and David K. Guilkey, "Persistent Advantage or Disadvantage? Evidence in Support of the Intergenerational Drag Hypothesis," *American Journal of Economics and Sociology* 60, no. 2 (April 2001): 439–40.

47. Darity, Dietrich, and Guilkey, 440.

48. Calvin Goldscheider and Alan S. Zuckerman, *The Transformation of the Jews* (Chicago: University of Chicago Press, 1984), 166.

49. Roger Daniels, "The Conference Keynote Address: Relocation, Redress, and the Report; A Historical Appraisal," in Roger Daniels, Sandra C. Taylor, and Harry H.L. Kitano, eds., *Japanese Americans: From Relocation to Redress* (Seattle: University of Washington Press, 1991), 3–4.

50. Masao Suzuki, "Success Story: Japanese Immigrant Economic Achievement and Return Migration," *Journal of Economic History* 35, no. 4 (December 1995): 889–901; Masao Suzuki, "Selective Immigration and Ethnic Economic Achievement: Japanese Americans before World War II," *Explorations in Economic History, no.* 39 (2002): 254–81.

51. Darity, Dietrich, and Guilkey, "Persistent Advantage or Disadvantage?," 440.

52. Data from the Reports of the Immigration Commission, in Suzuki, "Selective Immigration," 264–66.

53. Suzuki, 265.

54. Suzuki, 267.

55. Suzuki, "Success Story."

56. Suzuki.

57. Mitchell T. Maki, Harry H. L. Kitano, and S. Megan Berthold, *Achieving the Impossible Dream: How Japanese Americans Obtained Redress* (Urbana and Chicago: University of Illinois Press, 1999).

58. In Spike Lee's 1989 film classic *Do the Right Thing*, there is a stereotypical Korean grocer who operates a corner store in a black community in Brooklyn, New York, but has no black employees and lives elsewhere. At one point, it appears that the store will be destroyed by the wrath of enraged black residents after the police's brutal killing of one of the film's central characters.

59. Timothy Bates, *Race, Self-Employment, and Upward Mobility: An Illusive Dream* (Baltimore: Johns Hopkins University Press, 1997), 122.

60. Jennifer Lee and Min Zhou, *The Asian American Achievement Paradox* (New York: Russell Sage Foundation, 2015), 8, 30.

61. Lee and Zhou, 30–31.

62. Paul Bonner, "Women Bring Brazilian Snack to U.S.," *News and Record* (Greensboro, N.C.), June 13, 2004, https://www.greensboro.com/women-bring-brazilian -snack-to-u-s/article_f2b8a004-b03d-52d2-870a-f1959ecaa12d.html.

63. Eleanor Marie Brown, "The Blacks Who Got Their Forty Acres: A Theory of Black West Indian Migrant Asset Accumulation," *New York University Law Review* 89, no. 27 (2014): 38.

64. Brown, 39–40.

65. See Mosi Morrison [Ifatunji], "Are Black Immigrants a Model Minority? Race, Ethnicity and Social Mobility in the United States" (PhD diss., University of Illinois at Chicago, 2011).

66. Darity, Dietrich, and Guilkey, "Persistent Advantage or Disadvantage?"

67. U.S. Census Bureau, "Income."

68. Devah Pager, *Marked: Race, Crime, and Finding Work in an Era of Mass Incarceration* (Chicago: University of Chicago Press, 2007). In a more recent online experiment designed to test the effects of "ban the box" policies using employers in New Jersey and New York City, Amanda Agan and Sonja Starr did not find that black men without a felony conviction had lower callback rates than white men who did have a felony conviction. However, they still found huge discrepancies in callback rates, favoring white men, when blacks and whites were assigned criminal records and when they were not. In the absence of the check box indicating whether the individual had a criminal conviction, the disparity became dramatically worse; Agan and Starr conclude that this is due to "employers relying upon exaggerated impressions of real-world racial differences in felony conviction rates," or prejudice. Amanda Y. Agan and Sonja B. Starr, "Ban the Box, Criminal Records, and Statistical Discrimination: A Field Experiment," *Quarterly Journal of Economics* 133, no. 1 (February 2018): 191–235.

69. Marianne Bertrand and Sendhil Mullainathan, "Are Emily and Brenda More Employable Than Lakisha and Jamal?: A Field Experiment on Labor Market Discrimination," *American Economic Review* 94, no. 4 (September 2004): 991–1013.

70. Sonia Kang, Katherine A. DeCelles, Andras Tilcsik, and Sora Jun, "Whitened Résumés: Race and Self-Presentation in the Labor Market," *Administrative Science Quarterly* 61, no. 3 (March 2016), http://journals.sagepub.com/doi/abs/10.1177/0001839216639577.

71. Janelle Jones and John Schmitt, *A College Degree Is No Guarantee* (Washington, D.C.: Center for Economic and Policy Research, 2014), http://cepr.net/publications/reports/a-college-degree-is-no-guarantee.

72. Natalie Kitroeff, "Business School is Worth $22,000 More if You're White or Asian," Bloomberg, January 6, 2016, https://www.bloomberg.com/news/articles/2016-01-07/business-school-is-worth-22-000-more-if-you-re-white-or-asian.

73. Gaddis used Jalen, Lamar, and Daquan as black-sounding names and Caleb, Charlie, and Ronny as white-sounding names for men. He used Nia, Ebony, and Shanice as black names and Aubrey, Erica, and Lesley as white-sounding names for women. See S. Michael Gaddis, "Discrimination in the Credential Society: An Audit Study of Race and College Selectivity in the Labor Market," *Social Forces* 93, no. 4 (2015): 1451–79.

74. Donald Tomaskovic-Devey, Melvin Thomas, and Kecia Johnson, "Race and the Accumulation of Human Capital: A Theoretical Model and Fixed-Effects Application," *American Journal of Sociology* 111, no. 1 (July 2005): 58–89.

75. William Julius Wilson, *More Than Just Race: Being Black and Poor in the Inner City* (New York: W. W. Norton, 2009), 76–77; Peter Coy, "Inequality: The Plight of Young, Black Men Is Worse Than You Think," *Bloomberg Businessweek*, September 28, 2012, http://www.businessweek.com/articles/2012-09-28/the-plight-of-young-black-men-is-worse-than-you-think.

76. Darrick Hamilton, Algernon Austin, and William Darity Jr., "Whiter Jobs, Higher Wages: Occupational Segregation and the Lower Wages of Black Men" (Briefing Paper No. 288, Economic Policy Institute, Washington, D.C., February 28, 2011), http://www.epi.org/files/page/-/BriefingPaper288.pdf.

77. Hamilton, Austin, and Darity.

78. Fourth Annual Black Economic Summit, Howard University, Washington, D.C., February 1, 2013.

CHAPTER 3

1. Evelyn Brooks Higginbotham, foreword to *Complicity: How the North Promoted, Prolonged, and Profited from Slavery*, by Anne Farrow, Joel Lang, and Jenifer Frank (New York: Random House, 2005), xii.

2. Anne Farrow, Joel Lang, and Jenifer Frank, *Complicity: How the North Promoted, Prolonged, and Profited from Slavery* (New York: Random House, 2005).

3. See William B. Weeden, "The Early African Slave-Trade in New England," *Proceedings of the American Antiquarian Society* 5 (1887): 115–16. Circa 1856, enslaved persons also were transported in train baggage cars as human luggage; see Lyman Abbott, "Reminiscences: Politics," *Outlook*, May 23, 1914, 196–97.

4. Higginbotham, foreword, xvi. "By 1847, [New York Life, then known as Nautilus Mutual Life] insurance policies on slaves accounted for a third of the policies in a firm that would become one of the nation's Fortune 100 companies." See Michael Sean Quinn, "Slavery and Insurance: Examining Slave Insurance in a World 150 Years Removed," *Insurance Journal*, May 15, 2000, http://www.insurance journal.com/magazines/legalbeat/2000/05/15/21120.htm. See also Rachel L. Swarns, "Insurance Policies on Slaves: New York Life's Complicated Past," *New York Times*, December 18, 2016, https://www.nytimes.com/2016/12/18/us/insurance -policies-on-slaves-new-york-lifes-complicated-past.html; and "Aetna Acknowledges Issuing Slavery Policies during 1850s, Offers Apology, Denies Reparations," Democracy Now, March 14, 2000, https://www.democracynow.org/2000/3/14 /aetna_acknowledges_issuing_slave_policies_during.

5. Farrow, Lang, and Frank, *Complicity*, xviii.

6. Chester Himes, *Cotton Comes to Harlem* (New York: G. P. Putnam, 1965). Himes preferred the term "'domestic' fiction" over "'detective' fiction" to describe his books about "the slang, the daily routine and complex human relationships of Harlem." See John Ridley, "If He Hollers: Remembering Chester Himes," *Morning Edition*, National Public Radio, July 29, 2009, http://www.npr.org/templates/story/story .php?storyId=111210145.

7. Farrow, Lang, and Frank, *Complicity*, 4.

8. Farrow, Lang, and Frank, 4.

9. "Lehman Bros. Founded in Montgomery," *Huntsville Times*, September 2008. See also Encyclopedia of Alabama, s.v. "Lehman Brothers," by Herbert J. "Jim" Lewis, last updated August 30, 2018, http://www.encyclopediaofalabama.org/article/h-2160.

10. Farrow, Lang, and Frank, *Complicity*, 5.

11. Farrow, Lang, and Frank, 5.

12. While using the United Kingdom as a specific example, the general symbiotic relationship between slavery, the slave trade, and economic development in the Atlantic world was drawn most forcefully in Eric Williams, *Capitalism and Slavery* (Chapel Hill: University of North Carolina Press, 1944). In a part of his monumental *Caste, Class, and Race*, Oliver Cox made a similar argument about the centrality of slavery in capitalist economic development in Europe and the Americas. Like Williams, Cox argued that slavery and its accompanying economic exploitation produced antiblack racism, rather than vice versa; see Oliver Cromwell Cox, *Caste, Class, and Race: A Study of Social Dynamics* (New York: Monthly Review Press, 1948). See also Abram L. Harris, *The Negro as Capitalist: A Study in Banking and Business among American Negroes* (Philadelphia: American Academy of Political and Social Science, 1936), esp. the introduction and chap. 1; Wilson Elbe Williams, *Africa and the Rise of Capitalism* (Washington, D.C.: Howard University Studies in the Social Sciences, 1938); Walter Johnson, *River of Dark Dreams: Slavery and Empire in the Cotton Kingdom* (Cambridge, Mass.: Harvard University Press, 2013); Edward Baptist, *The Half Has Never Been Told: Slavery and the Making of American Capitalism* (New York: Basic Books, 2014); and Sven Beckert, *Empire of Cotton: A Global History* (New York: Vintage Books, 2014). We thank Samuel Schmerler for introducing us to Beckert's scholarship.

13. See Joseph E. Inikori and Stanley L. Engerman, eds., *The Atlantic Slave Trade: Effects on Economies, Societies and Peoples in Africa, the Americas, and Europe* (Durham, N.C.: Duke University Press, 1992), 218. See also Craig Steven Wilder, *Ebony and Ivy: Race, Slavery and the Troubled History of America's Universities* (New York: Bloomsbury, 2013), 159; Jacob Marcus Rader, "Rhode Island Refuses to Naturalize Aaron Lopez, March 1762," in *The Jew in the Medieval World: A Source Book, 315-1791* (Cincinnati: Hebrew Union College Press, 1999), 92–94; and Marilyn Kaplan, "The Jewish Merchants of Newport, 1749-1790," in *The Jews of Rhode Island*, ed. George M. Goodwin and Ellen Smith (Waltham, Mass.: Brandeis University Press, 2004), 21–22.

14. *Traces of the Trade: A Story from the Deep North*," directed by Katrina Browne (Point of View Documentary Films, 2008); Thomas Norman DeWolf, *Inheriting the Trade: A Northern Family Confronts Its Legacy as the Largest Slave Trading Dynasty in U.S. History* (Boston: Beacon Press, 2008).

15. Farrow, Lang, and Frank, *Complicity*, 95. Over a three-century period, vessels originating in Europe transported an estimated 11.5 million Africans that had been sold into slavery—645,000 of whom were brought to the American colonies.

16. See Jay Coughtry, *The Notorious Triangle: Rhode Island and the African Slave Trade 1700-1807* (Philadelphia: Temple University Press, 1981), 25–28, 95–96; and Farrow, Lang, and Frank, *Complicity*, 95, 101. The three authors said of the state's involvement in the slave trade: "While Rhode Island's neighbors, and Rhode Island itself, found ways to profit by trading first with the slave plantations of the West Indies and later with the cotton plantations of the American South, this smallest of states went even further, competing with European powers in the slave trade itself. Remote as it was, Rhode Island transported more slaves than any other of the original 13 states—North or South." It was Katrina Browne's idea to conduct research on the DeWolf family's involvement in the African slave trade and to invite her "kith and kin" to journey with her to Ghana, Cuba, and Bristol, Rhode Island, to begin to understand the breadth and meaning of that legacy. Her cousin Thomas Norman DeWolf was one of ten DeWolf family members who made the journey with Browne and chronicled the trip in his memoir; see DeWolf, *Inheriting the Trade*. For details on James DeWolf, the eighteenth- and nineteenth-century trader of enslaved Africans, see DeWolf, *Inheriting the Trade*, 148; James DeWolf Perry, personal correspondence with the authors, July 12, 2017.

17. For details on John Brown I, see Farrow, Lang, and Frank, *Complicity*, 101, 102–5, 109, 110, 111.

18. DeWolf, *Inheriting the Trade*, 45; Perry, personal correspondence.

19. Farrow, Lang, and Frank, *Complicity*, xxviii.

20. Bernard Bailyn, "Slavery and Population Growth in Colonial New England," in *Engines of Enterprise: An Economic History of New England*, ed. Peter Temin (Cambridge, Mass.: Harvard University Press, 2000), 254–55.

21. Bailyn, 253–60.

22. Jonathan Michael Square, "A Stain on an All-American Brand: How Brooks Brothers Once Clothed Slaves," Vestoj, http://vestoj.com/how-brooks-brothers-once-clothed-slaves. New Orleans clothier S. Hopkins Jr. pursued a similar, albeit a more specialized, business strategy to Brooks Brothers. A Hopkins advertisement

trumpeted provision of "plantation clothing" for both masters and slaves: head wraps, top hats and suits, livery coats, flannel shirts, blankets—"a single suit to one thousand!!" Erin Greenwald, ed., *Purchased Lives: New Orleans and the Domestic Slave Trade, 1808–1865* (New Orleans: Historic New Orleans Collection, 2015), published in conjunction with an exhibition of the same title, presented at the Williams Research Center, New Orleans, La., March 17–July 18, 2015, http://www.academia .edu/16710542/Purchased_Lives_New_Orleans_and_the_Domestic_Slave_Trade.

23. Anne Farrow, Joel Lang, and Jenifer Frank, "The State that Slavery Built: An Introduction," *Hartford Courant*, September 29, 2002, http://www.courant.com /courant-250/moments-in-history/hc-250-complicity-introduction-20140603-story .html; and Farrow, Lang, and Frank, *Complicity*, 193–94. See also Donald L. Malcarne and Brenda Milkofsky, "Ivory Cutting: The Rise and Decline of a Connecticut Industry," Connecticut History, June 17, 2019, http://connecticuthistory.org /ivory-cutting-the-rise-and-decline-of-a-connecticut-industry.

24. Farrow, Lang, and Frank, *Complicity*, 7. The authors note on the same page, "The numbers are almost impossible to grasp: in the season that ended on August 31, 1860, the United States produced close to 5 million bales of cotton, or roughly 2.3 *billion* pounds. Of that amount, it exported about half—or more than 1 billion pounds—to Great Britain's 2,650 cotton factories."

25. Farrow, Lang, and Frank, 49.

26. Farrow, Lang, and Frank, 49–51.

27. Farrow, Lang, and Frank, 51.

28. Farrow, Lang, and Frank, 53, 98.

29. Farrow, Lang, and Frank, 98.

30. Gavin Wright claimed the north generally was significantly more economically developed than the south on the eve of the Civil War; see Gavin Wright, *Slavery and American Economic Development* (Baton Rouge: Louisiana State University, 2006). Ironically, this suggests, in the longer run, that slavery practiced in the south had a greater positive effect on northern growth—although it functioned as a stimulus to growth in both regions. But it appears to be unambiguously the case that the possession of human property produced greater levels of personal wealth in the south. Samuel H. Williamson and Louis P. Cain report, based on Lee Soltow's research, that in 1860 the average total estate in the south was worth close to $4,000, while it was close to $2,000 in the north. See Samuel H. Williamson and Louis P. Cain, "Measuring Slavery in 2016 Dollars," Measuring Worth, https://www.measuringworth.com /slavery.php.

31. See esp. Lorenzo Johnston Greene, *The Negro in Colonial New England, 1620–1776* (New York: Columbia University Press, 1942); and Carter G. Woodson, "Review of *The Negro in Colonial New England*," *Journal of Negro History* 28, no. 4 (October 1943): 478–81. Also see the excellent essay by Ronald Bailey, "The Slave(ry) Trade and the Development of Capitalism in the United States: The Textile Industry in New England," *Social Science History* 14, no. 3 (Fall 1990): 373–414.

32.Craig Steven Wilder, *Ebony and Ivy: Race, Slavery and the Troubled History of America's Universities* (New York: Bloomsbury, 2013), 29.

33. Wilder, 42.

34. Wilder, 73.

35. "Northern Profits from Slavery," Slavery in the North, http://slavenorth.com /profits.htm.

36. Greene, *The Negro*, 319.

37. Wilder, *Ebony and Ivy*, 96–11. Wilder (101) also provides an extended description of the recruitment "brochure" advanced by the College of New Jersey's president, Rev. John Witherspoon, advocating for the superiority of his school over other American universities and British universities for the sons of West Indian slaveholders:

> "The very name of a West-Indian has come to imply in it great opulence,"
> wrote Rev. Witherspoon in a rhetorical bow before the white inhabitants of
> the British Caribbean. In 1772, the trustees approved a Caribbean campaign
> and appointed Witherspoon's son, James, who had graduated two years
> earlier, and the Reverend Charles Beatty as their West Indies agents. President
> Witherspoon's missive to the plantations laid out the appeal: It was safer for
> planters to send their children to New Jersey than to England, he cautioned,
> where unscrupulous men preyed upon privileged youngsters from the
> Americas. An education at Nassau Hall had other advantages. Princeton
> had all the comforts of urban life without "the many temptations in every
> great city, both to the neglect of study and the practice of vice." The latter
> comment was aimed especially at New York and Philadelphia, but also at
> New Haven and Cambridge. And if colonial colleges were dangerous, then
> British universities were damned. In the colonies, teachers lived on campus
> and supervised the students, he explained, while English universities were too
> large and too decentralized for instructors to properly guide the scholars. New
> Jersey was close enough to the Caribbean to allow parents to visit and expect
> regular communication, but distant enough to keep students from running
> home and becoming idle.

38. Wilder, 100.

39. Wilder, 98.

40. See Karl Watson, "Slavery and Economy in Barbados," BBC History, http:// www.bbc.co.uk/history/british/empire_seapower/barbados_01.shtml.

41. Watson.

42. Wilder, *Ebony and Ivy*, 98–99. Smith was a man of strong opinions. A critic of the military policy of Pennsylvania's elite Quaker governing body, he proposed that all Quakers be disenfranchised. If the withdrawal of suffrage from the Friends proved impossible, Smith argued, the state could "rid . . . our Assembly of Quakers" by requiring an oath of allegiance or "by cutting their Throats"; quote from Horace Wemyss Smith, *A Brief View of the Conduct of Pennsylvania, for the Year 1755* (London, 1756), 70. See also Wikipedia, s.v. "William Smith (Episcopal priest), https://en.wikipedia .org/wiki/William_Smith_(Episcopalian_priest).

43. Wilder, *Ebony and Ivy*, 99.

44. Wilder, 105. Wilder comments:

Founded to defend religious freedom, *the College of New Jersey under Witherspoon forged intimate ties to human slavery*. With high proportions of slaveholding families, Princeton was among the most welcoming places in the northern colonies to the sons of planters. A biographer [of Witherspoon] boasted of the minister's striking success at attracting the children of the colonial elite: Virginia's Washington, Randolph, Lee, and Madison lines; the Macon and Hawkins families of North Carolina; Reeds from Delaware; Livingstons, Stocktons, and Patersons from New Jersey; and the Morris and Van Rensselaer families of New York. The pattern of recruitment and enrollment at New Jersey conformed to the geography of American slavery. The percentage of young men from the South more than doubled during Witherspoon's tenure, while the proportion of students from elite background more than tripled. (Emphasis added.)

45. Wilder, 102–3. Elizabeth Boykin Witherspoon apparently was the victim of a small-scale insurrection conducted by some of her own slaves in September 1861.

46. Wilder, 122–23. This pattern, of course, was not unique to the College of New Jersey. As Wilder has observed in an interview:

Even after the end of slavery in the Northeast, even after the . . . Northern states had actually moved toward emancipation and finished their emancipation processes, they continued to have economic ties to the South and the West Indies. . . . One of the ways you can trace that is just by looking at who became the presidents of these [eight northern] universities. . . . And the presidents were virtually always the sons or the sons-in-law of merchant traders, people who were West India suppliers. And so, after the slave trade ends and after slavery ends in the Northern states, one of the businesses that continues is supplying the South and the West Indies with everything—all the provisions that they needed to run the plantations (Craig Steven Wilder, "Shackles and Ivy: The Secret History of How Slavery Helped Build America's Elite Colleges," interview by Amy Goodman, Democracy Now, October 30, 2013, http://www.democracynow.org/2013/10/30 /shackles_and_ivy_the_secret_history).

47. Wilder, *Ebony and Ivy*, 104. See also NCPedia, s.v. "Nash, Abner," by Jacqueline Drane Nash, http://www.ncpedia.org/biography/nash-abner; NCPedia, s.v. "Burgwin, George William Bush," by James Elliott Moore, http://www.ncpedia.org /biography/burgwin-george-william; NCPedia, s.v. "Burgwin, John Henry King," by James Elliott Moore, http://www.ncpedia.org/biography/burgwin-john-henry -king; NCPedia, s.v. "Witherspoon, John Knox," by Marie Claire Engstrom, http://www .ncpedia.org/biography/witherspoon-john-knox; and *Encyclopedia Britannica*, 11th ed. (1910–11), s.v. "Ramsay, David."

48. Benjamin A. Concannon-Smith, "The Black Vomit in Charleston: Dr. David Ramsay and the Reopening of the Slave Trade in Early National South Carolina," *NCSU Graduate Journal of History* 1 (2013).

49. Concannon-Smith. See also Jed Handelsman Shugerman, "The Louisiana Purchase and South Carolina's Reopening of the Slave Trade," *Journal of the Early Republic* 22, no. 2 (Summer 2002): 263–90.

50. Shugerman, "Louisiana Purchase."

51. Michael J. Hostetler, "David Ramsay and Louisiana: Time and Space in the Adolescent Rhetoric of America," *Western Journal of Communication* 20, no. 2 (2006): 134–46.

52. Rachel L. Swarns, "272 Slaves Were Sold to Save Georgetown: What Does It Owe Their Descendants?," *New York Times*, April 16, 2016, http://www.nytimes.com/2016/04/17/us/georgetown-university-search-for-slave-descendants.html.

53. Gerda Lerner, *The Grimké Sisters of South Carolina: Pioneers for Women's Rights and Abolition* (1967; repr., Chapel Hill: University of North Carolina Press, 2004), 3.

54. One of the authors of this book has urged the students to expand their efforts to lobby actively for congressional approval of a comprehensive national program of black reparations. See Jesús Rodriguez, "This Could Be the First Slavery Reparations Policy in America," Politico, April 9, 2019, https://www.politico.com/magazine/story/2019/04/09/georgetown-university-reparations-slave-trade-226581; and George Pierpoint, "The US Students Who Want to Pay Slavery Descendants," BBC News, April 10, 2019, https://www.bbc.com/news/world-us-canada-47886292.

55. Wilder, *Ebony and Ivy*, 95–96, 118, 121.

56. Wilder, 115. Washington College is now Washington and Lee University in Lexington, Virginia. Washington College began in 1782 as Liberty Hall, founded by former students of John Witherspoon at the College of New Jersey.

57. Wilder, 123.

58. Wilder, 100.

59. John K. "Yonni" Chapman, "Black Freedom and the University of North Carolina, 1793–1960" (PhD diss., University of North Carolina at Chapel Hill, 2006), 17–18, https://cdr.lib.unc.edu/indexablecontent/uuid:2ad37fba-c082-4e69-9a16-135c73aeedc9.

60. Chapman, 10.

61. "Spence-Dobbs Family Tree: Information about John Hogan," Genealogy, http://www.genealogy.com/ftm/s/p/e/Daniel-B-Spence-MN/WEBSITE-0001/UHP-0106.html; I. Randolph Daniel Jr., "A Preliminary Archaeological Assessment of the Meadowmont Property, the University of North Carolina at Chapel Hill," 2, Technical Report No. 23, May 1996, Research Laboratories of Anthropology, University of North Carolina at Chapel Hill, http://www.rla.unc.edu/Publications/pdf/TechRep/TechRep23.pdf. The comprehensive list of slave-owning land donors to the University of North Carolina at Chapel Hill is as follows: John Hogan, 200 acres; Benjamin Yeargin, 51 acres; Matthew McCauley, 150 acres; Christopher Barbee, 221 acres; Edmund Jones, 200 acres; Mark Morgan, 107 acres; Jonathan Daniel, 107 acres; Hardy Morgan, 125 acres; and William McCauley, 100 acres. See Nicholas Graham, "Original Donors to the University and the Myth of Free Tuition," *History on the Hill* (blog), University of North Carolina at Chapel Hill, https://blogs.lib.unc.edu/hill/index.php/2016/01/06/original-donors-to-the-university-and-the-myth-of-free-tuition.

62. Chapman, "Black Freedom," 26.

63. Chapman, 15. Smith became governor of North Carolina in 1810. His ancestor and plantation owner Thomas Smith had been one of the colonial governors of the Carolinas in 1693–94. NCpedia, s.v. "Smith, Benjamin," by Dorothy Fremont Grant, https://www.ncpedia.org/biography/smith-benjamin.

64. Chapman, "Black Freedom," 22–23.

65. "Buildings of South Carolina College," Slavery at South Carolina College, 1801–1865: The Foundations of the University of South Carolina, New University Library website, http://slaveryatusc.weebly.com.

66. "Buildings of South Carolina College"

67. Chapman, "Black Freedom," 29–30.

68. "Buildings of South Carolina College." While the university's website indicates that Lieber "owned slaves despite his convictions," we find that although he wrote about hiring the enslaved boy "Tom" from "his master" in an October 28, 1836, letter to Charles Sumner, there is no evidence that he personally owned any enslaved people. See Francis Lieber, *The Life and Letters of Francis Lieber* (Boston: James R. Osgood, 1882), https://archive.org/details/lifeandlettersfo1perrgoog. Lieber went on to write the Lieber Code, General Order No. 100: "Instructions for the Government of the Armies of the United States in the Field" (1863), a treatise for Union soldiers on the rules of engagement during armed conflict. The document became a precursor to the Hague and Geneva Conventions. Lieber opposed the execution of Confederate officers and operatives for treason, likening the practice to that of the Jacobins, who ordered the beheadings of perceived opponents during the French Revolution. See Aaron Sheehan-Dean, "The American Civil War: Total or Just?," Teaching History, http://teachinghistory.org/history-content/ask-a-historian/25245.

69. "Buildings of South Carolina College."

70. "Buildings of South Carolina College."

71. See Wilder, *Ebony and Ivy*, 235; and "Buildings of South Carolina College."

72. Farrow, Lang, and Frank, *Complicity*, xxvi. Farrow, Lang, and Frank (179–92) discuss in detail the case of physician Samuel Morton, one of the founders of the Philadelphia College of Medicine, whose investigations led him to conclude that Africans and Australian Aborigines had the smallest cranial capacity. See also Ibram X. Kendi, *Stamped from the Beginning: The Definitive History of Racist Ideas in America* (New York: Nation Books, 2016), 182, 187–90, 198–99, 332–33.

73. Wilder, *Ebony and Ivy*, 212–37, esp. 235.

74. See Charles B. Dew, *The Making of a Racist: A Southerner Reflects on Family, History, and the Slave Trade* (Charlottesville: University of Virginia Press, 2016), 101–2.

75. See "University of South Carolina Reconstruction Records," https://delphi.tcl.sc.edu/library/digital/collections/reconstruct.html; and John Roper, "Wade Hampton and Reconstruction," H-Net, October 2010, http://www.h-net.org/reviews/showrev.php?id=30609.

76. Theodore Kornweibel Jr., *Railroads in the African American Experience: A Photographic Journey* (Baltimore: Johns Hopkins University Press, 2010), 12.

77. Kornweibel, 26.

78. Kornweibel, 15.

79. Kornweibel, 22. Air brakes were developed by George Westinghouse in 1872 but not used on a widespread basis until the early 1900s.

80. Kornweibel, 89. To this day, blacks are crowded, disproportionately, into the most hazardous jobs. See Seth A. Seabury, Sophie Terp, and Leslie I. Boden, "Racial and Ethnic Differences in the Frequency of Workplace Injuries and the Prevalence of Work-Related Disability," *Health Affairs* 36, no. 2 (February 2017): 266–73; and John D. Leeth and Jon Ruser, "Safety Segregation: The Importance of Gender, Race, and Ethnicity on Workplace Risk," *Journal of Economic Inequality* 4, no. 2 (August 2006): 123–52.

81. Slave ownership persisted in the four border states—Delaware, Maryland, Missouri, and Kentucky—that remained with the Union, while, gradually, piecemeal abolition removed it from the twenty-one states mentioned here. Farrow, Lang, and Frank (*Complicity*, xxvii) observe, "In the eighteenth century, even after America won its freedom from Great Britain, even after the writing of the Declaration of Independence, tens of thousands of black people were living as slaves in the north. Earlier in that century, enslaved blacks made up nearly one-fifth of the population of New York City." Julia Grant, Gen. Ulysses S. Grant's wife, who was from Missouri, personally owned four slaves: "Eliza, Dan, Julia, and John belonged to me up to the time of President Lincoln's Emancipation Proclamation," she recorded in a narrative account. Julia Dent Grant, *The Personal Memoirs of Julia Dent Grant (Mrs. Ulysses S. Grant)* (Carbondale: Southern Illinois University Press, 1988), 83. Irving Wallace, David Wallechinsky, and Amy Wallace, *Significa* (New York: E. P. Dutton, 1983), 13. General Grant himself freed the single slave he had owned in 1859: "I Ulysses S. Grant . . . do hereby manumit, emancipate and set free from Slavery my Negro man William, sometimes called William Jones . . . forever." See "Slavery at White Haven," Ulysses S. Grant, National Park Service, https://www.nps.gov/ulsg/learn/historyculture/slaveryatwh.htm.

82. "Results from the 1860 Census," Civil War Home Page, http://www.civil-war.net/pages/1860_census.html. See also William Thorndale and William W. Dollarhide, *Map Guide to the U.S. Federal Censuses, 1790–1920* (Baltimore: Genealogical Publications, 1987).

83. Thorndale and Dollarhide, *Map Guide*. Slaves held by *free* blacks comprised a tiny proportion of the total number of enslaved persons. The best available estimates indicate that 3,000 free blacks owned 20,000 people in 1860, approximately .05 percent of the 4 million enslaved persons. The 3,000 slaveholding blacks themselves constituted less than 1 percent of the 477,000 free blacks in the United States. Louis Jacobson, "Viral Post Gets It Wrong about the Extent of Slavery in 1860," PunditFact, August 24, 2017, https://www.politifact.com/punditfact/statements/2017/aug/24/viral-image/viral-post-gets-it-wrong-extent-slavery-1860.

84. U.S. Census Bureau, "Statistics of Slaves," 1854, p. 136, table 65, https://www.census.gov/library/publications/1854/dec/1850c.html

85. "Because race bound all whites together as members of the master race, non-slaveholding whites took part in civil duties. They served on juries and voted.

They also engaged in the daily rounds of maintaining slavery by serving on neighborhood patrols to ensure that slaves did not escape and that rebellions did not occur. The practical consequence of such activities was that the institution of slavery, and its perpetuation, became a source of commonality among different economic and social tiers that otherwise were separated by a gulf of difference." "Wealth and Culture in the South," Lumen Learning, https://courses.lumenlearning.com /ushistory1os2xmaster/chapter/wealth-and-culture-in-the-south.

86. See Joseph T. Glatthaar, *General Lee's Army: From Victory to Collapse* (New York: Free Press, 2008), 19–20.

87. Nor were free blacks immune from being sold back into slavery. Harriet Jacobs's narrative provides a dramatic illustration in the following story she related about her own family: "I had also a great treasure in my maternal grandmother, who was a remarkable woman in many respects. She was the daughter of a planter in South Carolina, who, at his death, left her mother and his three children free, with money to go to St. Augustine [Florida], where they had relatives. It was during the Revolutionary War; and they were captured on their passage, carried back, and sold to different purchasers." Harriet Jacobs, *Incidents in the Life of a Slave Girl: Written by Herself* (Boston, 1861), http://docsouth.unc.edu/fpn/jacobs/jacobs.html.

88. Christopher Tomlins, "Reconsidering Indentured Servitude: European Migration and the Early American Labor Force, 1600–1775," *Labor History* 42, no. 1 (2001): 5–43.

89. David Galenson, "The Rise and Fall of Indentured Servitude in the United States: An Economic Analysis," *Journal of Economic History* 44, no. 1 (March 1984): 1–26. Digital History reports, "To meet planters' growing demand for slaves, the English government established the Royal African Company in 1672. After 1698, when Britain ended the Royal African Company's monopoly of the slave trade, the number of enslaved Africans brought into the colonies soared. Between 1700 and 1775, more than 350,000 African slaves entered the American colonies. By the mid-18th century, blacks made up almost 70 percent of the population of South Carolina, 40 percent in Virginia, 8 percent in Pennsylvania, and 4 percent in New England." "The Origins of New World Slavery," Digital History, http://www.digitalhistory.uh.edu/disp _textbook.cfm?smtid=2&psid=449.

90. U.S. Census Bureau, "Statistics of Slaves," 132.

91. Don Jordan and Michael Walsh's discussion of white indentured servitude in *White Cargo: The Forgotten History of Britain's White Slaves in America* (New York: New York University Press, 2008) tends to draw such an equivalence. Historian Liam Hogan has demonstrated that this is a false equivalence, and he has been especially vigorous in his critique of the "Irish slaves" version of this trope. See, e.g., Liam Hogan, "All of My Work on the Irish Slaves Meme (2015–19)," Medium, March 12, 2017, https://medium.com/@Limerick1914 /all-of-my-work-on-the-irish-slaves-meme-2015-16-4965e445802a.

92. Dominic Sandbrook, "The Forgotten History of Britain's White Slaves," *Telegraph*, May 3, 2007, http://www.telegraph.co.uk/culture/books/3664862/The -forgotten-history-of-Britains-white-slaves.html.

93. Reba McEntire explored her family's roots on a 2012 episode of the television program *Who Do You Think You Are?* (season 3, episode 4). The show invites celebrities to research their family genealogies. McEntire learned that she is descended from George Brassfield (or Brasfield or Braisfield—several spellings appeared in the consulted archival documents) on her mother's side; see "Reba McEntire, Who Do You Think You Are?," Tracingthetree, March 3, 2012, https://tracingthetree.wordpress.com/2012/03/03/reba-mcentire-who-do-you-are. We thank historian Harry Watson for providing information about McEntire's story; he was one of the scholars who did the genealogical research to recover her family history.

CHAPTER 4

1. "Introduction to Colonial African American Life," Colonial Williamsburg, http://www.history.org/almanack/people/african/aaintro.cfm; Tom Cowan and Jack Maguire, *Timelines of African-American History: Five Hundred Years of Black Achievement* (New York: Berkeley Publishing Group, 1994), 32. For population data see "Timeline of Slavery in America 1501–1865," Sharon Draper, http://sharondraper.com/timeline.pdf.

2. Edmund Morgan, *American Slavery, American Freedom* (New York: W. W. Norton, 1975). See also "African American Heritage and Ethnography: Laws that Bound and Laws in the Southern Colonies," Park Ethnography Program, National Park Service, https://www.nps.gov/ethnography/aah/aaheritage/contents.htm.which states, in part: "Seventeenth century Virginia laws defining occupational boundaries between *indentured servitude* and enslavement were flexible. Africans were as likely to be indentured (contracted as a servant to work for a set amount of time) as they were to be enslaved. The work of indentured servants, English or African, was much the same as the work of those enslaved. Social relationships between indentured servants and slaves were also fluid during this period." (Italics in the original.)

3. Niall Ferguson, *Colossus: The Price of America's Empire* (New York: Penguin Books, 2004), 2.

4. Customarily, 1619 has been taken as the signal year for the first importation of enslaved Africans to the North American colonies for sale or otherwise. However, there is some evidence that the British privateer Francis Drake may have left a large number of enslaved blacks and indigenous people at the Roanoke colony as early as 1586. Andrew Lawler, "Did Francis Drake Bring Enslaved Africans to North America Decades Before Jamestown?," *Smithsonian*, August 20, 2018, https://www.smithsonianmag.com/history/did-francis-drake-bring-enslaved-africans-north-america-decades-jamestown-180970075.

5. The Virginia Company of London, a joint-stock company that sold shares, was chartered in 1608 under the newly crowned King James I. Some twenty black indentured servants were brought to the colony in 1619, including Anthony (Antonio) Johnson, who procured his freedom by 1623 and imported five servants of his own by 1651, for which he obtained headrights of 250 acres of land. See Wikipedia, s.v. "History of slavery," http://en.wikipedia.org/wiki/History_of_slavery; and Workers of the WPA Writers' Program in the State of Virginia, *Virginia: A Guide to the Old*

Dominion (New York: Oxford University Press, 1940). Records from 1623 and 1624 list the Africans as "servants." See Nikole Hannah-Jones, "America Wasn't a Democracy Until African Americans Made It One," *New York Times Magazine*, August 14, 2019, https://www.nytimes.com/interactive/2019/08/14/magazine/black-history -american-democracy.html?mtrref=www.google.com&gwh=3EB2EC86FD 4299A62A33F3C3857A71BE&gwt=pay&assetType=REGIWALL. See also "Arrivals of First Africans to Virginia Colony 1619," *Africans in America: The Terrible Transformation*, PBS, https://www.pbs.org/wgbh/aia/part1/1p263.html, which states that "during their time as servants, they were fed and housed. Afterwards, they would be given what were known as 'freedom dues,' which usually included a piece of land and supplies, including a gun. Black-skinned or white-skinned, they became free."

6. Lerone Bennett Jr., "The 10 Biggest Myths about Black History," *Ebony*, February 1984, 26.

7. Don Jordan and Michael Walsh, *White Cargo: The Forgotten History of Britain's White Slaves in America* (New York: New York University Press, 2008). See also David W. Galenson, "The Rise and Fall of Indentured Servitude in the Americas: An Economic Analysis," *Journal of Economic History* 44, no. 1 (March 1984): 1–26.

8. William Darity Jr., "Africa, Europe, and the Origins of Uneven Development: The Role of Slavery," in Cecilia A. Conrad, John Whitehead, Patrick L. Mason, and James Stewart, eds., *African Americans in the U.S. Economy* (Lanham, Md.: Rowman and Littlefield, 2005), 16.

9. "Indentured servants agreed to work for a four or five year term of service in return for their transportation to the New World as well as food, clothing, and shelter. In certain respects, the status of white servants differed little from that of slavery. Like slaves, servants could be bought, sold, or leased. They could also be punished by whipping. Unlike slaves, however, servants were allowed to own property, and, if they survived their term of service, received their freedom along with a small sum of money known as 'freedom dues.' During the 17th century, indentured servants suffered an appalling death rate. Half of all white servants in the Chesapeake colonies of Virginia and Maryland died within five years of their arrival." "The Origins of New World Slavery," Digital History, http://www.digitalhistory.uh.edu/disp _textbook.cfm?smtid=2&psid=449. However, the source is not clear on an estimate of the indentured mortality rate, since vital statistics from the colonial period are sparse at best. The best available data indicates that death rates, especially infant mortality rates, generally were relatively high during much of the colonial era. Stephen J. Kurz, "Mortality Change in America 1620–1920," *Human Biology* 56, no. 3 (September 1984): 559–84.

10. "Indentured Servants," U.S. History: Pre-Columbian to the New Millennium, http://www.ushistory.org/us/5b.asp.

11. Morgan, *American Slavery*, 268.

12. Julia Ott, "Slaves: The Capital That Made Capitalism," Public Seminar, April 9, 2014, http://www.publicseminar.org/2014/04/slavery-the-capital-that-made -capitalism.

13. Ott.

14. Eric Foner, *Give Me Liberty!: An American History* (New York: W. W. Norton, 2009), 100. See also "Bacon's Rebellion," Historic Jamestowne, National Park Service, https://www.nps.gov/jame/learn/historyculture/bacons-rebellion.htm; and "Green Spring Plantation," Historic Jamestowne, National Park Service, https://www.nps.gov/jame/learn/historyculture/green-spring-plantation.htm.

15. The literal translation of *partus sequitur ventrem* is "that which is brought forth follows the womb." In 1664, Maryland passed a law that assigned the status of a child's father to his child. Directly conflicting with the Virginia law—for a brief period, mixed-race and mixed-legal-status couples fled to the state that gave them an advantage—the mandate was replaced with a facsimile of the original Virginia law later that year.

16. In 1670, a Virginia law was passed prohibiting blacks and Indians from owning Christian (that is to say, white) indentured servants. One by one all of the colonies along the Atlantic seaboard made slavery legal—as early as 1626 in New York, 1663 in Maryland, and 1664 in New Jersey.

17. Morgan, *American Slavery*, 331. Morgan refers to William Waller Hening, ed., *The Statutes at Large: Being a Collection of All the Laws of Virginia, From the First Session of the Legislature, in the Year 1619* (Richmond, Va.: Printed for the editor at the Franklin Press, 1809–23) 2:280; emphasis added by Morgan.

18. "October 1705-CHAP. XXII. An act declaring the Negro, Mulatto, and Indian slaves within this dominion to be real estate," in Hening, *Statutes at Large*, 3:333–35.

19. Encyclopedia Virginia, s.v. "'An Act Concerning Servants and Slaves' (1705)," http://www.encyclopediavirginia.org/_An_act_concerning_Servants_and_Slaves_1705.

20. Planters in Virginia alone were £2.3 million in debt. Encyclopedia.com, s.v. "British Debts," https://www.encyclopedia.com/history/dictionaries-thesauruses-pictures-and-press-releases/british-debts.

21. As the colonial economy grew and became more commercialized, banks and merchants began to circulate bills of exchange or credit with values that fluctuated. Britain, troubled by the destabilizing effects of the colonial currency, sought to put a stop to this practice and compel everyone to use the British pound.

22. Perhaps the earliest known document affirming the necessity of the abolition of the slave trade, the Germantown Quaker Petition Against Slavery was drafted in 1688 by Francis Daniel Pastorius. It was signed by three other members of the Quaker Meeting of the Religious Society of Friends on behalf of their community of faith. The Slavery Abolition Act of 1833 outlawed the institution throughout the United Kingdom, with the exception of the countries under the control of the East India Company—Ceylon Island and Saint Helena Island off the western coast of Africa. The institution was outlawed on those islands in 1843. Significantly, slavery was not outlawed in India itself until 1893.

23. An act to make slavery illegal was passed in 1735; however, pressure to repeal the act was relentless. Letters and petitions arguing for the economic necessity of slavery flooded the trustees. Following the example of South Carolina, Georgia adopted slave codes "for the better Ordering and Governing Negroes and other Slaves in this Province." The laws restricting the movement and autonomy of Africans in the

state were expanded in 1765 and 1770. Between 1750 and 1775, the state's enslaved population grew from fewer than 500 to over 18,000 people. See New Georgia Encyclopedia, s.v. "Slavery in Colonial Georgia," by Betty Wood, http://www.georgia encyclopedia.org/articles/history-archaeology/slavery-colonial-georgia.

24. New Georgia Encyclopedia, s.v. "Slavery in Colonial Georgia."

25. In *Somerset v. Stewart*, the English Court of King's Bench ruled that chattel slavery was not legal in England and Wales. The decision of Lord Chief Justice William Murray, First Earl of Mansfield, read, in part: "The state of slavery is of such a nature that it is incapable of being introduced on any reasons, moral or political. . . . The black must be discharged." See Stephen Usherwood, "The Black Must Be Discharged: The Abolitionists' Debt to Lord Mansfield," *History Today* 31, no. 3 (1981), http://www.historytoday.com/stephen-usherwood /black-must-be-discharged-abolitionists-debt-lord-mansfield.

26. In 1774, during the First Continental Congress, Jay, both a slaveholder *and* an abolitionist, wrote—with no apparent irony—an "Address to the People of Great Britain," asserting that the rights and liberties of English colonists were equivalent to those of slaves in the eyes of the British, concluding "that by having our lives and property in [Britain's] power, they may with the greater facility enslave *you*." (Italics in the original.)

For the text of the address, see "Address to the People of Great Britain," Wikisource, https://en.wikisource.org/wiki/Address_to_the_People_of_Great_Britain. The New York Manumission Society also provided support and legal counsel for free blacks who had been kidnapped or falsely accused of having been enslaved, and in 1799, when Jay was the governor of New York, the state passed legislation mandating gradual emancipation. Compensation was not provided to the formerly enslaved. See Roger G. Kennedy, *Burr, Hamilton and Jefferson: A Study in Character* (New York: Oxford University Press, 2000), 92.

27. During Clarkson's studies at Cambridge University, in 1785 he won an essay competition in which he argued against the institution of slavery on moral grounds. See *An Essay on the Slavery and Commerce of the Human Species, Particularly the African*, http://www.gutenberg.org/files/10611/10611-h/10611-h.htm#Part_204; italics in the original. Clarkson asked, "But how does the *slave* differ from his *master*, but by *chance*?"

When the British Parliament abolished slavery in 1833, it also reclassified enslaved persons as being in "slavish servitude"—meaning that they were no longer chattel property controlled by a "master" but "near slaves," or individuals whose status resided in servitude. Parliament also determined that all imported and escaped slaves who gained entry to the country would be automatically emancipated.

28. Martha Wayles Skelton's father was John Wayles. David McCullough, *John Adams* (New York: Touchstone Books, 2002), 115. See also Henry Stephens Randall, *The Life of Thomas Jefferson* (New York: Derby and Jackson, 1858), 1:64.

29. Morgan, *American Slavery*, 369.

30. McCullough, *John Adams*, 116. See also Randall, *Life of Thomas Jefferson*, 11.

31. During Jefferson's tenure, the House of Burgesses put forward resolutions condemning Britain's stationing of troops in Boston and taxation without

representation. In 1776, the House of Burgesses became the Virginia House of Delegates with the ratification of the Virginia Constitution.

32. McCullough, *John Adams*, 114. Jefferson characterized the escalation of taxes, restrictions on commerce and manufacturing, the issuing of land grants, and the expansion of government offices as "an instance of despotism to which no parallel can be produced in the most arbitrary ages of British history. . . . The true ground on which we declare these acts void, is, that the British Parliament has no right to exercise authority over us." (Italics in the original.) Randall, *Life of Thomas Jefferson*, 93.

33. The other delegates in the committee were John Adams (Massachusetts), Benjamin Franklin (Pennsylvania), Roger Sherman (Connecticut), and Robert Livingston (New York).

34. "(1776) The Deleted Passage of the Declaration of Independence," BlackPast, https://www.blackpast.org/african-american-history/declaration-independence -and-debate-over-slavery.

35. On Jefferson's possible ulterior motives for opposing the slave trade, see Ned and Constance Sublette, *The American Slave Coast: A History of the Slave-Breeding Industry* (Chicago: Lawrence Hill Books, 2016). During his first session as a burgess, Jefferson did introduce a bill giving slaveholders the right to manumit their slaves. The measure failed. It would pass in 1782 in the midst of the rebellion against England. Randall, *Life of Thomas Jefferson*, 58.

36. See "'Counter-Revolution of 1776': Was U.S. Independence War a Conservative Revolt in Favor of Slavery?," Democracy Now, June 27, 2014, http://www.democracy now.org/2014/6/27/counter_revolution_of_1776_was_us. See also Gerald Horne, *The Counter-Revolution of 1776: Slave Resistance and the Origins of the United States of America* (New York: New York University Press, 2014).

37. "Freedom and Bondage in the Colonial Era," *Africans in America: Revolution*, PBS, https://www.pbs.org/wgbh/aia/part2/2narr1.html.

38. Richard Sutch, "Breeding, Slave," in Randall M. Miller and John David Smith, eds., *Dictionary of Afro-American Slavery* (Westport, Conn.: Praeger, 1997), 82–86.

39. "Slavery FAQs—Property," Jefferson Monticello, https://www.monticello.org /site/plantation-and-slavery/property.

40. The rationale for the formation of the separate Republic of Texas was in fact the preservation of slavery:

> The Mexican Constitution of 1824 embraced a federal system of government and the creation of states. In 1827, the state constitution of Coahuila y Tejas provided for the gradual elimination of slavery by (1) prohibiting the further importation of slaves and (2) freeing, at birth, all children born to slaves. Two more state decrees that provided growing rights and freedom for slaves quickly followed. In 1829 Mexico's black President, Vicente Guerrero, abolished slavery and upon receiving news of the status of Texas from General Mier y Teran, passed The Law of 1830, which stopped all Anglo immigration to Texas. However, for most of 1833–34, Vice President Gomez Farias (in charge while Santa Anna was putting down rebellions in the Yucatan and Zacatecas) instituted various

measures favorable to Texas. These included (1) dividing Texas into three political districts, (2) accepting English for official purposes, (3) revising the court system, and (4) granting religious tolerance. But, Texas was not granted statehood from Coahuila (Maria Garza Lubeck, "The Colonization of Texas," June 30, 2015, volunteer educational document, Bullock Texas State History Museum, Austin, Texas).

See also Theodore G. Vincent, *The Legacy of Vicente Guerrero, Mexico's First Black Indian President* (Gainesville: University Press of Florida, 2001), 81.

41. British officer Lord Dunsmore, the former royal governor of Virginia, proclaimed on November 7, 1775, that all slaves and indentures that took up arms in support of England against the rebelling colonists would be freed at the end of the war. This declaration had a profound effect on the war as thousands of blacks joined the Loyalist cause while their owners, just as determinedly, sided with the rebels. Dunsmore commanded the Ethiopian Regiment, as the black militia was called, whose members wore uniforms with the words "Liberty to the slaves" stitched above their breasts. Thomas B. Allen, *Tories Fighting for the King in America's First Civil War* (New York: Harper, 2010), 154–55.

42. Philip Foner, *Blacks in the American Revolution* (Westport, Conn.: Greenwood Press, 1976), 75–76, 205.

43. Garry Wills, *"Negro President": Jefferson and the Slave Power* (Boston: Houghton Mifflin, 2003), 51–52.

44. Stanley Elkins, *Slavery: A Problem in American Institutional and Intellectual Life* (Chicago: University of Chicago Press, 1959).

45. See Harvey Wish, "American Slave Insurrections before 1861," *Journal of Negro History* 22, no. 3 (July 1937): 299–320; Hebert Aptheker, *American Negro Slave Revolts* (New York: International Publishers, 1974); and Henry Louis Gates Jr., "Did African-American Slaves Revolt?," African Americans: Many Rivers to Cross, http://www.pbs.org/wnet/african-americans-many-rivers-to-cross/history/did-african-american-slaves-rebel.

46. Wish, "American Slave Insurrections," 303–6.

47. Wish, 307–8.

48. Kai Wright, ed., *The African American Experience: Black History and Culture Through Speeches, Letters, Editorials, Poems, Songs, and Stories* (New York: Black Dog and Leventhal, 2009), 38.

49. Joyce D. Goodfriend, *Before the Melting Pot: Society and Culture in Colonial New York City, 1664–1730* (Princeton, N.J.: Princeton University Press, 1992), 123. Goodfriend (76) observes that slave ownership was commonplace across all white ethnic groups in New York City in the first decade of the eighteenth century. Forty-one percent of all households in the city owned at least one slave, distributed accordingly: 37 percent of Dutch households, 44 percent of English households, 50 percent of French households, and 75 percent of Jewish households. Therefore, the implications of the 1712 revolt were of widely shared concern among the city's white population.

50. Wright, *African American Experience*, 54. Wish ("American Slave Insurrections," 308) observed, "The retaliation showed an unusual barbarous strain on the part of the whites. Twenty-one Negroes were executed, some were burnt, others hanged, and one broken on the wheel."

51. Daniel Horsmanden, "The Trial of Cuffe and Quack," in Wright, *African American Experience*, 57.

52. Sven Beckert, *Empire of Cotton: A Global History* (New York: Random House, 2014), 96–97, contends that the explosive growth in cotton production above and beyond sugar production in Saint-Domingue intensified the already onerous burden of forced labor on the enslaved population. The additional pressures imposed by the growth in production accelerated the momentum toward revolution.

53. Claudia Sutherland, "Haitian Revolution (1791–1804)," BlackPast, July 16, 2007, https://www.blackpast.org/global-african-history/haitian-revolution-1791-1804; "Statistics of Wars, Oppressions, and Atrocities of the Eighteenth Century," Necrometrics, http://necrometrics.com/wars18c.htm.

54. For the classic study of the Haitian slave revolt, see C. L. R. James, *The Black Jacobins: Toussaint L'Ouverture and the San Domingo Revolution* (1938; New York: Random House, 1963).

55. Mary Turner, *Slaves and Missionaries: The Disintegration of Jamaican Slave Society, 1787–1834* (Urbana: University of Illinois Press, 1982), 121. For the text of the British Slavery Abolition Act of 1833, see "An Act for the Abolition of Slavery throughout the *British* Colonies; for Promoting the Industry of the Manumitted Slaves; and for Compensating the Persons hitherto Entitled to the Services of Such Slaves," William Loney RN (website), http://www.pdavis.nl/Legis_07.htm.

56. In 2007, more than 200 years after his execution, Prosser, whose name was simply "Gabriel," was pardoned by Virginia governor Timothy Kaine in recognition of "his devotion to the ideals of the American Revolution—it was worth risking death to secure liberty." Kaine continued, "Gabriel's cause—the end of slavery and furtherance of equality for all people—has prevailed in the light of history." See "Virginia Governor 'Pardons' Slave Who Led 'Gabriel's Rebellion,'" History News Network, August 31, 2007, http://historynewsnetwork.org/article/42380.

57. "A Map of Slave Revolts in the United States," The Slave Rebellion, http://slaverebellion.info/index.php?page=maps.

58. Juan Ignacio Blanco, "U.S.A. Executions—1607–1976: Index by State—Virginia—1801–1830," DeathPenaltyUSA, http://deathpenaltyusa.org/usa1/state/virginia3.htm.

59. John Fabian Witt, *Lincoln's Code: The Laws of War in American History* (New York: Free Press, 2012), 201.

60. This fiction still appears well into the twenty-first century. See Tera W. Hunter, "Putting an Antebellum Myth to Rest," *New York Times*, August 1, 2011, http://www.nytimes.com/2011/08/02/opinion/putting-an-antebellum-myth-about-slave-families-to-rest.html. See also Michael Kent Curtis, "The Curious History of Attempts to Suppress Antislavery Speech, Press, and Petition in 1835–37," *Northwestern University Law Review*, no. 89 (1994–95): 785–870. By 1827, it has been estimated there

were as many as 106 antislavery organizations with 6,625 members in the south, although only a quarter of those were "true abolitionists." The majority wanted the enslaved to be emancipated and transported to Africa. Many southern whites who were opposed to slavery simply migrated to the north. George McBride, "Were There White People in the South who Fought for Abolition before the Civil War?," Quora, updated June 27, 2015, https://www.quora.com/Were-there-white-people-in-the-South-who-fought-for-abolition-before-the-Civil-War.

61. The mental gymnastics required here were extraordinary. For example, the physician Samuel A. Cartwright invented a disease he called drapetomania, a psychological disease that would lead slaves to flee from their masters. Thus, for Cartwright, the flight to freedom was attributable to mental illness. See David Pilgrim, "Question of the Month: Drapetomania," Jim Crow Museum of Racist Memorabilia, November 2005, https://www.ferris.edu/HTMLS/news/jimcrow/question/2005/november.htm.

62. Kate Stone, *Brokenburn: The Journal of Kate Stone*, ed. John Q. Anderson (Baton Rouge: Louisiana State University Press, 1955), https://archive.org/stream/brokenburnthejou008676mbp/brokenburnthejou008676mbp_djvu.txt.

63. Stone, 11.

64. Stone, 6–7.

65. John Q. Anderson, introduction to Stone, xxii.

66. Thavolia Glymph, *Out of the House of Bondage: The Transformation of the Plantation Household* (Cambridge, Mass.: Cambridge University Press, 2008).

67. Stephany Jones-Rogers, "'She Could . . . Spare One Ample Breast for the Profit of Her Owner': White Mothers and Enslaved Wet Nurses' Invisible Labor in American Slave Markets," *Slavery and Abolition: A Journal of Slave and Post-Slave Studies* 38, no. 2 (2017), https://www.tandfonline.com/doi/full/10.1080/0144039X.2017.1317014.

68. Text from "A Nation Divided" panel, Gibbes Museum of Art, Charleston, South Carolina, March 2019.

69. Eric Muller and Sally Greene, "His Viciousness with Slaves Was Extreme, and His Portrait Dominates State's Top Court," *News and Observer* (Raleigh, N.C.), October 28, 2018, 15A; italics in the original. Judge Thomas Ruffin was a slaveholder and slave trader himself. See also North Carolina History Encyclopedia, s.v. "State v. Mann," by Jonathan Murray, http://northcarolinahistory.org/encyclopedia/state-v-mann.

70. Theodore Dwight Weld, Angelina Grimké Weld, and Sarah Grimké, *American Slavery as It Is: Testimony of a Thousand Witnesses* (New York: American Anti-Slavery Society, 1839), 14.

71. Weld, Weld, and Grimké, 14. An additional sample of the horrors of slavery catalogued in Weld, Weld, and Grimké appears in appendix 2.

72. Monique Prince, "Theodore Dwight Weld, 1803–1895," Documenting the American South, http://docsouth.unc.edu/neh/weld/summary.html.

73. Douglass, Reckless, and Forten were founding members of the Philadelphia Female Anti-Slavery Society.

74. Angelina Grimké's appeal read, in part:

But perhaps you will be ready to query, why appeal to *women* on this subject? We do not make the laws which perpetuate slavery. No legislative power is vested in us; *we* can do nothing to overthrow the system, even if we wished to do so. To this I reply, I know you do not make the laws, but I also know that you *are the wives and mothers, the sisters and daughters of those who do*; and if you really suppose you can do nothing to overthrow slavery, you are greatly mistaken. You can do much in every way: four things I will name. 1st. You can read on this subject. 2d. You can pray over this subject. 3d. You can speak on this subject. 4th. You can *act* on this subject" (Angelina Emily Grimké, *Appeal to the Christian Women of the South* [New York: American Anti-Slavery Society, 1836], http://utc.iath.virginia.edu/abolitn /abesaegat.html; italics in the original).

75. In her *Letters to Catherine Beecher*, Angelina Grimké also challenged the view of Harriet Beecher Stowe, her sister Catherine Beecher, and others that slavery should come to an end only if freed blacks are exiled to Liberia or some other foreign land. See also Laurel Thatcher Ulrich, *Well-Behaved Women Seldom Make History* (New York: Alfred A. Knopf, 2007), 135–38.

76. McBride, "Were There White People"; Stanley Harrold, *The Abolitionists and the South, 1831–1861* (Lexington: University of Kentucky Press, 1995). White southern abolitionists included Cassius Clay, William Bailey, Hinton Helper, Duncan Smith, William Dunlop, James Poage, and William Williamson.

77. Anthony's brothers, Daniel and Merritt, joined John Brown during the fight against slavery in "Bloody Kansas." In 1837, when she was sixteen years old, Anthony signed a petition opposing slavery as part of the resistance to the gag rule the House of Representatives had imposed on abolitionist appeals. Nearly thirty years later, she would help the Women's Loyal National League obtain 400,000 signatures from antislavery advocates, the largest effort of the type at the time. Harrold, *Abolitionists and the South*, 20–30, 105–42.

78. Stanton cautioned educated women of means that the franchise must be limited to "Anglo-Saxons," lest undeserving Americans, "the lower order of Chinese, Africans, Germans and Irish, with their low ideas of womanhood," be given the right to make "laws for you and our daughters." Ann D. Gordon, *The Selected Papers of Elizabeth Cady Stanton and Susan B. Anthony: Against an Aristocracy of Sex, 1866 to 1873* (New Brunswick, N.J.: Rutgers University Press, 2000). See also "Elizabeth Cady Stanton Quote," LibQuotes, https://libquotes.com/elizabeth-cady-stanton/quote /lbx5a60; "Susan B. Anthony's Suffrage Newspaper: The Revolution," Paperless Archives, http://www.paperlessarchives.com/susan-b-anthony-the-revolution. html; Ulrich, *Well-Behaved Women*, 138–41; and Michele Mitchell, "'Orders,' Racial Hierarchies, and Rights Rhetoric: Evolutionary Echoes in Elizabeth Cady Stanton's Thought during the Late 1860s," in *Elizabeth Cady Stanton, Feminist As Thinker: A Reader in Documents and Essays*, ed. Ellen Carol DuBois and Richard Candida Smith (New York: New York University Press, 2007), 129. Many women's rights leaders,

Elizabeth Blackwell, Julia Ward Howe, and Lucy Stone among them, disagreed with Stanton's "all or nothing" position. However, Stanton's vitriolic rhetoric carried the day. One consequence would be the decision on the part of many women activists to go their own way and establish an independent women's movement. Eric Foner, *Reconstruction: America's Unfinished Revolution* (New York: Harper and Row, 1988), 255–56.

79. E. Franklin Frazier, *The Negro in the United States* (New York: Macmillan, 1957), 109–10, provides two anecdotes that powerfully represent the ex-slaves' desire to be free. They are reported in appendix 3.

80. Frazier, 200–201.

81. Steven Nathaniel Dossman, review of *Drift toward Dissolution: The Virginia Slavery Debate of 1831–1832*, by Alison Goodyear Freehling, Virtual Office of Steven. E. Woodworth, http://personal.tcu.edu/swoodworth/GoodyearFreehling.htm.

82. Wish, "American Slave Insurrections," 299–320.

83. Daniel Rasmussen, *American Uprising: The Untold Story of America's Largest Slave Revolt* (New York: HarperCollins, 2011).

84. See "Immediate Abolition: David Walker, *Appeal to the Coloured Citizens of the World*, 1829," Nat Turner Project, http://www.natturnerproject.org/david-walker -appeal; and NCPedia, s.v. "David Walker's *Appeal*," by Crystal Walker, http://www .ncpedia.org/history/1776-1860/David-Walkers-Appeal. David Walker died under mysterious circumstances less than a year after the 1829 publication and circulation of the *Appeal*; there is speculation that he was poisoned.

85. John C. Hurd, *The Law of Freedom and Bondage in the United States* (Boston: Little, Brown, 1858), 1:307.

86. Encyclopedia Virginia, s.v. "Speech by Samuel McDowell Moore to the House of Delegates (January 11, 1832)," http://www.encyclopediavirginia.org/Speech _by_Samuel_McDowell_Moore_to_the_House_of_Delegates_January_11_1832; Encyclopedia Virginia, s.v. "The Virginia Slavery Debate of 1831–1832," by Erik S. Root, http://www.encyclopediavirginia.org/Virginia_Slavery_Debate_of_1831-1832_The.

87. See NCPedia, s.v. "Battle, James Smith (25 June 1786–18 July 1854)," by Elizabeth D. Battle, http://www.ncpedia.org/biography/battle-james-smith; and NCPedia, s.v. "Gaston, William (19 Sept. 1778–23 Jan. 1844)," by Charles H. Bowman Jr., http://www .ncpedia.org/biography/gaston-william.

88. NCPedia, s.v. "Moore, Bartholomew Figures," by Memory F. Mitchell, http:// www.ncpedia.org/biography/moore-bartholomew-figures; NCPedia, s.v. "*State v. Negro Will*," by Martin H. Brinkley, http://www.ncpedia.org/state-v-negro-will; Associated Press, "North Carolina Marker to Honor Slave Who Killed His Master," *Carolina Times*, June 10, 2017, A1; Josh Shaffer, "Slave Who Killed White Overseer in 1834 Honored with Marker," *News and Observer* (Raleigh, N.C.), June 10, 2017, A1–2.

89. Less than thirty years later, when the possibility of civil war loomed, Moore once again went against customary expectations when he refused to support secession and then ceased to bring cases to the federal court rather than taking the oath of allegiance to the Confederate government as was required. For details on the legal cases involving Gaston, see North Carolina History Project Encyclopedia,

s.v. "William J. Gaston (1778–1844)," by Ronnie W. Faulkner, http://www.north carolinahistory.org/commentary/45/entry; North Carolina History Project Encyclopedia, s.v. "State v. Negro Will (1834) and State v. Manuel (1838)," by Jonathan Martin, http://www.northcarolinahistory.org/encyclopedia/826/entry; and "William Joseph Gaston, 19 Sept. 1778–23 Jan. 1844," Documenting the American South, http://docsouth.unc.edu/browse/bios/pn0000574_bio.html. For details on Gaston's 1832 commencement speech given at the University of North Carolina at Chapel Hill, see William Gaston, "Address Delivered before the Philanthropic & Dialectic Societies at Chapel Hill," June 20, 1832," Civil War Era NC, https://cwnc.omeka.chass.ncsu .edu/items/show/36.

90. Larry E. Tise, *Proslavery: A History of the Defense of Slavery in America, 1701–1840* (Athens: University of Georgia Press, 1987).

91. Northwest Ordinance of 1787. The Missouri Compromise of 1820 had rendered Minnesota a free state.

92. Dred Scott v. Sandford, 60 U.S. 393 (1857). See also William Darity Jr., "The Class Character of the Black Community: Polarization between the Black Managerial Elite and the Black Underclass," *Black Law Journal* 7, no. 1 (1981): 21–31.

93. Harriet Jacobs, *Incidents in the Life of a Slave Girl: Written by Herself* (Boston, 1861), 193, http://docsouth.unc.edu/fpn/jacobs/jacobs.html.

94. Paul Finkelman, ed., *Encyclopedia of African American History, 1619–1895: From the Colonial Period to the Age of Frederick Douglass* (New York: Oxford University Press, 2006), 273. See also "Fugitive Slaves and Northern Racism," *Africans in America: Judgment Day*, PBS, https://www.pbs.org/wgbh/aia/part4/4narr3.html.

95. "Literacy from 1870 to 1979," excerpts from Tom Snyder, ed., *120 Years of American Education: A Statistical Portrait* (Washington, D.C.: National Center for Education Statistics, 1993), chap. 1, https://nces.ed.gov/naal/lit_history.asp.

96. Morgan, *American Slavery*, 4.

CHAPTER 5

1. See David S. Reynolds, *John Brown, Abolitionist: The Man Who Killed Slavery, Sparked the Civil War, and Seeded Civil Rights* (New York: Random House, 2005); and Gwyneth Swain, *Dred and Harriet Scott: A Family's Struggle for Freedom* (St. Paul: Minnesota Historical Society Press, 2004).

2. E. Franklin Frazier, *The Negro in the United States* (New York: Macmillan, 1957), 103.

3. Nor did Buchanan endorse the legitimacy of secession. Bruce Catton wrote in *The Coming Fury* (New York: Washington Square, 1961), 124: "[Buchanan] was torn by two deep emotions—a strong automatic sympathy for the South, and an unequally potent love for the unbroken Union of the States: a situation that left him feeling that to secede was illegal and that to prevent secession by force was equally illegal." Ultimately, he did nothing, and the hounds of war soon followed on the heels of his presidency.

4. See David Williams, *A People's History of the Civil War: Struggles for the Meaning of Freedom* (New York: New Press, 2005), 346–47.

5. Adele Logan Alexander, *Ambiguous Lives: Free Women of Color in Rural Georgia, 1789–1879* (Fayetteville: University of Arkansas Press, 1991), 117.

6. In 1855, Lincoln was elected to the Illinois General Assembly. Widely recognized for his leadership skills, he was his party's favorite to win the U.S. Senate seat from Illinois. As a U.S. congressman, Lincoln had championed the failed Wilmot Proviso, a rider on a bill specifying the terms dictating the resolution of the Mexican-American War that would have banned slavery in any territories acquired from Mexico during the war or thereafter. When he ran for president in 1860, Lincoln captured 180 votes in the Electoral College, compared to seventy-two for southern Democrat candidate John C. Breckinridge, thirty-nine for Union Party nominee John Bell, and only twelve for Democrat Stephen Douglas. Lincoln won 1,865,908 popular votes, compared to Breckinridge's 848,019 votes. Douglas actually ran second in the popular vote despite his distant last place in the Electoral College vote. See Wikipedia, s.v. "1860 United States Presidential Election," http://en.wikipedia.org/wiki/United_States_presidential_election,_1860.

7. In March 1837, Lincoln and fellow Springfield, Illinois, Whig and attorney Daniel Stone registered their protest of the ostensible antislavery resolution passed by the Illinois House of Representatives, of which they were members. In its denunciation of abolition societies, the elected body seemed to support the institution of slavery. Lincoln was one of only six representatives voting against the measure. The resolution echoed those already passed by several other states and met unanimous approval in the state senate.

The resolution Lincoln and Stone rejected read, in part, that "the right of property in slaves, is sacred to the slave-holding states by the Federal Constitution, and that they cannot be deprived of that right without their consent." For the text of the protest statement that Lincoln and Stone entered into the congressional record, see Roy Basler, ed., *Collected Works of Abraham Lincoln* (New Brunswick, N.J.: Rutgers University Press, 1953), 1:74, http://quod.lib.umich.edu/l/lincoln/lincoln1/1:101?rgn=div1;view=fulltext.

For a discussion of the inner workings of the Illinois legislature during this period, see "Illinois Legislature," Mr. Lincoln and Freedom, http://www.mrlincolnandfreedom.org/inside.asp?ID=7&subjectID=2.

8. "Abraham Lincoln's First Inaugural Address, Monday, March 4, 1861," *Atlantic*, https://www.theatlantic.com/past/docs/issues/99sep/9909linc1staddress.htm.

9. Don E. Fehrenbacher and Virginia Fehrenbacher, eds., *Recollected Words of Abraham Lincoln* (Stanford, Calif.: Stanford University Press, 1996), 277.

10. Joy Hakim, *Reconstructing America 1865–1890* (New York: Oxford University Press, 2003), 11.

11. H. B. Metcalf, "Lincoln's Attitude toward Emancipation with Compensation for Owners of Slaves," *Pacific Monthly*, August 1900, 152–53.

12. Under Lincoln's plan, children born to slave mothers after 1850 would receive an education at the expense of their mothers' owners as part of their preparation for emancipation. Harry S. Blakiston, "Lincoln's Emancipation Plan," *Journal of Negro History*, July 1922, 257–71.

13. The plan called for the immediate emancipation of all slaves over the age of thirty-five; all others would be freed in 1872. See Blakiston, "Lincoln's Emancipation Plan." The Delaware slavery figure is taken from the 1860 U.S. Census. Department of Commerce, *Negro Population 1790–1915* (Washington, D.C.: Government Printing Office, 1915), 57, table 6, https://www2.census.gov/library/publications /decennial/1910/black-population-1790-1915/00480330ch02.pdf.

14. See "Results from the 1860 Census," Civil War Home Page, http://www.civil -war.net/pages/1860_census.html.

15. Lincoln appointed Fisher to the Supreme Court of the District of Columbia, where, eventually, he presided over the trial of John H. Surratt, one of the alleged accomplices in the president's assassination. See Richard F. Miller, *States at War*, vol. 4, *A Reference Guide for Delaware, Maryland, and New Jersey in the Civil War* (Lebanon, N.H.: University Press of New England, 2015), 196.

16. The bill failed even though, in the words of opposition party member and Delaware senator Joseph A. Bayard, "slavery does not exist as a valuable source of prosperity." See "Slavery in Delaware," Slavery in the North, http://www.slavenorth .com/delaware.htm.

17. See, e.g., "Abolitionist Movement," History, October 27, 2009, http://www .history.com/topics/black-history/abolitionist-movement. For an analysis of the situation in Illinois in 1837, see "Illinois Legislature," Pre–Civil War, http://www .mrlincolnandfreedom.org/pre-civil-war/illinois-legislature.

18. Controversy over the absolute right of whites to possess claims to property in human chattel began to heat up during the mid- to late 1830s. During the summer of 1831, the nation—and especially the south—was stunned by the Nat Turner Rebellion in Southampton County, Virginia. On August 13, Turner and at least forty allies attacked and killed fifty-five whites in the early morning hours while they slept. Over a two-day period, whites retaliated by killing over 200 blacks. Turner eluded his pursuers for nearly three months. When he was captured, Turner was tried for "conspiring to rebel and making insurrection" and hanged. See "Slavery & Rebellion in Nat Turner's Virginia," Making History: Transcribe, Library of Virginia, http://virginiamemory .com/transcribe/collections/show/68; and "Nat Turner: A Troublesome Property," Independent Lens, http://www.pbs.org/independentlens/natturner/nat.html.

19. See NCPedia, s.v. "Battle, James Smith," by Elizabeth D. Battle, http://www .ncpedia.org/biography/battle-james-smith; and NCPedia, s.v. "Gaston, William," by Charles H. Bowman Jr., http://www.ncpedia.org/biography/gaston-william.

20. James M. McPherson, *The Struggle for Equality: Abolitionists and the Negro in the Civil War and Reconstruction* (Princeton, N.J.: Princeton University Press, 1964), 83–85. Organized by the Washington Lecture Association, based in Washington, D.C., the controversial series included antislavery advocates such as the poet and philosopher Ralph Waldo Emerson, author Henry Ward Beecher, and newspaper editor and politician Horace Greeley. Organizers had been allowed to use the hall on the condition that their presentations exclude "any subject connected with sectarianism, *discussions in Congress* and the political questions of the day." (Italics in the original.) Incensed that the Washington Lecture Association had ignored the directives for the

use of the hall, first Smithsonian secretary Joseph Henry blocked Frederick Douglass's inclusion among the series lecturers. The Smithsonian's terms for engagement are found in "Smithsonian Annual Report for 1857," *National Intelligencer*, December 12, 1861, 36, as quoted in "Joseph Henry: A Life in Science," Smithsonian Institution Archives, http://siarchives.si.edu/history/jhp/notes03.html.

21. Senator Charles Sumner, a leading Radical Republican, warned John Jay II, a Free Soil Party member and New York Republican Party co-organizer, that abolitionists should change their tactics and no longer insist that the war was being fought for the purpose of freeing the slaves. The more politic strategy, in Sumner's view, was to argue that arming black soldiers was a "military necessity." See McPherson, *Struggle*, 90.

22. See Francis Jackson Garrison, *William Lloyd Garrison, 1805–1879: The Story of His Life Told by His Children, 1861–1879*, vol. 4 (Boston: Houghton Mifflin, 1889), http://www.perseus.tufts.edu/hopper/text?doc=Perseus%3Atext%3A2001.05.0205%3A chapter%3D1%3Apage%3D35.

23. Metcalf, "Lincoln's Attitude," 152–53. See also "The District of Columbia Emancipation Act," America's Historical Documents, National Archives, https://www .archives.gov/historical-docs/dc-emancipation-act. In order to receive compensation, slaveholders had to provide proof of ownership, pledge loyalty to the Union, and file their claim within ninety days of the act's passage. See also Peter Zavodnyik, *The Rise of the Federal Colossus: The Growth of Federal Power from Lincoln to F.D.R.* (Westport, Conn.: Greenwood Press, 2011), 15.

24. Karl Reiner, *Remembering Fairfax County, Virginia* (Charleston, S.C.: History Press, 2006), 57. Douglass as quoted in "D.C. Emancipation Act, April 1862," Newspaper in Education, http://nie.washingtonpost.com/node/371.

25. Frederick Douglass, "The War and How to End It" (speech, Corinthian Hall, Rochester, N.Y., March 25, 1862), University of Rochester Frederick Douglass Project, http://www.lib.rochester.edu/index.cfm?PAGE=4394.

26. *Douglass' Monthly*, February 1861; *New-York Tribune*, January 19, 1861, as quoted in McPherson, *Struggle*, 40. *Douglass' Monthly*, one of four newspapers produced by Frederick Douglass to promote his antislavery position and other social reforms, was published from 1858 to 1863.

27. John Stauffer, *Giants: The Parallel Lives of Frederick Douglass and Abraham Lincoln* (New York: Twelve, 2008), 262.

28. Using 4 percent for a compound interest calculation, $750 in 1860 would be the equivalent of about $383,000 today.

29. Roger L. Ransom, "The Economics of the Civil War," https://eh.net /encyclopedia/the-economics-of-the-civil-war.

30. For estimates of the financial costs of the Civil War, see "Cost of the American Civil War," Shotgun's Home of the Civil War, https://www.civilwarhome.com /warcosts/html.

31. Peter Lindert and Jeffrey Williamson provide evidence that, apart from the enormous death toll, both north and south—especially the south—suffered immense losses in per capita income due to the Civil War. Peter Lindert and Jeffrey Williamson,

Unequal Gains: American Growth and Inequality Since 1790 (Princeton, N.J.: Princeton University Press, 2017), 142–65.

32. Metcalf, "Lincoln's Attitude," 152.

33. Metcalf, 152–53.

34. Metcalf, 153.

35. If $400 million had been paid to slaveholders at $300 each, the same rate paid to slaveholders in the District of Columbia, the sum would have been sufficient to emancipate approximately 1.33 million enslaved persons.

36. Metcalf, "Lincoln's Attitude," 153. The Hampton Roads Conference, a peace conference, took place on the *River Queen* steamboat in Hampton Roads, Virginia, two months before the war ended. In attendance, representing the Union, were President Abraham Lincoln and Secretary of State William A. Seward. The Confederacy was represented by Vice President Alexander H. Stephens, Senator Robert Mercer Taliaferro Hunter, and Assistant Secretary of War John A. Campbell. Metcalf, 154–55.

37. Sadly, the American black immigrants who settled in Liberia engaged in the worst excesses of settler colonialism themselves. Christina Spicer, "The Perpetual Paradox: A Look into Liberian Colonization," *Corvette* 3, no. 2 (2015–16): 36–52.

38. See Manisha Sinha, "Allies for Emancipation? Black Abolitionists and Abraham Lincoln," *History Now: The Journal of the Gilder Lehrman Institute*, http://www.gilderlehrman.org/history-by-era/african-americans-and-emancipation/essays/allies-for-emancipation-black-abolitionists. Other prominent supporters of the idea of repatriation of free African Americans to Liberia included Thomas Jefferson; Quaker colonization advocate Benjamin Lundy; Kentucky's Henry Clay; Virginia planter and congressman John Randolph, who manumitted over 100 of his slaves upon his death; and James Monroe, the fifth president of the United States, for whom Liberia's capital city, Monrovia, is named.

39. Frances Ellen Watkins Harper, "Mrs. Frances E. Watkins Harper on the President's Colonization Scheme," *Christian Recorder*, September 27, 1862, reprinted in Teresa Zackodnik, ed., *African American Feminisms, 1828–1923*, vol. 6, *Feminist Black Nationalism* (New York: Routledge, 2007), 110. See also Manisha Sinha, "The Other Frances Ellen Watkins Harper," *Common-Place: The Journal of Early American Life* 16, no. 2 (Winter 2016), http://common-place.org/book/the-other-frances-ellen-watkins-harper.

CHAPTER 6

1. Virginia state delegates voted to secede from the Union on April 17, 1861; the electorate concurred May 23, 1861. See Encyclopedia Virginia, s.v. "Virginia Convention of 1861," by Nelson D. Lankford, http://www.encyclopediavirginia.org/Virginia_Constitutional_Convention_of_1861.

Virginians were unequivocally committed to slavery. The state's economy and its way of life depended upon it. During Virginia's state convention of April 1861, when the question of secession was under consideration, a Mr. Holcombe argued that the state shared the south's "manufacturing, mining, agricultural, and commercial interests." Earlier, in January 1861, Virginia state representative D. C. De Jarnette addressed the Virginia House of Representatives, saying, "Where and how stands Virginia? I answer, with the South. Interest, honor, and inclination unite her fate with that of South Carolina, and her sister Southern States." See full text at D. C. De Jarnette, "Secession of South Carolina" (speech, House of Representatives of Virginia, January 10, 1861), Internet Archive, http://www.archive.org/stream/secessionofsouthoodeja /secessionofsouthoodeja_djvu.txt.

2. While the term "contraband" had a much earlier history, in August 1861, acting master William Budd, operator of the gunboat USS *Resolute*, used the term "contrabands of war" in a military record to refer to the new status of American slaves during the Civil War who had sought refuge with the Union army. See "Contraband (American Civil War)— Contraband Term First Used By William Budd," http://www.liquisearch.com/contraband_american_civil_war/contraband _term_first_used_by_william_budd.

3. Butler was an advocate for the rights of blacks and women throughout his political career. During his one-year term (1883–84) as governor of Massachusetts, Butler appointed the state's first black judges—Harvard Law School's first black graduate, George Lewis Ruffin, among them—and he appointed Clarissa "Clara" Harlowe Barton to head the Massachusetts Reformatory for Women. The appointment was the first executive office assigned to a woman. Butler became a "manager" of the impeachment proceedings against Lincoln's successor, Andrew Johnson; chaired the House Committee on Reconstruction; and authored the Civil Rights Act of 1871, known widely as the Ku Klux Klan Act. The act gave broad authority to federal agents to prosecute and dismantle the Klan. Butler also is remembered, notoriously, for allegedly entering into improper financial negotiations with Confederate plantation owners in the midst of the war, for personal profit. See William J. Simmons and Henry McNeal Turner, *Men of Mark: Eminent, Progressive, and Rising* (Cleveland, Ohio: G. M. Rewell, 1887), 740–43; "Clara Barton Chronology 1870–1912," Clara Barton, National Park Service, https://www.nps.gov/clba/learn/kidsyouth/chron3 .htm; and Chester G. Hearn, *When the Devil Came Down to Dixie: Ben Butler in New Orleans* (Baton Rouge: Louisiana State University Press, 1997), 3, 6, http:// books.google.com/books?id=emIg_jQ7Pu8C&printsec=frontcover&dq=Benjamin +Butler:+Civil+War:+Andrew+Butler&hl=en&sa=X&ei=2N8wU_flAomayQGfv4Cg Dw&ved=0CDYQ6AEwAA#v=onepage&q=Benjamin%20Butler%3A%20Civil%20 War%3A%20Andrew%20Butler&f=false.

4. Butler's declaration of the states in rebellion as a "foreign" power was difficult, if not impossible, to reconcile with Lincoln's rationale for deeming secession unconstitutional. From Lincoln's perspective, the southern states could not leave the Union and form a separate nation without congressional approval. Lincoln's justification for the contraband status of the refugees from slavery was premised on the principle of appropriation of any materials, human or otherwise, that could be used to support the rebellion.

5. On July 21, 1861, there were 3,000 casualties on the Union side in the north's crushing defeat at the First Battle of Bull Run (also called Manassas), in Prince William County, Virginia. Although casualties had claimed close to 10 percent of the troops, and nearly 40 percent of the men had sustained wounds, Lincoln still

was not prepared to authorize the arming of black troops. For First Battle of Bull Run casualty figures, see "First Battle of Bull Run," History, April 1, 2011 (updated June 6, 2019), https://www.history.com/topics/american-civil-war/first-battle-of -bull-run.

6. The Union's Western Department consisted of the troops occupying Kentucky, Ohio, Tennessee, Mississippi, Arkansas and the Indian territories west of the state, Nebraska, Colorado, and Dakota. Word of Frémont's actions was leaked to the *New-York Tribune*, edited by abolitionist Sydney Howard Gay, to activate support. See James McPherson, *The Struggle for Equality: Abolitionists and the Negro in the Civil War and Reconstruction* (Princeton, N.J.: Princeton University Press, 1964), 72. Frémont remained critical of Lincoln and ran against him for president in 1864, but rather than risk a victory for the Democratic candidate, Union general George McClellan, Frémont withdrew from the race and endorsed Lincoln eight weeks before the election. Lincoln had blamed the losses during the Virginia Peninsula Campaign on McClellan's caution and inaction and had relieved him of his duties in the fall of 1862. See Shelby Foote, *The Civil War: A Narrative* (New York: Random House, 1974), 3:17–18, 377, 559.

7. For the text of Lincoln's first annual address to Congress see "December 3, 1861: First Annual Message," University of Virginia Miller Center, https://millercenter .org/the-presidency/presidential-speeches/december-3-1861-first-annual-message.

8. In September 1861, members of the American Missionary Association placed their first teacher, Mary Smith Peake, at the former "Little Scotland" plantation near Fort Monroe, a major contraband camp (Elizabeth City County) that would become Hampton University. The organization positioned its publication, *American Missionary*, as a mouthpiece for the abolition of slavery.

9. McPherson, *Struggle*, 90.

10. *Douglass' Monthly*, July, August, September 1861, as quoted in McPherson, *Struggle*, 62–63. Text of the Emancipation Proclamation, January 1, 1863: "And upon this act, sincerely believed to be an act of justice, warranted by the Constitution, upon *military necessity*, I invoke the considerate judgment of mankind, and the gracious favor of Almighty God." (Emphasis added.)

11. See Lincoln, "First Annual Message."

12. McPherson, *Struggle*, 95. Lovejoy, a Congregationalist minister, abolitionist, and Underground Railroad conductor, dedicated his professional career to the antislavery cause after his brother, Elijah Parish Lovejoy, the publisher of an abolitionist newspaper in Illinois, was murdered in 1837 while attempting to protect his printing press from a white supremacist mob. The surviving brother, an 1854 member of the Illinois state legislature, who later served four terms in the U.S. House of Representatives beginning in 1856, pledged himself to the abolitionist cause with these words: "Beside the prostrate body of my murdered brother Elijah while fresh blood was oozing from his perforated breast, on my knees while along with the dead and with God, I vowed never to forsake the cause that was sprinkled with his blood." See "Owen Lovejoy," History Detectives, http://www.pbs.org/opb/historydetectives /feature/owen-lovejoy. Brooklyn, Illinois, is also known as Lovejoy, Illinois, in memory of Elijah Lovejoy.

13. The Department of the South was created for governance purposes as Union army troops occupied parts of Florida, Georgia, and South Carolina. For the text of Hunter's decree, General Order No. 11, see "David Hunter," Fort Pulaski, National Park Service, https://www.nps.gov/fopu/learn/historyculture/david-hunter.htm. On Frederick Douglass's call for arming blacks, see Frederick Douglass, "Fighting Rebels with Only One Hand," *Douglass' Monthly*, September 1861, in *The African American Experience: Black History and Culture through Speeches, Letters, Editorials, Poems, Songs, and Stories*, ed. Kai Wright (New York: Black Dog and Leventhal, 2009), 296–98. Despite intense lobbying from abolitionists and Republicans, huge numbers of white casualties, diminished white enlistment, and a growing consensus that freedmen also should be engaged in the fight for their freedom, it remained illegal for blacks to enlist in the Union army until August 1862.

14. For an illustration of a media account of Maj. Gen. David Hunter and General Orders No. 11 and the president's response see "General Hunter's Order No. 11 Freeing Slaves," *Civil War Harper's Weekly*, May 31, 1862, http://www.sonofthesouth .net/leefoundation/civil-war/1862/may/hunter-frees-slaves-order-11.htm.

15. Susan B. Anthony embarked on an extended lecture tour advocating the imminent end of slavery, and Angelina Grimké Weld collected signatures for her petition, "A Declaration of War on Slavery." McPherson, *Struggle*, 107–18.

16. The Second Confiscation Act, "an Act to Suppress Insurrection, to Punish Treason, and Rebellion," declared that Confederate slaves residing in Union-controlled territories could be appropriated in criminal proceedings if their owners did not surrender to the Union within sixty days of receiving a public warning. Anyone proved to have engaged in acts of rebellion could "suffer death . . . or imprison[ment] for not less than five years and [be] fined not less than ten thousand dollars." For the text of the Second Confiscation Act, see Wikipedia, s.v. "Confiscation Act of 1862," http:// en.wikipedia.org/wiki/Second_Confiscation_Act. See also "Black Soldiers in the U.S. Military during the Civil War," Educator Resources, National Archives, http://www .archives.gov/education/lessons/blacks-civil-war.

17. The states covered by the Emancipation Proclamation were Mississippi, Florida, Alabama, Georgia, Louisiana, Texas, Virginia, Arkansas, Tennessee, North Carolina, and South Carolina; slaveholding states whose jurisdictions were not covered were Missouri, Kentucky, Maryland, and Delaware.

18. McPherson, *Struggle*, 111, 117. The Battle of Antietam took place near Sharpsburg, Maryland, and Antietam Creek on September 17, 1862. During the war, an estimated one out of seven men died of complications from their wounds. At least 1,018 were thought to be missing or captured. See "Antietam: Sharpsburg," American Battlefield Trust, http://www.civilwar.org/battlefields/antietam.html.

There are some historians who believe the Union's ultimate victory was a matter of luck because Gen. Robert E. Lee's detailed battle orders and directives to his officers regarding the strategies they were to employ at Antietam and South Mountain, Virginia, as well as instructions for obtaining much needed supplies from the merchants in Frederick Town, Virginia, known as Special Order 191, were lost and discovered by Union soldiers. Maj. Gen. George McClellan, leader of the Union forces fighting to secure the Potomac, declared, "Here is a paper with which, if I cannot whip Bobby Lee, I will be willing to go home." See "General Robert E. Lee's 'Lost Order,'" American Battlefield Trust, http://www.civilwar.org/education/history/primarysources/lostorder.html; and Stephen W. Sears, *Landscape Turned Red: The Battle of Antietam* (Boston: Houghton Mifflin, 1983), 113.

19. From the early days of the republic, participation in a state-sanctioned militia was often a precondition for bearing arms. Each state specified who among the populace was eligible to participate in a militia. The Enrollment Act of 1863, also known as the Conscription Act of 1863 and the Civil War Military Draft Act, was universal and affected all black men. In the previous century, the measures individual states passed outlining their military recruitment standards varied greatly and were often contradictory, especially in the run-up to the American Revolution. In April 1775, Massachusetts's Provincial Congress made no mention of race or color exclusions when it set out to raise an army of 30,000 male volunteers from Massachusetts, New Hampshire, and Rhode Island. The colony of Rhode Island and Providence Plantations specifically extended the right to serve to blacks. Enslaved and free blacks had served in the state's militia as early as 1778, when they were recruited actively to meet the Continental Congress's quotas. Enslaved blacks who had served honorably "immediately [were] discharged from the service of [their] master or mistress, and [were] absolutely free." See Michael Lee Lanning, *African Americans in the Revolutionary War* (New York: Citadel, 2005), 205. New Hampshire, on the other hand, had excluded "Indians and Negroes" from its militias from 1679 to May 14, 1718, on the grounds that the militia represented the "nation" under arms and those people were not part of that body, and in April 1776, it excluded "Lunaticks, Idiots and Negroes" from its militia on the grounds that they were not citizens of the "United American COLONIES." Maryland initially required all "able-bodied freemen" to enroll in its militia in 1775, then excluded free blacks in 1777. See Robert Selig, "The Revolution's Black Soldiers," American Revolution, http://www.americanrevolution.org/blk.php.

20. For the comment about the severity of the riots, see Kenneth T. Jackson, "Kenneth Jackson Discusses the Colored Orphan Asylum," video, 5:00, Mapping the African American Past, http://maap.columbia.edu/video/25.html. Jackson is a professor of history at Columbia University and editor of *The Encyclopedia of New York City*.

21. Encyclopedia Brittanica s.v. "Horatio Seymour: American Politician," https://www.britannica.com/biography/Horatio-Seymour. For Seymour's July 4, 1863, declaration, see James Dabney McCabe, *The Life and Public Services of Horatio Seymour: Together with a Complete and Authentic Life of Francis Blair, Jr.* (New York: United States Publishing, 1868), 53. Seymour chaired the Democratic National Convention in 1868, became the Democratic Party nominee for president of the United States, and lost to Republican and former Union army general Ulysses S. Grant.

22. See Albon P. Man Jr., "Labor Competition and the New York Draft Riots of 1863," *Journal of Negro History* 36, no. 4 (October 1951): 375–405. Irish immigrant anti-black violence, motivated by the desire to exclude blacks from lines of work and to maintain black subordination, predated the famine. In Philadelphia, in particular,

seven mob uprisings took place between 1834 and 1838. In addition to direct assaults on blacks, the rioters frequently sought to destroy black-owned homes and properties that displayed any evidence of prosperity. See Noel Ignatiev, *How the Irish Became White* (New York: Routledge, 1995), esp. 106–43.

23. Jane E. Dabel, *A Respectable Woman: The Public Roles of African American Women in 19th-Century New York* (New York: New York University Press, 2008), 112–14. For details on New York's longshoremen and their strike history, see Charles Brinton Barnes and Pauline Dorothea Goldmark, *The Longshoremen* (Charleston, S.C.: Nabu Press, 2010), 93–94.

24. Leslie M. Harris, "The New York City Draft Riots of 1863," University of Chicago Press website, https://www.press.uchicago.edu/Misc/Chicago/317749.html &title=The+New+York+City+Draft+Riots+of+1863&desc=, excerpted from Leslie M. Harris, *In the Shadow of Slavery: African Americans in New York City, 1626–1863* (Chicago: University of Chicago Press, 2003).

25. Several historians, citing the absence of an investigation into the circumstances surrounding the New York rampage, believe that the official body count, including the number of black murder victims who were thrown into the river, is exceedingly low. For research that puts the death toll estimate at 500, see Linda Wheeler, "The New York Draft Riots of 1863," *Washington Post*, April 29, 2013, http://www .washingtonpost.com/lifestyle/style/the-new-york-draft-riots-of-1863/2013/04/26 /a1aacf52-a620-11e2-a8e2-5b98cb59187f_story.html; and "Draft Riots 1863 or Rampant New York Racism," Civil War Bummer, February 1, 2019, http://www.civilwar bummer.com/draft-riots-1863-or-rampant-new-york-racism-2. For research that puts the death toll estimate at 1,000, see "Draft Riots Continue to Rock New York City," This Day in History, History, November 13, 2009, http://www.history.com/this-day -in-history/draft-riots-continue-to-rock-new-york-city. Some whites, primarily German Americans, came to the aid of their black neighbors. See Robert C. Kennedy, "On This Day: How to Escape the Draft," HarpWeek, http://www.nytimes.com /learning/general/onthisday/harp/0801.html. See also Harris, "New York City Draft Riots." A "committee of merchants raised money to rebuild damaged property for both blacks and whites" and published a report detailing some of the "varied acts of violence during the riot," which are excerpted in "'His Body Was Left Suspended for Several Hours': The New York Draft Riot of 1863," in Wright, *African American Experience*, 312–14. In addition, see David M. Barnes, *The Draft Riots in New York: July 1863; The Metropolitan Police; Their Services during Riot Week; Their Honorable Record* (New York: Baker and Goodwin, 1863), 5–6, 12.

26. "The Riots on July 13–16," Mr. Lincoln and New York, http://www.mrlincoln andnewyork.org/new-york-politics/the-riots-on-july-13-16.

27. "Riots on July 13–16."

28. William O. Stoddard, *Lincoln's Third Secretary* (New York: Exposition, 1955), 183–85. Harris, *In the Shadow*, 279–88,

29. The COA, perhaps the first such institution in the country, was founded in 1836 by Quakers Mary Murray, Anna Shotwell, and Hannah Shotwell Murray. Dr. James McCune Smith, the country's first licensed black medical doctor, who

was educated in Scotland, became the COA's medical director in 1846. See Encyclopedia of New York City, s.v. "Colored Orphan Asylum," by Mike Sappol, https://virtualny.ashp.cuny.edu/EncyNYC/colored_orphan_asylum.html; and William Seraile, "Historic Harlem on My Mind, Part 2—Harlem's Colored Orphan Asylum," The Harlem Eye: Harlem One Stop, November 14, 2013, http://beatonthestreet harlem.blogspot.com/2013/11/historic-harlem-on-my-mind-part-2.html.

For details about the black child killed at the COA, see Wheeler, "New York Draft Riots."

30. Ultimately, New York City's draft was completed and, although their sentences were shamefully short, sixty-seven indicted rioters were convicted. See Kennedy, "On This Day." See also *Encyclopedia Britannica Online*, s.v. "Draft Riot of 1863," http://www.britannica.com/EBchecked/topic/170724/Draft-Riot-of-1863. John U. Andrews, a "Virginia lawyer and Peace Democrat," was convicted for giving an antidraft speech in front of the draft office and sentenced to "three years hard labor"; see "Court Cases Related to the New York City Draft Riots," Historical Society of the New York Courts, www.nycourts.gov/history/legal-history-new-york/legal-history -eras-04/history-new-york-legal-eras-draft-riot-cases.html.

31. See Kevin McGruder, "Black New York and the Draft Riots," *New York Times*, July 26, 2013, http://opinionator.blogs.nytimes.com/2013/07/26/black-new -york-and-the-draft-riots.

32. For a description of the March 6, 1863, Detroit Draft Riot in response to the Enrollment Act, see Adam Rozen-Wheeler, "Detroit Race Riot (1863)," BlackPast, January 8, 2018, https://www.blackpast.org/african-american-history/detroit-race -riot-1863.

33. Like the July 1863 riot in New York, Boston's riot was sparked by opposition to the Conscription Act and also disproportionately involved the Irish immigrant community. Unlike the New York horror, the crowd's focus did not shift to the city's black residents, and they were not specifically targeted. The Boston protesters' ire was directed at the conscription agents and the local police. "The Boston Draft Riot of 1863," *New England Historical Society*, http://www.newenglandhistoricalsociety .com/boston-draft-riot-1863.

34. One white bounty jumper managed to collect thirty-two separate cash awards before he was caught. See Byron Farwell, *The Encyclopedia of Nineteenth-Century Land Warfare: An Illustrated World View* (New York: W. W. Norton, 2001), 122.

35. In May 1863, Louisiana black soldiers were recruited into the Corps d'Afrique by Philadelphia abolitionist B. Rush Plumly, who would eventually fill five regiments—more than 12,000 men in all. An equally skillful recruiter, Adj. Gen. Lorenzo Thomas traveled widely across the Mississippi Valley and trumpeted the Union cause. He is credited with having recruited more than 76,000 black men over the course of the war, more than 40 percent of the nation's black military force.

36. Higginson, a Massachusetts-born Unitarian minister and the son of merchant, Harvard University trustee, and philanthropist Stephen Higginson, joined the Boston Vigilance Committee. The committee was founded after the passage of the 1850 Fugitive Slave Act to protect runaway enslaved persons from being remanded

to their owners, using violent resistance if necessary. The younger Higginson was also a member of the Secret Committee of Six, which contributed or raised funds for John Brown's Kansas Territory free state antislavery activities and the raid on the federal arsenal at Harpers Ferry.

37. Tubman escaped from slavery in Maryland in 1849. The quote from John Brown can be found in E. Franklin Frazier, *The Negro in the United States* (New York: Macmillan, 1957), 98. For Tubman's work in South Carolina, see Andrew Ward, *The Slaves' War: The Civil War in the Words of Former Slaves* (Boston: Houghton Mifflin, 2008), 216; and "Harriet Tubman: Civil War Spy, Daring Soldier," Liberty Letters, http://www.libertyletters.com/resources/civil-war/harriet-tubman-civil-war-spy.php. See also James McPherson, *The Negro's Civil War: How American Blacks Felt and Acted during the War for the Union* (New York: Vintage Civil War Library, 1993), 58; and Wayne Washington, "Harriet Tubman Work Uncovers South Carolina Site Where Raid Freed 700 Slaves," *Star Democrat* (Easton, Md.), November 6, 2005, https://www.stardem.com/news/harriet-tubman-work-uncovers-south-carolina-site-where-raid-freed/article_2d2363b5-b0a3-50ea-8784-4de9de6d1cb8.html.

38. The Emancipation Proclamation declared that all slaves in the Confederate territories were free. It did not apply to the four Union states where slavery was legal. There also were a number of U.S. territories that were not governed by the proclamation. For the full text of the document, see "The Emancipation Proclamation," Online Exhibits, National Archives, https://www.archives.gov/exhibits/featured-documents/emancipation-proclamation.

39. Andrew quoted in Willie Lee Rose, *Rehearsal for Reconstruction: The Port Royal Experiment* (Indianapolis: Bobbs-Merrill, 1964), 151; italics in the original.

40. See "Letter from George E. Stephens to the New York *Weekly Anglo-African*, March 6, 1864," Civil War Era NC, https://cwnc.omeka.chass.ncsu.edu/items/show/929.

41. Susan-Mary Grant, "Fighting for Freedom: African American Soldiers in the Civil War," in Susan-Mary Grant and Brian Holden Reid, eds., *Themes of the American Civil War: The War Between the States* (New York: Routledge, 2000), 201.

42. Shaw was a member of, first, the Seventh New York National Guard, then the Second Massachusetts Regiment, with which he fought at the Battle of Antietam. He was the second child and only son of Francis George and Sarah Blake (Sturgis) Shaw, who were well-known social reformers, public intellectuals, and founding members of the influential Unitarian Church of the Redeemer (formerly the United Independent Church of Stapleton, Staten Island, New York). Shaw took the command of the Fifty-Fourth Massachusetts at the suggestion of his father. He died leading his regiment at the assault at Fort Wagner in South Carolina on July 18, 1863. A *New York Times* editorial praised the "'gallant negroes' and their 'gallant Col. Shaw.'" A *New York Herald* opinion writer wrote: "I must [give] this regiment credit [for] fighting bravely and well. . . . Even if they were 'darkeys' . . . the Massachusetts negro regiment is evidently made of good stuff." Both editorials are referenced in Glenn David Brasher, "Striking the Blow at Fort Wagner," *New York Times*, July 18, 2013, https://opinionator.blogs.nytimes.com/2013/07/18/striking-the-blow-at-fort-wagner.

43. Differentials in pay and allowances for clothing and other essentials were baked in. The salary for the soldiers of the Fifty-Fourth Massachusetts was ten dollars per month—three of which were deducted to pay for clothing—while their white counterparts received thirteen dollars with no clothing deduction. See "African-American Soldiers during the Civil War," Library of Congress, http://www.loc.gov/teachers/classroommaterials/presentationsandactivities/presentations/timeline/civilwar/aasoldrs.

44. Harriet A. Jacobs, "Colored Refugees in Our Camps," *Liberator* (Boston), April 10, 1863, 60, http://docsouth.unc.edu/fpn/jacobs/support7.html.

45. The New York Society of Friends, established in the eighteenth century, is a community of Quakers. See New England Yearly Meeting of Friends, www.neym.org. The school that Jacobs and her daughter ran served 125 students, youths, and adults. There were no funds to hire any teachers, but Jacobs was fortunate to have the services of the convalescent soldiers who volunteered to teach the students. See Harriet Jacobs to Rev. J. Sella Martin, April 13, 1863, in *The Harriet Jacobs Family Papers*, ed. Jean Fagan Yellin (Chapel Hill: University of North Carolina Press, 2008), 2:478. For details on Jacobs's life and her involvement in the Civil War black relief effort, see William L. Andrews, "Harriet A. Jacobs (Harriet Ann), 1813–1897," Documenting the American South, http://docsouth.unc.edu/fpn/jacobs/bio.html. For details on the contrabands' desire for their children's education and their financial contributions to the Alexandria school, see Harriet Jacobs and Louisa Jacobs, "Letter from Teachers of the Freedmen," *National Anti-Slavery Standard*, April 16, 1864, https://docsouth.unc.edu/fpn/jacobs/support4.html.

46. Ulysses S. Grant, *Memoirs and Selected Letters: Personal Memoirs of U.S. Grant; Selected Letters 1839–1865* (New York: Library of America, 1990), 381; italics in the original. See also Earnest McBride, "The Battle of Milliken's Bend: Black Troops Made the Real Difference," *Jackson Advocate*, 1996, http://lestweforget.hamptonu.edu/page.cfm?uuid=9FEC3F93-EC44-5006-5B4FFBF627F409E2.

47. Benjamin Quarles, *The Negro in the Civil War* (Boston: Little, Brown, 1953), 114. See also Geoffrey C. Ward, *The Civil War: An Illustrated History*, with Ric Burns and Ken Burns (New York: Knopf, 1990), 247–48.

48. Pemberton, a northerner from Philadelphia and a West Point graduate who was married to Virginian Martha Thompson, was a Union officer when the war commenced (two of his brothers also fought for the Union cause), only to switch sides after Virginia seceded from the Union. Pemberton relinquished 2,166 officers and 27,230 men, 172 cannons, and nearly 60,000 muskets to Grant. See Foote, *Civil War*, 2:606–13; and John H. Eicher and David J. Eicher, *Civil War High Commands* (Stanford, Calif.: Stanford University Press, 2001), 423.

49. Milliken's Bend is located in the upper Mississippi Valley, about twelve miles from Vicksburg. Control of the Mississippi River would have enabled the Union to cut off Confederate supplies and troops coming into Texas, west Louisiana, Arkansas, and Missouri, in addition to giving it dominion over the river itself. The June 1863 battle became known as the siege of Vicksburg. The black regiments, which included the Ninth Louisiana Infantry, the Thirteenth Louisiana Infantry, and the

First Mississippi Infantry, fought alongside white troops mustered under the Tenth Illinois Cavalry and the Twenty-Third Iowa Infantry.

50. The black regiment, led by Col. John A. Nelson, included the First Louisiana Native Guard (formerly the Louisiana Native Guard, which comprised *gens de couleur* who previously had served under the Confederacy), the Second Louisiana Native Guard (free men of color of French descent)—both of which had black captains and lieutenants—and the Third Louisiana Native Guard (former slaves), which included both black and white officers. Over 600 casualties were sustained. This was the first regiment with a command that included African American officers. See Gregory J. W. Urwin, review of *The Louisiana Native Guards: The Black Military Experience during the Civil War*, by James G. Hollandsworth, H-Net, January 1996, http://www.h-net.org/reviews/showrev.php?id=252; and Hollandsworth, "The Louisiana Native Guards," USGenWeb Archives, http://files.usgwarchives.net/la/state/military/afriamer/natguard.txt.

51. For the *New York Times* editorial extolling the virtues of black troops, see "Negro Soldiers the Question Settled and Its Consequences," editorial, *New York Times*, June 11, 1863, http://www.nytimes.com/1863/06/11/news/negro-soldiers-the-question-settled-and-its-consequences.html.

A Republican, Banks had served as Speaker of the U.S. House of Representatives from 1856 to 1857 during the Franklin Pierce administration and as governor of Massachusetts from 1858 to 1861.

52. Massachusetts industrialist George Stearns and his wife, Mary Elizabeth Preston, were involved in a range of abolitionist projects that included providing financial support to the Emigrant Aid Company, which was organized to assist the antislavery homesteaders in the Kansas Territory. They were also the primary benefactors of revolutionary freedom fighter John Brown between 1857 and 1859. George Stearns was one of the Secret Committee of Six, wealthy and well-connected reformers who supported the Kansas Territory free state initiative and financed the raid on the federal arsenal at Harpers Ferry. The other members were Thomas Wentworth Higginson, Samuel Gridley Howe, Theodore Parker, Franklin Benjamin Sanborn, and Gerrit Smith. Tapping contacts in the abolitionist community, Stearns and Sanborn raised $48,000, which was used to purchase 200 Sharps rifles for Brown's men. See Evan Carton, *Patriotic Treason: John Brown and the Soul of America* (New York: Free Press, 2006), 13–15, 226–33.

53. Truth's grandson James Caldwell, a nineteen-year-old blacksmith from Battle Creek, Michigan, enlisted in the Fifty-Fourth Massachusetts Regiment on April 17, 1863, as a private, was captured July 16, 1863, and mustered out of the unit May 8, 1865. Over 1,500 black Americans served in the unit from March 1863 to April 1865. See "The 54th Massachusetts Regiment: C to H," National Gallery of Art, http://www.nga.gov/content/ngaweb/Collection/sculpture/fifty-fourth-regiment/fifty-fourth-c-h.html.

Douglass's sons Charles Remond (who was named for the abolitionist Charles Remond) and Lewis Henry enlisted in the Fifty-Fourth Massachusetts Infantry in April 1863. Charles Remond Douglass eventually became first sergeant of the Fifth Massachusetts Cavalry. Lewis Henry Douglass rose to the rank of sergeant major in the Fifty-Fourth Massachusetts and survived a wound during the Battle of Fort Wagner. Disabled by the wound, he was honorably discharged in 1866. See "Black Soldiers in the Civil War: Frederick Douglass' Sons," Educator Resources, National Archives, http://www.archives.gov/education/lessons/blacks-civil-war/douglass -sons.html.

54. For representations of the story of the Fifty-Fourth Massachusetts Regiment, see appendix 4.

55. A *New York Times* article from July 31, 1863, consisted entirely of a letter written from Beaufort, South Carolina, on July 22, 1863, by Edward L. Pierce. A guest of Gen. George Crockett Strong, who led one of the brigades backing Shaw and his men at Fort Wagner, Pierce praised the Fifty-Fourth Massachusetts's valiant efforts, saying, in part, that "they expressed their readiness to meet the enemy again, and they keep asking if Wagner is yet taken. Could any one from the North see these brave fellows as they lie here, their prejudice against them, if he had any, would all pass away." "The Siego [*sic*] of Fort Wagner; CONDUCT OF THE MASSACHUSETTS NEGRO REGIMENT," *New York Times*, July 31, 1863, http://www.nytimes.com/1863/07/31/news/the-siego -of-fort-wagner-conduct-of-the-massachusetts-negro-regiment.html.

56. Early in the assault at Fort Wagner, when the Union color-bearer was shot down, Carney, of Company C, grasped the Fifty-Fourth Massachusetts's flag and carried it across the fort's moat, which was strewn with bodies, sustaining bullet wounds to the head, chest, right arm, and leg in the process. Carney, the first African American to be awarded the Medal of Honor—the highest military recognition presented by the U.S. government—was one of twenty-five blacks who received the commendation for distinguished service during the Civil War. See "The Civil War's Black Soldiers," History E-Library, https://www.nps.gov/parkhistory/online_books /civil_war_series/2/sec1.htm.

57. Lincoln's praise for the black troops is included in a letter he wrote to his friend James C. Conkling. The letter was written to be read at a Union rally in Springfield, Illinois, in Lincoln's absence, on September 3, 1863. See Roy B. Basler, ed., *Collected Works of Abraham Lincoln* (New Brunswick, N.J.: Rutgers University Press, 1953), 1:408–10; and McPherson, *Negro's Civil War*, 212n57. See also "Letter to James C. Conkling," Abraham Lincoln Online, http://www.abrahamlincolnonline.org /lincoln/speeches/conkling.htm.

58. The Militia Act of July 17, 1862, specified the wage differential. McPherson, *Negro's Civil War*, 212. The women among the contraband who sought refuge at headquarters in Washington, D.C., at Duff Green's Row, were paid even less for their labors. As Harriet Jacobs noted, "Single women hire at four dollars a month; a woman with one child, two and a half or three dollars a month." See Harriet Jacobs, "Life among the Contrabands," *Liberator* (Boston), September 5, 1862, https://docsouth .unc.edu/fpn/jacobs/support5.html.

While the Congressional Committee on Pensions, authorized in 1883, could conceive of "no reason why the heirs of colored soldiers should not be put on the same footing as to bounty and pensions as the heirs of white soldiers and many reasons why they should," black veterans struggled to receive "fair and impartial" consideration for their claims with the pension bureau. A number of recent studies have found that "African Americans encountered more outright rejections and smaller pension awards than did whites." Researchers have identified "biased pension examiners and documentation rules that were more difficult for black veterans than white veterans to satisfy." See Larry M. Logue and Peter Blanck, "Benefit of the Doubt: African-American Civil War Veterans and Pensions," *Journal of Interdisciplinary History* 38, no. 3 (Winter 2008): 378–89.

59. In one instance, charges were initially brought against a Second U.S. Colored Cavalry soldier, Pvt. Sylvester Ray, when he complained that his wages were less than those of his white fellow troops. Ray's detachment muster roll, written later that month, specifies that he was to receive the "difference between white and colored soldiers pay due from Dec/63 to Feb 29/64." It is not known whether he actually received what he was owed. "Black Soldiers in the Civil War: Equal Pay," Educator Resources, National Archives, http://www.archives.gov/education/lessons/blacks-civil-war/equal-pay.html.

A significant percentage of the Freedmen's Branch of the Adjutant General's Office (1872–78) records are devoted to claims brought by black veterans and their heirs hoping to collect pensions, bounties, and arrears of pay claims. See "African American Records: Freedmen's Bureau," African American Heritage, National Archives, http://www.archives.gov/research/african-americans/freedmens-bureau.

From June 1874 to June 1875, the Freedmen's Bureau reviewed more than 13,000 inquiries involving black veterans' claims. At least 3,700 claims were settled, at a cost of approximately $390,000; see *Records of the Field Offices of the Freedmen's Branch, Office of the Adjutant General, 1872–1878* (Washington, D.C.: National Archives and Records Administration, 2006), http://www.archives.gov/research/microfilm/m2029.pdf.

60. When Douglass met with the president at the White House to discuss equal compensation for black soldiers, Lincoln cautioned that whites were not ready to accept the change. Douglass expressed his disappointment with Lincoln's views in a speech entitled "Our Work Is Not Done," given at the annual meeting of the American Anti-Slavery Society in Philadelphia, December 3–4, 1863. Douglass urged the society's members to rail against a policy where "black men fighting bravely for this country, are asked to take seven dollars per month, while the Government lays down as a rule or criterion of pay a complexioned one." Brooks D. Simpson, "Frederick Douglass Meets Abraham Lincoln, August 10, 1863," Crossroads, August 11, 2013, http://cwcrossroads.wordpress.com/2013/08/11/frederick-douglass-meets-abraham-lincoln-august-10-1863.

61. The prospect of immediate death upon capture was reduced when the U.S. Department of War made it known that for each Union soldier, black or white, summarily executed, the Union army would do the same with a Confederate prisoner. But black Union soldiers, once captured and stockaded, were treated far worse than white Union soldiers. In particular, they routinely were denied medicine and medical treatment—and therefore had a much greater likelihood of death while being held as prisoners of war. See Thomas J. Ward Jr., "The Plight of the Black P.O.W.," *New*

York Times, August 27, 2013, https://opinionator.blogs.nytimes.com/2013/08/27/the-plight-of-the-black-p-o-w.

62. Foote, *Civil War*, 3:106. Although Forrest was born into a poor family, "received virtually no education and earned money as a rail splitter," his uncle Jonathan Forrest owned a plantation in Hernando, Mississippi, and invited his twentysomething nephew to work with him. A few years later, the younger Forrest purchased his first human chattel. He eventually became the owner of several plantations and, by 1851, established his trade in human flesh with four of his brothers in Memphis. See John Stauffer, *Giants: The Parallel Lives of Frederick Douglass and Abraham Lincoln* (New York: Twelve, 2008), 283; and Samuel W. Mitcham Jr., *Bust Hell Wide Open: The Life of Bedford Forrest* (Washington, D.C.: Regnery, 2016).

63. Andrew Ward, *Slaves' War*, 176–77.

64. Foote, *Civil War*, 3:108–11.

65. Even two sympathetic Forrest biographers do not justify his actions at Fort Pillow. See Eddy W. Davidson and Daniel Foxx, *Nathan Bedford Forrest: In Search of the Enigma* (Gretna, La.: Pelican, 2007).

66. "The Fort Pillow Massacre: Tennessee, April 1864; Achilles Clark to Judith Porter and Henrietta Ray," Gilder Lehrman Institute of American History, https://www.gilderlehrman.org/sites/all/themes/gli/panels/civilwar150/April_2014.pdf. Nathan Bedford Forrest lived long enough to reconstruct himself. After the war he was an active member of the Pulaski, Tennessee, Ku Klux Klan in 1866–67 and may have served as its grand wizard. But in 1875, he was invited to address a gathering of black southerners whose mission was to reconcile hostilities between the races, and he displayed a vastly different attitude toward African Americans. Nevertheless, he did not issue an apology for his actions during the Civil War. The text of his presentation was printed in the *Memphis Daily Appeal*, a Confederate mouthpiece, on July 25, 1875, and read, in part: "I believe that I can exert some influence, and do much to assist the people in strengthening fraternal relations, and shall do all in my power to bring about peace. It has always been my motto to elevate every man—to depress none. (Applause.) I want to elevate you to take positions in law offices, in stores, on farms, and wherever you are capable of going." See Donald R. McClarey, "Nathan Bedford Forrest and Racial Reconciliation," American Catholic, August 6, 2010, https://www.the-american-catholic.com/2010/08/06/nathan-bedford-forrest-and-racial-reconciliation/; and "Death of Gen. Forrest," *New York Times*, October 30, 1877, http://www.nytimes.com/learning/general/onthisday/bday/0713.html.

67. See C. Vann Woodard, *The Burden of Southern History* (Baton Rouge: Louisiana State University Press, 1960), 82.

68. Andrew Ward, *Slaves' War*, 112.

69. Ward, 112. Chaseville is about twelve miles from Jacksonville, Florida, on the south side of the Saint Johns River.

70. Ward, 194–95. The report was written by officer Thomas J. Morgan, colonel of the Fourteenth U.S. Colored Infantry and commander of a brigade of four black regiments that fought in the Battle of Nashville. See McPherson, *Negro's Civil War*, 232–37.

71. McPherson, *Negro's Civil War*, 160. The executive branch of government commands the U.S. Armed Forces.

72. During the Civil War, there were 40,000 black deaths among the U.S. Colored Troops, *more than 20 percent* of the total number who had served. In contrast, about 15 percent of troops in white Union regiments died during the conflict. The black mortality rate was 33 percent higher than the white rate for Union soldiers. See "Civil War Facts," American Battlefield Trust, http://www.civilwar.org/education/history /faq; and "The Civil War by the Numbers," American Experience, http://www.pbs .org/wgbh/americanexperience/features/general-article/death-numbers.

73. Historian David Hacker published the new estimates using newly available digitized census data made available by the Minnesota Population Center; see David Hacker, "A Census-Based Count of the Civil War Dead," *Civil War History* 57, no. 4 (2011): 306–47. The previous estimate relied heavily on muster rolls, pension records, and battlefield records written by military officers that were later tabulated by veterans of the war.

CHAPTER 7

1. Harriet Beecher Stowe, *Dred: A Tale of the Great Dismal Swamp* (1856; repr., Chapel Hill: University of North Carolina Press, 2006), 50. However, not all white abolitionists held the view that ex-slaves would have to be trained for freedom. In 1775, Anthony Benezet—a French-born Huguenot who joined the Religious Society of Friends, or Quakers, and cofounded the nation's first antislavery organization, the Pennsylvania Society for Promoting the Abolition of Slavery and for the Relief of Free Negroes Unlawfully Held in Bondage, in Philadelphia, with Benjamin Franklin and Thomas Paine—saw no need for special "training for freedom." The antislavery organization was incorporated in 1789 as the Pennsylvania Abolition Society. See Richard S. Newman, "The PAS and American Abolitionism: A Century of Activism from the American Revolutionary Era to the Civil War," Historical Society of Pennsylvania, http://hsp.org/history-online/digital-history-projects /pennsylvania-abolition-society-papers/the-pas-and-american-abolitionism -a-century-of-activism-from-the-american-revolutionary-era-to-the-c.

2. For an excellent study of black communal communities, see Jessica Gordon Nembhard, *Collective Courage: A History of African American Cooperative Economic Thought and Practice* (University Park: Pennsylvania State University Press, 2014).

3. During her time at the Northampton commune, Truth changed her name from Isabella Van Wagner to Sojourner Truth. See Nell Irvin Painter, "Representing Truth: Sojourner Truth's Knowing and Becoming," *Journal of American History* 81, no. 2 (September 1994): 461–92.

4. The Northampton Association of Education and Industry community, which was located in present-day Florence, Massachusetts, had been home to some 200 people, white and black. It disbanded in 1846.

5. "Timbuctoo," Adirondack.net, https://www.adirondack.net/history/timbuctoo.

6. Black settlers in the Adirondacks commune "had previously held jobs as cooks, barbers, and domestic workers," not employments that gave them the skills required for "cutting down evergreens, clearing rocks," planting, and harvesting.

As an additional complication, the settlers had difficulty "securing money to pay taxes on the land." Many simply abandoned the commune not long after arrival. See "Timbuctoo."

7. See appendix 5 for more particulars about additional black settlement undertakings.

8. The Nashoba Commune, built on a plan of compensated emancipation—slave owners would be paid to relinquish their human chattel—was home to thirty slaves, some of whom had been given to Wright, while others she had purchased with an inheritance from her father, James Wright, a political radical and prominent linen manufacturer in Dundee, Scotland. Slaves were expected to earn their keep and to purchase their freedom and passage to their eventual homelands in Liberia or Haiti. When the commune closed in 1828 due to ineffective management, controversy over its promotion of interracial cohabitation, and a lack of financial support, Frances Wright freed the slaves and arranged for their transport to Haiti, where slavery had been declared illegal in 1804. See Tennessee Encyclopedia, s.v. "Nashoba," by John Egerton, https://tennesseeencyclopedia.net/entries/nashoba.

9. William H. Pease and Jane Pease, *Black Utopia: Negro Communal Experiments in America* (Madison: State Historical Society of Wisconsin, 1963), 3–6, 38–41.

10. Nembhard, *Collective Courage*, 40–44.

11. Nembhard, 40–44.

12. By 1855, the number of black mutual-aid societies in Philadelphia had increased to 108. Nembhard, 40–44.

13. James McPherson's magisterial *The Struggle for Equality: Abolitionists and the Negro in the Civil War and Reconstruction* (Princeton, N.J.: Princeton University Press, 1964), 178–79, provides the relevant documentation. McPherson's primary sources include *National Anti-Slavery Standard*, July 27, 1861; John Jay to Charles Sumner, January 4, 1862, Sumner Papers, Houghton Library, Harvard University, Cambridge, Massachusetts; and Rev. William J. Potter's passionate plea on behalf of the freedmen in a sermon at New Bedford, Massachusetts, in July 1861.

14. McPherson, *Struggle*, 178–79. The actual jurisdiction of the eventual Freedmen's Bureau was a matter of great controversy. Sumner believed the most important part of the bureau was the provision pertaining to settling the newly freed slaves on confiscated lands. As confiscated lands came under the control of the Treasury Department, Sumner argued, the Freedmen's Bureau should be placed under that same jurisdiction.

15. The administrators to whom the questionnaires were distributed were U.S. Army and Treasury agents in the District of Columbia, Virginia, South Carolina, Arkansas, and Missouri.

16. Julie Roy Jeffrey, *The Great Silent Army of Abolitionism: Ordinary Women in the Movement* (Chapel Hill: University of North Carolina Press, 1998), 214; McPherson, *Struggle*, 178–81.

17. Karen Whitman, "Re-evaluating John Brown's Raid at Harpers Ferry," *West Virginia History* 34, no. 1 (October 1972): 46, http://www.wvculture.org/history/journal_wvh/wvh34-1.html. Robert E. McGlone provides a thoughtful assessment of the claim that John Brown suffered from mental illness, arguing that he probably was

a victim of malaria—and the symptoms of that disease were mistaken for evidence of insanity. See McGlone, "The Madness of John Brown," HistoryNet, http://www.historynet.com/john-brown.

18. Louis A. DeCaro, *"Fire from the Midst of You": A Religious Life of John Brown* (New York: New York University Press, 2002), 237.

19. The biographical information on John Brown reported here has been extracted from Oswald Garrison Villard, *John Brown 1800–1850: A Biography Fifty Years After* (London: Constable, 1910); and David S. Reynolds, *John Brown, Abolitionist: The Man Who Killed Slavery, Sparked the Civil War, and Seeded Civil Rights* (New York: Random House, 2005).

20. "John Brown's Last Speech," *History Is a Weapon*, https://www.historyisaweapon.com/defcon1/johnbrown.html.

21. W. E. B. Du Bois, *Black Reconstruction in America 1860–1880* (1935; repr., New York: Free Press, 1998).

22. Of the confluence of events that produced the general strike, Du Bois (63–64) wrote: "Transforming itself suddenly from a problem of abandoned plantations and slaves captured while being used by the [southern] enemy for military purposes, the movement became a general strike against the slave system on the part of all who could find opportunity. The trickling streams of fugitives swelled to a flood. Once begun, the general strike of black and white went madly and relentlessly on like some great saga."

23. On the incorporation and early years of settlement of Jamestown(e) see "The Records of the Virginia Company of London," Library of Congress, https://www.loc.gov/item/06035006.

24. Virginia had ratified its secession ordinance against the United States on April 17, 1861. Like other Union commanders, Gen. Benjamin Franklin Butler had turned away escaped slaves that sought refuge within his encampment and even returned some to their masters. At the direction of their owner, Shepard Mallory, Frank Baker, and James Townsend had been loaned out in May 1861 to the Confederacy to erect artillery battery at Sewell's Point, Virginia, not far from Norfolk, under the direction of the 115th Virginia Militia, whose battle flag bore the motto "Give me liberty or give me death." When they realized their owner, Col. Charles Mallory, planned to send them to North Carolina, away from their families, to further Confederate aims there, the men resolved to present themselves to the commanding officers at Fort Monroe in hopes of winning their freedom. Their appeal is thought to have been the catalyst that led Lincoln to reverse the existing policy and to grant refugees from slavery safe haven within military fortifications as contrabands of war. For details on the three men, see Adam Goodheart, "How Slavery Really Ended in America," *New York Times Magazine*, April 3, 2011, and Contraband Historical Society, https://contrabandhistoricalsociety.com.

See also notes from Edward L. Pierce, "The Contrabands at Fortress Monroe," *Atlantic Monthly* 8 (November 1861): 626–40.

Brig. Gen. John W. Phelps is said to have played a role in convincing Lincoln of the cruelty and shortsightedness of the military's practice of sending defenseless escaped slaves back to their masters when, in all likelihood, if they were not beaten or killed for their impertinence, they would be put to work aiding the Confederate cause. See Andrew Ward, *The Slaves' War: The Civil War in the Words of Former Slaves* (New York: Houghton Mifflin, 2008), 111.

25. The process of creating breastworks—cutting the trees, preparing the logs, and dragging them to the selected site and constructing reinforcement walls standing breast high, a height calculated to provide cover to soldiers while they fired on the enemy—required tremendous strength and skill.

26. For these and other observations of blacks' treatment at Fort Monroe, see Ward, *Slaves' War*, 185.

27. Joelle Jackson, "Port Royal Experiment (1862–1865)," BlackPast, June 23, 2011, https://www.blackpast.org/african-american-history/port-royal-experiment -1862-1865.

28. As quoted in Adam Goodheart, "How Slavery Really Ended."

29. Confident that the south had a surefire weapon that would protect it from northern incursions, Senator James Henry Hammond (D-S.C.), an unreconstructed slavery advocate who, together with his wife, Catherine Fitzsimmons, at one time owned over twenty-two square miles of land that included several houses and plantations and enslaved more than 300 people, proudly declared to the U.S. Senate in March 1858, in his speech "On the Admission of Kansas, Under the [Proslavery] Lecompton Constitution": "Would any sane nation make war on cotton? Without firing a gun, without drawing a sword, should they make war on us, we could bring the whole world to our feet. . . . What would happen if no cotton was furnished for three years? . . . England would topple headlong and carry the whole civilized world with her to save the South. No, you dare not to make war on cotton. No power on the earth dares to make war upon it. *Cotton is King.*" James Hammond, "Cotton is King," Teaching American History, http://teachingamericanhistory.org/library/document /cotton-is-king; emphasis added.

30. Edward L. Pierce, "The Negroes at Port Royal: Report of E. L. Pierce, Government Agent, to the Hon. Salmon P. Chase, Secretary of the Treasury," 1862, Wikisource, http://en.wikisource.org/wiki/The_Negroes_at_Port_Royal:_Report _of_E._L._Pierce,_Government_Agent,_to_the_Hon._Salmon_P._Chase,_Secretary _of_the_Treasury.

31. In 1860, the seven U.S. counties with black population ratios higher than that of Beaufort, South Carolina, were located in South Carolina (Georgetown County), Mississippi (Bolivar, Washington, and Issequena Counties), and Louisiana (Madison, Tensas, and Concordia Counties).

32. Cotton was "experimentally undertaken" in South Carolina as early as 1733 as an ornamental garden plant. Negligible amounts were produced in North America until 1784, when eight bags of the fibrous plant were seized in Liverpool. By 1786, the blossoming of the "culture of cotton" prompted James Madison to declare in a speech at the Meeting of Commissioners to Remedy Defects in the Federal Government, which met in Annapolis, Maryland, that "there was no reason to doubt the United States would one day become a great cotton growing country." Robert

Iacobacci, *Fabric of a Nation* (Morrisville, N.C.: Lulu Press, 2019), 123. Also see "The Market Revolution," Lumen: Boundless U.S. History, https://courses.lumenlearning .com/boundless-ushistory/chapter/the-market-revolution.

33. Sven Beckert, *Empire of Cotton: A Global History* (New York: Vintage Books, 2014), 102. Elsewhere, even higher estimates of possible levels of cotton processing with the aid of Whitney's cotton gin have been reported: the "labor of one man could clear for market a thousand pounds of cotton instead of the four or six pounds by the usual hand process." By any measure, Whitney's invention was a boon to the cotton industry.

34. Beckert, 117.

35. Pierce addressed a group of about 2,000 blacks in Hilton Head, South Carolina, and reported that he said the following to them:

> Mr. Lincoln, the President or Great Man at Washington, had the whole matter in charge, and was thinking what he could do for them; that the great trouble about doing anything for them was that their masters had always told us, and had made many people believe, that they were lazy, and would not work unless whipped to it; that Mr. Lincoln had sent us down here to see if it was so; that what they did was reported to him, or to men who would tell him; that where I came from all were free, both white and black; that we did not sell children or separate man and wife, but all had to work; that if they were to be free, they would have to work, and would be shut up or deprived of privileges if they did not; that this was a critical hour with them, and if they did not behave well now and respect our agents and appear willing to work, Mr. Lincoln would give up trying to do anything for them, and they must give up all hope for anything better, and their children and grand-children a hundred years hence would be worse off than they had been (Pierce, "Negroes at Port Royal").

36. Pierce.

37. Pierce.

38. *The Freedmen of Port Royal, South Carolina: Official Reports of Edward L. Pierce* (New York: Rebellion Record, 1863), 32.

39. Rations were items provided for the men's subsistence.

40. *Freedmen of Port Royal*, 309.

41. James McPherson, *The Negro's Civil War: How American Blacks Felt and Acted during the War for the Union* (New York: Vintage Civil War Library, 1993), 165–67.

42. Claude F. Oubre, *Forty Acres and a Mule: The Freedmen's Bureau and Black Land Ownership* (Baton Rouge: Louisiana State University Press, 1978), 8.

43. See Pease and Pease, *Black Utopia*, 125.

44. The *National Anti-Slavery Standard* was the official weekly newspaper of the American Anti-Slavery Society, an abolitionist association founded in 1833 by William Lloyd Garrison and Arthur Tappan. The society trained seventy agents and lecturers in 1836 alone and sought audiences across the north for their antislavery message. Lydia Child and her husband, David, established the *Standard* in 1840 and

each spent time editing the paper over its thirty-year run. Lydia Child edited and penned the preface for *Incidents in the Life of a Slave Girl* (1861), the memoir of formerly enslaved North Carolinian Harriet Jacobs, who wrote under the pseudonym Linda Brent. See *Encyclopedia Britannica Online*, s.v. "American Anti-Slavery Society," http://www.britannica.com/topic/American-Anti-Slavery-Society.

45. Willie Lee Rose, *Rehearsal for Reconstruction: The Port Royal Experiment* (Indianapolis: Bobbs-Merrill, 1964), 240.

46. McPherson, *Struggle*, 167.

47. McPherson, 251–53.

48. Jackson, "Port Royal Experiment."

49. Philbrick's reference to the "manufacturing interests of the North" appeared in his letter to the Boston *Daily Advertiser* on July 20, 1864, quoted in Elizabeth Ware Pearson, ed., *Letters from Port Royal: Written at the Time of the Civil War* (Boston: W. B. Clarke, 1906), http://www.gutenberg.org/files/24722/24722-h/24722-h.htm. For his comment about the Sea Islands going to "the negroes and wild hogs," see Philbrick to William Channing Gannett, April 18, 1864, in Pearson.

50. McPherson, *Struggle*, 251.

51. McPherson, 251–53. "Mr. Philbrick has bought in all thirteen plantations [two of the thirteen were merely leased], at an expense of about $7000: three places for R., two for Wells, two for Hull on Ladies [*sic*] Island, six places within five miles of this place." Letter from C.P.W. to unidentified recipient March 14, 1863, in Pearson, *Letters from Port Royal*, 172. C.P.W. is identified as one of the "New Englanders and antislavery people . . . just out of college."

52. Pease and Pease, *Black Utopia*.

53. Oubre, *Forty Acres*, 9; Edward S. Philbrick, letter to the editor, *Evening Post* (Boston), February 24, 1864.

54. Rose, *Rehearsal for Reconstruction*, 294.

55. This is a quotation from a letter published January 1, 1864, in the *Liberator*, the weekly newspaper founded in 1831 in Massachusetts by internationally renowned abolitionist William Lloyd Garrison. The following year, in January 1832, Garrison and Arthur Tappan founded the New England Anti-Slavery Society. By 1834, the *Liberator* had amassed over 2,500 paid subscribers, 75 percent of whom were free blacks. See *Liberator* (Boston), February 5, 1864, Newspapers.com, http://www.newspapers.com/newspage/35042866.

56. This letter from a correspondent in Port Royal, South Carolina, dated February 3, 1864, appears in McPherson, *Struggle*, 246–47.

57. McPherson, 249.

58. McPherson, 249. Formerly a Whig, a Free Soil Party member, and a Democrat, Julian was a delegate to the 1856 Republican National Convention, campaigned on the Republican ticket in 1860, and was elected to the Thirty-Seventh, Thirty-Eighth, Thirty-Ninth, Fortieth, and Forty-First U.S. Congresses, serving from March 1861 to March 1871. In 1862 he pushed to repeal the Fugitive Slave Act, which lost by a vote of 66–51. The measure was repealed two years later.

59. McPherson, 249.

60. Pease and Pease, *Black Utopia*, 125–26.

61. For the report of the Department of the South originating in Beaufort, South Carolina, on May 11, 1862, see "Correspondence 2, 3, 4, 5 on Impressment of Freedmen for 1st South Carolina," May 11, 1862, in *The War of the Rebellion: A Compilation of the Official Records of the Union and Confederate Armies* (Washington, D.C.: Government Printing Office, 1899), ser. 3, 49:50, https://www.loc.gov/item/03003452, and L. D. Phillips to Edward L. Pierce, in *War of the Rebellion*, ser. 3, 49:60.

62. Phillips to Pierce. See also Pierce to Chase No. 1, May 12, 1862, *War of the Rebellion*, ser. 3, 49:60.

63. See Pierce to Hunter No. 6, May 13, 1862, *War of the Rebellion*, ser. 3, 49:60.

64. Saxton's parents were Miranda Wright, a celebrated author and feminist, and Jonathan Ashley Saxton. Rufus Saxton received the Medal of Honor, the country's highest military distinction, for his role as a defender of the Harpers Ferry Federal Arsenal during the Civil War battle that took place there in September 1862. "Rufus Saxton, Awards by Date of Action: Medal of Honor," The Hall of Valor Project, https://valor.militarytimes.com/hero/2818.

65. *Hearings before Joint Committee on Reconstruction*, 39th Cong. (1866) (statement of Rufus Saxton, special agent to the Treasury), http://chnm.gmu.edu/courses/122/carr/saxton.htm. Saxton was asked, "If the Negro is put in possession of all his rights as a man, do you apprehend any danger of insurrection among them?"

66. "Rufus Saxton Argues That Land Should Be Set Aside for Freedpeople," After Slavery: Educator Resources, Lowcountry Digital History Initiative, http://ldhi.library.cofc.edu/exhibits/show/after_slavery_educator/unit_three_documents/document_one.

67. Emancipation League questionnaire respondent Capt. E. W. Hooper voiced this opinion in 1863. See Heather Freud, "A War for Freedom: Slavery and the Emancipation Proclamation," *Oshkosh Scholar*, no. 1 (April 2006): 115–28, http://minds.wisconsin.edu/bitstream/handle/1793/6691/War%20for%20Freedom.pdf.txt; italics in the original.

68. In Britain, the formerly public "commons" were enclosed and declared private property between 1604 and 1801. See Gregory Clark and Anthony Clark, "Common Rights to Land in England," *Journal of Economic History* 61, no. 4 (December 2001): 1009–36.

69. Commission members were Dale Owen, James McKaye, and Samuel Gridley Howe, all committed abolitionists and champions of black civil and political equality. Howe, a physician, was the leader of the Boston Vigilance Committee organized in 1841 to assist and protect runaway slaves and, after the passage of the Fugitive Slave Act of 1850, to actively resist the recapture of escaped slaves, with violence if necessary. In Boston in 1850, Howe, together with Thomas Wentworth Higginson and Theodore Parker, attempted to rescue Anthony Burns, who had been enslaved in Virginia, from confinement. Howe also played a key role in the Emancipation League's 1862 campaign to convince the federal government to make concrete plans for the soon-to-be-liberated enslaved populations. See Eric H. Walther, *The Shattering of the Union: America in the 1850s* (Lanham, Md.: Rowman

and Littlefield, 2004), 47–48. Howe also was one of the Secret Committee of Six, which raised funds for John Brown's antislavery initiatives. Evan Carton, *Patriotic Treason: John Brown and the Soul of America* (New York: Free Press, 2006), 224. See also Tom Colarco, *The Underground Railroad in the Adirondack Region* (New York: MacFarland, 2004), 121.

70. See, for example, the statement of Harry McMillan: "Testimony of a South Carolina Freedman before the American Freedmen's Inquiry Commission (June, 1863)," Freedmen and Southern Society Project, http://www.freedmen.umd.edu /mcmilln.htm and Ward, *Slaves' War*, chap. 7, sec. 3.

71. Congressman Thomas Eliot (R-Mass.), chair of the Committee on Freedmen's Affairs, introduced a bill during the 1862–63 session placing the Freedmen's Bureau under the jurisdiction of the War Department, where it would benefit from the force of the military. Originally called the Bureau of Emancipation, the agency's name was changed to reflect its broader scope—freedmen and all refugees would be eligible for services—a move legislators hoped would broaden its appeal. See "The Freedmen's Bureau," EH.net, https://eh.net/encyclopedia/the-freedmens-bureau.

The measure failed; however, a similar bill, which benefited from the endorsement of President Lincoln and the intense lobbying efforts of abolitionists Levi Coffin, Francis George Shaw, and J. Miller McKim, passed during the subsequent session. Shaw, an early antislavery advocate and eventual president of the Freedmen's Bureau, was the father of Col. Robert G. Shaw, the commander of the black Fifty-Fourth Massachusetts Regiment who was killed in the battle at Fort Wagner. McKim was one of the investors in the *Nation*, an early publication (1865–present) dedicated to the interests of the freedman. The failed bill that Senator Charles Sumner sponsored in support of the Freedmen's Bureau situated the agency within the Treasury Department because, Sumner reasoned, the abandoned and confiscated lands fell under the agency's control.

72. During the March 1863 U.S. Direct Tax Commission land auction, the "aggregate price paid for 64 [houses] . . . was $32,927." The remaining properties, six or so "house-lots," brought $40,000. See Jackson, "Port Royal Experiment."

73. Jackson.

74. Howard was the first and only commissioner of the Freedmen's Bureau. For his comments on the many obstacles to black education, see Oliver O. Howard, *Autobiography of Oliver Otis Howard* (New York: Baker and Taylor, 1908), 2:375. See also Harry G. Robinson III and Hazel Ruth Edwards, *The Long Walk: The Placemaking Legacy of Howard University* (Washington, D.C.: Moorland-Spingarn Research Center, Howard University, 1996); and Robert B. Moore, *Reconstruction: The Promise and Betrayal of Democracy* (New York: CIBC, 1983). W. E. B. Du Bois also detailed the ferocity of white southern resistance to black education in the same period, including documentation of "'official reports from those who have charge of the schools that upon the withdrawal of the military from the parishes of St. Mary and Lafourche the freedmen's school-houses in those parishes were, before night, burnt or pulled down, the schools disbanded, and the teachers frightened away.'" See Du Bois, *Black Reconstruction*, 529–31.

75. The Second Freedman's Bureau Bill read in part:

And be it further enacted, That the President is hereby authorized to reserve from sale or from settlement, under the homestead or pre-emption laws, and to set apart for the use of freedmen and loyal refugees, male or female, unoccupied public lands in Florida, Mississippi, Alabama, Louisiana, and Arkansas, not exceeding in all 3 millions of acres of good land; and the Commissioner, under the direction of the President, shall cause the same from time to time to be allotted and assigned, in parcels not exceeding forty acres each, to the loyal refugees and freedmen, who shall be protected in the use and enjoyment thereof for such term of time and at such annual rent as may be agreed on between the Commissioner and such refugees or freedmen.

76. See Frederick Douglass, "What Shall Be Done with the Slaves If Emancipated?," *Douglass' Monthly*, January 1862, https://www.lib.rochester.edu/index.cfm?PAGE=4386.

CHAPTER 8

1. Of the 241 members of the Twenty-Fifth Congress present for the roll call on the measure on February 4, 1839, 51 percent cast their votes to table the resolution, 18 percent voted to discuss it in the House, and 31 percent abstained. Govtrack, https://www.govtrack.us/congress/votes/25-3/h427.

2. Under Lincoln's 1849 plan, children born to enslaved mothers after January 1, 1850, would be attached to "a tentative system of apprenticeship" and, thereafter, freed from slavery. Harry S. Blakiston, "Lincoln's Emancipation Plan," *Journal of Negro History*, July 1922, 259.

3. See Lee to Madison, April 3, 1790, Birth of the Nation: The First Federal Congress 1789–1791, https://www2.gwu.edu/~ffcp/exhibit/p14/p14_1text.html. Henry Lee III became the ninth governor of Virginia. His son, Robert E. Lee, was born in 1807.

4. Before its relocation to Washington, D.C., in 1800, the federal government had been based in New York City, Philadelphia, and Annapolis, Maryland. Washington, D.C., was formed from land ceded by both Virginia and Maryland. The Residence Act of 1790, or more formally, "an Act for establishing the temporary and permanent seat of the Government of the United States," specified that the laws of Maryland would apply to residents living east of the Potomac River, with Virginia law applying to those to the west. When Congress gained full authority of the District in 1800, it adopted the laws of Maryland for the federal district. Alexandria, Virginia, was part of the land that comprised the District. It was also the site of one of the largest slave-trading companies in the country, Franklin and Armfield, cofounded by Isaac Franklin and John Armfield and operating from 1828 to 1836, which relocated over 1,000 enslaved African Americans annually to their slave markets in New Orleans and Natchez, Mississippi. Keeping slavery legal would be in their best interest. In 1846, Congress approved a petition from Virginia residents to retrocede their land from the District to their home state. One significant consequence of the retrocession was the end of public education for free District blacks. Shuttered for the next

fifteen years, black schools of learning were reopened when the Union army occupied Alexandria.

5. Craig Steven Wilder, *Ebony and Ivy: Race, Slavery and the Troubled History of America's Universities* (New York: Bloomsbury, 2013), 52–53, 86–87, 96–101.

6. See, for example, the remarks of the eventual president of the Confederacy, Jefferson Davis, made in defense of slavery in 1850 while he was a U.S. senator from Mississippi, reproduced in appendix 6.

7. By 1838, the American Anti-Slavery Society's membership had grown to 250,000. See *Encyclopedia Britannica Online*, s.v. "American Anti-Slavery Society," http://www.britannica.com/topic/American-Anti-Slavery-Society. For the full text of the society's manifesto, see William Lloyd Garrison, "Constitution of the American Anti-Slavery Society," Teaching American History, http://teachingamericanhistory .org/library/document/manifesto.

8. See caution poster by Benjamin Franklin Roberts dated April 24, 1851, in "African American Heritage Trail—Benjamin Franklin Roberts," Mount Auburn Cemetery, February 1, 2013, https://mountauburn.org/aaht-roberts; italics in the original.

9. This was not the first law the U.S. Congress passed that affirmed the right of slaveholders to reclaim their escaped slaves. George Washington had signed the Fugitive Slave Act of 1793. The penalty for any citizen that should "harbor or conceal such person after notice that he or she was a fugitive slave from labor" was $500, or about $47,000 today. The 1793 law was unevenly enforced and northern states passed "personal liberty laws," which provided some protection to both resident runaway slaves and free blacks and further diminished the law's effectiveness. In 1842, the U.S. Supreme Court ruled that the federal government must enforce the Fugitive Slave Act of 1793. Between the passage of the initial measure to police the movements of blacks and the law of 1850, some northern states passed laws designed to limit the effectiveness of the federal act, ranging from providing for jury trials upon appeal (Indiana, 1824, and Connecticut, 1828) to providing attorneys for fugitives (New York and Vermont, 1840). Others passed laws making it illegal for state authorities to assist in the capture and return of fugitives. See *Encyclopedia Britannica Online*, s.v. "Personal-liberty laws," http://www.britannica.com/topic /personal-liberty-laws.

10. "'Cornerstone Speech' by Alexander Stephens in Savannah, Georgia, March 21, 1861," Iowa.gov, Iowa Department of Cultural Affairs, https://iowaculture .gov/history/education/educator-resources/primary-source-sets/civil-war /cornerstone-speech-alexander.

11. "Speech of Hon. James H. Hammond, of South Carolina, On the Admission of Kansas, Under the Lecompton Constitution: Delivered in the Senate of the United States, March 4, 1858," Washington, D. C., 1858 [*Often referred to as the 'Cotton is King' Speech*]," American Antiquarian Society Online Resource, https://www.americananti quarian.org/Freedmen/Manuscripts/cottonisking.html.

12. James McPherson, *Battle Cry of Freedom: the Civil War Era* (Oxford: Oxford University Press, 1988), 244.

13. Judah P. Benjamin, "Slavery Protected by the Common Law of the New World" (speech to the U.S. Senate, Washington, D.C., March 11, 1858), https://archive.org

/details/DKC0146; italics in the original. See also Owen Peterson's sympathetic account of Benjamin's orations on the floor of the U.S. Senate, Owen Peterson, "Judah P. Benjamin's Senate Speeches on Slavery and Secession," *Southern Speech Journal* 23, no. 1 (1957): 10–20; and Maury Wiseman, "Judah P. Benjamin and Slavery," *American Jewish Archives Journal* (2007): 107–14, http://americanjewisharchives.org /publications/journal/PDF/2007_59_01_02_wiseman.pdf.

14. Judah P. Benjamin, "You Never Can Subjugate Us" (speech to the U.S. Senate, Washington, D.C., December 31, 1860), Civil War Causes, http://civilwarcauses.org /judah.htm; emphasis added.

15. Quoted in Adam Serwer, "The Myth of the Kindly General Lee," *Atlantic*, June 4, 2017, https://www.theatlantic.com/politics/archive/2017/06/the-myth-of-the -kindly-general-lee/529038. Serwer also provides evidence that Lee was an especially brutal slaveholder who, during the course of the war, permitted his troops to engage in atrocities, including the massacre of black Union soldiers seeking to surrender at the Battle of Crater in 1864 and the abduction of free blacks in Pennsylvania who then were enslaved and taken south. Lee's postwar behavior was sufficiently obdurate that Ulysses Grant observed in 1866 that Lee's posture was "setting an example of forced acquiescence so grudging and pernicious in its effects as to be hardly realized."

16. Serwer ("Myth") informs us that during the postwar period, Lee served as president of Washington College (now Washington and Lee University) until his death in 1870. He did nothing to prohibit students at the college from seizing and raping black schoolgirls in the area or from attempting to lynch blacks.

17. C.S. Const., art. I, § 9, Avalon Project, http://avalon.law.yale.edu/19th_century /csa_csa.asp.

18. Christopher Hamner, "Booth's Reason for Assassination," Teaching History, http://teachinghistory.org/history-content/ask-a-historian/24242.

19. Remorseful Rebels who applied to reclaim their landholdings could gain ownership of that property only if it had not been sold outright by the Direct Tax Commission.

20. See Max Siollun, "Nigeria's Civil War Reconciliation," Nigeria Village Square, January 26, 2009, http://www.nigeriavillagesquare.com/articles/nigerias-civil -war-reconciliation.html; and "The Gowon Regime and the Nigerian Civil War, 1966–1975," Online Nigeria, https://onlinenigeria.com/military/?blurb=677.

21. See William Darity Jr., "From Here to Full Employment," *Review of Black Political Economy* 40, no. 2 (June 2013): 115–20.

22. Douglas A. Blackmon, *Slavery by Another Name: The Re-enslavement of Black Americans from the Civil War to World War II* (New York: Random House, 2008).

23. David Blight, *Race and Reunion: The Civil War in American Memory* (Cambridge, Mass.: Harvard University Press, 2002).

24. Johnson not only wanted blacks kept out of the American polity but at times, expressed the desire that they be removed from the United States altogether. Scott Malcomson has written:

Johnson had himself once been in the servile class, as a tailor's apprentice. He believed that putting the black and white poor on equal footing would enrage the latter, just as it enraged him. For this he blamed blacks, who he saw as representing, in a sense, the white rich. Blacks were the rich man's laboring tool for keeping poor whites down. And rage being something one tends to direct, in practical terms, at the near rather than the far and the defenseless rather than the protected, Johnson the former apprentice, directed a share of his at blacks. The obvious alternative to poor whites' hatred of blacks was an alliance of the two groups against their common class enemy, the rich. This was just what [Frederick] Douglass proposed to Johnson, a channeling of southern class conflict into democratic, nonracial politics. To this, Johnson, an insecure, self-educated ex-apprentice faced with the imposing, self-educated ex-slave, responded, "You touch right upon the point there. There is this conflict, and I suggest emigration" (Scott Malcomson, *One Drop of Blood: The American Misadventure of Race* [New York: Farrar, Straus and Giroux, 2000], 208).

25. Malcomson has observed, "The Northern radicals in Congress believed that the white South would never extend full citizenship, or even something close to it, to black people unless forced to do so. They were probably correct in this assumption." Actually, they *were* correct in this assumption. Malcomson (209, 340) himself acknowledges that "it became clear that the price of peace for the nation was an acceptance that blacks could not be equal to whites."

26. Malcomson, 340; emphasis added.

27. Danielle Allen and Emily Sneff demonstrate that the Webster-Lincoln view that the national government takes primacy over the states—"that the basis of the new government lay in popular sovereignty, not in the sovereignty of the 13 states"— anchored on the content of the Declaration of Independence, was not unprecedented or fabricated from whole cloth. Indeed, it was expressed most strongly by James Wilson, one of the participants at the Constitutional Convention, in 1787. Wilson, one of only six men to sign both the Declaration and the Constitution, perhaps borrowing from Patrick Henry's rhetoric, observed at the convention, "If we mean to establish a national Govt. the states must submit themselves as individuals—the lawful Government must be supreme—either the Genl. or the State Government must be supreme. We must remember the language with wh. we began the Revolution, it was this, Virginia is no more, Massachusetts is no more—we are one in name, let us be one in Truth & Fact." Allen and Sneff discovered a parchment version of the Declaration of Independence at the Sussex County Record Office in Chichester, United Kingdom; they contend that the document probably was commissioned by Wilson "as support for his persistent argument that the new nation rested on the authority of a unitary national people, not a federation of states." See Danielle Allen and Emily Sneff, "Golden Letters: James Wilson, the Declaration of Independence, and the Sussex Declaration," *Georgetown Journal of Law and Public Policy* 17, no.1 (2019): 193–230.

28. It is worth noting that, unlike the conditions that have to be met for the adoption of a constitutional amendment, the U.S. Constitution stipulates that Congress, and Congress alone, has the authority to create new states by establishing them on newly acquired territory or by reconfiguring the boundaries of existing

states. No approval from the states themselves is needed for Congress to alter the number or size of individual states. See Edward L. Rubin, "If the States Had Been Sovereign," *Constitutional Commentary* 16, no. 3 (Winter 1999): 555.

29. See Garry Wills's excellent treatment of these issues in *Lincoln at Gettysburg: The Words That Remade America* (New York: Simon and Schuster, 1992), 121–47. One important consequence of the Union victory was to win the day for the Webster-Lincoln constitutional interpretation. Wills (145) provides the following evocative description of its impact: "Up to the Civil War, 'the United States' was invariably a plural noun: 'The United States are a free country.' After Gettysburg, it became a singular: 'The United States is a free country.' This was the result of a whole mode of thinking Lincoln expressed in his acts as well as his words, making union not a mystical hope but a constitutional reality."

30. "De-Confederatization" is the term we have coined to describe the initiative on the part of the Radical Republicans to eliminate Confederate ideology and practices from post–Civil War America.

31. Excerpt from Stevens's speech delivered September 1, 1862. See Beverly Wilson Palmer and Holly Byers Ochoa, eds., *The Selected Papers of Thaddeus Stevens*, vol. 1, *January 1814–March 1865* (Pittsburgh, Pa.: University of Pittsburgh Press, 1997), 322.

32. For the text of the Ironclad Oath, see "An Act to prescribe an Oath of Office, and for other Purposes," Public Act No. 37-128, 2d Sess., 12 Stat. 502 (July 2, 1862), https://www.loc.gov/law/help/statutes-at-large/37th-congress/session-2/c37s2ch128.pdf.

33. While the term "lustration" was not used in the 1860s, the relevance of the concept to the Radical Republicans' plans for Confederate leadership has been drawn explicitly in George P. Fletcher, *Our Secret Constitution: How Lincoln Redefined American Democracy* (New York: Oxford University Press, 2001), 83–84.

34. When a U.S. president receives a bill during a congressional recess and elects to neither actively veto nor sign the measure, the chief executive is said to have allowed the bill to die by "pocket veto." This is the maneuver Lincoln employed to block the Wade-Davis Bill.

35. Fletcher, *Our Secret Constitution*, 87. See also "Confederate President Jefferson Davis Captured by Union Forces," This Day in History, May 10, 1865, http://www.history.com/this-day-in-history/jefferson-davis-captured. In this instance, the "rump government" was all that formally remained of the Confederate States of America.

36. See David O. Stewart, *Impeached: The Trial of President Andrew Johnson and the Fight for Lincoln's Legacy* (New York: Simon and Schuster, 2009), 17.

37. "Reconstruction: Hon. Thaddeus Stevens on the Great Topic of the Hour; An Address Delivered to the Citizens of Lancaster, September 6, 1865," *New York Times*, September 10, 1865, http://www.nytimes.com/1865/09/10/news/reconstruction-hon-thaddeus-stevens-great-topic-hour-address-delivered-citizens.html. At 4 percent interest, the dollar value of $10,000 in 1865 was approximately $4,198,887 in 2019.

38. "Reconstruction: Hon. Thaddeus Stevens."

39. "Reconstruction: Hon. Thaddeus Stevens."

40. "Reconstruction: Hon. Thaddeus Stevens."

41. "Reconstruction: Hon. Thaddeus Stevens." In the same speech, Stevens offered the following catalog of Confederate atrocities as justification for trials of Rebel leaders:

> This war had its origin in treason without one spark of justice. It was prosecuted before notice of it, by robbing our forts and armories, and our navy-yards; by stealing our money from the mints and depositories, and by surrendering our forts and navies by perjurers who had sworn to support the constitution. In its progress our prisoners, by the authority of the government, were slaughtered in cold blood. Ask Fort Pillow and Fort Wagner. Sixty thousand of our prisoners have been deliberately starved to death because they would not enlist in the rebel armies. The graves at Andersonville have each an accusing tongue. The purpose and avowed object of the enemy "to found an empire whose corner-stone should be slavery," rendered its perpetuity or revival dangerous to human liberty.

42. The unit of forty acres harkened to the Northwest Ordinance of 1787: "Townships were each divided into 36 sections of a mile square (640 acres)." Forty acres was a "quarter-quarter" lot.

43. Sherman was the commander of the Military Division of the Mississippi of the U.S. Army. On January 16, 1865, he issued Special Field Orders No. 15 in Savannah, Georgia, mandating that 400,000 acres of confiscated land were to be divided into forty-acre parcels and redistributed to 18,000 recently emancipated families and other blacks living in the Sea Islands area of South Carolina. The orders were carried out immediately, with contrabands and Port Royal Experiment residents given priority for "peaceable agricultural settlement" on tillable ground. Former human captives living in and around Beaufort and Hilton Head, South Carolina; Savannah, Georgia; and Fernandina Beach, St. Augustine, and Jacksonville, Florida, were to be allowed to settle in their current places of residence. Four months later, on April 14, 1865, President Abraham Lincoln was assassinated, and his vice president, Andrew Johnson, who had long affirmed that his loyalty was to the Union and not to the abolition of slavery, ascended to the presidency. Johnson moved quickly to withdraw all reparations and restore the land the freedmen had improved to its former owners. Although he himself owned slaves, Johnson professed deep hostility toward plantation owners on social-class grounds. Frederick Douglass, the great orator and advocate for full black citizenship, who had himself escaped enslavement, picked up on Johnson's racism toward blacks during Lincoln's second inaugural address. Douglass said that when Lincoln pointed out Vice President Johnson to him, "the first expression which came to his face, and which I think was the true index of [Johnson's] heart, was one of bitter contempt and aversion." Douglass then recalled saying to Mrs. Thomas J. Dorsey, with whom he was standing, "Whatever Andrew Johnson may be, he certainly is no friend of our race." Frederick Douglass, *Life and Times of Frederick Douglass* (London: Forgotten Books, 2018), originally published

1881), 442. In sum, Johnson's disdain for blacks far superseded his disdain for the planter class. Arguably, he was envious of the latter.

44. "Newspaper Account of a Meeting between Black Religious Leaders and Union Military Authorities," Freedmen and Southern Society Project, http://www.history.umd.edu/Freedmen/savmtg.htm.

45. "Newspaper Account of a Meeting."

46. "Newspaper Account of a Meeting."

47. "Newspaper Account of a Meeting."

48. "Newspaper Account of a Meeting."

49. For the text of Sherman's Special Field Orders No. 15, see *The War of the Rebellion: A Compilation of the Official Records of the Union and Confederate Armies* (Washington, D.C.: Government Printing Office, 1895), ser. 1, 48(2):60–62. The distance from Savannah, Georgia, to Charleston, South Carolina, is 107 miles; from Savannah to Jacksonville, Florida, is 139 miles; and the Saint Johns River runs ninety-five miles from its source, near Jacksonville, to Daytona Beach, for a total of 341 miles.

50. This is a new formulation we have calculated based on a reexamination of Special Field Orders No. 15. For an example of the mistaken interpretation of Sherman's orders, see New Georgia Encyclopedia, s.v. "Sherman's Field Order No. 15," by Barton Myers, http://www.georgiaencyclopedia.org/articles/history-archaeology/shermans-field-order-no-15. The error was propagated further in Henry Louis Gates Jr., "The Truth Behind '40 Acres and a Mule,'" African Americans: Many Rivers to Cross, http://www.pbs.org/wnet/african-americans-many-rivers-to-cross/history/the-truth-behind-40-acres-and-a-mule.

51. The Republic of New Afrika and the speculative fiction writer Terry Bisson conceive of this coastal region as the foundation for a separate black nation in the south; see Terry Bisson, *Fire on the Mountain* (1988; repr., Oakland, Calif.: PM Press, 2009). But full execution of Special Field Orders No. 15 would have created a separate black region *within* the United States.

52. A "ghetto" need not be a "slum." All-white communities in the United States—white ghettos—typically are not characterized as economically depressed neighborhoods. If black Americans had comparable levels of wealth to whites, all-black communities would not necessarily be sites of deprivation. The tendency to overemphasize residential segregation rather than asset poverty in and of itself as the source of the black-white wealth gap is characteristic of works like Richard Rothstein's generally admirable *The Color of Law: A Forgotten History of How Our Government Segregated America* (New York: Liveright, 2017).

53. "Counterfeit governments like the Virginia, Louisiana, Tennessee, Mississippi and Arkansas pretenses, will be disregarded by the sober sense of the people." Thaddeus Stevens, "'Reconstruction, September 6, 1865, Lancaster," in *The Selected Papers of Thaddeus Stevens: Vol. 2, April 1865–August 1868*, ed. Beverly Wilson Palmer and Holly Byers Ochoa (Pittsburgh: University of Pittsburgh Press, 1998), 22. When Johnson selected Pierpont as provisional governor in May 1865, an incredulous Stevens wrote to Charles Sumner, "Virginia is recognized. I fear before Congress meets [the president] will have so bedeviled matters as to render them incurable." Hans L. Trefousse, *Andrew Johnson: A Biography* (Norwalk, Conn.: Easton Press, 1989), 216–17.

Predictably, many southern newspapers—the Petersburg, Virginia, *Daily News* among them—were delighted to see that the president was not "likely to stand idle, while black stars were substituted for white in the banner of the Union."

54. Trefousse, *Andrew Johnson*, 217. Article 1, section 5, of the U.S. Constitution states: "Each House shall be the judge of the elections, returns, and qualifications of its own members, and a majority of each shall constitute a quorum to do business, but a smaller number may adjourn from day to day, and may be authorized to compel the attendance of absent members, in each manner, and under such penalties as each House may provide." Consequently, members of the Senate and House of Representatives can refuse to recognize, or even bar outright, the election or appointment of a new representative or senator.

55. Lustration was an important feature of the transitional justice measures adopted in central Eastern Europe vis-à-vis former Communist Party officials after the collapse of the Soviet Union. Elazar Barkan, *The Guilt of Nations: Restitution and Negotiating Historical Injustices* (New York: W. W. Norton, 2000), esp. chap. 6.

56. Dan Malouf, "In 1861 Maryland Almost Annexed Virginia," Greater Washington, March 1, 2016, http://greatergreaterwashington.org/post/29874/in-1861-maryland-almost-annexed-virginia.

57. Malouf.

58. Malouf; italics in the original.

59. Rubin, "If the States," 556–58.

60. Johnson was no friend of the abolition movement, but before his presidency, he appeared to reserve his deepest hatred for the planter class. James McPherson, *The Struggle for Equality: Abolitionists and the Negro in the Civil War and Reconstruction* (Princeton, N.J.: Princeton University Press, 1964), 317.

61. Eric Foner, *Reconstruction: America's Unfinished Revolution* (New York: Harper and Row, 1988), 132.

62. Foner, 114.

63. Trefousse, *Andrew Johnson*, 232.

64. Trefousse, 233.

65. Whitelaw Reid, *After the War: A Southern Tour May 1, 1865 to May 1, 1866* (London: Sampson Low, Son and Marston, 1866), 219–20.

66. Randall M. Miller, "The Freedmen's Bureau and Reconstruction: An Overview," in *The Freedmen's Bureau and Reconstruction: Reconsiderations*, ed. Paul Alan Cimbala and Randall M. Miller (New York: Fordham University Press, 1999), xiii. We preserve the original spelling in Private Holly's statement.

67. Miller, xiii.

68. The man Perry fatally wounded, Turner Bynum, who was the editor of the *Southern Sentinel*, a pro-state sovereignty newspaper in Greenville that was closely aligned with John C. Calhoun, was an ardent nullificationist in 1832. Perry, editor of the pro-Union *Greenville Mountaineer* had challenged Bynum to a duel over the content of one of Bynum's editorials attacking Perry's position. See "Turner Bynum (c1808-c1832)," in "The Line of 1.1.1 William Bynum (c1690–c1760), grandson of John Bynum," Bob's Genealogy Filing Cabinet, 13, http://www.genfiles.com/bynum-files/3-Line-of-William-Bynum-(c1690-c1760).pdf; and "Perry-Bynum

Duel," *Sacramento Daily Union*, October 18, 1897, https://cdnc.ucr.edu/cgi-bin
/cdnc?a=d&d=SDU18971018.2.53.

69. Mississippi did not ratify the Thirteenth Amendment until February 18, 2013.

70. *Journal of the House of Representatives: Eleventh Legislature, State of Texas*
(Austin: Office of the *State Gazette*, 1866), 22, http://www.lrl.state.tx.us/scanned
/govdocs/James%20W%20Throckmorton/1866/IA_Throckmorton_8.9.1866.pdf;
David Minor, "Throckmorton, James Webb," TSHA: Texas State Historical Association,
https://tshaonline.org/handbook/online/articles/fth36.

71. Carl H. Moneyhon, *Republicanism in Reconstruction Texas* (Austin: University of Texas Press, 1980), 49; Richard B. McCaslin, "Great Hanging at Gainesville,"
TSHA: Texas State Historical Association, https://tshaonline.org/handbook/online
/articles/jig01; James Alex Baggett and Joseph G. Dawson III, "Griffin, Charles," TSHA:
Texas Historical Association, https://tshaonline.org/handbook/online/articles
/fgr60.

72. John Townsend Trowbridge, *The South: A Tour of the Battle-Fields and Ruined
Cities* (Hartford, Conn.: L. Stebbins, 1866), 189.

73. Ruth Smalley, *An Interview with Andrew Johnson, Seventeenth President of
the United States* (Johnson City, Tenn.: Overmountain Press, 2003), 70.

74. Smalley, 232.

75. Trefousse, *Andrew Johnson*, 230.

76. The accusation against Johnson was that he had removed Edwin McMasters
Stanton, the secretary of war, from office and selected Brevet Maj. Gen. Lorenzo
Thomas to replace him, in violation of the Tenure of Office Act. The U.S. Constitution
required a two-thirds majority Senate vote for conviction. Johnson avoided conviction by a single vote.

77. Malcomson, *One Drop of Blood*, 209.

78. Foner, *Reconstruction*, 442.

79. Malcomson, *One Drop of Blood*, 209.

80. Foner, *Reconstruction*, 442, 444.

81. For many years the conventional wisdom has had it that Smalls's estimate
was a gross overinflation, but recent scholarship is demonstrating that Smalls's estimate apparently is accurate. See Douglas Egerton, "Terrorized African Americans
Found Their Champion in Robert Smalls," *Smithsonian*, September 2018, https://
www.smithsonianmag.com/history/terrorized-african-americans-champion
-civil-war-hero-robert-smalls-180970031.

CHAPTER 9

1. Again, as noted in chapter 8, Alexander Stephens, vice president of the Confederacy, speaking in Savannah, Georgia, on March 21, 1861, asserted that beliefs
that "rested upon the assumption of the equality of races" were "fundamentally
wrong." The "corner-stone" of the government of the new Confederacy, he continued, "rests upon the great truth that the negro is not equal to the white man; that
slavery—subordination to the superior race—is his natural and normal condition.
This, our new government, is the first, in the history of the world, based upon this
great physical, philosophical, and moral truth." "'Cornerstone Speech' by Alexander

Stephens in Savannah, Georgia, March 21, 1861," Iowa.gov, Iowa Department of Cultural Affairs, https://iowaculture.gov/history/education/educator-resources /primary-source-sets/civil-war/cornerstone-speech-alexander.

2. From "A Declaration of the Immediate Causes Which Induce and Justify the Secession of the State of Mississippi from the Federal Union," approved January 29, 1861, Avalon Project, http://avalon.law.yale.edu/19th_century/csa_missec.asp.

3. The Mississippi River flowed through Arkansas and offered the Union the opportunity to intercept Confederate troops and supplies sent downriver by Missouri. If the Union controlled the state it also would have a strategic advantage over Mississippi and Louisiana and the Indian territories out west. In April 1861, Lincoln demanded that Arkansas send troops to help with the Union war effort. The state's governor, Henry Rector, refused and instead sent troops to retake Fort Smith from Federal control. By May, when the state's constitutional convention met for the second time, fewer than 10 percent of the delegates supported the Union, and the Hempstead Rifles, a volunteer militia company of the Eighth Arkansas Militia Regiment, became Company B, Third Regiment, Arkansas State Troops, and reported to the Confederate States of America. *The War of the Rebellion: A Compilation of the Official Records of the Union and Confederate Armies* (Washington, D.C.: Government Printing Office, 1888), ser. 1, 22(1):468, http://texashistory.unt.edu/ark: /67531/metapth154600/m1/471/?q=Etter.

4. In 1868, Arkansas became the second state to gain readmission to the Union—after Tennessee in 1866—and was closely followed by Louisiana, Florida, North Carolina, South Carolina, and Alabama. Mississippi, Georgia, Texas, and Virginia were not readmitted to the United States of America until 1870.

5. In some ways, it is a misnomer to describe the steps required for the formerly enslaved to acquire full citizenship as "reconstruction." Reconstruction, or as Lincoln referred to it, "re-inauguration of the national authority," implies that a preexisting foundation is being rebuilt. However, the ex-slaves were starting from ground zero. A more apt term might have been "construction."

6. David O. Stewart, *Impeached: The Trial of President Andrew Johnson and the Fight for Lincoln's Legacy* (New York: Simon and Schuster, 2009), 17. Among Stevens's colleagues were Galusha A. Grow (R-Pa.), Speaker of the House from 1861 to 1863, John C. Frémont (R-Calif.), Charles Sumner (R-Mass.), John A. Logan (R-Ill.), Edwin Stanton (R-Ohio), Ulysses S. Grant (R-Ill.), and Benjamin Butler (R-Mass.).

7. Johnson was elected mayor of Greeneville, Tennessee, in 1834, became a state representative in 1835, and was reelected in 1839, after having been defeated for re-election in 1837. He became a state senator in 1841, purchased two slaves—Dolly and Sam—in 1842, was elected as a U.S. representative in 1843 for five consecutive terms, and remained loyal to the Union when the Civil War commenced.

8. Johnson's state and national political history was the following: fifteenth governor of Tennessee, October 17, 1853–November 3, 1857; member of the U.S. House of Representatives from Tennessee's First District, October 17, 1853–November 3, 1857; U.S. senator from Tennessee, October 8, 1857–March 4, 1862, and March 4–July 31, 1875; military governor of Tennessee, March 12, 1862–March 4, 1865; sixteenth vice president of the United States, March 4–April 15, 1865; seventeenth president of the

United States, April 15, 1865–March 4, 1869. See Wikipedia, s.v. "National Union Party (United States)," https://en.wikipedia.org/wiki/National_Union_Party_%28United _States%29; and Wikipedia, s.v. "Robert Jefferson Breckinridge," https://en.wikipedia .org/wiki/Robert_Jefferson_Breckinridge. See also Hans L. Trefousse, *Andrew Johnson: A Biography* (Norwalk, Conn.: Easton Press, 1989), 179–80.

9. The National Union Party was the name the Republican Party coined for the countrywide ticket in the 1864 presidential election to represent its coalition with the "War Democrats," members of the Democratic Party who had been more critical of the Confederacy and had sided with Lincoln after the Civil War began. The party held its national convention in Baltimore, Maryland, June 7–8, 1864.

10. Wikipedia, s.v. "National Union Party (United States)"; Wikipedia, s.v. "Robert Jefferson Breckinridge." See also Trefousse, *Andrew Johnson*, 179–80. There were other times when Johnson's actions caused members of the Republican Party to question his suitability for public office at the highest levels. Vice President Johnson consumed several glasses of whiskey the night preceding Lincoln's second inauguration, and he continued to drink on the morning of the event. He delivered an incoherent speech that prompted Senator Zachariah Chandler (R-Mich.)—a supporter of black civil rights, a financial supporter of the Underground Railroad in Detroit, where he served as mayor 1851–52, and a founder of the Republican Party—to say of the proceedings, "The inauguration went off very well except that the Vice President Elect was too drunk to perform his duties & disgraced himself & the Senate by making a drunken foolish speech. I was never so mortified in my life, had I been able to find a hole I would have dropped through it out of sight." Jonathan R. Allen, "Andrew Johnson Drunk at Lincoln's Second Inaugural," Civil War: Civil War History and Stories, http://www.nellaware.com/blog/andrew-johnson-drunk-at-lincolns -second-inaugural.html.

11. Early in his political career, Johnson had been a member of the Whig Party. In 1839, when the party split over antislavery legislation, Johnson sided against the abolitionists and joined the Democrats, quickly becoming a party favorite. In another ominous sign, he had also considered becoming Stephen A. Douglas's vice-presidential running mate in 1860. See Trefousse, *Andrew Johnson*, 123–24. On the other hand, members of the Republican Party may have been confused, reasonably, by his steadfastness when the "Confederate's most talented cavalry leaders," Nathan Bedford Forrest and John Hunt Morgan, attacked Tennessee throughout Johnson's term as military governor and threatened Nashville itself on several occasions. See Trefousse, 158.

12. James Graham, *Vessels of Rage, Engines of Power: The Secret of Alcoholism* (Lexington: Aculeus Press, 1994), 154.

13. From a speech to Davidson County citizens, March 22, 1862, and a speech at Nashville, July 4, 1862, in McPherson, *Struggle*, 165.

14. Before Lincoln was renominated by the newly formed National Union Party, Johnson was named his running mate, replacing Hannibal Hamlin. For the text of Johnson's speech, see "October 24, 1864: Moses of the Colored Man Speech," Almost Chosen People, https://almostchosenpeople.wordpress.com/2014/10/24 /october-24-1864-moses-of-the-colored-man-speech.

15. Abraham Lincoln, "Last Public Address" (speech, Washington, D.C., April 11, 1865), Abraham Lincoln Online, http://www.abrahamlincolnonline.org/lincoln/speeches/last.htm.

16. Confederate supporters could be reinstated by a two-thirds vote from each house of Congress.

17. Eric Foner, *Reconstruction: America's Unfinished Revolution, 1863–1877* (New York: Harper and Row, 1988), 131–32.

18. The phrase "Lost Cause" originally was deployed to characterize the intentions of the white women and men who campaigned for and raised funds to erect romanticized monuments to the Confederacy during the first quarter of the twentieth century, but it applies equally well to the actions of the late nineteenth-century southern legislatures. See Catherine W. Bishir, "Memorial Observances," *Southern Cultures* 15, no. 2 (Summer 2009): 61–85. In one of many books on the subject, one author redefines the Rebels' efforts as "self-defense [not] treason." Duval Porter, *Lyrics of the Lost Cause* (Danville, Va.: J. T. Townes, 1914), https://archive.org/details/lyricsoflostcaus00port/page/n11. Correcting the Lost Cause narrative about the genesis of the Civil War and the character of Reconstruction was W. E. B. Du Bois's primary objective in writing *Black Reconstruction in America 1860–1880* (1935; repr., New York: Free Press, 1998).

19. Encyclopedia Virginia, s.v. "The Lost Cause," by Caroline E. Janney, https://www.encyclopediavirginia.org/lost_cause_the#start_entry.

20. Bob Neale, "Query: Lost Cause Memorial Plaques," ed. Wayne Homren, *E-sylum: An Electronic Publication of the Numismatic Bibliomania Society* 11, no. 32 (August 10, 2008), https://www.coinbooks.org/esylum_v11n32a10.html. We first saw the poem on display at the Confederate Museum in Charleston, South Carolina.

21. In the same year, following his successful campaign for the American presidency, William McKinley "made a victory tour of the South with a Confederate badge on his lapel." The Confederate flag "became standard decoration in the military." Jedediah Britton-Purdy, "Infinite Frontier," *Nation*, April 1, 2019, https://www.thenation.com/article/greg-grandin-end-of-the-myth-frontier-border-wall-book-review. Indeed, white U.S. troops from the South raised the banner of the Confederacy in Cuba in 1898; at Okinawa, Japan, in June 1945; during the Korean War in the early 1950s; in Vietnam in the early 1970s; and in Iraq in the early twenty-first century. Greg Grandin, "What Was the Confederate Flag Doing in Cuba, Vietnam, and Iraq?," *Nation*, July 17, 2015, https://www.thenation.com/article/what-was-the-confederate-flag-doing-in-cuba-vietnam-and-iraq.

22. Saeed Ahmed, "There Are Certain Moments in US History When Confederate Monuments Go Up," CNN, August 16, 2017, https://www.cnn.com/2017/08/16/us/confederate-monuments-backlash-chart-trnd/index.html. The original documentation was conducted by the Southern Poverty Law Center in 2016.

23. Ethan J. Kytle and Blain Roberts, *Denmark Vesey's Garden: Slavery and Memory in the Cradle of the Confederacy* (New York: New Press, 2018), 130–31.

24. Jacquelyn Dowd Hall, "'You Must Remember This': Autobiography as Social Critique," *Journal of American History* 85, no. 2 (September 1998): 449.

25. Charles Dew, *The Making of a Racist: A Southerner Reflects on Family, History, and the Slave Trade* (Charlottesville: University of Virginia Press, 2016). See also Richard M. Smith, *The Confederate First Reader: Containing Selections in Prose and Poetry, as Reading Exercises for the Younger Children in the Schools and Families of the Confederate States* (Richmond, Va.: G. L. Bidgood, 1864).

26. Bishir, "Memorial Observances," 81.

27. The Freedmen's Bureau's mandate was derived from the report of the American Freedmen's Inquiry Commission, discussed at greater length in chapter 7. For the specifics of the mandate, see "Law Creating the Freedmen's Bureau: An Act to Establish a Bureau for the Relief of Freedmen and Refugees," United States, *Statutes at Large, Treaties, and Proclamations of the United States of America*, vol. 13 (Boston 1866), 507–9, http://www.freedmen.umd.edu/fbact.htm.

28. Claude F. Oubre, *Forty Acres and a Mule: The Freedmen's Bureau and Black Land Ownership* (Baton Rouge: Louisiana State University Press, 1978), 54. See also *Reconstruction: The Second Civil War*, part 2, directed by Llewellyn M. Smith (Boston: WGBH, 2004), American Experience, aired January 12, 2004, on PBS, https://www.youtube.com/watch?v=SoGvRBW9N2w.

29. Oubre, *Forty Acres*, 46–71.

30. Philipp Ager, Leah Platt Boustan, and Katherine Eriksson, "The Intergenerational Effects of a Large Wealth Shock: White Southerners after the Civil War" (Working Paper No. 25700, National Bureau of Economic Research, Cambridge, Mass., March 2019).

31. Law Creating the Freedmen's Bureau, § 4.

32. *Life, Speeches, and Services of Andrew Johnson, Seventeenth President of the United States* (Philadelphia: T. B. Peterson and Brothers, 1865), 118, 120.

33. Confederate officers and owners of estates valued at or about $20,000 could appeal to the president for a pardon.

34. Trefousse, *Andrew Johnson*, 236, citing Eric L. McKitrick, *Andrew Johnson and Reconstruction* (Chicago: University of Chicago Press, 1960), 184, which included an excerpt from the *Cincinnati Enquirer*, September, 30, 1865, in which Johnson's letter to Fletcher is quoted.

35. In his speech to the Senate on December 18, 1865, days before the body was scheduled to recess for several weeks, Andrew Johnson asserted that his efforts to "induc[e] a resumption of the functions of the States comprehended in the inquiry of the Senate" had led "the people of North Carolina, South Carolina, Georgia, Alabama, Mississippi, Louisiana, Arkansas, and Tennessee [to reorganize] their respective State governments" and that they "are yielding obedience to the laws and Government of the United States." He further stated that, in fact, there has been "no official information" from Mississippi but that "in nearly all of [the other seven states] measures have been adopted or are now pending to confer upon freedmen the privileges which are essential to their comfort, protection, and security." For the full text of Johnson's speech, see Edmund G. Ross, *History of the Impeachment of Andrew Johnson, President of the United States, by the House of Representatives, and His Trial by the Senate, for High Crimes and Misdemeanors in Office, 1868* (Santa Fe: New Mexican Printing Company, 1896), chap. 3, https://avalon.law.yale.edu/19th_century/john_chap_03

.asp. Johnson conveniently omitted the states of Florida, Texas, and Virginia, and in fact, at the point that he affirmed that black Americans were being well treated in seven states, none of the eleven former Confederate states where Freedmen's Bureaus were located had produced comprehensive reports on the status of the freedmen. The commissioners Johnson had authorized to investigate the Freedmen's Bureau had not yet submitted their findings, and the agencies in Georgia and North Carolina—the only southern states where blacks could hold a political meeting legally—had not yet held their freedmen's conventions. See James Barrett Steedman and J. S. Fullerton, *The Freedmen's Bureau: Reports of Generals Steedman and Fullerton on the Condition of the Freedmen's Bureau in the Southern States* (Augusta, Ga.: Printed at the office of the *Loyal Georgian*, 1866), https://www.loc.gov/item/92838840; and *Minutes of the Freedmen's Convention, Held in the City of Raleigh, on the 2nd, 3rd, 4th and 5th of October, 1866* (Raleigh, N.C.: Standard Book and Job Office, 1866), http://docsouth.unc.edu/nc/freedmen/freedmen.html. Consequently, any information Johnson had received would not have included the views of the freedmen.

36. Swing Around the Circle was the name given to the ill-advised speaking tour Johnson conducted between August 27 and September 15, 1866, in advance of the midterm elections to garner support for his Reconstruction plan and the political candidates he was backing. At the time, no president had ever taken to the campaign trail to rally the public. Many of Johnson's colleagues thought this an unfortunate precedent that demeaned the office. During the early stages of what would become an eighteen-day, twenty-stop tour that began in Washington, D.C., and moved north to upstate New York, west as far as Indiana, and back south, completing the "circle" in Washington, D.C., Johnson's remarks were well received. In Cleveland, Ohio, however, hecklers attacked the president's Reconstruction plan and shouted him down. Johnson, unable to rise above the fray, lost his composure and yelled back. His lack of decorum triggered a backlash within the Republican Party and among the members of the press. Johnson's public relations ploy had backfired ominously. See Foner, *Reconstruction*, 264–65; and Trefousse, *Andrew Johnson*, 262–66, 270, 318. Edward Baptist's terse and scathing characterization of Johnson casts him as "an alcoholic racist bent on undermining Reconstruction." Edward Baptist, *The Half Has Never Been Told: Slavery and the Making of American Capitalism* (New York: Basic Books, 2014), 407.

37. Shelby Foote, *The Civil War: A Narrative* (New York: Random House, 1974), 3:1031.

38. Johnson's call for the abolition of slavery was not insignificant, however. Historian James Oakes has estimated that only 15 percent of the south's slaves had attained freedom at the time of General Lee's surrender. See Aaron Astor, "When Andrew Johnson Freed His Slaves," *New York Times*, August 9, 2013, https://opinionator.blogs.nytimes.com/2013/08/09/when-andrew-johnson-freed-his-slaves.

39. Trefousse, *Andrew Johnson*, 226–27.

40. This exchange was recorded in an 1865 Freedmen's Bureau report documenting the abuses freedmen were subjected to by recalcitrant whites. See "Statement of Albert Brooks" and "Statement of Wm. Ferguson," in *The African American*

Experience: Black History and Culture through Speeches, Letters, Editorials, Poems, Songs, and Stories, ed. Kai Wright (New York: Black Dog and Levanthal, 2001), 363–64.

41. Philip Henry Sheridan, *Personal Memoirs of P. H. Sheridan: General United States Army*, vol. 2, pt. 5 (New York: Charles L. Webster, 1888), http://www.bookrags.com/ebooks/5858/39.html.

42. Sheridan.

43. Sheridan.

44. Sheridan. For details on Anthony Paul Dostie, see Jeffrey C. Holtz, "Biography of Dostie, Anthony Paul, 1821–1866," USGenWeb Archives, http://files.usgwarchives.net/la/orleans/bios/d-000048.txt.

45. Michael Stolp-Smith, "New Orleans Massacre (1866)," BlackPast, April 7, 2011, https://www.blackpast.org/african-american-history/new-orleans-massacre-1866.

46. Donna L. Dickerson, *The Reconstruction Era: Primary Documents on Events from 1865 to 1877* (Westport, Conn.: Greenwood Press, 2003), 139.

47. Allen W. Trelease, *White Terror: The Ku Klux Klan Conspiracy and Southern Reconstruction* (New York: Harper and Row, 1971), 8.

48. Lorraine Boissineault, "The Deadliest Massacre in Reconstruction-Era Louisiana Happened 150 Years Ago," *Smithsonian*, September 28, 2018, https://www.smithsonianmag.com/history/story-deadliest-massacre-reconstruction-era-louisiana-180970420.

49. Unlike the Ku Klux Klan, which staged its attacks at night, the villainous White Leagues in Louisiana, the Rifle Clubs in Mississippi, and the Red Shirts in South Carolina brazenly executed their crimes in the light of day—frequently in the presence of witnesses. They torched municipal buildings, battered and assassinated Republican officials, and murdered black voters at will. See Bettye Stroud, *The Reconstruction Era (Drama of African American History)*, with Virginia Schomp (Tarrytown, N.Y.: Marshall Cavendish Benchmark, 2007), 63; and Trelease, *White Terror*, 550–51.

50. For a discussion of the membership of the Ku Klux Klan and its activities, see Foner, *Reconstruction*, 432, 426–27. A son born to Emanuel Fortune and his wife, Sarah Jane Fortune, Timothy Thomas Fortune, became the editor of the influential black newspaper the *New York Age* and the cofounder of the National Afro-American League. Thomas Fortune played a key role in the career of a fellow journalist and political activist, the fearless Ida Bell Wells Barnett (frequently remembered as Ida B. Wells). In 1892, after Wells penned an editorial about the lynching of her friend and People's Grocery co-owner Thomas Moss and two others, white terrorists destroyed the printing press and the furnishings of the Memphis *Free Speech and Headlight*, which Wells owned with the Beale Street Baptist Church and its founding publisher, the Reverend Taylor Nightingale. Fortune came to Wells's aid and supported her work documenting the lynching of black Americans. See Foner, 287, 426, 608; "The Lynch Mob's Thread-Bare Lie," in Wright, *African American Experience*, 381–86; and Paula J. Giddings, *Ida, a Sword among Lions: Ida B. Wells and the Campaign against Lynching* (New York: Amistad, 2008), 150, 154–55, 174–87, 210–14.

51. Radical Republican Albion W. Tourgee wrote Senator Joseph Carter Abbott (R-N.C.) on May 24, 1870, to tell him Stephens had been "foully murdered by the Ku-Klux [at the Caswell County, North Carolina] Court House." Tourgee reported that Stephens "had been stabbed five or six times, and then hanged on a hook in the Grand Jury room." Stephens, a champion of black rights who was active in Caswell County politics, had been on record as having said, "3,000 poor ignorant colored Republican voters had stood by [me] and elected [me] at the risk of persecution and starvation, and that [I have] no idea of abandoning them to the Ku-Klux." Tourgee to Abbott, May 24, 1870, Civil War Era NC, https://cwnc.omeka.chass.ncsu.edu/files /original/24708c4c818c4d2b2758fed529146356.pdf.

52. See Douglas Harper, "Exclusion of Free Blacks," Slavery in the North, http:// slavenorth.com/exclusion.htm.

53. In January 1866, the Georgia state legislature elected two U.S. senators— Alexander Stephens and Herschel Johnson, formerly the vice president of and a senator in the Confederacy, respectively.

54. Brooks D. Simpson, "Ulysses S. Grant and the Freedmen's Bureau," in *The Freedmen's Bureau and Reconstruction: Reconsiderations*, ed. Paul Alan Cimbala and Randall M. Miller (New York: Fordham University Press, 1999), 11–12.

55. Hamilton's speech, in which he also informed the state's residents that President Andrew Johnson had appointed him provisional governor of the state of Texas, was delivered in Galveston, Texas, on July 25, 1865, and was published in full in the *New York Times*. See "TEXAS: Proclamation of Provisional Governor Hamilton," *New York Times*, August 9, 1865, http://www.nytimes.com/1865/08/09/news/texas -proclamation-of-provisional-governor-hamilton.html. Texas's 1866 constitutional convention, which was composed of an all-white delegation, refused to ratify the Thirteenth and Fourteenth Amendments, depriving blacks of the right to vote and to hold public office. Freedmen were given the right to protection of their person and property, and they could enter into contracts. Blacks also were granted the right to bring their grievances to court as whites did, and they could present testimony against other blacks. In addition, if the courts deemed it necessary, they also could testify against whites. During the 1868–69 convention, which included ten blacks among its ninety delegates, black suffrage was finally granted and funds were appropriated for the creation of public schools for blacks. In the days before the measure was passed, proponents for and against the black vote made their cases in the media. The *Houston Telegraph* published an open letter "To the Colored Voters" on December 11, 1868, advising blacks to refuse the franchise because it was only a matter of time before their widespread abuse of the privilege would result in its being taken from them. Black convention delegate Charles W. Bryant of Harris County, Texas, a minister and former slave who worked as a Freedmen's Bureau agent, responded in the progressive *Weekly Austin Republican*. "If a free man can live so well in a free country without a voice in the government," Bryant countered, "why not try it yourself for awhile?" Charles W. Bryant, "Good Advice, but We Decline to Take It," *Weekly Austin Republican*, December 23, 1868; for excerpts, see "1860s: The 1868–69 Constitutional Convention," Texas State Library and Archives Commission, https://www .tsl.texas.gov/exhibits/forever/freedom/page6.html.

56. For the narrative written by captain and sub-assistant commander Samuel C. Sloan to Lieutenant Madden asserting that Texas's white supremacists sought to reenslave the freedmen, see Barry A. Crouch, "'To Enslave the Rising Generation': The Freedmen's Bureau and the Texas Black Code," in Cimbala and Miller, *Freedmen's Bureau and Reconstruction*, 261.

57. N.C. Gen. Stat. § 25-1-101 (1866), http://ushistoryscene.com/article/excerpts -north-carolina-black-codes-1866.

58. "(1866) Texas Black Codes," BlackPast, http://www.blackpast.org/primarywest /1866-texas-black-codes.

59. "(1866) Texas Black Codes."

60. Sloan's report appears in his correspondence to Lieutenant Madden, the acting assistant adjutant general, who was then based in Galveston, Texas. See Sloan to Madden, September 7, 1866, Freedmen's Bureau Online, http://www.freedmens bureau.com/texas/millicanoutrages.htm.

Millican, Texas, which is located fifteen miles from present-day Texas A&M University in Bryan Station, had been a training site for 5,000 members of the Confederate army during the Civil War. In 1868, George Brooks, the pastor of the local Methodist church, a Union army veteran, and a Union League organizer, was killed in a race riot that was covered by media outlets around the world. See Christina L. Gray, "Millican, TX," Texas State Historical Association, https://tshaonline.org /handbook/online/articles/hlm71; "A Regular War," *Hickman (Ky.) Courier*, August 15, 1866, https://millican.omeka.net/items/show/184; and "The Galveston News Says That the Body of Brooks," *South-western* (Shreveport, La.), August 19, 1868, https://millican.omeka.net/items/show/186.

61. Oliver Otis Howard, *Autobiography of Oliver Otis Howard, Major General United States Army* (New York: Baker and Taylor, 1907), 2:218, https://archive.org /details/autobiographyofoo2howa.

62. Howard, 2:291–92.

63. Howard, 2:385–86.

64. Colonel Whittlesey was referring to the Morant Bay Rebellion, which took place in Morant Bay, Jamaica, on October 11, 1865. When several hundred black laborers armed with sticks and stones marched to the courthouse to register their displeasure with the prevailing low wages, high poll taxes, and deplorable living conditions, they were attacked by an armed volunteer militia. After seven laborers were gunned down, the protesters burned the government building and several other properties. Clashes lasted for several days and the eventual death toll exceeded 400. See Howard, 2:279.

65. See "An Act concerning Servants and Slaves (1705)," in *The Statutes at Large: Being a Collection of All the Laws of Virginia, From the First Session of the Legislature, in the Year 1619*, ed. William Waller Hening (Richmond, Va.: Printed for the editor at the Franklin Press, 1823), 447–63.

66. "Alabama Slave Code of 1833," http://alabamaslavecode.blogspot.com.

67. See "Alabama Black Code 1866," from Edward McPherson, "Legislation Respecting Freedmen," in *The Political History of the United States of America during the Period of Reconstruction (from April 15, 1865 to July 15, 1870)*, 2nd ed. (Washington,

D.C.: Solomon and Chapman, 1875), 83, https://archive.org/stream/political historo1mcphg00g#page/n50/mode/1up. McPherson was clerk of the U.S. House of Representatives from 1863 to 1875, and he served again in that capacity from 1881 to 1883 and 1889 to 1891.

68. Catherine W. Bishir, *Crafting Lives: African American Artisans in New Bern, North Carolina, 1770–1900* (Chapel Hill: University of North Carolina Press, 2013), 173–74. Bishir is curator of Architectural Special Collections at North Carolina State University.

69. An Act to Establish and Regulate the Domestic Relations of Persons of Color and to Amend the Law in Relation to Paupers and Vagrancy, S.C. Stat. Act No. 4733, § 34 at 274, (1875), http://www.teachingushistory.org/pdfs/BlackCodes_000.pdf.

70. *The Statute-at-Large of South Carolina*, 12:269–85.

71. Douglas A. Blackmon, *Slavery by Another Name: The Re-enslavement of Black Americans from the Civil War to World War II* (New York: Random House, 2008), 62–63.

72. *The Statute-at-Large of South Carolina*, 12:269–85. The price of an artisan's license in South Carolina in 1865 was $100. While this amount may not seem significant to contemporary readers, it was not trivial. At a 4 percent interest rate in today's currency an artisan would pay about $41,908 for the license, a handsome sum.

73. See Act to Establish and Regulate, § 55. The value of $2,200, adjusting for a long-term rate of U.S. inflation, is approximately $61,000, a stunning levy on the head of any individual who deigned to aid a black person in obtaining more lucrative employment.

74. Mississippi Black Codes, *Laws of Mississippi*, 1865, 82, http://web.mit.edu /21h.102/www/Primary%20source%20collections/Reconstruction/Black%20codes .htm. The value of five dollars in 1866, adjusted for inflation alone, now is about seventy-five dollars.

75. See Act to Establish and Regulate, Act No. 4733, § 34 at 274.

76. "(1866) Mississippi Black Codes," BlackPast, chap. 3, sec. 1, https://www .blackpast.org/african-american-history/1866-mississippi-black-codes.

77. Occasionally, fines were levied to pay the "witnesses" to their alleged crimes. See Blackmon, *Slavery by Another Name*, 53–54, 120–21.

78. See Act to Establish and Regulate, § 50.

79. Joe M. Richardson, "Florida Black Codes," *Florida Historical Quarterly* 47, no. 4 (April 1969): 366n5. See also Foner, *Reconstruction*, 200; and Cong. Globe, 39th Cong., 1st Sess., 443 (1866), http://memory.loc.gov/cgi-bin/ampage?collId=llcg&file Name=070/llcg070.db&recNum=548.

80. "(1866) Mississippi Black Codes," chap. 4, sec. 3; emphasis added. At a 4 percent rate of interest, the values of $10 and $100 are about $4,198 and $41,988, respectively, today.

81. See the excerpt of Thomas's congressional testimony at http://chnm.gmu .edu/courses/122/recon/thomas.htm.

82. See Steedman and Fullerton, *Freedmen's Bureau*, 9–13.

83. Steedman and Fullerton, 9–13.

84. Cable was a New Orleans–born journalist turned novelist, whose work featured descriptions of Creoles that were read widely. See Trelease, *White Terror*, xvi.

85. Trelease, xvi.

86. For the text of Johnson's February 19, 1866, veto, see "Veto of the Freedmen's Bureau Bill," Teaching American History, http://teachingamericanhistory.org/library/document/veto-of-the-freedmens-bureau-bill.

87. Second Freedmen's Bureau Bill, Public Act No. 39-200, 2d Sess., 14 Stat. 173 (1865), http://oll.libertyfund.org/titles/frohnen-the-american-nation-primary-sources.

88. "Reconstruction: Hon. Thaddeus Stevens on the Great Topic of the Hour; An Address Delivered to the Citizens of Lancaster [Pennsylvania], September 6, 1865," *New York Times*, September 10, 1865, http://www.nytimes.com/1865/09/10/news/reconstruction-hon-thaddeus-stevens-great-topic-hour-address-delivered-citizens.html.

89. Foner (*Reconstruction*, 273) examines the promises and the deficiencies of the congressional Reconstruction plan.

90. John Pool, as cited in Foner, 272.

91. Harold Holzer and Norton Garfinkle, *A Just and Generous Nation* (New York: Basic Books, 2015), 169.

92. See U.S. Const., art. I, § 2. The compromise that enabled the south's enslaved population to be counted guaranteed the region a larger representative voice. From 1797 until the Civil War, slaveholding states controlled the presidency, the designation of the Speaker of the House of Representatives, and the appointment of the U.S. Supreme Court.

93. The Thirteenth Amendment to the U.S. Constitution was ratified December 6, 1865. Louisiana's Black Codes were approved December 21, 1865. One stipulation of Louisiana's Code Noir read, "We forbid negroes to sell any commodities, provisions, or produce of any kind, without the written permission of their masters, or without wearing their known marks or badges, and any persons purchasing any thing from negroes in violence of this article, shall be sentenced to pay a fine of 1500 livres." See "(1724) Louisiana's Code Noir," art. 15, BlackPast, http://www.blackpast.org/primary/louisianas-code-noir-1724#sthash.S3kCktjP.dpuf. A similar law regarding the policing of freedmen was passed 141 years later, in 1865: "No freedman should sell, barter or exchange any articles of merchandise or traffic within the limits of the town without permission in writing from his employer, the mayor, or president of the police board." See Byne Frances Goodman, "The Black Codes, 1865–1867" (bachelor's thesis, University of Illinois, 1912), https://archive.org/stream/blackcodes18651800good/blackcodes18651800good_djvu.txt.

94. The Memphis riot took place May 1–3, 1866. One of the two white police officers who were killed died of a self-inflicted gunshot wound. Kevin R. Hardwick, "'Your Old Father Abe Lincoln Is Dead and Damned': Black Soldiers and the Memphis Race Riot of 1866," *Journal of Social History* 27, no. 1 (Autumn 1993): 21–123; James G. Ryan, "The Memphis Riots of 1866: Terror in a Black Community during Reconstruction," *Journal of Negro History* 62, no. 3 (1977): 249; Altina L. Waller, "Community, Class, and Race in the Memphis Riot of 1866," *Journal of Social History* 18, no. 2 (1984): 250.

95. Foner, *Reconstruction*, 262–63. Foner's report on the number of casualties in the 1866 New Orleans riot is far below more recent estimates. See Stolp-Smith, "New Orleans Massacre." Wells, a Whig turned Democrat and a Louisiana native, was the rare southern slaveholder who advocated compensated emancipation. He was also an ardent Unionist and a supporter of northern Democrat Stephen A. Douglas for president, positions that ran afoul of Wells's family and political allies. During the Civil War, Wells was arrested by Confederates for his beliefs; in 1864, he was championed by both moderate and Radical Republicans for the position of Louisiana lieutenant governor; and in 1865 he was elected governor. As governor, Wells confounded his party when he reinstated former Confederates to power while simultaneously advocating black suffrage and the elimination of the Black Codes. Not content with their reprieve, the rebels vowed to attack the Louisiana constitutional convention delegates who had declared their intention to enfranchise blacks and to shatter, once and for all, the Radicals' plans to expand black rights. At least thirty blacks and three whites were killed during the July 30, 1866, New Orleans massacre. Gen. Philip Sheridan, commander of the district, held Wells responsible for the violence and the general unrest and removed him from his post in June 1867.

96. Trelease, *White Terror*, 133. Trelease said Dunn recruited 243 white men and 130 blacks to the police force.

97. *Report of the Joint Select Committee to Inquire into the Condition of Affairs in the Late Insurrectionary States*, 42nd Cong., 13:330–31 (1872) (statement of A. M. Merrick, chairman, Board of Registration, Lafayette County, Arkansas), http://onlinebooks.library.upenn.edu/webbin/metabook?id=insurrection1872. For details on the extent and location of Mississippi's Klan activity, see Trelease, *White Terror*, 274–301. That section encompasses chapters 17 and 18, titled "Mississippi, Tennessee, and Kentucky" and "Mississippi: The Campaign against Schools," respectively.

98. Many blacks believed there was good reason to feel hopeful about Grant's election. In 1863, after the Mississippi plantations of Jefferson Davis and his brother Jackson Davis had been captured, formerly enslaved blacks began to develop the 10,000-acre property known at the time as Davis Bend. The following year, under orders from President Lincoln, General Grant authorized the new inhabitants to create an independent community, essentially "a refuge for displaced freedmen." For several years, the community produced profitable cotton harvests. In 1864, as many as "seventy-five freed people working plots of five to one hundred acres showed profits of $500 to $1,000 at season's end." The following year, after diversifying their crops to include vegetables, the families harvested "12,000 bushels of corn" and "1,736 bales of cotton" and reaped profits of $159,200 on earnings of $397,700. While Grant was acting on orders from the president, many Union officers refused to follow similar directives, and some actively subverted the president's plans for the freedmen. As it turned out, blacks' optimism about Grant's election was misplaced. See Michael T. Martin and Marilyn Yaquinto, eds., *Redress for Historical Injustices in the United States: On Reparations for Slavery, Jim Crow, and Their Legacies* (Durham, N.C.: Duke University Press, 2007), 42, 226. The freedmen's profits would be valued at about $4.4 million and their earnings at about $11 million if generated in today's currency.

99. Foner, *Reconstruction*, 337.

100. For a description of contemporary views on Grant's character, see Ronald C. White, *American Ulysses: A Life of Ulysses S. Grant* (New York: Random House, 2016).

101. Trelease, *White Terror*, 131–34. This New Orleans massacre began on September 22, 1868. In 1870, New Orleans's white male population was approximately 32,000 people; membership in the Knights of the White Camelia was approximately 15,000 in 1868. When the local metropolitan police force—operating at a great disadvantage with only 550 men—lost control, Governor Warmoth summoned federal commander Gen. Lovell H. Rousseau, who petitioned Washington and received permission to install Gen. J. B. Steedman as military force commander.

102. For Gibbs's account of the murders at the hands of ex-Confederates that he gave in Jacksonville, Florida, on November 13, 1871, and for a fuller account of Florida's Reconstruction-era Klan activity, see *Report of the Joint Select Committee*, 13:222. Gibbs's testimony was noted in Paul Ortiz's important study *Emancipation Betrayed: The Hidden History of Black Organizing and White Violence in Florida from Reconstruction to the Bloody Election of 1920* (Berkeley: University of California Press, 2005), 11, 24. Ortiz quotes a white Republican official speaking in 1874 about capitalists' motivation in keeping blacks' wages low: "Colored labor is the cheapest, and therefore just the kind suited to the South in its present condition. This fact must have weight also with capitalists, for other things being equal, the returns from investment must increase in proportion to the cheapness of the labor employed." For biographical information about Gibbs, a Philadelphia-born black missionary and Presbyterian minister who moved to Florida in 1867, held the office of secretary of state from 1868 to 1871 and was appointed state superintendent of public instruction in 1872, see Marvin Dunn, *The Beast in Florida: A History of Anti-Black Violence* (Gainesville: University Press of Florida, 2013), 49–52.

103. David C. Cecelski, *The Fire of Freedom: Abraham Galloway and the Slaves' Civil War* (Chapel Hill: University of North Carolina Press, 2012), 206. Cecelski apparently reported the senator's name incorrectly as R. G. Robbins.

104. This report was given to Congress by A. P. Huggins during its investigation of the "Ku-Klux Conspiracy" in July 1871. Huggins was a black former Union officer who held the posts of Monroe County school superintendent and assistant assessor of internal revenue for five Mississippi counties (Monroe, Itawamba, Prentiss, Alcorn, and Tishomingo) at the time of Dupree's assassination. Huggins related the confession of Joseph Davis, a member of the gang that killed Dupree and had turned state's evidence. On February 10, 1871, Huggins testified, "some sixty disguised men took [Dupree] . . . from his bed out into the yard, stripped him of his shirt and drawers, and the clothing he had on, and beat him." Dupree's wife had just given birth to twins, and the couple also had a one-year-old child. The gang took him to remote woods, "some five miles" out from Aberdeen, where they beat him again "until he was nearly dead. . . . They then cut him open from the throat to the straddle, took out all his insides, and then threw his body into McKinley's Creek." Huggins himself suffered a severe beating at the hands of the Ku Klux Klan a month later, in March 1871. See *Report of the Joint Select Committee*, 11:265–68, 270–72. See also Trelease, *White Terror*, 287; and "Jack Dupree, Murder Victim (1871)," in *The Encyclopedia of Unsolved Crimes*, ed. Michael Newton (New York: Infobase, 2009), 112.

105. See Trelease (*White Terror*, 149–74) for details on the Ku Klux Klan's reign of terror during the 1868 presidential election in Arkansas. For his reporting on the terrorists' attacks on blacks in Mississippi, see Trelease, 274–76, 287–88, 299.

106. Foner, *Reconstruction*, 428.

107. For details on the Republican Party and the rise of the White Leagues of Mississippi, see Foner, 558–60.

108. Foner, 558–60. See Zuzanna Wisniewska, "Charles Caldwell (ca. 1831–1875)," BlackPast, https://www.blackpast.org/african-american-history/caldwell-charles-c-1831-1875/ and Steven J. Niven, "Reconstruction-Era Voting Rights Activist Claimed by an Assassin's Bullet," The Root, https://www.theroot.com/reconstruction-era-voting-rights-activist-claimed-by-an-1790858903.

109. Punishment for conviction would have led to a fine of $500–$2,500, imprisonment for six months to six years—possibly under "hard labor"—or both, at the will of the courts. See Enforcement Act of 1871, Public Act No. 17-22, 1st Sess., 42 Stat. 18 (1871), http://legisworks.org/sal/17/stats/STATUTE-17-Pg13.pdf. The first Enforcement Acts was enacted in 1870; two more were enacted in 1871. For a discussion of the political environment that gave rise to the passage of the first Enforcement Act (1870), see E. Franklin Frazier, *The Negro in the United States* (New York: Macmillan, 1957), 135–39.

110. See John Y. Simon, William N. Ferraro, and Aaron M. Lisec, eds., *The Papers of Ulysses S. Grant: 1875* (Carbondale: Southern Illinois University Press, 2003), 26:312.

111. For details on the financial crisis and its consequences for the Freedmen's Bank, see appendix 7.

112. Trelease (*White Terror*, 154) notes that Hinds "was shot and killed from ambush in Monroe County [Arkansas] on October 22 [1868]." See also Foner, *Reconstruction*, 342. The three South Carolina legislators who were assassinated were freeborn minister and former Union army chaplain Benjamin F. Randolph from Orangeburg; Irish immigrant James Martin from Abbeville, who was killed in front of the county courthouse; and Solomon George Washington Dill of Camden. See Julie Saville, *The Work of Reconstruction: From Slave to Wage Laborer in South Carolina, 1860–1870* (Cambridge: Cambridge University Press, 1996), 159; Lerone Bennett Jr., "Black Power, Part VIII: The First White Backlash; Counter-Revolutionary Campaign of Terror in 1870's Doomed Democracy in the South," *Ebony*, December 1966, 50; and Lerone Bennett Jr., "The People's Convention: South Carolina Meeting Was the First Official State Assembly in America with Black Majority," *Ebony*, February 1976, 70.

113. Justin A. Nystrom, "Reconstruction," 64 Parishes, https://64parishes.org/entry/reconstruction.

114. Foner, *Reconstruction*, 561.

CHAPTER 10

1. Ta-Nehisi Coates, "The Case for Reparations," *Atlantic*, June 2014, https://www.theatlantic.com/magazine/archive/2014/06/the-case-for-reparations/361631.

2. William Darity Jr. and Dania Frank, "The Economics of Reparations," *American Economic Review* 93, no. 2 (May 2003): 326–29.

3. Wikipedia, s.v. "Stagville," https://en.wikipedia.org/wiki/Stagville.

4. NCPedia, s.v. "Cameron, Paul Carrington," by Charles Richard Sanders, http://ncpedia.org/biography/cameron-paul-carrington.

5. Justin Loiseau, "Does Your Home Live Up to the American Average?," DailyFinance, June 18, 2014, http://www.dailyfinance.com/on/average-us-home-size-features (article no longer available).

6. Claude Oubre has observed, "During the first thirty-five years of freedom 25 percent of the black farmers in the South acquired land. Since the assistance provided by the [Freedmen's B]ureau only helped to counteract the negative aspects of slavery and in no way altered the prevailing racial attitude, their success represents a personal triumph against overwhelming odds." Claude F. Oubre, *Forty Acres and a Mule: The Freedmen's Bureau and Black Land Ownership* (Baton Rouge: Louisiana State University Press, 1978), 197–98. Tragically, those personal triumphs were reversed, comprehensively, in the subsequent thirty-five years.

7. Leah Douglas, "African American Have Lost Untold Acres of Land Over the Last Century," *Nation*, June 26, 2017, https://www.thenation.com/article/african-americans-have-lost-acres.

8. Antonio Moore, "#BlackWealthMatters: The 5 Largest U.S. Landowners Own More Land Than All of Black America Combined," HuffPost, October 28, 2015, http://www.huffingtonpost.com/antonio-moore/ted-turner-owns-nearly-14_b_8395448.html.

9. Moore.

10. Todd Lewan and Dolores Barclay (Associated Press), "Black Americans' Farmland Taken through Cheating, Intimidation, Even Murder," pt. 1 of "Torn from the Land," Hartford Web Publishing, December 2, 2001, http://www.hartford-hwp.com/archives/45a/393.html.

11. Douglas, "African Americans Have Lost."

12. In addition to interviewing the descendants of affected blacks, the Associated Press team also spoke with "lawyers, title searchers, historians, land archivists and public officials," examined "deeds, mortgages, tax records, estate papers, court proceedings, oil leases and Freedmen's Bureau archives," and obtained Farmers Home Administration records through the Freedom of Information Act. Todd Lewan (Associated Press), "Taking Away the Vote—and a Black Man's Land," pt. 2 of "Torn from the Land," Authentic Voice, https://theauthenticvoice.org/mainstories/tornfromtheland/torn_part4; *Report of the Joint Select Committee to Inquire into the Condition of Affairs in the Late Insurrectionary States*, 42nd Cong. 12:718, 1055 (1872), http://onlinebooks.library.upenn.edu/webbin/metabook?id=insurrection1872.

13. Lewan, "Taking Away the Vote."

14. Lewan; "Historic Sandfield Cemetery," USGenWeb Archives, http://files.usgwarchives.net/ms/lowndes/cemeteries/historicsandfieldcemetery.txt.

15. See *Report of the Joint Select Committee*, 12:718–728 (statement of Robert Gleed, Mississippi politician). The thirteen-volume publication included testimony regarding outrages in North Carolina, South Carolina, Georgia, Alabama, Mississippi, and Florida. South Carolina and Alabama each take up three volumes and over 2,000 pages.

16. *Report of the Joint Select Committee*, 12:724.

17. *Report of the Joint Select Committee*, 12:718–19, 720.

18. *Report of the Joint Select Committee*, 12:720.

19. *Report of the Joint Select Committee*, 12:721.

20. *Report of the Joint Select Committee*, 12:722.

21. *Report of the Joint Select Committee*, 13:222 (statement of Jonathan C. Gibbs).

22. See, e.g., "Defamation of Character and Criminalization of Black People in the United States," TeleSUR, August 18, 2014, https://www.telesurenglish.net/analysis/Deation-of-Character-and-Criminalization-of-Black-People-in-the-US—-20140818-0036.html.

23. *Report of the Joint Select Committee*, 12:1056.

24. Melissa Fussell, "Dead Men Bring No Claims: How Takings Claims Can Provide Redress for Real Property Owning Victims of Jim Crow Race Riots," *William and Mary Law Review*, no. 57 (2015–16): 1915.

25. Fussell, 1915.

26. Jae Jones, "Mississippi: White Men Kill Black Minister and Steal Over 270 Acres of Land," Black Then, August 10, 2016, https://blackthen.com/mississippi-white-men-kill-black-landowner-minister-and-steal-over-270-acres-of-land.

27. For an excellent discussion of coerced black land loss, see esp. Thomas W. Mitchell, Stephen Malpezzi, and Richard K. Green, "Forced Sale Risk: Class, Race and the 'Double Discount,'" *Florida State University Law Review*, no. 37 (2009–10): 589–658.

28. See esp. Ira Katznelson, *When Affirmative Action Was White: An Untold History of Racial Inequality in Twentieth-Century America* (New York: W. W. Norton, 2005); Richard Rothstein, *The Color of Law: A Forgotten History of How Our Government Segregated America* (New York: Liveright, 2017); and Gary Dymski, Jesus Hernandez, and Lisa Mohanty, "Race, Power, and the Subprime Mortgage/Foreclosure Crisis: A Mesoanalysis" (Working Paper No. 669, Levy Economics Institute of Bard College, Annondale-on-Hudson, N.Y., May 2011), http://www.levyinstitute.org/pubs/wp_669.pdf.

29. Josie Spencer Roberts Walls, "The Negro in Meriwether County, Georgia as Reflected in the Meriwether Vindicator, 1873–1910," 1971, p. 18, paper 1166, ETD Collection for Atlanta University Center, Robert W. Woodruff Library, Atlanta, Georgia.

30. Lerone Bennett Jr., "Black Power in Dixie," *Ebony*, July 1962, 90.

31. Bennett, 90.

32. Guy B. Johnson, "Patterns of Race Conflict," in *Race Relations and the Race Problem: A Definition and An Analysis*, ed. Edgar T. Thompson (Durham, N.C.: Duke University Press, 1939), 138.

33. Bennett, "Black Power in Dixie," 90.

34. In his famous study, the historian C. Vann Woodward argued that the regime of legal segregation in the south did not crystallize until the 1890s. Obviously, we think otherwise; we identify the onset of the regime with the adoption of the Black Codes. Regardless of whether the antiblack atrocities associated with the collapse of Reconstruction and the period immediately following are labeled as Jim Crow practices, they certainly produced immense harms for freedmen and merit

inclusion in a bill of particulars for reparations. C. Vann Woodward, *The Strange Career of Jim Crow* (New York: Oxford University Press, 1955).

35. For example, Oregon kept a law on its books excluding blacks from the state from 1843 until 1926. Fortunately, it was enforced relatively weakly. Oregon Encyclopedia, s.v. "Black Exclusion Laws in Oregon," by Greg Nokes, http://oregon encyclopedia.org/articles/exclusion_laws/#.VwDpVUoUXIU.

36. Bryan Stevenson, *Just Mercy: A Story of Justice and Redemption* (New York: Spiegel and Grau, 2014), 59.

37. On the Memphis riot of 1866, see Stephen Ash, *A Massacre in Memphis: The Race Riot That Shook the Nation One Year after the Civil War* (New York: Farrar, Straus and Giroux, 2013). On the massacre of 1873 in Colfax, Louisiana, see LeeAnna Keith, *The Colfax Massacre: The Untold Story of Black Power, White Terror and the End of Reconstruction* (New York: Oxford University Press, 2009); and Charles Lane, *The Day Freedom Died: The Colfax Massacre, the Supreme Court, and the Betrayal of Reconstruction* (New York: Henry Holt, 2008). The Coushatta massacre is documented comprehensively in *Reconstruction: The Second Civil War*, directed by Llewellyn M. Smith (Boston: WGBH, 2004), American Experience, aired January 12, 2004, on PBS; see also "Southern Violence," American Experience, http://www.pbs.org/wgbh /amex/reconstruction/kkk/ps_marston.html. Some estimates put the number of blacks murdered at Coushatta at over 100.

These massacres were motivated by white supremacist desires to root out black political participation, influence, and authority. The Danville riot of 1883 is treated in depth by Jane Dailey in "Deference and Violence in the Postbellum Urban South: Manners and Massacres in Danville, Virginia," *Journal of Southern History* 63, no. 3 (August 1997): 553–90. For Thibodaux, see John DeSantis, *The Thibodaux Massacre: Racial Violence and the 1887 Sugar Cane Strike* (Charleston, S.C.: History Press, 2016). On the Wilmington massacre, see H. Leon Prather, *We Have Taken a City: The Wilmington Racial Massacre and Coup of 1898* (Rutherford, N.J.: Fairleigh Dickinson University Press, 2006); David Cecelski and Timothy B. Tyson, eds., *Democracy Betrayed: The Wilmington Race Riot of 1898 and Its Legacy* (Chapel Hill: University of North Carolina Press, 1998); Sheila Smith McKoy, *When Whites Riot: Writing Race and Violence in American and South African Cultures* (Madison: University of Wisconsin Press, 2001), 31–70; LeRae Umfleet, *A Day of Blood: The 1898 Wilmington Race Riot* (Raleigh: North Carolina Office of Archives and History and the African American Heritage Commission, 2009); Larry Reni Thomas, "A Study of Racial Violence in Wilmington, North Carolina Prior to February 1, 1971" (master's thesis, University of North Carolina at Chapel Hill, 1980); and the excellent documentary film *Wilmington on Fire*, directed by Christopher Everett (Laurinburg, N.C.: Speller Street Films, 2015), 89 min., DVD.

38. South Carolina Encyclopedia, s.v. "Phoenix Riot: November 8, 1898," by Matthew H. Jennings, http://www.scencyclopedia.org/sce/entries/phoenix-riot.

39. Gregory Mixon, *The Atlanta Riot: Race, Class, and Violence in a New South City* (Gainesville: University Press of Florida, 2005).

40. Jan Voogd, *Race, Riots, and Resistance: The Red Summer of 1919* (New York: Peter Lang, 2008); Robert Whitaker, *On the Laps of Gods: The Red Summer of 1919 and the Struggle for Justice That Remade a Nation* (New York: Three Rivers, 2009); Cameron McWhirter, *Red Summer: The Summer of 1919 and the Awakening of Black America* (New York: Henry Holt, 2011).

41. Scott Ellsworth, *Death in a Promised Land: The Tulsa Race Riot of 1921* (Baton Rouge: Louisiana State University Press, 1982); Tim Madigan, *The Burning: Massacre, Destruction, and the Tulsa Riot of 1921* (New York: Thomas Dunne Books, 2001); Alfred L. Brophy, *Reconstructing the Dreamland: The Tulsa Race Riot of 1921, Race, Reparations, and Reconciliation* (New York: Oxford University Press, 2002).

42. Paul Ortiz, *Emancipation Betrayed: The Hidden History of Black Organizing and White Violence in Florida from Reconstruction to the Bloody Election of 1920* (Berkeley: University of California Press, 2005); Marvin Dunn, *The Beast in Florida: A History of Anti-black Violence* (Gainesville: University Press of Florida, 2013).

43. Unconfirmed stories persist that the entire 1,200-man black 364th Infantry Regiment was annihilated at 30,000-man Camp Van Dorn in Mississippi in 1943. Robert Suro and Michael A. Fletcher, "Mississippi Massacre, or Myth? Army Tries to Put to Rest Allegations of 1943 Slaughter of Black Troops," *Washington Post*, December 23, 1999, A4; Geoffrey F. X. O'Connell, "The Mysterious 364th," My CityPaper, May 17–24, 2001, https://mycitypaper.com/articles/051701/cs.coverstory1.shtml; and Geoffrey F. X. O'Connell, "The Mysterious 364th, Part 2," My CityPaper, May 17–24, 2001, https://mycitypaper.com/articles/051701/cs.coverstory2.shtml.

44. See W. H. Harris, "Federal Intervention in Union Discrimination: FEPC and West Coast Shipyards During World War II," *Journal of Labor History*, 22, no. 3 (1981): 325–47; and "White Workers Riot After Black Workers Promoted in Mobile," EJI: A History of Racial Injustice, https://calendar.eji.org/racial-injustice/may/25.

45. See Harvard Sitkoff, "Racial Militancy and Interracial Violence in the Second World War," *Journal of American History* 58, no. 3 (December 1971): 661–81; and Elliott R. Barkan, "Vigilance versus Vigilantism: Race and Ethnicity and the Politics of Housing, 1940–1960," *Journal of Urban History* 12, no. 2 (February 1986): 181–84.

46. Keisha L. Bentley-Edwards, Malik Chase Edwards, Cynthia Neal Spence, William A. Darity Jr., Darrick Hamilton, and Jasson Perez, "How Does It Feel to Be a Problem? The Missing Kerner Commission Report," *Russell Sage Foundation Journal of the Social Sciences* 4, no. 6 (September 2018): 20–40.

47. See *Lynching in America: Confronting the Legacy of Racial Terror* (Montgomery, Ala.: Equal Justice Initiative, 2015), https://eji.org/sites/default/files/lynching-in-america-second-edition-summary.pdf; and Mark Berman, "Even More Black People Were Lynched in the United States Than Previously Thought, Study Finds," *Washington Post*, February 20, 2015, https://www.washingtonpost.com/news/post-nation/wp/2015/02/10/even-more-black-people-were-lynched-in-the-u-s-than-previously-thought-study-finds.

48. Dolores Barclay, Todd Lewan, and Allen G. Breed, "Prosperity Made Blacks a Target for Land Grabs: Specter of Lynching Boosted Lesser Threats," *Los*

Angeles Times, December 9, 2001, http://articles.latimes.com/2001/dec/09/news/mn
-13043.

49. See "Lynchings: By State and Race, 1882–1968," Famous Trials: The Trial of Sheriff Joseph Shipp et al. (website), http://law2.umkc.edu/faculty/projects/ftrials/shipp/lynchingsstate.html; and Douglas Egerton, "Terrorized African Americans Found Their Champion in Robert Smalls," *Smithsonian,* September 2018, https://www.smithsonianmag.com/history/terrorized-african-americans-champion-civil-war-hero-robert-smalls-180970031.

Sociologists Robert DeFina and Lance Hannon provide evidence suggestive of additional long-term consequences of the lynching trail. They find that, at the Metropolitan Statistical Area level, past lynching rates with black victims in the south are associated strongly with current levels of residential segregation. See Robert DeFina and Lance Hannon, "The Legacy of Black Lynching and Contemporary Segregation in the South," *Review of Black Political Economy* 38, no. 2 (June 2011): 165–81. Using superior measures of residential segregation, Lisa Cook, Trevon Logan, and John Parman find an even stronger association between lynchings of blacks and contemporary patterns of residential segregation in the south. See their "Racial Segregation and Southern Lynching," *Social Science History* 42, no. 4 (Winter 2018): 635–75.

50. Jerome Karabel, "Police Killings Surpass the Worst Years of Lynching, Capital Punishment, and a Movement Responds," HuffPost, November 4, 2015, http://www.huffingtonpost.com/jerome-karabel/police-killings-lynchings-capital-punishment_b_8462778.html.

51. Karabel.

CHAPTER 11

1. Rachel L. Swarns, "Insurance Policies on Slaves: New York Life's Complicated Past," *New York Times,* December 18, 2016, https://www.nytimes.com/2016/12/18/us/insurance-policies-on-slaves-new-york-lifes-complicated-past.html. Our estimates of monetary differences in the value assigned to black and white lives was prompted by questions raised by Noel King, now host of National Public Radio's Morning Edition, when the Black Lives Matter movement first came into prominence.

2. For the hospital bed estimates, see Cheryl Lynn Greenberg, *To Ask for an Equal Chance: African Americans in the Great Depression* (Lanham, Md.: Rowman and Littlefield, 2009), 94.

3. For the per pupil expenditure estimates, see Gerald Jaynes and Robin Williams, eds., *A Common Destiny: Blacks and American Society* (Washington, D.C.: National Academy of Sciences, 1989), 58, table 2-1.

4. "32 Cents per Capita for the Education of Negro Children; $15 for White Students," *Liberator* (Los Angeles), April 19, 1912, 1.

5. Ivy Morgan and Ary Amerikaner, *Funding Gaps: An Analysis of School Funding Equity across the U.S. and within Each State* (Washington, D.C.: Education Trust, 2018), https://edtrust.org/resource/funding-gaps-2018.

6. Harold O. Levy, "Discrimination in Gifted Education Must End," *Education Week,* January 4, 2017, https://www.edweek.org/ew/articles/2017/01/04/discrimination-in-gifted-education-must-end.html.

7. Frank Edwards, Michael H. Esposito, and Hedwig Lee, "Risk of Police-Involved Death by Race/Ethnicity and Place, United States, 2012–2018," *American Journal of Public Health* 108, no. 9 (September 2018): 1241–48, https://ajph.aphapublications .org/doi/abs/10.2105/AJPH.2018.304559.

8. Emily Badger, "Why a Housing Scheme Founded in Racism Is Making a Resurgence Today," *Washington Post*, May 13, 2016, http://www.washingtonpost .com/news/wonk/wp2016/05/13/why-a-housing-scheme-founded-in-racism -is-making-a-resurgence-today.

9. Ta-Nehisi Coates, "The Case for Reparations," *Atlantic*, June 2014, https://www .theatlantic.com/magazine/archive/2014/06/the-case-for-reparations/361631. A study conducted by a research team at the Samuel DuBois Cook Center on Social Equity at Duke found that, under the constraints of discriminatory lack of access to federally insured loans, at least 75 percent of home sales to blacks in Chicago in the 1950s and 1960s were made under contract. The study reported that contract selling led to the extraction of $3.2 to $4 billion in wealth from blacks in Chicago transferred to whites. See Samuel George, Amber Hendley, Jack McNamara, Jasson Perez, and Alfonso Vaca-Loco, *The Plunder of Black Wealth in Chicago: New Findings on the Lasting Toll of Predatory Contracts* (Samuel DuBois Cook Center on Social Equity at Duke University, May 2019), https://socialequity.duke.edu/sites/socialequity.duke .edu/files/The%20Plunder%20of%20Black%20Wealth%20in%20Chicago.pdf.

10. Preston Lauterbach, "Memphis Burning," *Places*, March 2016, https://places journal.org/article/memphis-burning.

11. Lauterbach. Boss Crump was the white architect of a political machine that dominated Memphis politics throughout the first half of the twentieth century.

12. Lauterbach.

13. Justin Juozapavicius (Associated Press), "Tulsa's Former Black Wall Street Tries to Remake Itself," *U.S. News and World Report*, February 22, 2017, https:// www.usnews.com/news/oklahoma/articles/2017-02-22/tulsas-former-black -wall-street-tries-to-remake-itself.

14. Michael Bates, "The 1921 Tulsa Race Riot and the 90 Years That Followed," BatesLine: Tulsa Straight Ahead, May 30, 2011, http://www.batesline.com/archives /2011/05/the-1921-tulsa-race-riot-and-the.html.

15. Mohl lists Nashville, Tennessee; New Orleans, Louisiana; Montgomery and Birmingham, Alabama; Kansas City, Missouri; St. Paul, Minnesota; Miami, Tampa, Saint Petersburg, Jacksonville, and Orlando, Florida; Atlanta, Georgia; Columbia, South Carolina; Los Angeles, California; Camden, New Jersey; Charlotte, North Carolina; and Milwaukee, Wisconsin, among the cities where black business districts and stable black communities effectively were destroyed by the choice of location for an interstate highway. In some cities political opposition to the location of new freeways was successful in preventing their placement in black neighborhoods, but this was in a minority of cases, and usually the initial phase of the projects already had damaged communities. See Raymond Mohl, "Urban Expressways and the Central Cities in Postwar America," in *The Interstates and the Cities: Highways, Housing, and the Freeway Revolt* (Washington, D.C.: Poverty and Race Research Action Council, 2002), 29–39, http://www.prrac.org/pdf/mohl.pdf.

16. Mohl, 29.

17. Mohl, 29.

18. Mohl, 30.

19. Alan Pyke, "Top Infrastructure Official Explains How America Used Highways to Destroy Black Neighborhoods," Think Progress, March 31, 2016, https://think progress.org/top-infrastructure-official-explains-how-america-used-highways -to-destroy-black-neighborhoods-96c1460d1962.

20. Pyke.

21. "Durham's Hayti Community: Urban Renewal or Urban Removal?," Carolina K–12, NC Civic Education Commission: Program in the Humanities and Human Values, April 2012, https://civics.sites.unc.edu/files/2012/04/Hayti1.pdf.

22. In somewhat of a cheerleading commentary, Kelsey Campbell-Donaghan enthusiastically described the "A New Dallas" plan as a progressive move to improve traffic conditions in the city and to create alternative uses for "land too valuable to justify rebuilding it [I-345]." She did not seem to be aware of the circumstances under which the freeway first was built, nor did she seem to be concerned about whether there will be an opportunity to rejuvenate the black businesses and community shattered by the highway's construction. Kelsey Campbell-Donaghan, "Dallas Is the Latest City to Propose Tearing Down Huge Urban Freeways," Gizmodo, November 13, 2013, http://gizmodo.com/dallas-is-the-latest-city-to-propose-tearing-down -huge-1463627161. In contrast, George Battle III displays an acute awareness of the historical context but is strangely optimistic about the benefits of the "A New Dallas" plan for Dallas's African American population. George Battle III, "Why Tearing Down I-345 Matters to South Dallas—and the Rest of the City," *Dallas Morning News*, March 17, 2015, http://www.dallasnews.com/opinion/latest-columns/20150317-george -battle-iii-why-tearing-down-i-345-matters-to-south-dallas.ece.

23. Margaret Kimberly, "Gentrification and the Death of Black Communities," Common Dreams, May 29, 2015, http://www.commondreams.org/views/2015/05 /29/gentrification-and-death-black-communities.

24. Kimberly.

25. Junia Howell and Elizabeth Korver-Glenn, "Neighborhoods, Race, and the Twenty-First-Century Housing Appraisal Industry," *Sociology of Race and Ethnicity* 4, no. 4 (2018): 473–90.

26. Andre M. Perry, Jonathan Rothwell, and David Harshbarger, *The Devaluation of Assets in Black Neighborhoods: The Case of Residential Property* (Washington, D.C.: Brookings Institution, 2018), https://www.brookings.edu/research /devaluation-of-assets-in-black-neighborhoods.

27. Derald Wing Sue, *Microaggressions in Everyday Life: Race, Gender, and Sexual Orientation* (Hoboken, N.J.: John Wiley and Sons, 2010).

28. Samuel DuBois Cook, "Political Movements and Organizations," *Journal of Politics* 26, no. 1 (February 1964): 135.

29. Cook, 135.

30. Cook, 145. Cook (139) described the White Citizens' Councils as the "master of Mississippi politics" by the early 1960s. The impunity (and hypocrisy) with which

whites excluded black voters is reflected in the following ironic description of conditions in Colfax, Louisiana—the same Colfax where the white massacre of blacks took place in 1873:

> The editor of the Colfax *Chronicle*, of Grant Parish, Louisiana, on October 12, 1956, made a rather astonishing observation. He said that members of the local Citizens Councils had re-examined the voter rolls and had removed the names of many Negro voters. The President of the local Council, W. B. Jones, was reported to have said that his group voted unanimously to purge Negro voters and an estimate was made that 90 per cent of the Negro registrants were challenged. The *Chronicle*'s editor checked the first one hundred registrants' cards and found only one that would meet the exacting standards set for Negroes. He reported that not a single member of the Citizens Council Committee had filled out his card correctly by the Council's standards (Thomas D. Clark, *The Emerging South* [New York: Oxford University Press, 1961], 215).

31. Taylor Branch, *Parting the Waters: America in the King Years 1954–63* (New York: Simon and Schuster, 1988), 712–13.

32. By the 1950s, "white people in Greenwood made up 33 percent of the population but owned 90 percent of the land. Just 2 percent of eligible black voters were registered. Black residents held not a single elected office. In 1964, 10 years after the Supreme Court's Brown v. Board of Education decision, Mississippi was the only state in the country where not a single black child attended a school with a white child." Nikole Hannah-Jones, "Ghosts of Greenwood," ProPublica, July 8, 2014, https://www.propublica.org/article/ghosts-of-greenwood.

33. Blanche K. Bruce (R-Miss.) and Hiram Rhodes Revels (R-Miss.), who served from 1870 to 1871, were the nation's only black senators for the next eighty-six years, until Edward Brooke (R-Mass.) was elected in 1967.

34. In 1896 Vardaman founded the *Greenwood Commonwealth*, which is still published today. See also James K. Vardaman, "A Governor Bitterly Opposes Negro Education," February 4, 1904, Teaching American History, https://teachingamerican history.org/library/document/a-governor-bitterly-opposes-negro-education.

35. Theodore Roosevelt Mason Howard, activist, fraternal organization leader, entrepreneur, and surgeon, founded the Regional Council of Negro Leadership in 1951 to advance school equality, black civil rights, business ownership, and strategies for wealth accumulation through the education of community leaders. Civil rights leader Medgar Evers worked for the Regional Council of Negro Leadership. See Charles M. Payne, *I've Got the Light of Freedom: The Organizing Tradition and the Mississippi Freedom Struggle* (Berkeley: University of California Press, 1995), 49; and Wikipedia, s.v. "Regional Council of Negro Leadership," https://en.wikipedia.org/wiki /Regional_Council_of_Negro_Leadership.

36. See Frederick Knight, "Voter ID Laws: Why Black Democrats' Fight for the Ballot in Mississippi Still Matters," Conversation, August 22, 2016, https://theconver sation.com/voter-id-laws-why-black-democrats-fight-for-the-ballot-in-mississippi -still-matters-63583.

37. See Payne, *I've Got the Light*, 36; and Mississippi Encyclopedia, s.v. "Gus Courts," by William P. Hustwit, https://mississippiencyclopedia.org/entries/gus -courts.

38. Payne, *I've Got the Light*, 37.

39. Over 1,000 people attended Reverend Lee's funeral. His widow, Rosebud Lee, elected to have his coffin open at the service. Emmett Till's mother, Mamie Carthan Till-Mobley, would do likewise four months later, when her son was brutally murdered in Leflore County, Mississippi.

40. See Knight, "Voter ID Laws."

41. Wesley C. Hogan, *Many Minds, One Heart: SNCC's Dream for a New America* (Chapel Hill: University of North Carolina Press, 2007), 80.

42. Robert E. Baker, "Greenwood Is Symbol of Negro Vote Hopes," *Washington Post (Times Herald)*, April 1, 1963.

43. King was the immediate successor of Dexter Avenue Baptist Church's activist minister Vernon Johns, who had been subjected to death threats in Birmingham.

44. "Civil Rights Martyrs," Southern Poverty Law Center, https://www.splcenter .org/what-we-do/civil-rights-memorial/civil-rights-martyrs.

45. "Interposition" refers to a state's claim to the right to oppose the operations of the federal government if it deems those operations unconstitutional. Those states are said to "interpose" themselves between the federal government and the people of that state. "Nullification" refers to a state's claim to the right to reject, or "nullify," laws its officials deem unconstitutional; the laws would not be enforced within the state's borders.

46. Horace Mann Bond, *The Education of the Negro in the American Social Order* (New York: Prentice-Hall, 1934).

47. Robert Margo, *Race and Schooling in the South, 1880–1950: An Economic History* (Chicago: University of Chicago Press, 1990), 61–64.

48. Hans L. Trefousse, *Andrew Johnson: A Biography* (Norwalk, Conn.: Easton Press, 1989), 236; emphasis added. We suspect that Johnson would have been even more satisfied with a *widening gap* in white and black educational attainment.

49. Jonathan Kozol, *Savage Inequalities: Children in America's Schools* (New York: Random House, 1991). Also see the moving description of the contemporary operation of school segregation and uneven access to funding in New York City in Nikole Hannah-Jones, "Choosing a School for My Daughter in a Segregated City," *New York Times Magazine*, June 6, 2016, https://www.nytimes.com/2016/06/12/magazine /choosing-a-school-for-my-daughter-in-a-segregated-city.html.

50. Jason Grissom and Christopher Redding, "Discretion and Disproportionality: Explaining the Underrepresentation of High-Achieving Students of Color in Gifted Programs," *AERA Open* 2, no. 1 (January–March 2016): 1–25, http://news.vanderbilt .edu/files/Grissom_AERAOpen_GiftedStudents1.pdf. See also William Darity Jr. and Alicia Jolla, "Desegregated Schools with Segregated Education," in *The Integration Debate: Competing Futures for American Cities*, ed. Chester Hartman and Gregory Squires (New York: Routledge, 2010), 99–114.

51. Nick Buffie, "The Black-White Unemployment Gap Isn't Really about Education," Center for Economic and Policy Research Blog, March 4, 2016, http://cepr.net/blogs/cepr-blog/the-black-white-unemployment-gap-isn-t-really-about-education.

52. Janelle Jones and John Schmitt, *A College Degree Is No Guarantee* (Washington, D.C.: Center for Economic and Policy Research, 2014), http://cepr.net/publications/reports/a-college-degree-is-no-guarantee.

53. Douglas A. Blackmon, *Slavery by Another Name: The Re-enslavement of Black Americans from the Civil War to World War II* (New York: Random House, 2008), 7. It is pertinent to note that the brief Thirteenth Amendment to the Constitution, the amendment prohibiting slavery in the United States, includes an important exception clause: "Neither slavery nor involuntary servitude, *except as a punishment for crime whereof the party shall have been duly convicted*, shall exist within the United States, or any place subject to their jurisdiction." (Emphasis added.)

54. Blackmon, 49.

55. "Sugar Land, TX," Data USA, https://datausa.io/profile/geo/sugar-land-tx.

56. Kathryn Eastburn, "Texans Share History of Convict Leasing, Unearthed Remains," Texas News, April 5, 2019, https://www.nbcdfw.com/news/local/Texans-Share-History-of-Convict-Leasing-Unearthed-Remains-508193061.html. See also Michael Hardy, "Blood and Sugar," *Texas Monthly*, January 2017, https://www.texasmonthly.com/articles/sugar-land-slave-convict-labor-history; and "Edward Hall Cunningham," Lost Texas Roads, November 18, 2014, http://losttexasroads.com/people/34-cunningham-edward-h.

57. As quoted in Jeffrey Toobin, "The Milwaukee Experiment: What Can One Prosecutor Do about the Mass Incarceration of African-Americans?," *New Yorker*, May 11, 2015, https://www.newyorker.com/magazine/2015/05/11/the-milwaukee-experiment, from Michelle Alexander, *The New Jim Crow: Mass Incarceration in the Age of Colorblindness* (New York: New Press, 2010).

58. Michelle Alexander, "Roots of Today's Mass Incarceration Crisis Date to Slavery, Jim Crow," interview by Amy Goodman, Democracy Now, March 4, 2015, https://www.democracynow.org/2015/3/4/michelle_alexander_roots_of_todays_crisis.

59. Jeffrey S. Sartin, "J. Marion Sims, the Father of Gynecology: Hero or Villain?," *Southern Medical Journal* 97, no. 5 (2004), http://www.medscape.com/viewarticle/479892_1. See also Ibram X. Kendi, *Stamped from the Beginning: The Definitive History of Racist Ideas in America* (New York: Nation Books, 2016), 185–86.

60. James H. Jones, *Bad Blood: The Tuskegee Syphilis Experiment* (New York: Free Press, 1981).

61. Nelson summarizes cases explored in detail in Harriet Washington, *Medical Apartheid: The Dark History of Medical Experimentation on Black Americans from Colonial Times to the Present* (New York: Doubleday, 2006). See Alondra Nelson, "Unequal Treatment," review of Washington, *Medical Apartheid, Washington Post*, January 7, 2007, http://www.washingtonpost.com/wp-dyn/content/article/2007/01/05/AR2007010500180.html.

62. Rebecca Skloot, *The Immortal Life of Henrietta Lacks* (New York: Random House, 2010).

63. Lutz Kaelber, "Eugenics: Compulsory Sterilization in 50 States" (presentation at the Social Science History Association Meeting, Vancouver, Canada, 2012), http://www.uvm.edu/~lkaelber/eugenics.

64. Kaelber. On North Carolina, see also Gregory Price and William Darity Jr., "The Economics of Race and Eugenic Sterilization in North Carolina, 1958–1968," *Economics and Human Biology* 8, no. 2 (July 2010): 261–72.

65. Dorothy Roberts, "Forum: Black Women and the Pill," *Perspectives on Sexual and Reproductive Health* 32, no. 2 (March/April 2000), https://www.guttmacher.org/about/journals/psrh/2000/03/forum-black-women-and-pill.

66. Bryce Covert, "Environmental Racism," *Nation*, March 7, 2016, 5.

67. Covert, 5.

68. Heather Rogers, "Erasing Mossville," Intercept, November 4, 2015, https://theintercept.com/2015/11/04/erasing-mossville-how-pollution-killed-a-louisiana-town. The 2019 documentary film *Mossville: When Great Trees Fall*, directed by Alexander John Glustrom, provides a view of the deep personal losses associated with the erasure of the town.

69. Rogers, 5.

70. Ishaan Tharoor, "U.S. Owes Black People Reparations for a History of 'Racial Terrorism,' Says U.N. Panel," *Washington Post*, September 27, 2016, https://www.washingtonpost.com/news/worldviews/wp/2016/09/27/u-s-owes-black-people-reparations-for-a-history-of-racial-terrorism-says-u-n-panel.

CHAPTER 12

1. Noah Millman, "Reparations Could Widen, Rather Than Heal, Racial Rifts," *New York Times*, June 8, 2014, https://www.nytimes.com/roomfordebate/2014/06/08/are-reparations-due-to-african-americans/reparations-could-widen-rather-than-heal-racial-rifts.

2. The arguments addressed in this chapter have been extracted from criticisms raised by a variety of opponents of reparations. Of particular significance are David Horowitz, *Uncivil Wars: The Controversy over Reparations for Slavery* (San Francisco: Encounter Books, 2003); Richard Epstein, "The Case against Black Reparations," *Boston University Law Review*, no. 84 (2004): 1177–99, http://chicagounbound.uchicago.edu/cgi/viewcontent.cgi?article=2323&context=journal_articles; Peter Flaherty and John Carlisle, *The Case against Slave Reparations* (Falls Church, Va.: National Legal and Policy Center, 2004); and Juan Williams, *Enough: The Phony Leaders, Dead End Movements, and the Culture of Failure That Are Undermining Black America—and What We Can Do about It* (New York: Three Rivers Press, 2006). Note that the Flaherty and Carlisle article is dated 2004, but it refers to events that took place in 2005. It provides perhaps the most comprehensive list of complaints generally made against reparations for black Americans—all of them considered in this chapter.

3. Zora Neale Hurston, *Barracoon: The Story of the Last "Black Cargo,"* ed. Deborah G. Plant (New York: Amistad, 2018).

4. Sandra E. Garcia, "She Survived a Slave Ship, the Civil War, and the Depression: Her Name Was Redoshi," *New York Times*, April 3, 2019. Redoshi's life is chronicled in an article by a researcher at Newcastle University in Britain; see Hannah Durkin, "Finding Last Middle Passage Survivor Sally 'Redoshi' Smith on the Page and Screen," *Slavery and Abolition*, March 23, 2019, https://doi.org/10.1080/01440 39X.2019.1596397. The *Clotilde* (also *Clotilda*) was the last known schooner to transport African captives illegally to the United States in order to sell them into slavery. The longest-living survivor of that brutal institution may have died in 1971; Sylvester Magee maintained he was nineteen years old when Hugh Magee, owner of the Lone Star plantation in Covington, Mississippi, purchased him at an Enterprise, Mississippi, slave auction house. Sylvester had become the chattel property of Florence, Mississippi, planter Victor Steen when he escaped to fight for the Union during the Civil War. Ellen Ciurczak, "Miss. Man Claimed to Be 130-Year-Old Last Slave," *USA Today*, September 26, 2016, https://www.usatoday.com/story/news /nation-now/2016/09/26/miss-man-130-year-old-last-slave/91140564.

5. Martha Quillin, "Civil War Saga: Black Re-enactors Tell Their Side of the Story," *News and Observer* (Raleigh, N.C.), January 25, 2015, https://www.news observer.com/news/local/article10231829.html.

6. Hortense McClinton, interviews by the authors, September 4, 2014, Durham, North Carolina, and November 2, 2019, Silver Spring, Maryland. See also Hortense McClinton, "A First Black Professor Remembers Her Segregated Education," interview by Lynn Neary, *Weekend Edition*, National Public Radio, May 18, 2014, http://www .npr.org/2014/05/18/313471434/a-first-black-professor-remembers-her-segregated -education. The NPR site correctly indicates that McClinton's father's parents were born into slavery, but it does not reveal that her father, Sebrone Jones King, was himself born a slave on January 14, 1865. Ms. McClinton was born August 27, 1918.

7. Amazingly, we encountered a second person alive in 2014 who was also the daughter of an enslaved person. Mattie Clyburn Rice, who was ninety-one years old when she died in High Point, North Carolina, in September 2014, made headlines in part because her father, Weary (also known as Wary and Worry) Clyburn, who was born in 1841 and was in his ninth decade when Mattie was born, had supported the Confederate effort during the Civil War. Clyburn, who had lived his first twenty-five years as a slave, was one of eighteen human chattel owned by the Thomas Lorenzo Clyburn family on the Uriah Clyburn plantation in Kershaw District, Lancaster County, South Carolina, a property that spanned more than 20,000 acres in 1900. See Martha Waggoner (Associated Press), "Confederate Pomp amid Burial of Slave's Daughter," *Carolina Times*, October 18, 2014, http://www.thetimesnews.com /news/region-state/confederate-pomp-amid-burial-of-slave-s-daughter-1.388344. In a strange and rare case, Weary Clyburn accompanied his owner's son and near age-mate, Thomas Frank Clyburn, to the battleground when Thomas became a captain with the Twelfth South Carolina Confederate corps. Weary Clyburn's own statement to the South Carolina pension board and an affidavit provided by attorney J. P. Richards of Lancaster County dated January 22, 1926, both contended that Weary had been Captain Clyburn's bodyguard and personal servant and that the enslaved man

had "performed personal services" for Robert E. Lee. Between 1863 and 1865 the two men had been engaged at a training camp in Columbia, South Carolina, and with the Twelfth Battalion in Charleston, Morris Island, and Pages Point. Later, "at Hilton Head, while under fire of the enemy, [Weary Clyburn] carried [Thomas Clyburn] out of the field of fire on his shoulder." When Weary died in 1930, he was remembered in an obituary published April 1, 1930, on the front page of South Carolina's *Monroe Journal* as "Uncle Weary Clyburn," "a white man's darkey," who had been buried "in the Confederate uniform of gray." Before the 1930s, Confederate soldiers and their dependents were eligible to receive pensions only from their state governments. When Weary's February 1, 1926, application for support was approved, he became one of the first blacks living in Union County, North Carolina, to receive a Confederate pension. His pension records indicate that "his services were meritorious and faithful toward his master and the cause of the Confederacy." See "Weary Clyburn," Find a Grave, http://www.findagrave.com/cgi-bin/fg.cgi?page=gr&GRid=60770561; and Jessica Jones, "After Years of Research, Confederate Daughter Arises," *Weekend Edition Sunday*, WUNC Radio, August 7, 2011, http://www.npr.org/2011/08/07/138587202/after-years-of-research-confederate-daughter-arises. When Weary Clyburn's family requested support from the federal government, however, their petition was denied on the grounds that no black man—slave or free—had served as a soldier in the Confederacy. The Sons of the Confederate Veterans, which made arrangements for Mattie Clyburn Rice's funeral, and the United Daughters of the Confederacy—two organizations that were, unsurprisingly, sympathetic to the family's claims—played active roles in Rice's burial ceremony. In the eyes of the United Daughters of the Confederacy, Rice, the daughter of "a Confederate soldier," was a "Real Daughter."

However, to the extent that Clyburn served voluntarily on behalf of the Confederacy, he was a far outlier among black southerners. See Kevin Levin, *Searching for Black Confederates: The Civil War's Most Persistent Myth* (Chapel Hill: University of North Carolina Press, 2019).

8. In an interview, Stevenson related the story passed down in his family of his great-grandfather John Baylor, born into slavery in the late 1840s, who managed to learn to read at age six. The keeper of the Baylor family's history was Stevenson's maternal grandmother, Victoria Baylor Golden—his mother, Alice Golden, was her youngest child—who was born in Bowling Green, Virginia, in 1889 and lived with Stevenson's family in Milton, Delaware, when he was a child. As early as 1785, the Virginia General Assembly had made it illegal for the Office of the Poor to bind out blacks or mulattoes to masters whose intent was to teach them to read, write, or do arithmetic. By 1833—two years after the Nat Turner Rebellion—the state had made it a criminal offense to teach slaves, free blacks, and mulattoes to read or write. Those found guilty of helping blacks acquire literacy could be subjected to penalties of up to twenty lashes of the whip, two months of imprisonment, and fines not to exceed $100. Baylor's parents were proud of their son's ability, Stevenson said, but his precocity also put them in a precarious position, which compelled them "to keep it secret. [John Baylor's] parents were terrified that he had figured out how to read" and that his secret would become known to others. Nonetheless, Stevenson said, "they wanted him to use that skill to help them figure things out when Emancipation came."

And "even after Emancipation, my grandmother [told] me . . . he did not like people to know that he could read, but he desperately wanted [his wife, Mary,] to read." References include "One Lawyer's Efforts to Save Young Blacks and *Just Mercy*," Bryan Stevenson interview, *Fresh Air*, National Public Radio, October 20, 2014; Meg Grant, "Bryan Stevenson: Stubborn Lawyer Stands Alone between Death and His Clients," *People*, November 27, 1995; the Bryan Stevenson extended interview, featured on *The Daily Show with Jon Stewart*, October 14, 2014; and Bryan Stevenson, "We Need to Talk about an Injustice," March 12, 2012, TED Talk, 23:26, http://www.ted.com/talks/bryan_stevenson_we_need_to_talk_about_an_injustice. See also *Supplement to the Revised Code of the Laws of Virginia* (Richmond, Va., 1833), chap. 186; Rudolph Lewis, comp., "Up from Slavery: A Documentary History of Negro Education," ChickenBones, http://www.nathanielturner.com/educationhistorynegro6.htm; and Bryan Stevenson, personal correspondence with one of the authors, January 18, 2015.

9. Constance E. G. N. Edwards (1944–2016). See Shana Farrell, "Advanced Oral History Summer Institute Alum Spotlight: Kelly Navies," *Berkeley Library Update* (blog), University of California at Berkeley Library, November 7, 2018, https://update.lib.berkeley.edu/2018/11/07/advanced-oral-history-summer-institute-alum-spotlight-kelly-navies; and Kelly Navies, personal correspondence with one of the authors, November 9, 2018.

10. Kenneth Lewis, interview by the authors, June 2013, Durham, North Carolina.

11. The "delay until death" tactic has been deployed in other contexts. For example, the state of Oklahoma has never compensated even the few remaining living victims of the Tulsa massacre of 1921. When all are dead, the position that reparations must go to direct victims will be a convenient barrier to making payments for the riot. In 2011, Cathryn Young, the spouse of the ninety-four-year-old Wess Young, who had to flee the Greenwood neighborhood as a child with his family during the white riot, commented, "I think they [white Oklahomans] are trying to keep this hidden. . . . Don't talk about it, don't do nothing about it until all these people are dead." However, she added, "Then they think it'll be over with. But it won't." A. G. Sulzberger, "As Survivors Dwindle, Tulsa Confronts Its Past," *New York Times*, June 19, 2011, http://www.nytimes.com/2011/06/20/us/20tulsa.html.

12. Jessica Snethen, "Queen Nzinga (1583–1663)," BlackPast, https://www.blackpast.org/global-african-history/queen-nzinga-1583-1663.

13. For an excellent dissection of the "model minority" trope, see Jennifer Lee and Min Zhou, *The Asian American Achievement Paradox* (New York: Russell Sage Foundation, 2015).

14. Malcolm X, Television interview, March 1964, http://www.notable-quotes.com/x/x_malcolm.html.

15. Steve Valocchi, "The Racial Basis of Capitalism and the State, and the Impact of the New Deal on African Americans," *Social Problems* 41, no. 3 (August 1994): 347–62.

16. Ira Katznelson, "When Affirmative Action Was White," *History and Policy*, November 10, 2005, http://www.historyandpolicy.org/policy-papers/papers/when-affirmative-action-was-white.

17. Katznelson. See also Ira Katznelson, *When Affirmative Action Was White: An Untold History of Racial Inequality in Twentieth-Century America* (New York: W. W. Norton, 2005), for a more detailed exegesis. While 28 percent of white World War II veterans went to college on the GI Bill, only 12 percent of black World War II veterans did so. Shannon Landers-Manuel, "The Inequality Hidden within the Race-Neutral G.I. Bill," JSTOR Daily, September 18, 2017, https://daily.jstor.org/the-inequality-hidden-within-the-race-neutral-g-i-bill.

18. Landers-Manuel, "Inequality Hidden." Landers-Manuel draws on Edward Humes, *Over Here: How the G.I. Bill Transformed the American Dream* (Orlando, Fla.: Harcourt, 2006), for the material quoted here. For more on Rankin, see Kenneth Wayne Vickers, "John Rankin: Democrat and Demagogue" (master's thesis, Mississippi State University, 1993). Limited space at historically black colleges and universities due to low funding under the dual system of higher education constrained black enrollment.

19. William Darity Jr., "Confronting Those Affirmative Action Grumbles," in *Capitalism on Trial: Explorations in the Tradition of Thomas E. Weisskopf*, ed. Jeannette Wicks-Lim and Robert Pollin (Cheltenham, UK: Edward Elgar, 2013), 215–23.

20. Ross Douthat, "A Different Bargain on Race," *New York Times*, March 14, 2017, https://www.nytimes.com/2017/03/04/opinion/sunday/a-different-bargain-on-race.html.

21. Charles Krauthammer, "A Grand Compromise," *Washington Post*, April 6, 2001, https://www.washingtonpost.com/archive/opinions/2001/04/06/a-grand-compromise/884f9488-ed4f-4978-8226-0074b5e2529b.

22. In a response to Krauthammer's op-ed, Martin L. Brown has observed that the figure of $50,000 per family "is awfully cheap." He observed, "One measure of this injustice, itself only partial, is the difference in household net wealth accumulated by middle age. Data from the U.S. Health and Retirement Survey indicate this difference to be at least $100,000 on average, double Charles Krauthammer's recommended payment. This figure itself underestimates the true difference because it is expressed in 1994 dollars and because it does not take into account both the much higher percentage of African American families with negative net wealth and the higher percentage of white families with very large amounts of net wealth, which tends to be under-measured by standard government statistics." Martin L. Brown, "Evaluating Reparations," *Washington Post*, April 10, 2001, https://www.washingtonpost.com/archive/opinions/2001/04/10/evaluating-reparations/525b4171-8795-493f-80da-1817e2e5c0b8.

23. Claude Oubre, in a fine study of the original development of the forty-acres policy, says that the ministers expressed a desire to live separately from whites at least as a "temporary" condition. See Claude F. Oubre, *Forty Acres and Mule: The Freedman's Bureau and Black Land Ownership* (Baton Rouge: Louisiana State University Press, 1978), 18. But there is no intimation of a desire for the arrangement to be "temporary" in the official report of the Savannah conversation. "Newspaper Account of a Meeting between Black Religious Leaders and Union Military Authorities," Freedmen and Southern Society Project, http://www.freedmen.umd.edu/savmtg.htm.

24. *Proceedings of the Freedmen's Convention of Georgia* (Augusta, Ga.: Printed at the Office of the *Loyal Georgian*, 1866), https://archive.org/stream/proceedings offreo1free#page/n3/mode/2up; *Minutes of the Freedmen's Convention, Held in the City of Raleigh, on the 2nd, 3rd, 4th and 5th of October, 1866* (Raleigh, N.C.: Standard Book and Job Office, 1866), https://docsouth.unc.edu/nc/freedmen/freedmen.html. We thank David A. Gamson for alerting us to the existence of records from several freedmen's conventions.

25. Eric Foner, *Reconstruction, 1863–1877: America's Unfinished Revolution* (New York: Harper and Row, 1988), 96–97.

26. See Patrick L. Mason, "Race, Culture, and Skill: Interracial Wage Differentials among African Americans, Latinos, and Whites," *Review of Black Political Economy* 25, no. 3 (Winter 1997): 5–39; William Mangino, "Race to College: The 'Reverse Gap,'" *Race and Social Problems*, no. 2 (December 2010): 164–78; William Mangino, "Why Do Whites and the Rich Have Less Need for Education?," *American Journal of Economics and Sociology* 71, no. 3 (July 2012): 562–602; and William Mangino, "The Negative Effects of Privilege on Educational Attainment: Gender, Race, Class, and the Bachelor's Degree," *Social Science Quarterly* 95, no. 3 (September 2014): 760–84.

27. M. C. Black, K. C. Basile, M. J. Breiding, S. G. Smith, M. L. Walters, M. T. Merrick, J. Chen, and M. R. Stevens, *The National Intimate Partner and Sexual Violence Survey: 2010 Summary Report* (Atlanta: National Center for Injury Prevention and Control of the Centers for Disease Control and Prevention, Division of Violence Prevention, 2010), http://www.cdc.gov/violenceprevention/pdf/nisvs_report2010-a.pdf.

28. Researchers at the Organization for Economic Cooperation and Development analyzed member countries' "Better Life Index" in 2013, which takes into account factors ranging from income and health to life satisfaction and physical security, and concluded that the top five countries were Australia, Sweden, Canada, Norway, and Switzerland. See Megan Willett, "The 15 Countries with the Highest Quality of Life," Business Insider, May 28, 2013, http://www.businessinsider.com /top-countries-on-oecd-better-life-index-2013-5.

29. Cedric Johnson, "An Open Letter to Ta-Nehisi Coates and the Liberals Who Love Him," *Jacobin*, February 3, 2016, https://www.jacobinmag.com/2016/02/ta -nehisi-coates-case-for-reparations-bernie-sanders-racism; Cedric Johnson, "Reparations Isn't a Political Demand," *Jacobin*, March 7, 2016, https://www.jacobinmag .com/2016/03/cedric-johnson-brian-jones-ta-nehisi-coates-reparations.

30. William Darity Jr., Darrick Hamilton, Patrick Mason, Gregory Price, Alberto Dávila, Marie Mora, and Sue Stockly, "Stratification Economics: A General Theory of Intergroup Inequality," in Andrea Flynn, Susan Holmberg, Dorian Warren, and Felicia Wong, eds., *The Hidden Rules of Race: Barriers to an Inclusive Economy* (New York: Cambridge University Press, 2017), 41.

31. William Darity Jr., Darrick Hamilton, Mark Paul, Alan Aja, Anne Price, Antonio Moore, and Caterina Chiopris, *What We Get Wrong about Closing the Racial Wealth Gap* (Durham, N.C.: Samuel DuBois Cook Center on Social Equity, Duke University; Oakland, Calif.: Insight Center for Community Economic Development, 2018).

32. Imari Z. Smith, Keisha Bentley-Edwards, Salimah El-Amin, and William Darity Jr., *Fighting at Birth: Eradicating the Black-White Infant Mortality Gap* (Durham, N.C.: Samuel DuBois Cook Center on Social Equity, Duke University; Oakland, Calif.: Insight Center for Community Economic Development, 2018), 4.

33. Olga Kazhan, "In One Year, 57,375 Years of Life Were Lost to Police Violence," *Atlantic*, May 8, 2018, https://www.theatlantic.com/health/archive/2018/05/the -57375-years-of-life-lost-to-police-violence/559835; Frank R. Baumgartner, Derek A. Epp, and Kelsey Shoub, "The Fears of Driving While Black in NC Are True: The Data Prove It," *News and Observer* (Raleigh, N.C.), July 29, 2018, 13A.

34. Peter C. Myers, *Frederick Douglass: Race and Rebirth of American Liberalism* (Lawrence: University Press of Kansas, 2008), 143–44. For the quotations in the origi-nal, see Frederick Douglass, "Blessings of Liberty and Education (September 3, 1894)," in John Blassingame and John McKivigan, eds., *The Frederick Douglass Papers* (New Haven, Conn.: Yale University Press, 1992), 5:624; Frederick Douglass, "Salutory (Sep-tember 8, 1870)," in Blassingame and McKivigan, 4:225; and Frederick Douglass, "The White People of This Country Can Never Do Too Much for Us," in Blassingame and McKivigan, *Frederick Douglass Papers*, 5:557.

35. Myers, *Frederick Douglass*, 144.

CHAPTER 13

1. When reparations supporter Ta-Nehisi Coates appeared on *The Colbert Report*, Stephen Colbert famously asked him whether it would be satisfactory if he simply cut Coates a personal check. See Ta-Nehisi Coates, "Ta-Nehisi Coates," interview with Stephen Colbert, *The Colbert Report*, Comedy Central, June 16, 2014, http:// www.cc.com/video-clips/n3etz1/the-colbert-report-ta-nehisi-coates. While Col-bert meant the offer tongue in cheek, the notion that individual whites might make payments to individual blacks as reparations deflects attention from the more se-rious and fundamental issue at stake: the national debt to African Americans as a whole. We are not concerned about personal guilt; we are concerned with national responsibility.

2. See Roy L. Brooks, "The Age of Apology," in *When Sorry Isn't Enough: The Con-troversy Over Apologies and Reparations for Human Injustice*, ed. Roy L. Brooks (New York: New York University Press, 1999), 3–11. Brooks also insists, like we do, that the demand for reparations be put in the hands of legislators, not judges.

3. John Tateishi, a Japanese American Citizens League activist who had been incarcerated at Manzanar, California, for three years, says of the wartime "intern-ment": "You can make this mistake, but you have to correct it—and by correcting, hopefully not repeat it again." Retribution payments to 82,219 eligible claimants to-taled $1.6 billion. In addition, the enabling legislation for Japanese American repa-rations provided for the establishment of the Civil Liberties Public Education Fund, directed to inform the public about the incarceration of Japanese Americans. A total of $50 million was allocated in 1988 "to sponsor research and public education ac-tivities"; however, an antispending lobby put the education program on hold until 1994, when funding was reduced to $5 million. President Bill Clinton appointed an advisory board in 1996, and the Civil Liberties Public Education Fund initiated the

program in 1997–98. In 1998, a curriculum conference was held in San Francisco, and the Smithsonian Institution hosted an exhibition, *Days of Remembrance*, to recollect Franklin Delano Roosevelt's signing of Executive Order 9066, which authorized the incarceration. The Japanese American National Museum in Los Angeles is the repository for the Civil Liberties Public Education Fund grant program records. See Bilal Qureshi, "From Wrong to Right: A U.S. Apology for Japanese Internment," *Code Switch*, National Public Radio, August 3, 2013; and Densho Encyclopedia, s.v. "Civil Liberties Public Education Fund," by Sharon Yamato, http://encyclopedia.densho .org/Civil_Liberties_Public_Education_Fund.

4. Mari J. Matsuda emphasizes the importance of careful and comprehensive documentation of the relevant injustices in "Looking to the Bottom: Critical Legal Studies and Reparations," *Harvard Civil Liberties–Civil Rights Law Review*, no. 22 (1987): 323, 363–97.

5. Corinne Ruff, "Many Colleges Profited from Slavery: What Can They Do about It Now?," *Chronicle of Higher Education*, April 19, 2016.

6. See Henrietta Verma, "Rooted in Research," *Library Journal* 141, no. 8 (May 2006): 26–31; and Lisa Peet, "Growing the Family Tree," *Library Journal* 141, no. 8 (May 2006): 27, 31.

7. "The Mormons: Genealogy and the Mormon Archives," American Experience, PBS, http://www.pbs.org/mormons/etc/genealogy.html.

8. The State Library of North Carolina provides a website with instructions for exploring slave records; see "How to Find Slave Records," State Library of North Carolina, https://statelibrary.ncdcr.gov/ghl/genealogy/finding-slave-records.

9. We employ an interest rate of 4 percent because 3 percent provides a conservative estimate of the historical annual return on an investment and 1 percent is a conservative estimate of the long-run inflation rate. We then use 5 and 6 percent to accommodate less conservative estimates of the rate of return and/or higher rates of inflation.

10. Roger Ransom and Richard Sutch, "Who Pays for Slavery?," in *The Wealth of Races: The Present Value of Benefits from Past Injustices*, ed. Richard F. America (Westport, Conn.: Greenwood Press, 1990), 31–54.

11. Larry Neal, "A Calculation and Comparison of the Current Benefits of Slavery and the Analysis of Who Benefits," in America, *Wealth of Races*, 91–106.

12. Thomas Craemer, "Estimating Slavery Reparations: Present Value Comparisons of Historical Multigenerational Reparations Policies," *Social Science Quarterly* 96, no. 2 (June 2015): 639–55. In the jargon of economists, the hypothetical non-slave-labor wage can be construed as the "shadow" wage for labor in the absence of slavery.

13. James Marketti, "Estimated Present Value of Income Directed during Slavery," in America, *Wealth of Races*, 107–24.

14. Judah P. Benjamin, "You Can Never Subjugate Us" (speech to U.S. Senate, Washington, D.C., December 31, 1860), Causes of the Civil War, http://civilwarcauses .org/judah.htm. "Four thousand million dollars" is another way of saying $4 billion.

15. Walter Fleming, "'Forty Acres and a Mule,'" *North American Review* 182, no. 594 (May 1906): 731.

16. Anuradha Mittal and Joan Powell, "The Last Plantation," *Food First* 6, no. 1 (Winter 2000): 1–8.

17. Fleming, "'Forty Acres,'" 733.

18. There were an estimated 31 million persons in the American population as a whole at the close of the Civil War, so the formerly enslaved constituted about 13 percent of the national population.

19. William Darity Jr., "Forty Acres and a Mule in the 21st Century," *Social Science Quarterly* 89, no. 3 (September 2008): 656–64.

20. Paul Alan Cimbala, "The Freedmen's Bureau, the Freedmen, and Sherman's Grant in Reconstruction Georgia, 1865–1867," *Journal of Southern History* 55, no. 4 (November 1989): 597–632.

21. Note that there is a significant typographical error on page 662 of Darity, "Forty Acres." The estimate of the per person allocation of funds from the present value estimate of forty acres, at the time of the article, is overstated by a full decimal place at $400,000; it should be $40,000.

22. Bernadette Chachere and Gerald Udinsky, "An Illustrative Estimate of the Present Value of the Benefits from Racial Discrimination 1929–1969," in America, *Wealth of Races*, 163–68.

23. David Swinton, "Racial Inequality and Reparations," in America, *Wealth of Races*, 153–62.

24. U.S. Census Bureau, "Selected Characteristics of People 15 Years and Over by Total Money Income, Work Experience, Race, Hispanic Origin, and Sex," issued 2018, https://www.census.gov/data/tables/time-series/demo/income-poverty/cps -pinc/pinc-01.html. Federal statistics that limit the calculation of per capita income to persons fifteen years of age or older reduce the racial income gap, since the black population is relatively younger than the white population in the United States.

25. Lisa J. Dettling, Joanne W. Hsu, Lindsay Jacobs, Kevin B. Moore, and Jeffrey P. Thompson, "Recent Trends in Wealth-Holding by Race and Ethnicity: Evidence from the Survey of Consumer Finances," with assistance from Elizabeth Llanes, FEDS Notes, September 27, 2017, https://www.federalreserve.gov/econres/notes/feds -notes/recent-trends-in-wealth-holding-by-race-and-ethnicity-evidence-from-the -survey-of-consumer-finances-20170927.htm.

26. If medians are used instead of means, the gap would be $153,400 per family and about $38,350 per person in 2016, leading to a total estimated bill of a more modest $1.5 trillion. We use means here instead of medians because we seek to estimate the magnitude of the bill that would eradicate the entire black-white wealth disparity. *Ninety-seven percent* of white wealth is held by white households above the white median net worth, so targeting median net worth ignores a vast amount of white-owned wealth. See William Darity Jr., Fenaba Addo, and Imari Smith, "A Subaltern Middle Class: The Case of the 'Black Bourgeoisie' in America" (paper presented at the Renewing the Promise of the Middle Class conference, Board of Governors of the Federal Reserve, Washington, D.C., May 10, 2019).

27. An argument has been circulating that universal programs like the "baby bonds" (or child trust accounts) policy could accomplish the same objectives

without being targeted exclusively at black America. The policy has been put forward in the form of Senator Cory Booker's Opportunity Accounts Bill, designed in part by one of the coauthors of this book. However, the "baby bonds" policy aims to move all Americans closer to the national median level of wealth. Once fully executed, even if it achieves its aim, the associated $1.5–$2 trillion increase in black wealth would fall far short of the sum necessary to close the racial wealth gap.

28. "US Household Net Worth Almost $107 Trillion in Second-Quarter 2018," Reuters, September 20, 2018, https://www.reuters.com/article/us-usa-economy -wealth/u-s-household-net-worth-almost-107-trillion-in-second-quarter-2018 -idUSKCN1M02KN.

29. We must be clear here. We *do not* advocate eliminating the racial wealth gap by taxing away white wealth until white net worth reaches the low existing levels of black wealth. We *do* advocate raising the assets held by blacks to meet higher existing levels of white wealth.

30. William Darity Jr. and Dania Frank, "The Economics of Reparations," *American Economic Review* 93, no. 2 (May 2003): 327–28.

31. This potential use of reparations monies came to mind in a conversation with Lawrence Carter, dean of the Martin Luther King Jr. International Chapel at Morehouse College, September 2017. See also Darrick Hamilton, Tressie McMillan Cottom, Alan A. Aja, Carolyn Ash, and William Darity Jr., "Still We Rise," *American Prospect*, November 9, 2015, http://prospect.org/article/why-black-colleges-and -universities-still-matter.

32. Of course, reparations payments would not be subject to taxation.

33. See V. P. Franklin, "Introduction—African Americans and the Movement for Reparations: From Slave Pensions to the Reparations Superfund," *Journal of African American History* 97, no. 1–2 (Winter–Spring 2012): 1–12; and Mary Frances Berry, "We Need a 'Reparations Superfund,'" *New York Times*, June 9, 2014, http:// www.nytimes.com/roomfordebate/2014/06/08/are-reparations-due-to-african -americans/we-need-a-reparations-superfund.

34. Berry, "'Reparations Superfund.'"

35. Matthew Yglesias, "Slavery Reparations Are Workable and Affordable," Vox, May 23, 2014, http://www.vox.com/2014/5/23/5741294/slavery-reparations -are-workable-and-affordable.

36. Jordan Malter, "Bernie Sanders' 2016 Economic Adviser Stephanie Kelton on Modern Monetary Theory and the 2020 Race," CNBC Business News, March 2, 2019, https://www.cnbc.com/2019/03/01/bernie-sanders-economic-advisor-stephanie -kelton-on-mmt-and-2020-race.html.

37. Here we explicitly embrace the premises of modern monetary theory. See, e.g., Pavlina Tcherneva, "PAYGO Is Based on a Fallacy," *In These Times*, January 3, 2019, http://inthesetimes.com/article/21658/PAYGO-government-spending-raising -taxes-modern-monetary-theory-pelosi.

38. The Office of Redress Administration carried out the mandate of the Civil Liberties Act of 1988 to provide reparations payments for Japanese Americans who were incarcerated by the federal government during World War II. The NRB would

constitute a parallel agency responsible for fulfilling the mandate of enabling legislation for reparations for black Americans.

39. The agency can maintain and disseminate a "Swindler's List."

40. This suggestion was made to one of the coauthors by Toby Grytafey on Twitter on April 6, 2016.

41. It will be essential that textbooks do not sanitize, distort, or obscure the history of slavery as do several that have been used in Texas public schools. Ellen Bresler Rockmore, "How Texas Teaches History," *New York Times*, October 21, 2015, http://www.nytimes.com/2015/10/22/opinion/how-texas-teaches-history.html.

42. Matsuda, "Looking to the Bottom."

43. On the relationship between major American universities and the slave system in the first half of the nineteenth century, again, see esp. Craig Steven Wilder, *Ebony and Ivy: Race, Slavery, and the Troubled History of America's Universities* (New York: Bloomsbury, 2013).

44. Reparations are central to the black agenda advanced by the #ADOS movement; see American Descendants of Slavery, https://ados101.com. The Black Youth Project 100 has also developed a policy platform that includes reparations as a key element. See "Our Agenda," Agenda to Build Black Futures, http://agendatobuild blackfutures.org/our-agenda.

APPENDIX 2

1. Theodore Dwight Weld, Angelina Grimké Weld, and Sarah Grimké, *American Slavery as It Is: Testimony of a Thousand Witnesses* (New York: American Anti-Slavery Society, 1839), 72. An electronic version of the book can also be found at the Documenting the American South website, http://docsouth.unc.edu/neh/weld/weld.html#p14.

2. Weld, Weld, and Grimké, 73; italics in the original.

3. Weld, Weld, and Grimké, 65–68.

APPENDIX 3

1. E. Franklin Frazier, *The Negro in the United States* (New York: Macmillan, 1957), 109–10.

APPENDIX 4

1. Donald Bogle, *Toms, Coons, Mulattoes, Mammies and Bucks: An Interpretive History of Blacks in American Films* (New York: Continuum Books, 1994), 300, 309–10.

2. See "Robert Gould Shaw and the 54th Regiment," Boston African American, National Park Service, http://www.nps.gov/boaf/historyculture/shaw.htm.

3. See Barbaranne E. Mocella Liakos, "Their Civil Rights in Popular Prints: Kurz and Allison's Civil War Series," *Montage*, no. 2 (2008): 65–70, http://www.uiowa.edu/~montage/issues/2008/04_Liakos.pdf (article no longer available).

APPENDIX 5

1. See William H. Pease and Jane Pease, *Black Utopia: Negro Communal Experiments in America* (Madison: State Historical Society of Wisconsin, 1963), 38–41; and Charles Clark, "Augustus Wattles," Kansas Bogus Legislature, http://kansasbogus legislature.org/free/wattles_a.html.

2. For details on Gist's early life in England, see "Samuel Gist," Ohio History Central, http://www.ohiohistorycentral.org/w/Samuel_Gist. See also the text of the wills of Samuel Gist and his son-in-law William Anderson, respectively, at "Gist," RootsWeb, http://www.rootsweb.ancestry.com/~ohafram/gist; and William Buckner McGroarty, "Exploration in Mass Emancipation," *William and Mary Quarterly* 21, no. 3 (July 1941): 208–26, http://www.jstor.org/discover/10.2307/1919821. For details on the destiny of Gist's 1,000 former slaves in Ohio, see C. A. Powell, B. T. Kavanaugh, and David Christy, "Transplanting Free Negroes to Ohio from 1815–1858," *Journal of Negro History* 1, no. 3 (July 1916): 302–17; and Henry Howe, *Historical Collections of Ohio in Two Volumes: An Encyclopedia of the State* (Cincinnati: State of Ohio, 1907).

APPENDIX 6

1. Jefferson Davis, "Slavery in the Territories" (speech to the U.S. Senate, Washington, D.C., February 13–14, 1850), 26–27, https://babel.hathitrust.org/cgi /pt?id=loc.ark:/13960/t13n2840d; emphasis added.

APPENDIX 7

1. Eric Foner, *Reconstruction, 1863–1877: America's Unfinished Revolution* (New York: Harper and Row 1988), 467.

2. Abram L. Harris, *The Negro as Capitalist: A Study of Banking and Business among American Negroes* (Philadelphia: American Academy of Political and Social Science, 1936), 28, 34.

3. See Garrett Peck, *The Smithsonian Castle and the Seneca Quarry* (Charleston, S.C.: History Press, 2013); and John Stauffer, *Giants: The Parallel Lives of Frederick Douglass and Abraham Lincoln* (New York: Twelve, 2008), 309–10. See also William C. Harris, "Blanche K. Bruce of Mississippi: Conservative Assimilationist," in *Southern Black Leaders of the Reconstruction Era*, ed. Howard N. Rabinowitz (Urbana: University of Illinois Press, 1982), 21–22; Foner, *Reconstruction*, 69, 531–32; and esp. Abram L. Harris, *Negro as Capitalist*, 25–45.

Index

ARC (acknowledgment, redress, and closure). *See* acknowledgment; closure; redress

Arkansas, 66, 101, 162, 169, 196, 199, 200, 203–4, 217, 331n6, 332n17, 337–38n49, 343n15, 350n75, 396n53, 359nn3–4, 362–63n35, 369n97, 371n105

Asian Americans, 26, 32, 34, 41–42, 45, 245, 385n13; Asian Indians, U.S., 32; Koreans, U.S., 41–42, 304n57

assassinations. *See* terrorism, white

Astor, John Jacob, 54

Atlantic coast and Atlantic economy, 22–23, 51, 158–59, 161, 169, 306n12, 317n16

atonement, 3, 269, 289n3

atrocities, 1–3, 4, 13, 16–21, 150, 179, 201, 207, 209–18, 231–36, 256, 277–80, 334n25, 352n15, 355n41, 370n104, 373–74n34, 376n49, 385n11; convict leasing, 231–33; forced labor camps (re-enslavement), 104, 231–32; whippings, 85, 210, 278–80, 316n9. *See also* terrorism, white

Australia, 387n28; aborigines, 312n72; stolen generations, 289n1

Aycock, Charles B., 20, 296n57

back-to-Africa solution. *See* repatriation

Bacon's Rebellion, 71–72

Bailyn, Bernard, 51, 56

Baker, Ella, 1

Balloch, George W., 287

Banks, Nathaniel P., 115–16, 197, 338n51

banks and banking, 14–15, 20, 22–23, 53–54, 201–2, 265–67, 287, 317n21

"ban the box" policies, 304n67

Baradaran, Mehrsa, 9, 302n7. *See also* banks and banking

Barbados, 58–59

Barbee, Christopher, 61, 311–12n61

Bates, Timothy, 41–42, 302n39

Battle, James Smith. See *State v. Negro Will*

Battle of Antietam, 107, 120, 332n18, 336n42

Baxter, Richard, 89

Beaufort, South Carolina, 130–33, 339n50, 345n31, 348n61, 355n43

Beckert, Sven, 131

Beech, Malcolm, 239

Beecher, Catherine, 323n75

Beecher, Henry Ward, 327–28n20

Belinda (enslaved person), 291n13

Bell, John, 326n6

Benneton, Luciano, 293n33

Benezet, Andrew, 342n1

Benjamin, Judah P., 149–50, 261, 351–52n13, 352n14, 389n143

Bennett, Lerone, Jr., 70, 207, 213

Berry, Mary Frances, 265–66

Bertrand, Marianne, 45

Bethune Cookman College, 18, 295n49

Better Life Index, 387n28

Birmingham, Alabama, 230, 377n15, 380n43

Bishir, Catherine, 35, 61, 175, 187

Bisson, Terry, 292n25, 356n51; *Fire on the Mountain*, 292n25

Bittker, Boris, 5, 263

Black Codes, 145–46, 154, 178, 180–94, 197, 214–15, 367n74, 367n77, 367n80, 368n93, 369n95, 373–74n34

black dysfunction (black pathology), 29–30, 33, 137, 234, 299n4; racial cultural determinism in economics, 299n6

Black Economic Research Center, 15

Blackedge, Ann, 35

Blackedge, William, 35

black land loss, 17–18, 136, 208–9, 277

black lives, devaluation of, 5, 217, 219–21, 225–26, 231, 234, 236, 376n1; Black Lives Matter, 26, 219, 270, 376n1. *See also* atrocities

Black Manifesto, 14

Blackmon, Douglas, 188, 231–33

Black Panthers, 13–14

black settlements, 124–26, 235, 241, 284–85

black slave owners, 313n83

black soldiers and veterans: Camp Van Dorn, 375n43; Civil War, 12, 112–20, 181, 198, 246–47, 283, 291n14, 328n21, 335n35, 337–38n49, 339–40n49, 340nn59–60, 386n17; *Glory*, 283; Revolutionary War, 79–81, 333n19; World War I, 12, 16; World War II, 247–48, 386n17

Black Star Publications, 15

Black Youth Project, 392n4

Blackwell, Elizabeth, 323–24n78

Blanchflower, David G., 38

Bloomberg News, 45

Bond, Horace Mann, 230

Booker, Cory, 15

Booth, John Wilkes, 151–52

Booth, Lionel F., 118

border states, 100–102, 160, 313n81. *See also* Cameron, Simon

Borges, Ana, 42

Boston, Massachusetts, 52, 69, 74, 77, 88, 112–13, 127, 131–37, 147, 193, 283, 318–19n31, 335n33, 347n49, 348–49n69

bounty jumpers (American Civil War draft evaders), 112

Brassfield, George (grandfather and grandson), 67–68, 315n93; and Reba McIntire, 67, 315n93

Breckinridge, John Cabell, 171, 326n6

Breckinridge, Robert Jefferson, 170–71

Brinkley, Martin H., 324n88

Britain, 4, 55, 57, 58, 67, 70–73, 73–78, 79–80, 83, 313n81, 314n89, 315n4, 317n21, 318nn26–27, 318n31, 319n32, 348n48; British Army, 79; British High Court, 75, 78; British royal charter, 75; colonial finances, 71–74, 317nn20–21; Royal African Company, 314n18; textiles industry, 56–57, 308n24; Townshend Acts, 74. *See also* West Indies

Brooke, Edward, 379n33

Brooks, Albert, 179–80, 326n6

Brooks, George, 366n60

Brooks, Roy L., 5, 388n2

Brooks Brothers, 22, 56, 307–8n22

Brophy, Alfred L., 256, 277

Brown, Eleanor Marie, 43–44

Brown, Harrison, 229

Brown, John, 88, 95, 113, 125–28, 292n25, 323n77, 335–36n36, 336n37, 338n52, 343–44n1, 348–49n69

Brown, John, I, 55–56

Brown, Michael, 218

Brown, Neill S., 171

Brown, Oscar, Jr., 293n33

Brown, William Wells, 116

Browne, Katrina, 55

Browne, Robert, 15; Black Economic Research Center, 15

Brown v. Board (1954), 6, 21, 25, 225–26, 228, 231, 379n32

Bruce, Blanche K., 227, 379n33

Bryant, Charles W., 365n55

Buchanan, James, 95–96, 128, 325n3

Budd, William, 330n2

Burdette, Martha, 241

Burleson, Albert S., 12

Burns, Anthony, 348–49n69

Butler, Benjamin Franklin, 104–5, 214, 330nn3–4, 344n24, 359n6

Butler, Patrick, 111

Cabarrus, Stephen, 61

Cable, George Washington, 194, 368n84

Cade, Ebb, 234

Caldwell, Charles, 201

Caldwell, James, 338n53

Caldwell, Joseph, 60

Caldwell, Sam, 201

Calhoun, John C., 146–47, 357n68

California, 22, 45–46, 63, 96, 277; Los Angeles freeway, 377n15; Manzanar, 388n3; University of California at Berkeley, 63. *See also* sterilization, involuntary

Cameron, Simon, 160

Cameron-Bennehan plantation (Stagville), 208; owner Paul Carrington Cameron, 208

Campbell, John A., 329n36

Canada, 1–2, 125–26, 127, 140, 239, 187n28

capitalism, 9, 56–57, 65, 306–7n12, 370n102

Carlisle, John, 239

Carney, William H., 116, 339n56

Carr, Julian Shakespeare, 20–21

Carter, Lawrence, 391n31

Carter, Sam, 16

Carthagena and Carthage, 284

Cartwright, Samuel A., 322n61

Castro, Julián, 26

caution poster, 147; Benjamin Franklin Roberts, 351n8

Chachere, Bernadette, 262–63, 390n22

Chandler, Zachariah, 360n10

Chaney, James, 229

Chapman, John K., 61, 62

Charleston, South Carolina, 59, 69, 83, 85, 86, 97, 116, 158, 174–75, 217, 322n68, 356n49, 361n20, 383–84n7

Chase, Salmon, 130

Cheatham, Henry Plummer, 295n54

Cheatham, Richard B., 171

Cheever, George B., 99–100

Chestnut, J. L., Jr., 277

Chetty, Raj, 34

Chicago, 12–13, 221, 228, 283, 292nn19–20, 377n9; Chicago Commission on Race Relations, 13, 292nn19–20; contract selling scam, 221, 377n9; massacre of 1919, 12–13, 216–17, 292nn18–20; riot of 1947, 217

Christianity, 2, 64, 69, 70, 73, 78, 82, 86, 150–51, 195, 317n16, 323n74

Church, Robert, 221–22

civil rights, 5, 99, 162, 165–66, 185, 195, 207, 236, 257, 360n10; Civil Rights Act of 1866, 195; Civil Rights Act of 1871, 330n3; Civil Rights Act of 1875, 203,

214; Civil Rights Act of 1964, 30, 215, 221, 243; civil rights movement, 1, 5, 6, 30, 225–31, 235, 243, 277, 379n35; Freedom Summer, 229; voter registration, 227–30; Voting Rights Act of 1965, 169

Civil War, Nigeria. *See* secession: Biafran

Civil War, U.S., 1–5, 9, 11, 12, 52–53, 55–56, 61, 65–67, 69, 84, 89, 91, 95, 97, 143–66, 169–75, 182, 186, 319–20n40, 322n60, 324–25n89, 328n30, 328–29n31, 330n2, 333n19, 339–40n58, 340n59, 345n45, 348n64, 354n30, 358n56, 359n7, 360n9, 361n18, 366n60, 368n92, 369n95, 383n4; draft riots, 108, 109, 112, 114, 334nn24–27, 335nn29–33; Enrollment Act of 1863 (Conscription Act of 1863), 108, 333, 335n32; "lost order," 332–33n18; Militia Act of 1862, 117, 339n58

Clark, Achilles, 119

Clarkson, Thomas, 76, 318n27

Clinton, Bill, 18, 388–89n3

closure, 2–4

Clyburn, Weary, 383–84n7; Mattie Clyburn Rice (daughter), 383–84n7

Coates, Ta-Nehisi, 24, 207, 219, 221; and Stephen Colbert, 388n1

Cochran, Johnnie, 277

Coffin, Levi, 349n71

Cole, Johnnetta, 277

Cole, Sharon, 277

Colfax massacre (Louisiana), 215, 374n37, 378–79n30

College of William and Mary, 57, 64, 77

Collins, Addie Mae, 230

Comer, James, 277

compensated emancipation, 4, 79, 95–103, 106–7, 113, 144–45, 155, 246, 343n8, 369n95; District of Columbia Compensated Emancipation Act of 1862, 100, 106–7. *See also* Hampton Roads Conference

Compromise of 1790, 145

DeWolf, James, 55–56, 306n16
Dill, Solomon George Washington, 371n112
discrimination, 1–6, 12, 17, 25–26, 28, 29, 30, 38, 42–47, 79–80, 117–18, 230–31, 239, 243–52, 257, 262–64, 292n24, 337n43, 339n58, 340nn59–60; antidiscrimination measures, 6, 25, 248–49; in business ownership, 37–38; in Canada, 125–26; during Civil War, 114, 117–18, 339n58; and contract-selling scheme, 221, 312n68; in employment, 44–47, 216–17, 339n58, 340n59; estimates of cost of, 262–63; and field experiments, 45–46; in housing, 221, 377n9; in school expenditures and education, 220, 225–26, 230–31; sundown towns, 225
dismemory, 173–74
District of Columbia (Washington, D.C.), 97–98, 99, 100–101, 106–7, 115, 131, 144–46, 160, 195–96, 216–17, 277, 202n21, 293n33, 305n77, 327–28n20, 328n23, 329n35, 343n15, 346n35, 350n4, 361n15, 363n36, 370n101; Compensated Emancipation Act of 1862, 100; Georgetown University, 60, 256–57, 258, 311n54; Howard University, 28, 141, 349n74; Howard University Law School, 214
Dolly (person enslaved by Andrew Johnson), 359n7.
Dombrowski, James, 230
Dostie, Anthony Paul, 180, 364n44
Douglas, Stephen A., 326n6, 360n11
Douglass, Frederick, 1–2, 100, 116, 117, 125, 142, 254–55, 322n73, 327–28n20, 328nn24–26, 331n10, 332n13, 338–39n53, 340n60, 352–53n24, 355–56n43, 388n34; *Douglass' Monthly*, 101, 328n26, 331n10, 332n13, 350n76; Charles Remond Douglass (son), 338–39n53; Lewis Henry Douglass (son), 338–39n53
Douglass, Sarah Mapps, 86

Dozier, Oscar, 13
Drake, Francis, 315n4
drapetomania, 322n61
Dred Scott v. Sandford, 325n92
Du Bois, W. E. B., 128, 167, 168, 292n19, 344n22, 349n74, 361n18
Dunn, Marvin, 294
Du Pont, Samuel F., 130
Dupree, Jack, 200, 370n14
Durban, South Africa, 23, 292n24
Durham, North Carolina, 20, 42, 173, 223, 242, 289n4, 383n6, 385n10; Duke University, 20, 45; Durham Freeway, 223; Hayti, 223, 378n21

Eastern Europe, 39–40, 357n55
East India Company, 74, 317n22
Eastland, James O., 226, 230
Easton, Hosea, 291n13
Eaton, D. L., 287
Edisto Island, South Carolina, 123, 133, 193
Edmund Pettus Bridge, 277
Elaine massacre (Arkansas), 217
Electoral College, 81, 96, 326n6
Eliot, Thomas D., 349n71
Eliza (person enslaved by Julia Dent Grant), 313n81
Elkins, Stanley, 81
Ellis, Kimberly, 277
Ellis, Littleberry. See sugar and sugar cane: Imperial Sugar Company
Ellsworth, Elijah, 278–79
emancipation, Emancipation Leagues, 127, 348n67, 348–49n69; Emancipation Proclamation, 107, 110, 113–14, 124, 146, 152, 157, 171–72, 188, 191–92, 246, 269, 313n81, 331n10, 331n17, 336n38
Emerson, John, 90
Emerson, Ralph Waldo, 327–28n20
England, 58, 63, 67, 70, 74, 75, 78, 146, 284–85, 309n37, 318n25, 319n35, 320n4, 345n29, 348n68, 393n2 (appendix 5). *See also* Britain
Ethridge, J. I. "Bose," 216

Europe, 12, 16, 39–40, 51, 67, 70, 72, 75–76, 84, 130–31, 139, 202, 287, 290–91n10, 306–7n12, 307n15, 357n55

Evers, Medgar, 229, 379n35

exception clause. *See* Thirteenth Amendment

Fair Deal, 247–48

Farmer-Paellmann, Deadria, 23–25, 297–98n68

Farrow, Anne, 51–55

Feagin, Joe, 6

Federal Bureau of Investigation (FBI), 229

Federal Reserve (Board of Governors of the Federal Reserve), 36, 266

fen-phen (fenfluramine), 234, 277

Ferguson, Missouri, 218, 233

Fifteenth Amendment, 91–92, 165, 168, 203–4

Fifty-Fourth Massachusetts Regiment, 114, 116, 119, 283, 336n42, 337n43, 338–39n53, 339nn54–56, 349n71. *See also* black soldiers and veterans; Civil War, U.S.

Fitzsimmons, Catherine, 345n29

FleetBoston Financial, 23, 297–98n68

Fleming, Walter, 256, 289n2

Fletcher, George, 155–56, 354n33, 354n35

Fletcher, Thomas C., 177, 362n34

Flint, Michigan, 235

Florida, 16–17, 24, 36–37, 66, 69, 97, 98, 119, 157–59, 166, 182, 191, 196, 200, 203, 207, 211–12, 213, 217, 223, 251, 294n37, 294n40, 294n43, 295n49, 314n87, 332n13, 341n69, 350n75, 355–56n49, 359n4, 362–63n35, 370n102, 372n15, 377n15. *See also* Miami

Florida massacres. *See* Florida

Foner, Eric, 165, 203, 287

Foner, Philip, 320n42

food relief, 226

Footman, Pamela, 242; Alison Footman (daughter), 242; John Wallace Footman (father), 242; Wallace

Roby (great-uncle), 242; Essex Shaw (great-grandfather), 242

forgiveness, 3, 158, 289n3. *See also* atonement3, 269, 289n3

Forman, James, 14

Forrest, Jonathan, 341n62

Forrest, Nathan Bedford, 118–19, 341n62, 341nn65–66

Forten, Charlotte, 86, 322n73

Fort Monroe, Virginia, 105, 129–31, 331n8, 344n24, 345n26

Fort Pillow, Tennessee, 118–19, 181, 341nn65–66, 355n41. *See also* Forrest, Nathan Bedford

Fort Sumter, South Carolina, 97, 112–13, 130

Fortune, Emanuel, 182, 364n50; Sarah Jane Fortune (wife), 364n50; Timothy Thomas Fortune (son), 364n50

Fort Wagner, South Carolina, 116, 119, 283, 336n42, 338–39n53, 339nn55–56, 349n71, 355n41

Fortune 500, 37, 302n37

forty acres, 2, 5, 9, 13, 43, 142, 156–59, 170, 176, 207–8, 213, 243, 256, 261–62, 293n33, 350n75, 355n2, 386n23, 390n21; 40 Acres and a Mule film company, 15; Special Field Orders No. 15, 156, 175–76, 196, 251, 355–56n43, 356nn49–51; Spike Lee, 15. *See also* Metcalf, H. B.; Sherman, William Tecumseh

Fourteenth Amendment, 87, 165, 168, 196, 215, 365n55, 374n36

Foxx, Anthony, 223

Frank, Jennifer, 51–55

Franklin, Abraham, 111

Franklin, Benjamin, 145, 319n33, 342n1

Franklin, Isaac, 350–51n4

Franklin, John Hope, 18, 95; Buck "Charles" Colbert Franklin (father), 18

Franklin, V. P., 265–66

fraud, 12, 161, 188, 202, 203, 221, 267, 268, 291n17; and mail fraud, 12, 291n17

Frazier, E. Franklin, 281–82

Grimké, Angelina Emily, 35–36, 60, 85–87; *American Slavery as It Is*, 85, 278–79; John Faucheraud Grimké (father), 86

Grimké, Sarah, 35–36, 85–87; *American Slavery as It Is*, 85, 278–79; John Faucheraud Grimké (father), 86

Grow, Galusha Aaron, 359n6

Guerrero, Vicente, 319–20n40

Hahn, George Michael Decker, 180–81

Haiti, 82, 102–3, 125, 131, 146, 180, 343n8

Haitian Revolution, 78, 82, 83, 88, 131, 146, 286, 321n54

Hall, Jacquelyn Dowd, 175

Hamilton, Andrew Jackson, 183–85, 365n55

Hamlin, Cyrus, 198

Hamlin, Hannibal, 198, 360n14

Hammond, James Henry, 149, 345n29; mudsill theory, 149

Hampton, Wade, 64

Hampton Roads Conference (Virginia), 102, 129, 329n36, 331n8. *See also* compensated emancipation

Harper, Douglas, 365n52

Harper, Frances Ellen Watkins, 103, 329n39

Harpers Ferry, Virginia, 88, 95, 292n25, 335–36n36, 338n52, 343–44n17, 349n69

Harris, Ira, 155

Hartford Courant, 52, 318n23

Harvard University, 57, 58, 64, 277; Harvard Business School, 19, 45; Harvard Law School, 19, 277

Hatch, Ann B., 35

Hatch, Richard B., 35

Hayes, Rutherford B., 166, 203

Hazelwood, Janell, 302

headright system, 67–68, 71–72, 315–16n55

Hendrick, Bernard W., 209–10

Henry, Charles P., 239, 290–91n10

Hester, Clifton E., 229

Hicks, Jacob, 210

Higginbotham, Evelyn Brooks, 51, 305

Hilton Head, South Carolina, 133, 138, 346n35, 355n43, 384n7

Himes, Chester, 306n6; *Cotton Comes to Harlem*, 52–53

Hinds, James M., 203, 371n112

Hixson, Richard, 16

Hodgson, Adam, 85

Hogan, John, 61, 311n61

Hogan, Liam, 314n19

Holcombe, James P., 329–30n1

Holly, Calvin, 162

Holzer, Harold, 196

Hood, John Bell, 120

Hooper, Edward W., 348n67

Hopkins, S., Jr., 307–8n22

Horne, Gerald, 78

Horowitz, David, 23

hospital beds, 220, 376n2

House, Callie D. Guy, 11–12, 18; and Isaiah Dickerson, 11; and National Ex-Slave Mutual Relief, Bounty, and Pension Association (MRBP), 11–12

Houston, Charles Hamilton, 277

Houston, Samuel R., 253

Houston, Ulysses, 123

Howard, Oliver Otis, 141, 172, 176, 185, 287, 349n74, 366nn61–63

Howard, Theodore Roosevelt Mason, 379n35

Howe, Julia Ward, 323–24n78

H.R. 40, 15–16, 257–58; and Steve Cohen, 26–27; and John Conyers, 15, 25, 257, 294n36; and Sheila Jackson Lee, 15, 257; and Commission to Study and Develop Proposals for Reparations for African Americans, 258. *See also* Booker, Cory

Huger, Mary Esther, 174

Huggins, A. P., 370n104

human chattel, 2, 22, 43, 65, 70, 76, 83, 97, 100, 105, 144, 147, 152, 156, 176, 131,

Johnson, Herschel, 365n53
Johnson, James Weldon, 292n18
Johnson, Lyndon Baines, 44
Johnston, Joseph Eggleston, 161, 173
Johnston, Samuel, 61
Jonas, Sidney Alroy, 173
Jones, Edmund, 311–12n61
Jones, James H., 45, 46
Jones, W. B., 378–79n30
Jones, William (victim of New York draft riots), 111
Jones, William (person enslaved by Ulysses S. Grant), 313n81
Jones, Willie, 61
Julia (person enslaved by Julia Dent Grant), 313n81
Julian, George Washington, 136–37, 167, 195, 347n58

Kansas, 95, 127–28, 147, 323n77, 335–36n36, 338n52, 345n29, 351n11; "Bleeding Kansas," 147; Kansas-Nebraska Act, 127–28, 147
Katznelson, Ira, 247–48; *When Affirmative Action Was White*, 373n28, 385n16, 386n17
Kelton, Stephanie, 391n36
Kennedy, John, 110
Kennedy, John F., 229
Kennedy, Robert F., 229
Kentucky, 10, 98, 100–101, 102, 105, 106, 118, 163
Ker, David, 70
Keynesian economics, 290–91n10
Kiddoo, Joseph Barr, 163, 185
King, Martin Luther, Jr., 167, 230, 391n31; Dexter Avenue Baptist Church, 230, 380n43; and Vernon Johns, 380n43
King, Sebrone Jones, 241, 383n6
Kitroeff, Natalie, 46
Kluge, John, 21
Knights of the White Camelia, 181, 182, 198, 200, 370n101
Know-Nothings, 170, 171

Kollock, Susan Davis, 59
Korean War, 361n21
Kornweibel, Theodore, Jr., 64–65
Kossola, Oluale (Cudjo Lewis), 240
Ku Klux Klan, 16, 165–66, 182, 194, 199–204, 210, 213–14, 226, 232, 295–96n55, 330n3, 341n66, 364n49–51, 370n104, 371n105; and Civil Rights Act of 1871, 330n3; and hearings of the Joint Select Committee to Inquire into the Condition of Affairs in the Late Insurrectionary States, 210–11

land speculators. *See* forty acres; Philbrick, Edward
Lang, Joel, 51–55
Langston, John Mercer, 116, 214
Lake Michigan, 12–13
lateral mobility hypothesis, 40–44
Lawlor, Jan S., 301n27
Lawlor, Michael Syron, 301n27
law of the womb, 317n15
LeConte, John and Joseph, 63
Lee, George Washington, 228
Lee, Henry, III ("Light Horse Harry"), 145, 350n3
Lee, Herbert, 229
Lee, Jennifer, 42
Lee, Robert E., 66–67, 110–11, 113, 128, 150–51, 179, 332–33n18, 350n3, 383–84n7; Army of Northern Virginia, 66
Leflore County, Mississippi, 226, 228, 380n35
Lehman Brothers, 22, 53–54
Lethrbury, Peregrine, 289–90n1
Levine, Philip B., 38
Lewis, Kenneth, 242–43, 385n10; Amelia Stewart Winstead (grandmother), 242
Liberator, The, 125, 136, 347n55
Liberia, 103, 253, 323n75, 329nn37–38
Lieber, Francis, 62–63, 312n68
Lincoln, Abraham, 9, 91, 95–103, 105–7, 109–10, 112–17, 124, 128, 136, 141–42, 145–56, 157–58, 160–71, 178–79, 182,